THE PUBLIC NATURE OF PRIVATE PROPERTY

Law, Property and Society

Series Editor:
Robin Paul Malloy

The Law, Property and Society series examines property in terms of its ability to foster democratic forms of governance, and to advance social justice. The series explores the legal infrastructure of property in broad terms, encompassing concerns for real, personal, intangible, intellectual and cultural property, as well as looking at property related financial markets. The series is edited by Robin Paul Malloy, and book proposals are welcome from all interested authors.

Robin Paul Malloy is E.I. White Chair and Distinguished Professor of Law, and the Kauffman Professor of Entrepreneurship and Innovation at Syracuse University College of Law, USA. He is Director of the Center on Property, Citizenship, and Social Entrepreneurism. He is also Professor of Economics (by courtesy appointment) in the Maxwell School of Citizenship and Public Affairs, Syracuse University. Professor Malloy writes extensively on law and market theory and on real estate transactions and development. He has authored eight books (one now in its third edition and another in its second edition), and edited seven additional books. He has also written more than 30 scholarly articles, and contributed to 12 other books. His recent books include: LAW AND MARKET ECONOMY (2000, in English and translated into Spanish and Chinese); LAW IN A MARKET CONTEXT (2004); and REAL ESTATE TRANSACTIONS 3RD EDITION (with James C. Smith, 2007).

The Public Nature of Private Property

Edited by

ROBIN PAUL MALLOY
Syracuse University College of Law, USA

MICHAEL DIAMOND,
Georgetown University Law Center, USA

Routledge
Taylor & Francis Group
LONDON AND NEW YORK

First published 2011 by Ashgate Publishing

2 Park Square, Milton Park, Abingdon, Oxon OX14 4RN
711 Third Avenue, New York, NY 10017, USA

Routledge is an imprint of the Taylor & Francis Group, an informa business

First issued in paperback 2016

British Library Cataloguing in Publication Data
The public nature of private property. -- (Law, property and society)
1. Right of property.
I. Series II. Malloy, Robin Paul, 1956- III. Diamond, Michael R.
346'.04-dc22

Library of Congress Cataloging-in-Publication Data
The public nature of private property / by Robin Paul Malloy and Michael Diamond.
p. cm. -- (Law, property and society)
Includes bibliographical references and index.
ISBN 978-0-7546-7951-6 (hardback)
1. Right of property--United States. I. Malloy, Robin Paul, 1956- II. Diamond, Michael R.
KF562.P83 2011
346.7304'2--dc22

2011003270

ISBN 978-0-7546-7951-6 (hbk)
ISBN 978-1-138-25197-7 (pbk)

Contents

List of Contributors *vii*
Preface – Michael Diamond *ix*
Acknowledgements *xiii*

1 The Public Nature of Property Rights and the Property Nature of Public Law 1
J. Peter Byrne

2 Explaining the Persistent Myth of Property Absolutism 13
David Fagundes

3 Shared Equity Housing: Cultural Understanding and the Meaning of Ownership 37
Michael Diamond

4 Crisis and the Public–Private Divide in Property 65
Nestor M. Davidson and Rashmi Dyal-Chand

5 Eviction and the Public Interest: The Right to Respect for Home in English Law 89
Lorna Fox O'Mahony

6 Opening Neighborhoods to People with Mobility Impairment: Property, Disability and Inclusive Design Housing 133
Robin Paul Malloy

7 Who Should Fix the Sink?: Addressing Maintenance and Repairs in Limited Equity Cooperatives 153
Jennie O'Flanagan

8 Preserving Public Peace, Protecting Private Property 185
Susan S. Kuo

9 Adult Adoption of Lovers and Spouses to Help Ensure Their Inheritance: Fair or Foul? 209
Terry L. Turnipseed

Table of Cases *229*
Table of Statutes and Legislative Material *233*
Bibliography *237*
Index *257*

List of Contributors

J. Peter Byrne, Professor of Law, Georgetown University Law Center

Nestor M. Davidson, Associate Professor of Law, Fordham Law School

Michael Diamond, Professor of Law, Georgetown University Law Center

Rashmi Dyal-Chand, Professor of Law, Northeastern University School of Law

David Fagundes, Associate Professor, Southwestern Law School.

Susan S. Kuo, Associate Professor, University of South Carolina School of Law

Robin Paul Malloy, E.I. White Chair and Distinguished Professor of Law, Kauffman Professor of Entrepreneurship and Innovation, College of Law, Syracuse University

Jennie O'Flanagan, staff attorney and Adjunct Professor, the Harrison Institute for Housing and Community Development at Georgetown University Law Center

Lorna Fox O'Mahony, Professor of Law, Durham University, England, U.K.

Terry L. Turnipseed, Associate Professor of Law, Syracuse University College of Law.

Preface

Michael Diamond

What, exactly, is private property? Or, to ask the question another way, what rights to intrude does the public have in what is generally accepted as private property? The answer, perhaps surprisingly to some, is that the public has not only a significant interest in regulating the use of private property but also in defining it, establishing its contour and texture. Thus, there is a range of views on both the meaning of private property and on the ability, some might say the requirement, of the state to regulate it. This volume includes a selection of several papers presented at a workshop at Georgetown Law entitled The Public Nature of Private Property. The workshop was jointly sponsored by Georgetown and the Center on Property, Citizenship, and Social Enterpreneurism of the Syracuse University College of Law. The authors included in this volume discuss the public's interest in private property from widely disparate perspectives. We hope that the discussion provokes thought and inquiry into this fundamental but only modestly articulated area of research.

We begin the volume with Peter Byrne's keynote address. In his chapter, Byrne presages several of the themes that are addressed in this volume. He looks at the nature of property and the ways in which the law has changed the meaning of the term. Byrne locates the traditional meaning of property in a Blackstonian common law but asks why such common law rules should have normative precedence over legislation or regulation. Byrne argues that they should not. He points out that as society and the economy change, property law must also change to accommodate societal realities and that this can be accomplished more efficiently, more comprehensively and more fairly through statutory or regulatory innovation rather than through common law development. Byrne argues that such positive law must be understood and accepted as part of the overall law of property. This "elementary" principle, that statutes displace pre-existing common law rules, has not been fully accepted into the lay lexicon, nor even by certain judges. Nevertheless, Byrne sees "no barriers between the private and public dimensions of property." This argument, in both its positivist and normative sense, is reasserted in various ways throughout the remaining chapters.

David Fagundes, in the second chapter, examines the disconnect between what *is* the law of property and the general public's perception of it. While the popular myth hearkens back to Blackstone's "despotic dominion," the reality is considerably different. Fagundes seeks to explain "the persistent myth of property absolutism" by examining three possible explanations for it; law and economics, behavioralism, and sociobiology. While he finds each of these explanations insufficient on their own, Fagundes concludes by constructing a tentative explanation made up of elements of all three of these narratives. He points out that while the concept of property includes many aspects designed to augment the well-being of a property owner, that is not the only characteristic that property is designed to enhance. It also has as a goal the improvement of society as a whole. Thus, certain restraints on individual well-being would be appropriate.

Michael Diamond continues this theme in the next chapter. Diamond examines the meaning of property from both cultural and historical perspectives. He argues that property and ownership are culturally constructed concepts that are understood differently in different cultures and even in the same culture over time. Diamond then focuses on the legal/political history of the United States and argues that there have been in America, from colonial days to the present, at least two competing strains of property theory; the Blackstonian absolutist model and what Gregory Alexander has termed the "proprietarian" model that sees property as being used to secure societal good, however that is defined. Diamond applies the proprietarian model in justifying limiting the equity that may be required of low income homeowners as a condition of obtaining highly subsidized public financing for their property.

Two themes discussed earlier in this volume, those of legislation and regulation as an essential element of property law and the nature of private property in the American historical context, are continued in Nestor Davidson and Rashmi Dyal-Chand's chapter on the relationship between crisis and substantive legal change. Recognizing the American law of property as a stable and relatively conservative institution, Davidson and Dyal-Chand nevertheless point out that crisis can, and, in our history, has, sped up the normal, slow evolutionary change in property law. The public intervention during such crises into traditional property conceptions has raised the question about the very nature of private property. The authors use the current economic crisis to examine various tensions "along the perennial public/private fault lines" and the "relevance of public versus private decisions in response to the crisis."

The nature of property is raised in a different context in Lorna Fox O'Mahoney's chapter concerning eviction and the right to respect for one's home under English law. O'Mahoney examines Article 8(1) of The European Convention on Human Rights and its application to English law. Article 8(1) requires respect for one's "private and family life, his home and his correspondence." The question O'Mahoney asks is whether this implies merely a right to privacy in one's home or, more expansively, respect for one's home, itself. If the latter interpretation were to prevail, it would have significant implications, for example, in situations where a public authority sought to evict a resident from publicly owned housing. If there was an underlying human right to housing, this would create new property rights in a tenant that might be offset against pre-existing rights of the public. Such rights, if created by the European Convention, are reminiscent of Peter Byrne's call for legislative modifications of traditional property concepts.

Robin Paul Malloy takes yet another approach to the public/private distinction. Malloy examines the physical obstacles imposed on persons with disabilities from full participation in civil society by a lack of accessibility—he calls it *visitability*—in private structures. He argues that such limitations are not only losses to the individuals restricted from full participation but also to the society that loses the benefits to be derived from broader participation by all members of the community. He also argues that market imperfections have resulted in a shortage of housing units with an "inclusionary design," a design that invites use by those with mobility impairments. He explains this imperfection by pointing out that while any particular home-owner resides in a home for a relatively short time, the home itself continues to exist for a much longer period. As such, it imposes ongoing costs on the public through the long-term limitation of accessible housing. Malloy argues that these shortcomings can be addressed by national regulation of accessibility standards and points to some factors in the public's involvement in the single family housing market that were previously used as the basis for national accessibility regulation of public accommodations.

In the seventh chapter, Jennie O'Flanagan, drawing from her experience in working with tenant groups seeking to develop their own properties (typically in the form of limited equity cooperatives) examines an element that, she argues, could increase the likelihood that these endeavors will succeed as permanent tenant-owned affordable housing. Housing Cooperatives are treated by law as a form of ownership rather than as a rental. That being the case, the cooperative corporation that owns the building may transfer maintenance obligations, in whole or in part, to the members of the cooperative. O'Flanagan argues that transferring to the member the obligation to maintain his or her apartment achieves two salutary purposes. First it reduces the cost of maintenance to the cooperative and places it on the occupant of the unit. This helps to reduce profligacy and free-rider problems and can improve the overall quality of maintenance in the building. Moreover, it helps to instill in members the sense of ownership and responsibility that is often not present in rental situations. Finally, O'Flanagan suggests techniques that can be built in to the structure of the cooperative to protect very low income members from the potential hardship such cost-shifting might impose.

The next group of chapters looks at issues a bit further from the core of traditional property discourse. They illustrate some of the ways in which public and private rights and interests interact in unexpected property milieus.

Continuing the exploration of property concepts in non-traditional contexts, Susan Kuo, in our penultimate chapter, explores the link between preserving the public peace and the public's obligations to protect private property. Kuo examines historic Riot Acts in England and the United States. These laws imposed on the public "communal responsibility for riot harm." These Acts provided a means of incentivizing the public to prevent (or to attempt to minimize) the harm that would result from a riot and also provided a means of compensating the victims of riots. While these Acts have been generally repealed in the United States and consigned to the status of relics where they continue to exist, Kuo argues that something important has been lost to society through their demise. She suggests the possibility of instituting redesigned Riot Acts that would restore an element of the communal interdependence among residents that characterized former periods, periods before the bureaucratization of preserving the public peace and the protection of private property.

The volume concludes with a chapter by Terry Turnipseed in which he explores the state's involvement in the disposition of one's property upon death. We are all generally familiar with the statutory schemes involved in intestate succession. What is less well known is the practice of a person with property adopting his or her lover better to insure their lover's ability to inherit their property upon their death. This is particularly significant in jurisdictions that do not recognize same-sex marriages. In particular, the adoption of a same-sex lover provides a vehicle for the lover to claim property under intestate descent laws. While there are several contract-based methods for "higher-net-worth partner" to provide for their lover, these are subject to claims of other potential heirs who wish to challenge such contracts. This problem is not present in adoption situations. Since the adopted "child" is the legal heir to the exclusion of parents, siblings and other distant relatives, and since adoption is final and conclusive, none of these relatives would have the standing to challenge the inheritance. Such adoptions, however, also raise a variety of other problems, not the least of which is criminal prosecution for incest. Turnipseed goes on to examine the constitutional dimensions after *Lawrence v. Texas* of laws that criminalize sexual relations between an adult and his or her consenting-adult adopted "child."

Our goal in producing this volume was to draw attention to the widespread and deep involvement of the public in what has traditionally been called private property. It was also to suggest that the contours of property as a concept go beyond what most people, and, indeed, many scholars have thought of as encompassed within the term. We hope that the chapters in this volume have added to the theoretical, doctrinal and practical discourse.

Acknowledgements

Thanks and appreciation are gratefully extended to Zack Baisley, Lesley Germanow, Melissa Schreiber-Stahl, John Stevens, and Sheila Welch for their invaluable assistance in the preparation of THE PUBLIC NATURE OF PRIVATE PROPERTY. I also thank Dean Hannah Arterian for supporting the efforts of our Center on Property, Citizenship, and Social Entrepreneurism.

I dedicate this book to the memory of my dear friend and colleague of 20 years, Rod Surratt. Rod devoted some 34 years of his professional teaching career to Syracuse University, and made a genuine and lasting contribution to our College of Law and to the lives of countless students. Rod's witty conversation and gentle laughter will be greatly missed. I am proud to have called Rod my friend.

RPM

In recognition of those who struggle to obtain or retain property and to those who help them do so.

MD

Chapter 1
The Public Nature of Property Rights and the Property Nature of Public Law

J. Peter Byrne

This chapter, 'The Public Nature of Property Rights', argues that statutes adjusting the terms of ownership should be considered to be part of property law just as fully as are common law rules. As a description of positive law, this may seem a mere truism. That statutes displace the common law is an elementary principle of state constitutional law.[1] Moreover, statutes create many forms of property rights; federal copyright and patent, for example, are nearly entirely statutory. But for more traditional assets, such as land or goods, the law of which has been rooted in the common law, judges and scholars seem often to treat legislation as a second-class and suspect form of law. We are accustomed to think of traditional property rights of possession, use, exclusion, and transfer as being largely created by the common law but subsequently limited by legislation and regulations that shrink the domain of property.

My claim will be that there is no essential difference between what we may term the private law and the public law of property. Property law creates rights and duties in regard to resources regardless of whether it originates in the common law or in local, state, or federal legislation. Legislation that limits or conditions earlier established property rights is as much part of property law as is legislation that creates or enhances the capacity to exclude or convey. Common law has no normative precedence. The opposite impression reflects our historically situated perspective and the ideological struggles of our time.

I hope that I am saying something more than reiterating the "bundle of sticks" argument. From Morris Cohen to Laura Underkuffler, fine scholars have disaggregated property and considered the distribution of interests as conscious policy choices.[2] This approach has always made sense to me, because the persistence of private property depends upon the continuing consent of the community, which protects and gives endurance to specific private interests in resources because it

1 *See, e.g.*, 3 Norman J. Singer & J.D. Shambie Singer, Sutherland Statutes and Statutory Construction §61 (7th ed. 2008).

2 *See, e.g.*, Laura Underkuffler, The Idea of Property: Its Meaning and Power (2003); Thomas C. Grey, *The Disintegration of Property*, in Richard A. Epstein, ed., Modern Understandings of Liberty and Property (2000); Morris R. Cohen, *Property and Sovereignty*, 13 Cornell L.Q. 8 (1927).

enhances human welfare more generally (even if not in every specific case). Some scholars have brought to the foreground arguments about what values property should advance: autonomy, efficiency, stability, human flourishing, and equality. Legal realists' insistence on the bundle of sticks approach reflects their support for regulation of use resisted by claims that such regulation violated property rights enshrined in the common law. Although normative arguments can be compelling, I do not plan to enter that fray here. My concern rather is with legal technology, advances in which have made it possible to recognize and shape interests in assets that the common law system simply lacked the capacity to conceive or implement. Common law came earlier in time, but rapidly changing social conditions conjured legislation and regulations to increase our legal capacity to deal with new demands and values.

Take contemporary local historic preservation regulation, for a preliminary example. Such laws recognize the interest of a community resident in preventing the demolition of an old, lovely building that she passed with pleasure twice every day for twenty years on her walk to and from the bus stop, while preserving the owner's exclusive right to propose a plan to redevelop the site.[3] One might argue that historic preservation has some kind of common law core, that the community resident acquires a prescriptive easement in perpetuating the visible aspects of the significant building based on her cognitive or cultural bonding with it over time. The problems with such an approach are legion. The law we actually have is much more efficient and fair. An administrative agency, aided by an expert staff, evaluates the historic significance of the buildings and appropriateness of what the owner proposes, as well as the concerns of interested persons, in a process aiming at balance and accommodation.[4] Both the resident and the owner have interests or rights that count, although of differing characters and strengths. The common law lacks the resources in rule formation and in administrative decision making to recognize both interests without creating holdouts, a massive anti-commons, and stalemate. Courts could not recognize the validity of each resident's interest without conceptualizing it as some kind of prescriptive servitude that would create an indeterminate number of vetoes on an owner's desired project, essentially destroying the owner's use rights.

Despite the greater efficiency and fairness of regulatory approaches to many asset uses, some courts give normative precedence to the common law of property and treat legislation as its antithesis. While this stance may have ideological roots, it takes a jurisprudential form. Judicial invigoration of the regulatory

3 Not all historic preservation ordinances prohibit demolition of privately-owned historic structures, but the stronger ones do. *See, e.g.*, Historic Landmark and Historic District Protection Act, D.C. Code § 6 – 1101, *et seq*. Alterations and new construction can be proposed only by an owner, but are subject to review by the Historic Preservation Review Board.

4 *See* J. Peter Byrne, *Hallowed Ground: The Gettysburg Battlefield in Historic Preservation Law*, 22 Tul. Envtl. L.J. 203 (2008).

takings doctrine, for example, highlighted by *Lucas*,[5] sought to use constitutional legerdemain and no little natural law to bar new legislative limits on property rights of use without paying just compensation, which would have made them impracticable. While the prospect of a robust regulatory takings doctrine is troubling on constitutional and policy grounds,[6] some of the supporting reasoning also is puzzling on jurisprudential grounds. *Lucas* itself privileges "background principles" of common law against legislation. Justice Scalia's opinion structures its analysis to preclude consideration of the public interests served by the challenged legislation. Some proponents embrace the Blackstonian precept that property *means* absolute dominion, arguing that environmental or other use regulations destroy property. A robust exposition of this perspective was given by then Justice Janice Brown of the California Supreme Court, dissenting from her court's upholding of a San Francisco ordinance requiring mitigation payments for eliminating affordable housing:

> But private property, already an endangered species in California, is now entirely extinct in San Francisco. The City and County of San Francisco has implemented a neo-feudal regime where the nominal owner of property must use that property according to the preferences of the majorities that prevail in the political process—or, worse, the political powerbrokers who often control the government independently of majoritarian preferences. Thus, "the lamb [has been] committed to the custody of the wolf." (6 The Works of John Adams, *supra*, at p. 280.) San Francisco has redefined the American dream. Where once government was closely constrained to increase the freedom of individuals, now property ownership is closely constrained to increase the power of government. Where once government was a necessary evil because it protected private property, now private property is a necessary evil because it funds government programs. (citation omitted)[7]

Even with generous allowance for poetic license, this is so wrong: the market for land and buildings in San Francisco remains one of the most desirable in the country, which is what makes the mitigation payments system possible. That system was designed to support the retention or replacement of property interests of low-income residents. Moreover, feudalism was a property regime—indeed, the origin of our own. And legislative innovations have contributed to the evolution of property law over its entire history.[8] Justice Brown, like other property zealots,

5 Lucas v. South Carolina Coastal Council, 505 U.S. 1003 (1992).

6 *See* J. Peter Byrne, *Ten Arguments for the Abolition of the Regulatory Takings Doctrine*, 22 Ecology L.Q. 89 (1995).

7 San Remo Hotel, L.P. v. City and County of San Francisco, 41 P.3d 87, 120 (Cal. 2002) (Brown, J., dissenting).

8 Looking over the broad stretch of English land law, Holdsworth opined that "the Legislature has had a larger share in shaping the land law than it has had in shaping any

uses the term "property" to describe the common law property rules extant at the end of the nineteenth century.

Property law certainly has changed in modern times, adopting new legislative approaches to adapt to new economic, political, and environmental problems. What after all was the legal difference between a common law nuisance doctrine protecting the neighboring property owners and a legislative rule specifying what uses you cannot pursue? The main features of the legislative fix through zoning are prospective clarity and some over-inclusivity, the filtering of a wide range of interests and concerns of voters (not just neighboring land owners), decisionmaking by democratically responsible officials rather than by judges, and less encouragement to rely upon a perpetuation of current rules. No court could have created this system through common law adjudication. The blend of legislation, planning, administrative adjudication, and political voice constitute a new legal technology. My focus just now is not the merits of any a particular land use policy or allocation of rights, but that legislation and administrative oversight create new opportunities to recognize a variety of rights and duties, none of which should be considered "outside" property law. As a property innovation, zoning may increase or decrease the scope of free action of any interested party and contemplates a "public interest" mediating many individual interests through various public processes.

To develop my claim and test whether it has any explanatory power, I now want to consider two examples at greater depth. The first example of public regulation adjusting the scope of property rights we might consider is the successful transformation of creditor interests in a debtor's commercial property from fraudulent conveyances to property rights. Grant Gilmore gave an exhaustive account of the various hesitating steps in this process for different forms of collateral in his classic treatise, *Security Interests in Personal Property.* But the basic story line is simple. Early in the nineteenth century, courts generally held that a conveyance of title to goods while retaining possession of them was fraudulent as to the seller's creditors. "The law will not and ought not to permit the owner of personal property to create an interest in another, either by mortgage or absolute sale, and still to continue to be the ostensible owner."[9] Chancellor Kent's view of the matter was slightly less absolute: "Delivery of possession is so much of the essence of the sale of chattels, that an agreement to permit the vendor to keep possession is an extraordinary exception to the usual course of dealing, and requires a satisfactory explanation."[10] The concern in all these cases is that ordinary unsecured creditors will erroneously but naturally believe that a merchant owns

---

other branch of private law." Moreover, "at all periods in the history of the land law, statutes have been the parents of a great many of its fundamental principles, and the starting-points of new epochs in its development." W.S. Holdsworth, An Historical Introduction to the Land Law 325 (1927).

9 Clow v. Woods, 5 Serg. & Rawle 275, 279 (Pa. 1819).

10 Sturtevant & Keep v. Ballard, 9 Johns. Ch. 337, 339-40 (N.Y. 1812).

the goods in his possession and thus will overestimate his creditworthiness. If the merchant failed or entered bankruptcy, the unsecured creditors would find that the debtor's assets were claimed as property by the secret transferee. This legitimate concern led courts routinely to invalidate such arrangements to protect the reliance of ordinary creditors.

As markets expanded and financing became more sophisticated, however, commercial interests argued for greater leniency to facilitate secured lending on the basis of equipment, inventory, and accounts receivable.[11] It made no commercial sense to take these commercial assets out of the possession of the borrower, who needed them to conduct his business and generate the revenue to repay the debt. A Virginia court admitted that such transactions were not actually fraudulent but objectionable because deceptive in fact. "A preventive of the evil may be found in requiring the parties to give notoriety to the transaction; but that is a matter beyond the province of judicial recognition, and requires the aid of legislative enactment."[12] State legislatures soon enacted diverse statutes that allowed creditors to obtain nonpossessory interests in certain of their debtor's property, provided they file a specific form of public notice. Interestingly, courts suspicious of such a legislative innovation sometimes invalidated chattel mortgages and other security interests on technicalities to protect the more familiar rights of unsecured creditors.[13] After many false starts and an accumulation of experience with various forms of collateral, these acts were superseded by the mid twentieth century by the general security interest in personal property provided by Article Nine of the Uniform Commercial Code.

This innovation decreased the rights of unsecured creditors and enhanced the rights of secured creditors. Under the common law approach, all the unsecured creditors together enjoyed a limited commons of sorts in the debtor's assets, consisting of a conditional right to appropriate them upon a court finding default by the debtor and obtaining exclusive rights through the process of levy and execution. Facilitating security interests worked a form of enclosure, under which the secured creditors' collateral was "walled off" from the debtor's general remaining assets, beyond the reach of the unsecured creditors' capture. These

---

11 Gilmore attributed the demand for secured credit to budding industrialism. "The unprecedentedly rapid expansion of industrial facilities created an equally unprecedented demand for credit....As industrialization progressed, personal rather than real property came to be the principal repository of wealth....[T]he medieval institution of pledge [could not] suffice to take up the slack: share certificates and bonds could be conveniently pledged but obviously the equipment of the factory, the rolling stock of the railroad, the stock in trade of the merchant could not be. And yet all this property which could not be pledged because it had to be used in the borrower's business represented a nearly inexhaustible source of prime collateral for loans." Grant Gilmore, Security Interests in Personal Property 25 (1965).

12 Davis v. Turner, 45 Va. (4 Gratt.) 422, 436 (Va. 1848).

13 Douglas G. Baird & Thomas H. Jackson, Security Interests in Personal Property 34-36 (2d ed. 1987).

security interests are property rights. When perfected by filing or otherwise, they are good against the whole world, respected in bankruptcy and protected by the Takings Clause. Unsecured creditors encountered a new obligation to check these records to determine if their debtor's assets were encumbered, depriving them of their traditional reliance on assets visibly in the debtor's possession. The filing system itself is a form of public property, which all can access, but which can charge a user's fee to those filing notices.

The creation of security interests in personal property required legislation. The new rules establishing the rights of secured creditors had to be promulgated comprehensively, synchronically, and prospectively. Court adjudication of individual cases might have evolved over time away from precedents treating nonpossessory security interest as fraudulent, although at real cost in confusion and unfairness, but could never have solved the notice problem. Only legislation and appropriations could create offices to receive and manage publicly available notices of creditor interests. Nor could courts create comprehensive legal systems to specify how such property interests could be created, perfected, and enforced, so that lenders would have confidence in the efficiency of the new devices. The emergence of security interest required changes in economic needs and legal attitudes, but also an advance in legal technology that made new rights and duties feasible. It now would be anachronistic to claim that security interests are not property because they depend on legislation and bureaucratic management, or because they limit the rights or frustrate traditional expectations of unsecured creditors. One may still criticize aspects of security interests as inefficient or unfair, even as "neo-feudal," but not competently argue that they are not property, despite their legislative origins and administrative operation.

Security interests do not involve obvious, ongoing discretionary judgments by public officials about the rights of the respective parties (leaving aside bankruptcy valuation). My second example thus pushes my argument further. Here I want to contrast the common law's inability to protect a property owner's interest in securing adequate light and air with the easy success of zoning in doing so prospectively through legislation and regulation. My claim will be that courts could not find a doctrinal path to protect reasonable sharing of the burden between neighbors to provide each other the benefit of adequate light and air not because they did not think it desirable but because of the limited lawmaking capacity of common law adjudication.[14]

Students of property law are familiar with the fact that American courts in the nineteenth century rejected the English "ancient lights" doctrine. Under that rule,

---

14 In an interesting contrast, several American jurisdictions provided another solution to the basic problem of compatible urban growth through enactment of party wall statutes, which amended the common law to allow either party to build a single wall on the property line that could be shared as could the costs and duties of repair. The party-wall rules for Washington, DC, were included in the building regulations promulgated by President Washington in 1791. *See* Miller v. Elliot, 17 F. Cas. 315 (C.C.D. D.C. 1839).

a landowner with windows overlooking his neighbor's land acquired an easement of light over his neighbor's land if he enjoyed uninterrupted access to the light for 20 years.[15] The consequence of establishing a right to ancient lights was to require the defendant to build back from his lot line or limit the height of his building so as not to block the plaintiff's windows. As such, of course, it protects the interest of the first window owner in preserving valuable natural light. Securing access to natural light for the interior of buildings was an important economic asset before electric lighting and chancy in early urban areas characterized by rapid and spotty development. We can understand it as an early device to manage urban growth so as to protect existing investments.

After some early reception, American courts came to reject the ancient lights doctrine decisively. In 1898, one treatise writer declared: "An easement in the unobstructed passage of light and air cannot be acquired by prescription. This is the rule now established in all the American states, with a single exception."[16] Courts offered a variety of reasons for this nearly unanimous conclusion, but can be grouped under both conceptual and policy arguments.

The conceptual arguments centered on the nature of prescription, which was viewed the sole legitimate means (other than consent) by which a court could restrict the later builder's height or lot coverage. The problem was that for the court to find a prescriptive right to light and air for the first builder, the second builder would had to have had a legal recourse against the first builder's invasion. As a New York court observed in an influential case, the owner whose neighbor's windows looked upon his land possesses no such legal remedy:

> Most of the cases on the subject we have been considering relate to ways, commons, markets, water-courses, and the like, where the use or enjoyment, if not rightful, has been an immediate and continuing injury to the person against whom the presumption is made. His property has either been invaded, or his beneficial interest in it has been rendered less valuable. The injury has been of such a character that he might have immediate redress by action. But in the case of windows overlooking the land of another, the injury, if any, is merely ideal or imaginary. The light and air which they admit are not the subjects of property beyond the moment of actual occupancy; and for overlooking one's privacy no action can be maintained.…If one commit a daily trespass on the land of another, under a claim of right to pass over, or feed his cattle upon it; or divert the water from his mill, or throw it back upon his land or machinery; in these and the like cases long continued acquiescence affords strong presumptive evidence of right. But in the case of lights, there is no adverse user, nor, indeed,

15 *See, e.g.*, Kevin Gray & Susan Francis Gray, Elements of Land Law 663-64, 707 (4th ed., 2005); Stephen Bickford-Smith & Andrew Francis, Rights of Light: the Modern Law 59-72 (2d ed. 2007).

16 Leonard A. Jones, A Treatise on the Law of Easements 465 (1898). The exception was Delaware.

> any use whatever of another's property; and no foundation is laid for indulging any presumption against the rightful owner.[17]

It was entirely permissible for the first builder to erect a house with windows looking over his neighbor's land; he did not thereby invade any legal right of the neighbor. Neither owned the ambient light and air. There being no trespass that the defendant could previously have sued to stop, the court had no basis to recognize a prescriptive right to light in the plaintiff. Without some ground in legally cognizable harm or consent, any adjustment of use rights would be viewed as illegitimate. "This right of the injured party is a cardinal fact that must exist, else all statutes of limitation, and all rules of prescription or of presumption, of license or grant, would be but rules of spoliation or robbery."[18] A similar set of concerns can be traced regarding judicial rejection of arguments for implied easement to light and air from earlier grants.[19]

Courts also advanced policy arguments for rejecting the ancient lights doctrine. They repeatedly expressed concerns that the rule would stifle development in "the growing cities and villages of this country."[20] The first building would obtain rights that could prevent or hinder subsequent building. The Illinois Supreme Court wondered whether such a first-in-time doctrine "has any adaptation at all to a country in the infancy of its improvements, containing hundreds of embryo cities and villages and thousands of vacant lots, waiting the demands of future population, for dwellings and other buildings for habitation and business."[21] The Texas Supreme Court made a similar point, worrying that the consequence would be "that the occupants of low and inferior houses, such as are usually the first erected in new towns, at the end of a few years, would acquire rights without any act of adverse possession, which might render useless and waste the most valuable lots for business purposes or residences in our growing towns and cities."[22]

Courts also worried that the ancient doctrine would encourage premature or wasteful construction by owners on vacant lots seeking to avoid become a servient estate. The Supreme Court of Pennsylvania observed that the doctrine of "ancient lights…should be introduced with caution. Many vacant lots in our towns and cities are owned by persons who reside at a distance, and who are either unable or unwilling to improve them. It would be inconvenient to compel them to do so, on the penalty of forfeiting a valuable right by neglect."[23] Some courts seemed particularly concerned about the demands the rule would place on small holders

17 Parker & Edgartonv. Foote, 19 Wend. 309, 316-17 (N.Y. 1838).

18 Mitchell v. Mayor and City Council of Rome, 49 Ga. 19, 26 (Ga. 1873). Contrast English approach to easements.

19 *See, e.g.*, Keats v. Hugo, 115 Mass. 204 (Mass. 1874).

20 Parker & Edgarton v. Foote, *supra* note 17, 19 Wend. at 318.

21 Gerber v. Grabel, 16 Ill. 217, 223 (Ill. 1854).

22 Klein v. Gehrung, 25 Tex. 232, 243 (Tex. 1860).

23 Hoy v. Sterrett, 2 Watts 327, 331 (Pa. 1837).

of modest means. Moreover, courts also were concerned that the doctrine would promote the unneighborly construction of "dead walls," erected only to defeat claims of prescription. One court speculated that an owner of an undeveloped lot would seek to save his rights "by some churlish or expensive appropriation of his property to uses or purposes hurtful to himself and offensive to his neighbor."[24]

So, to summarize, the courts rejected the doctrine of ancient lights because the first windowed house could not be understood to have invaded the rights of the neighboring lot owner, who should not be forced through legal fictions to sue his neighbor or erect a dead wall to protect his future capacity to develop fully. Recognition of a prescriptive right to light and air would have imposed serious barriers to rational development, giving existing building owners a right to block new, larger buildings in dynamic but scruffy cities. The courts understood the interest in securing natural light. But they had no institutional means to create a rule or institutions that could protect light without stunting future urban development.

Legislation and regulation largely solved these institutional problems (with a nice dollop of help from electricity). Although a variety of buildings and land use laws accomplished these ends,[25] for present purposes, I will concentrate on simple zoning law. More generally, zoning laws prospectively separated uses, imposed limitations on height, and mandated various set backs and limits on lot coverage that gave most buildings needed light and air. The institutional advantages of zoning to achieve this end over common law easements are legion. First, zoning acted prospectively to eliminate the inefficiency and unfairness of the first-in-time rule and the arbitrariness of the prescription period. Second, zoning imposed limits on all new construction creating a reciprocity of advantage and of burden, eliminating the zero-sum nature of prescriptive rights. Third, zoning provided certainty by specifying height and lot coverage limitations rather than leaving the parties to the vagaries of litigation and standards of reasonableness. Fourth, zoning could vary limitations by use and location, so that natural light could be protected more where most wanted or least expensive and not at all in dense commercial settings, unlike easements that would provide universal rights to all property owners irrespective of location. Fifth, zoning limits could be changed as conditions or needs changed, or adjusted in specific cases through variances or site specific alternative procedures, such as a Planned Unit Development.

The difference in outcomes regarding light and air does not reflect primarily normative disagreement about how land should be developed. Common law courts were not unsympathetic with the goals of parties arguing for securing natural light, but could not recognize their interests within their conceptual frame and without creating consequences putting beneficial development capriciously at risk. Finding for the plaintiff would give him too much control over the defendant. The ancient

24 Mitchell v. Mayor and City Council of Rome, 49 Ga. at 26.

25 Tenement laws, for example, beginning with New York's 1879 Tenement House Act, effectively required new multi-family buildings to have light and air shafts. 1879 N.Y. Laws ch. 504, § 3, *amended by* 1901 N.Y. Laws ch. 334.

lights doctrine seemed unwieldy and unfair. Zoning overcame these institutional barriers by acting prospectively, comprehensively, and mutually. It gave each lot owner both rights and duties that secured mutual advantage, encouraging development within a protective framework. It could recognize the interest in light without excessively burdening the neighbor. Common law courts had no doctrine by which they could restrict height and lot coverage without a finding of fault.

This aspect of zoning was recognized early on, even by Justice Sutherland in *Euclid.* His opinion for the Court contains a notorious passage in which he explained how an apartment building could be a nuisance to a single family house. He argued against the location near single family houses of apartment buildings, "interfering by their height and bulk with the free circulation of air and monopolizing the rays of the sun which otherwise would fall upon the smaller houses,"[26] Sutherland's nuisance analysis is fatally undermined by his using an argument for height and bulk regulations in support of an argument for use regulations (apartment buildings can and often have been built under height and set back limits, so as to be physically compatible with single family homes). But his more basic claim is certainly correct: zoning protects a resident's interests in light and air in a way that the common law could not.[27]

Zoning height and lot coverage regulations create new property rights. I have a right that my neighbor not build on more than some percentage of her lot, in order to maintain my enjoyment of light and air in my backyard. My rights do not depend on the priority or duration of my backyard but on sensible uniform requirements. I enforce my rights not by litigating against completed construction but by showing up at a local agency hearing to oppose my neighbor's permit. And we might have an argument or a compromise about a variance. But it seems deeply misleading to see this process as something external to the property system; rather it *is* the modern property system, adopted because the nineteenth-century version ceased to meet modern needs. None of this is to claim that zoning or other land use regulations do not pose numerous problems that cause legitimate unhappiness, but that solutions to these problems cannot come from liberating property from external shackles. We should not confuse the institutional limitations of common law judges (or the social imperatives of a sparsely settled country rich in land resources) with natural law.

Legislative innovations like zoning and security interests do not destroy or restrict property, they change the rules and institutions within which the property system operates. If I am right, why do traditional notions of property as pre-political rights persist? First, deeply ingrained notions of individual political and economic liberty grew up in the U.S. alongside expansive notions of private property, at least for white men. This is a complex subject, but sufficient for

26 Village of Euclid v. Ambler Realty Co., 272 U.S. 365, 394 (1926).

27 The development of solar energy presents new challenges for access to sunlight that requires new legal institutions. *See* Sara C. Bronin, *Modern Lights*, 80 Colo. L. R. 101 (2009).

now to posit that this reflected the economic and political ideology of a time of ample resources, small-scale enterprise, and rapid development. The property law for that time emphasized individual action. Small scale governments left large scope for judicial governance. Regulation came later with industrialization, immigration, and urbanization. These large social changes and the legal response to them were viewed by some as threatening the established order. Anxieties today about economic insecurity and impersonal forces draw on the powerful rhetoric of property rights to evoke a phantasm of secure liberty.

Second, legislation generally changes more rapidly than the common law evolves, thus threatening to upend established understandings and stable reliance that support both rational investment and personal autonomy. Regulatory takings law long has been viewed as judicial supervision of abrupt legal changes that unfairly destroy reasonable investment-backed expectations.[28] But the risk of unexpected change would seem to present a separate concern from the mode of law making. More fundamentally, law does not want to permit absolute reliance on legal stability but encourage owners to estimate the risks of and adjust prospectively to legal change, in order to avoid waste.[29] Moreover, legislative changes more often are predictable in a political process in which Owner A can participate, as opposed to a judicial change as a result of litigation in which the Owner A has no voice.[30] Finally, the regulatory takings doctrine provides some protection against legislative changes, but as of yet, no protection against judicial changes in common law rules.

Third, property rights rhetoric draws on an outsized concern about democratic politics being only a valueless scramble for self-interest.[31] According to the standard claim of law and economics, the legislative process is dominated by rent-seeking interests, while courts seek efficiency. But even bracketing the adequacy of this account, "There are a number of features of legislative decisionmaking that make it relatively more attractive than common-law decisionmaking as a basis for modifying or creating categories of property rights."[32] The features discussed in

28 The approach was theorized in Frank I. Michelman, *Property, Utility, and Fairness: Comments on the Ethical Foundations of "Just Compensation" Law*, 80 HARV. L. REV. 1165 (1967), and canonized in Penn Central Transportation Co. v. City of New York, 438 U.S. 104 (1978).

29 *See, e.g.*, Louis Kaplow, *An Economic Analysis of Legal Transitions*, 99 HARV. L. REV. 509 (1986).

30 *See* District Intown Properties v. District of Columbia, 198 F.3d 874 (D.C. Cir. 1999) (property owner should have foreseen designation of his property as an historic landmark).

31 Richard Epstein's view of the Takings Clause makes it the substantive regulator of all legislative decisions in place the essentially procedural rules of democracy specified in federal and state constitutions. *See generally* RICHARD EPSTEIN, SUPREME NEGLECT: HOW TO REVIVE CONSTITUTIONAL PROTECTION FOR PRIVATE PROPERTY (2008).

32 Thomas W. Merrill & Henry E. Smith, *Optimal Standardization in the Law of Property: The* Numerus Clausus *Principle*, 110 YALE L J. 1, 61 (2000).

this chapter are prospectivity, flexibility, capacity to create and fund institutions, democratic participation in rule formation, and the inclusion of more diffuse interests. The legislative innovations associated with security interests and with zoning lowered the governance costs required to accommodate and coordinate more interests in an asset compared with what the common law could achieve.[33]

Moreover, it seems fair to note the vast public support for protecting private property across our political spectrum. Indeed, much contemporary legislation seeks to harness private property to address social issues. The wide political embrace of a "cap and trade system" to reduce emissions of greenhouse gases provides an example. Michael Diamond's work, described elsewhere in this volume, developing affordable limited equity cooperative housing, provides another example. His projects create new opportunities for home ownership for low income residents, while limiting the amount of wealth any resident can accumulate in her home, in order to balance the wholesome incentives of ownership with maintenance of affordable housing.[34] Both examples exemplify the reasonable belief that private decisionmaking concerning assets, within a public normative framework, can advance the public interest more efficiently and with greater personal freedom than can governmental commands.

What follows from my argument in this chapter? Property measures, whatever their institutional form, should be evaluated on their capacities to enhance human welfare, including liberty and economic incentives, without tired rhetorical invocation of property rights. There are no barriers between the private and public dimensions of property. The test for legal innovation can only be whether it makes people better off in regard to relevant social goals. Property scholars need not have a bad conscience about blending the public and the private; they should be creative in imagining rights and duties in crafting new arrangements to meet new needs. We live in a world of tradable pollution permits and digital property commons licenses. It is property all the way down. Let creative proposals begin.

Acknowledgement

My thanks for research assistance go to Peter Amaro and Brett Marston.

33 *See* Henry E. Smith, *Exclusion Versus Governance: Two Strategies for Delineating Property Rights*, 31 J. Legal Stud. S453 (2002) (arguing that choices between exlusion and governance delineations of property rights vary with costs and benefits of each).

34 For a broader discussion of how limited equity coops fit into affordable housing policy, *see* J. Peter Byrne & Michael Diamond, *Affordable Housing, Land Tenure, and Urban Policy: the Matrix Revealed*, 34 Fordham Urb. L. J. 527 (2007).

Chapter 2

Explaining the Persistent Myth of Property Absolutism

David Fagundes

Introduction

Few Supreme Court decisions in recent years have generated as much public ire as 2005's *Kelo v. City of New London*.[1] Commentators across the political spectrum went apoplectic when the Court approved a Connecticut town's exercise of its eminent domain power to confiscate several homes as part of a comprehensive urban redevelopment plan,[2] and their reaction was mirrored in public sentiment.[3] Legislators reacted to the uproar by passing a series of sternly worded (though questionably effective) statutes designed to limit state eminent domain powers.[4] At the height of the public backlash, some anti-*Kelo* activists even spawned a movement to have Justice Souter's home in Keene, New Hampshire house

1 545 U.S. 469 (2005).

2 Rush Limbaugh, *Liberals Like Stephen Breyer Have Bastardized the Constitution*, Radio Transcript, Oct. 12, 2005, *available at* http://www.freerepublic.com/focus/f-news/1501453/posts (visited Dec. 20, 2006) (claiming that because of *Kelo*, "Government can kick the little guy out of his and her homes and sell those home to a big developer who's going to pay a higher tax base to the government. Well, that's not what the takings clause was about. It's not what it is about. It's just been bastardized, and it gets bastardized because you have justices on the court who will sit there and impose their personal policy preferences rather than try to get the original intent of the Constitution."); Ralph Nader, *Statement*, June 23, 2005, *available at* http://ml.greens.org/pipermail/ctgp-news/2005-June/000507.html (visited Dec. 21, 2006) (claiming that "The U.S. Supreme Court's decision in *Kelo v City of New London* mocks common sense, tarnishes constitutional law and is an affront to fundamental fairness.").

3 Michael Allan Wolf, *Hysteria versus History: Public Use in the Public Eye*, *in* Private Property, Community Development, and Eminent Domain 15, 16-22 (Robin Paul Malloy ed., 2008) (detailing the media and public backlash against *Kelo*).

4 *See The Castle Coalition—Citizens Fighting Eminent Domain Abuse*, *available at* http://www.castlecoalition.org/legislation/states/index.asp (compiling a list of state statutes designed to constrain eminent domain power); *see* Ilya Somin, *The Limits of Backlash: Assessing the Response to* Kelo, 93 Minn. L. Rev. 2100 (2009) (questioning the efficacy of these statutes).

condemned and converted into a site where libertarians and their friends could lament lost liberty.[5]

In contrast to the emotional public reaction to *Kelo*, few property commentators found the decision surprising (though many objected to its substance[6]). For most legal specialists, *Kelo* represented an unambitious and straightforward application of well-established Supreme Court precedent.[7] Indeed, the *Kelo* majority was phrased in terms of classic common-law minimalism, stressing the importance of both stare decisis and deference to democratically elected state governments.[8] While many commentators criticized *Kelo* as following a line of flawed precedent,[9] the decision itself merely reapplied principles that had been announced decades earlier and applied countless times since.[10] The gulf between the public's outraged reaction to *Kelo* and specialists' sense that the decision was predictable illustrates the more general point that specialist and lay conceptions of property differ substantially. This gap frames the question that lies at the core of this chapter: Why do lay instincts about property diverge so starkly from lawyers' understanding of the field?

That the institution of property has a public dimension comes as no surprise to those with formal legal training. While property exists primarily to facilitate and protect private ownership, these values exist in symbiosis with public-regarding elements. Examples abound. Zoning ordinances limit the scale and aesthetics of land development in accordance with public preferences. Easements and running covenants constrain owners' use of their land, even where the conditions were originally agreed to by their predecessors. And the state possesses authority to buy out landowners (even against their will) so long as it does so for public use. Though lawyers and academics reasonably disagree about the efficiency of these limitations on property owners' rights, these examples illustrate that the positive

5 *See* Wikipedia, *The Lost Liberty Hotel*, *available at* http://en.wikipedia.org/wiki/Lost_Liberty_Hotel (describing this failed effort).

6 Richard A. Epstein, *Blind Justices; the Scandal of* Kelo v. New London, Wall St. J., July 3, 2005, at Opinion. Epstein, like many *Kelo* critics, objected to the entire foundation of takings jurisprudence from which the case followed. From this perspective, *Kelo* was wrongly decided but not a surprising result.

7 *See* Marcilynn A. Burke, *Much Ado About Nothing:* Kelo v. City Of New London, Babbit v. Sweet Home, *and Other Tales From the Supreme Court*, 75 U. Cin. L. Rev. 663, 683 (2006) ("Perhaps the only surprising part of the [*Kelo*] decision was Justice Sandra Day O'Connor's scathing dissent[.]").

8 545 U.S. at 480-82 (invoking controlling prior precedent, and stressing "our long policy of deference to legislative judgments in this field").

9 *E.g.*, Epstein, *supra* note 6.

10 *E.g.*, Berman v. Parker, 348 U.S. 26 (1954) (holding that private property can be taken for public purposes, such as urban renewal, consistently with the Just Compensation Clause of the Fifth Amendment to the U.S. Constitution; Hawaii Housing Auth. v. Midkiff, 467 U.S. 229 (1984) (approving a state plan that enabled confiscation and redistribution of land held by highly concentrated private owners).

law of property exists not only to preserve the ownership rights of private parties, but attends also to the public good.

But as the popular outrage over *Kelo* illustrates, the lay public's understanding does not reflect any of this public/private tension. Just the contrary: The "conversational" view of property tends much more toward Blackstone's "despotic dominion" caricature, a binary conception that property is a simple matter of mine versus yours.[11] Well-worn clichés like "a man's home is his castle" illustrate the public's instinct that ownership rights have few if any limits, and this absolutist conception of possession extends beyond the real property setting, animating owners' attitudes toward taxation and intellectual property.[12]

This gap between the practical reality of property and popular conceptions of the institution is puzzling. Law normally guides social norms and beliefs, at least to a large extent. And property law has long embodied this tension between private interests and the public good, from early restrictions on the forms of estates in land to modern reconceptualizations of property as a system of social relations. One would think that in light of law's frequent indications about the ambivalence at the core of property, lay intuitions would follow suit and lead to a more balanced public understanding of the legal character of ownership. Yet the myth of property rights as absolute remains dominant in the popular imagination, persistent and sticky despite law's signals to the contrary.

I use this puzzle—the persistent myth of property absolutism—to frame the exploration that follows. What explains the divergence between specialist and popular conceptions of property? Is it possible to tell a story that makes sense of this gap? To answer these questions, I consider three such narratives—welfarism, essentialism, and behavioralism—and examine how each might (and might not) explain this puzzle. My aim is not to argue that any one of these narratives provides the sole or even the best solution to this puzzle, but rather to draw from different fields to find a multi-textured explanation for the lawyer/layperson variance.

This chapter proceeds as follows. Part I examines the divergence between popular conceptions of property and its legal reality, and explains why this disparity is particularly puzzling in light of our expectations about how law and social beliefs interact. Part II identifies three narratives drawing from different fields—law and economics, biology and psychology, and behavioral economics—and shows how each of them play a part in explaining this puzzle. The Conclusion discusses the implications of this investigation for the regulation of real property, and sounds a cautionary note about the seductiveness of unitary theoretical explanations of complex phenomena.

---

11 *See* Stephen L. Carter, *Does It Matter Whether Intellectual Property Is Property?*, 68 CHI.-KENT L. REV. 715, 717 (1993) (referring to the lay understanding of property as a simple matter of mine versus yours as "conversational property").

12 *See* sources cited *infra* notes 36-37.

Part I: The Puzzling Persistence of Property Absolutism

Lawyers and Laypeople: Two Understandings of Property

William Blackstone famously described property as "that despotic dominion that one man claims and exercises over the things of the world,"[13] and based on this well-worn observation, the term "Blackstonian" has come to refer to a simplistic, absolutist view of property. Yet this is more than a little unfair to Blackstone, whose views on property were actually much more complex and nuanced than the standard narrative lets on. Indeed, Blackstone spent the 518 pages of his *Commentaries* that follow the hoary "despotic dominion" phrasing disabusing readers of the notion that property is absolute, and cataloguing limitations on owners' rights.[14]

Correctly understood, Blackstone's *Commentaries* provide an early, apt example of law specialists' deeply conflicted view of property. Though much writing is devoted to understanding the nature of law's regulation of ownership, each attempt seems to exaggerate rather than resolve lawyers' and legal academics' internally discordant sense of the institution of legal ownership. The property literature is rife with fundamental disagreements about the nature of property itself. Writers in a libertarian vein emphasize the character of property as an atomizing institution that preserves a bulwark of personal autonomy against state interference.[15] Other scholars point to property's capacity to create and maintain communal bonds, suggesting that ownership is a deeply social, and socially contingent, institution, rather than a solely individualist one.[16] Some authors tend to regard property as a natural right that pre-exists the state, and that its essential elements (e.g., the right to exclude) should be protected from interference even by democratic means.[17] Others take the positivist view that property amounts to whatever the state says it is. This is the familiar

---

13 2 William Blackstone, Commentaries on the Laws of England 2 (facsimile ed. 1979) (1765-69) ("There is nothing which so generally strikes the imagination, and engages the affections of mankind, as the right of property; or that sole and despotic dominion which one man claims and exercises over the external things of the world, in total exclusion of the right of any other individual in the universe.").

14 Joan Williams, *The Rhetoric of Property*, 83 Iowa L. Rev. 277, 281 (1989) (observing that Blackstone's *Commentaries* focus largely on limits on private ownership); Richard A. Epstein, *Intellectual Property: Old Boundaries and New Frontiers*, 76 Ind. L.J. 802, 805 (2001) (calling Blackstone's "despotic dominion" phrasing an "injudicious overgeneralization").

15 *See, e.g.*, Milton Friedman, Capitalism and Freedom 7-21 (1962); F.A. Hayek, The Constitution of Liberty 139-41 (1960).

16 *See, e.g.*, Eduardo Penalver, *Property as Entrance*, 91 Va. L. Rev. 1889, 1894 (2005).

17 For arguments critical of robust use of the eminent domain power, see Richard A. Epstein, Takings: Private Property and the Power of Eminent Domain (1986). *Cf. also* Thomas W. Merrill, *Property and the Right to Exclude*, 77 Neb. L. Rev. 730, 730

"bundle of sticks" conception, according to which property is merely a socially constructed relation of ownership between persons with respect to things,[18] so that government can define—and take away—ownership interests however it sees fit.[19]

The positive law of property evinces similar tensions. While the protection of private ownership lies at its core, property law also exhibits a litany of limitations on and exceptions to these rights. Some of these limits are designed to mediate between competing possessory interests. Easements and covenants that run with the land, for example, cabin owners' rights in order to facilitate use and development by neighbors, and can be enforced even against owners who are not parties to the original agreement. Other constraints on owners' rights are public-regarding. Zoning ordinances and the eminent domain power curb land development and enable forced sales in the public interest. Law also restricts private property rights in order to preserve easements for access to public lands[20] and in order to allow the exercise of basic freedoms.[21] Incorporeal property is subject to similar prescriptions. Sales of stocks, intrafamilial transfers, and estate inheritance are typically subject to mandatory federal taxation. And ownership

(1998) (arguing that "the right to exclude other is more than just 'one of the most essential' constituents of property—it is the sine qua non").

18 Restatement (1st) of Property *Introductory Note* (1936) (defining property as a "legal relation[] between persons with respect to a thing"); *see also* Morris Cohen, *Property and Sovereignty* 13 Cornell L.Q. 8, 13 (1927); A.M. Honoré, *Ownership*, *in* Oxford Essays in Jurisprudence 107, 128-30 (A.G. Guest ed., 1961) (emphasizing that ownership describes relations between persons and other persons, not between persons and objects of ownership).

19 Joseph Singer, Entitlement: The Paradoxes of Property 95-139 (2000) (discussing property as a "system [of] social relations" that accounts for the rights of owners as well as the interests of non-owners); Stephen Munzer, *Property as Social Relations*, *in* New Essays on the Legal and Political Theory of Property 36-37 (Stephen Munzer, ed., 2001) (surveying the work of writers who conceive of property as a constructed system of social relations rather than solely as ownership and exclusion).

20 *See* Matthews v. Bay Head Improvement Ass'n, 471 A.2d 355 (N.J. 1984) (upholding creation of easement by public necessity over privately owned land to allow access to public beach); Raleigh Ave. Beach Ass'n v. Atlantis Beach Club, Inc., 879 A.2d 112, 121-24 (N.J. 2005).

21 *See, e.g.*, PruneYard Shopping Center v. Robins, 447 U.S. 74 (1980) (upholding California Supreme Court's construing state constitution to require owners of private shopping centers to allow certain kinds of speech on the premises).; State v. Shack, 277 A.2d 369, 371 (N.J. 1971) (holding that property owners' rights were limited by needs of resident workers to receive social services).

of intellectual property exists subject to a host of constraints, such as the fair use defense[22] and the first sale doctrine.[23]

In this chapter, I take no position on the substance of these debates about the nature of property or the appropriate balance of public and private interests in the regulation of ownership. I mention them only to illustrate that specialists' views of property reflect consciousness of deep divisions and disagreement about the character of the institution. In fact, if we can say that property has an essential nature, it may lie in that very tension. It is an institution that enshrines individualism and binds society together, all at the same time.[24] I mention law specialists' understanding of property also to illustrate how much lay conceptions of property differ from it. Lay views of property are as simple and monist as specialist views of property are nuanced and pluralist. As numerous commentators have observed, the public tends to regard property as a straightforward matter of mine versus yours,[25] without reflecting much if any consciousness of the various limits that positive law places on ownership rights.[26] While specialists (including enthusiasts of strong property rights) understand that property cannot be reduced to

---

22 Copyright and trademark are both subject to different variations of a fair use defense, permitting use of protected works or marks under certain conditions. *See* 17 U.S.C. § 107(2010) (creating a four-factor test for fair use of copyrighted works of authorship); Century 21 Real Estate Corp. v. LendingTree, Inc., 425 F.3d 211 (3d Cir. 2005) (discussing the trademark doctrine of nominative fair use).

23 The first sale doctrine, forms of which exist in copyright, trademark, and patent law, permits resale of legitimately purchased copies of protected intellectual property. *See* 17 U.S.C. § 109 (2010) (copyright first-sale doctrine); Quanta Computer, Inc. v. LG Elecs., Inc., 553 U.S. 617 (2008) (patent first-sale doctrine); Champion Spark Plug Co. v. Sanders, 331 U.S. 125 (1947) (trademark first-sale doctrine).

24 Carol Rose, Mahon *Reconsidered: Why the Takings Issue is Still Such a Muddle*, 57 S. Cal. L. Rev. 561, 593-97 (1984) (observing that "[o]ur traditional discourse envisions property as serving quite divergent purposes").

25 *See* Vincent Chiappetta, *The (Practical) Meaning of Property*, 46 Willamette L. Rev. 297, 312-13 (2010) (describing the "instinctive 'mine not yours' view of property" generally shared by the lay public); Thomas Grey, *The Disintegration of Property*, *in* XXII Nomos: Property 69 (J. Roland Pennock & John W. Chapman, eds.) ("Most people, including most specialists in their unprofessional moments, conceive of property as things owned by persons. To own property is to have exclusive control of something—to be able to use it as one wishes, to sell it, give it away, leave it idle, or destroy it. Legal restraints on the free use of one's property are conceived as departures from an ideal conception of full ownership.").

26 *See* Jeremy Waldron, The Right to Private Property 27 (1988) (noting this distinction between lay perceptions and specialized definitions of property); Grey, *supra* note 25, at 69 ("In the English-speaking countries today, the conception of property held by the specialist (the lawyer or economist) is quite different from that held by the ordinary person."); Bruce Ackerman, Private Property and the Constitution 97-100, 113-67 (1977) (distinguishing perceptions of property held by "ordinary observers" from those held by "scientific policymakers").

a "despotic dominion,"[27] that phrasing roughly describes the property absolutism that prevails among the lay public.[28]

This popular property absolutism may not actually track the reality of the positive law, but its prevalence is apparent in the deeply emotional reactions laypeople have to any perceived incursion on their property rights. As we have seen, the strident public reaction to *Kelo v. City of New London*[29] derived to a large extent from powerful moral intuitions about the wrongfulness of state takings of private property,[30] even though the law of eminent domain has long historical roots. Owners have chained themselves to their (former) homes upon foreclosure, even where the bank's repossession is an agreed-upon and legal incident of failure to make mortgage payments.[31] Feuding neighbors use their land as sites to express antipathy for one another by building elaborate spite structures,[32] even though law does not permit their construction.[33] Entire communities have demonstrated in anger to protest legally valid acquisitions by one landowner of a neighbor's land via adverse possession.[34] Landowners often engage in apparently disproportionate violence to protect the security of their homes against intruders (often with law's blessing[35]). Popular critics deride even longstanding marginal

27 *E.g.*, Richard A. Epstein, *Intellectual Property: Old Boundaries and New Frontiers*, 76 Ind. L.J. 802, 805 (2001) (calling Blackstone's "despotic dominion" phrasing an "injudicious overgeneralization").

28 Williams, *supra* note 14 at 285-86 (1989) (discussing popular property absolutism).

29 545 U.S. 469 (2005) (upholding a state court determination that a city's taking of private homes for the purpose of economic development did not offend the U.S. Constitution's "public use" requirement).

30 *See* Thomas W. Merrill & Henry E. Smith, *The Morality of Property*, 48 Wm. & Mary L. Rev. 1849, 1882 (2007) (observing that the public reaction to *Kelo* resided in "basic moral intuitions, not pragmatic balancing or cost-benefit analysis").

31 *See, e.g.*, Steve Rode, *Woman Chains Self to Home to Prevent Foreclosure*, *available at* http://getoutofdebt.org/2533/woman-chains-self-to-home-to-prevent-foreclosure. *See also generally* Jeannie Suk, *Taking the Home*, 20 L. & Literature 291, 295-98 (2008) (discussing the distinctive psychological importance of the home). *But cf.* Stephanie Stern, *Residential Protectionism and the Legal Mythology of Home*, 107 Mich. L. Rev. 1093 (2009) (citing psychological data suggesting that home ownership does not increase individual well-being).

32 *See e.g.*, Mike Industries, *When Your Neighbor Builds a Jackass Home*, *available at* http://www.mikeindustries.com/blog/archive/2008/07/when-your-neighbor-builds-a-jackass-home.

33 *See* Jesse Dukeminier et al., Property 645 (6th ed.) (2006) (observing that most jurisdictions find nuisance liability for the construction of spite fences).

34 *See* John Aguilar, *Hard Feelings on Hardscrabble Drive*, Daily Camera, Nov. 19, 2007, *available at* http://www.dailycamera.com/news/2007/nov/19/protest-draws-hundreds-hard-feelings-on-drive/; David Harsanyi, *Property Right Wrongly Taken*, Denver Post, Nov. 19, 2007, *available at* http://www.denverpost.com/harsanyi/ci_7501264.

35 *See, e.g.*, State v. Carothers, 594 N.W.2d 897, 901, 903-04 (Minn. 1999) (reasoning that one has no duty to retreat before using deadly force to prevent a felony in the home); *see also* Richard A. Posner, *Killing or Wounding to Protect a Property Interest*, 14 J.L.

taxes on only the very wealthy as unconscionable incursions on sacred ownership prerogatives.[36] Copyright and patent owners invoke the sanctity of their property when seeking ever broader ownership rights, refer even to licit uses of their works and inventions as "theft."[37] This is not to say that the public remains unaware of *any* limits on property rights.[38] Everyone understands that they must pay property taxes (however much they may dislike it), and it is probably generally accepted that property rights are not so extreme that they would permit, say, killing any trespasser.[39] These marginal exceptions do not, however, diminish the force of the general observation that lay attitudes about property presume a much less limited suite of entitlements than the law actually creates.[40]

My repeated references to the lay public raise an obvious definitional question, and so I pause here to delimit that term. For the purposes of this chapter, I use "lay public" to refer generally to prevalent contemporary American ideas and attitudes. Other cultural and ethnic groups may well not have understood property in absolute terms. Many Native Americans, for example, thought about property in a way that rejected the idea of atomized ownership outright.[41]

& ECON. 201, 204 (1971) (justifying this rule by arguing that the fact of home invasion connotes greater risk than other kinds of robberies).

36 *E.g.*, Kenn Jacobine, *U.S. Property Rights in Line with Tenets of Communism*, *available at* http://blogcritics.org/politics/article/us-property-rights-in-line-with/ (lamenting estate tax as an offense to property rights) (last visited Aug. 9, 2010).

37 *E.g.*, Ronald A. Cass, *Patent Remedy*, WALL ST. J., Aug. 28, 2007, *available at* http://online.wsj.com/article/SB118824874547610202.html (stating that those who endorse compulsory patent licenses "oppose protection of all property rights"); *see also* David Fagundes, *Property Rhetoric and the Public Domain*, 94 MINN. L. REV. 652, 661-67 (2010) (discussing invocations of property rhetoric in defense of expanded IP rights).

38 And public perceptions of property rights may change situationally. An owner may adopt a more absolutist posture when their own property rights are threatened, and a more cabined conception of ownership when they stand to benefit from limits on ownership entitlements. Some scholars have suggested that social norms (separately from positive law) reflect this more accommodating view of property rights. *See* Gregory Alexander, *The Social-Obligation Norm in American Property Law*, 94 CORNELL L. REV. 745 (2009).

39 Some state laws come closer to this than one might imagine. In Florida, for example, real property owners are permitted to kill home intruders without any obligation to retreat. Fla. Stat. Ann. § 776.013(4) (West Supp. 2008); *see also Florida Legislation—The Controversy Over Florida's New "Stand Your Ground" Law—Fla. Stat. 776.013 (2005)*, 33 FLA. ST. U. L. REV. 351, 355 (2005).

40 Even some specialists espouse something approaching absolutism when characterizing property. *Cf., e.g.*, RICHARD PIPES, PROPERTY AND FREEDOM xv (1999) (characterizing property as "the right of the owner or owners, formally acknowledged by public authority, both to exploit assets to the exclusion of everyone else and to dispose of them by sale or otherwise").

41 PETER MATHIESSEN, INDIAN COUNTRY 118 (Penguin 1994) ("[W]hen we speak of land, we are not speaking of property, territory, or even a piece of ground upon which our houses sit and our crops are grown, we are speaking of something truly sacred.") (quoting Jimmie Durham, Eastern Band of Cherokees).

Historically, slaves in the United States responded to their dispossession and disenfranchisement by rejecting the idea of property's sanctity, often manifesting in an indifference or even hostility to the notion of ownership.[42] And some Western European nations exhibit a more communitarian attitude toward property than the absolutism that tends to prevail in the United States.[43] Thus it may be that that property absolutism is a distinctly American phenomenon, perhaps because lay strong-property instincts derive from a Wild-West "frontier mentality" (whether real or idealized).[44]

The Unusual Stickiness of Property Absolutism

The persistence of popular notions of property absolutism is puzzling. While harmless social or cultural beliefs like folk tales may continue thanks to word of mouth,[45] law is (or at least should be) different. Sources of positive law provide an external referent against which belief about the scope of rights can be objectively measured. Law's regulatory signals are often simple and clear, as where signs tell drivers that they may not drive faster than 65 miles per hour on a freeway, employers that they may not fire people solely on the basis of race and gender, and politicians that they may only accept capped amounts of political donations from donors. While individuals may object to the content of these and other laws, the state nevertheless places an affirmative duty on citizens to be cognizant of these demands, as the familiar maxim *ignorantia legis neminem excusat*[46] expresses.

Nor is the social impact of law limited to notifying the public of the legality of specific, easily defined conduct, such as the speed limits and campaign donation caps. Less crystalline fields, such as constitutional law, possess a teaching function

42 *See* Remembering Slavery: Africans-Americans Talk About Their Personal Experiences of Slavery and Emancipation 192-94, 249-51 (Iral Berlin, Marc Favreau & Steven Miller eds., 1998) (collecting oral testimony from slaves indicating willingness to steal their owners' chattel property under certain circumstances). Thanks to Kali Murray for helping me develop this point.

43 *Cf.* Benito Arrunada & Veneta Andonova, *Common Law and Civil Law as Pro-Market Adaptations*, 26 Wash. U. J.L. & Pub. Pol'y 81, 114 (2008) (illustrating that continental European legal systems and attitudes reflect ambivalence about property rights).

44 *See* Thorstein Veblen, Absentee Ownership and Business Enterprise in Recent Times: The Case of America ch.7 (1923) (arguing that property fetishism is particularly strong in America due thanks to our frontier mentality); J.B. Ruhl, *Ecosystem Services and the Common Law of the "Fragile Land System,"* 20 Natural Resources & Environment 3, 8 (observing that "property law was influenced by our nation's boundless frontier mentality").

45 For a fascinating account of one kind of persistent folk belief—rumors of pernicious conspiracies that are common in African-American communities—see Patricia A. Turner, I Heard It Through the Grapevine: Rumor in African-American Culture (1993).

46 "Ignorance of the law excuses no one."

that has the capacity to shape social norms.[47] The antidiscrimination reforms of the post-World War II era epitomize law's capacity to change even emotionally charged, deeply engrained social beliefs. For example, while *Brown v. Board of Education*[48] was resisted substantially in the first years following its issuance, the federal government's insistence on the moral decrepitude of segregation eventually led to integration in schools and other public institutions. And while it would obviously be premature to suggest that America's race problems have been solved,[49] today's nation is much more integrated and tolerant than it was in the Jim Crow era—in its attitudes as well as its institutions—to a large extent because of law's demanding a baseline of racial equality.

And in light of the malleability of social beliefs and norms in the face of legal reforms, the persistent myth of property absolutism presents a vexing exception.[50] As Blackstone's discussion of the institution in his commentaries suggest,[51] property has from its inception been an institution that limits as well as protects private owners.[52] Indeed, the English crown issued edicts limiting owners' rights to transfer at least as far back as the thirteenth century. And during the last century, the ambivalence surrounding the public/private dialectic within property has only increased. From legal realism in the early part of the twentieth century[53] to

47 *See* Scott L. Cummings & Deborah L. Rhode, *Public Interest Litigation: Insights from Theory and Practice*, 36 Fordham Urb. L.J. 603, 606-25 (2009) (describing law's capacity to effect social change); *cf.* Jack M. Balkin & Reva B. Siegel, *Principles, Practices, and Social Movements*, 154 U. Pa. L. Rev. 927 (2006) (discussing law's capacity to effect change in concert with social movements).

48 Brown v. Bd. of Educ. of Topeka, 347 U.S. 483 (1954).

49 For example, the Supreme Court has moved away from its mid-century holdings in favor of school integration, in some instances even refusing to permit reassignment on the basis of race in order to achieve integration. *See, e.g.*, Parents Involved in Community Schools. v. Seattle School District No. 1, 551 U.S. 701 (2007) (prohibiting assignment of students to public schools solely for the purpose of achieving racial integration, and declining to recognize racial balancing as a compelling state interest).

50 Criminal law scholarship provides one exception. Work in that field both observes several divergences between lay instincts about punishment and positive law, *see generally, e.g.*, Norman J. Finkel, Commonsense Justice: Juror's Notions of the Law (1995), and explores how the state's punitive strategies diverge from these instincts, *see, e.g.*, Paul H. Robinson & John Darley, *Intuitions of Justice: Implications for Criminal Law and Justice Policy*, 81 S. Cal. L. Rev. 1, 8-10 (2007).

51 *See supra* text at note 14.

52 *See* The Statute of Westminster the Second (*De Donis Conditionalibus*) (1285) (c. 1), *available at* http://www.statutelaw.gov.uk/content.aspx?activeTextDocId=1517444 (English statute responding to judicial construction of fees simple conditional by creating the fee tail).

53 *See, e.g.*, Felix S. Cohen, *Dialogue on Private Property*, 9 Rutgers L. Rev. 357, 361 (1954).

the New Property many decades later,[54] the notion of property underwent basic changes in the past hundred years, and the judicial and legislative product of this has been a institution that, more than ever, seeks to calibrate private profit with the public good. Yet despite the passage of zoning and environmental laws that restrict development, increased exercise of the state's eminent domain power, and countless other visible and evident limits on owners' rights, popular conceptions of property appear not to have budged from their Blackstonian baseline.[55] Rather, property remains simple matter of absolute rights in the public consciousness. Why have lay beliefs about legal ownership proven distinctively impervious to law's signals to the contrary? In the following Part, I examine three theories that may shed light on this question.

Part II: Explaining the Persistent Myth of Property Absolutism: Three Conjectures

A Welfarist Story

One way to think about the law, most commonly associated with the law and economics school, is that regulation should be organized around core principles

---

54 *See generally* Charles A. Reich, *The New Property*, 73 YALE L.J. 733 (1963-64) (articulating a broad vision of property that would extend to intangibles like labor or state entitlements, not only real property and chattels).

55 There are instances where lay instincts about strong property rights accord with the law. For example, most lay people have instincts about first possession that line up with common law principles about acquisition. Ori Friedman, *First Possession: An Assumption Guiding Inferences About Who Owns What*, 15 PSYCHONOMIC BULL. & REV. 290 (2008). Recent work has also shown that the author-protective moral rights principles of the Visual Artist Rights Act accord with lay intuitions about control over one's property. Barbara Spellman & Frederick Schauer, *Symposium: A Psychological Perspective on Property Law: Artists' Moral Rights and the Psychology of Ownership*, 83 TUL. L. REV. 661, 674-76 (2009). Some research also indicates that accession doctrine, and in particular the reluctance to extend property rights to bad-faith value-adders, matches with laypersons' instincts. Jay Hook, *Judgments About the Right to Property from Preschool to Adulthood*, 17 L. & HUM. BEHAV. 135, 144 (2002).

These studies are consistent with, rather than contradictory of, the notion that there is a general divergence between lay perceptions and expert understandings of property, because they illustrate that in the many instances where law creates owner-friendly rules, those rules match with lay strong-property assumptions. Where law deviates from strong ownership norms, popular perceptions tend not to follow. *See* Janice Nadler & Shari Seidman Diamond, *Eminent Domain and the Psychology of Property Rights: Proposed Use, Subjective Attachment, and Taker Identity*, 5 J. EMPIRICAL LEGAL STUD. 713 (2008) (showing that actors' attachment to their homes correlated positively with the length of home ownership, even though eminent domain law does not reflect this factor in valuing just compensation awards).

of welfare maximization. Two central tenets of this law-and-economics approach, in its simplest form, are the assumption that humans rationally seek to maximize their individual utility, and that efficiency (in a roughly Benthamite utilitarian sense of creating the greatest good for the greatest number) should be law's core organizing principle.[56] This narrative, which I will call the welfarist story[57] for the purposes of this chapter, provides a baseline from which to begin exploring the persistence of property absolutism. Indeed, two of the most foundational law and economics theories of the later twentieth century have property at their core. Coase famously showed that, in the absence of transaction costs, actors will redistribute entitlements (including property rights) to the owner that values them most highly, regardless of initial legal baselines.[58] Demsetz argued that property emerges as (and because) resources become more privately valuable.[59] Each of these stories about property share a common theme: actors acquire, possess, and trade things in order to maximize their welfare, and property law exists primarily to enable the ownership and transfer of entitlements in those things.

The welfarist account provides a parsimonious explanatory framework for the pervasiveness of lay property absolutism. In a nutshell, the story is that laypeople cling to a Blackstonian vision of property because that vision of property is most likely to maximize their own wealth. Here's why: The rational-actor assumption states that what primarily drives human behavior is the maximization of individual welfare.[60] Property entitlements enable individual wealth accretion by allowing actors to extract value from the things they own.[61] By contrast, limits on those

56 Richard Posner, Economic Analysis of Law 3-10 (6th ed. 2003) (baseline assumptions animating economic analysis of law). Whether these assumptions hold up in a broader sense has been brought into question by numerous studies showing that actors' conduct is not nearly as rationally utility-maximizing as law-and-economics would predict. *See, e.g.*, Ward Farnsworth, *Do Parties to Nuisance Cases Bargain After Judgment? A Glimpse Inside the Cathedral*, 66 U. Chi. L. Rev. 373 (1999) (showing that people do not engage in economically rational bargaining following judicial allocation of entitlements simply because, as a result of litigation, they dislike each other).

57 The phrasing is imperfect and deployed as an operational definition rather than in an attempt to equate welfarism with law and economics. There are other normative organizing principles that rely on measures of social welfare but use different analytical tools or value systems than those endemic to law and economics. The behavioral variation on law and economics furnishes one such example.

58 Ronald Coase, *The Problem of Social Cost*, 3 J. L. & Econ. 1 (Oct. 1960). Less familiar than the standard summary of this traditional "Coasean" insight is that *The Problem of Social Cost* stressed the extent to which transaction costs are ubiquitous, so that idealized reallocation around initial baselines would be unlikely to occur.

59 Harold Demsetz, *Toward a Theory of Property Rights*, 79 Am. Econ. Rev. Proc. 347 (1967).

60 *See* Posner, *supra* note 56, at 3.

61 Whether such limits also diminish social welfare presents a harder case. Limits on property rights may be suboptimal because they sap actors' incentives to engage in socially productive behavior. On the other hand, limits on property rights may enhance net welfare

property entitlements—the panoply of statutory or common law limits on rights of use, exclusion, and transfer—diminish the value of things to their owners by limiting their ability to derive value from them. An owner of an unzoned parcel can use their land for whatever purpose they value most highly—they can build a factory, open up a convenience store, or construct a seven-room McMansion with driveway space for many HumVees. Or they can choose to sell, and will have a wide variety of buyers at their disposal, creating more demand and driving up the land's price. By contrast, the owner of land designated only for residential development (with accompanying setback and height limitations as well as aesthetic zoning restrictions) may be able to extract value from their parcel, but on average will find that value to be lower than the unconstrained owner, because use limitations tend to drive down demand for real property.

Perhaps, then, all we need to unlock the puzzle of popular property absolutism is a good dose of simple welfarist analysis. Maybe lay people cleave to a belief in the absolute character of property rights because it is a product of innate self-interest. Broader property entitlements give rights-holders greater ability to extract value from the things they own, so a rational utility maximizer will instinctively gravitate toward a broad vision of property because that will tend to enhance individual welfare. On this view, then, property absolutism is a predictable strategic choice designed to maximize individual welfare by creating private wealth. Examined more closely, though, questions emerge that take away from the explanatory force of this narrative.

First, this basic welfarist approach lacks explanatory breadth. It may account for why lay people who own substantial amounts of property (and thus stand to gain from broad entitlements) gravitate toward absolutism, but it does not explain why virtually *all* lay people adopt this approach. About 60% of Americans own real property (typically a personal residence),[62] but what the welfarist story cannot explain is that even individuals who are not property owners share a belief in property absolutism.[63] The puzzle grows when we broaden the definition of property beyond land. Wealth in the United States remains highly stratified, with

---

by correcting market failures that would go unremedied in the absence of law. *Compare* Robert Cooter & Thomas Ulen, Law and Economics 51 (1988) (arguing that social welfare can be measured simply by adding up individual welfare) *with* Wendy Gordon, *Fair Use as Market Failure*, 82 Colum. L. Rev. 1600 (1982) (arguing that fair use is a necessary limit on copyright owners' entitlements because it enables socially valuable expression that would otherwise be precluded due to transaction costs).

62 About two-thirds of Americans owned their homes as of 2008, though these figures do not take into account the full impact of the housing crash of the late 2000s, and the vast majority of these homes are owned subject to a substantial mortgage, and increasingly with very little equity. *see* Wikipedia, *Home Ownership in the United States, available at* http://en.wikipedia.org/wiki/Homeownership_in_the_United_States (last visited Aug. 10, 2010).

63 To take just one example, 2008's political flavor of the month, Joe "the Plumber" Wurtzelbacher, staunchly opposed President Obama's proposed tax increases as redistributionist, even though Wurzelbacher (who had twice been on welfare) did not

about 10% of the population enjoying about 90% of the country's wealth.[64] These kinds of disparities mean that the welfarist story actually predicts the *opposite* of what we see: Pure self-interest should drive many people to want a weak vision of property that enables redistribution of income in their direction.[65]

Second, the welfarist story lacks explanatory depth because it does not explain the real puzzle of property absolutism: Why lay attitudes about property remain Blackstonian despite law's longstanding signals to the contrary. In the vast majority of instances, we understand what the law requires of us (even if we opt not to comply), even if we do not like it. I may want to drive fast, and I may even feel as though I should be legally entitled to do so, but this does not change the fact that I am well aware of the general 65 miles per hour speed limit. The puzzle of property absolutism is not a puzzle about why people want strong property rights, but about why people continue to perceive ownership rights as absolute even though positive law does not comport—and has never comported—with this impression. Welfarism, and in particular, simple self-interest, may account for why laypeople desire a property system that allows them to create as much private individual wealth as possible, but it does not explain why laypeople still have a broader notion of their ownership entitlements than law actually creates.

These latter two points do not take away entirely from the explanatory force that the welfarist story brings to bear on the myth of property absolutism. In many individual cases, lay beliefs in Blackstonian property may be inspired by nothing more than good old selfishness. But welfarism lacks sufficient breadth and depth to explain the phenomenon across the entire lay population, so it remains necessary to look further to complete the story.

An Essentialist Story

As the above subpart explains, welfarism provides a helpful starting place for exploring the persistent myth of property absolutism, but one of its failings is that it lacks explanatory breadth. That is, it cannot explain the universality of the lay strong-property instinct in a society characterized by substantial disparities in wealth and ownership. This shortcoming requires us to seek an explanation that looks to qualities possessed by all actors. This points to another possible

---

remotely earn enough money to have his taxes raised by Obama's plan. *See* Wikipedia, *Joe the Plumber*, *available at* http://en.wikipedia.org/wiki/Joe_the_Plumber.

64 Arthur B. Kennickell, "A Rolling Tide: Changes in the Distribution of Wealth in the U.S., 1989-2001," U.S. Federal Reserve Board, August 2003, http://www.federalreserve.gov/pubs/oss/oss2/papers/concentration.2001.10.pdf.

65 To take one salient example, some evidence indicates that American slaves, who were both treated as someone else's property and disenfranchised from possessing anything of their own, occasionally refused to respect the institution of ownership. *See* Remembering Slavery, *supra* note 42. The prevalence of property absolutism in the face of wealth concentration may also say a lot about contemporary Americans' persistent belief in their future wealth, regardless of the reasonableness of such a belief.

story, which I refer to as an essentialist one.[66] Perhaps property absolutism is not a conscious, strategic choice made in order to maximize individual wealth, but a product of pre-legal inclinations that we all share, whether as a result of biological predispositions or strongly engrained social norms.

Scholars have long claimed that property instincts are engrained in human consciousness. Centuries ago, James Kent observed that "[t]he sense of property is inherent in the human breast."[67] Recent social science has provided some support for these assertions. For this essentialist account to work, there must some evidence that people have strong possessive instincts that drive popular beliefs in property absolutism. And in fact, some researchers have found suggestions that property instincts do have biological roots.[68] One study showed that speckled wood butterflies and swallowtail butterflies behave consistently with the first-possession instinct. They are relatively more aggressive in defending resources that they have acquired first, and relatively deferential in defending resources that they acquired as subsequent possessors.[69] Perhaps more surprisingly, animals' property-like instincts even include other-regarding preferences. When a rogue bird seeks to occupy a nest that rightly belongs to a particular raven, that bird will be attacked not only by the nest-owning raven, but also by other, unrelated ravens who perceive the attacks as a usurpation of the preexisting "ownership" regime.[70] Other work seems to indicate that when it comes to property, chimpanzees exhibit some of the same cognitive biases that humans do, valuing owned objects in a manner consistent with the endowment effect.[71]

It goes without saying that humans are not ravens or monkeys, so merely showing that nonhuman animals possess qualities of acquisitiveness that remind us of our legal rules concerning ownership does not tell us enough—or perhaps even anything at all—about whether property rules inhere in *homo sapiens*.[72] The results of these animal studies, though, have been replicated to an extent in

---

66 As with "welfarism," I pause to specify the operational definition of "essentialism" for the purpose of this chapter. I use the term to include all pre-legal inclinations that might lead actors to adopt Blackstonian views of property, whether the product of biological predisposition or responses to social cues and norms. My use of the term "essentialist" should not be taken to imply that property instincts possess an exclusively biological cause.

67 James Kent, Commentaries on American Law 319 (1836). Thanks to Art McEvoy for pointing me in the direction of Kent's *Commentaries*.

68 *See* Jeffrey Evans Stake, *The Property Instinct*, 359 Phil. Trans. R. Soc. Lond. 1763, 1763 (2004) (suggesting that "fundamental principles of property are encoded in the human brain").

69 *See id.* at 1764.

70 *See id.* at 1767.

71 Sara Brosnan, et al., *Endowment Effects in Chimpanzees*, 17 Current Biology 1704, 1706 (2007).

72 *See* Brian Leiter & Michael Weisberg, *Why Evolutionary Biology Is (So Far) Irrelevant to Legal Regulation*, 29 L. & Phil. 31, 63-65 (2010) (arguing that non-human animal studies show little or nothing about human behavior).

work about humans. For example, experiments showed that young (two- to three-year-old) children tend to follow a first-possession rule structure when ascribing ownership of objects.[73] Adults have, in a number of experiments, also been shown to exhibit similar instincts with respect to first possession.[74]

Research on lay intuitions about property remains preliminary. These studies show relationships between popular conceptions of property in only a handful of doctrinal areas, and leave open the much harder question whether these popular conceptions of property are the product of biological hard-wiring or social norms. Still, this work suggests that intuitions about property—and in particular, strong ownership instincts toward personal property—have their source in qualities of human biology or psychology that exist separately from and prior to law. This essentialist story suggests that property, rather than being merely a state-imposed regulatory regime, reflects and satisfies a basic desire to assert control over objects in our immediate surroundings. As Margaret Radin argued, "to be a person…an individual needs some control over resources in the external environment."[75] This conjecture is consistent with studies showing a correlation between the sense of self-determination actors believe they possess over their environment and their sense of well-being.[76] And if property intuitions do have some pre-legal foundation, this also helps to explain why we object even to formal violations of property rights that exact no meaningful costs.[77] Such trivial incursions effect dignitary harms by transgressing boundaries that are central to our sense of control and identity.[78]

Taken together, this work suggests an essentialist narrative that accounts for the persistence of property absolutism by looking to widely shared predilections about possession and ownership. This propensity may derive from biological

73 Ori Friedman & Karen Neary, *Determining Who Owns What: Do Children Infer Ownership from First Possession?* 107 Cognition 829 (2008); Friedman, *supra* note 55.

74 Ori Friedman & Karen Neary, *First Possession Beyond the Law: Adults' and Young Children's Intuitions About Ownership*, 83 Tul. L. Rev. 679 (2009).

75 Margaret J. Radin, *Property and Personhood*, 34 Stan. L. Rev. 957, 957 (1982).

76 Daniel Gilbert, Stumbling on Happiness 21-25 (2005) (summarizing psychological experiments showing an elemental relationship between a sense of well-being and a belief in one's control over the external environment).

77 A slap in the face may only sting a little, but the profound lack of respect it expresses may well be enough to trigger a fight or long-standing ill will. Intentionally touching another person's car or tossing trash on their land may have just as powerful an effect, demonstrating disdain even in the absence of any physical or financial harm. *Cf.* Merrill & Smith, *supra* note 30 at 1851 ("'No taking' is the analogue of 'no punching.'").

78 *E.g.*, Jacque v. Steenberg Homes, Inc., 563 N.W.2d 154 (Wis. 1997) (reinstating a lower-court punitive damages award of $100,000 for a trespass that caused no tangible economic harm to the plaintiffs); *see also* Lee Anne Fennell, *Taking Eminent Domain Apart*, 2004 Mich. St. L. Rev. 957, 962-67 (2004); Nicole Stelle Garnett, *The Neglected Political Economy of Eminent Domain*, 105 Mich. L. Rev. 101, 106-10 (2006) (each discussing the dignitary harms inflicted by involuntary taking of property via state eminent domain power).

hard-wiring, psychological reactions to social norms, or perhaps some of each.[79] Regardless, the essentialism story seeks to explain lay property absolutism as largely unrelated—and in fact prior—to law. Just as lay people understand that murder is wrong before they are aware of criminal prohibitions against unlawful killing, so it may be that lay people come to believe in a broad vision of property even before they know that law regulates ownership, or how it does so.

This essentialist story about property adds something that the previous welfarist narrative lacked. Welfarism, with its rational-actor and utility-maximizing assumptions, can explain why owners strongly prefer property absolutism, but it cannot explain why non-owners (or at least, those who own significantly less property) also do so. Looking to biology and psychology, by contrast, provides a way of explaining why property absolutism is sticky all the way down, and not just among those who are relatively wealthy. Research from these fields suggests that strong-property beliefs are a characteristic feature of human behavior that affects all of us, regardless of how much property one has.

So while essentialism helps construct a plausible account of lay property absolutism because it possesses explanatory breadth, it is still lacking, because it lacks explanatory depth. It helps us see why owner and non-owner alike gravitate toward a strong vision of property, but it does not explain (as the welfarist account did not) why actors do so even in the face of law's constant indications to the contrary. Humans may share a universal, instinctive strong-property baseline, but this does not mean that these beliefs and attitudes cannot change. It is the persistence of lay property absolutism—particularly in the face of law's signals about the limits on ownership and the conflicted character of property itself—that requires explanation. And so we must look still further to find a complete solution to this puzzle.

A Behavioralist Story

The pervasiveness of property absolutism among laypeople is puzzling because it does not square with the way the law actually works. Far from being purely Blackstonian, property law contains both a public dimension that limits private ownership prerogatives in the interest of both fairness and efficiency, as well as its more familiar private dimension that enables individual wealth accumulation. Given this, then, why is property absolutism so distinctively sticky in the public consciousness? We have seen that people begin from a strong-property baseline thanks to simple self-interest or some pre-legal instinct, but this does not solve the puzzle completely because it does not explain why people do not move away from these initial baselines when law gives them clear signals to the contrary.

---

79 The variance of attitudes toward property in different cultural traditions, *see supra* notes 41-43 (challenges the idea that property attitudes could be solely attributable to hard-wired biological factors).

Because this final element of the puzzle is ultimately about a gap in perception, its solution may lie in recent work that identifies ways in which we make systematic cognitive errors in perceiving and interpreting the world around us. Work in this field—cognitive psychology, and the related behavioralist variation on traditional rational choice theory—has shown that conduct frequently deviates from what standard rational-actor assumptions would predict, and that these deviations take place in a systematic way that can be explained by identifiable heuristics and biases.[80] Several of these biases can help to explain the stickiness of the lay public's Blackstonian vision of property law.

This behavioralist story begins by considering status quo bias. Cognitive psychological research has shown that people display a strong tendency against moving from initial baselines.[81] This tendency emerges in daily behavior in our tendency to leave in place default options even when it is not optimal to do so.[82] For example, while workplaces typically offer employees the opportunity to change their 401k retirement savings plans at least once a year, the majority of such plans have the same basic features that they did when they were first elected by an employee (including many default options that have become disadvantageous for the account holder).[83]

This insight begins to help forge an explanation for the distinctive stickiness of lay property absolutism. Assuming that we tend to begin with strong-property instincts (as the welfarism and essentialism stories each indicate), then status-quo bias suggests that it's very hard to move people away from that baseline. Beliefs in absolute property are, like any other starting point, overly determinative of where we are likely to end up. This is not to say that it is impossible to move away from baselines generally, or from a Blackstonian vision of property in particular. Taking three years of law school, and having a 1L professor repeatedly hammer home law's numerous limits on ownership rights and the public/private tensions within

80 The title of behavioral economist Dan Ariely's wonderful book Predictably Irrational (2008) neatly captures the somewhat counterintuitive thrust of work in this field. For a good overview of the implications of behavioralism for law, see Christine Jolls, Cass Sunstein, & Richard H. Thaler, *A Behavioral Approach to Law and Economics*, 50 Stan. L. Rev. 1471 (1998).

81 A seminal account is William Samuelson & Richard J. Zeckhauser, *Status Quo Bias in Decision Making*, 1 J. of Risk & Uncertainty 7 (1988).

82 Cass Sunstein & Richard Thaler, Nudge: Improving Decisions About Health, Wealth, and Happiness 83 (2008) ("[I]f, for a given choice, there is a default option …, then we can expect a large number of people to end up with that option, whether or not it is good for them.").

83 *Id.* at 34-35. I am embarrassed to admit that this is true of my 403(b) retirement plan, which I have not modified meaningfully since first establishing it upon starting to work at Southwestern Law School several years ago. I am slightly less embarrassed about this because even writers who have observed, and critiqued, status quo bias, have also fallen victim to it. *Id.* at 35 (observing that Cass Sunstein still subscribes to magazines that he stopped reading years ago).

property itself causes law specialists to move away from the strong-property starting points they had upon entering law school. But this is not an experience the average member of the general population has had (perhaps thankfully so), so laypeople remain very likely to stick with the property-maximalist baseline from which we all tend to begin.

Second, consider the endowment effect. Cognitive psychology has shown that our perception of the value of goods depends to a large extent on whether we are the owners of those goods at the time we are asked to assess their worth.[84] Ask me to estimate the value of a coffee mug, and I'll likely give it a lower value than if you asked me to estimate the value of *my* coffee mug.[85] Another way to understand this phenomenon is that people perceive the costs of losses to be greater than the benefits of equivalent gains, perhaps because the experience of loss is distinctively unpleasant.[86] These reactions also depend to a large extent on whether different options are framed as gains or losses. In fact, there is evidence that actors react to legal rules that they perceive as inflicting losses much more negatively than they will to rules that they perceive as causing gains—even when the two rules have the same actual effect.[87]

The endowment effect also helps explain how people—at least those who are property owners[88]—will react to perceived changes in the entitlements created by property law, and in particular why they cling so strongly to property absolutism. To reiterate, most laypeople start from a starting conception of property as nearly absolute. When actors are apprised of about the limits law actually imposes on their ownership entitlements, they perceive it as a loss—a subtraction from the ideal, broad set of rights they thought they had. Coming to understand the contours of property law requires laypeople to accept that what they believed were nearly absolute entitlements to extract value from their owned goods are in reality more

---

84 A classic early account is Daniel Kahneman, Jack L. Knetsch & Richard H. Thaler, *Experimental Tests of the Endowment Effect and the Coase Theorem*, 98 J. Polit. Econ. 1325, 1329 (1990).

85 *See id.* at 1329-30 (showing that experiment subjects who were asked to estimate the value of a coffee mug that they owned consistently gave a higher estimate of its value than they did when asked to estimate the value of an equivalent mug that they did not own).

86 *See* Richard Thaler, *Toward a Positive Theory of Consumer Choice*, 1 J. Econ. Behav. & Org. 39, 43-47 (1980).

87 *See* Edward J. McCaffery, Daniel J. Kahneman & Matthew L. Spitzer, *Framing the Jury: Cognitive Perspective on Pain and Suffering Awards*, 81 Va. L. Rev. 1341 (1995) (showing that test subjects had a positive response when asked to evaluate a "credit card surcharge" but a positive one when asked to evaluate a "bonus for using cash", even though the two options were functionally identical).

88 The endowment effect may still help to explain property absolutism among even those who possess relatively little property. Such owners may be particularly disinclined to accept losses, because they have less wealth, and are disproportionately strongly affected by (real or perceived) diminishments of their entitlements. Thanks to Stephanie Stern for helping me to develop this point.

modest. This is, of course, only a *perceived* loss. The absolutist baseline from which laypeople tend to anchor their expectations about property law overstates the actual scope of their entitlements. But this does not diminish the force of the point, because the endowment effect applies as much to ideal losses as it does to actual ones.[89]

The third heuristic that helps to illuminate the persistence of property absolutism is confirmation bias. Numerous studies have shown that people do not reason about the world by dispassionately sifting through all available evidence and then coming to the most plausible conclusion. Instead, we tend to select and emphasize evidence that confirms our preexisting ideas,[90] especially when those ideas are self-serving. This bias works in two directions. People are more likely to identify and emphasize evidence that confirms beliefs they already hold,[91] and are also more likely to ignore and deemphasize evidence that disconfirms beliefs different from those beliefs.[92] Importantly, confirmation bias does not operate only when actors want to confirm their existing beliefs.[93] Instead, the bias arises

89 The endowment affect applies as much to ideas that we hold dear as it does to physical objects that we own. *See* Dan Ariely, Predictably Irrational: The Hidden Forces that Shape Our Decisions 177-78 (rev. ed. 2009) ("Ownership is not limited to material things. It can also apply to points of view. Once we take ownership of an idea—whether it's about politics or sports—what do we do? We love it perhaps more than we should. We prize it more than it is worth. And most frequently, we have trouble letting go of it because we can't stand the idea of its loss. What are we left with then? An ideology—rigid and unyielding.").

90 *See* Robert Prentice, *Enron: A Brief Behavioral Autopsy*, 40 Am. Bus. L.J. 417, 424 (2003) ("[P]eople tend to be subject to the confirmation bias in that they seek out and process information in such a way as to confirm preexisting beliefs rather than in a more optimally neutral manner.").

91 Dan M. Kahan, *The Cognitively Illiberal State*, 60 Stan. L. Rev. 115, 121 n.26 (2007) ("[C]onfirmation bias...refers to the tendency of persons to seek out and assign more weight to evidence that confirms a prior belief or hypothesis than to evidence disconfirming it.").

92 Michael A. McCann, *It's Not About the Money: The Role of Preferences, Cognitive Biases and Heuristics Among Professional Athletes*, 71 Brook. L. Rev. 1459, 1460 (2006) ("[B]ecause of confirmation bias, individuals are subject to ignore or discount information that challenges existing beliefs.").

93 Behavioralist work has identified a close cousin of confirmation bias, self-serving bias, pursuant to which actors tend to choose conclusions that benefit them. *See* Linda Babcock & George Loewenstein, *Explaining Bargaining Impasse: Self-Serving Biases*, 11 J. Econ. Perspectives 109 (1997) (observing that people typically "conflate what is fair with what benefits oneself"). Numerous scholars have discussed the implications of self-serving bias in a legal setting. *See, e.g.*, Sean Williams, *Sticky Expectations: Responses to Persistent Over-Optimism in Marriage, Employment Contracts, and Credit Card Use*, 84 Notre Dame L. Rev. 733, 767-72 (2009).

Self-serving bias may also help to explain the persistence of property absolutism, insofar as people who own property would tend to prefer a Blackstonian vision of ownership, and

regardless of the content of the preexisting idea,[94] perhaps because the utility of confirming entrenched opinions is almost always greater than the disutility of disrupting well-settled belief systems.

Confirmation bias may also help to explain why the lay public tends to assume that property is nearly absolute, despite law's frequent signals to the contrary. While owners' rights may not be as capacious as lay instincts would have them, property law is still substantially (though by no means completely) characterized by solicitude for private rights of possession.[95] There is thus plenty of evidence in blackletter law that is consistent with a vision of property as absolute, and confirmation bias suggests that people will identify and emphasize these features of property law when forming an understanding of the field. There is also, of course, plenty of evidence in blackletter law to undermine and complicate an absolutist understanding of property as well. But confirmation bias helps to explain why popular perceptions of property tend not to register provisions of property law that limit owners' rights. These provisions do not comport with preexisting conceptions of property, so people are likely to discount or simply ignore them.

This behavioralist story concludes with consideration of the simplicity heuristic. Research has shown that actors express a strong tendency to reduce complex ideas to simple, easily understood sound bites. After all, we do not have infinite time when forming perceptions and making decisions, so it is useful to have quick-reference versions of the ideas that we need to quickly make decisions and understand the world around us.[96] This is not necessarily a product of bias or self-interest, but simple convenience. The world is highly complex, and given the proliferation of information that could be processed with respect to any given choice, we tend (understandably and in many cases, optimally) to use cognitive shortcuts as soon as we have sufficient information to make decisions or reach conclusions.[97] Voting supplies a familiar example. Ballots often present citizens with tens of different candidates and policy options, and sifting through and

---

so would tend to understand property law by emphasizing its elements that enshrine private ownership, and deemphasizing those that limit it.

94 Keith A. Findley & Michael S. Scott, *The Multiple Dimensions of Tunnel Vision in Criminal Cases*, 2006 Wis. L. Rev. 291, 311 (2006).

95 *E.g.*, Grey, *supra* note 25 at 69 (informally defining property as composed of broad rights of use, exclusion, and transfer); *cf.* Lior Strahilevitz, *The Right to Destroy*, 114 Yale L.J. 781 (2005) (considering whether property entitlements also include a right to destroy). *See also* examples discussed *supra* note 55 (showing that property law contains numerous substantive provisions that comport with lay strong-property instincts).

96 G. Gigerenzer & D.G. Goldstein, *Reasoning the Fast and Frugal Way: Models of Bounded Rationality*, 103 Psychological Review 650 (1996) (showing that actors tend to decide based on simple, readily available heuristics rather than by carefully assessing all available evidence).

97 D.S. Levine & L.I. Perlovsky, *Neuroscientific Insights on Biblical Myths: Simplifying Heuristics versus Careful Thinking: Scientific Analysis of Millennial Spiritual Issues*, 43 Zygon: J. of Sci. & Religion 797 (2008) (summarizing research showing that

carefully analyzing all of them would take more time than the average voter can afford to spend on this process, especially given the infinitesimally small chance that any single vote will affect an election outcome.[98] Most people thus use a simple, binary heuristic—Democrat or Republican—that roughly aligns with their political preferences and allows them to make political decisions much more simply and quickly.

This simplicity heuristic provides some final explanatory leverage in explaining the puzzle of property absolutism. Law specialists have the time and professional exigencies that allow (and require) them to understand property at a high level of complexity, which explains why this group tends to have a nuanced understanding of how law regulates ownership. Lay people, by contrast, lack the time (and, usually, any real reason) to create similarly elaborated understandings of property. "Mine, not yours" may be a simplified vision of how possession works, but it plausibly suffices as a basic understanding of the institution. And given the doctrinal ambivalence and academic disputes that make property law distinctively complex, it is easy to comprehend why laypeople tend to adopt the simplifying heuristic of absolutism as a cognitive shortcut for making sense of the field.

Behavioralist insights combine with welfarism and essentialism to provide a multitextured explanation of the persistent myth of property absolutism, one that possesses explanatory breadth and depth. According to the welfarist story, simple self-interest suggests that at least some humans have a strong tendency to prefer an absolutist vision of property. The essentialist story broadens this proposition, showing that we all tend to start thinking about property with absolutist presuppositions. Yet neither of these stories accounts for why people tend to cleave to this Blackstonian baseline when the positive law sends consistent signals to the contrary. The behavioralist story fills in the final piece of the puzzle. Evidence from numerous studies shows that actors tend to cling to initial baselines, resist losses, prioritize information consistent with preexisting beliefs, and prefer simple explanations to complex ones. These heuristics help us understand why the strong-property baseline from which laypeople start is so distinctively sticky, and provides a complete explanation for the persistence of property absolutism.

"[w]e tend to employ heuristics (that is, short cuts or rules of thumb) that enable us to employ minimal cognitive effort in decision making.").

98 Anthony Downs first observed the puzzle that individual voting appears inconsistent with rational choice theory because the costs of voting are far greater than the benefits in terms of electoral influence. *See* Anthony Downs, An Economic Theory of Democracy (1957).

Conclusion

In this chapter, I have sought to proffer a plausible explanation for the persistence with which lay people tend to believe in an absolute vision of property, even though law itself does not square with these intuitions. This is primarily a descriptive project that seeks to explain a puzzling phenomenon rather than to prescribe a given course of action.[99] In concluding, though, I offer a brief gesture at the practical implications of this inquiry for the law of property itself.

The persistence of property absolutism reflects on how lay people conceive of property, but it also has implications for how law should regulate ownership. Property is not solely an institution designed to make private individuals richer, but also one that creates and regulates public entitlements with the aim of maximizing overall social welfare for owners and non-owners alike.[100] Yet popular understandings of property do not reflect—or at least understate—this aspect of law's regulation of ownership. This may pose a practical problem, not just an academic puzzle. Propounding ideas that seek to enhance and refine the public side of property may not succeed in their implementation if they are at odds with lay conceptions of ownership. This is because legal reform can engender backlash when it falls too far out of step with lay expectations.[101] The gap between lay conceptions of property and its practical reality is thus not just an matter for intellectual inquiry, but one that is inextricably linked to law's efficacy, and in particular the efficacy of laws that limit ownership rights for public-regarding reasons. While public resistance alone does not necessarily justify avoiding laws that are otherwise fair or efficient, the potential hurdles raised by distance between popular attitudes toward law must be part of the discussion when deciding how to regulate ownership. Understanding how and why the public side of private property does not resonate with the public represents a first step in overcoming these hurdles.

---

99 Adam Kolber's stellar analogy captures this aim: "[I]ntuitions are like stars in the sky, and theorists draw constellations around the stars to more or less capture the locations of the stars and make the connections between the stars seem sensible, elegant, and sometimes even beautiful." Adam J. Kolber, *How to Improve Empirical Desert*, 75 Brook. L. Rev. 433, 434 (2009).

100 *See* Fagundes, *supra* note 37 ("Property law does not only acknowledge that greed is good, it also attends to the common good.").

101 *See, e.g.*, Ilya Somin, *The Limits of Backlash: Assessing the Response to* Kelo, 93 Minn. L. Rev. 2100, 2114-2153 (2009) (describing how public outrage in reaction to *Kelo* led to a strong, though debatably effective, legislative backlash); Merrill & Smith, *supra* note 30 at 1854 (observing instances, such as mining claims on federal lands in nineteenth-century California and online filesharing in the past decade, in which divergence between blackletter property law and social norms led to widespread noncompliance); *cf.* Paul Robinson & Robert Kurzban, *Concordance and Conflict in Intuitions of Justice*, 91 Minn. L. Rev. 1829, 1880-83 (2007) (arguing, in the criminal law context, that popular intuitions about fairness have to accord with the substance of law in order to possess efficacy).

Acknowledgment

Thanks to Bill Araiza, Al Calnan, Michael Diamond, Mike Dorff, Steve Eagle, Brian Galle, Andy Hessick, Carissa Hessick, Paul Horwitz, Roman Hoyos, Rob Kar, Erik Knutsen, Zak Kramer, Christine Lorillard, Dan Markel, Caleb Mason, Jonathan Masur, Art McEvoy, Kali Murray, Bob Popovich, Marc Poirier, Gowri Ramachandran, Angela Riley, Gary Rowe, Ira Shafiroff, Sonja Starr, Stephanie Stern, Lesley Wexler, and Sean Williams, as well as participants in the Fifth PrawfsFest! Workshop on Public Law & Legal Theory at the Florida State University College of Law, the Junior Property Professors Works-in-Progress Panel at the AALS 2010 Annual Meeting, and the Southwestern Law School Faculty Workshop for helpful comments on earlier drafts; and to Danielle Foster and Genevieve Younce for outstanding research assistance.

Chapter 3
Shared Equity Housing: Cultural Understanding and the Meaning of Ownership

Michael Diamond

Property is a culturally constructed concept. The prevalent Western view of property, particularly real property, involves substantial domination over it by an owner who, in classical theory, is able to use it more or less as he or she chooses.[1] One of the central elements in this model of domination is that the owner is entitled to maximize the financial rewards that may be extracted from the property through its exploitation or sale. This classical concept of dominance is not, however, the only possible view of property or of ownership. Many other cultures and many theorists and philosophers have viewed property quite differently from the prevailing Western view. In fact, the current state of real property ownership in the United States diverges markedly from what the prevailing view would suggest. Nevertheless, the classical view remains prevalent in much of our current public discourse.

Property, or, more precisely, the absence of property, itself plays a central role in the definition of poverty. One of the traditional strategies to combat poverty has been to assist poor individuals and families in their wealth-building activities, in increasing their assets.[2] Historically, one of the most effective ways of doing this has been through homeownership. Based on this theorem, many governmental programs have been established to aid low income families in becoming homeowners.[3] There is, however, a hidden flaw imbedded in the

---

1 J.W. Ehrlich, Erlich's Blackstone 113 (1959).

2 Michael A. Stegman et al., *The Wealth-Creating Potential of Homeownership: A Preliminary Assessment of Price Appreciation among Low-Income Homebuyers*, *in* Chasing the American Dream, New Perspectives on Affordable Homeownership 171 (William M. Rohe & Harry L. Watson eds., (2007) (the majority of home buyers realize substantial gains in paper wealth as a result of their transition from renting to owning. "Housing policies that increase homeownership also have the potential to create and to democratize wealth."); *See also* Thomas P Boehm et al., *Housing and Wealth Accumulation: Intergenerational Impacts, Low Income Homeownership*, *in* Examining the Unexamined Goal 407 (Nicolas P. Retsinas & Eric S. Belsky eds., 2002) (Homeownership has the positive effect of increasing the likelihood a child will also become a future homeowner).

3 *See* Tenant Opportunity to Purchase Act, D.C. Code §42-3404.02 (2001) (giving tenants the opportunity to buy residential rental housing when it is offered for sale); Housing

possibility of wealth creation through homeownership for the poor. To the extent that poor homeowners are able to maximize wealth creation through the economic exploitation of their home, they do so at the social cost of making those homes less affordable to (or unaffordable for) subsequent low income buyers or renters.

In this chapter, I examine the intersection of property rights and the ongoing availability of affordable housing. In particular, I explore the relationship between wealth creation through homeownership for lower income homeowners and the preservation of affordability for future potential buyers of that housing. This intersection arises most directly in the context of what is known as shared equity housing.[4] This is housing in which the equity build-up in a home (the appreciation in its value and the reduction of the mortgage obligation through amortization) does not go solely to the nominal owner of the property but is shared with other individuals or entities. As such, shared equity housing removes one of the major sticks from the theoretical bundle of sticks normally thought in Western mythology to be part of the concept of ownership. Therein lies the essence of a widespread, but, so far as I have been able to determine, as yet unpublished critique of shared equity housing.[5]

The problem is more intricate than merely defining what is meant by ownership, although that, itself, is a complex subject. It involves what I have previously called the conflict of competing goods.[6] This concept relates to a situation in which highly desirable (at least for many people) social goals are in competition with each other but cannot each be maximized at the same time. The problem of wealth creation and preservation of affordability is one of those incommensurable situations. Maximizing wealth creation for a particular low income homeowner through the unrestricted realization of equity will often eliminate a previously affordable unit from the affordable housing stock. Conversely, preserving affordability through equity restrictions often eliminates (or at least places significant restrictions on) the maximization of wealth creation.

Production Trust Fund, D.C. Code § 42-2802 (2001) (establishing a dedicated fund for the development of affordable housing).

4 John Emmeus Davis, *Shared Equity Homeownership, The Changing Landscape of Resale-Restricted, Owner-Occupied Housing* (Nat'l Hous. Inst. 2006), *available at* http://www.nhi.org/pdf/SharedEquityHome.pdf.

5 Duncan Kennedy, *The Limited Equity Coop as a Vehicle for Affordable Housing in a Race and Class Divided Society*, 46 How. L.J. 85 (2002). As had Duncan Kennedy, I have heard several advocates of wealth creation for the poor through ownership criticize the limited equity model of homeownership as providing something less than standard, or what they believe are full, property rights.

6 Michael Diamond, *Affordable Housing and the Conflict of Competing Goods: A Policy Dilemma*, given as the keynote address at a workshop on Affordable Housing and Public-Private Partnerships at the University of Colorado Law School on October 19-20, 2007 and compiled in Affordable Housing and Public Private Partnerships, (Nestor M. Davidson & Robin Paul Malloy eds., 2009).

Independently of ascertaining the means by which society should choose among these incommensurable goals, advocates for the poor and for affordable housing preservation often exhibit a significant difference of opinion about the substantive dichotomy. For many of those who favor using homeownership as a means of creating wealth for low income residents, any restriction on the equity that the homeowner may extract from the property is a deprivation of a fundamental property right, a relegation of the poor to second class homeownership.[7] Those who hold this position do not credit, or at least do not credit highly, any interest that other low income individuals might have in the continued availability of decent, affordable housing in the future. Alternatively, those who, given the dilemma posed by the conflict of competing goods, favor the preservation of affordable units by restricting equity extraction do not credit (or at least do not credit highly) the benefits of wealth creation for low income families.

Nevertheless, my goal in this chapter is not to develop an overarching definition of property or to suggest that we adopt the definition offered by the other cultures or by the theorists to whom I will refer. What I do propose is that the ability to extract wealth from the use or transfer of real property should belong, in certain situations, not only to the nominal owner of that property but to a combination of interests and entities composed of that nominal owner, a group of future, as yet unknown, potential owners and to society as a whole. I argue that this normative prescription is well within the concept of property as it is currently (and has been historically) implemented in American society.

My hypothesis is straightforward. There is not today a sufficient number of affordable housing units and the pace at which new affordable units enter the market is insufficient to meet current demand. Moreover, the demand for such units continues to grow due to a growing number of households in need.[8] To further exacerbate the problem, there is an increasing number of affordable units being lost to the existing stock due to market conditions, deterioration, or owner choice.[9] Since the gap between supply and demand is growing, it is critically important for society to preserve the existing stock of affordable units while simultaneously working to increase the supply. Use restrictions are one method of preserving affordable units. The concomitant reduction of owner equity is not a significant departure from currently accepted restrictions on property and is justified by the legitimate expectations of society and lower income individuals that decent, affordable housing will be available to those who need it.

In Part 1 of this paper, I briefly address the idea of property as a culturally constructed concept and I suggest how the prevailing notion of property in

---

7 *See e.g.*, Benita Jones, The Property Paradox: Limited Equity Housing Cooperatives and the Challenge of African-American Wealth Creation (Apr., 2007) (unpublished paper, Georgetown Law, on file with author).

8 U.S. Dep't. of Hous. and Urban Dev., Affordable Housing Needs 2005: Report to Congress 36 (2005), *available at* http://www.huduser.org/publications/pdf/Affhsgneeds.pdf.

9 *Id.* at 37.

the United States does not reflect the reality of property ownership. In Part 2, I explain some of the ways in which government and non profit organizations fund the development and preservation of affordable homeownership, including a discussion of limited or "shared" equity. Because these concepts have been criticized as depriving low income homeowners of an important element of homeownership, wealth creation, I offer in Part 3 a response to the critics. In Part 4, I draw conclusions and offer some policy recommendations.

Part I: Property as Cultural Construction

Many, perhaps most, people consider the definition of property as clear, fixed and immutable.[10] Societal understandings of property, however, have varied from culture to culture and, within cultures, from time to time. While it is not my purpose in this chapter to analyze the various understandings of property and ownership, I do want to emphasize that there has been, over time and across cultures, a wide range of generally accepted understandings. Several brief examples will be sufficient to illustrate the point.

Non-Western Views of Property

Throughout history, many non-Western cultures and thinkers have considered the meaning and nature of property and the rights of ownership. In this section, I will address three such views, each of which departs significantly from the prevailing Western understanding of property and property rights. These are not offered as complete analyses of the views presented or even to suggest that they were the predominant view during the period of their appearance. They are offered instead to demonstrate the wide range of views of property that are different from the dominant view of property in the United States today.

Confucius and Mensius As early as the sixth century BCE, Confucius (Kong fuzi) had developed a complex concept of private property that included many elements of what would later become the foundation of capitalist market economies.[11] Nevertheless, Confucius believed that each person had a moral

10 *But see*, Bruce Ackerman arguing to the contrary: "[O]nly the ignorant think it meaningful to talk about owning things free and clear of further obligation...More precisely, the law of property considers the way rights to use things may be parceled out amongst a host of competing resource users." BRUCE A. ACKERMAN, PRIVATE PROPERTY AND THE CONSTITUTION 26 (1977).

11 Daniel A. Bell, *Confucian Constraints on Property Rights*, *in* CONFUCIANISM FOR THE MODERN WORLD 218 (Daniel A. Bell and Hahm Chaibong eds, Cambridge Univ. Press 2003). Bell states that Confucius opposed "heavy-handed government control." The goal of the rulers was to foster the moral development of the people.

right to subsistence, a right that permitted (or even required) the government to intervene on his or her behalf. This more welfarist view of governance obliged the rulers to secure for the people the basic means of subsistence.[12] He supported, for example, a controlled distribution of goods monitored and, if necessary, implemented, by the state.[13]

Several generations later, Mensius (Mengzi), a follower of Confucianism, while he supported the concept of private property, went further than Confucius concerning the people's right of subsistence. Mensius argued that the government should control the distribution and use of land so that individual households can make productive use of it and insure their subsistence.[14] His *well-field* theory called for households to share nine squares of land with each of eight households to be responsible for one square. The ninth square was to be jointly cultivated with the crop from this square used to provide for the needy. The obligation of the eight households was to cultivate and harvest the ninth square before they tended their own land. In addition, each of the eight households was obliged to each other household to help support any of them that fell into need.[15]

Islamic conceptions of property

> The concept of dual ownership is one of the special features of the Islamic doctrine of economics. Islam protects and endorses the personal right to own what one may freely gain, through legitimate means....Yet human ownership is tempered by the understanding that everything...belongs to God...What appears to be ownership is in fact a matter of trusteeship, whereby we have temporary authority to handle and benefit from property.[16]

---

12 Confucius said, for example, that "...the gentleman helps out the needy but does not contribute to the upkeep of the rich." The analects of confucius (Watson trans., 2007), (hereinafter, *The Analects*), 6:4; And further, "When Yuan Si was given the post of steward, he was offered an allotment of nine hundred measures of grain, but he declined it. The Master said, Oh, no! You could have shared it with your neighboring communities, couldn't you?" *The Analects*, 6:5.

13 *Id.*

14 *Id.* In fact, Mensius wanted local land to be divided into nine "squares" of which eight would be privately owned and the ninth would be a public field. The public field would have to be cultivated before the eight private fields could be tended.

15 Joseph Chan, *Giving Priority to the Worst Off: A Confucian Perspective on Social Welfare*, *in* Confucianism for the Modern World 239 (Daniel A. Bell & Hahm Chaibong eds., 2003).

16 Muhammad Abdul Rauf, quoted in Siraj Sait & Hilary Lim, Islamic land theories and its (sic) applications, Paper 1 *in* UN-Habitat islam, land and property research series 8 (2005) (hereinafter Habitat Islam).

The traditional Islamic view of property rights conceived of a dual ownership between a human being and Allah. The land was thought to be a sacred trust that must be used productively but without exploitation or hoarding.[17] The land owner may benefit from his or her land but only within a circumscribed range. The concept was clearly not one of unlimited dominion.

In the traditional Islamic legal system property rights were essentially either public, state, or private. Private rights depended on use and public lands might be converted to the private realm by the productive use of such land. On the other hand, private land that went unused might revert to the state.

A further restriction on obtaining the full benefit of private land was the traditional Islamic requirement that landowners pay a levy of a part of their earnings from the land for the benefit of the poor. This levy, known as *zakat*, was not viewed as voluntary charity but as a social obligation and, correlatively, as a right of the poor to receive.[18]

Similarly, the traditional culture provided for an endowment, known as *waft*, by which an owner could provide income or other benefits of property to named beneficiaries. While this often meant that the donor provided for his or her family and their descendants, it was also often used for the purpose of providing charity to the poor. The concept involves more than a voluntary gift and is the result of long established cultural norms of sharing the benefits of property with others.[19]

Native American conceptions of property

> What is this you call property? It cannot be the earth. For the land is our mother, nourishing all her children, beasts, birds, fish, and all men. The woods, the streams, everything on it belongs to everybody and is for the use of all. How can one man say it belongs to him only?[20]

Various Native American Nations traditionally have viewed property rights differently than those of the archetypal Western model, although there is some debate as to whether this is a function of culture, religion or economic condition.[21] While most Native American nations recognized individual rights in personal property, their view of rights in land varied widely. Many did not recognize

17 Siraj Sait & Hilary Lim, Land, Law & Islam: Property and Human Rights in the Muslim World, Habitat Islam, *supra* note 16, at 11.

18 *Id.* at 12-14.

19 *Id.* at 10.

20 Massasoit, protesting after several Native Americans were arrested for hunting on land previously "sold" to Miles Standish. From Frank Waters, Brave are my people, *quoted in* Bruce E. Johansen, The Encyclopedia of Native American Economic History, 211 (1999).

21 *Id.*

individual property interests in land. In some cases this was because tribes were nomadic and such interests were not important to their existence or were even adverse to it.[22] Others had a more communal or even spiritual sense about the land. They viewed the land as belonging to all and no individual could exercise complete dominion over it.[23] While individuals who occupied particular land could have the fruits of their labor, they had an obligation to preserve the land for future generations. They merely used the land in trust.

In a somewhat related vein, William Cronon has pointed out that

> [w]hat the Indians owned-or, more precisely, what their villages gave them claim to-was not the land but the things that were on the land during the various seasons of the year.[24]

This vision of use, coupled with a strong norm concerning the preservation of the land, was the forerunner of the modern view of stewardship.

Even for items of personal property, there was often an approach that was quite different from contemporary Western notions of ownership and use. The Kwakuitl Indians utilized a method of property distribution known as *potlatching*.[25] While Bruce Johnson argues that the potlaching system was a method to preserve property rights of the various kinship groups, the fact of the matter is that it was groups, rather than individuals who held these rights and the groups understood that redistribution of property was the social norm. The failure to redistribute fairly through the potlatch resulted in various social sanctions:

> The kinship group that attempted to free ride by holding few or meager potlatches would have found itself descending in the potlatch ranking, ultimately leading to the reduction of the potlatch gifts it later received from other kinship groups.[26]

---

22 Carol M. Rose, *Possession as the Origin of Property*, 52 U. Chi. L. Rev. 73 (1985). *See also* Paul H. Carlson, The Plains Indians (1998).

23 Paul H. Carlson, The plains Indians 111 (1998).

24 William Cronon, changes in the land: indians, colonists and the ecology of new england 65 (1983).

25 Under this system, kinship groups had, as a group, fishing and hunting rights to particular hunting or fishing areas. As part of the recognition of these exclusive rights, each group that had had a good hunting or fishing seasons gave to other groups that had not been successful, a portion of their catch. *See* D. Bruce Johnson, *The Formation and Protection of Property Rights Among the Southern Kwakiutl Indians*, 15 J. Legal Stud. 41, 42 (1986). *See also* Jennifer Roback, *Exchange, Sovereignty, and Indian-Anglo Relations* 9, *in* property rights and indian economies (Terry L. Anderson ed., 1992).

26 *Id.*

What emerges is a sense of property that clearly views a form of common ownership and sharing of property, not only with current clan members but also with future generations to whom current members owe obligations.

Western Views of Property

Western legal and political thinkers have also had varying views of property. They run from classical Greek conceptions of property to Christian-humanist views; from classical liberal views to the collectivist views of Marx and the socialists. Moreover, modern writers have identified and discussed concepts of personhood and propriety. I offer here only a brief sample of the historic diversity in Western thought about property.

Platonic and Aristotelian conceptions of property There was a wide range of views concerning the meaning and purpose of property during the classical Greek era. Plato, for example, believed that property was a basis of jealousy and conflict. Since he wanted the state governed for the common good, he rejected the concept of private property for the rulers, the Guardians. He argued instead for commonly owned property to be held for the common good.[27] The property of the non rulers was to be limited to what one needed. Commerce and wealth accumulation were to be minimized.[28] Moreover, Plato, as all Greeks of the period, viewed property as family rather than individual property:

> ...The Greeks set out from a different starting point. In their early world of tribes and brotherhoods and families, no one thought of his own 'rights' or questioned the claims of society. Practically everything he had belonged to his kin.[29]

Plato elaborated on the distribution of property in the *Laws.* There he spoke of an allocation of property among citizens according to a lottery system. Plato would impose a maximum allocation of four times an individual allocation and create a minimum allotment of one share. Any property above the maximum allowance would be confiscated.[30]

> The form of law which I would propose...would be as follows: in a state which is desirous of being saved from the greatest of all plagues...there should exist among the citizens neither extreme poverty, nor, again, excess of wealth... Let the limit of poverty be the value of the lot;...But if a person have yet greater riches...which is in excess of the measure, if he give back the surplus to the state

27 Plato, The Republic 161-63 (H.D.P. Lee trans., 1962).
28 Alan Ryan, property 11 (1987).
29 *Id. Quoting* Zimmern, at 10.
30 Plato, Laws 127 (Benjamin Jowett trans., 2008).

> and to the Gods…he shall suffer no penalty…but if he disobeys [he shall forfeit the excess].[31]

Aristotle disagrees with Plato's view of commonly owned property and strongly favors private ownership. He believes that private ownership is necessary if anyone is to care for the property. He thinks that Plato's goal of commonly owned property would result in no one caring for it.[32]

Aristotle's model was founded on idea that households were the backbone of the state and that good household management was required for a just and prosperous population.[33] He also made an important and rather subtle distinction between ownership and use. While property could be owned, it should not be used in an "unnatural" way, that is, for making profit.[34] He thus supported the idea of farming for use rather than for trade and believed in moderation rather than excess.

In a related vein, Aristotle desired a distribution of property so that the gradations between richer or poorer citizens would not be so stark. This would lead, he believed, to the reduction of conflict which he thought to be the inevitable condition of the population.[35] In fact, Aristotle says that "…the better system is that under which property is privately owned but is put to common use."[36] This, despite the conspicuous differences between Aristotle and Plato, is quite reminiscent of Plato's call for a quota on property ownership found in the Laws.

Theological views

> …go sell what you own and give the money to the poor and you will have treasure in heaven.[37]

The traditional Christian belief is that all things were created by and belong to God. Since people were created in God's likeness, all people have a claim to the benefits of the earth. Those in rightful possession of land, for example, may exercise dominion over it but only to the extent of their need for sustenance and growth. Beyond that, they must care for the land and provide their community and for future inhabitants.[38]

---

31 *Id.*

32 Ryan, *supra* note 28, at 16. *See also*, Garrett Hardin, *The Tragedy of the Commons*, 162 SCIENCE 1243, 1243-48 (Dec. 13, 1968).

33 ARISTOTLE, THE POLITICS 4 (Ernest Barker trans., 1962).

34 *Id.* at 28.

35 *Id.* at 48.

36 *Id.* at 50.

37 Jesus talking to a man who asked how to obtain eternal life. The Gospel of Mark 10:20. THE NEW OXFORD ANNOTATED BIBLE (Michael D. Coogan ed., 1991).

38 Peter W. Salsich Jr., *Property Law Serves Human Society: A First-Year Course Agenda*, 46 ST. LOUIS U. L.J. 617 (2002). Salsich goes on to say "The landowner, as steward, will ultimately be asked to give an accounting of that use to God, the Master." *Id.* at 618.

Other, more radical views concerning property also had their foundation in Scripture. Several mendicant and monastic orders in the Middle Ages forswore the ownership of property or possessions beyond their daily needs. They asserted "… that property and possessions stand as barriers to the grace of God."[39]

Among the great religious thinkers of medieval and renaissance Europe, both Thomas Aquinas and Thomas More considered the meaning and uses of property. Aquinas, who supported the idea of individual ownership of property, nevertheless believed that

> God has sovereign dominion over all things: and he, according to His providence, directed certain things to the sustenance of man's body. For this reason, man has a natural dominion over things, as regards the power to make use of them.[40]

This distinction between ownership and use is another forerunner of the concept of stewardship that has been associated with traditional Native American beliefs and with environmental activists today.

Thomas More went even further. He argued in the *Utopia* for common ownership of property in order to foster a just society. There, he said

> …to tell you candidly my heart's sentiments, it appears to me that wherever you have private property and all men measure all things by cash values, there it is scarcely possible for a commonwealth to have justice or prosperity—unless you think justice exists where all the best things flow into the hands of the worst citizens or prosperity prevails where all is divided among very few—and even they are not altogether well off, while the rest are downright wretched.[41]

In a contemporary context, Frank Alexander has discussed the private ownership of property as analogous to "the theological depiction of the human condition in light of the fall…"[42] The idea of "property as mine" is "the elevation of individual human self-centeredness over and against the omnipotent creator."[43] He moves on to discuss "property as ours and concludes by stating that "…Christians have proclaimed in a strong voice that property does not belong to the individual but rather that the community holds 'all things in common' (Acts 4:32-35)."[44]

---

39 Frank S. Alexander, *Property and Christian Theology in* CHRISTIANITY AND LAW 206 (John White & Frank S. Alexander eds., 2008) (hereinafter *Property*).

40 THOMAS AQUINAS THE SUMMA THEOLOGICA, II –II Q 55, art. 1, 1476 (1947). For an interesting discussion of Acquinas' views and their relationship to Aristotle and Cicero, *see* David Lametti, T*he Objects of Virtue, in* PROPERTY AND COMMUNITY (Gregory S. Alexander & Eduardo M. Penalver eds., 2009).

41 THOMAS MORE, UTOPIA 52 (Edward Surtz, S.J. ed., 1964).

42 Alexander, *supra* note 39, at 210.

43 *Id.* at 209.

44 *Id.* at 214.

Classical liberal (and other) conceptions The English Liberals have lent their individualistic philosophy to the modern American idea of property. The man generally thought to have been the progenitor of that philosophy concerning property and property rights is John Locke. His view was that property rights predated the advent of the state which was created to protect such rights.[45] Property was created by mixing the labor of the first user with the natural bounty of the earth.[46] The involvement by individuals in the creation of property eventually led Blackstone to make his famous pronouncement:

> Property is that sole and despotic dominion which one man claims and exercises over the external things of the world, in total exclusion of the right of any other individual in the universe.[47]

While this concept of property became theoretically dominant in seventeenth and eighteenth century England, even Locke placed important limitations on one's dominion over property. While labor is the "unquestionable property of the labouror, [and] no man but he can have a right to what that is once joined to," nevertheless there must be "enough and as good left in common for others."[48] Locke goes on to say:

> The same Law of Nature that does by this means give us property, does also bound that property, too. "God has given us all things richly"....But how far has he given it to us? To enjoy. As much as any one can make use of to any advantage of life before it spoils....Whatever is beyond this, is more than his share and belongs to others.[49]

Later, John Stuart Mill, commenting on the nature and meaning of property, further limited Locke's views of dominion. One such limitation involved Mill's denial of the right of inheritance. While he accepted the idea of one's dominion over things on which one has expended labor, including the right to bequeath that thing to another, Mill denies the right of inheritance:

> If it may be said...that those who have inherited the savings of others have an advantage which they may have in no way deserved, over the industrious whose predecessors may not have left them anything: I not only admit, but strenuously contend, that this unearned advantage should be curtailed, as much as is consistent

45 John Locke, The Second Treatise on Government, §45, at 143 (1947) (1690).

46 Id. §§26-29, at 134.

47 J.W. Ehrlich, Erlich's Blackstone 113 (1959).

48 *Id.* §27 at 134.

49 *Id.* §31 at 136.

> with justice to those who thought fit to dispose of their savings by giving them to their descendants.[50]

In fact, in Mill's perfect state, all people start out equally, with compensation to those with disadvantages in order to give them an equal opportunity to compete.[51]

The second major limitation that Mill placed on the despotic dominion is based upon land being different from other forms of property. Land, itself, as opposed to the fruits of the land, is not the product of labor. Therefore,

> [w]henever…the proprietor, generally speaking, ceases to be the improver, political economy has nothing to say in defense of landed property….In no sound theory of private property was it ever contemplated that the proprietor of land should be merely a sinecurist quartered on it.[52]

The limitations that Locke had conceived and those that Mill would conceive were among the philosophical foundations of the Diggers, or Levelers, who were active in England at about the time that Locke was writing. Far from supporting the idea of private property, the Diggers and their leader, Gerrard Winstanley, argued that subsistence of the people was a fundamental right of freedom. Therefore, they argued against the enclosure of the land by the wealthy and for communally owned property to provide the subsistence of the people.[53]

Karl Marx and socialist conceptions

> …you are lost if you forget that the fruits belong to all and the earth to no one[54]

As the Industrial Revolution took firm hold of the economic life of the Western world, a different social order emerged, one with great disparities between the rich and the poor. The poor endured great suffering as manufacturing gave rise to urban centers with great concentrations of low wage workers. The conditions of the urban poor drew the attention of philosophers, economists and reformers.

---

50 John Stuart Mill, Principles of political economy with some of their applications to social philosophy, *quoted in* C.B. MacPherson, property: mainstream and critical positions, 86 (1978).

51 *Id.* at 78.

52 *Id.* at 94.

53 Laura Brace, The Politics of Property: Labour, Freedom and Belonging 14 (2004).

54 Jean-Jacques Rousseau, discourse on the origin and foundations of inequality, *in* The Social Contract and discourses 235 (G. D. H. Cole trans.,1950) (hereinafter The Social Contract).

Approximately one hundred years before the Communist Manifesto, Rousseau recognized this disparity and wrote about the natural and contrived inequalities among people and the resulting maldistribution of labor, goods and land. He said:

> Do you not know that numbers of your fellow creatures are starving from want of what you have too much of? You ought to have had the express and universal consent of mankind before appropriating more of the common subsistence than you needed for your own maintenance.[55]

Rousseau believed that this inequality would lead to disorder in which the wealthy would further enslave the poor. It could, however, be cured by the coming together of individuals under a social compact which would substitute a "moral and legitimate" equality under which individuals might "...become every one equal by convention and legal right."[56] During the same period, the Utopian Socialists also wrote of these inequalities and offered a variety of suggestions, many of which included common ownership of goods and the means of production.[57]

A century after Rousseau, Karl Marx again pointed out the inequalities associated with privately owned property. He argued that the nature of societal production determined the property relations in society and the nature of production changes over time with the advent of new systems and new technologies.[58] Moreover, the means of production has a dispositive impact on the distribution of income, property and wealth. His theory of surplus value (based on the excess of the selling price of a commodity over the cost of the labor required to create the commodity) placed the laboring class in constant struggle with the capital class, a struggle that inevitably led to the exploitation of the worker.[59]

Marx argued that the only solution to this inequality could "be summed up in a single sentence: Abolition of private property."[60] He goes on to say that

> ...labor-levelled down, parceled, and thus unfree labor-is taken as the source of the *perniscíousness* of private property and its humanly alienated existence.[61]

---

55 *Id.* at 250. It is interesting to note here the implicit agreement with Locke's admonition to property owners to leave "enough and as good" for others.

56 *Id.*

57 *See e.g*, ROBERT L. HEILBRONER, THE WORLDLY PHILOSOPHERS 102-30 (4th ed., 1972).

58 This is in contrast to Edmund Burke's assertion that "the laws of commerce...are the laws of Nature, and consequently the laws of God." Quoted in Joseph Cropsey, *Karl Marx, in* LEO STRAUSS & JOSEPH CROPSEY, HISTORY OF POLITICAL PHILOSOPHY 805, (3rd ed. 1987) (hereinafter POLITICAL PHILOSOPHY).

59 He based his theory on the inherent "...antagonism of capital and wage-labor." KARL MARX & FREDERICH ENGELS, THE COMMUNIST MANIFESTO 35 (1998).

60 *Id.* at 52.

61 Karl Marx, *Feuerbachian Criticism of Hegel, in* WRITINGS OF THE YOUNG MARX ON PHILOSOPHY AND SOCIETY 301 (Lloyd D. Easton & Kurt H. Guddat eds. & trans., 1967) (emphasis in original). Cropsey has described Marx' position as by saying "All historic

This exploitation of the propertyless by those with capital had to be "overcome" and would be overcome by the communalization of property.

> When, therefore, capital is converted into common property, into the property of all members of society, personal property is not thereby transformed into social property. It is only the social character of the property that is changed. It loses its class-character.[62]

Marx sought a classless, humane society in which work was the release of human and creative energy rather than the means of subsistence. His idea of property and ownership could be summed up in his now famous aphorism "from each according to his [her] ability and to each according to his [her] need."[63]

Common law and current theories of property In the previous sections, I have surveyed a range of societies and a range of time to demonstrate the cultural and temporal variations in the concept of property. These and other variations are reflected as well in modern common law theory. These modern variations add further support to the idea of limited equity housing for the poor being well within the mainstream of historic concepts of property.

Thus, while the common law has generally accepted the idea of private property, common law theories about the ways in which individuals gain property rights have undergone several permutations over time. Many of the traditional theories have been criticized by modern commentators. For example, an old common law theory cites possession as the basis of such rights. While this theory has been influential, Morris Raphael Cohen has pointed to several of its flaws. The first is that most property is not discovered or found but is the result of an ongoing process of creation, typically by many people. Secondly, a rule that permits a finder to have rights of possession against the rest of the world tells us nothing about the restrictions that might be applied to that property's use or disposition.[64]

John Locke's labor theory of property rights[65] has also been criticized as being too loosely conceived. For example, when several people's labor has contributed to the creation of some thing, which one has the ownership rights? While the

---

modes of production have had one feature in common, and that feature has in turn affected all the corresponding societies: control of the means of production has not been shared by all men, but in each age some have been owners or possessors while many more have had to give of themselves, *i.e.*, of their capacity for work....Thus, in all previous history the act of production has brought many men into dependence upon the few." Political Philosophy, *supra* note 58, at 806.

62 Marx, the communist manifesto note 59 supra, at 53.

63 Karl Marx, *Critique of the Gotha Program* (1875), *in* Marx & Engels: Basic Writings on Politics and Philosophy 119 (Lewis S. Feuer ed., 1959).

64 Morris Raphael Cohen, *Property and Sovereignty*, 13 Cornell L.Q. 8 (1927).

65 John Locke, The Second Treatise of Government: An Essay Concerning the origin, extent and end of civil government (1690).

common law has created several forms of common ownership (tenants in common, joint tenancies or condominium associations), these are not the typical resolution to conflicting claims to a particular piece of property.

There have been several more novel views of property in the mid to late twentieth century. Again, these views are presented to demonstrate the broad range of meaning for the concept of property offered by influential thinkers and commentators. For example, in 1964, Yale Law Professor Charles Reich wrote an influential paper entitled The New Property.[66] In it he argued that

> One of the most important developments in the United States during the past decade has been the emergence of government as a major source of wealth....
>
> The valuables dispensed by government take many forms, but they all share one characteristic. They are steadily taking the place of traditional forms of wealth—forms which are held as private property.[67]

Reich was discussing government largesse and traced the increase in the forms of such bounty. He lamented the concomitant incursions of government that accompanied the granting of such benefits.[68]

In order to protect against these incursions, Reich wants to do away with what he believes is an artificial distinction between privileges or gratuities and rights. He argues that the dispensation of wealth by the government "is not much different from the absolute right of ownership that private capital once invoked..." and ought to be treated as what he terms a "new property."[69]

More recently, Margaret Radin has expounded on yet another theory of property. She is concerned with the idea of "personhood" and her premise is that "...an individual needs some control over resources in the external environment. The necessary assurances of control take the form of property rights."[70] That is, one's right to act as a free individual must be supported by elements allowing self assertion. Radin examines how personhood has and should influence property law and traces concepts of personhood from Locke, through Hume, Kant, Hegel, Marx and others to argue that the law has and should give added protection to property that involves some personal relationship between a person and the property (as distinguished from what she calls *fungible* property).[71] Morris Cohen, writing

66 Charles A. Reich, *The New Property*, 73 YALE L.J. 733 (1963-64).

67 *Id.*

68 Reich calls on us "to remember what the framers of the Constitution knew so well-that 'a power over a man's subsistence amounts to a power over his will.'" *Id.* at 787.

69 Id.

70 Margaret Jane Radin, *Property and Personhood*, 34 STAN. L. REV. 957 (1981-82).

71 Id. at 959. Radin gives as an example a wedding ring stolen from a jewelers being replaceable with another ring or with money. This is fungible property. Alternatively, a wedding ring stolen from a "loving spouse" cannot be so easily replaced. This is property in which one has some personal tie, in which one has part of his or her identity entangled.

long before Radin, criticized the personhood theory and suggested that such personal property rights would typically include the right to exclude others. This, he thought, could potentially deprive the excluded of their right of self assertion, thereby diminishing their own personhood.[72]

Another theory, adopted by the law and economics analysts, derives from Adam Smith. It utilizes economic efficiency as a basis for property rights. Private ownership promotes efficient use of property in one's self interest. This, in turn, redounds to the benefit of society, Adam Smith's "invisible hand" writ large. Once again, Morris Cohen offers a cogent critique. He argues that efficiency theories fail to look out for the overall societal good. He denies the efficacy of the invisible hand as applied to individuals being beneficial to society. Private property cannot, Cohen claims, be sacrosanct and free of government restriction:

> The issue before a thoughtful people is therefore not the maintenance or abolition of private property; but the determination of the precise lines along which private enterprise must be given free scope and where it must be restricted in the interest of the common good.[73]

This admonition regularly has been heeded by modern societies. Consider the scope of the restrictions that are now accepted by virtually everyone in industrialized societies.[74] Zoning rules tell us how large buildings may be and to what uses they may be put. Building and housing codes tell us how buildings must be constructed and what amenities they must contain. Warranties of habitability and rent control laws restrict landlord behavior and income. Environmental laws limit uses and emissions of and from buildings. Taxes deprive the owner of some of the value of land and different uses produce different tax obligations, thereby steering behavior.[75]

Shared equity housing raises many of these questions about the meaning of ownership and property rights. The views briefly cataloged in this and previous sections should at least suggest the malleable and indeterminate nature of our understanding of property rights. In the next section, I discuss the state of

---

72 Cohen, *supra* note 64, at 18-19.

73 *Id.* at 21. Of course, this concept is not necessarily inconsistent with an idea of efficiency. The question, as Cohen suggests, is what goal is to be maximized. Both Smith and, I take it, the modern law and economic scholars, seek to maximize financial gains rather than more social outcomes. In this way I believe Cohen is arguing against the Smithian model of efficiency.

74 Of course, the scope and wisdom of many of these regulations is contested. What is not contested, except on the margins, is the state's power to regulate.

75 There is, in addition to those already mentioned, a rich and varied body of current views about the meaning and nature of property. An interesting compendium of such views can be found in a special issue of the Cornell Law Review addressing Property and Obligation. 94 Cornell L. Rev. (2008-09). In this issue, commentators on both the left and the right address the role of property in society.

affordable housing in the United States today. I look at some of the issues faced by low income people in finding decent housing they can afford and those faced by society in attempting to assure that decent, affordable housing exists for lower income individuals and families.

Part II: Shared Equity Housing

Affordable housing means, at its most basic level, housing that is affordable to residents with low and very low incomes. It means, however, much more than that. Housing provides many of the important elements of a social existence. It provides shelter and security, recreation and social interaction. It affects the health and psychological well-being of its occupants. It also often provides a vehicle for the creation of wealth.[76] Of course, if the housing is inadequate or too expensive, its influence on the factors I just mentioned is more likely to be negative. Better quality, more affordable housing is more likely to produce socially beneficial outcomes.

Currently there is throughout the United States a severe shortage of decent affordable housing for low and very low income residents.[77] Moreover, the gap between the demand for and supply of such units is growing.[78] In an effort to curtail this crisis, the federal government as well as several state and local governments have instituted programs designed to produce or to preserve decent, affordable rental and homeownership units.[79]

I will focus here on one model, that of shared equity housing, as a method of preserving and improving the existing stock of affordable homeownership. Shared equity housing is simply a form of homeownership in which the equity in a home, that is, the difference between the value of the home and the amount of debt secured by it at any particular time, is shared between someone called the owner of the property and some other person or entity. In the context of affordable housing, this limitation on equity raises for some observers the specter of a less-

76 *See, e.g.*, J. Peter Byrne & Michael Diamond, *Affordable Housing, Land Tenure, and Urban Policy: The Matrix Revealed*, 34 Fordham Urb. L.J. 527 (2007).

77 Keith Wardrip et. al., *Out of Reach 2009*, National Low Income Housing Coalition (2009).

78 Preliminary Assessment of American Community Survey Data Shows Housing Affordability Gap Worsened for Lowest Income Households from 2007-2008, Danilo Pelletiere, Nov. 30, 2009, National Low Income Housing Coalition.

79 26 USCS § 42 (2009) (Low Income Housing Tax Credit. Provision in the tax code that requires housing built through the low income tax credit to lease to low income tenants for at least 15 years, and maintain the low income housing as such for an extended period of fifteen years.); 110 P.L. 289 (2008) (The National Housing Trust Fund was established as a provision of the Housing and Economic Recovery Act of 2008. The housing trust fund will, once capitalized, provide communities with funds to build, preserve, and rehabilitate affordable housing.)

than-full-ownership interest because the low income home buyer, as a condition of obtaining the financing to permit her to purchase the home, is required to share the equity with others, often future generations of low income home buyers.[80] It is this limitation of the ability to extract the equity from one's home that conflicts with the common vision of ownership.

The concept of shared equity housing is not new and it has taken many forms over time. In a standard market arena, there have been many instances of an investor providing assistance, often down payment assistance, to a potential home buyer in exchange not for an interest payment on the advance but, instead, for a share of the equity attained by the property over time. These arrangements usually call for a sale of the property (or at least a buy-out of the investor's interest) at a particular point in time. Here, the shared equity is delineated between clearly defined participants, each of whom receives a clearly defined benefit as a result of the agreement. In this arm's length, commercial transaction the investor takes a certain risk in exchange for a potential reward and the buyer gives up part of a potential future benefit for a current benefit that he or she could not obtain without the assistance of the investor.[81]

The concept also has a history in situations quite distant from the standard investment model. In these situations, an investor, often a local government or a non-profit corporation, provides funding for a low income individual or groups to purchase a building to be used as their residence.[82] The goal of the investors in such situations is not primarily financial gain from the investment. Instead, such investors have one or more social goals that provide the impetus to invest. Typically, that goal is the long term preservation of affordable housing. In the following section, I briefly discuss the nature of the investment made by these social investors. I will then examine how they achieve their social goals. I conclude this part by discussing the impact on the recipients of the social investments.

---

80 There is a resemblance between the idea of restrictions on equity and other, socially created property rights and restrictions such as fishing or game quotas or tradable emissions permits. Each restriction is designed to provide for others a benefit that could be depleted by current overuse of a resource.

81 Andrew Caplin et al., *Shared-Equity Mortgages, Housing Affordability, and Homeownership*, 2007 Fannie Mae Foundation, *available at* http://cess.nyu.edu/caplin/SEM2007.pdf. *See also*, Michael Diamond, *The Meaning and Nature of Property: Homeownership and Shared Equity in the Context of Poverty* 29 St. Louis Pub. L. Rev. 85 at 102 (2009).

82 In this discussion I will focus on multi-family buildings, although the conceptual underpinnings are essentially the same whether the property is a single family residence or a multiple dwelling. The reason for this focus is the economies of scale associated with a multiple dwelling; lower per unit land costs, one heating and cooling system for multiple units, one roof rather than many, etc.

The Nature of Social Investments

Social investments typically come in one of three forms: loans, grants or equity investments. Each has the ability to make affordable housing feasible and each can provide the social investor with a means of achieving its ends. I will briefly discuss these forms as they apply to the preservation of affordable housing.

Loans Many local governments and non profit corporations have loan programs with flexible and beneficial terms for low income borrowers seeking to purchase a residence. The nature of the loans, however, differs dramatically depending on whether the lender is a governmental entity or a non profit community lender. Community lenders, that is, organizations or community development financial institutions (CDFIs),[83] are usually intermediaries who get their funds from grants, loans from other institutions or from governments. They re-lend these funds usually at rates more favorable than those that might be obtained from commercial lenders but at rates far higher than those of many governmental programs.

The funds held by theses community lenders are usually limited in amount and often the donors to the community lender limit the duration of their commitments. Thus, the amount of any loan from a community lender is constrained and the term of such loans is normally limited to no more than three to five years. In addition, while community lenders are often quite efficient in processing applications, they normally have up front fees that increase the cost of their loans, although such costs are still less than those of commercial lenders. In part this is because community lenders have no certain way of acquiring capital (such as deposits) and therefore they need to protect their resources while at the same time achieving their social mission.

On the positive side, community lenders will often capitalize their interest, that is, they will calculate the amount of interest that will be due during the life of the loan and add it to the loan amount. This relieves the borrower from coming up with out-of-pocket cash for the interest but does increase the size of the loan, and thus the total interest that will be paid. The lender will hold the excess amount, that portion loaned for the payment of interest, and draw it down at appropriate intervals to pay themselves the interest owed to that point.[84] The entire loan, including the amount of capitalized interest, will have to be repaid when the loan comes due. The borrower's goal would be to repay it with funds obtained from a lower interest rate, longer term government loan.

83 12 USCS §§ 4701-4718 (2008) (Section entitled "Assistance Provided by the Fund").

84 The advantage of capitalizing interest is that the borrower will not have to make payments out of operating funds, which can be used to operate the building during the early stages of ownership. The interest will be paid back when the loan of the community lender is repaid later with permanent financing.

Governmental lenders do not have the same constraints as community lenders. They have a constant supply of capital through taxation (although the uses of tax revenue are often highly contested) and can therefore be more committed to mission. Loans from government entities can be at very low interest rates and for very long terms.[85] In addition to favorable length and interest rates, local governments have often been very flexible in permitting deferred payments or allowing loans to be repaid only out of net cash flow rather than at a fixed amortization rate. This flexibility allows buyers to weather difficult periods and to make projects that appear unfeasible at the early stages (as being too expensive) grow into successful developments that both provide decent, affordable housing and permit the repayment of the loans to the local government.

Each of these types of loans often includes restrictions in the loan agreement on the use and disposition of the property. The documents will give the lenders monitoring rights and, in some cases, receivership rights, if the loan agreement is breached.

Grants Grants, to the extent they are available, are infusions of funds without repayment requirements and without the expectation by the grantor of financial returns. Governments, both federal and local, have grant programs that help low income residents buy, renovate and/or operate their buildings. Charitable organizations also make grants for these purposes. Some of the grants are for general use by the purchaser of property while others are for specific purposes such as energy conservation, lead removal or handicap accessibility. While grants are beneficial because of the absence of a repayment requirement, they are difficult to obtain, the application process often takes a significant amount of time and effort and monitoring and reporting costs can be high. The grants often have long term restrictions as to the use of the funds as well as to the ongoing use or disposition of the property.

Equity investments Equity investments in affordable housing can look much like the standard market investment where an investor provides capital in exchange for a share of the equity in a building. Such investments may also be in the form of capital contributions in exchange for tax benefits provided by the federal government.[86] Perhaps the most unusual type of investment is that made by organizations known as community land trusts (CLT). Community land trusts are non profit organizations that acquire land for the purpose of providing and preserving affordable housing. Their funding often comes from grants,

85 In the District of Columbia, for example, the Department of Housing and Community Development has been able to offer (prior to the current economic crisis) 40 year, one half of one per cent loans to tenant groups seeking to purchase and renovate their buildings.

86 *See, e.g.*, the Federal Low Income Housing Tax Credit program, 26 USCS § 42 (2009).

contributions and loans from mission driven lenders and from commercial lenders seeking Community Re-investment Act credit.[87]

The CLT acquires lands and buildings (or, sometimes, will buy the land simultaneously with a low income purchaser buying the building) with its own or with borrowed funds. If the CLT has purchased both the land and the improvements, it will re-sell the buildings, but not the land, to eligible low income residents.[88] It often will help the residents obtain the financing for the purchase, which will be less expensive since the value of the land will not be included in the price. The CLT will then enter into a ground lease by which the resident will have the right to use the land for an extended period, typically 99 years, subject to a ground rent, a payment for the use of the land. The ground lease will also contain a set of rules and obligations as to the use of the land and the disposition of the building.

In each of these forms of social investments, the rules contained in the transaction documents (the ground lease, the covenants in the loan agreements and the restrictions in the grant agreements) are the bases upon which the social investors can control the use and re-sale price of the housing. It is these limitations that raise the question as to whether low income residents subject to a social investment with such restrictions has been deprived of rights essential to considering them the owners of the property.

The Nature of the Restrictions

Because of the shortage of affordable housing, and the growing gap between supply and demand, social investors who provide subsidies to low income home buyers often require that the equity that the buyer can extract from the property on resale be limited so that the subsequent low income buyers will be able to afford the property when the current buyer desires to sell it. In other words, a part of the equity built up in the property stays with the property for the benefit of the community and future low income buyers. The restrictions normally manifest themselves in one of two ways. The first method restricts the first buyer and each succeeding buyer in what he or she can charge when selling the property. The amount is determined by a formula that is part of the loan or grant agreement or the ground lease. The restriction and formula are also often recorded among the

87 12 USCS § 2901 (2008). The community Re-investment Act is a federal stature that encourages federally chartered banks to make loans and other investments in the communities in which they have branches. The benefit is a good CRA rating while the penalty for inadequate performance is the threat of negative action on expansion requests, merger applications and the like. It should be noted that while CRA has led to a good deal of new community investment, the sanctions of the Act have not been formally imposed to date.

88 It is also possible that a joint closing will be had whereby the CLT purchases the land, the tenants purchase the improvements and the CLT gives a ground lease to the tenants permitting them to use the CLT's land for an extended period.

land records of the jurisdiction as a covenant that runs with the land. The formula can be very simple or quite intricate. It normally will permit the return to the buyer (market conditions permitting) of his or her down payment, the depreciated value of any improvements he or she has made to the property, some portion of the equity built up due to the pay down of the mortgage debt, and a percentage of the total of these items (often one or two per cent) for each year the buyer has owned and occupied the property.

The second common way of restricting equity is that there is a limitation on who the buyer may sell to. This is often manifested as a requirement that the property can only be sold (and must be affordable) to a person who is at or below a certain percentage of the Area Median Income (AMI). This means that the cost of the property must be affordable to a buyer who spends no more than 30% of his or her income (this is the federal standard for affordability) for housing costs. If there is a cap on the income of the buyer, this translates into a cap on the sale price although this cap is softer than a formulaic cap on equity.

Both types of restrictions typically run with the land and continue to operate, in the case of loans or grants, for anywhere from 20 to 40 years from the initiation of the investment.[89] "Running with the land" means that the restriction will survive the pre-payment of the loan or repayment of the grant. Beyond the restrictions on extracting equity, the other restrictions placed on recipients of these investments are not significantly different than those normally imposed on any other buyer. There are often financial reporting requirements, limitations on committing or permitting waste and the availability of inspection rights. These and other restrictions protect the interests of the social investor and, while an imposition, often inure to the benefit of the buyer, as well, because they tend to preserve the value of the property.

The rationale behind the restriction on equity is more complex than may at first appear. Most obviously, it reflects a desire on the part of the social investor to preserve the scarce affordable units for future generations of low income home buyers. Without the restriction, it is likely that these units quickly will pass out of the affordability range. The desire for preservation, however, is not the only socially valuable choice available to the social investor. Homeownership of any sort offers the opportunity for wealth creation which, in turn, offers significant potential benefits to the home owner and his or her family. The equity from a home can provide the foundation for the further education of children, the ability to take business opportunities, and the possibility of intergenerational wealth transfers. These factors can permanently remove a family from the deprivations of poverty and may lead to the reduction of the social costs often associated with poverty.

However, there is a finite amount of subsidy available for low income homeownership and a demand for the subsidy that far exceeds the supply. On a purely economic level, is it more efficient to provide for a one time subsidy

89 The restrictions in a ground lease run for the duration of the lease.

with the subsidy's benefit going to the initial buyer or to spread the benefit to a larger number of potential buyers while limiting the economic gain of each? There may be empirical measures of the costs and benefits of either approach but there are many subjective, difficult to value, elements of the choice. For example, there is a fundamental question of whether one has a communal or an individualist set of values in relation to societal benefit. The difference in values will lead to widely disparate values assigned to various elements of one choice or the other.

One might refer, in thinking about this choice, to Garrett Hardin's essay, "The Tragedy of the Commons."[90] Hardin wrote about the problems resulting from population growth in a world of finite resources. He was concerned with the world's ability to provide for a growing population where technology is unable to increase the pool of available resources. The "commons" in pre-revolutionary times was a village's common grazing area. Since each resident had no additional cost to graze an additional animal on the commons, each had an incentive to maximize his or her herd. At some point, Hardin postulates, the demand on the commons would exceed its ability to provide. Assume, in this discussion, that the pool available for housing subsidies is the commons and that the pool is finite. To the extent that the pool is depleted by excess demand it will, at some point, deteriorate to the point of vanishing. If resale restrictions to preserve affordability are not in place the pool will have been transferred from the community to a relatively few select individual beneficiaries. This is an example of the conflict of competing goods that I mentioned earlier. Society cannot, in a world of finite resources, maximize for both the preservation of affordable housing and for the provision through homeownership of maximum wealth creation to low income owners.

The Impact of Equity Restrictions on Low Income Homeowners

The argument has been made by many that there is an inherent unfairness in depriving subsidized, low income homeowners of the equity buildup that is available to other homeowners. It deprives this group of a major opportunity to escape poverty. Such a deprivation has been said to be creating a second class form of homeownership.[91] While the argument of the critics of shared equity housing has a certain resonance, it is, in my view, misguided for at least two reasons. First, it attempts to measure shared equity homeownership with non-shared-equity

90 Hardin, *supra* note 32.

91 *But see* Deborah Kenn, *Paradise Unfound: The American Dream of Housing Justice for All*, 5 B.U. Pub. Int. L.J. 69 (1995). "Community land trusts can function to support comprehensive access to the resource of land; not as second class homeownership for the poor, but as opportunities for everyone to decent housing. The value of land converts from individual profit-making to community profitsharing. Viewed as a community resource and justly distributed among all individuals, land held in trust benefits common goals." *Id.*

homeownership. This comparison would be apt if the poor had the choice between the two and were forced into the shared equity model. This is very unlikely to be the choice actually available to the poor who are more likely to have a choice, if at all, between shared equity homeownership and tenancy in a rental situation. Typically, the costs in the unsubsidized market are too high and the underwriting requirements of lenders too stringent for most of the poor to be able to buy in such a market.

The second reason I believe the criticism of shared equity homeownership is misguided is that it assumes a definition of homeownership that is neither essential nor even descriptive. As I stated at the beginning of this chapter, the idea of property is a culturally specific constructed concept. In the United States, the understanding of property has undergone changes over time. Today, property in the United States is highly regulated and the reality of property rights is very different from the concept in any of the classical Western models.

The pertinent comparison of tenure choices We have already discussed the problem of the shortage of affordable housing for low income residents. There is not enough decent affordable housing to meet the demand and some of the existing stock of such housing leaves the market each year without being replaced. The growing gap between supply and demand for decent affordable housing will continue to cause a variety of social problems ranging from homelessness to poor health to disengagement from civil society.[92] The concept of shared equity housing must be viewed in this context. It is a palliative that slows the disintegration of the existing affordable stock.

To set the stage, shared equity housing is only one of many models of housing tenure on the housing market. Who is likely to choose this form of housing over the other possible tenures? Typically the answer is the poor but that answer leaves far too much unexplained.

Who among the poor are faced with the prospect of sharing equity? In general, they fall into one of two groups: tenants who have the opportunity of homeownership using a program subsidized by a social investor or homeowners who are seeking to refinance their homes using such a program. Owners need refinancing generally because they have encountered financial difficulties during their non-shared-equity tenure.[93] I will not say much here about homeowners in financial difficulty. They had made a choice of tenure and found, for whatever

92 *See*, Byrne & Diamond, *supra* note 76.

93 In this latter category, the evidence of financial among low income homeowners is significant. Many are not able to operate their homes on 30% of their income and of these, many devote more than 50% of their income to housing costs. Moreover, many low income first time home buyers revert to renting and do not purchase another home. For a comprehensive study of these issues, *see* Josephine Louie, Eric S. Belsky, & Nancy McArdle, *The Housing Needs of Low-Income Homeowners*, Joint Center for Housing Studies (1998).

reason, that it was not feasible for them to continue in that tenure. Their choices then were to return to renting, which many did, or to choose another form of ownership tenure where that was available to them.

The choice confronting renters is quite different. Typically, they do not have the opportunity to acquire non-shared-equity housing. Income, housing prices, lenders requirements and interest rates may make this option unrealistic. Thus, to argue that shared equity housing imposes a second class form of homeownership misses the point. First, this form of tenure is typically not imposed by outside forces. Where available, it may be offered to tenants who may choose it or not. Second, it provides renters with an opportunity for homeownership, for a change in tenure from renter to owner with all of the attributes of market ownership, including the possibility of equity creation (albeit, most likely to a reduced degree). That is the choice that must be examined.

In examining that choice we must examine what is offered to tenants who choose shared equity homeownership and what may be withheld. We also must return to the question of what we mean by ownership. As I stated earlier, ownership of real property involves a range of rights benefiting a range of stakeholders. It offers the buyers, for example, security of tenure, control over living environment, a stake in community, a sense of identity and, of course, a possibility of wealth creation.

Shared equity homeownership offers most of these features in a degree equal to any other form of ownership. What it lacks is the full extent of wealth extraction that might be available in non-shared-equity homeownership. It is this specific lack that motivates critics to label shared equity as a second class form of ownership. Yet in other areas normally associated with shared equity housing, there is evidence of benefits to the individual residents and to the community. In a comprehensive study of shared equity housing for the National Housing Institute, John Emmeus Davis examined several performance standards in order to evaluate shared equity housing.[94]

Davis examined the performance of shared equity housing in the areas of affordability, stability, involvement and improvement as well as wealth creation.[95] While in some cases the evidence was mixed or inconclusive, he did find evidence of good performance in these areas, particularly when considering limited equity cooperatives. Other research has shown some of the many indirect benefits associated with homeownership which are also available to the limited equity owner: better health of occupants, better achievement in school of the children of homeowners, and a greater level of civic involvement.[96]

---

94 Davis, *supra* note 4. The National Housing Institute, 2006. In the interest of full disclosure, the author of this essay was on the advisory committee for this study.

95 *Id.* at 89-117.

96 *See generally*, Byrne & Diamond, *supra*, note 76.

Even on the issue of wealth creation, Davis has found that owners of shared equity housing do accumulate wealth. The question for him is not whether there is wealth creation but whether the amount of wealth created is sufficient.[97] The answer to this question depends on what is meant by sufficient. For example, if the limited return is commensurate with what the open market would have provided, the question has little meaning. If it is less than what the market would have provided, the question is whether the limitations on equity are at least balanced by the gains to the society and the individual shared equity owner. This, of course, brings us back to the question of what we mean by property and property rights. In the shared equity model, other residents, social investors and the public have interests that are worthy of recognition and protection. How to balance those interests with the interests of homeowners in maximizing wealth creation is the problem. Unfortunately, it is a problem that has not received enough attention from scholars and advocates. It is an area in need (and worthy of) of further elaboration.

Conclusion

Property, as I said at the outset of this chapter, is a constructed and contested concept. The bundle of rights that may have made up a classical understanding of property has long since been adapted to modern needs and modern views of property and societal needs. One might go further and say that the classical Western view has been abandoned in favor of a more regulatory approach that has the goal of enhancing overall societal wellbeing while accommodating a certain level of private rights concerning property.

Among the important societal goals of the day are the creation and preservation of decent affordable housing for lower income households. Such housing fills a moral obligation of society but also serves instrumental purposes by reducing social costs. One of the ways in which such housing is maintained over the long period is through restrictions on its resale or use of property only to or by households within the targeted income limits. These restrictions, while contrary to the Blackstonian view of dominion, are consistent with a wide range of restrictions on the use and transfer of property today. The limitation on equity in publicly subsidized housing is merely one of numerous restrictions on use and benefit imposed on private property by modern societies. It should be understood as no different from the zoning, fair housing, taxation and environmental regulations prevalent, and widely accepted, throughout societies today.

97 Davis, *supra*, note 4, at 103.

Acknowledgment

I want to thank my friend and colleague, Peter Byrne for his extremely helpful comments on various drafts of this article. I'd also like to thank Daniel Park for tireless and imaginative research assistance. In addition, I owe a debt of gratitude to the participants at the Georgetown workshop on The Public Nature of Private Property for their thoughtful and provocative comments.

Chapter 4

Crisis and the Public–Private Divide in Property

Nestor M. Davidson and Rashmi Dyal-Chand

As our current financial crisis—the deepest since the Great Depression—has taken its toll in human terms, it has also generated significant anxiety about deep-seated property norms. At base, the crisis started in the housing market, arising in no small measure from the veneration of homeownership opportunities and a regulatory environment that privileged unfettered risk and reward. The government's response—pumping hundreds of billions of dollars into financial markets, nationalizing major enterprises, and unleashing a stimulus program touching almost every sector of the economy—has in turn been shaped by contested norms of ownership. As bailouts, stimulus plans, housing-market rescue efforts and other interventions have emerged, the appropriate boundaries of interference with the property tied up in distressed sectors of the economy have become significant flashpoints.[1] In short, this is a crisis grounded in and evocative of property, underscoring the interconnected nature of the institution and highlighting the potential for contagion that our system of property cannot long tolerate.

Times of economic and social crises throw into stark relief perennial tensions in the discourse of property around the balance between the individual and the community. No crisis ever really generates a final synthesis that resolves these underlying tensions, and the cycle continues. This chapter accordingly examines patterns of crisis and equilibrium in property and what the current crisis reveals in terms of contemporary property theory. It is too early to draw definitive conclusions about the residue the current crisis will leave on property doctrine. As with others before, there are already important legal changes emerging in the regulatory response that may prove lasting in areas such as mortgage law, bankruptcy, access to credit, and others. On the deeper structure of property law and the culture of property however, the crisis has already left its mark.

1 *See, e.g.*, Raymond J. Ahearn, Cong. Research Serv., The Global Economic Downturn and Protectionism 9 (2009); James R. Barth et al., The Rise and Fall of the U.S. Mortgage and Credit Markets: A Comprehensive Analysis of the Market Meltdown 269–74 (2009); Baird Webel, Cong. Research Serv., Ongoing Government Assistance for American International Group (AIG) 1–2 (2009).

Stasis and Disruption in Property

Property law generally develops through the slow, common-law resolution of individual conflicts and marginal legislative changes. This inherent conservative tendency is hardly surprising, given what the institution represents in terms of settled expectations. Crisis, however, tends to upset this accretive process, generating moments of what can be described—borrowing from Bruce Ackerman's exploration of transformational constitutional realignments—as "property moments."[2]

Evolutionary theory provides fruitful metaphors for understanding the role of crisis in the development of property law. Classic evolutionary theory assumed generally that changes at the species level reflect a steady accumulation of incremental differentiation. As natural selection reinforced these changes, species gradually evolved. Niles Eldredge and Stephen Jay Gould, however, argued that the fossil record contains frequent examples of long-term and relatively undisturbed stasis punctuated by massive change in relatively short order.[3] They thus hypothesized that when a relatively steady equilibrium is disrupted by some significant exogenous force, rapid adaptation occurs and a new equilibrium emerges.[4]

These two modes of change—steady state gradualism and rebalancing to equilibrium through crisis—can be found in social institutions no less than in nature. Law, political order, the policy landscape, even the structure of scientific thought,[5] witness hydraulic change that is occasionally punctuated by some confluence of factors (economic crisis, technological revolution, war) causing social or legal disruption that forces institutions to change rapidly in ways that parallel Eldredge and Gould's phyletic paradigm shifts.

The legal literature has proven congenial to theories of steady state incremental development versus punctuated equilibrium.[6] Ackerman's work on constitutional

---

2 *See* Bruce Ackerman, We The People: Foundations (1991) [hereinafter Ackerman, Foundations]; Bruce Ackerman, We The People: Transformations (1998) [hereinafter Ackerman, Transformations] (discussing significant historical moments of constitutional change); *Cf.* Giovanni Capoccia & R. Daniel Keleman, *The Study of Critical Junctures: Theory, Narrative, and Counterfactuals in Historical Institutionalism*, 59 World Pol. 341, 350 n. 36 (2007) (discussing the terminology of "moments" to describe critical junctures of significant institutional change).

3 The modern paleontological literature on punctuated equilibria traces to Niles Eldredge & Stephen Jay Gould, *Punctuated Equilibria: An Alternative to Phyletic Gradualism, in* Models in Paleobiology 82 (Thomas J. M. Schopf ed., 1972); *see generally* Michael Shermer, The Borderlands of Science: Where Sense Meets Nonsense (2001).

4 Eldredge & Gould, *supra* note 3.

5 *Cf.* Thomas Kuhn, The Structure of Scientific Revolutions (1962).

6 *See, e.g.*, Oona A. Hathaway, *Path Dependence in the Law: The Course and Pattern of Legal Change in a Common Law System*, 86 Iowa L. Rev. 101, 113-17 (2001) (discussing evolutionary path dependence and punctuated equilibrium as paradigms for evaluating

crisis and realignment, for example, outlines several distinctive periods in American history of popular constitutionalism, during which "We the People" have acted in a kind of higher lawmaking capacity to amend the existing constitutional order.[7] Focusing on the Revolutionary era, the Civil-War realignment, and the New Deal, Ackerman argues that at each of these junctures, a process of popular upheaval literally changed the meaning of the federal Constitution.[8] Ackerman's thesis has been as controversial as it has been influential,[9] but it does highlight the role of crisis in opening up a legal discourse beyond the frames that institutional stasis generally imposes.

It is possible to see a pattern in American history of similar repeated disjunctions in property law. As noted, property as an institution tends to be reactive, and relatively stable, with a number of forces reinforcing incrementalism in legal change. The nature of property as repository of individual and collective investment means that an array of social institutions tends to protect that investment.[10] Even if the state were inclined to challenge those expectations, the resources available to the state to influence private ordering can slow how property law develops.[11] Likewise, the institutional and individual capacity of actors in the legal system to instantiate change, whether in terms of limitations of the judicial enterprise or the scope of the regulatory state, limits creativity and reifies a certain degree of conservatism in existing norms. And hydraulic pressures that economic and social forces exert on a variety of other mediating institutions, including lawyers, judges, legislators, and increasingly the apparatus of the modern regulatory state, tend to hold existing

---

legal change); *cf.* Herbert Hovenkamp, *Evolutionary Models in Jurisprudence*, 64 TEX. L. REV. 645 (1985) (tracing the influence of Darwinian evolutionary theories on the history of jurisprudence).

7 *See* ACKERMAN, FOUNDATIONS, *supra* note 2, at 6-7; ACKERMAN, TRANSFORMATIONS, *supra* note 2, at 20 (arguing for a model of popular constitutional change that begins with constitutional impasse, moves to an electoral mandate, followed by a challenge to dissenting institutions, a judicial validation of the new order (a "switch in time"), and, finally, a consolidating election); *see also* Walter Dean Burnham, *Constitutional Moments and Punctuated Equilibria: A Political Scientist Confronts Bruce Ackerman's We The People*, 108 YALE L.J. 2237 (1999) (discussing the parallels between Ackerman's theory and the political-science literature on critical realignments).

8 *See generally* ACKERMAN, TRANSFORMATIONS, *supra* note 2 (charting fundamental constitutional realignments at each of these transformative "constitutional moments").

9 *See, e.g.*, Colin Gordon, *Rethinking the New Deal*, 98 COLUM. L. REV. 2029 (1998); Larry Kramer, *What's a Constitution for Anyway? Of History and Theory, Bruce Ackerman and the New Deal*, 46 CASE W. RES. L. REV. 885 (1996).

10 *Cf.* Abraham Bell & Gideon Parchomovsky, *A Theory of Property*, 90 CORNELL L. REV. 531 (2005).

11 *See, e.g.*, LAWRENCE M. FRIEDMAN, A HISTORY OF AMERICAN LAW 77 (1985) (arguing that during the Colonial era, "the desire to rule, and rule broadly, was tempered by the modest means, in taxes and staff, that rulers had at their command. Regulation tended to be local, and as cheap in money and men as possible").

institutional arrangements in relative stability.[12] These forces generate relative stasis in ordinary times, with property more so than many areas of law representing significant path dependency.[13]

Repeatedly throughout American history, however, property law and property norms have undergone moments of significant contestation, confronting our political and legal culture with a kind of punctuated equilibrium that raises fundamental questions about the nature of property. One need not delve far into debates about Charles Beard's argument that the federal Constitution, particularly its protections for contract and property, enshrined the economic power of the Founding Fathers[14] to recognize that fundamental questions about the nature of property were actively contested in the Revolutionary and early Federal period.[15] Early American history saw conflicts over the confiscation of Loyalist property, skirmishes over slavery, rebellions and populist arguments about redistribution, and debt crises, among other crucibles at the formation of our property law.[16]

Within a generation after the Founding, then, an uneasy stasis was to be found that largely lasted until the Civil War. That crisis and its legal aftermath, most notably in the Thirteenth, Fourteenth, and Fifteenth Amendments, represented another moment of significant disjunction and unstable resolution in the structure of property.[17] The Civil War Amendments not only barred slavery, but also ironically laid the foundation for the eventual constitutionalization of broad protection for property in the Fourteenth Amendment. Again, after crisis, the pendulum swung. Late nineteenth-century formalism can hardly be said to grow directly in response to state intervention in property rights.[18] However, the ideological and rhetorical

12 *Cf.* William Weston Fisher III, The Law of the Land: An Intellectual History of American Property Doctrine, 1776-1880, at 1–4 (Oct. 1, 1991) (unpublished doctoral thesis, Harvard University) (describing the interaction between legal discourse and related discourses in social theory, economics, popular discourse, and others).

13 *Cf.* Hathaway, *supra* note 6, at 113-17.

14 *See* Charles A. Beard, An Economic Interpretation of the Constitution of the United States (1913).

15 *See, e.g.*, Stuart Bruchey, *The Impact of Concern for Security of Property Rights on the Legal System of the Early American Republic*, 1980 Wisc. L. Rev. 1135.

16 *See* Gordon S. Wood, The Radicalism of the American Revolution (1992) (discussing doctrinal developments in property law arising out of the Revolution); *see also* Fisher, *supra* note 12, at 4 (describing "watershed" moments in the development of American property law, bookended by the Revolution and Reconstruction).

17 *See* James W. Ely, Jr., The Guardian of Every Other Right: A Constitutional History of Property Rights 82-83 (3d ed. 2008) (discussing ways in which the exigencies of the Civil War led to significant reordering of existing property rights, including the abolition of slavery in the Thirteenth Amendment and the Confiscation Acts during the war).

18 Developments in conceptions of property rights in the nineteenth century raise interesting questions about the public/private divide, and the role of the state in fostering a uniquely American property law. For example, Willard Hurst has argued that a prevailing vision in the early nineteenth century was of property as a dynamic source of productive potential, rather than a static barrier against the state. *See* Willard Hurst, *The Release of*

foundations of pre-New Deal substantive due process protections for property rights were in some sense forged in the crisis of the mid-nineteenth century.

Tensions between Classical Liberal and Civic Republican visions of property again came to dominate the discourse during the Great Depression, an economic and social crisis not entirely unlike the one we are now experiencing, although (so far) of much greater magnitude. The New Deal and the revolution it spawned in constitutional jurisprudence—rejecting *Lochner*ian judicial oversight of basic economic regulation—was perhaps predictably attacked as the dawning of collectivization and communism.[19] And it is no coincidence that the work of the Legal Realists in attacking formalist conceptions of property, although generally predating the New Deal, took hold largely against this backdrop.[20]

This crisis and response revealed deep anxieties about what the Supreme Court was doing to property rights, but nonetheless confirmed the constitutional validity of the modern regulatory state. At the same time that a constitutional revolution was underway, the ground-level law of property was changing in response to crisis as well. Exercising power the Court affirmed after initial doubts, the New Deal transformed the housing market through standardizing and insuring 30-year fixed mortgages.[21] Regulatory intervention also sowed the first seeds of modern consumer rights law.[22]

American history has witnessed any number of other, less momentous, crises and financial panics up to (and now beyond) the Savings and Loan Crisis of the 1980s.[23] Similar stories can be told about public outrage, institutional reordering, and reflexive response that raise questions about the nature of property as an institution and legal force.[24] What this brief overview highlights is that a series of

---

Energy, *in* AMERICAN LAW AND CONSTITUTIONAL ORDER: HISTORICAL PERSPECTIVES 109-20 (Lawrence M. Friedman & Harry N. Scheiber eds. 1988). And Harry Scheiber has ably chronicled the many ways in which an array of sectors were increasingly granted sweeping powers, notably the power of eminent domain, to alter property arrangements as a means of fostering infrastructure and industrial development. *See* Harry N. Scheiber, *Property Law, Expropriation, and Resource Allocation by Government, 1789-1910*, *in* AMERICAN LAW AND CONSTITUTIONAL ORDER, *supra*, at 132-41.

19 *See* ELLEN SCHRECKER, MANY ARE THE CRIMES: MCCARTHYISM IN AMERICA (1998).

20 *See, e.g.*, Morris R. Cohen, *Property and Sovereignty*, 13 CORNELL L.Q. 8 (1927).

21 *See* Richard K. Green & Susan M. Wachter, *The American Mortgage in Historical and International Context*, 19 J. ECON. PERSP. 93, 94-96 (2005) (discussing New Deal era structural interventions in the mortgage market).

22 For an illuminating history of these developments, see LIZABETH COHEN, A CONSUMERS' REPUBLIC: THE POLITICS OF MASS CONSUMPTION IN POSTWAR AMERICA 18-61 (2003) (discussing the Depression and the rise of the "citizen consumer").

23 *See* CHARLES P. KINDLEBERGER & ROBERT Z. ALIBER, MANIAS, PANICS AND CRASHES: A HISTORY OF FINANCIAL CRISES 2 (5th ed. 2005).

24 Lawrence Friedman outlines, for example, a perennial cycle of debtor-creditor struggles in the terms of mortgage law that has flared repeatedly in times of crisis. *See* FRIEDMAN, *supra* note 11, at 245. As early as the Panic of 1819, which led the state of New

critical junctures throughout our history provoked fundamental questions about the nature of property and intensified long-standing tensions in property law.

This pattern of crisis reflects an ongoing debate about the balance between public and private in property. On the one hand, the association of property with possessive individualism and unfettered alienability have been deep and interconnected property norms since the Founding. Theorists who track this side of the divide focus on ownership as a spectrum that starts with "public" or common holding of a given resource, moves towards greater exclusivity and individual control, and arrives at the other end with something like Blackstone's sole and absolute dominion.

Competing with this conception, however, have always been communitarian or Civic Republican ideals that emphasize the social construction of property and property's role in social ordering.[25] From this perspective, property is less a bulwark against the state and more a reflection of complex personal relationships and power dynamics.

Neither ideal type has ever existed in pure form in American law, but the larger discourse of property tends to gravitate between them. And these ever-competing norms have been placed in starkest light in times of upheaval, where the necessity, or perhaps bare reality, of the state role in what is otherwise considered private ordering through property becomes most visible.

These are disparate vocabularies to describe similar tensions, tensions that still strongly inform not only disputes over land and property rights, but at a deeper level, popular reaction to the role of the regulatory state. These tensions have played out primarily in the structure of constitutional property, although that structure in turn enables much underlying doctrine. Thus, in the pre-New Deal *Lochner* era,[26] the Court actively policed a balance between state power and the claimed sanctity of property, giving foundational weight at times to a common-law driven vision of the latter.[27] More recently, the same tension has played out in the endless jurisprudential conflict over the definition of a regulatory taking.[28] Similar balancing certainly informs the many daily disputes that the law of property resolves, if more as a set of background norms.

The tension between public and private in property is a particular example of larger intractable ambiguities over the relationship between the state and

York to legislate a one-year grace period for hard-pressed debtors, doctrinal shifts have followed economic upheaval. *Id.*

25 *See generally* GREGORY S. ALEXANDER, COMMODITY & PROPRIETY: COMPETING VISIONS OF PROPERTY IN AMERICAN LEGAL THOUGHT 1776-1970 (1997).

26 Lochner v. New York, 198 U.S. 45 (1905).

27 *See, e.g.*, Cass R. Sunstein, *Constitutionalism After the New Deal*, 101 HARV. L. REV. 421, 437-38 (1987).

28 *See, e.g.*, Bradley C. Karkkainen, *The Police Power Revisited: Phantom Incorporation and the Roots of the Takings "Muddle"*, 90 MINN. L. REV. 826 (2006).

the individual in private ordering.[29] In this sense, the question is not formal ownership—public, private, or any number of hybrid approaches[30]—but rather the nature of legal property itself. Is property primarily a recognition by the state of *a priori* private relations, as in cruder versions of the Lockean narrative? Or is the state the essential force that defines the nature of property rights and mediates individual relationships through conscious or default choices to privilege one set of entitlements over another? The relative valence of these ideological poles remains contested in the historiography,[31] and our purpose here is simply to note the deep resonance of these competing conceptions.

In short, moments of crisis seem less to represent fundamental realignments in the way that Ackerman describes his examples of popular constitutional amendment (however contested), although they do at times take place in the context of larger legal change that filters through to property doctrine.[32] What they represent more immediately are times when seemingly quiet questions about the balance of individual autonomy and state authority, the role of the state in regulating property, and the role of property in social ordering rise to the cultural and legal surface. This is not to say that property law and the tension between public and private is silent outside of crisis—in the long arc of change, Classic Liberal property norms have hardly gone unchallenged in American history in the best of times. It is rather that sharp moments of economic uncertainty provoke anxiety and ferment about the nature of ownership itself. Although time and again the pendulum seems to swing back toward more privatized visions of property, the residue of crisis remains.

The Great Recession: Housing Crisis, Economic Shock, and Emerging Response

Divining the precise causes of the current crisis, dubbed by many the Great Recession, will provide scholars with ample work for some time.[33] However, it

---

29 *Cf.* Bernard E. Harcourt, Neoliberal Penality: The Birth of Natural Orders, The Illusion of Free Markets (2008).

30 *See, e.g.*, A Fourth Way? Privatization, Property, and the Emergence of New Market Economies (Gregory S. Alexander & Graznya Skapska, eds. 1994).

31 *See* William Weston Fisher III, *Stories about Property*, 94 Mich. L. Rev. 1776, 1786-87 (1996) (discussing historiographic developments in visions of the ideology of property); *id.* at 1788 (noting the increasing scholarly critique of a simple bi-polar perspective).

32 Thus, for example, the New Deal Court's ratification of an expanded scope of federal regulatory power has had profound effects on the operation of property law in practice, even if that ratification operated at one step removed from most of the doctrinal questions that frame common-law aspects of property law.

33 Some commentators have focused on one or a few determinants, such as the startling decline in home values in 2007, *see* Christopher L. Foote et al., *Subprime Facts: What (We*

is possible to chronicle, even as the crisis continues to play out, critical events that took shape throughout much of the decade, a period in which innovations in the credit market for housing fueled a major housing bubble. It is useful to begin with the Federal Reserve's interest-rate responses after the dot-com crash in the early part of this millennium. As mortgage interest rates fell, credit began to flow to housing consumers. Favorable economic conditions, innovations within the industry, and regulatory promotion of homeownership produced an environment in which underwriting standards dropped and borrowers with lower incomes and riskier profiles received mortgage loans.[34]

"Subprime" lending—a category that defies easy definition, but generally involves higher risk loans and less creditworthy borrowers[35]—increased significantly, peaking in 2006 at over six hundred billion dollars in originations.[36] The riskier nature of subprime loans was only partially a corollary of spottier borrower credit histories. As lenders loosened underwriting standards, underwriting processes in the subprime market also changed, moving away from lending norms established during the New Deal.[37]

As housing prices rose in markets across the country and homebuilders turned deserts into cities seemingly overnight, the cycle of borrowing was fueled by increasingly sophisticated securitizations.[38] Indeed, subprime securitizations relied on this very housing market appreciation for their underlying value.[39] In contrast

---

Think) We Know about the Subprime Crisis and What We Don't 3 (Fed. Reserve Bank of Boston: Pub. Policy Discussion Papers, Paper No. 08-2, 2008), *available at* http://ssrn.com/abstract=1153411, or systemic failures to assess risk, *see* Steven L. Schwarcz, *Systemic Risk*, 97 Geo. L.J. 193 (2008), or the illusion of liquidity, *see* Anastasia Nesvetailova, *The End of a Great Illusion: Credit Crunch and Liquidity Meltdown* (Danish Inst. for Int'l Studies, Working Paper No. 2008/23, 2008), *available at* http://www.diis.dk/graphics/Publications/WP2008/WP2008-23_Credit_Crunch_and_Liquidity_Meltdown.pdf.

34 Gary B. Gorton, *The Panic of 2007* 5–7 (Yale Sch. of Mgmt. and Nat'l Bureau of Econ. Research, Working Paper No. 08-24, 2008), *available at* http://papers.ssrn.com/sol3/papers.cfm?abstract_id=1255362.

35 Kathleen C. Engel & Patricia A. McCoy, *A Tale of Three Markets: The Law and Economics of Predatory Lending*, 80 Tex. L. Rev. 1255, 1261 (2002). Subprime and "Alt-A" loans are marked in the industry by some general characteristics, including lower borrower FICO scores, borrower credit problems, and failure to conform to Fannie Mae and Freddie Mac underwriting standards. *See* Gorton, *supra* note 34, at 8.

36 L. Randall Wray, *Lessons from the Subprime Meltdown* 30 (The Levy Econ. Inst. of Bard Coll, Working Paper No. 522, 2007), *available at* http://ssrn.com/abstract=1070833; *see also* Gorton, *supra* note 34, at 3.

37 Michael H. Schill, *The Impact of the Capital Markets on Real Estate Law and Practice*, 32 J. Marshall L. Rev 269, 270-76 (1999).

38 *See generally* Adam J. Levitin, *Resolving the Foreclosure Crisis: Modification of Mortgages in Bankruptcy*, 2009 Wis. L. Rev. 565.

39 Danielle DiMartino & John V. Duca, *The Rise and Fall of Subprime Mortgages*, Econ. Letter (Fed. Reserve Bank of Dallas, Dallas, Tex.), Nov. 2007, at 1, 5-6; Gorton, *supra* note 34, at 12, 19.

to its long experience with the traditional loan terms that still largely characterize prime lending, the industry had no experience in valuing the risks associated with the exotic loan terms underlying subprime mortgage-backed securities.[40] Moreover, the market participants best positioned to value risk had little incentive to do so, given that mortgage originators received higher fees for imposing more onerous terms on borrowers, but then sold the loans and often also the servicing function to third parties.[41] Nonetheless, it appears that the most exotic loans were also the most securitized.[42]

In late 2006, two events interrupted the expanding bubble in the primary and secondary mortgage markets: the rise in interest rates and the flattening (and in some areas of the country, falling) of home values.[43] The consequence was what would turn out to be only the first wave of interest-rate resets, mortgage defaults, and foreclosures.[44] By mid-2007, secondary market investors had begun to lose confidence.[45] Unable to sell loans in the secondary market, subprime lenders originated fewer loans.[46] The slow-down in the primary market was exacerbated by increasing demands among secondary market investors that subprime lenders buy back some of the riskiest securities.[47] By late 2007, credit markets began to tighten, and more than twenty subprime lenders had already filed for bankruptcy or gone out of business.[48] Meanwhile, another wave of interest rate resets and defaults hit.[49]

The stock market started to drop in early 2008, with the year beginning with the kind of volatility that has since come to seem normal. Throughout the spring and summer, some of Wall Street's largest financial institutions were forced to write off billions of dollars in assets related to what had become essentially worthless subprime securities.[50]

---

40 DiMartino & Duca, *supra* note 39, at 4; Wray, *supra* note 36, at 22–23; *see also* Gorton, *supra* note 34, at 49–61.

41 *See* Wray, *supra* note 36, at 46–47; *see also* Charles D. Anderson et al., *Deconstructing a Mortgage Meltdown: A Methodology for Decomposing Underwriting Quality* (May 29, 2009) (unpublished working paper), *available at* http://ssrn.com/abstract=1411782.

42 Wray, *supra* note 36, at 30–31.

43 Barth et al., *supra* note 1, at 73–74.

44 *Id.* at 74–99.

45 DiMartino & Duca, *supra* note 39, at 5–6.

46 Allan N. Krinsman, *Subprime Mortgage Meltdown: How Did It Happen and How Will It End?*, J. Structured Fin., Summer 2007, at 16–17.

47 Wray, *supra* note 36, at 34.

48 *See* Leslie Earnest, *Pink Slips Litter Loan Industry: The Turmoil in the Sub-Prime Mortgage Sector Hits Some Workers As Hard As Borrowers*, L.A. Times, Apr. 6, 2007, at C1; Knowledge@Wharton, The Subprime Crisis: A Timeline, http://knowledge.wharton.upenn.edu/special_sections/subprime/timeline.cfm# (last visited Feb. 2, 2010); *see also* Krinsman, *supra* note 46, at 16.

49 Barth et al., *supra* note 1, at 135–41.

50 *Id.* at 4–5, 106, 235.

The first major response to the crisis occurred in the summer of 2008, when Congress passed the Housing and Economic Recovery Act ("HERA").[51] In a multifaceted effort to address weaknesses in the housing market that moved well beyond the enhanced disclosures and tax breaks characteristic of recent legislation targeting homeowners, HERA authorized the FHA to insure $300 billion worth of mortgages by means of voluntary refinancings, and it also changed certain FHA lending requirements.[52] The legislation provided new oversight for Fannie Mae and Freddie Mac and gave the Treasury Department authority to purchase an equity interest in both entities.[53]

In one watershed month—September, 2008—the federal government placed Fannie Mae and Freddie Mac in conservatorships, committing up to $100 billion to each entity in the event of capital shortfalls,[54] Bank of America bought Merrill Lynch at a fire sale, the storied firm Lehman Brothers filed for bankruptcy,[55] the Federal Reserve agreed to loan the then-staggering sum of $85 billion to insurance giant American International Group (A.I.G.),[56] and the largest bank failure in American history occurred with the emergency sale of Washington Mutual to JP Morgan Chase.[57]

Over the next few weeks, the magnitude of the lockup of credit markets around the world—and the resulting fall-out—became clear.[58] Globally, investors shifted investments to Treasury bills and other relatively safe havens, thereby raising the cost of borrowing.[59] In late October, currencies around the globe plummeted.[60] That same month, unemployment in the United States reached a 14-year high.[61]

In the midst of this pivotal moment, as banks became increasingly reluctant to loan given the uncertainty of their own subprime-infected portfolios, the Bush

51 Pub. L. No. 110-289, 122 Stat. 2654 (2008).

52 *See* 12 U.S.C.A. §§ 1701, 1709, 1715z-23(m) (2009).

53 *See id.* §§ 1455, 4501–4526, 1719.

54 BARTH ET AL., *supra* note 1, at 253–55.

55 *See* Andrew Ross Sorkin, *Merrill is Sold: Failing to Find Buyer, Lehman Set to File for Bankruptcy*, N.Y. TIMES, Sept. 15, 2008, at A1.

56 BARTH ET AL., *supra* note 1, at 64, 235–37.

57 *Id.* at 269.

58 *See* Arthur E. Wilmarth, Jr., *The Dark Side of Universal Banking: Financial Conglomerates and the Origins of the Subprime Financial Crisis*, 41 CONN. L. REV. 963, 967–68 (2009).

59 *See* BARTH ET AL., *supra* note 1, at 78, 352; *see also* Eamonn K. Moran, *Wall Street Meets Main Street: Understanding the Financial Crisis*, 13 N.C. BANKING INST. 5, 71–76 (2009).

60 Mark Landler & Vikas Bajaj, *Some Currencies Plunge as Stocks Sink Worldwide*, N.Y. TIMES, Oct. 25, 2008, at A1.

61 Bureau of Labor Statistics, Labor Force Statistics from the Current Population Survey, *available at* http://data.bls.gov/PDQ/servlet/SurveyOutputServlet?data_tool=latest_numbers&series_id=LNS14000000 (last visited June 1, 2010). Since November, 2008, unemployment rates steadily increased from 6.9% to a peak of 10.1% in October 2009. *Id.*

Administration moved to unfreeze credit markets, proposing what eventually became a $700 billion bailout package.[62] The bailout plan began with a proposal to buy up hundreds of billions of dollars worth of distressed mortgages, theoretically stanching the uncertainty that was blocking lending out of fear of the inability to value assets backed by this so-called "toxic" debt.

As the crisis spread across the globe, the Treasury shifted gears in response to early indications that purchasing toxic debt was unlikely to calm the markets.[63] In mid-October, the Treasury announced that it would use the almost limitless authority granted under the Act's Troubled Asset Relief Program (TARP) to buy up to $250 billion in bank stock, thereby taking equity in a mix of large and regional banks.[64] In November, Secretary Paulson changed course again, proposing to extend his program of equity injections to include consumer lenders, such as credit card companies and auto finance companies, which eventually came to fruition as the Term Asset-Backed Securities Loan Facility (TALF).[65] The Federal Reserve Board eventually proposed expanding the TALF to as much as $1 trillion, with a particular focus on stimulating economic growth among households and small businesses.[66] This initiative is part of the current administration's multi-pronged Financial Stability Plan, which includes a "Financial Stability Trust" and a "Public-Private Investment Fund."[67] Prominently among the supports offered by the Trust is a capital assistance program which provides preferred stock, convertible to common stock, in return for capital, as well as a mandatory "stress test" for major banking institutions and the promise of greater coordination among the key regulatory agencies.[68] Meanwhile, the public–private investment fund is intended to include private capital alongside public funds for bailing out troubled banks.[69]

President Obama has thus far departed from his predecessor's position on consumers and homeowners. His administration's Homeowner Affordability and Stability Plan (HASP) was designed to help at least nine million families modify or refinance their mortgages. The plan seeks to accomplish these measures by means of a mix of mandates and incentives, including promised opportunities to refinance loans owned or guaranteed by Fannie or Freddie, mandated reductions in

---

62 Barth et al., *supra* note 1, at 257.

63 Lucian A. Bebchuk, *Buying Troubled Assets*, 26 Yale J. on Reg. 343, 346–47 (2009).

64 Barth et al., *supra* note 1, at 258–59.

65 *Id.* at 240.

66 Press Release, Bd. of Governors of the Fed. Reserve Sys., Federal Reserve is Prepared to Expand the Term Asset-Backed Securities Loan Facility (TALF) (Feb. 10, 2009), *available at* http://www.federalreserve.gov/newsevents/press/monetary/20090210b.htm.

67 In connection with this initiative, the Obama administration established a publicly accessible website providing information about the new programs as well as opportunities to track public expenses in connection with the program. *See* U.S. Dep't of the Treasury, Fact Sheet: Financial Stability Plan, http://www.financialstability.gov/docs/fact-sheet.pdf.

68 *Id.*

69 *Id.*

interest rates, matching funds for this purpose, and financial incentives to lenders to modify terms and to borrowers to comply with terms.[70] Notably also, the plan provides $1.5 billion in relocation funds to renters displaced by foreclosure and $2 billion in "neighborhood stabilization funds."[71]

On February 17, 2009, President Obama signed into law the American Recovery and Reinvestment Act, a $787 billion package, approximately one-third of which took the form of tax cuts, many of them for middle-class taxpayers. The Act also provides financial aid to states, and financial incentives for home purchases as well as basic consumer purchases.[72]

By most accounts, the recent crisis brought the American economy to the brink of a second Great Depression, and the governmental reaction has been swift if not always certain. Not since the New Deal has the government spent so much money, nor intervened so intrusively in the private sectors of housing, banking, and finance.

The Crisis and the Public–Private Divide in Property

No two crises in our history have been exactly alike, although some echoes recur with eerie similarity—the bursting of seemingly irrational economic bubbles, chronicles of financial deaths that in hindsight could have been foretold, and broad regulatory and cultural changes that never completely solve underlying structural problems. The current crisis recapitulates elements of many earlier crises, but perhaps more than many, deeply evokes tensions in how we think about property along perennial public–private fault-lines.

Crisis as a Rebalancing Force

Our current moment has brought to the fore conceptions of property that highlight interconnection and the distributional consequences of unfettered risk. First, the crisis has underscored what might be considered the unity of property, a unity emphasized in theoretical terms by social relations and ecological conceptions of property. Conceptually, this is a central strand of the debate between Lockean-individualist and more communitarian, proprietarian visions of property.[73] In this context, the debate plays out between a kind of physicalized Blackstonian

---

70 Such reductions are to last for a period of five years. *See* U.S. Dep't of the Treasury, Homeowner Affordability and Stability Plan: Fact Sheet, http://www.treasury.gov/initiatives/eesa/homeowner-affordability-plan/FactSheet.pdf.

71 *Id.* at 7.

72 American Recovery and Reinvestment Act of 2009, Pub. L. No. 111-5, 123 Stat. 115 (2009).

73 *See supra* Part I.

isolation as a descriptive and normative baseline, and conceptions of property that stress holistic interconnection.[74]

On one level, the unity of property revealed by the current crisis is eminently practical. Land is tied to debt; debt is tied to complex financial instruments like mortgage-backed securities and collateralized debt obligations; those instruments are tied to personal holdings for investors. When one thread in this web becomes "toxic"—to use a way of describing debt that has entered the popular consciousness in this crisis—the entire interrelated system can be compromised. Retirees in Arizona see the value of their 401(k) retirement plans evaporate because of lending practices in Maine and appetite for debt tranches in Bahrain. At a more local level, the crisis is demonstrating the broad consequences of our neighbors' debts—a view of property that transcends the externalities-driven focus of the isolationist conception. We have always known that foreclosures, as devastating as they might be for an individual borrower in immediate terms, have an impact on others. This is a "spillover," in the classic sense, but still fairly localized. As the scale of foreclosures has reached levels not seen since the Great Depression, however, entire communities are being devastated.[75] In the light of crisis, the interdependence of the value of individual property holding becomes inescapable.

A second, and perhaps more explicitly normative, debate brought to the fore in the current crisis is tension between property as opportunity versus property as an instrument of egalitarianism and material redistribution. American property law has generally privileged the inchoate promise that property ownership leads to ever greater opportunities—for wealth, income, and other rewards. This orientation elevates certain policy choices. For example, as some commentators have noted approvingly,[76] the property-as-opportunity paradigm permeates regulatory support for transactions in credit and other opportunities to leverage assets such as one's home. The connotation is that the "right" to assume debt must be preserved as a means of leveraging opportunity.[77]

Indeed, the hyper-expansive layering of securities and credit transactions on the residential real estate market is a reminder that the oldest and most traditional objects of property remain foundational as potential sources of market access

74 *See, e.g.*, Joseph L. Sax, *Takings, Private Property and Public Rights*, 81 YALE L.J. 149, 152 (1971) ("Particular parcels are tied to one another in complex ways, and property is more accurately described as being inextricably part of a network of relationships that is neither limited to, nor usefully defined by, the property boundaries with which the legal system is accustomed to dealing.").

75 *See, e.g.*, David Streitfeld, *Almost Entire Town Is Drowning in Debt as Home Values Plunge*, N.Y. TIMES, Nov. 11, 2008, at A1.

76 *See, e.g.*, HERNANDO DE SOTO, THE MYSTERY OF CAPITAL: WHY CAPITALISM TRIUMPHS IN THE WEST AND FAILS EVERYWHERE ELSE (2000).

77 Indeed, in the globalizing trend toward increased rights to credit, the founder of the Grameen Bank, who recently won the Nobel Peace Price, has repeatedly declared that "credit is a fundamental human right." *See* Randeep Ramesh, *Credit is a Basic Human Right*, GUARDIAN WEEKLY (U.K.), Jan. 5, 2007, at 28.

at a time when scholars are increasingly announcing the ascendancy of various "modern" forms of property.[78] In this crisis, the humble single-family house—so venerated in our culture in contemporary suburban echo to the Jeffersonian tradition of the yeoman farmer and even older echo of the cultural power of land—turns out to be central to the entire global economy.[79]

This opportunity-enhancing viewpoint generates a corresponding stake in the infrastructural public–private debate. The role of both market and state in protecting property rights is to protect access to ownership opportunities, in the classically liberal or neo-liberal sense of regulating in the event of market failure.[80] As constitutional drafters in other parts of the world make markedly different choices about positive rights in recognition of explicit distributional objectives, the American standard has remained reactive rather than prospective, incremental rather than all-inclusive.

Yet as the current crisis has deepened, it has exposed anew drawbacks of conceptualizing property as the locus for primarily individual opportunity. Given the extent to which the crisis has touched so many people's retirement accounts, savings, and investments—not to mention homes, jobs, and schools—the distributional consequences of crisis are difficult to ignore. It has also become clear that spreading opportunity widely can result in widespread pain and loss. The recent scholarly discussions of property as a tool of egalitarianism, "human flourishing," and "development and dignity" provide a rich basis for elaborating alternatives to the negative-rights focused orientation of property as opportunity.[81] Some of these conceptions view property law as the appropriate mechanism for

---

78 *See, e.g.*, Scott R. Cleere, *Intellectual Property: The Capital of the Information Age*, ADVOCATE, June 2005, at 10; Lee G. Meyer, *Intellectual Property in Today's Financing Market*, 19 AM. BANKR. INST. J., Mar. 2000, at 20.

79 Perhaps the most obvious lesson for property scholars that the current crisis evinces is the tenacity of certain reflexive images of property in the private realm. It may be that our supposed service economy was, until the current crisis, increasingly creating wealth out of ever-more creative financial structures, and it is certainly true that property now extends to even the most abstract and novel of creations. *See, e.g.*, Joshua A.T. Fairfield, *Virtual Property*, 85 B.U. L. REV. 1047 (2005). Our point is not that traditional forms of property are on some pragmatic or normative metric more important than intellectual property or other emerging property types. It is instead an observation that, in an era in which intangibles and intellectual property dominate the discourse, this crisis reminds us that the most traditional forms of property—indeed, land—remain important.

80 *See* BRIAN Z. TAMANAHA, ON THE RULE OF LAW: HISTORY, POLITICS, THEORY 118–19 (2004).

81 Gregory S. Alexander et al., *A Statement of Progressive Property*, 94 CORNELL L. REV. 743, 743–44 (2009) [hereinafter Alexander et al., *A Statement of Progressive Property*]; *see also* Gregory S. Alexander & Eduardo M. Peñalver, *Properties of Community*, 10 THEORETICAL INQUIRIES L. 127 (2009); Eduardo M. Peñalver, *Land Virtues*, 94 CORNELL L. REV. 821 (2009).

elucidating a framework that recognizes "moral and political conceptions of just social relationships, just distribution, and democracy."[82]

Thus, even while almost viscerally reacting against a negative image of "redistribution," some parts of the public discourse have begun to contemplate the possibility that the government ought more systematically to moderate the likelihood of such losses being suffered again. Indeed, the current administration's most recent initiatives suggest a serious deliberation over government's role in establishing a distributional baseline—which has in turn generated anxiety in response.

A third, closely related, tension in conceptions of property that the current crisis has put into stark relief is the role of property as a repository for investment, in the classic sense of either reward for labor or security of expectation.[83] The Classical Liberal emphasis on individual labor retains deep cultural relevance in the reflexive preference for market mechanisms that are supposed to price risk accurately, and a corresponding conception of property as the locus of residual value.[84] The current crisis—and particularly the scale and breadth of federal, state, and local interventions to respond to cascading market-failures related to property—put real pressure on the idea that property is a neutral vessel to align risk and reward.

At a local level, one of the ironies of the crisis is that the push to promote the ur-privatized vision of ownership and a culture that increasingly venerated reward for risk-taking were in no small measure responsible for a global economic collapse. There are at least some documented benefits for ownership as a tenure model that can undergird our cultural preference for homeownership.[85] But there are countervailing costs, not the least of which include the real economic and psychological consequences of the *loss* of homeownership—costs that are becoming acutely understood in light of the current level of foreclosures.[86]

---

82 Alexander et al., *A Statement of Progressive Property*, *supra* note 81, at 743.

83 *See, e.g.*, Richard A. Posner, Economic Analysis of Law § 3.1 (7th ed. 2007). As Gregory Alexander has noted, the foundational modern economic account of property rights offered by Harold Demsetz "holds that property rights maximize aggregate social wealth by encouraging people to take into account the costs and benefits of how they use their property." Alexander, *supra* note 25, at 379–80 (discussing Harold Demsetz, *Toward a Theory of Property Rights*, 57 Am. Econ. Rev. 347 (1967)).

84 *See, e.g.*, John Armour & Michael J. Whincop, *The Proprietary Foundations of Corporate Law*, 27 Oxford J. Legal Stud. 429, 437–38 (2007) (discussing conceptions of property rights in which "'Ownership' is defined as the entitlement to exercise 'residual rights of control'").

85 *See, e.g.*, Rachel D. Godsil & David V. Simunovich, *Protecting Status: The Mortgage Crisis, Eminent Domain, and the Ethic of Homeownership*, 77 Fordham L. Rev. 949, 970–73 (2008).

86 *See generally* Lorna Fox O'Mahony, *Homeownership, Debt, and Default: The Affective Value of Home and the Challenge of Affordability*, in Affordable Housing and Public-Private Partnerships 169 (2009).

In the other heart of the crisis, the financial sector, a long arc of regulatory change in the past quarter-century reduced monitoring and supervision of financial markets, justified by the argument that risk-taking should be encouraged and rewarded. The consequence of this excessive risk-taking in an era of privatized regulatory structures is that the nature of the underlying asset base is becoming increasingly seen as a bewildering failure—something of a global Ponzi scheme (or, perhaps now, a global Madoff scheme). Direct intervention thus becomes critical to shore up confidence in a number of arenas, often explicitly to avoid a psychological herd effect of cascading doubt.

One of the many reminders from this crisis of risk's unpredictability is the echo in the crisis-torn financial sector of the anticommons fragmentation problem at a large scale.[87] Securitization in the subprime sector entailed an acute level of decomposition of ownership in the classic sense, in which multiple owners were granted rights of exclusion, producing an atmosphere of instability, insecurity, and inability to exercise predictable and productive rights of use.[88] As with Michael Heller's Moscow storefronts, in this case of too much property, the interdependence of property rights resulted in an opaque decision-making structure and a failure to rescue property ownership from a downward spiral of insecurity.[89]

As a result, in complex global financial markets no less than in single-family housing, conceptions of the balance between risk and reward instantiated in property are being recalibrated to account for the reality of an active (if still unproven) safety net. Property's function as a font of security now more clearly highlights the centrality of the state in bolstering that very security. This is nothing new in our culture, but is a central aspect of the current crisis nonetheless.

Public versus Private as a Framework for Regulatory Response

While this crisis has evoked—and challenged—the traditional balance between public and private in property, the public–private dichotomy has also powerfully influenced regulatory responses to the crisis. To the extent that crisis-regulation could have revealed the artificiality of the dichotomy, that opportunity was not at the core of the response. Instead, at different levels of intervention, regulation reified core features of this age-old tension. On the one hand, regulatory responses to the subprime mortgage meltdown reactively preserved a Demsetzian vision of property as creating private ownership opportunities at all levels of market

87 Frank I. Michelman, *Ethics, Economics and the Law of Property*, 24 Nomos 3 (1982); Michael A. Heller, *The Tragedy of the Anticommons: Property in the Transition from Marx to Markets*, 111 Harv. L. Rev. 621, 622–23 (1998).

88 Heller, *supra* note 87, at 664–67.

89 *See id.* at 673. David A. Dana discusses some of the implications, including the impossibility of loan modifications, in his article, *The Foreclosure Crisis and the Anti-Fragmentation Principle in State Property Law*, 77 U. Chi. L. Rev. 97 (2010).

participation in anticipation of incentivizing industry-driven market correction. Regulation at the core thus embodied the relatively more isolationist, opportunity-oriented, risk-rewarding view of ownership. On the other hand, in the response to failures in wider financial markets, the Civic Republican vision of property arguably liberated regulatory intervention. At this level, regulators adopted the property norms that come to the fore in times of crisis, including a more interconnected, distribution-protective, stability-oriented, and coordinated view of property. The regulatory choice of new norms at this level of crisis response resulted in a new role for government as a coercive owner of property that had previously been perceived as inaccessibly private.

As a whole, the property story that emerges from the response invokes the particular version of the age-old public/private debate in which large-scale rhetoric and massive public intervention combine to restore and protect private rights of ownership. Consider two notable responses to the subprime mortgage meltdown. At the rhetorical level, the title of the "Housing and Economic Recovery Act" (HERA) signaled its focus on housing as the stabilizer of markets and the originator of economic recovery. But neither HERA nor the other early responses to the meltdown sought to renegotiate the vision of property as a bulwark of private ownership and control. Thanks in part to the voluntary nature of the refinancing program, the statute's primary impact appears to have been rhetorical. Very few refinancings under the statute actually occurred.[90] Moreover, of the range of possible choices, HERA's two regulatory targets, lenders and the government-sponsored entities, historically have been the most regulated and, not coincidentally, the least associated with traditional rights of ownership. Particularly in light of this and other limitations on federal mortgage refinancing programs, the property story that emerges from HERA is a singular focus on the importance of ownership, combined with a restrained regulatory balancing of ownership opportunities.[91]

President Obama's HASP seems to attempt to convert HERA's rhetoric to tangible protections for homeowners, most conspicuously by mandating some of the protections that HERA merely incentivized. Viewed as a property story, however, the program is consistent with HERA in protecting private ownership, if a bit more emphatically. The image of homeownership as an important means of individual wealth accumulation pervades this program.

90 Brian Grow et al., *The Home Foreclosure Fiasco: How the Banking Industry is Undermining Efforts to Keep People in Their Houses*, Business Week, Feb. 23, 2009, at 34, 36 ("Hope for Homeowners—which Bush officials and banks promised last fall would shield 400,000 families from foreclosure—has so far produced only 25 refinanced loans.").

91 The refinancing program, licensing requirements, and monitoring of capitalization levels evince a cautious regulatory interest in protecting homeownership. Also evident, particularly in the reforms aimed at the government-sponsored entities, is a clear interest in protecting the ownership interests in the secondary market for mortgage-backed securities. The limitations in the provisions aimed at protecting homeowners reveal the balancing of lenders' and investors' property interests.

In short, the government's response thus far to the crisis at the level of primary mortgage markets has tilted quite heavily toward the Blackstonian rather than the Civic Republican orientation in property. Property manifests as a negative right of access to credit and ownership opportunities. It serves as a powerful tool of wealth accumulation. Even under more recent interventions, refinancing of debt (for the purpose of restoring opportunity) takes primacy over foreclosure relief. The latter would be a more obvious means of establishing a distributional baseline. Importantly in this property story, strident rhetoric about the dignity, primacy, and social worth of ownership underpin regulatory reaction and incrementalism. In response to failures in disclosure and incentive-based regimes, this conception of property proposes more enticing incentives—refinancing rather than reductions in debt through "cram-downs."

At this level of regulatory intervention, property also symbolizes risk taking rather than mere subsistence or even security. Property is a tool of individual choice. At bottom, property signifies access to the free market, and indeed to freedom itself. In this property story, the isolationist vision of property materializes as an obsession with privacy. Thanks to industry innovations, FICO credit scores now substitute for face-to-face meetings with loan officers[92] Little or no documentation is required to obtain a loan. Contracts, in lieu of intrusive regulation, govern rights in private relationships.

Finally, this incrementalist vision carries with it the sense that the current crisis is an anomaly rather than a foreseeable event that could happen again. The regulatory response has not been reactive only because of the unpredictability of the crisis. It has also been reactive because regulators have assumed that at the local level, the market does not need a more permanent form of correction or coordination.

In contrast to the restrained property story emanating from the government's response to failures in the primary mortgage market, property has had a far more public, even communitarian face in the response to broader financial market failures. At the forefront, in dollars, commentary, and press, was the Treasury Department's decision to take equity stakes in private firms. Regulation in the face of the understandably pervasive sense of distrust in private decision-making by financial firms took the form of a counter-balancing governmental *ownership* interest. In its use of TARP funds, the federal government pointedly thrust aside traditional protections buttressing private ownership—at least on a temporary basis. It deliberately chose to disrupt the august vision in liberal economies of corporations as bastions of private ownership, contracts, relationships, and risk taking.[93]

92 *See* Wray, *supra* note 36, at 48.

93 *See, e.g.*, Melvin A. Eisenberg, *The Conception That the Corporation is a Nexus of Contracts, and the Dual Nature of the Firm*, 24 J. Corp. L. 819 (1999); Michael C. Jensen & William H. Meckling, *Theory of the Firm: Managerial Behavior, Agency Costs and Ownership Structure*, 3 J. Fin. Econ. 305 (1976); *see also* United States v. Jon-T Chems., Inc., 768 F.2d 686, 690 (5th Cir. 1985) ("Under the doctrine of limited liability, the owner

If only at the level of rhetoric, this move crossed important property boundaries between public and private. It is striking that as Fannie Mae, Freddie Mac, and potentially significant portions of the banking industry come into forms of public ownership, there have been no modern *Steel Seizure* cases,[94] or even much popular outcry. In the immediate aftermath, companies deemed "too large to fail" seemed to be lined up for similar intervention, beginning with General Motors and Chrysler. The pendulum has already begun to swing back again, with companies starting to reduce their dependence on federal aid, but at an institutional level, this wave of state control puts pressure on conceptions of property rights feeding opportunity, risk, and reward that vilify the role of the state in creating the conditions under which individual entrepreneurship can take place.

In the response to the broader economic crisis, then, the idea of property as relational is enjoying a moment of ascendance. Regulation of the financial markets in this crisis may for generations be the paradigmatic example of the Legal Realists' claim that property exists to serve relationships.[95] The globalized ripple effects from the subprime meltdown forced a set of regulatory responses that strongly refuted Blackstonian absolutism: property rights had to be limited to protect the property rights of others.

Although property retained its rhetorical connection with power, here the power was public, collective, and even at times coercive in its effect. It was public both because the government's involvement included the increasingly meaningful right to control and because of the transparency of the Treasury's actions.[96] Rather than serving as a tool of individual opportunity, property ownership in this response became a means of collective action against the broad distributional consequences of unrestrained private behavior.[97] In these aspects of the regulatory response, the

---

of a corporation is not liable for the corporation's debts. Creditors of the corporation have recourse only against the corporation itself, not against its parent company or shareholders. It is on this assumption that 'large undertakings are rested, vast enterprises are launched, and huge sums of capital attracted.'" (citing Baker v. Raymond Int'l, 656 F.2d 173, 179 (5th Cir. 1981), *cert. denied*, 456 U.S. 983 (1982); Anderson v. Abbott, 321 U.S. 349, 362 (1944))).

94 Youngstown Sheet & Tube Co. v. Sawyer, 343 U.S. 579 (1952) (limiting the power of the President to seize private property during times of emergency).

95 *See generally* Joseph William Singer, Entitlement: The Paradoxes of Property (2000); Cohen, *supra* note 20; Robert L. Hale, *Bargaining, Duress, and Economic Liberty*, 43 Colum. L. Rev. 603 (1943).

96 *See, e.g.*, Press Release, U.S. Dep't of the Treasury, Treasury Announces TARP Investment in GMAC (Dec. 29, 2008), *available at* http://www.treas.gov/press/releases/hp1335.htm; Joint Press Release, Bd. of Governors of the Fed. Reserve Sys., Fed. Deposit Ins. Corp. & U.S. Dep't of the Treasury, Joint Statement by Treasury, Federal Reserve, and the FDIC on Citigroup (Nov. 23, 2008), *available at* http://www.federalreserve.gov/newsevents/press/bcreg/20081123a.htm.

97 *See, e.g.*, Peter S. Goodman, *Chilly Review From Experts*, N.Y. Times, Sept. 23, 2008, at A1 ("'It absolutely has to be punitive,' Mr. Baker said. 'If they sell us the junk, then we own the company.'").

image of property as a set of duties, not just rights, has come to the fore. In this sense, nationalization recognizes that the assets at stake included pensions, homes, and savings accounts. This was a moment of stabilizing, indeed even subsistence, rather than risk taking. In an extraordinary inversion of prevailing property norms, property ownership served briefly as a locus for efforts to achieve stability, more in the nature of a safety net than a risk enabler, within the free market.

Finally, the current crisis has brought longstanding tensions to the surface of American property law about what exactly the prescriptive role of the state should be when it does intervene. A striking example emerges from the government's partial nationalization of banks. While European social democracies have long been accustomed to the notion that government can legitimately serve to coordinate property rights and market relationships among private firms, such a notion is both foreign to most in this country and repugnant to many.[98] In our putatively Classic Liberal market economy, the state's role is theoretically to protect the integrity of market interactions.[99] State intervention beyond this point raises deep questions of legitimacy, dilution of competition, and the natural hierarchies that are popularly thought to flow from the rough-and-tumble world of the free market. Fundamental in this conceptualization is the notion that private firms and individuals have the freedom to engage in a broad range of competitive behavior, with property rights serving as a source of freedom. This orientation of private firms vis-à-vis each other, the market, and the state creates an atmosphere in which state intervention in private structures of ownership is not only unwelcome, but a signal of abnormal, troubled times.

It could be argued, of course, that such interventions occur with regularity.[100] Indeed, recent regulatory efforts to cap executive compensation and otherwise control significant corporate decisions could simply be viewed as those of a controlling shareholder demanding compliance with a new business model. But against a conceptualization in which the government's role is viewed neither as a market coordinator nor – at least not comfortably – as a private owner of property such as this, the acquisition of property rights by the state seems coercive rather than collaborative, aggressive rather than supportive. Partial or complete nationalization sends a message that the state has been required to settle affairs and relationships that private firms can no longer manage.[101]

98 *Compare* Varieties of Capitalism: The Institutional Foundations of Comparative Advantage 6–66 (Peter A. Hall & David Soskice eds., 2001) *with* the sentiments of then-Treasury Secretary Henry Paulson early in the crisis, when he stated that "Government owning a stake in any private U.S. company is objectionable to most Americans—me included." Press Release, U.S. Dep't of the Treasury, Statement by Secretary Henry M. Paulson, Jr. on Actions to Protect the U.S. Economy (Oct. 14, 2008), *available at* http://www.treas.gov/press/releases/hp1205.htm.

99 *See* Varieties of Capitalism, *supra* note 98, at 49, 251.

100 *See id.* at 8, 251.

101 We thank Lorna Fox O'Mahony for supplying the familiar adage (for her, from the British context) "capitalized profit, socialized loss" to the American crisis.

Indeed, the primary purpose of state ownership rights may be its signaling effect. After all, the government at first proceeded by taking preferred stock in these private entities, with no voting rights and without the kind of control traditionally associated with equity.[102]

Against this backdrop of unwelcome coercion, the particular regulations accompanying partial nationalization have generated a novel image of property—that of property as an instrument of punishment. When, after taking preferred stock in certain lenders, the government moved to cap executive compensation paid out by those lenders, it came to seem less the actions of a prudent investor and more a popular response to the excesses that required intervention.[103] Although there may be excellent reasons to limit executive compensation and require other concessions in exchange for state investment, in the context of crisis, they take on an undertone of sanction rather than regulation. In response to the public outcry against corporate misbehavior, the government chose ownership almost as a path toward retribution.

Implicit in this emergent property story, then, is a reliance (however uncomfortable) on regulation to protect the structure of opportunity. In contrast to responses targeted at preserving homeownership, this was not an incentive program to promote more accurate assessment of risk. It was a large-scale "cram-down" of sorts to mandate responsible behavior. It was the seizure of temporary governmental control for the purpose of managing risk. Governmental involvement conceded both the need for coordinated action at times of economic crisis and the reverberating public consequences of private, corporate decision-making. It is in this respect that property's drift toward the coordination among firms in more socialized economies is most apparent—and the corresponding public response equally telling.

Conclusion: Tracking the Pendulum

It is too soon to predict whether and to what extent this particular crisis will resolve any of the longstanding tensions associated with the public–private divide in property theory. The pendulum is still swinging. On the one hand, we may see a more widespread acceptance of an active state role in property regulation. For

102 Such a move may also have been influenced by federal regulations governing the adequacy of capital maintained by national banks. *See* 12 C.F.R. pt. 3, app. A (2009). The government's cap on executive compensation belies the merely rhetorical nature of the government's ownership interest, however, as does the recent move to convert some preferred stock to common stock.

103 Paula Cruickshank, *Treasury Issues New Restrictions on Executive Compensation Paid by Financial Institutions*, CCH Fin. Crisis News Ctr., Feb. 4, 2009, *available at* http://www.financialcrisisupdate.com/2009/02/treasury-issues-new-restrictions-on-executive-compensation-paid-by-financial-institutions.html.

example, our culture may come to recognize that state action that seems to cut deeply into traditional notions of property can be as stabilizing as state inaction (or at least less visible action).[104] This is so less because individual expectation must always be paramount, but rather because it falls at times to the state to backstop and mitigate what would be harshest about a system that venerates individual expectation—and risk taking and reward—above all else. In many ways, a central thrust of the current response is aimed as much at the psychology of the market as it is at the underlying economic fundamentals. In this respect, it sends a strong signal about the unique power of the state to rectify broad-scale collapse. If the state is often seen as a threat to individual liberty—with property standing as a bulwark against arbitrary action—then the ability of the state to respond to crisis can act as a perennial reminder of the opposite proposition.

Normatively, this may lead to a greater willingness to embrace an ethic of mutual responsibility around property.[105] Thus, if the prevailing conception of property is one of the Classical Liberal vision of isolation, where externalities are an aberration to be responded to on a grudging basis, then conceptions of the common good hold little traction. By contrast, if property is understood as deeply interconnected, woven into an inextricable web, then there is nothing more natural than a role for the community in modulating the consequences of what happens in that web. Whether the community will accept a more overtly redistributive impulse once the crisis subsides is another question.

On the other hand, as has occurred regularly in American history, it seems just as possible that the valence of property rights will return to something closer to the possessive individualist vision. Advocates can and often do react hyperbolically to any change in the structure of property rights that might represent some unalterable turn towards collectivization or laissez-faire absolutism. But in the broad sweep, there seems to be something of a regression to the mean in the dialectic of individual and state. Perhaps more than any other signal, the familiar echo of strident rhetoric surrounding a core veneration of ownership portends a pendulum swing back toward the individualist vision. In this respect, there is a marked consistency in the evolving regulatory response. Perhaps also one of

---

104 One of the more influential concerns articulated about the state's role in property rights is Frank Michelman's idea that certain types of state action give rise to what he described as "demoralization costs." Frank I. Michelman, *Property, Utility, and Fairness: Comments on the Ethical Foundations of "Just Compensation" Law*, 80 Harv. L. Rev. 1165, 1214–16 (1967). These costs derive from the uncertainty and disaffection that people feel when faced with interference with their expectations about their entitlements. Bruce A. Ackerman, Private Property and the Constitution 60–64 (1977). His idea has been invoked to justify minimalism in how the state approaches the terms of ownership, *see, e.g.*, David A. Dana & Thomas W. Merrill, Property: Takings 36 (2002), and has added a powerful undergirding for the long-standing argument that stability of expectation is a paramount virtue for any property system.

105 *See* Gregory S. Alexander, *The Social-Obligation Norm in American Property Law*, 94 Cornell L. Rev. 745, 818–19 (2009).

the more enduring lessons from the discourse of institutional evolution would be to understand whether this consistency is part of the cycle between steady state change and punctuated equilibrium—a buffering system of sorts, that the institution builds in for crises such as this.

Acknowledgment

Portions of this chapter appeared as *Property in Crisis*, 78 FORDHAM LAW REVIEW 101 (2010). The authors wish to thank participants in the Washington University School of Law faculty colloquium.

Chapter 5

Eviction and the Public Interest: The Right to Respect for Home in English Law

Lorna Fox O'Mahony

Introduction

Notwithstanding the popular belief that the English legal system regards 'an Englishman's home as his castle',[1] the idea of an enforceable 'right to respect for home' is not one which sits easily within English law. Historically, references to respect for home have tended to revolve around the idea of *privacy* at home, and particularly with the extent to which the state can lawfully impinge upon a citizen's private dwelling.[2] While Article 8(1) of the European Convention on Human Rights states that 'Everyone shall have the right to respect for his private and family life, his home and his correspondence', the reference to 'respect for home' in this paragraph is clearly embedded in the overall context of Article 8. For example, in *London Borough of Harrow v. Qazi*,[3] the first landmark decision of the House of Lords on the right to respect for home, Lord Hope noted that: '[m]ost international human rights instruments recognize a right to privacy. That is the concept which underlies Article 8 of the Convention.'[4] Thus, the references in Article 8 to the right to respect for family life, for home and for correspondence are often viewed conjunctively, as aspects of the right to private life,[5] and the right to respect for home in Article 8 has tended to be narrowly interpreted as meaning the right to *privacy* from the state's gaze within one's home.[6]

---

1 The expression 'An Englishman's home is his castle' is a misquotation from the decision in Semayne's Case, (1604) 77 Eng. Rep. 194, 195 (K.B); 5 Co. Rep. 91a, 91b, when Coke CJ commented that: '...the house of everyone is to him as his castle and fortress'.

2 Entick v. Carrington, (1765) 95 Eng. Rep. 807 (K.B.); Malone v. Commissioner of Police for the Metropolis (No 2), [1979] 2 All E.R. 620, Ch 344 (Eng.).

3 2003] UKHL 43 (appeal taken from Eng.).

4 [2003] UKHL 43, at [49] (appeal taken from Eng.).

5 van Dijk and van Hoof have noted that: '[a]s a collective noun designating the rights involved in Article 8, the "right to privacy" is often used nowadays'; PIETR. VAN DIJK & FRIED VAN HOOF, THEORY AND PRACTICE OF THE EUROPEAN CONVENTION ON HUMAN RIGHTS 489, [8.1] (3rd edn, 1998),

6 For example, work to develop more robust criminal and civil responses to domestic violence within the home in England had to overcome the additional challenges associated

That this perspective has prevailed in English law is undoubtedly, in part at least, a result of the instinctive view that:

> 'Human rights' are seen as being concerned with matters at the heart of the human condition, such as liberty, freedom of speech, a right to privacy; [while] protection for private property rights does not have the same emotive appeal.[7]

This led Howell to observe that: '[h]istorically, property lawyers have tended to ignore any possible human rights aspects to their work'.[8] Yet, in recent years the House of Lords has been challenged to re-visit its restrictive interpretation of those aspects of Article 8 which recognize a 'right to respect for home', and to consider (and reconsider) the argument that the right to respect for home in Article 8 demands a more substantive interpretation, with greater focus on the home occupier's ability to defend herself against eviction, for example, at the hands of a landlord.

This chapter analyses the line of cases between two landmark decisions of the House of Lords: *London Borough of Harrow v. Qazi*,[9] and *Doherty v. Birmingham City Council*,[10] which deal with the eviction of occupiers from public authority properties. The cases deal primarily with public sector tenants (where the local authority is the landlord), although in some cases the courts have drawn analogies between public sector tenants and other evictees, such as private sector tenants and defaulting mortgagees. This chapter considers the development of the right to respect for home within the context of English legal culture, with its emphases on 'respect for home' as 'respecting privacy at home', and (in the absence of a significant constitutional property jurisdiction before the Human Rights Act 1998) the strong tradition of property law as the *sine qua non* of private law.

In the decade since the enactment of the Human Rights Act 1998 these cases have shaped the content of the right to respect for home in English law. Indeed, the jurisprudence of the House of Lords, interspersed with some intervening decisions from the European Court of Human Rights, tells a fascinating story of the development of human rights discourse within English housing law, of the strategies adopted and employed to negotiate through the Article 8 obligation, and of judicial resistance to the idea of a right to respect for home which goes beyond the traditionally accepted idea that Article 8 merely obliges the state to respect

---

with policing offences with the private space of the home, *see* , S.S.M. Edwards, Policing 'Domestic' Violence: Women, the Law and the State (1989).

7 J. Howell, *The Protection of Rights of Property in Land under the Human Rights Act, in* The Human Rights Act 1998 – What it Means 167 (L Betten, ed. 1999).

8 J. Howell, *Land and Human Rights* 63 Conv. & Prop. Law. (N.S.) 287 (1999).

9 *Qazi, supra* note 3.

10 [2008] UKHL 57 (appeal taken from Eng.).

the privacy of the occupier's activities within the home.[11] In each of these five landmark cases[12] a particular question – 'whether rights under article 8 represent a reservoir of entitlement upon which the occupier of a home can draw in order to resist an order for possession when domestic law leaves him defenceless'[13] – has been scrutinized repeatedly by both the House of Lords and the European Court of Human Rights.

While it is recognized that in the realm of housing law, states enjoy a wide margin of appreciation under the Convention,[14] the chapter argues that the differences in approach between the European Court of Human Rights and the House of Lords in these cases go beyond a state's own judgment about the balance struck between competing interests, but rather reflect a more fundamental issue concerning the content of Article 8 and the necessary steps in the court's reasoning when scrutinizing actions which potentially breach a Convention right. The response of the English courts to the 'right to respect for home' also highlights several important features for human rights law more broadly after the 1998 Act, including the meaning of 'proportionality'; and the extent to which the harm occasioned by the violation of individual rights *for that individual* is a relevant factor for a court when determining whether an actionable breach has occurred. The very intimate and personal nature of the connection that exists between an occupier and her home brings the issue of individual facts, circumstances, and harms into sharp relief. However, it is these very features which, across the arc of cases, militated against the application of Article 8 of the European Convention in an expansive manner in this context – at least so far as the English courts are concerned.

Peter Byrne, in this collection, has reflected on how statutory law can modify traditional property rights, and this is echoed in relation to the right to respect for home in the UK. Of course, since these cases all concerned actions brought by public authorities as landowners, they already required applications of the public/private hybrid of common law property rights as overlaid by the additional rights and responsibilities set out in statutory public housing provisions. In addition, however, while it is not suggested that the possibility that a court might

11 *See* London Borough of Harrow v. Qazi, [2003] UKHL 43 (appeal taken from Eng.), when Lord Hope noted that: '[m]ost international human rights instruments recognise a right to privacy. That is the concept which underlies Article 8 of the Convention.'. *Id.* at [49], Lord Hope.

12 *Qazi, supra* note 3; Kay v. Lambeth LBC; Price v. Leeds CC, [2006] UKHL 10 (appeal taken from EWCA (Civ))(U.K.); Connors v. U.K., App. No 66746/01, Eur. Ct. H.R. at [82] (2004), *available at* http://cmiskp.echr.coe.int/tkp197/view.asp?action=html&documentId=699671&portal=hbkm&source=externalbydocnumber&table=F69A27FD8FB86142BF01C1166DEA398649; McCann v. U.K., App. No. 19909/04, 21 Eur. Ct. H.R. 97 (2008); and, *Doherty, supra* note 10.

13 Patel v. Pirabakaran, [2006] EWCA (Civ) 685, [41], Wilson LJ.

14 James and Others v. UK, 8 Eur. H.R. Rep. 123 (1986); Buckley v. UK, App. No. 203848/92, 23 Eur. H.R. Rep. 101 (1997).

find an unlawful interference with respect for home would, or should, amount to a supervening 'property right' for the occupier (the discretionary nature of the court's review is too contingent to be described as a property 'right' in the traditional sense), the right to have the court take account of 'home' factors would constitute an additional, 'non-property', public law right, which could impact on the ability of the landlord to recover the land. Of course, the idea that private property rights are subject to the boundaries of a public law framework is not new: private property rights can never be regarded as absolute but must be balanced against wider 'public' considerations, and the Human Rights Act in the UK has explicitly transformed the landscape of public law by making Convention Rights directly enforceable against public authorities in domestic courts (for example, by requiring legislation, so far as it is possible to do so, to be interpreted compatibly with the Convention Rights, section 3(1); and by requiring public authorities to act compatibly with Convention Rights, section 6(1))).

Yet, although the human rights framework – and particularly the proportionality doctrine – seems inherently suitable for conducting the balancing exercise which is often required when a *home* interest comes into conflict with another (usually property) claim, judicial reluctance to bestow real content on the right to respect for home within English law, and to carry out that balancing exercise in a meaningful way, has important implications for the potential usefulness of the human rights framework as a means of recognizing the importance of the home as the site of everyday life for its occupiers.[15] While the House of Lords appears to have now reached a resolution (for the time being at least) in *Doherty v. Birmingham City Council*, compromises have had to be made on both sides (that is, for public authority landowners and for occupiers). This chapter reviews the journey to the decision in *Doherty* and evaluates the position which appears to have been finally reached on this much-litigated aspect of Article 8.

Article 8 and the Right to Respect for Home

Article 8 of the European Convention on Human Rights states that:

> 8(1) Everyone has the right to respect for his private and family life, his home and his correspondence.
>
> 8(2) There shall be no interference by a public authority with the exercise of this right except such as is in accordance with the law and is necessary in a democratic society in the interests of national security, public safety or the economic well-being of the country, for the prevention of disorder or crime,

---

15 For a detailed discussion of the importance of home as a site of everyday life for its occupiers, *see* Lorna Fox, Conceptualising Home: Theories, Laws and Policies (2006) (especially ch. 4).

> for the protection of health or morals, or for the protection of the rights and freedoms of others.

A first important point of note in relation to Article 8 of the Convention is that it is directed at protecting citizens against interferences with their established home; Article 8 does *not* provide for a *right to a home*. This was clearly established shortly after the Convention was adopted, in the decision of the European Commission on Human Rights in *X v. Germany*.[16] The Commission, which rules on the admissibility of claims brought under the Convention, rejected the argument that Article 8(1) imposed a duty on the state to provide citizens with a home.[17] Indeed, in several subsequent cases, the European Court of Human Rights has repeatedly confirmed that Article 8 does not give the right to be provided with a home, nor does it give a right to have one's housing problem solved by the state.[18]

Rather, Article 8 is concerned with protecting citizens against interferences with their *existing* homes (as well as protecting against interference with private and family life, and with correspondence). It has already been noted that the right to respect for the home in Article 8 is clearly embedded in the overall context of Article 8, which is strongly associated with *privacy*,[19] and the references in Article 8 to the right to respect for family life, for home and for correspondence are often viewed conjunctively, as aspects of the right to private life. For example, in *Marckx v. Belgium*,[20] Sir Gerald Fitzmaurice set out the reductionist interpretation of the right to respect for home when he stated that: '…the main, if not indeed the sole, object and intended sphere of application of Article 8 was that of what I will call the "domiciliary protection" of the individual'.[21] It is also significant that this 'domiciliary protection' was primarily conceived of as a protection against *state* intrusion into one's privacy within the home.[22]

---

16 1 Y.B. 202 (1956).

17 The Commission held that the right to an adequate standard of living and the right to suitable accommodation were not in principle among the rights and freedoms safeguarded by the Convention. *See*, for example, PRIVACY AND HUMAN RIGHTS 79 (A.H. Robertson, ed., 1973).

18 Chapman v. U. K., 33 Eur. H.R. Rep. 399, 427 [99] (2001); Marzari v. Italy, App. No. 36448/97, 28 Eur. H.R. Rep. Comm'n Dec. 175, 179 (1999); O'Rourke v. U. K., App. No. 39022/97, Eur. Ct. H.R. 889 (2001).

19 This approach to Article 8 was re-emphasized in *London Borough of Harrow v. Qazi*, [2003] *supra* note 3 – considered at length below – when Lord Hope noted that: '[m] ost international human rights instruments recognise a right to privacy. That is the concept which underlies Article 8 of the Convention.'. *Id.*, at [49] (Lord Hope).

20 App. No. 6833/74, 2 Eur. H.R. Rep. 330 (1979).

21 *Id.* at [7].

22 Fitzmaurice went on to state that, in light of the right to respect for 'private and family life, home and correspondence' in Article 8: 'He [the citizen] and his family were no longer to be subjected to the four o'clock in the morning rat-a-tat on the door; to domestic intrusions, searches and questionings; to examinations, delayings and confiscation of

The Article 8 cases considered in this chapter are not concerned with 'the four o'clock in the morning rat-a-tat on the door', but with a different – and arguably more fundamental – type of interference with the right to respect for home: where an action has been brought to evict an occupier, by a landowner (indeed, in each of the landmark cases, by a public authority landowner). Since, on the facts of each case, there was no doubt that the public authority landowner had a superior right to recover possession of the property under domestic private law principles:

> ...the cases...address the question whether rights under article 8 represent a reservoir of entitlement upon which the occupier of a home can draw in order to resist an order for possession when domestic law leaves him defenceless.[23]

Even if the answer to this question was affirmative, any such 'reservoir of entitlement' would, of course, necessarily be *qualified*, as even when an interference with an Article 8 right has been established, that interference may be justified under Article 8(2), if it can be shown to be:

> ...in accordance with law and necessary in a democratic society in the interests of national security, public safety or the economic well-being of the country, for the prevention of disorder or crime, for the protection of health or morals, or for the protection of the rights and freedoms of others.

Consequently, in considering whether there has been a breach of Article 8, it would appear evident that the court must consider (1) whether Article 8 is 'engaged'; (2) whether there has been an 'interference' with the occupier's right to respect for home within the meaning of Article 8(1); and (3) if so, whether that interference was justified under Article 8(2). In working through the justification limb of Article 8(2), there are again three steps which must typically be followed: to be justified, the interference must be (a) in accordance with law; (b) have a legitimate aim and (c) be necessary in a democratic society (in pursuit of the legitimate aim). Finally, the court must consider whether the interference is a *proportionate* means of achieving the aim – that is, that it does not go any further than is necessary in order to pursue the legitimate aim, balancing the harms to both parties, and occasioning the minimum interference necessary to achieve the legitimate aim.

---

correspondence; to the planting of listening devices (bugging); to restrictions on the use of radio and television; to telephone-tapping or disconnection; to measures of coercion such as cutting off the electricity or water supply; to such abominations as children being required to report upon the activities of their parents, and even sometimes the same for one spouse against another – in short, the whole gamut of fascist and communist inquisitorial practices such as had scarcely been known, at least in Western Europe, since the eras of religious intolerance and oppression, until (ideology replacing religion) they became prevalent in many countries between the two world wars and subsequently.'. *Id.*

23 *Patel*, *supra* note 13, at [41] (Wilson LJ) (Eng.).

Although the principle of 'proportionality' is not explicitly set out in the Convention, the need to strike a balance between the protection of the individual rights under consideration and the needs of the community at large is a prominent feature in analysis relating to the qualified rights. The principle is rooted in the need to ensure a fair balance between the competing claims: in order for the balance struck to be *fair*, any interference with Convention rights will only be justified so long as it is proportionate to the legitimate aim it pursues:

> In other words, even where it is clear that there is a legitimate purpose for restricting a Convention right, the authorities must still show that the actual restriction employed does not go beyond what is strictly necessary to achieve that purpose.[24]

The proportionality principle provides a mechanism to: '...enable the Court to balance all the relevant interests and factual circumstances, and also to take into account the intensity of the infringement as well as the question whether the essence of the right has been infringed'.[25] The more serious the infringement of the right in question, the more justification is needed in order to avoid a breach of the claimant's rights: it therefore appears to be an important aspect of the judicial process of reasoning through Article 8 (or any other qualified right). The story of the case law on the meaning and content of the right to respect for home under Article 8 is about the journey towards this final question, that is, towards addressing the proportionality of interferences with the right when occupiers are evicted from their homes. In charting that journey, the five key cases from *Qazi* to *Doherty* are of central importance.

The Eviction Cases

The question of 'whether rights under article 8 represent a reservoir of entitlement upon which the occupier of a home can draw in order to resist an order for possession when domestic law leaves him defenceless'[26] has been the cause of extensive litigation in the English courts, and on appeal to the European Court of Human Rights, since the first landmark decision of the House of Lords on the question was handed down in the case of *London Borough of Harrow v. Qazi*,[27] in 2003. The principles elucidated in *Qazi* were subsequently developed through the House of Lords decision in *London Borough of Lambeth v. Kay; Leeds City*

24 K. Starmer, European Human Rights Law: The Human Rights Act 1998 and the European convention on Human Rights 170 (1999). *See* H. Fenwick & G. Phillipson, Media Freedom under the Human Rights Act chs. 2 & 16 (2006).

25 van Dijk & van Hoof, *supra*, note 5, at 8.8.1.

26 *Patel*, *supra* note 13, at [41] (Wilson LJ).

27 *Qazi*, *supra* note 3.

Council v. Price (*Kay & Price*)[28]; and, most recently, have been 'refined' yet again in *Doherty v. Birmingham City Council* (*Doherty*).[29]

Section 2 of the Human Rights Act 1998 requires the UK's domestic courts, when considering a matter falling under the Convention, to take account, where relevant, of 'Convention jurisprudence', that is, of decisions of the European Court of Human Rights, the Committee of Ministers and the European Commission of Human Rights. It is interesting, therefore that between the House of Lords' decisions in *Qazi* in 2003, and *Doherty* in 2008, the European Court also considered this very question – the meaning and content of the right to respect for home in Article 8 when invoked by an occupier against a landowner – on two separate occasions, both involving appeals against decisions of the UK's House of Lords, firstly in *Connors v. UK*[30] and later in *McCann v. UK*.[31] These five decisions (within five years) have moulded the meaning given to 'respect for home' within Article 8 by the European Court of Human Rights and the extent to which the UK courts are prepared to recognize this meaning, after filtering Convention jurisprudence through the 'margin of appreciation'. The cases portray important differences in the extent to which the courts have worked through the stages of an Article 8 analysis, particularly with regard to the treatment of the proportionality principle in relation to Article 8(2), and so require a case-by-case analysis to map the shifting approach of the House of Lords over the five year period.

London Borough of Harrow v. Qazi

The decision in *London Borough of Harrow v. Qazi*[32] provided the first and perhaps the most extreme example of judicial resistance to the right to respect for home in a decision of the House of Lords. The case concerned Mr Qazi's attempt to defend a possession action against his home following termination of his tenancy. Mr and Mrs Qazi had been joint tenants of a secure tenancy under the Housing Act 1980. Following the breakdown of their relationship and the departure of Mrs Qazi and their daughter from the property, Mrs Qazi served a notice to quit on the housing authority which was, in accordance with domestic law, effective to terminate their joint tenancy. Mr Qazi, who wished to continue living in the property, applied for a sole tenancy, but his application was rejected on the basis that the property provided family sized accommodation and so, in accordance with the authority's allocation policy, could not be (re-)granted to a single individual. When Mr Qazi appealed this decision, he revealed that he was, by this stage, living in the property with his new wife and her son, and that the second Mrs Qazi was pregnant with another child. The Court of Appeal held that Mr Qazi was entitled to remain in

28 *Kay & Price*, *supra* note 12.
29 *Doherty*, *supra* note 10.
30 *Connors*, *supra* note 12.
31 *McCann*, *supra* note 12.
32 *Qazi*, *supra* note 3.

the property by virtue of his right to respect for his home under Article 8, but the Council appealed this decision to the House of Lords.

Was the property Mr Qazi's home? The first hurdle for Mr Qazi was to establish that the disputed property was his 'home' for the purposes of Article 8. It is interesting to note that, on this question, all five judges sitting in the House of Lords were satisfied that the property was Mr Qazi's 'home' within the meaning of Article 8, even though he did not, by the time the possession order was sought, have any proprietary or contractual rights in the property. Lord Bingham stated that:

> On a straightforward reading of the Convention, its use of the expression 'home' appears to invite a down-to-earth and pragmatic consideration whether the place in question is that where a person 'lives and to which he returns and which forms the centre of his existence', since 'home' is not a legal term of art and article 8 is not directed to the protection of property interests or contractual rights.[33]

Lord Bingham explicitly acknowledged the affective significance of 'home' when he commented that: '[n]ot surprisingly, the need for some protection of the home was recognized in the Convention, since few things are more central to the enjoyment of human life than having somewhere to live...'[34] This definition of 'home' was 'non-technical' in the sense that it did not depend on demonstrating that the occupier had any legal or equitable ownership interest in the property. The court recognized the property as Mr Qazi's 'home' on the basis of his *de facto* relationship with the property, that is, his occupation of the property *as a home*. Lord Bingham concluded that: '[w]hen the possession proceedings were issued Mr Qazi had lived at 31 Hutton Lane continuously for eight years. The house had been his home and he had no other.'[35] His Lordship concluded that: '[t]he expiry of his wife's notice to quit brought his right to occupy the house as a tenant to an end, but it did not bring his occupation to an end. The house continued to be the place where he lived and so his home.'[36] This view was consistently adopted, with all five members of the House of Lords who sat as Lords of Appeal in this case (and who delivered separate speeches) agreeing that the property was Mr Qazi's 'home' within the meaning of Article 8 at the time that the possession proceedings were issued.[37] So, on the first question of whether Article 8 was 'engaged' it clearly

---

33 *Id.* at [8] (Lord Bingham).

34 *Id.*

35 *Id.* at [11] (Lord Bingham).

36 *Id.*

37 Lord Hope claimed that: '[w]here an individual's right to respect for his private and family life is in issue, the application of a narrow or technical test as to what this part of his life comprises would plainly be inappropriate. The same is true of the word "home" when it is used in the same context.', *Qazi, supra* note 3, at [67]; Lord Millett agreed that:

established that it was not necessary for the claimant to fall within a strictly defined legal category of 'home' in order for Article 8 to be relevant: the property was his home as a matter of fact, and so article 8 was engaged.

Was the possession order an 'interference'? Since the court accepted that the property in question was Mr Qazi's 'home' for the purposes of Article 8, and following the sequence of questions set out above, the next issue to be considered was whether, by taking possession of the property, the Council had interfered with Mr Qazi's right to 'respect for home' under Article 8(1). It was at this hurdle that the majority of the House of Lords found that Mr Qazi's case failed. Although the five Law Lords each gave different reasons for their positions on this issue, the speeches can be grouped, broadly, into two clusters: while Lord Bingham and Lord Steyn argued that the granting of a possession order against the property constituted a prima facie interference with home under Article 8(1), and proposed that the question of whether the interference could be justified within the terms of Article 8(2) should be remitted to the county court, Lord Hope, Lord Millett and Lord Scott were of the view that the council had not interfered with Mr Qazi's right to respect for his home, and so there was no need to justify the eviction under Article 8(2).

In deciding so, the majority of the House of Lords thereby supported an interpretation of Article 8 that effectively stripped the right to 'respect for home' of any content so far as eviction and the defence of possession actions was concerned. In fact, the decision suggested that, where a dispute required the court to resolve a clash of interests between the occupier's *home* interest and the contractual and proprietary interests of a landlord within the framework of Article 8, it would not even be necessary for the court to balance the competing claims within the human rights framework. Rather, the home interest would be automatically defeated on the basis that 'the proposition that there was a violation of Article 8 was unarguable',[38]

'[c]onsidered as a question of fact, the premises were Mr Qazi's home at all material times. They were his home when he lived there with his former wife, and they continued to be his home after she left him. They did not cease to be his home when his tenancy came to an end. The most that can be said is that he no longer had a legal right to remain in occupation which he could maintain against the council, though he could maintain it against anyone else. He was liable to be evicted at the suit of the council; but while he lived there it was still his home. It was his home when the council brought proceedings against him, and it was still his home when the recorder made a possession order against him. It would not have ceased to be his home until he left possession or was evicted by the bailiffs. This has not happened. He lives there to this day, now with his second wife and two children. It is still his home.', *Id.* at [96]; Lord Scott agreed that the property was Mr Qazi's 'home' within the meaning of Article 8, since the decision of the Commission in *Buckley v. U.K.*, had: '… eliminated the unlawfulness of the occupation as a relevant factor, let alone a determinative factor, in deciding whether the occupation was of a "home"', Buckley v. U.K. [1997] 23 EHRR 101, [133].

38 *Qazi*, *supra* note 3, at [77] (Lord Hope).

that 'no such balancing exercise need be conducted when its outcome is a foregone conclusion',[39] and that 'Article 8 was not, in these circumstances, applicable'.[40]

Was the interference justified? In reaching its conclusion in *Qazi*, the House of Lords avoided considering the balance struck between the right to respect for home in Article 8(1) and the qualifying factors set out in Article 8(2): that the interference is (a) in accordance with law; (b) has a legitimate aim and (c) is necessary in a democratic society (in pursuit of the legitimate aim). This interpretation also dealt a severe blow to the prospect of applying the proportionality principle in relation to justification under Article 8. The House of Lords held, by a majority of three to two, that the reference to 'respect for home' in Article 8 was effectively limited to actions concerning privacy and intrusion by the state. Article 8 provided no basis for defending possession proceedings when the party seeking possession[41] was entitled to possession under domestic law, based on their contractual and proprietary rights. The major impact of the decision in *Qazi* was the truncation of the reasoning process required in relation to the occupier's right to respect for home under Article 8, thus circumventing the need to justify the possession action under Article 8(2), or to analyse the proportionality of the measure sought. In fact, the decision of the House of Lords in *London Borough of Harrow v. Qazi* appeared to close off the possibility that occupiers facing eviction would be able to raise successful Article 8 arguments in relation to possession actions against their homes in the future.

Themes from the majority speeches A number of key themes from their Lordships' speeches provide interesting clues to the reasoning behind this position. One of these themes was the interpretation of Article 8 as an article concerned only with privacy within the home – that is, with the state's powers of 'search-and-seizure', or other intrusions into the citizen's privacy from the state's gaze.[42] Lord Hope, for example, reasoned that, since the other limbs of Article 8 – the right to respect for private and family life and correspondence – were concerned with privacy, the reference to respect for home in Article 8 was simply another aspect of the more general right to privacy afforded by Article 8.[43] Article 8 was delineated as a provision conferring rights with respect to privacy in the home, but not with

---

39 *Id.* at [103] (Lord Millett).

40 *Id.* at [149] (Lord Scott).

41 Although the decision in *Qazi* itself concerned a public authority tenancy, the House of Lords claimed that their reasoning on the scope of Article 8 also applied by analogy to mortgage possession actions.

42 For a discussion of these aspects of the 'home' interest in the U.S. context, *see* D.B. Barros, *Home as a Legal Concept* 46 SANTA CLARA L. REV. 255, 255-306 (2006).

43 'The emphasis is on a person's home as a place where he is entitled to be free from arbitrary interference by the public authorities. Article 8(1) does not concern itself with the person's right to peaceful enjoyment of his home as a possession or as a property right.' *Qazi*, *supra* note 3, at [50].

any of the other aspects associated with occupying the property as a home. Lord Millett also emphasized the idea that Article 8 was directed towards privacy at home rather than protection of home. His Lordship described a person's 'home' for the purposes of Article 8 as:

> …the place where he and his family are entitled to be left in peace free from interference by the state or agents of the state. It is an important aspect of his dignity as a human being, and is protected as such and not as an item of property.[44]

Lord Millett agreed that the property was still Mr Qazi's 'home'; but he rejected the proposition, asserted by Lord Steyn, that the views of the majority that no Article 8(2) justification was necessary where the party seeking possession was entitled to possession under domestic law based on their contractual and proprietary rights 'emptied Article 8 of virtually any meaningful content'. The content of Article 8 in such circumstances was, however, delineated as protection against interferences by the state *in respect of privacy issues*, for example, an unlawful search of the premises without a warrant.

Secondly, the majority judges took notice of the public policy arguments on the side of the (public authority) landlord: that is, with the potential impact of a decision in favour of Mr Qazi on the broader scheme of public housing policies and procedures. Lord Hope was concerned that, if the court accepted that possession proceedings amounted to a *prima facie* 'interference' with the occupier's right to respect for home, such that the court was required to consider the justifications for evicting occupiers under Article 8(2), including whether the interference was proportionate, that this would have detrimental implications for landlords. His Lordship claimed that:

> The point of automatic possession proceedings is generally to provide a quick and reliable way of evicting tenants whose leases have by the operation of law been terminated. A procedure which gives a discretion to the court by requiring it to consider whether having regard to article 8(2) the making of the order would be proportionate is inimical to that purpose…[45]

It was clear that, as a matter of policy, Lord Hope was disinclined to require the court – in this case, or as a matter of precedent – to justify the grant of a possession order under Article 8(2).

All three majority judges emphasized the weight that they attached to the position in domestic law, and their reluctance to allow Article 8 arguments to prevail over the rights of the parties at domestic law. Thus, while Lord Hope recognized that, for the occupier: '…his removal from his home is bound to interfere with his

44 *Id.* at [89] (Lord Millett).
45 *Id.* at [38] (Lord Hope).

enjoyment of that right at least to some extent';[46] thereby accepting that article 8 was 'applicable'; that: '[i]t is not irrelevant to [Mr Qazi's] case'; and that: '[i]n that sense the article is 'engaged';[47] for Lord Hope the case turned on the fact that *under domestic law*, Mr Qazi's tenancy had been terminated as a result of Mrs Qazi's notice to quit and the terms of the lease and that: '[i]n domestic law the making of an order for possession follows automatically'.[48] Lord Hope emphasized the importance of the position under domestic law: '...in view of the fundamentally subsidiary role of the Convention, which gives special weight to the domestic policy maker'.[49] In acknowledging that the Convention affords domestic policy makers a degree of discretion, Lord Hope indicated that he regarded the decision to evict in this case as falling within the margin of appreciation.[50] Yet, the consequence in *Qazi* was not merely the conclusion that domestic law and policy *justified* the eviction, but that it was not necessary to consider whether or not the decision to evict was justifiable (and proportionate), in light of the position under domestic law.[51]

The margin of appreciation – which is used to indicate 'the measure of discretion allowed the Member State in the manner in which they implement the Convention's standards, taking into account their own particular national circumstances and conditions'[52] – has been identified as particularly relevant in respect of the 'personal freedom rights', under Articles 8-11 and the right to property under Article 1 of the First Protocol.[53] But while the margin of appreciation allows states to: '...have some space in which they can balance for themselves conflicting public goods';[54] it is important to recognize that even a wide margin of appreciation does not obviate the requirement that the state apply Article 8,

46 *Id.* at [70] (Lord Hope).

47 *Id.* at [71].

48 *Id.* at [74] (Lord Hope).

49 *Id.*

50 That is, within: '...the latitude a government enjoys in evaluating factual situations and in applying the provisions enumerated in international human rights treaties...'; Y Arai-Takahashi, The Margin of Appreciation Doctrine and the Principle of Proportionality in the Jurisprudence of the European Convention on Human Rights 2 (2002).

51 Lord Hope accepted that Article 8(1) *was* engaged, but concluded that, in cases in which domestic law afforded an unqualified right to possession, Article 8(2) *was* met on proof that the tenancy had been terminated in accordance with domestic law. Lord Hope accepted that a tenant might have an arguable case for justification under Article 8(2) in 'wholly exceptional' circumstances, but concluded – with Lord Millett and Lord Scott in agreement – that: 'contractual and proprietary rights to possession cannot be defeated by a defence based on article 8'; *Qazi, supra* note 3, at [84] (Lord Hope).

52 Arai-Takahashi, *supra* note 50, at 2.

53 *See id.*, at 8-9; Howard Charles Yourow, The Margin of appreciation Doctrine in the Dynamics of European Human Rights Jurisprudence 22-23 (1996).

54 James Sweeney, Margins of Appreciation: Cultural Relativity and the European Court of Human Rights in the Post-Cold War Era, 54 ICLQ 459, 462 (2005).

including reasoning through Article 8(2) and the proportionality requirement.[55] As Yourow has noted, an:

> ...important methodological mainstay...is the place of the principle of proportionality, and its relation to other of the Court's tests...the very components of supervisory function and margin doctrine analysis...come into prominent play in all of the 'Personal Freedoms' articles cases...The key tests of the validity of state action in restricting rights involving the 'Personal Freedoms' articles entail legitimacy of aim ('prescribed by law') and necessity within the context of 'a democratic society'. The state must meet the burden of proof concerning proportionality.[56]

In a detailed analysis of Convention jurisprudence concerning Article 8, and specifically the right to respect for home within that article, Arai-Takahashi has argued that: '[d]espite the express reference to the "margin of appreciation", the Strasbourg organs have carried out a strict examination of the merits with respect to any restriction on the right to respect for home'.[57] This is because, notwithstanding the margin of appreciation: '...[w]hen applying the proportionality test, they must closely balance the overriding importance of public objectives and the nature of the right involved'.[58] Arai-Takahashi went on to claim that: 'For the purpose of proportionality appraisal, [the Strasbourg organs] have required Member States to adduce both "relevant and sufficient" reasons justifying interference with private premises.'[59] For example, in *Gillow v. UK*, the court emphasized – in the context of the right to respect for home – the inter-relationship between the margin of appreciation and the doctrine of proportionality when it stated that: '[t]he importance of such a right to the individual must be taken into account in determining the scope of the margin of appreciation allowed to the government'.[60]

Yet, by excluding the need to consider Article 8(2) or the proportionality of any interference, the *Qazi* approach did not allow for such considerations. While Lord Millett accepted that Article 8 was 'applicable'; he added that: '...it does not follow that it was even arguably infringed'.[61] Lord Millett claimed that: '[i]n my opinion article 8 is not ordinarily infringed by enforcing the terms on which the applicant occupies premises as his home'.[62] It is interesting to note, however, that, although Lord Millett expressed himself as in agreement with Lord Hope and Lord Scott, he did adopt a slightly different approach, which allowed for a little more

55 Arai-Takahashi, *supra* note 50, at 214 *et seq*.
56 Yourow, *supra* note 53, at 31.
57 Arai-Takahashi, *supra* note 50, at 83.
58 *Id.*
59 *Id.*.
60 Gillow v. U.K, 109 Eur. Ct. H.R. (ser. A.) at 22, §55 (1986).
61 *Id.* at [100] (Lord Millett).
62 *Id.*

scope for considering the justifications under Article 8(2) cases of this nature in the future, when he claimed that the question of infringement under Article 8(1) could not be understood in isolation, but must be considered alongside Article 8(2), since: '...article 8(2) gives meaning to that concept and limited the scope of the article'.[63] Lord Millett thus allowed for the fact that 'interferences' with the right to respect for home must not be arbitrary and must be in accordance with law; he also noted that: 'the interference must also be justified'.[64] It would thus appear that it was only the proportionality consideration which was excluded from his conception of Article 8 in respect of home.

Lord Millett's speech also emphasized the importance of the public interest of the landowner in considering whether to work through the Article 8(2) justification. His Lordship claimed that:

> In most cases article 8(2) calls for a balance to be struck between the applicant's right to 'respect' for his home and *some competing public interest*, such as national security, public safety, the prevention of disorder or crime, the protection of health and morals, and so on...article 8(2) also permits interference with the right where it is necessary 'for the protection of the rights and freedoms of others'. *Those others include but are not limited to private citizens. They include land owners whether they are private citizens or public authorities.*[65]

A crucial element in Lord Millett's discussion of Article 8(2) was his view that: '[c]onsideration of the question whether interference with the right is "necessary for the protection of the rights and freedoms of others" may also call for a balance to be struck, but it need not do so'.[66] Lord Millett claimed that in most circumstances the balancing exercise under Article 8(2) has already been carried out, within the application of the domestic law provision. In such cases, His Lordship claimed that: '[p]rovided that [the court] carries out the exercise properly and in accordance with the ordinary law, there is no need to give separate consideration to article 8'.[67]

Within the framework of Convention rights, particularly when it comes to 'qualified rights', or to balancing competing Convention rights, the principle of proportionality provides a means by which the impact of any 'interference' can be taken into account. However, Lord Millett's judgment in *Qazi* demonstrated judicial reluctance to employ the framework of Article 8 to this end. Although Lord Millett recognized the court's role in conducting a balancing exercise in the context of the qualified rights, he claimed that: '...no such balancing exercise need be conducted where its outcome is a foregone conclusion'.[68] Since the housing authority was

63 *Id.*
64 *Id.* at [101] (Lord Millett).
65 *Gillow*, *supra* note 60 (emphasis added).
66 *Id.* at [102] (Lord Millett).
67 *Id.*
68 *Id.* at [103] (Lord Millett).

entitled to possession as a matter of domestic law, Lord Millett claimed that: '...there was simply no balance to be struck'.[69] This effectively closed off any consideration of the nature of any 'public interest' justification, as well as avoiding any evaluation of the proportionality of the balance struck between the competing interests.

The minority speeches The minority judges, although also finding against Mr Qazi, took a different route through Article 8, which is important to note in light of its re-emergence in subsequent cases. When Lord Bingham came to consider the question of whether there had been any 'interference' with Mr Qazi's right to respect for home, he claimed that since: '[t]he simple, untechnical test of "home" which I have described...is easily understood and easily applied to facts arising in the different member states...I would expect a similarly simple and untechnical test to be applied to "respect" and "interference".'[70] Lord Bingham considered the fact that the tenancy had been terminated according to the terms of the contract, but he concluded that this was not relevant to the issue of 'interference'. Thus:

> [d]etails of the bargain made between owner and occupier, and the provisions of national law governing that bargain, are likely to be crucial in deciding the issue of justification under article 8(2) if that stage is reached, but it would seem to me to undermine the broad international application at which the Convention aims if matters of this kind are treated as determinative when considering whether there has been interference or a lack of respect.[71]

Although Lord Bingham described this approach as his 'instinctive' reaction, he also found support by reference to a range of cases in which the Commission and the Court appeared to accept that eviction from one's home *was* an 'interference' under Article 8(1).[72] Although it was noted that the interferences identified in

69 *Id.*

70 *Id.* at [12].

71 *Id.*

72 Lord Bingham noted that although, in each of the cases to which he had referred, the claimants had no legal right to remain in the property, neither the European Court nor the Commission had ever based its decision on that fact. Rather, they had consistently treated the eviction or possession action as an 'interference', which then fell to be justified under Article 8(2). Lord Bingham also referred to three decisions of the English Court of Appeal, which had also treated eviction orders and possession proceedings as an 'interference' with the occupier's right to respect for home under Article 8(1), but which had found that the interference was justified under Article 8(2). In *Sheffield City Council v. Smart*, Laws LJ held that, in cases concerning possession actions, it was: '...inescapable that those orders amounted to an interference with the appellants' right of respect of their homes. I have said that the case is all about Article 8; more precisely, it is all about Article 8(2).' [2002] EWCA (Civ) 04, [26]. *See also* R (McLellan) v. Bracknell Forest Borough Council, [2001] All E.R. 214 (Eng.); Reigate and Banstead Borough Council v. Benfield, [2001] EWCA (Civ)

these cases were generally justified under Article 8(2),[73] this approach did require the court to work through Article 8(2), and to consider proportionality.[74] Lord Bingham also referred to the decision in *Sheffield City Council v. Smart*, when Laws LJ adopted a purposive approach to Article 8, reasoning that:

> [t]he court has to arrive at a judicial choice between two possibilities, a choice which transcends the business of finding out what the legislation's words mean. The first choice...would entail a judgment that the Convention requirement was met at the Article 8(1) stage...[and that] there was no want of respect for the appellants' homes. The second choice (accepting a *prima facie* violation of Article 8(1)), which I prefer, entails a judgment that the more rigorous and specific standards set out in Article 8(2) have to be met if the court is to hold that the evictions are compatible with the appellants' Convention rights.[75]

Laws LJ concluded that: '[t]he Convention is, as it were, much more remotely engaged in the fabric of our domestic law if the first, rather than the second, choice is taken'.[76]

While the majority speeches did not limit the applicability of their approach to cases involving public authority landlords (i.e., the *public* landowner), Lord Bingham's more expansive approach *was* limited to cases in which the landlord was a 'public authority': although Lord Bingham did not express any view as to what principles should be adopted in respect of 'any landlord or owner which is not a public authority', his comments were clearly restricted to actions by public authorities against public sector rented properties.[77] Lord Bingham acknowledged the potential practical implications raised by his view of Article 8, especially in

---

1510 (Eng.); Central Sunderland Housing Company Ltd v. Wilson, [2002] EWCA (Civ) 04 (Eng.).

73 Di Palma v. U.K., 10 Eur. H.R. Rep. 159 (1986); P. v. U.K., App. No. 14751/89, 67 Eur. Comm'n H.R. Dec. & Rep. 264 (1990); Ure v. U.K., App. No. 28027/95, Eur. H.R. Rep. (1996) (unreported), *available at* http://cmiskp.echr.coe.int/tkp197/view.asp?action=html&documentId=667561&portal=hbkm&source=externalbydocnumber&table=F69A27FD8FB86142BF01C1166DEA398649; Wood v. U.K., App. No. 32540/96, 24 Eur. H.R. Rep. CD 69 (1997); *Marzari*, *supra* note 18.

74 '...these authorities...give somewhat more help to Mr Qazi than to the council. They reveal a tendency to assume an interference or a lack of respect and then to consider justification, an issue decided against the applicant in all the cases except *Larkos*, where the complaint was of discrimination in conjunction with article 8'; *Qazi*, *supra* note 3 at [20] (Lord Bingham).

75 *Id.* at [27].

76 *Id.* Finally, Lord Bingham suggested that: '...the vindication and fulfilment of the Convention rights, for which purpose HRA was enacted, require that the domestic law procedures involved in these appeals should be subjected to scrutiny for conformity with the Article 8(2) standards. Such a process is demanded by the fullness of our municipal law of human rights.' *Id.*

77 *Id.* at [23] (Lord Bingham).

relation to the litigious burden and the 'expense and delay' that housing authorities would be subjected to as a result of his conclusion that a possession order was a *prima facie* interference with an occupier's home. However, he concluded that, at the end of the day, the circumstances in which the court would decline to order possession at the request of a housing authority (that is, the circumstances in which the interference with the occupier's rights would not be justified within Article 8(2)) would be 'very highly exceptional'. Finally, although Lord Bingham expressed the view that the case should be remitted to the County Court to consider the justification under Article 8(2), he did not anticipate that Mr Qazi would ultimately be successful; rather, his concern was with the structure that the court's reasoning should follow when applying Article 8 in the context of possession orders. Indeed, Lord Steyn, in broad agreement with Lord Bingham, added that: '[i]t would be surprising if the views of the majority on the interpretation and application of article 8...withstood European scrutiny'.[78]

Connors v. UK

It was not long before Lord Steyn's comment was vindicated, and the *Qazi* approach came under criticism from the European Court of Human Rights. In *Connors v. UK*[79] – a case in which the occupier had no proprietary or contractual right, and the claimant was entitled to possession – the European Court of Human Rights indicated that reasoning through Article 8(2) must form a key aspect of the court's analysis, particularly with reference to whether the eviction was justified as 'necessary in the interests of a democratic society'. In *Connors* the parties had agreed that the eviction of the claimant – a gypsy living on a local authority site by licence, who was evicted by a bare notice to quit – disclosed an interference with his right to respect for his private life, family life and home; and they also agreed that the interference was in accordance with law, and pursued a legitimate aim. This meant that the main question to be considered by the Court was the final stage of Article 8(2): whether the interference was 'necessary in a democratic society' in pursuit of that aim.

The Strasbourg court applied a proportionality test to consider whether the interference with Mr Connors' right to respect for home (the eviction) was justified under Article 8(2). The court also emphasized the significance of the particular

78 *Id.* at [27] (Lord Steyn). Lord Steyn described the majority's position as: '... contrary to a purposive interpretation and application of article 8 read against the structure of the Convention...inconsistent with the general thrust of the decisions of the European Court of Human Rights, and of the Commission...contrary to the position adopted by the United Kingdom Government on more than one occasion before the European Court of Human Rights.' It does not accord to individuals 'the full measure of the [protection] referred to...On the contrary, it empties article 8(1) of virtually any meaningful content.' *Id.*, at [27] (Lord Steyn).

79 *Connors*, *supra* note 12.

facts of the case in reviewing the 'margin of appreciation' in this context, on the basis that:

> Where general social and economic policy considerations have arisen in the context of Article 8 itself, the scope of the margin of appreciation depends on the context of the case, with particular significance attaching to the extent of the intrusion into the personal sphere of the applicant.[80]

The importance of the proportionality analysis in determining this margin of appreciation was also emphasized in the subsequent paragraph, when the court indicated that:

> The procedural safeguards available to the individual will be especially material in determining whether the respondent State has, when fixing the regulatory framework, remained within its margin of appreciation. In particular, the Court must examine whether the *decision-making process* leading to measures of interference was fair and such as to afford due respect to the interests safeguarded to the individual by Article 8.[81]

This emphasis on scrutiny of the decision-making process from a proportionality perspective has re-emerged more recently in the decision of the House of Lords in *Doherty*,[82] and is discussed further below. It was clear, however, that the court in *Connors* regarded the question of whether the domestic legal framework provided sufficient procedural protection for Mr Connors' right to respect for home as a key consideration in determining whether the domestic decision had exceeded the margin of appreciation.

The court held that there could be no 'public interest' in allowing public authorities to interfere with an occupier's home interests without being required to offer *reasons* for the decision to evict: '[t]he power to evict without the burden of giving reasons liable to be examined as to their merits by an independent tribunal has not been convincingly shown to respond to any specific goal'.[83] This raises an important point in relation to the accountability of the local authority as representative of the 'public interest', and the function of the European Convention (and by extension the Human Rights Act) as a tool to keep the state 'in check', and to ensure that the 'public interest' is not permitted to override individual rights, unless the interference is (a) in accordance with law; (b) has a legitimate aim and (c) is necessary in a democratic society (in pursuit of the legitimate aim).[84] The decision in *Connors* provided an important reminder of the need for the court to

80 *Id.*, at [82].
81 *Id.* at [83], emphasis added.
82 *Doherty, supra* note 10.
83 *Id.* at [94].
84 This issue is discussed further below, in relation to the decision in *Doherty*.

work through Article 8, including, Article 8(2), if the individual's private right to respect for home is to be properly balanced against the public interest of the community at large, including the public interest as represented by the public authority landlord.

Kay v. London Borough of Lambeth; Leeds City Council v. Price

It was not long before this issue was reconsidered in the English courts, the following year in the Court of Appeal in *Price v. Leeds City Council*,[85] and then in the House of Lords when the appeal against *Price* was conjoined with *Kay v. London Borough of Lambeth*, another case also raising the same question in relation to Article 8. In the Court of Appeal in *Price*, Lord Phillips, MR recognized that:

> [t]he decision in Connors is unquestionably incompatible with the proposition that the exercise by a public authority of an unqualified proprietary right under domestic law to repossess its land will *never* constitute an interference with the occupier's right to respect for his home, or will *always* be justified under Article 8(2).[86]

Counsel for the local authority argued that the decision in *Connors* could be distinguished as being confined to the treatment of gypsies as a minority group, but the Court of Appeal was not persuaded and held that the approach adopted by the European Court of Human Rights was not so restricted; but rather that *Connors* was authority for the fact that the issues of justification and proportionality must be considered under Article 8(2), even where the party seeking a possession order has an absolute right to possession under domestic law.

Lord Phillips emphasized the importance of having a process to hold public authorities in check, claiming that: '[s]tatutory regimes that govern obtaining possession of land must be open to scrutiny'.[87] The Court of Appeal recognized that: '[t]he decision in Connors does not exclude the possibility that a particular statutory regime may itself achieve the balance required by Article 8(2), so that, if the judge complies with it, the requirements of Article 8(2) will be satisfied'.[88] However, it also added that:

> Equally, however, the decision in Connors does not exclude the possibility that, if a statutory regime is to comply with the Convention, it must require a public authority to weigh in the balance the impact of its actions on the individual affected

85 [2005] EWCA Civ 289 (Eng.).
86 *Id.* at [26].
87 *Id.* at [29].
88 *Id.*

> and permit the individual affected to challenge in the courts the conclusion reached by the public authority.[89]

Faced with conflicting decisions of the European Court of Human Rights and the House of Lords, and with the domestic authority of the House of Lords bearing heavily upon it, the Court of Appeal opted to follow the House of Lords decision in *Qazi* but to give leave for the applicant to appeal to the House of Lords, thus providing an opportunity to reconsider the *Qazi* approach in light of the decision in *Connors* and, if it so wished, for the House to overrule itself.

The conjoined appeals of *Kay v. London Borough of Lambeth* and *Leeds City Council v. Price*[90] raised some discrete issues: in Kay, the defendant was lawfully in possession of property belonging to the local authority before his rights of occupation were terminated and a possession order was sought, while in Price the defendants were gypsies who had entered the local authority's property unlawfully, and had remained there for only two days before the local authority issued proceedings for possession of the property. It was accepted, however, that both cases raised an important common issue concerning the scope and application of the right to respect for home under Article 8.[91] The House of Lords, this time sitting as an Appellate Committee of seven, handed down six substantive opinions; the majority view on the implications of Article 8 for possession proceedings can be found in the speeches of Lord Hope, Lord Scott, Baroness Hale and Lord Brown. The relevance of their judgments for the full range of cases in which occupiers (licensee, tenant, owner-occupier) are evicted by landowners with rights at domestic law was alluded to in Lord Hope's leading judgment, when he stated that the questions set out in the appeal: 'are important questions, as the answers to them will affect all cases in which the owner of land seeks to recover possession from someone who has no right under domestic law to remain there'.[92] Yet, although their Lordships' discussion on Article 8 was to some extent generic, much emphasis was laid on a common and specific issue at stake in both cases: the effects of interfering with local authority housing policies in light of the role of the local authority in managing public sector housing pursuant to the democratic will of Parliament, and as expressed in the housing legislation.

The Occupier's Individual Interest: Are Personal Circumstances Relevant? Although the House of Lords 'clarified' the ratio of Qazi to recognize that the eviction of an occupier could potentially constitute an 'interference' with the occupier's right to

89 *Id.*

90 *Kay & Price, supra* note 12.

91 Lord Bingham's judgment also addressed the important issue of precedent between decisions of the House of Lords and the European Court of Human Rights following the Human Rights Act 1998: *see* especially, *Kay & Price, supra* note 12, at [40]–[45].

92 *Id.* at [64].

respect for home under Article 8,[93] the majority agreed that, in making an order for possession, the court was entitled to assume for the purposes of Article 8(2) that the domestic law had struck the right balance between the competing interests at stake – the occupiers' interests in the property as their home and the local authority landlords qua the 'public interest'. The main point of departure for the minority speeches[94] concerned the opportunities afforded to an occupier to argue that the Article 8(2) justifications were not met in any given case. All of the judges agreed that in the vast majority of cases the fact that the landlord was entitled to possession as a matter of domestic law would automatically supply the justification required under Article 8(2). All of the judges agreed that the public authority landlord could not be required, from the outset, to plead and prove that the possession order was justified, as '[t]hat would, in the overwhelming majority of cases, be burdensome and futile'.[95] However, Lord Bingham argued that:

> where a public authority seeks to evict a person from premises which he occupies as his home, that person must be given a fair opportunity to contend that the excepting conditions in article 8(2) have not been met on the facts of his case . . . If the occupier wishes to raise an article 8 defence to prevent or defer the making of a possession order it is for him to do so and the public authority must rebut the claim if, and to the extent that, it is called upon to do so.[96]

Lord Bingham added that '[i]n the overwhelming majority of cases this will be in no way burdensome. In rare and exceptional cases it will not be futile'.[97]

The majority position, in contrast, was that it was not necessary to afford such opportunity to individual occupiers in individual cases; rather, while it was important to ensure that, where there was a 'live question' in relation to a Convention right there would be some process in place for the question to be dealt with appropriately, Lord Hope claimed that 'a system which provides for all other cases where possession is sought to be dealt with simply and summarily will not be objectionable'.[98] The important distinction between the two positions was that the majority did not consider a 'merits review' – or even the opportunity of conducting such an analysis – to be necessary in every case. Lord Hope alluded to the underlying systemic issues at stake when he reasoned that:

> if it were to be open to a defendant to raise this issue in the county court in every case where the premises are occupied as his home, this would have serious

93 *Id.* at [113].
94 Lord Bingham and Lord Nicholls, with whom Lord Walker agreed.
95 *Kay & Price*, *supra* note 12, at 29 (Lord Bingham).
96 *Id.*
97 *Id.*
98 *Id.* at [70].

> consequences for the system which Parliament has chosen for dealing with possession cases.[99]

Lord Hope emphasized the importance of going no further than the Strasbourg case law required ('no more and no less'), and concluded that this obviated any defence based on the occupier's personal circumstances which did not challenge the law under which the possession order was being sought as incompatible. The only possibilities envisaged as exceptions to this principle were 'two gateways' to Article 8(2), set out in paragraph 110 of Lord Hope's speech:

> (a) if a seriously arguable point is raised that the law which enables the court to make the possession order is incompatible with article 8, the county court in the exercise of its jurisdiction under the Human Rights Act 1998 should deal with the argument in one or other of two ways: (i) by giving effect to the law, so far as it is possible for it to do so under section 3, in a way that is compatible with article 8, or (ii) by adjourning the proceedings to enable the compatibility issue to be dealt with in the High Court; (b) if the defendant wishes to challenge the decision of a public authority to recover possession as an improper exercise of its powers at common law on the ground that it was a decision that no reasonable person would consider justifiable, he should be permitted to do this provided again that the point is seriously arguable.[100]

It is this paragraph which has been latterly identified as providing the core ratio of *Kay & Price*, and has become the focus of subsequent debate.

Beyond paragraph 110, the task of divining the ratio of *Kay & Price* was complicated, as was the case in *Qazi*, by the fact that each of their Lordships' speeches adopted a slightly different emphasis. For example, on the issue of whether or not the personal circumstances of the individual occupier could be taken into account, Lord Scott acknowledged that there were some inconsistencies in the Strasbourg case law with regard to the relevance of personal circumstances in landlord and tenant disputes: in *Ure v. UK*[101] and *Marzani v. Italy*,[102] the European Commission and the European Court of Human Rights had taken account of the personal circumstances of the individual occupiers – for example, medical conditions – when determining whether an eviction was 'necessary in a democratic society' for the purposes of Article 8(2).[103] Nevertheless, Lord Scott was satisfied that the broad thrust of the Strasbourg case law – before and after *Connors* – was consistent with the approach adopted by Lord Hope

---

99 *Id.* at [85].

100 *Id.* at [110]. These propositions, described as the two 'gateways' of *Kay & Price*, would later become the focus of the decision in *Doherty*.

101 *Ure*, *supra* note 73.

102 *Marzari*, *supra* note 18.

103 *Kay & Price*, *supra* note 12, at [156].

and with the decision in *Qazi*:[104] that in a case in which the occupier had no contractual or proprietary right to remain in possession as against the owner of the property, an Article 8 defence which was based on no more than the personal circumstances of the occupier could not succeed.[105] Even Lord Bingham, who was more liberal on the importance of affording the opportunity to occupiers to bring a claim under Article 8, was adamant that it was only in highly exceptional circumstances that Article 8 was likely to avail an occupier defending possession proceedings, and that he:

> [did] not, however, consider that problems and afflictions of a personal nature should avail the occupier where there are public services available to address and alleviate those problems... if under the relevant social legislation the occupier is specifically disentitled from eligibility for relief it will be necessary to consider the democratic judgment reflected in that provision.[106]

Kay & Price therefore appeared to determine that the personal circumstances of the occupier were not relevant to questions of impact and proportionality under Article 8(2).

Article 8(2) and proportionality Even if the individual circumstances of the occupier could not be taken into account, the views of the majority in Kay & Price allowed, at least in principle, for the possibility that the overall balance struck by a legal provision or, indeed, a common law doctrine could be called into account under Article 8.[107] While there was broad agreement that, in the vast majority of cases, the public authority landlord's right to possession in domestic law would automatically supply the justification required by Article 8(2), the House of Lords did admit the possibility that in certain (albeit exceptional) circumstances, the law governing possession actions could be found to be incompatible with Article 8: that the possession action itself could be recognized to be an 'interference' and, in certain exceptional cases, the argument that the domestic law was incompatible with Article 8 was: 'theoretically available'.[108]

Once it is accepted that an eviction can, in principle, amount to an Article 8 'interference', the focus of attention naturally shifts to the question of justifying that interference, in accordance with the qualifications set out in Article 8(2). When it came to analysing the Article 8(2) justifications, Lord Hope delineated the three-pronged test: (1) that the interference must be 'in accordance with law'; (2) that it was in pursuit of a legitimate aim; and (3) that it was 'necessary in a democratic

104 *Id.* at [167] (Lord Scott).
105 *Id.* at [172].
106 *Id.* at [38].
107 *Id.* at [110] (Lord Hope); [185] (Baroness Hale); at [198] (Lord Brown).
108 *Id.* at [200].

society'.[109] It was readily recognized that the first limb would be satisfied whenever the possession proceedings complied with domestic law, such compliance ensuring, at least, that the proceedings were not arbitrary. Regarding the second element of justification, it was also readily accepted that the: '[s]atisfaction of the housing needs of others is regarded as a legitimate aim…because it was intended to promote "the economic well-being of the country" and "the protection of the rights of… others"'.[110] In fact, it was the third limb of Article 8(2) – that the 'interference' was 'necessary in a democratic society' – which prompted more detailed analysis. Lord Hope expanded on this requirement by noting that the notion of 'necessity': 'implies a pressing social need, and the measure employed must be proportionate to the legitimate aim pursued'.[111]

The task of balancing competing claims, where both parties have legitimate, albeit irreconcilable, interests is always complex, as it clearly requires the court to make a value judgement, in this case between the individual rights of the occupier on the one hand, and the 'community' or 'public' interest represented by the (local authority) landlord on the other. Yet, this type of judicial activity is inherent in human rights discourse. As Lord Bingham recognized in *Kay & Price*:

> …inherent to the whole Convention is the search for balance between the rights of the individual and the wider rights of the society to which he belongs, neither enjoying any absolute right to prevail over the other.[112]

Indeed, it is in assessing whether an appropriate balance has been struck between the protection of the individual rights under consideration and the needs of the community at large that the doctrine of proportionality plays a crucial role. When conducting a proportionality analysis, it is necessary to weigh the interests at stake on both sides, taking account of the extent of any interference, the justificatory factors and the degree of harm done to the right (in this case, the right to respect for home) by granting the possession order. In addition, a proportionality analysis requires the court to assess whether the proposed interference is no more than the minimum interference necessary to achieve the legitimate aim pursued.[113] Furthermore, the measure of what was 'necessary': 'depend[ed] not only on the aim of the interference but also, where the right to respect for home is involved, the importance of that right to the individual'.[114] Thus, while the personal

109 *Id.* at [66].

110 *Id.*

111 *Id.* at [66]; *see* Blecic v. Croatia, App. No. 59532/00, 41 Eur. H.R. Rep. 185 (2004).

112 *Id.* at [32]. Indeed, Lord Bingham even went so far as to assert that '[i]t is unnecessary to cite authority for propositions so well established and understood'. *Id.*

113 *See supra* notes 24-25 and associated text.

114 *Kay & Price*, *supra* note 12 at [66] (Lord Hope).

circumstances of the occupier could not be taken into account by the court,[115] this analysis appeared to suggest that the importance of the right to respect for home – described in *Connors v. UK* as referring to: '…rights of central importance to the individual's identity, self-determination, physical and moral integrity, maintenance of relationships with others and a settled and secure place in the community'[116] – was a relevant factor when considering the proportionality of an interference, in those exceptional circumstances (gateway (b)) where *the law* governing possession actions might be found to be incompatible with Article 8.

The public housing context: Local authority landlords While all six substantive opinions delivered in Kay & Price placed a strong emphasis on the special role of the local authority landlord, there was some difference of approach once again as to whether their Lordships' reasoning applied only to cases involving local authority landlords or (potentially at least) to all eviction cases. This is significant since many of the issues discussed in the speeches are also relevant in any other eviction case (possession proceedings brought by a private landlord or a mortgagee): for example, concerns regarding the effects of any decision on the scope and applicability of Article 8 on the conduct of cases in the county courts, with particular regard to the risk of increasing workloads and delays,[117] as well as debates around the efficient use of resources and the wider policy impact of the court's decision. Yet across the speeches there was also broad support for the proposition that the implications of the decision on public authority housing policies and practices were important when considering whether an interference was 'necessary in a democratic society'.[118] Baroness Hale placed particular emphasis on the political context of the housing legislation and the competing demands on resources which characterize public housing disputes:

> This is an area of the law much trampled over by the legislature as it has tried to respond to shifting and conflicting social and economic pressures. If there were enough suitable and affordable housing to share amongst those who needed it there would be no problem. But there is not, so priorities have to be established,

115 *See id.*, at [38] (Lord Bingham).

116 *Connors*, *supra* note 12, at [82].

117 Lord Bingham claimed that the practical effects of their decision on 'the conduct of housing claims in the county court', on 'local authority housing policies and budgets' and on the 'important compromises inherent in our property law and housing legislation' were 'an important aspect of these appeals, and one that has caused the House much concern'; *Kay & Price*, *supra* note 12, at [31].

118 The House of Lords referred at length to the complexity of the legislation that regulates public housing, and they were, by and large, willing to accept that the legislature had already made every effort to strike a fair and appropriate balance between the competing interests at stake.

> either by Parliament or by the public sector landlord, who has to allocate this scarce resource in accordance with the priorities set by Parliament.[119]

Similarly, Lord Nicholls argued that 'elaborate steps [had been] taken by Parliament to strike an appropriate balance between the competing interests of all those who are in need of homes. The country's housing stock is finite', and that 'Parliament's decisions on this extremely difficult and intricate social problem are to be respected'.[120]

Although the minority judges in *Kay & Price* (Lord Nicholls and Lord Bingham, with whom Lord Walker concurred) adopted a slightly more generous construction of Article 8 than the majority, they also distinguished the facts of this case as bearing only upon disputes involving public authorities. The minority speeches claimed that the decision in this case was concerned with a local authority landlord, and said nothing about private landlords or other private owners (such as mortgagees) who do not have the status of public authorities.[121] This was attributed, in part, to their statement that the question of horizontal effect between a private citizen and an occupier did not arise for decision in these appeals and was 'best left for consideration in a case where it arises'.[122] Nevertheless, although Lord Nicholls recognized that private landlords (and presumably private creditors) were not public authorities, and so were outside the scope of section 6 of the HRA,[123] he also noted that '[t]he court of course is itself a public authority. Courts are bound to conduct their affairs in a way which is compatible with Convention rights. The court's own practice and procedures must be Convention compliant.'[124] Again, however, Lord Nicholls noted that this point did not call for a decision in these cases.[125] In contrast, the majority judges were much more willing to include cases involving private individuals within the scope of their analysis. Although Lord Hope agreed that the issue of private landlords did not stand to be addressed in the present case, his Lordship claimed that he '[did] not think that it can be left out of account as we explore the wider implications of the argument'.[126] Lord Hope was more robust in his observations concerning the court's standing as a public authority, and the indirect horizontal effect of the Human Rights Act, when he

119 *Kay & Price*, *supra* note 12, at [185] (Baroness Hale).

120 *Id.* at [53] (Lord Nicholls).

121 '[N]othing in this opinion should be understood as applying to any landlord or owner which is not a public authority'. *Id.* at [28] (Lord Bingham); '[t]hese brief observations on section 6 are directed solely at local authorities and other landlords which are public authorities within the meaning of section 6. I say nothing about private landlords'. *Id.* at [61] (Lord Nicholls).

122 *Id.* at [28] (Lord Bingham).

123 *See* G. Phillipson, *The Human Rights Act, 'Horizontal Effect' and the Common Law: A Bang or a Whimper*? 62 Mod. L. Rev. 824 (1999).

124 *Kay & Price*, *supra* note 12, at [61] (Lord Nicholls).

125 *Id.*

126 *Id.* at [64] (Lord Hope).

indicated that: 'The article 8(1) right to respect for the home does not distinguish between public authorities and private landlords and landowners. Private landlords and landowners too must obtain an order from the court, and the court itself is a public authority.'[127]

Of course, many of the specific arguments made in respect of the local authority landlord may not, in fact, be relevant in a private sector context. For example, the House of Lords laid considerable emphasis on the prospect that, by allowing an occupier of local authority property to remain in possession, the court was obliging the landlord to continue providing a home for that occupier when it was not required to do so under domestic law, and, crucially, denying another prospective (and possibly more deserving, according to the criteria set out in the domestic legislation) tenant of that property as a consequence.[128] A further factor raised by the court was the assumption that it was likely that a public authority landlord would already have shown considerable forbearance towards a defendant occupier. When Lord Brown supported the position of the majority by suggesting that he 'doubt[ed] whether the legal regimes of many contracting states are more sensitive than ours to the rights of residential occupiers',[129] he appeared to be expressing his faith in the values of the public sector housing regime, as a safeguard against any unjustified interference with a tenant's right to respect for home.

A final distinction to consider in this regard concerns the role of local authority landlords as public authorities, as compared to private landlords or secured creditors as private entities. In the context of horizontal effect, this difference in status appears to favour the public sector tenant, since – in light of the obligation set out in section 6 of the Human Rights Act 1998 – there is clear authority on which to bring a complaint based on an alleged breach of a Convention right against a public authority, as opposed to a private creditor. It is interesting, however, that in *Kay & Price* the local authority's status as a 'public authority' was also considered relevant in the context of the substantive consideration of Article 8(2), where much was made of the fact that the local authority had been entrusted by Parliament with the responsibility of managing public sector housing.[130] Private landlords and creditors, on the other hand, have not been entrusted with their role by Parliament but, rather, operate within the free economic market. Yet, considering the outcome for the occupier, it would be ironic if private landlords, who have not been entrusted by Parliament to carry out housing allocations, and who are not seeking possession in order to recover the property for re-letting to another household in accordance with their allocation policy in a social welfare framework, are given

127 *Id.*

128 *Id.* at [187] (Baroness Hale). Similarly, Lord Brown reasoned that: '[t]he rights and interests of others too, however, are at stake – and not merely landlords but the many others who also require Homes – and the law as a whole has been developed to give effect to these as well'. *Id.* at [205] (Lord Brown).

129 *Id.* at [187].

130 *Id.* at [33] (Lord Bingham); at [185], [187] (Baroness Hale).

a freer hand in evicting their tenants and debtors than the public sector landlords. Rather, applying a strong indirect horizontal effect,[131] one might think that these distinctions raise a stronger case in support of a 'merits review' of the existing domestic law governing eviction by the private landlord or creditor.

McCann v. UK

While the House of Lords in *Kay & Price* took account of the decision in *Connors v. UK*, and purported to shift its position some way from the *Qazi* approach – where the majority held that an eviction was no interference – there remained some considerable gap between the approach of the European Court in *Connors v. UK*, which emphasized the importance of the proportionality analysis, and the majority view in *Kay & Price*, that an eviction was an interference but that (with the exception of the two gateways) it was always justified, so that a proportionality analysis would not be required. The inconsistencies between the domestic position and the Convention jurisprudence were sufficient to trigger a further round of litigation, and in May 2008 the European Court of Human Rights published its judgment in *McCann v. UK*.[132] In this case, the local authority landlord had sought to evict Mr McCann, having ended the joint tenancy he held with his estranged wife by procuring a notice to quit from Mrs McCann, without making her aware of the consequences for her former husband.[133]

Although this chapter focuses on the *process* by which the court works through its Article 8 analysis, it is worth noting that a common feature of all the landmark Article 8 cases is the problem of weak facts: in *Kay & Price*, the House of Lords noted that the specific facts of the two cases were particularly weak,[134] and this is

131 *See* Phillipson, *supra* note 123 for a discussion of 'strong' and 'weak' models of horizontal effect.

132 See Southampton Port Health Authority v. Seahawk Marine Foods Ltd, [2002] EWCA (Civ) 54 (Eng.). *See also* Huang v. Secretary of State for the Home Department, [2007] UKHL 11 (appeal taken from EWCA (Civ))(U.K.).

133 The decision of *Hammersmith and Fulham London Borough Council v. Monk*, [1992] 1 A.C. 478 (appeal taken from Eng.), established the common law proposition that, where a valid notice to quit is given by one joint tenant, it has the effect of bringing the joint tenancy to an end, whether or not the other joint tenant knew of or consented to the service of the notice to quit.

134 Baroness Hale claimed that '[e]ach of the cases before us is a classic example of one in which a defence based upon article 8 would have no real prospect of success'. *Id.* at [193]; while Lord Scott, although suggesting that 'the Lambeth . . . seems to me a very good test case', *id.* at [130], claimed that '[i]n my opinion, the Leeds case was a very bad one to choose for the purpose of revisiting the correctness of Qazi since, whether the appellants' arguments be right or wrong, it is grotesque to suppose that the Maloneys could claim that the commencement by Leeds of possession proceedings to recover its recreation ground was an interference with their right to respect for a "home" that they had established on Leeds' land'. *Id.* at [130]. Lord Scott claimed that '[w]hen the article 8(2) balance is struck

borne out particularly strongly in *McCann*, as Mr McCann could not have been viewed as a litigant likely to evince much natural sympathy from the court.[135] Mr McCann was, with his wife, joint tenant of a three-bedroom property rented from the local authority. After their marriage broke down, Mrs McCann moved out of the house with their two children, before an ouster order was granted to remove Mr McCann from the property, with a non-molestation order to enable Mrs McCann to return to the family home with their children. Nine days after these orders were granted by the court, the court was told that Mr McCann returned to the home with a crowbar which he used to force entry, before allegedly assaulting Mrs McCann and her friend. Criminal proceedings were brought against Mr McCann, but his wife elected not to give evidence against him. He was acquitted of the charges.

Mrs McCann asked the local authority to re-house her on grounds of domestic violence, and subsequently returned the keys of the house with a note indicating her intention to give up the tenancy. Mrs McCann and the children were re-housed in another local authority property, allocated in accordance with the local authority's domestic violence policy. On an inspection of the former family home the local authority discovered that most of the fixtures had been removed, leading the local authority to conclude that the property was uninhabitable. Mr McCann later returned to the house, did some renovations to make it habitable, and, his relationship with Mrs McCann having improved, applied with her support to exchange the property for a smaller home in the area, as his contact visits with the children were dependent on his having a suitable home. On the same day, the local authority's agent visited Mrs McCann and procured her signature on a notice to quit against the former family home, without advising her that by signing the document she would extinguish any claim her former husband had to either live in the former family home or to exchange it for another property. Mr McCann claimed that the local authority had acted in breach of his Article 8 right to respect for home, particularly in light of the surreptitious manner in which Mrs McCann's notice to quit had been obtained.

The Court of Appeal applied the *Qazi* approach, and concluded that the case was not 'wholly exceptional', and so no consideration of Article 8(2) was necessary. Mr McCann then requested a judicial review of the local authority's decision to procure notice to quit from his wife, and this application was refused, the court finding that the local authority had acted within its powers, that the methods employed by the local authority landlord were not unlawful and that they were not outside the range of decisions properly open to the local authority in all the circumstances. Mr McCann's application for leave to appeal to the Court of Appeal against this decision was refused, at which point he had exhausted his domestic remedies, and so applied to the European Court of Human Rights to

in a case with facts like those in the Leeds case the balance must at once come down with a resounding clank in favour of the local authority'. *Id.* at [173].

135 For details of the facts of the case as reported to the European Court of Human Rights, *see McCann*, *supra* note 12, at [6–18].

consider whether the decision of the domestic court to limit its consideration to 'bare property law issues'[136] meant that the state had acted in breach of his Article 8 right to respect for home.

The European Court of Human Rights worked through the steps of Article 8: (1) whether Article 8 is 'engaged'; (2) whether there has been an 'interference' with the occupier's right to respect for home within the meaning of Article 8(1); and (3) if so, whether that interference was justified under Article 8(2), that is, that interference must be (a) in accordance with law; (b) for a legitimate aim and (c) necessary in a democratic society (in pursuit of the legitimate aim). The court concluded firstly that the former family home was Mr McCann's home within the meaning of Article 8, as a question of fact, since it remained the place where he lived (regardless of the lawfulness of the occupation under domestic law).[137] Secondly, the court found that the effect of the notice to quit, with the subsequent possession proceedings brought by the local authority to evict Mr McCann, was an interference with his right to respect for his home.[138] It was accepted that the eviction was (a) in accordance with law, and (b) 'pursued the legitimate aim of protecting the rights and freedoms of others',[139] both in respect of the landowner's right to regain possession against someone who was now a trespasser (a factor which would apply in all eviction cases), and additionally in 'ensuring that the statutory scheme for housing provision was properly applied'.[140] The particular public interest dimension of the public sector housing cases, in which the eviction of one (undeserving?) tenant is likely to be followed by the reallocation of the property to another (deserving?) tenant, according to the local authority's allocation principles, was noted with the court's comment that: 'the "others" in such a case are the intended beneficiaries of the complex arrangements set up by, amongst others, the Housing Acts. The Court accepts that it is only by limiting the protection of the Acts to the categories to which it applies that the policy underlying the Acts can sensibly be implemented.'[141]

The main focus of the court's attention was with question (3)(c), whether the local authority's interference with Mr McCann's right to respect for home was proportionate to the aim pursued, and therefore 'necessary in a democratic society'. The court cited its own earlier decision in *Connors v. UK*,[142] stating clearly that the approach set out in *Connors* was not confined to cases involving gypsies or to cases in which the applicant sought to challenge the law itself rather than its application in her particular case.[143] It held that Article 8 connotes procedural as

---

136 *McCann, supra* note 12, at [32].
137 *Id.* at [46].
138 *Id.* at [47].
139 *Id.* at [48].
140 *Id.*
141 *Id.*
142 *See* discussion, *supra.*
143 *McCann, supra* note 12, at [50].

well as substantive obligations, and that procedural fairness in this case required that an independent tribunal be allowed to examine the proportionality of the interference with Mr McCann's right to respect for home *on the facts of the individual case*. In what rapidly became the most-quoted section of the judgment, the court stated that:

> The loss of one's home is a most extreme form of interference with the right to respect for home. Any person at risk of an interference of this magnitude should in principle be able to have the proportionality of the measure determined by an independent tribunal in light of the relevant principles under Article 8 of the Convention, notwithstanding that, under domestic law, his right of occupation has come to an end.[144]

In making this statement, the court appeared to indicate that if there is an Article 8(2) defence on the merits of the case, the court must consider it, thus considerably widening the 'two gateways' for Article 8(2) consideration, as set out in *Kay & Price*.[145]

Although the court recognized the importance of the public sector housing context, it was noted that, had the local authority sought to evict Mr McCann under statutorily justified grounds for eviction, rather than by procuring a notice to quit from Mrs McCann, it would have been necessary for the landlord to establish that it was reasonable to make the order, and:

> ...it would have been open to the applicant to ask the court to examine, for example, whether his wife had really left the family home because of domestic violence and whether in his personal circumstances, including his need to provide accommodation for his children during overnight visits several times a week, it was reasonable to grant the possession order.[146]

In opting instead to bypass the statutory scheme, the court concluded that: '[i]t does not appear that the authority...gave any consideration to the applicant's right to respect for his home'.[147] With an interesting reference to the relevance of the applicant's personal circumstances, the court added that although there had been the possibility for Mr McCann to seek judicial review of the local authority's decision to seek possession (as the local authority is a public authority), that:

> ...the 'procedural safeguards' required by Article 8 for the assessment of the proportionality of the interference were not met by the possibility for the applicant to apply for judicial review and to obtain a scrutiny by the courts of the

144 *Id.*

145 *See supra* note 99 and associated text.

146 *McCann*, *supra* note 12 at [51].

147 *Id.* at [52].

> lawfulness and reasonableness of the local authority's decisions. Judicial review procedure is not well adapted for the resolution of sensitive factual questions which are better left to the County Court responsible for ordering possession. In the present case, the judicial review proceedings, like the possession proceedings, did not provide any opportunity for an independent tribunal to examine whether the applicant's loss of his home was proportionate under Article 8(2) to the legitimate aims pursued.[148]

In addition, the court was not prepared to accept that requiring an independent tribunal to consider proportionality where an 'arguable case' had been successfully raised would present significant problems for the functionality of the system, since it would only be exceptionally that this would be likely to occur.[149] The decision in *McCann v. UK* appeared to set out very clearly the reasoning process required when domestic courts reasoned through Article 8 in eviction cases, and, as a result, to require that the decisions of the House of Lords in *Kay & Price*, which had set out the structured reasoning to be applied in UK courts, be revisited. And indeed, once again it was not long before the House of Lords was provided with a further opportunity to comment, this time with the case of *Doherty v. Birmingham City Council*,[150] which was already under consideration by the House when the judgment in McCann was published on 13 May 2008, and on which their Lordships handed down judgment on 30 July 2008.

Doherty v. Birmingham City Council

The decision in *Doherty v. Birmingham City Council* provides the final instalment, for the time being at least, in the trail of litigation which has sought to unravel the meaning and content of the Article 8 right to respect for home for occupiers facing eviction. Mr Doherty and his family were travellers who for 17 years occupied a designated local authority site under a licence from Birmingham City Council, until the Council took the decision to re-deploy the site. The local authority issued Mr Doherty with a notice to quit,[151] but he defended the possession proceedings on various grounds, including his right to respect for home under Article 8. The question for the court to consider, once again, was the impact of Article 8 on whether a local authority land owner could obtain a summary order for possession against the occupier of a site. There was no question that Mr Doherty's licence to occupy the site had come to an end, and that he had no enforceable right to remain there under English property law, so the only ground available to defend the possession action was Article 8.

148 *Id.* at [53].

149 *Id.* at [54].

150 *Doherty, supra* note 10.

151 In accordance with the Caravan Sites Act 1968, which requires that such a notice allow at least 4 weeks before taking effect.

The Doherty litigation was strongly intertwined with the four key cases discussed above, not least in terms of the timing, as the local authority commenced proceedings against Mr Doherty in Birmingham County Court on the same day the European Court of Human Rights gave its judgment in *Connors v. UK*.[152] In light of the doubt that the decision in *Connors* had cast on the House of Lords' judgment in *Qazi*, Mr Doherty was given the opportunity to apply for judicial review of the decision to seek possession against him,[153] although he declined this opportunity, preferring to pursue the apparent incompatibility between *Qazi* and *Connors*, and was subsequently given leave to appeal directly to the House of Lords, reflecting the extent to which the question raised in the appeal was recognized as a 'live' issue in need of resolution.[154] However, before this appeal could be heard, the conjoined cases of *Kay & Price*[155] were given leave to appeal to the House of Lords, and – in the belief that this would resolve the substantive issues around the application of Article 8 in this type of case – the Doherty case was remitted to the Court of Appeal to apply the principles that would emerge from *Kay & Price*. When the Court of Appeal concluded that: (a) there was no arguable basis for finding that the decision of the local authority to seek possession could have been successfully challenged under the domestic law; and (b) the decision made by the local authority to seek possession fell well within margin of appreciation, Doherty appealed to the House of Lords on the basis that the Court of Appeal had: '... failed to appreciate the guidance that was offered in *Kay* and *Price* and how that guidance should be applied in this case'.[156]

The House of Lords heard the case as a five judge appellate committee, with a majority position of four agreed between Lord Hope, Lord Walker, Lord Rodger and Lord Mance.[157] The composition of the Committee was important, since the issue had previously been considered by a seven-strong committee in *Kay/ Price*: thus, Lord Scott stated that: '[y]our Lordships' function on this appeal is to consider whether the circumstances of this case do enable the appellant to rely on paragraph 110. Anything more would involve the unacceptable spectacle of a committee of five presuming to revise the considered opinion of a committee of seven.'[158] However, the speeches in *Doherty* did mark a shift from what had become a pattern of judicial reluctance to recognize the role of *proportionality* analysis in working through Article 8, towards a stronger focus on *judicial review* as the

152 *See* discussion above.

153 Although the deadline for making such an application had passed five months previously; *see Doherty*, *supra* note 10, at [6] (Lord Hope).

154 Mr Doherty was given leave to appeal directly to the House of Lords from the High Court, when the more usual route to the House of Lords is through the Court of Appeal.

155 *See* discussion above.

156 *Doherty*, *supra* note 10, at [7] (Lord Hope).

157 Lord Rodger did not deliver a full opinion, but agreed with Lord Hope and Lord Walker.

158 *Doherty*, *supra* note 10, at [61] (Lord Scott).

mechanism for testing the procedural propriety of the decisions of local authority landlords through gateway (b) – bringing with it, in turn, a resultant narrowing of the scope of the debate to focus only on cases involving public authority landlords – and so excluding private landowner eviction actions (whether private landlord or mortgagor).

From the outset, the Doherty litigation emphasized the importance of the procedural aspects of Article 8, as identified by the European Court of Human Rights in *Connors v. UK*. As Lord Hope later noted, the decision in *Connors* was concerned that:

> ...while a legitimate aim was being pursued by the local authority, the eviction of the applicant and his family could not be regarded as necessary in pursuit of that aim as it was not attended by procedural safeguards that would enable the applicant to challenge the factual basis on which the local authority decided to serve the notice. They had been evicted on the ground that they were troublemakers, and it was asserted that they had breached the licence agreement. The applicant disputed these allegations, but he was not given the opportunity to challenge them in court.[159]

In Doherty's case, the local authority claimed that its decision was motivated by public policy considerations relating to the underutilization of the site, because: '...genuine travellers...were currently deterred from going on the site because of the presence there of the appellant and his family';[160] and because this resulted in unauthorized encampments elsewhere, the local authority maintained that its decision was: 'not based on any allegation of misconduct on the part of the appellant or any members of his family';[161] but on the best strategy to achieve optimum use of the land.

The House of Lords reiterated the three points at which the legal framework would intervene on Article 8 grounds in an eviction case: firstly, that where the framework provided for 'personal circumstances' to be taken into account, and there had not been fair opportunity for the arguments for the occupier to be presented; and secondly, through the two gateways of *Kay & Price*: (a) the seriously arguable point that the law itself is incompatible; and (b) if the defendant wished to challenge the local authority's decision as an improper exercise of its powers 'on the ground that it was a decision that no reasonable person would consider justifiable he should be permitted to do this provided again that the point is seriously arguable...'; that is, through judicial review of the local authority's decision to seek possession.

The idea of using judicial review as the arbitrator of procedural safeguards when assessing the proportionality of interferences with the right to respect for

159 *Id. at* [3].
160 *Id.* at [4].
161 *Id.* at [4].

home was a feature of the decisions in *Connors v. UK* and *McCann v. UK*, although in both cases the European Court held that the possibility for the applicant to apply for judicial review did not provide a sufficient safeguard in the circumstances.[162] Yet, in *Doherty* the House of Lords continued to promote judicial review as the means by which the justification in Article 8 could be tested, rather than allowing for a HRA-proportionality analysis. For one thing,[163] the judicial review approach was seen as allowing for a measure of objectivity that their Lordships seemed to find lacking in a more general proportionality approach. In what reads as a damning indictment, Lord Hope claimed that a HRA-proportionality approach: '…suffers from a fundamental defect which renders it almost useless in the domestic context. It lacks any firm objective criterion by which a judgment can be made as to which cases will achieve this standard and which will not.'[164] Of course, this also enabled Lord Hope to maintain that paragraph 110 of his speech in *Kay & Price* (the two gateways) continued to apply, with the greater emphasis on gateway (b) in the *Doherty* decision explicitly allowing for judicial review of the procedural aspects of the decision making process. Lord Hope added that: '…I would be the first to acknowledge that the way that the formula works in a case of this kind requires further explanation. To some extent too it needs to be modified.'[165] Lord Hope now described gateway (b) as: 'designed to leave open the possibility of a challenge on public law grounds that the public authority's decision to bring the claim was so unreasonable as to be unlawful'.[166]

It is interesting to note that gateway (b) as it was presented in *Doherty* was honed to appear *not* as a HRA gateway, but simply as an application of the general process of seeking judicial review of public authority decisions: that it is '… limited to what is conveniently described as *conventional judicial review*'.[167] Yet,

162 *See Connors*, *supra* note 12, at [53]; *McCann*, *supra* note 12, at [17].

163 The House of Lords also dedicated considerable space to discussion of the appropriate mechanisms for dealing with incompatibility where it arises in primary legislation, with extensive analysis of section 6(2)(b) of the 1998 Act, including the protection afforded to public authorities under s6(2)(b) when exercising a discretion (even when their actions employ common law methods such as the action to recover possession) which is available within the statutory scheme; *see* for example, Lord Hope's speech, paras 39-40. While this aspect of the case will be of interest for HRA/Parliamentary sovereignty scholarship, it did not relate directly to the content (substantive or procedural) of Article 8, so is not discussed further in this chapter.

164 *Doherty*, *supra* note 10, at [20]. Lord Hope added that '[u]nless parameters or guidelines are set down, the judgment in each case will be a subjective one. Every solicitor who is asked to advise an occupier will have to consider whether it is arguable that the decision to seek his eviction was not proportionate. If he decides to raise this argument the court will have to examine the issue. The whole point of the reasoning of the majority was to reduce the risks to the operation of the domestic system by laying down objective standards on which the courts can rely.' *Id.*

165 *Id.* at [36].

166 *Id.* at [44].

167 *Id.* at [52], (emphasis added).

Lord Hope went on to indicate that the exercise of judicial review in this context was not restricted to a consideration of *Wednesbury* unreasonableness,[168] but could include other contextual considerations, for example, the length of time the Doherty family had been living on the site.[169] Crucially, Lord Hope emphasized that this did not mean that gateway (b) permitted a merits review: '…the requisite scrutiny would not involve the judge substituting his own judgment for that of the local authority…';[170] rather, the test of reasonableness remained the traditional question of: '…whether the decision to recover possession was one which no reasonable person would consider justifiable'.[171]

Thus, while the European Court in *McCann* had emphasized the need to carry out a proportionality analysis in working through Article 8, the House of Lords in *Doherty* rejected that approach in favour of a judicial review model, albeit a model which could include consideration of contextual factors. While their Lordships' were keen to assert that this remained faithful to the authority of the '2 gateways' approach in *Kay & Price*, by articulating a '*Wednesbury plus*' approach to judicial review, as well as enhancing the claimant's procedural rights by allowing that this review take place within the summary action for possession rather than requiring a separate judicial review hearing, the *Doherty* approach can be regarded as a small step forward into engagement with Article 8-type considerations in eviction cases, presented as a way of giving 'practical recognition' to the European Court of Human Rights while still resisting the call in *McCann* (and previously in *Connors*) for a proportionality review. The final section considers the current resting point of the House of Lords on this much-litigated issue, locating the *Doherty* approach within the broader framework of UK domestic law concerning judicial review and proportionality after the Human Rights Act 1998.

Conclusions

In tracing the development of the House of Lords' approach to eviction cases under Article 8 it is clear that, alongside the gradual shift towards engaging with a justificatory analysis under Article 8(2) (albeit through the lens of judicial review rather than HRA proportionality), one of the significant consequences of the *Doherty* judicial review approach is a resolution of the debate concerning

---

168 That is, that a decision taken by an administrative body is so unreasonable that no reasonable authority could have made the decision, *see* Associated Provincial Picture Houses v. Wednesbury Corporation [1948] 1 K.B. 223 (Eng.); alternatively described as a decision: '[s]o outrageous in its defiance of logic or accepted moral standards that no sensible person who had applied his mind to the question to be decided could have arrived at it.'; Council of Civil Service Unions v. Minister for the Civil Service, [1985] A.C. 374, 410 (Lord Diplock) (appeal taken from Eng.).

169 *Doherty*, *supra* note 10, at [55].

170 *Id.*

171 *Id.*

the applicability of reasoning under Article 8 in eviction cases beyond local authority landowners, to private landlords or mortgagees.[172] While the landmark cases considered in this chapter have, on their facts, all concerned local authority landlords – who are public authorities and so subject to the section 6 duty under the HRA – some speeches in the House of Lords have entertained the possibility that the right to respect for home under Article 8 would also be actionable against private landowners on the basis of the court's own role as a public authority.[173] However, by 'substituting' the public law mechanism of judicial review for a proportionality analysis, *Doherty* has made some concession to the consideration of contextual factors in local authority cases, while excluding consideration of such issues in cases concerning eviction by a private landowner. Furthermore, while this facilitated the House of Lords in answering the case before it in *Doherty*, without being seen to do violence to the authority of the seven-judge Appellate Committee of the House of Lords in *Kay & Price*, it is important to recognize the remaining gap between the *Doherty* approach and that advocated by the European Court of Human Rights in *McCann*.

One further question which this position leads to is concerned with when a landowner will be designated to be a 'public authority' for the purposes of Article 8. This issue has been examined in other contexts, where it has been noted that for the purposes of section 6(3)(b) of the Human Rights Act 1998, there are:

> ...two types of public authority – 'core' public authorities who are to be so regarded in relation to all their functions and 'hybrid' persons with functions both of a public and of a private nature who are only to be so regarded when the nature of their particular act under consideration is public rather than private...[174]

In *YL v. Birmingham City Council* the House of Lords indicated that a 'private' body's interference with Convention rights could engage UK responsibility before Strasbourg if it was carrying out delegated state or government functions, so that it would be designated as a 'hybrid' body performing a public function for the purposes of Convention rights – including the right to respect for home under Article 8. The designation of 'private' bodies involved in the provision of housing as 'public authorities' was examined in *Regina (Weaver) v. London & Quadrant Housing Trust*,[175] in which a registered social landlord (RSLs are independent, non-governmental housing organizations which are registered with the Housing Corporation under the Housing Act 1996) was designated as a 'public authority' on the basis that it was performing functions of a 'public nature'. The RSL was

172 *See* discussion *supra*, notes 117-31 and associated text.

173 *See* comments from Lord Nicholls and Lord Hope in *Kay & Price*, discussed *supra*, notes 123-27 and associated text.

174 YL v. Birmingham City Council, [2007] UKHL 27, [81], Lord Mance (appeal taken from Eng.).

175 [2008] EWHC 1377 (Admin).

deemed a 'hybrid' public authority on the grounds that it performed a delegated function in the development of affordable housing; was permeated by state control and influence; the nature and extent of public subsidy involved; and its role in the implementation of government policy, following the voluntary transfer of housing stock from the public sector to RSLs.

In considering, then, which occupiers will potentially be able to rely on the right to respect for home under Article 8 after *Doherty*, it is worth noting that UK housing stock is currently distributed across (a) the 'social sector' (18%), comprised of local authority landlords (9.75% of households) and Registered Social Landlords (8.25% of households); (b) private landlords (12%); and (c) the owner-occupied sector (70%).[176] The decision in *Doherty* would appear to suggest that the Article 8 right to respect for home is only relevant in eviction cases in the social sector, although some interesting questions remain to be explored in relation to the nationalization of banks – for example, Northern Rock, the UK's fifth largest mortgage lender which went into 'temporary public ownership' in February 2008, and other partially nationalized lenders – following the credit crunch which began in 2007.

The focus on possession proceedings brought by public authorities can also be seen as determinative of the decision to opt for judicial review rather than a HRA-proportionality analysis. The relationship between judicial review and HRA proportionality, and, specifically, the difficulties of applying a proportionality approach in cases involving the exercise of administrative discretion by a public authority, have been scrutinized in some detail in recent years. When considering the reasoning of the European Court in *McCann* concerning proportionality and Article 8 in the eviction cases, which emphasized the importance of allowing an opportunity for the court to consider the personal circumstances of Mr McCann,[177] it is useful to note the distinctions between HRA proportionality review, judicial review in HRA cases, and 'ordinary judicial review'. In *R (Daly) v. Secretary of State for the Home Department*,[178] Lord Steyn noted that, while it was recognized that while judicial review in HRA cases might involve: '...heightened scrutiny in cases involving fundamental rights as formulated in [Smith]';[179] there remained: '...a material difference between the *Wednesbury* and *Smith* grounds of review and the approach of proportionality applicable in respect of review where convention rights are at stake';[180] with a proportionality review requiring: '...the reviewing court to assess

176 *Social Trends 39* (2009), *available at* http://www.statistics.gov.uk/downlo.ads/theme_social/Social_Trends39/Social_Trends_39.pdf.

177 *See* discussion, *supra* notes 146-48 and associated text.

178 [2001] 2 W.L.R. 1622.

179 *R v. Ministry of Defence, Ex p Smith* [1996] Q.B. 517, [554E-G], (Sir Thomas Bingham MR).

180 *Ex parte Daly*, *supra* note 178, at [26].

the balance which the decision maker has struck, not merely whether it was within the range of rational or reasonable decisions'.[181]

Yet, while this approach – the 'easier' application of proportionality[182] – applies in any case 'in which the exercise of discretion impinges upon, or clashes with, a recognized fundamental right',[183] there appears to be a tension in the House of Lords' application of HRA-proportionality where such an exercise of discretion falls within the category of an exercise of 'administrative discretion'.[184] Craig has noted that: 'The application of a proportionality test may be more difficult in this type of case…in part because many administrative decisions involve balancing, which is the essence of many political determinations and administrative choices.'[185] Since public authorities are entrusted by Parliament to balance competing interests before exercising their discretion, it has been suggested that, in deference to the executive power of Parliament: 'It cannot therefore be right for the judiciary to overturn a decision merely because the court would have balanced the conflicting interests differently. This would amount to substitution of judgment by any other name.'[186] While it is not suggested that proportionality has no role to play in such cases, the 'intensity' of the review appears to be determined according to at least two factors: (1) whether the review is focused on a particular administrative decision, or whether it challenges the policy strategy, with challenges to particular decisions more likely to require a broader approach;[187] and (2) the nature of the right impinged upon by the exercise of the discretion. Leigh and Masterman have noted that: '…by the time the HRA came into force *Wednesbury* had become in effect a variable standard: the more fundamental the right interfered with, the greater the need for justification'.[188]

---

181 *Id.* at [27].

182 P. Craig, Administrative Law (6th ed., 2008), [19-015].

183 *Id.*

184 Leigh & Masterman have noted that: 'Lord Steyn's twin concerns in *Daly* of setting out a more intensive test than *Wednesbury* (commending "something close to an autonomous merits decision") but adjuring merits review are plainly in tension…the courts have nevertheless justified a more deferential approach, post-*Daly*…through use of the fact-finding/policy distinction in relation to Art 6; "indirect deference" to Parliament; and use of the different stages of proportionality analysis'; I. Leigh & R. Masterman, Making Rights Real: The Human Rights Act in its First Decade 159 (2008).

185 Craig, *supra* note 182, at 19-017.

186 *Id.*

187 *Id.* at 19-017; *see* Southampton Port Health Authority v Seahawk Marine Foods Ltd, [2002] EWCA (Civ) 54 (Eng.). *See also* Huang v Secretary of State for the Home Department, [2007] UKHL 11 (appeal taken from EWCA (Civ))(U.K.), which explained the: '…bar on the primary review by the courts of *policy*. This opens the possibility that there could and should be primary review of factual determinations'; Leigh & Masterman, *supra* note 184, at 166.

188 Leigh & Masterman, *supra* note 184, at 135. Leigh & Masterman later add that: '…there is a spectrum of intensity of review, with unqualified rights at the more intense end, rather than a total difference in approach to qualified rights cases'. *Id.* at 157.

This raises, once again, the importance of delineating the content of Article 8, in order for the court to be in a position to apply its own tests. It is reasonable to assert that, after *Doherty*, it will be possible for a claimant to seek to defend an eviction – albeit in an 'exceptional case' – on the basis that the application of a local authority's policy in the particular decision to evict him from his home has failed to strike a 'fair balance'; and that the local authority may, in responding to such a claim, be required to provide reasons for its decision.[189] It is also reasonable to suggest that the articulation of this approach in *Doherty* represents some advance in the House of Lords' engagement with Article 8 in eviction cases, both in terms of the explicit emphasis placed on contextual factors, and by facilitating the requirement that the local authority may be called to account for its reasons, if not in respect of policies themselves, in taking particular decisions to implement those policies that might not strike a fair balance between the interests of the community and the individual occupier. In both respects, this can be seen to be in line with the general trend of House of Lords' decisions in respect of proportionality, judicial review and administrative discretion. Thus: '...while it has involved a general intensification of the standard of review in human rights cases...[it] nevertheless falls short of review of the merits as such';[190] and it is consistent with a post-HRA approach which has: 'accelerate[d] a pre-existing tendency to treat review as context-specific'.[191]

Nevertheless, it is also noteworthy that, in line with this broader trend, the decision in *Doherty* has stopped some way short of applying HRA-proportionality when reviewing the justification for interferences with an occupier's Article 8 right to respect for home through a decision to evict by the local authority. As Lord Steyn clearly acknowledged in *ex parte Daly*,[192] the proportionality test is 'more precise and more sophisticated'[193] than the *Wednesbury plus* test of conventional judicial review with contextual factors, in three important respects. While the *Doherty* approach remains focused on whether the local authority's decision was within the range of rational or reasonable decisions, a proportionality test would require the court to assess the balance which had been struck in making the decision; while the proportionality test might require the court to consider the relative weight accorded to interests and considerations, this does not form part of the judicial review test; and finally, while the structure of the reasoning required to apply the proportionality test under Article 8 would include assessing not only whether the interference was justified, but whether it was the minimum interference needed to give effect to the pressing social need – that is, whether it was proportionate to the legitimate aim pursued, such a consideration is not

189 On the strengthening trend towards a duty to give reasons for decisions, *see* Stefan v. General Medical Council, [1999] 1 W.L.R. 1293, 1301, n.14 (Lord Clyde) (Eng.).

190 Leigh & Masterman, *supra* note 184, at 133.

191 *Id.* at 168.

192 *Ex parte Daly*, *supra* note 178.

193 *Id.* at [27].

required in the context of judicial review. Indeed, in *ex parte Daly*, Lord Steyn emphasized that while the outcome, having applied the proportionality test or a judicial review test, might well be the same in many cases, it may not always be so, and it remains: '…important that cases involving Convention rights must be analysed in the correct way'.[194]

The arc of cases from *Qazi* to *Doherty* can be viewed as a struggle to capture the appropriate role for the Article 8 right to respect for home in eviction cases. In doing so, the House of Lords is setting important parameters to the treatment of Article 8 in the lower courts. In the early stages of this journey, the House of Lords concerned itself with the scope of the right to respect for home, specifically whether there had been an interference with the occupier's right by ordering possession in favour of a landlord who was entitled to possession under principles of domestic private law. However, the focus of analysis then shifted somewhat, after the decisions of the European Court of Human Rights in *Connors* and *McCann* found the UK to be in breach of Article 8 for failing to take adequate account of the occupier's right to respect for home, leading the House of Lords firstly to accept that eviction can amount to an interference with the right to respect for home, and secondly, that such an interference will not always be justified on the basis that it gives effect to rights at domestic private law. The third and final stage of this journey, played out in *Doherty v. Birmingham City Council*, has concerned the 'fair balance' test, which the House of Lords has designated as 'judicial review with contextual factors' rather than a HRA-proportionality test; indeed, Lord Hope went so far as to assert that HRA-proportionality: '…suffers from a fundamental defect which renders it almost useless in the domestic context. It lacks any firm objective criterion by which a judgment can be made as to which cases will achieve this standard and which will not.'[195]

In this respect, the Article 8 eviction cases can also be seen to play an important role in the broader framework of House of Lords decisions addressing the application of the proportionality test in cases involving both fundamental rights, on the one hand, and administrative discretion, on the other. While the *Doherty* decision does not go as far as the European Court of Human Rights appeared to require in both *Connors* and *McCann*, when it was explicitly stated that judicial review was not an adequate mechanism by which to resolve sensitive factual questions such as those raised in respect of the balance struck in the eviction cases, this remains consistent with the UK jurisprudence on this question more generally. The decision in *Doherty* can be viewed as marking a shift in the analytical framework on Article 8, which is moving slowly towards a more justifiable approach in theory at least and perhaps to some extent in practice. The real focus of any Article 8 inquiry must be around the proportionality of interference, to ensure that it does not go beyond what is required to achieve its 'legitimate aim'. Although it is likely to be still only exceptionally that an arguable case can be made, the decision in *Doherty* suggests

194 *Id.* at [28].

195 *Doherty, supra* note 10, at [20]; *see supra* note 164 and associated text.

that the House of Lords are finally beginning to move towards a proper reasoning process, and one which better reflects the values of the HRA 1998. The role of the House of Lords in this process is to establish the approach to be applied by the lower courts in applying section 8(2) in the content of an eviction proceeding. Crucially, in practice, the decision in *Doherty* means that local authorities will not be permitted to bypass their own statutory schemes and procedures, and that, for 'public authority' cases at least, the question of proportionality can now be raised at county court level through the mechanism of judicial review, including a broad consideration of all the facts of case, including oral evidence, the conduct of the local authority, the public interest justification, the impact of the eviction, without the need for a separate judicial review hearing. Nevertheless, it is important to note that, in reaching this theoretical position, the House of Lords has been nudged along by findings of breach by the European Court of Human Rights each step of the way. It remains to be seen to what extent this development in the reasoning process will result in differences in the practice of eviction cases, or whether there will be any further litigation to test whether the House of Lords can be pressed any further towards the fuller HRA-proportionality test in this context.

Acknowledgment

This paper was originally presented for this collection in November 2008 and the final version accepted for publication in 2009. Since then, the UK's Supreme Court (which has replaced the House of Lords as the highest court of appeal) has handed down two further decisions on this point, Manchester City Council v Pinnock [2010] UKSC 45 and Hounslow LBC v Powell [2011] UKSC 8. In these cases, the Supreme Court accepted the core argument advanced in this chapter, that the structure of Article 8 requires at least the theoretical possibility of a 'proportionality' analysis in these eviction cases. The application of this principle in the lower courts, which routinely deal with housing evictions, will be crucial in determining the extent to which this theoretical development translates into enhanced 'respect for home' for occupiers threatened with eviction.

Chapter 6
Opening Neighborhoods to People with Mobility Impairment: Property, Disability and Inclusive Design Housing

Robin Paul Malloy

Introduction

While much progress has been achieved in making *public/common* spaces more accessible, residential housing remains largely unable to be freely visited by people with mobility impairment. This is a significant problem because it truncates the socio-economic relationships of a large, diverse, and growing population within our community. The problem is not simply localized; it is national because barriers to accessible housing are present in the vast majority of "private" single-family residential housing units in the United States.

My own tri-level home, for instance, is difficult to access and navigate. Not only are all three entrances to my home subject to access barriers, once a person enters my home she has to deal with a sunken living room (two steps down from the entrance hall), a two step rise to my dining room, a small first floor powder room with a door and interior space too narrow for a wheelchair or walker, a seven step rise to an otherwise accessible master bathroom and a 14-step barrier to our lower level family and activity room. The exclusionary design that makes my home difficult to navigate for family, friends, and colleagues is replicated in the houses of most of my neighbors, and in residential communities across our country.

A significant reason for the failure to adopt nationwide standards of inclusive design for all residential housing, even while improved accessibility in public accommodations has become pervasive, is related to an erroneous framing of the situation in the discourse of legal institutions. For the most part, the legal system frames the discourse of accessibility to residential housing in terms of a false dichotomy between the private and public spheres, with the home understood as private space—a space of intimate relationships, a space easily hidden from public view, and a space carrying high expectations of privacy. In this context, law seems to view residential housing in terms that affirm the voluntary and contractual undertakings of numerous discrete and autonomous individuals;

individuals presumed to be empowered by market forces to bargain for socially optimal housing outcomes.

The underlying assumption of this viewpoint is that private parties bargaining in the marketplace can achieve results that simultaneously maximize both private and public benefits. This assumption traces its roots all the way back to Adam Smith and his famous metaphor of the invisible hand.[1] Adam Smith suggested that private individuals acting in their own self interest promote the public good even though it is no part of their original intention.[2] This means that private and public benefits are invariant.[3] As we learn, however, from counter examples such as the tragedy of the commons, the prisoner's dilemma, and the problem of transactions costs more generally, variance between private and public interest is often observed.

Relying on this dominant frame of reference for addressing the need for inclusionary design in residential housing is problematic. It is problematic in several respects, including: the failure to understand that while a home may be private space, the housing unit (as a physical structure) is a quasi-public place; a failure to fully appreciate the imperfections of present market operations which result in variance between optimal private and social outcomes; and, a failure to comprehend mobility impairment as a disability with implications for families and communities, and not just for discrete and identifiable individuals.

By way of introduction, therefore, it is important to understand the current framework and to appreciate its shortcomings. The shortcomings produce harmful results by excluding people with mobility impairment from full participation in the everyday activities of community life, and market imperfections result in an undersupply of fully accessible units. Inadequate supplies of residential housing with inclusionary design limit choices for the mobility impaired and constrain their ability to safely visit and interact with family, friends, and community members. It also burdens the housing market for people seeking to relocate, and raises potential difficulty in responding quickly to emergency re-housing needs in the wake of disasters such as Hurricane Katrina.[4] Emergency relocation is made more difficult than it could be because so few housing structures are currently accessible to people with mobility impairment. This makes it hard for families to exercise self help since many family members have houses without inclusive

1 Robin Paul Malloy, Law in a Market Context: An Introduction to Market Concepts in Legal Reasoning 27-30 (2004).

2 *Id.*

3 *Id.* Thus, it is assumed that marginal private costs equal marginal public costs and marginal private benefits equal marginal public benefits. *See also* Nicholas Mercuro & Steven G. Medema, Economics and the Law: From Posner to Post-Modernism 14-19 (1997).

4 Robin Paul Malloy, *Inclusion by Design: Accessible Housing and Mobility Impairment*, 60 Hastings L.J. 699, 736-38 (2009) [hereinafter *Inclusion by Design*].

design and their homes may pose problems for a relocated family member with mobility impairment.

With this in mind, this chapter discusses the public aspects of private single-family residential housing by considering the need for inclusive design and the idea of open and accessible neighborhoods. It does this in terms taking a narrowly tailored look at the need to reframe several underlying assumptions concerning the market for private single-family residential housing. While one might examine these issues in terms of civil rights and anti-discrimination law, this chapter takes a decidedly narrower view. In this context, I start by defining an open neighborhood as one in which everyone can safely visit any other person without confronting exclusionary barriers to use of the built environment. In pursuing this discussion the chapter proceeds in several steps. First, it identifies several factors suggesting a need to reframe the basic assumptions about the "private" in private single-family homes. Second, it addresses background information on inclusive design and demographics. And third, it discusses the nature of our national housing stock with implications for the inability of private parties to bargain for socially optimal design outcomes in the open marketplace.

Reframing Basic Assumptions

This part of the chapter suggests that the current legal framework for thinking about the requirements for inclusive design is less than satisfactory. The current framework excludes and minimizes inclusive design requirements in single-family residential housing because it predicates regulation on the degree of "publicness" attributed to a structure. Thus, for instance, a post office can be regulated for inclusive design as can a department store, as a place of public accommodation. It is the public aspect of such places, and of publicly funded housing that makes them easier to regulate. As a consequence, the private market for single-family housing is very weakly regulated with respect to inclusive house design.

In this section of the chapter I explore several initial reasons for identifying a significant public aspect to private residential housing.

First, I address the mistaken view of residential housing as a simple private and local undertaking. While residential construction is local, housing markets are not. Just because we see housing units constructed on local lots, the market supporting this construction is national and international in scope. The funding for construction and for residential home mortgages is funneled through fully integrated and global financial markets.[5] America would be greatly under-housed but for the financial resources that are brought into local markets by complex secondary mortgage market and financial market operations. Realtors and a variety of other service providers for locally built housing construction also operate on a national scale. Likewise, the production of the construction supplies

5 *Id.* at 705-07.

and equipment needed for building residential housing is national in scope and not simply local. Understanding the integrated nature of housing is important to appreciating the macro-economic scale of residential housing markets. Local construction activities are fully integrated into non-local markets and are heavily dependent upon institutions expressing strong public characteristics, such as banks, mortgage markets, and networks of interstate commerce.

Second, despite assumptions to the contrary, our residential housing stock should be considered a quasi-public good for two primary reasons. The first relates to government support and subsidy of housing markets, and the later to the durability of housing that stays in service long beyond the occupation of the first resident owner.

Housing in the United States is heavily subsidized, indirectly, if not directly.[6] There would be far less private housing in the United States if the public did not subsidize and support it. Government and government related entities support mortgage markets and the development of uniform mortgage documentation. The government also supports programming such as VA (Veterans Administration) and FHA (Federal Housing Administration) lending, and the government built the infrastructure needed for a strong and efficient primary and secondary mortgage market. In addition, homeowners are assisted in their efforts by subsidies extended via the mortgage interest rate deduction on their federal income tax returns. Private housing markets also benefit from government bailouts of lenders. The most recent example of this being the current sub-prime mortgage disaster,[7] and another not so distant example includes the bailout of the savings and loan industry in the 1980s.[8] All of this suggests a strong public element to so-called private housing in the United States.

Another significant reason for finding the idea of private housing to be a misnomer is that housing units stay in the housing stock much longer than the occupation time of any given owner. While an average home owner may occupy a home for seven to ten years, the average age of a unit in our national housing stock is 30-40 years old, with some 25% of housing being in excess of 70 years old.[9] This means that the individual home buyer, contracting in his or her own self interest with a private developer, fails to account for the long-term social consequences of personal design choices, primarily because these costs and benefits will accrue to others in a later time period. Thus, private parties, acting out of self interest in the housing market, miscalculate the costs and benefits of inclusive design housing, and such housing ends up being under produced.

Third, the impact of mobility impairment is underestimated in a system that frames the matter in terms of the number of discrete individuals with such

---

6 *Id.*

7 Robin P. Malloy, *Mortgage Market Reform and the Fallacy of Self-Correcting Markets*, 30 Pace L. Rev. 79, 80 (2009).

8 *Inclusion by Design, supra* note 4, at 705-07.

9 *Id.* at 723-29.

a disability.[10] People with mobility impairment do not live and should not live lonely and isolated lives, even if those lives are lived out in individual housing units equipped to meet their needs. People have relationships, people visit other people, people have friends and families, and people connect with others outside of the workplace and outside of places of public accommodation. The proper way to think about accessible housing is not in terms of how many individual units need to be built to match the number of individuals with mobility impairment but rather to think in terms of all units being accessible to the extent that every indivdiual can at least visit the home of any other individual. Mobility is a family and a community issue, not simply a private and individual one.

Fourth, housing accessibility is a public concern for at least two additional considerations. The first being that we need a housing stock that is more capable of providing re-housing during a major emergency.[11] In an emergency situation we need to be able to quickly re-house people without having to sort out people with special needs and expend valuable time figuring out which housing units will meet their needs. A more fungible design strategy on questions of accessibility will make emergency response time more effective and efficient. It will also make it possible for more friends and families to assist in self help efforts at providing shelter and re-housing. And, second, we have to look at the issues of accessibility in terms of our national policy in favor of inclusion. We would not exclude people from residential housing on the basis of race, religion, or ethnicity, for example, yet we permit easily corrected design features to serve as a proxy to prevent people with mobility impairment from having equal access to neighborhoods.

The barriers to civic participation in residential neighborhoods are invisible because the barriers are expressed within seemingly private space; the private residential home. The invisibility of these barriers, however, makes them no less exclusionary, and their location within a housing unit makes them no less subject to public scrutiny. Residential housing does not naturally feature exclusionary design elements such as multiple steps rather than ramps leading to the entranceway, and doorways and hallways too narrow for wheelchair accessibility – in housing construction, exclusion is by design, and we can readily change it; just as we do with building codes and other structural regulations.

In suggesting a need to rethink the legal framework on private homes to include recognition of housing units as quasi-public places, I do not want to be misunderstood. This chapter does not suggest that people must let uninvited guests into their homes to further a policy of inclusion of people with mobility impairment, but rather argues in favor of requiring all homes to be designed so

10 *Id.* at 720-23.

11 *Id.* at 736-38. The idea being that a general policy of building inclusive design housing provides additional benefits by creating a larger stock of more fungible inclusive design housing units; units that can be safely and easily used by people with mobility impairment when confronted with an emergency housing situation.

that they can be safely and easily visited by all *invited* quests without regard to mobility impairment.[12]

Background on Inclusive Design, and Demographics

Full inclusion of people into the fabric of everyday life is important. In order to be a full participant in one's community, however, one must be able to enjoy reasonable access to the spaces and places that make up and compose civic life. This means that public buildings, commercial venues, streets, transportation systems, and communication networks need to be navigable by people with disabilities. It also means that neighborhoods should be open and accessible so that people may enjoy the full benefits of community life.

There are many types of disability one might address, but in this chapter I focus on mobility impairment and residential housing. While most public spaces, shopping areas, places of employment, and educational and government institutions have been made reasonably accessible, our residential neighborhoods have generally avoided close scrutiny. Many neighborhoods consist of homes that cannot be easily visited by a person with mobility impairment. This should be unacceptable. We have millions of people who can not easily and safely visit family, enjoy socializing with neighbors, or engage in the requisite home party networking that is crucial to success in many work environments.

Being a member of a neighborhood—of a community—means being fully able to participate in the normal and everyday rhythms of community life. Being tucked away in one's own house, even if it has been personally modified for accessibility, is a lonely thing when all of one's neighbors, friends, colleagues, and extended family live in homes that cannot be easily and safely visited. In such a situation, one can not just drop by the home of a family member, friend, or colleague for a visit, and invitations to home-based events become scarce. People on all sides of the relationship begin to view the entire process as a chore. Under such circumstances it is difficult for people with mobility impairment to fully participate in community life and to feel like an equally dignified citizen in the important networks of one's own neighborhood.

12 In this regard, this chapter expresses three important ideas. First, it emphasizes the fact that much of our residential housing is designed in an exclusionary way, making it difficult for people with mobility impairment to navigate their own homes as well as those of friends and family that they might wish to visit. Second, it recognizes that exclusion is by design and thus volitional. Hence it can easily be made inclusionary by simply changing our design choices. Third, the idea of open neighborhoods draws attention to the fact that accessibility is not just an issue for a particular housing unit occupied by a specific individual with mobility impairment. People live in communities and have social networks of friends, family, and colleagues. Unless entire neighborhoods are open and accessible in housing design these social networks will be truncated for the mobility impaired because they will be unable to freely visit and interact with others.

Through exclusion by design, our residential housing structures re-enforce a negative image of people with mobility impairment. Our housing design policy treats people with mobility impairment as isolated and detached from normal family relationships. It imprisons the mobility impaired in housing situations that take them out of normal friendship and community networks while signaling that each mobility impaired individual presents the broader community with a discrete housing "problem" to be dealt with as an exception to the norm. Instead of making low-cost changes to housing design to benefit everyone, our residential housing policy suggests that it is an injustice for housing costs to rise a very small amount in order to make all homes inclusive. This view is based on a misunderstanding of the number of families and social relationships affected by mobility impairment and by thinking in terms of discrete individuals rather than in terms of communities and social networks.

In getting at the accessibility problem in residential housing, this section of the chapter addresses two points. First, it discusses several standards of inclusive design. Second, it presents basic demographic information on the nature and scope of mobility impairment in the United States.

Two generally referenced standards of inclusive design are those of *universal design* and *visitability*.[13]

Universal design standards are generally quite pervasive and applied throughout an entire structure. One way to quickly grasp the basic idea of universal design is that everything within a structure is designed to be readily accessible to a person in a wheelchair. Thus, doorways and hallways are wider (36-inch width recommendation), and have entrances that are barrier free. Bathrooms include appropriate grab bars, are bigger in size to accommodate the turning radius of a wheelchair, and include showers designed for easy roll in and out with a wheelchair. Throughout the home light switches are placed lower, and traditional round doorknobs give way to lower positioned levers. Storage shelves and cabinets are lower, and counter tops are lower with "cut outs" so that a wheelchair user can push close enough to have the chair frame fit under the counter, thus permitting the user to be positioned to make full use of the counter space. In addition, the residential living unit is generally designed on a single level layout, and provides appropriate means for ready access to the entire unit and to any common property. These universal accessibility design criteria are applied to every room, and every element throughout the home.

The visitability standard is much less pervasive. The general idea behind this standard, as applied to residential housing, is one of making it possible for every home to be easily and safely visited by anyone in the community. In other words, if I am hosting a neighborhood party at my house it should be possible for all of my neighbors to be included and to feel that they are full participants

13 *Inclusion by Design*, *supra* note 4, at 710-20 (this section of the chapter on universal design and visitability are based substantially on the indicated pages of the Hastings article).

in the social life of the neighborhood, without regard to mobility impairment. In order for this to readily happen my home would have to meet some minimal inclusionary design standards. The entrance to my home would have to have a zero step elevation through the doorway and appropriate grade of incline from street level to the entrance. And, my entrance doorway and hallway should be at least 36 inches wide (consistent with that of universal design). The main portions of my entertainment area need to be on one level floor, no drop living rooms or raised dinning rooms for instance. In addition, for all of my guests to feel equally comfortable I should have a bathroom on the main floor of the home and it needs to be sized to permit entrance and appropriate turning radius for a wheelchair. Ideally, the bathroom will also have light switches and a sink at appropriate levels (slightly lower than the traditional non accessible levels). Round doorknobs would be replaced with lever style door openers placed at the appropriate height (these are easier to open). This would be a minimal visitability standard imposing very little cost on the design requirements of a housing unit. I refer to this standard as a Level I Visitability Standard.

Going a step further than the Level I standard would involve the need for at least one bedroom to be located on the main floor of the home (could be a bedroom/den) and a bathroom on the main floor which would have a roll-in shower and grab bars. These additional features would make the home visitable by anyone, such as a close friend or family member with mobility impairment, who is staying for a day or more as a house guest. It also makes the housing unit more fungible and therefore more readily accessible in the event of an emergency resulting in a rapid loss of a significant part of a community's housing stock; as in the circumstances of New Orleans after Hurricane Katrina. The greater the fungibility of accessible housing, the more effective and efficient can be emergency responses to providing safe and sanitary re-housing for people in need of shelter. I refer to this standard as a Level II Visitability Standard.

From an aesthetic perspective, issues sometimes arise concerning the "look" of inclusionary housing. Young people sometimes feel that a home with grab bars in the bathroom, for instance, signifies that they are living in an "old person's home." Consequently, they often react by removing such devices in an effort to make the premises signify that a cooler and more hip younger resident has moved in to occupy the space. There are two logical responses to this concern. First, as more and more homes incorporate these accessibility features we can expect them to be manufactured in styles and colors that go beyond the typical cold steel ones often found in today's housing structures. Second, as the presence of these features becomes pervasive they will lose their signification of old age and will disappear into the realm of the "ordinary", in the same way that the soap dish and tooth brush holder have become ordinary fixtures in the current customary bathroom. Moreover, the accessibility standard might be met by simply building the home with the necessary reinforced bathroom walls needed as a prerequisite to affixing grab bars. With the walls properly reinforced to bear the weight, grab bars might be installed at a later date or made removable so that they can be put on and taken off as desired.

A second set of aesthetic concerns relate to the front view of the home; the "curb appeal" of the property, as some real estate sales people might say. The inclusionary design standard that requires a zero elevation entranceway to permit an easy roll in on a wheelchair constrains some designs for front porches and patios. Again, these design features are in large part influenced by expectations of what is perceived as a norm in the housing market. Design norms can be changed and inclusionary housing design can be made pleasing to the eye. Acceptability depends not so much on the entrance door itself but on the planning that goes into integrating other home design features and landscaping with the view of the accessible point of entry. In new construction housing this issue can be readily addressed with good inclusive design work done up front.

With remodeling of existing structures and with properties designated with historical significance some compromises may be needed. There are ways to design residential housing changes to provide aesthetically pleasing front views of the entrance while providing a side riser to the porch or patio. In addition to creative use of landscaping to eliminate a need for steps, a raised front patio might include a side ramp permitting access to the same front door but without being positioned as the primary focal point of the front yard. In the alternative, for situations in which remodeling and rehab work make costs prohibitive, it is often possible to construct a reasonably equal alternative point of access to the premises. This less desirable approach of using an alternative entranceway for accessibility might be a reasonable accommodation (or a permitted variance in zoning terminology) in cases where it can be demonstrated that historic preservation needs or remodeling costs make it prohibitive to properly rebuild a particular front entrance. The calculus involved in such a situation is not one of using a simple cost and benefit analysis. The individual benefits need not outweigh the costs, as there are significant public benefits to be gained by opening neighborhoods to readily accessible housing. The key point, with respect to both new housing and remodeling, is that thoughtful planning and design can make most any feature attractive, just as poor design and lack of planning can make most any construction feature look out of place and distracting.

As to Level I and Level II Visitability standards, the cost of meeting these design features is estimated at between $0 and $1,500 in most cases of new construction for single-family residential housing.[14] It is mostly a matter of up front planning and design. And, costs should decline as inclusionary standards become the norm rather than the exception in building design. Normalizing certain design features permits mass production and economies of scale. This can apply, for example, to a change in the "standard size" door, or in moving from round doorknobs to lever style door openers. As inclusionary features are made the norm, the new design elements become cheaper because of the economies of scale associated with being

14 *Id.* at 715-20, 733-36, 746-48 (discussing costs).

an "off the shelf" product, as opposed to being a special order item. Thus, special order cost considerations for many accessible design features disappear once the accessibility feature is implemented as the new norm.

From a legal perspective, regulation of aesthetic features of design has been permitted for some time.[15] Local government zoning codes have covered aesthetic matters and have been regularly upheld by the courts.[16] A rationale for this is that the exterior of the home and its landscaping are "quasi-public," rather than private. Exterior design and the space surrounding buildings are public in the sense of having a significant impact on others. The structural design, colors, and placement of landscaping address themselves to others beyond the owners. Thus, the exterior presents a classic example of an externality, with spillover effects that go beyond the immediate parties—beyond the current occupant of the house. Good design and landscaping may provide a positive externality to neighbors and the community. In contrast, poor design and landscaping may impose a negative externality. Since, as is often said, "beauty is in the eye of the beholder," regulation has been permitted as one means of mediating the tension between private and public evaluations of such aesthetic matters.

The idea of considering the exterior surface and space of a structure as "public" is one found in architecture and in law. It is also consistent with the enforceable regulations of many planned communities and subdivisions. Architectural design controls, particularly as applied to things visible from off the property, are regularly upheld as valid and enforceable.[17]

Importantly, it needs to be noted that at the time of writing this chapter the only major national requirement for residential housing accessibility is that 5% of new housing units funded or operated as "public housing" under programs of the Department of Housing and Urban Development (HUD) need to be fully accessible (meet a general standard that is similar to universal design).[18] This is a very small subset of our national housing stock and it completely misses privately owned

---

15 *See* Julian Conrad Juergensmeyer & Thomas E. Roberts, Land Use Planning and Development Regulation Law, 787-814 (2d ed., Practitioner's Treatise Series 2007). *See also* Daniel R. Mandelker, Land Use Law, §§ 6.39-6.52, 11.01-11.12 (5th ed. 2003 & Supp. 2008)

"The Concept of the public welfare is broad and inclusive. … The values it represents are spiritual as well as physical, aesthetic as well as monetary. It is within the power of the legislature to determine that the community should be beautiful as well as healthy, spacious as well as clean, well-balanced as well as carefully patrolled."

Id. at § 11.05 (alteration in original) (quoting Berman v. Parker, 348 U.S. 26, 33 (1954)) (noting that this represents the majority view in the United States).

16 *See supra* note 15.

17 *See generally*, James Charles Smith, *Restrictions on Freedom of Expressions Imposed by Servitudes* 16 Digest 1 (2009); Also things like zoning regulation of fences and good side faces out, sheds, etc.

18 *Inclusion by Design*, *supra* note 4, at 708. Other current legislation fails to cover private single family homes and includes:

single-family residential housing that does not otherwise function as offering public accommodation. This policy is seemingly based on misunderstanding the mobility impaired as discrete and disconnected individuals and then attempting to reasonably match the number of public housing units to the perceived needs (number) of people with mobility impairment in a given population. In other words, the view seems to be that there is not a universal need for all housing to be inclusive because only a small percentage of people have serious mobility impairment. This approach ignores the neighborhood and network effect of human relationships. In response, Congress is considering the Inclusive Design Housing Act which, if passed, will make all

---

Architectural Barriers Act of 1968. The Architectural Barriers Act (ABA) requires that buildings and facilities designed, constructed, altered, or leased *with certain federal funds* after September 1969 must be accessible to and useable by handicapped persons. Private market construction of single-family housing is not covered by the ABA. 42 U.S.C. §§ 4151-4157 (2006).

Section 504 of the Rehabilitation Act of 1973. Section 504 prohibits discrimination based on disability in any *program or activity receiving federal financial assistance*. To the extent that Section 504 applies to housing it covers housing programs receiving federal funding and not privately funded single-family residential housing. 29 U.S.C. §§ 701 et seq. (2006).

Title II of the Americans with Disabilities Act of 1990. Title II prohibits discrimination based on disability in programs, services, and activities provided or *made available by public entities*. HUD enforces Title II when it relates to state and local *public housing*, housing assistance and housing referrals. Title II sets standards of accessibility for public facilities and programs, not for private residential housing. 42 U.S.C. §§ 12131-12181 (2006).

Title III of the Americans with Disabilities Act of 1990. Title III prohibits discrimination based on disability in the provision of goods, services, facilities, privileges, advantages, or accommodations of any place *of public accommodation* by any person owning, leasing, or operating a place *of public accommodation*. Single-family residential housing is not considered a place of public accommodation. 42 U.S.C. §§ 12181-12213 (2006).

Executive Order 13217. Executive Order 13217 requires federal agencies to evaluate their policies and programs to determine if any can be revised or modified to improve the availability of *community-based living* arrangements for persons with disabilities. Community-based living arrangements might include senior housing developments and group homes but not single-family residential housing. Exec. Order. No. 13217, June 18, 2001.

Fair Housing Amendments Act of 1988. The Fair Housing Amendments Act applies to access to *multi-family* housing and it outlaws discrimination against people with disabilities. Fair Housing Act, 42 U.S.C. § 3601 et seq. (2008). It also provides mandates for all new multi-family housing to meet specific inclusive design standards; including guidelines for entranceways, hallways, light switches, grab bars, spacing to accommodate use of a wheelchair, and other design elements. The anti-discrimination and inclusive design criteria do not apply to single-family residential housing.

public housing accessible.[19] Private single-family residential housing will still have its own guidelines of under inclusiveness.

To better appreciate the need for open neighborhood design standards we can consider some demographic information.[20] According to the 2000 census, the total number of families in the United States was 72.3 million.[21] Of this number, approximately 20.9 million families had at least one member with a disability,[22] and of this group over 12 million had at least one member with a *physical* disability.[23] For these purposes, a physical disability was defined as "a condition that substantially limited one or more basic physical activities such as walking, climbing stairs, reaching, lifting, or carrying."[24] Thus, when we stop thinking in terms of atomistic individuals with discrete mobility impairment problems, we see that 16.6% of families in the United States are potentially affected by exclusionary design in residential housing. When we think in broader terms, including social networks of family, friends, and colleagues we begin to appreciate that perhaps 20-25% or more of Americans are potentially touched by issues of concern to people with mobility impairment.

The network implications of mobility impairment multiply quickly. As our population ages we will confront increasing demands for open neighborhood housing. As of the year 2000, the total number of people in the United States aged 65 and over was 35 million.[25] This is a 12% increase over the year 1990 when the number of people 65 and over totaled 31.2 million.[26] The 35 million people over age 65 represented 12.4% of the population in 2000.[27] Furthermore, in 2000 there were 18.4 million people ages 65-74,[28] and people age 75-84 numbered 12.4 million.[29] Many of these Americans aged 65 and over must deal with disability. In fact, according to an American Community Survey performed by the census bureau,

19 Inclusive Home Design Act of 2007, H.R. 4202, 110th Cong. (2007-08).

20 *Id.* at 720-23.

21 Qi Wang, U.S. Dep't of Com., Report No. CENSR-23, *Disability and American Families: 2000, at* 3 tbl.1. (2005), *available at* http://www.census.gov/prod/2005pubs/censr-23.pdf.

22 *Id.*

23 *Id.*

24 *Id.* at 4. This definition referred to "substantial" limitations, so there are probably many more people who have physical limitations.

25 Lisa Hetzel & Annetta Smith, U.S. Dep't of Commerce, Brief No. C2KBR/01-10, *The 65 Years and Over Population: 2000*, at 4 (2001), *available at* http://www.cenus.gov/prod/2001pubs/c2kbr01-10.pdf.

26 *Id.*

27 *See* Jon Pynoos et al., *Aging in Place, Housing, and the Law*, 16 Elder L.J. 77, 78 (2008).

28 Helzel & Smith, *supra* note 25.

29 *Id.*

40.5% of Americans 65 and older have a disability.[30] The elderly are one of the fastest growing segments of our population, and we are just now starting to deal with the fact that there are 76 million "baby boomers" adding to their ranks[31]

Finally, we have to be mindful of the fact that accessibility is not just a question with respect to current occupants. Current occupants may not even have mobility impairment but they may have friends, relatives, grandparents, or neighbors with mobility impairment. And, at some point in the future they may develop a temporary or permanent impairment as the result of an accident or other incident that puts them in a wheelchair, or requires them to use a walker, crutches, or a cane. Our housing stock must, therefore, be designed and built for a dynamic population over time. It must respect the individuals occupying the home while also facilitating social networks crucial to open neighborhoods and healthy human relationships.

Private Homes and Our National Housing Stock

The housing market in the United Sates consists of a very large private sector and a much smaller but significant public sector. Both sectors must be responsive to regulation related to accessibility for the mobility impaired. As in other areas of American life, however, the government expresses a greater degree of comfort in its ability to regulate housing in which public funding and resources are used for construction and operations than it does with respect to housing in the "private" sector. This is particularly true with respect to the market for so called private residential home ownership.

This section of the chapter explores the potentially misplaced deference to private preferences in the private home ownership market. In proceeding, I first explore the basic contours of our housing markets, and then address the market implications for under production of inclusive design housing.[32]

Home ownership has long been a public policy goal in the United States. Adequate and affordable housing is important. Currently approximately 70% of Americans own their own homes. This means, of course, that 30% do not. For those that do not currently own a home there may be multiple reasons. These reasons may include the voluntary choice to be a renter or it maybe that private

30 United States and States — R1803. Percent of People 65 Years and Over with a Disability (2005), http://factfinder.census.gov/servlet/GRTSelectServlet?ds_name=ACS_2005_EST_G00_&_lang=en&_ts=254773591968 (follow the link to the right of "R1803" under "Aging").

31 *See* Pynoos et al., *supra* note 27 at 79 (using the number 75 million rather than 76 million and defining boomers as those born between 1946 and 1964); Judy Stark, *And Access for All*, St. Petersburg Times (Fla.), June 8, 2002, *available at* http://www.sptimes.com/2002/06/08/Homes/And_access_for_all.shtml.

32 *Inclusion by Design*, *supra* note 4, at 720-38 (This part of the chapter is substantially based on the material covered in the identified pages in the Hastings article).

housing is too expensive. Many people find that they are involuntary renters. They are in rental housing because they lack the income, employment history, savings, and access to credit necessary to become an owner. Even with an adequate monthly income it is difficult for some people to save enough for the down payment and closing costs. In fact, many home buyers are people that already own a home and who are simply moving on to buy a different one. The most difficult hurdle to homeownership, therefore, is the ability to move from renting (or residing for free with a friend or family member) to owning a first home.

While the average rate of home ownership in the United States is around 70%, home ownership rates differ by race, with a significant disparity between whites and Asians on the high end, and blacks and Latinos on the low end. Correspondingly, mortgage application approval and denial rates also reveal similar disparities, although gains in each area have been made by people of color over the past few years.[33]

In many instances people may be home owners and yet find themselves underhoused or in housing of poor quality, or located in undesirable areas (areas of urban decay or rural poverty). The overwhelming majority of housing in both the rental and ownership markets is private. In addition to the private sector, we also have a much smaller, yet significant number of people living in public and publicly subsidized housing. Public housing is directly owned, regulated, or subsidized by the government. The primary focus of this chapter is on physical accessibility with respect to the private home ownership market.

In the private home ownership market, developers often build products assumed to meet the personal preferences of their buyers, and the assertion is made that to the greatest extent possible, private homes should reflect individual preferences rather than government dictates. For the most part, however, these private preferences are expressed in the context of prefabricated housing units or pre-construction design templates. In other words, people are not going into the process asking to have inaccessible doorways and homes. They are being shown inaccessible designs and housing products and are selecting based on preferences for other elements such as layout, colors, and construction materials. Thus, core accessibility issues are driven not so much by intentional consumer preferences as by pre-packaged and prefabricated housing designs.

The argument in favor of protecting private preferences is also problematic in as much as private housing markets have a significant public dimension. First, each new housing unit becomes a part of our national housing stock, and the housing stock lasts much longer then the time in which any particular units is occupied by a given owner. Second, private home ownership is subsidized through the tax system, through the mortgage markets, and to some extent through the insurance markets. Thus, private home ownership is really a misnomer. We really have a system of publicly supported housing units that are temporarily occupied for a

---

33 Some of these gains may be wiped out after accounting for the sub-prime mortgage foreclosure problems.

period less than the useful life of the structure. Consequently, there is a legitimate public interest in the type of housing being built and in the implications of such housing on the long-term housing stock.

In this context it is important to note that in the United States the age of the housing stock varies considerably. Over 25% of the housing stock was built prior to 1950.[34] However, over 25% of the housing stock is much newer, having been built since 1980.[35] A significant number of homes, nearly 50%, were built between 1950 and 1980.[36] The median age of housing units in the United States, as of 2000, was 30 years.[37] Thus, we see that housing units enter the market and stay in service for a long number of years. Each of these units becomes part of our national housing stock. Significantly, while individual housing units remain in the national housing stock for 20, 40, 70, or even 100 years, the typical American moves once every seven to ten years. In this respect we have a situation in which private parties are building and buying housing units based on private individual design preferences which create potentially negative long-term path dependent implications for future potential users of our long-term national housing stock.

In a market where private home ownership represents a short time period in the life of a unit that will be in the public housing stock for years to come, it is unclear that private preferences should be given significant weight in the balancing of public policy respecting inclusive design for the mobility impaired. The design implication of a national commitment to visitability and open neighborhoods imposes a nominal cost on construction while delivering significant benefits to individuals, families, and communities. And, even with accessible design requirements, homes can be built with numerous decorating and design features capable of expressing the personal tastes and preferences of the occupant. This is no different than designing houses that otherwise incorporate particular building code and land use requirements.

In response to the clear need for more accessible housing, and the lack of Federal leadership, some individual counties have created ordinances aimed at forcing homebuilders to build housing that is more accessible.[38] Pima County, Arizona, for instance, passed the first ordinance in the country to require a zero-step entrance.[39] It also required doors to be at least 32 inches wide, lever style door handles, reinforced walls in ground floor bathrooms so grab bars could be

34 *How We Are Housed: Results from the 1999 American Housing Survey*, http://www.huduser.org/periodicals/ushmc/fall00/summary-2.html (last visited Mar. 23, 2009).

35 *Id.*

36 *Id.*

37 *Id.*

38 *Inclusion by Design*, *supra* note 4, at 728-31.

39 *See* Pima County Visitability Ordinance (Dec. 23, 2003), http://www.accessiblesociety.org/topics/housing/pimacoruling.html; World Visitability Legislation, Sample U.S. State and Local Ordinances, http://www.concretechange.org/policy_legislative_local.aspx (last visited Mar. 23, 2009).

easily installed, switches no higher than 48 inches, and hallways 36 inches wide throughout the main floor.[40]

In *Washburn v. Pima County*, the ordinance was challenged on several grounds by homebuilders and a homebuilder's association.[41] First, the plaintiffs claimed that the county lacked statutory authority to adopt the ordinance.[42] The plaintiffs also claimed the ordinance violated their right to privacy and their equal protection rights.[43] The court did not accept the plaintiff's arguments. Instead, the court held that the county was authorized, pursuant to an Arizona statute, to adopt individual building design criterion for the purpose of developing codes in enacting its ordinance.[44] The court also held that the county's ordinance did not unconstitutionally infringe on the homebuilders' right to privacy because the ordinance was a proper exercise of the county's police power. Finally, the court held that the ordinance did not violate the homebuilder's equal protection rights because the county advanced the legitimate government interest of increasing the number of accessible homes.[45]

Significantly, Judge Eckerstrom stated in the majority opinion:

> The uncontested evidence established that approximately one percent of the population is confined [*sic*] to wheelchairs, but the county points out that a much larger percentage will suffer [*sic*] a disability at some point in their lives. Although all age groups are affected by disability, the county introduced evidence that approximately forty-one percent of people over the age of sixty-five have some form of disability. Disability is a growing problem both nationally and locally, and the county also introduced evidence that Arizona's population of people over the age of sixty is expected to triple by 2025. Although many of these disabled people will not be confined [*sic*] to wheelchairs, the county concluded from these figures that the number of people confined [*sic*] to wheelchairs is rising. For these reasons, the county addressed a legitimate governmental interest when it adopted a building code designed to increase the number of homes accessible to those in wheelchairs.[46]

The judge observed that wheelchairs are not the only reason that accessible housing should be required. He pointed out that much more than 1% of the population will suffer a disability at some point in their lives, and also noted that the aging population suffers from a much higher prevalence of disability. Following up on the judge's point, it is important to keep in mind that the proper frame of reference

40 *Id.*
41 81 P.3d. 10301, 1030 (Ariz. Ct. App. 2003).
42 *Id.* at 1033.
43 *Id.* at 1038-39.
44 *Id.* at 1038.
45 *Id.* at 1039-40.
46 Washburn v. Pima County, 81 P.3d. at 1039 (citation omitted).

is not just the individual with mobility impairment but the web of relationships of each such person. The accessibility issue in residential housing is really about families and communities. Looking only at meeting housing needs of a small fraction of our population misses the point; people do not live in isolated shelters, they live in communities and share their homes with family and friends.

Since the time that Pima passed its ordinance to promote accessibility, other communities have also enacted laws regarding visitability.[47]

Another interesting development has taken place in Georgia. In 2003, the directors of the National Association of Home Builders passed a policy resolution in favor of voluntary visitability programs and opposing mandatory programs.[48] The Home Builders Association of Georgia took this guidance and created a voluntary program called "Easy Living."[49] The problem with such voluntary efforts is that they leave too many housing units out of the system and they fail to account for market imperfections that result in the underproduction of fully accessible units.

There are several reasons for this underproduction.[50] As previously discussed, housing units are quasi-public goods and, as such, we observe the same kind of under production as we do with other public goods. In the case of public goods, the parties to the transaction do not capture or internalize all of the costs and benefits of their activities and thus, too few of the desired products are produced; in this case we under produce housing units with open neighborhood design. Another way to look at this involves the problem of having the parties internalize the true cost of their design choices. The individuals involved in a given purchase and sale transaction do not take account of the full social costs of adding exclusionary housing units to the long-term housing stock. Thus, we over produce exclusionary housing units and underproduce housing that is fully accessible to the mobility impaired.

In addition to these reasons for underproduction of open neighborhood design housing, some developers just do not want to update their building work because they are resistant to change and prefer to follow path dependent designs of the past. Inertia is a powerful defender of the status quo. Another more likely reason, however, for resisting inclusive designs in residential housing has to do with what I call "amenity pricing." Because developers may believe that price and profit can

---

47 Jordana L. Maisel, Ctr. For Inclusive Design & Envtl. Access (IDEA), *Visitability as an Approach to Inclusive Housing Design and Community Development: A Look at Its Emergence, Growth and Challenges* 20-23 (2005) [hereinafter *Vistability as an Approach*]. Katie Spegal & Phoebe Liebig, *Visitability: Trends, Approaches, and Outcomes* (2003), (unpublished manuscript), *available at* http://www.usc.edu/dept/gero/nrcshhm/research/pages/VA%20PAPER.pdf. For information on some communities *see* World Visitability Legislation, Sample U.S. State and Local Ordinances, *supra* note 39.

48 *NAHB Supports Voluntary "visitability,"* NATION'S BUILDING NEWS ONLINE, May 26, 2003, http://www.nbnnews.com/NBN/issues/2003-05-26/Seniors+Housing/2.html.

49 *Id.*

50 *Inclusion by Design*, *supra* note 4, at 730-35.

be enhanced by allocating scarce square footage inside the housing unit to features other than accessibility, they are reluctant to sign on to a national standard for open neighborhood design. Many developers would rather offer an exclusionary design with one and one half bathrooms than an inclusionary one with only one bathroom. More bathrooms add market value; whereas wider hallways and bigger bathrooms simply allocate more precious square feet to what is already there. When hallways and bathrooms are kept small and exclusionary, some square footage can be reallocated to other defined amenities with higher consumer appeal (another bathroom, a bigger kitchen with a breakfast nook, an additional closet, etc.). After all, builders and realtors generally sell houses by advertising amenities such as one and one half baths, and not by advertising 36-inch wide hallways. The problem with this, of course, is that self-interested consumers are drawn to these other amenity options because they do not absorb the full cost of adding to our exclusionary housing stock and they do not account for the externality of generating truncated social networks for the mobility impaired.

Some builders and developers have opposed inclusive design standards because they think it will drive up their costs.[51] Of course, many building code features can be opposed for similar reasons. While costs are important to keeping housing affordable, cost alone is not the only value factor to consider when building safe and socially desirable housing. Housing costs are probably less significant to most developers than loss of control with respect to flexible allocation of square footage to enhance amenity pricing inside the unit. In contrast to developers who express concern about housing costs, we find that others have willingly adopted visitability standards because they have found it to be another marketing tool in some markets, which may outweigh any added costs. There are other complaints about inclusionary housing standards. In addition to cost based complaints, some developers assert that inclusionary features are impractical, go beyond the scope and purposes of building codes, and unfairly restrict consumer choice. These concerns seem to be outweighed by the negative implications of exclusionary housing and by the reality of the market imperfections upon which they are based. Likewise, they under appreciate the health and safety issues of non-inclusive design housing.

As to the cost of achieving a visitability standard of inclusion, there is some debate. Some of the debate likely stems from the fact that houses can be built in a variety of ways in an infinite number of locations. These variables obviously affect the cost. Despite these many variables, some numbers may be less difficult to determine. A paper by the Center for Inclusive Design and Environmental Access stated that the cost of a zero-step entrance would only add $150 to the cost of a new construction.[52] Additionally, the cost of having wider interior doors could be

---

51 *Id.* at 732-35.

52 *Visitability as an Approach*, *supra* note 47. Costing considerations are also more fully discussed in; *Inclusion by Design*, *supra* note 4, at 715-6; and in AFFORDABLE HOUSING

as little as $50 if they are put in during construction.[53] Adding these features later on is significantly more costly. For example, the cost of having a no-step entrance added later would be around $1,000.[54] Also, the cost of widening the doors later on could be as much as $700.[55] These costs, while not high, are not insignificant and they emphasize the importance of having the correct design at the outset. There is no reason to believe that wider hallways and larger bathrooms would add any costs.

Pima County, Arizona, before implementing its visitability ordinance, did a study on the cost of visitability. The court noted the study in its opinion. The results of the study corroborated the numbers stated above. The study found that implementing the visitability standards [in the Pima County ordinance] would only cost about $100.[56] Specifically, the court stated, "The Board of Supervisors could have rationally concluded that the benefit to the community in providing for the disabled justified the comparatively minimal cost of implementing the required design features."[57]

The key here is to build visitability and inclusionary standards into the construction process to avoid the added costs of doing rehab work at a later date. With a national standard all developers will face the same design constraints and thus would have incentives to develop attractive ways of integrating accessible design features into the homes they build.

Conclusion

This chapter suggests that while much progress has been made in making public places more inclusive, there is still much work to be done in our residential neighborhoods. The chapter has taken a focused and narrowly tailored look at one important part of the housing market; the market for so called single family private residential homes. It suggests a reframing of key underlying assumptions so that the need for regulatory reform can be more readily understood. While change might be implemented by expansion of coverage under the Fair Housing Act or the Americans with Disabilities Act, it may also be implemented through local zoning laws.[58] The key is that change in whatever form is more likely to come about when people understand the public nature of our private housing stock.

AND PUBLIC-PRIVATE PARTNERSHIPS 207-17 (Nestor M. Davidson & Robin Paul Malloy eds. 2009)

53 *Id.*

54 *Id.*

55 *Id.*

56 Washburn v. Pima County, 81 P.3d. 1030, 1040, 1039 (Ariz. Ct. App. 2003); *see also* Pima County Visitability Ordinance, *supra* note 39.

57 Washburn v. Pima County, 81 P.3d at 1040.

58 The Fair Housing Act and the Americans with Disabilities Act have so far avoided covering these inclusive design concerns in private single-family residential housing. The

Acknowledgment

This book chapter is based on a much longer article titled *Inclusion by Design: Accessible Housing and Mobility Impairment*, 60 HASTINGS L.J. 699 (2009). The author has permission to use in full or in part, any and all material from the article.

---

focus of this chapter has not been on addressing the details of those Acts but rather to address the reframing of assumptions that when properly understood might make reform possible; either through revision of those Acts or in some other way.

Chapter 7

Who Should Fix the Sink?: Addressing Maintenance and Repairs in Limited Equity Cooperatives

Jennie O'Flanagan

As a lawyer representing tenant groups attempting to purchase their multifamily buildings in the District of Columbia, it is easy to enjoy a client's acquisition closing.[1] A tenant purchase closing marks the successful end of an intense, statutorily-defined period of tenant organization, education and decision making, which often includes securing often multi-million dollar financing. The tenant groups I have worked with usually consist of a mix of elderly and younger residents.[2] Most residents are lifelong renters. Usually, all have incomes that qualify as low-income for the Washington, D.C. area. When the closing, accomplished with the participation of the District government, is complete, the tenants have become homeowners, something they may have thought impossible just over a year before. And they have done it using a sophisticated and unusual ownership form that, before the process started, they likely did not know existed—through shared equity homeownership,[3] specifically the limited equity cooperative ("LEC").

The tenant purchase is possible because of two elements of public involvement. First, the District has a longstanding tenant opportunity to purchase law (known as the Tenant Opportunity to Purchase Act, or TOPA)[4] that is a proven mechanism for

---

1 As a fellow and staff attorney at the Harrison Institute for Housing and Community Development at Georgetown Law, I have worked with a number of tenant groups that have formed and are operating as limited equity cooperatives.

2 The residents and LECs discussed herein are drawn from actual projects I have worked on or am aware of in the District of Columbia.

3 Shared equity ownership also is referred to as third sector housing, limited equity housing or perpetually affordable housing. *See* John Emmeus Davis, *Shared Equity Homeownership* 2 (Nat'l Hous. Inst. 2006), *available at* http://www.nhi.org/pdf/SharedEquityHome.pdf. The best known forms are limited equity cooperatives, community land trusts and deed-restricted homes; all are housing that is owner-occupied, resale-restricted, and affordable long term. *Id.* at 13.

4 Rental Housing Conversion and Sale Act of 1980, D.C. Code Ann §42-3404.01 et seq. (2010). TOPA is the comprehensive successor statute to the Rental Housing Act of 1977, which initially established a right of first refusal for tenants.

preserving as affordable multifamily properties occupied by low-income residents.[5] Second, for low-income residents to take advantage of this opportunity,[6] many tenant groups secure below market rate financing from the District for acquisition (and rehabilitation). The District and the residents bring their various goals and interests to the table; in many cases,[7] the result is that is that the tenants purchase[8] and operate their building as a limited equity cooperative, a well-established form of multifamily shared equity housing.[9]

The triumph of any tenant purchase closing is quickly tempered by the fact that it is just the beginning of the hard work that the residents will undertake as LEC shareholder-members. They are responsible for operating a complex business entity that is also their home. The LEC (run by a board of directors and membership drawn from its residents) must make a number of structural and operational governance decisions that ultimately determine whether the LEC succeeds or fails. These decisions determine the financial viability of the LEC, and further, whether the residents' (and the District's) goals and aspirations for the LEC are met.

One such decision is how LECs will allocate the costs of maintenance and repairs of individual units.[10] Soon after closing, mundane though often expensive problems arise for the LEC members—a leaky faucet, a broken air conditioner on a

---

5 *See* Coal. for Nonprofit Hous. and Econ. Devt., *A Study of Limited-Equity Cooperatives in the District of Columbia* (2004) [hereinafter CNHED], *available at* http://www.cnhed.org (follow "CNHED's Limited-Equity Coop Study" hyperlink) (empirical study detailing the history and current condition of LECs in the District).

6 The TOPA rights and process discussed herein are those applicable to all sales of residential buildings in the District with more than four units. The rights are the same regardless of resident income levels. My work and this discussion addresses only buildings where the majority if not all of the tenants are low-income, defined as household annual income less than 80% Area Median Income ("AMI"). *See HPTF Limits Effective 3/19/09*, http://dhcd.dc.gov/dhcd/cwp/view,a,1242,q,646929.asp (hereinafter *HPTF Limits*) (listing maximum income levels based on household size for categories of Extremely Low (0-30% of AMI), Very Low (31-50% of AMI) and Low (51-80% of AMI)).

7 Some affordable housing advocates argue that shared equity housing including LECs is too often the affordable housing option used in the District. *See, e.g.*, Manna's Response to NCB Capital Impact's Papers on Shared Equity Ownership (SEO), on file with author (arguing against "pigeonholing" low income homeownership into the shared equity model and for limiting its role in the continuum of housing options). I agree that affordable housing must be a continuum of choices but I believe that for the right tenant group, an LEC is the best option and does not function to "keep low-income residents in poverty." *Id.* at 1.

8 The timing of TOPA and the residents' decision-making process may be such that the acquiring entity is the tenant association, with a commitment in place to the transfer and operate as a LEC, consistent with District law.

9 *See* Davis, *supra* note 3, at 27 (estimating 425,000 LEC units nationwide).

10 Some other examples include selecting and managing a management company, creating house rules, addressing delinquencies and other resident violations, and allocating board and membership authority.

hot summer day, a crumbling ceiling. For the traditional single-family homeowner, these problems are the homeowner's to address. However, the answer is not so clear for LEC members. An LEC is a hybrid form of affordable housing that has characteristics generally associated with each of rental and homeownership, as well as with public and private ownership. The equity and income limitations as well as the cooperative form[11] signal a departure from the bundle of rights and responsibilities associated with fee simple single-family homeownership. Yet neither the LEC corporate form nor the negotiated financing documents dictate whether the LEC or the individual residents will be responsible for maintenance and repairs of individual units. The nature of the LEC as both a home for and business operated by its low-income shareholder-residents makes this issue a complex and interesting one to consider.

In contrast to the rental model that I have found to be more pervasive among LECs, I believe that shifting responsibility and costs to the residents is the better model because it best meets the goals that the residents and the District sought to achieve with the LEC. First and foremost, it can help to assure the financial viability of the LEC. Second, it can help to preserve the physical condition of the LEC's asset, the multifamily building. Finally, this model preserves the experience of housing (and the expected individual and community benefits) that the residents and the District desire.

In this chapter, I consider why this governance decision is crucial to the overall success of the LEC and why a model that approximates the market-rate cooperative allocation of responsibilities is preferable. In Part I of this chapter, I discuss the LEC generally and the current DC model as part of the shared equity housing framework. In Part II, I discuss the problem of maintenance and repairs for individual units, and two models—one similar to the allocation of responsibility and cost in a rental context, the other to a market-rate cooperative—that an LEC can use for allocating responsibilities and rights. In Part III, I consider the private and public interests and goals involved in the LEC. Finally, in Part IV, I explore how the market-rate cooperative model of individual resident responsibility for maintenance and repair best meets these goals and suggest some proposals for addressing the potential concerns that the market-rate cooperative model might pose for low-income members.

11 Stuart S. Moskowitz, *Cooperative Apartments: The Enforceability of Transfer Restrictions and the Impact of Bankruptcy*, 18 Real Estate L.J. 142, 142 (1989) (discussing "hybrid nature" of cooperatives and shareholder interest that "does not fit neatly into traditional property classifications").

Part I: Limited Equity Cooperatives in the District of Columbia

Preservation of affordable housing is a continuing challenge in the District of Columbia.[12] The District is a total of just over sixty square miles of land[13] that has experienced numerous waves of gentrification that have limited the available supply of affordable housing. Similar to many other metropolitan areas, the District is experiencing reduced public subsidies for affordable housing,[14] decreased private lending for home purchases[15] and a high unemployment rate (significantly higher than the surrounding region and the national average).[16] Even now, single-family homes and condominiums remain quite expensive,[17] and the affordability gap

---

12 There are two scenarios common in preservation of affordable housing projects in the District. The first is preserving affordable housing in rapidly gentrifying neighborhoods that otherwise imminently will have little to no affordable housing. The second is preserving affordable housing in less rapidly-changing neighborhoods that tend to be poorer, have fewer amenities and less desirable locations. Even in the second category, homeownership is still not attainable for many low- to moderate-income residents.

13 The District of Columbia's land area is 61.40 square miles. U.S. Census Bureau, State and County Quick Facts, http://quickfacts.census.gov/qfd/states/11000.html

14 *See* Testimony of Jenny Reed, Policy Analyst, D.C. Fiscal Policy Inst., at the Public Hearing on the Fiscal Year 2010 Budget Oversight Hearing for the Dept. of Hsg. and Community Devt., D.C. Committee on Hsg. and Workforce Devt., Apr. 8, 2009, *available at* http://dcfpi.org/?p=390 (stating that the District's Housing Production Trust Fund ("HPTF"), the source of most District affordable housing funds in recent years "has seen a sharp decline in support from the substantial slow down in DC's real estate market and is now expected to receive just $18 million in FY 2010 and will be at its lowest level since 2003"); and Ed Lazere, D.C. Fiscal Policy Inst., and Robert Pohlman, Coal. for Nonprofit Hsg. and Econ. Devt., *Affordable Housing in the District Depends on a Stable Housing Production Trust Fund* (Oct. 20, 2008), *available at* http://dcfpi.org/wp-content/uploads/2008/10/10-20-08stablehptfreport.pdf (listing HPTF levels from 2003 — 2008, with a 2007 high of $58.7 million). For further explanation of the HPTF, *see* note 24.

15 Federal Reserve Bank of Kansas City, *Financial Industry Perspectives*, Dec. 2009, *Trends in Residential Mortgage Loan Originations and their Impact on Community Vanks*, *available at* http://www.kc.frb.org/banking/bankingpublications/prs09-12.pdf (58% decline in number of 2008 loan originations for home purchase as compared to 2005).

16 The District's unemployment rate was approximately 12% for February 2010, compared to 9.7% nationwide. D. C. Dep't of Employment Services, *District of Columbia Jobless Rate 11.9 Percent*, *available at* http://newsroom.dc.gov/show.aspx/agency/does/section/2/release/19560/year/2010/month/3. However, certain areas of the District, particularly lower-incomes ones, have been hit much harder, as shown by the 28.5% unemployment figure cited for the District's Ward 8 based on December 2009 statistics. V. Dion Haynes, *DC Unemployment Rate Increases Overall Number for Washington Metro Area*, Wash. Post Feb. 3, 2010, *available at* http://www.washingtonpost.com/wp-dyn/content/article/2010/02/02/AR2010020202258.html.

17 According to a recent D.C. Fiscal Policy Institute study, low-cost homeownership options in the District have rapidly declined since 2000, and despite recent declines in home values, home prices remain much higher than a decade ago. Ed Lazere, *Nowhere to*

remains wide. Many low- to moderate-income families who want to own their homes are not able to buy in the private market due to income, wealth or credit constraints,[18] making it crucial to think creatively about how to create and preserve enduring, quality affordable homeownership.

The District's Role in the Creation of LECs

In recent times, many tenant groups have concluded that purchasing and operating as an LEC is the best option they had to move towards what they want from their housing tenure. Since the late 1970s,[19] LECs in the District of Columbia most often were formed in connection with the District's Tenant Opportunity to Purchase Act ("TOPA"), which gives DC tenants in multi-family buildings the opportunity to purchase when the owner of their building offers it for sale.[20] Under TOPA, when the owner of a multi-family rental building offers the building for sale, the owner is required to notify the residents, and the residents collectively have the right to attempt to purchase the building.[21] Upon receiving an offer of sale from the owner, residents then

---

Go: As Affordable Housing Costs Rise, Residents Are Left with Fewer Affordable Options, http://dcfpi.org ("The number of D.C. homes values at $250,000 or less fell from 58,000 to 15,000 between 2000 and 2007. Homes valued at this level represented more than half of the owner-occupied units in 2000 but just one-sixth in 2007… Median sales prices at the end of 2008 were roughly double the median sales price from the late 1990s.") National Association of Realtors numbers for the Washington, D.C. Metropolitan Area Prices remain high. See Nat'l Association of Realtors, *Metropolitan Median Prices*, *available at* http://www.realtor.org/research/research/metroprice (median price for fourth quarter 2009: single-family $306,200, condo/ coop $239,000); and prices for the District alone are cited as even higher. *See* Alejandro Lazo, *A Trying Year, By the Numbers*, Wash. Post, Mar. 28, 2009, at F01 (stating 2008 median single-family sales price of $520,000); DC Home and Condo Prices, *available at* http://www.dchousingprices.com/2009/03/wapo-smackdown-district-sales-full-year.html (Mar. 30, 2009) (criticizing *Washington Post* analysis and asserting 2008 median condominium and single-family sales price of $375,000).

18 Terry Lewis & Lindley R. Higgins, *The Advantages and Disadvantages of Cooperative Housing as an Affordable Alternative*, *available at* http://www.ncbcapitalimpact.org/documents/Advantagesanddisadvantages.pdf, at 4-5 (discussing income and wealth barriers to home purchase).

19 I do not by any means offer here a comprehensive history of TOPA or LECs in the District, but rather mention a few salient developments to provide context for the discussion of the public and private interests and goals involved in the formation and operation of LECs. For a historical perspective on LECs in the District, *see* CNHED, *supra* note 5, at 5-6, and Davis, *supra* note 3, at 26.

20 D.C. Code §42-3404.02 (2010). For an explanation of the tenant purchase process under D.C. law, *see* Richard C. Eisen, *The Rental Housing Conversion and Sale Act: A Practitioner's Roadmap to Tenant Ownership*, 2 D.C. L. Rev. 1, 93-111 (1993).

21 D.C. Code §42-3404.03, §42-3404.08 (2006) (outlining owner obligations and tenant rights). See Eisen, *supra* note 20, for a thorough discussion of TOPA in practice.

have a defined period of time to register as a tenant organization, go to contract, secure financing and close.[22] For tenant groups that have decided to form an LEC, the tenant group also must convert to a cooperative through an election process required by D.C. law.[23]

Where the purchase price of a multifamily building is high and the incomes and wealth of the residents are low, tenant groups hoping to buy their buildings have looked to DC's Department of Housing and Community Development ("DHCD") for some or all of the financing for acquisition and rehabilitation.[24] For some tenant purchase projects, the District has offered far more favorable loan terms—for example, 1% or 2% loans with 30 to 40-year terms and initial interest-free or deferral periods[25]—than what, if anything, would have been available to these borrowers, together or as individuals, in the private market.[26] In exchange, DHCD has required ongoing affordability[27] with the District loan thereby subsidizing the

22 D.C. Code §42-3404.11 (2010) (detailing time frames for tenant association registration, negotiating a sales contract, securing financing and closing).

23 D.C. Code §42-3402.02 et seq. (2010); D.C. Mun. Regs. tit. 14 § 4700 et seq. (2010). Depending on the timing of the TOPA process and the decision making process of the tenant organization, the acquiring entity may be the tenant association or the (pre-conversion) cooperative corporation. The formal conversion under D.C. law takes place after the tenants have acquired the property.

24 Prior to the recent residential real estate downturn, DHCD had provided the majority of the permanent acquisition and rehabilitation financing for many tenant groups represented by the Harrison Institute. Since 2003, the source of much of this financing has been the District's Housing Production Trust Fund ("HPTF"), which provides financing for, inter alia, rehabilitation or preservation of existing housing and site acquisition for targeted populations. The HPTF is funded from 15% of the residential real property transfer tax and deed recordation tax. D.C. Code §42-2802 et seq. (2010). The drastic reduction in HPTF funding, *see supra* note 14, means that the HPTF is no longer a readily available source of funds for affordable homeownership projects requesting DHCD funding for acquisition and rehabilitation. Federal funding, community lenders and commercial banks also are important sources of bridge or permanent financing for tenant groups.

25 *See* loan documents on file with author.

26 Because LEC acquisition and rehabilitation financing is blanket financing based on the property's projected financials, lack of individual resident credit-worthiness will not doom a project. However, the financial profiles of the prospective LEC members, as well as the cooperative as a whole, are relevant to the mortgage underwriting process. Accordingly, the District requires income information for all prospective members to both demonstrate that the residents are low-income and that the project is financially viable. To the extent that a prospective LEC member has to personally secure financing, it would be only for that member's share price. In practice, often the initial LEC share price is so low (ranging from several hundred to several thousand dollars) that the LEC member does not use outside private financing.

27 The Housing Production Trust Fund statute defines "continuing affordability" as a period of at least 40 years for rental units, and at least ten or 15 years from for-sale units. D.C. Code §42-2801 (1C) (2010). In current practice, cooperatives, although not rental, often have 40-year mortgages held by the District and 40-year covenants running with the

creation of long-term low-income homeownership units. To secure this long-term affordability, the District commonly has required as a financing condition that a tenant group agree to operate the building as an LEC.[28]

The Form of LECs in the District

LECs are an established form for providing affordable housing through shared equity ownership.[29] Shared equity ownership, as thoroughly discussed by John Emmeus Davis, seeks to "balance individual and community interests" by providing owner-occupied, resale-restricted housing that is affordable for the present generation of low-income buyers and for future generations.[30] While each LEC has its own unique history and structure, every LEC created through the efforts of tenants and the District government balances individual and community interests; and LECs in the District have endured, with some exceptions, as a form of affordable resident ownership.[31]

In terms of individual interests, LECs are cooperative associations under District law,[32] as are market-rate housing cooperatives.[33] The LEC owns the property and is governed by a board of directors and officers drawn from the

---

land, which run regardless of prepayment of the DHCD loan. In contrast, some earlier loans made to tenant groups, for example in the 1980s, did not include explicit restrictions or had restrictions that terminated upon payment in full of the blanket mortgage. Some of those properties still remain affordable (often taking on long-term covenants through subsequent borrowing); others do not. *See* CNHED, *supra* note 5, at 10 (of 81 LECs formed in the District since 1977, 22 changed from limited equity ownership).

28 That is not to say that no other ownership (e.g., deed-restricted condominiums) or participation (e.g., LIHTC) models are funded by the District. However, LECs were the prevalent form for tenant purchase projects. In an LEC project, because the property cannot be converted until after acquisition, this requirement would be evidenced by a corporate resolution stating intent to convert to an LEC and related covenants in the loan documents.

29 *See* Davis, *supra* note 3, at 27 (estimating 425,000 LEC units nationwide), at 23-31 (surveying the LEC model). *See generally* Duncan Kennedy, *The Limited Equity Coop as a Vehicle for Affordable Housing in a Race and Class Divided Society*, 46 How. L.J. 85, 85 (2002). Jim Gray, *Shared Equity Gains Acceptance in Affordable Multifamily Development*, Commercial Mortgage Insight (May 2008) at 18, *available at* www.cmi-online.com.

30 Davis, *supra* note 3 at 3-4.

31 The best source of comprehensive information about LECs was compiled by CNHED for its 2004 report, which has not been updated. *See* CNHED, *supra* note 5, at 10, 13 (finding 81 LECs formed in the District since 1977; 57 consisting of 2269 units in operation as of 2004; of 24 LECs providing sufficient information to the study, 79% were in stable or excellent financial condition).

32 Most LECs physically located in the District choose to incorporate in D.C, under D.C. Code §29-901 et seq. (2010).

33 An LEC shares the general characteristics of the housing cooperative form: ownership of shares of stock in the cooperative corporation, rather than ownership of a unit; exclusive right to occupy a unit detailed in an occupancy agreement; and responsibilities

shareholder-members.[34] Every head of household[35] is a member of the LEC. The LEC's structure and governance documents (including articles, bylaws, subscription agreements, occupancy agreements and house rules) are drafted, approved, and amended as needed, by the board or the membership, usually with the assistance of legal counsel or other professionals.

The "community interest" and defining difference for LECs as compared to market-rate housing cooperatives is the limitation of the equity a member can realize upon transfer or sale of her share. The "buy-in" price for original TOPA tenants usually is very affordable.[36] At resale, the LEC member shares her equity in the asset, the cooperative share, with, depending on how broadly it is viewed, the subsequent low-income buyer (by providing a housing unit at a below-market price) or the District (by ensuring enduring affordable housing stock). The upside potential of the home appreciation is separated, in whole or part depending on the LEC structure,[37] from the LEC member's housing experience.[38] There are many ways to calculate the resale formula designed to maintain affordability over time.[39]

---

and rights as between the cooperative and the shareholder detailed in the cooperative's corporate documents.

34 D.C. Code §29-918 (requiring that the Board of Directors consist of members of the association, except in certain cases in the first ten years of a cooperative's existence where a nonprofit sponsoring organization can appoint directors who are not members). While District law allows for outside participation on an LEC board in limited circumstances, this participation is time-limited and not usual among LECs I have worked with.

35 The LECs I have worked with generally operate with a certain number of shares allocated to each particular unit, based on the square footage of the unit. The shares allocated to a unit can be held jointly by one or more adult members of the household. Each unit, regardless of number of shares, must vote unanimously.

36 For example, residents who are part of an original TOPA group generally buy their shares with a small financial investment (often ranging from zero to several thousand dollars per household). Share prices of several hundred to several thousand dollars are common for residents who join later; however I am aware of at least one D.C. LEC where share resale prices remain in range of tens of thousands of dollars, including a mid-2009 share sale for $45,000.

37 In practice, the resale formula may be structured to result in an amount equivalent to either a departing renter's security deposit or a fee simple homeowner selling at a modest profit. *See* Davis, *supra* note 3, at 65 (noting the debate among share equity housing advocates about what constitutes a "fair" or "reasonable" return for departing residents).

38 *See* discussion of residents' prioritization of elements of the homeownership experience ahead of wealth accumulation through resale, *infra.* at 168-171 and note 74. For a broad-ranging discussion of the possibilities presented by this separation of elements of homeownership, *see* Lee Anne Fennell, *Homeownership 2.0*, Nw. U. L. Rev. 1047, 1064-9 (2008) (discussing existing models for allocating offsite risk of homeownership including limited equity cooperatives).

39 *See* Davis, *supra* note 3, at 65-69 (describing four general approaches — indexed formulas, itemized formulas, appraisal-based formulas and mortgage-based formulas).

In my experience in recent years,[40] DHCD has assured long-term affordability through a mortgage-based formula that caps the resale price at the maximum price that a buyer at a certain level of income can afford. For example, in a 2008 loan by the District to a tenant association purchasing its building, DHCD required that the property be operated as continuously affordable housing exclusively for low-income residents, with all units[41] leased at carrying charge levels that are affordable[42] to residents with a household income not exceeding 80% of the Washington, D.C. AMI.[43] This affordability and equity restriction runs for forty years, regardless of prepayment of the mortgage obligation or change of owner.

Part II: Why Maintenance and Repairs Matters

In any multifamily housing cooperative, the issue of maintenance and repairs involves both common and individual areas and elements of the property. Common, or building-wide, maintenance and repairs, vary based on the specifics of the property and include repairs in common areas (hallways or staircases),

40 In contrast, some older D.C. LECs used an itemized formula based on the initial share price, accounting for longevity through an annual interest rate applied thereto, and including some compensation for pre-approved improvements. *See, e.g.*, D.C. Code § 42-3402.02 (2010) ("nonprofit cooperatives," which limit transfer value to the annual rate of inflation applied to initial share price and pre-approved improvements). An itemized formula often is coupled with an obligation or standard practice of the LEC to repurchase the share(s) of any departing member. *See generally* Davis, *supra* note 3, at 66-67.

41 I note that in some cases all or a certain number of units are reserved for households falling in lower income brackets, e.g., the 30% or 50% AMI bracket.

42 Exactly how this cap would be calculated depends on the standards and definitions negotiated up front and enforced over time by the LEC and the District. One reasonable approach is that the sum of monthly carrying charge (each unit's pro rata portion of monthly operating expenses and blanket debt service), monthly utilities (not included in carrying charge) and individual monthly share loan payment cannot exceed 30% of the household's average monthly income.

43 Through May 2011, for projects using DC Housing Production Trust Fund funds, the maximum annual income for a one-person household at 80% AMI is $57,960 and the maximum one-bedroom rent (for LECs, carrying charge) limit is $1656.00. *HPTF Limits*, *supra* note 6. Therefore an LEC member selling her share to a single person household can charge a share price such that the share loan monthly payment plus carrying charges and utilities does not exceed $1656.00. Currently, most LEC carrying charges plus utility payments are much less than $1643.00 per month. *See* CNHED, *supra* note 5, at 16-17 (analyzing 2003 data and generally finding that LEC carrying charges in the District remain very low over time as compared to market rents). Assuming the market for LEC shares would support it and share loan financing (particularly subsidized low-income homeownership programs) were available, that gap of up several hundred dollars per month would allow for a significant share price, and therefore significant equity to the departing LEC member. However, those two assumptions usually are not borne out for LECs in the District.

to the building's envelope (roof, foundation) or common systems (expensive elements such as heating, ventilating, and air conditioning systems). Costs of common maintenance and repairs are paid directly by the LEC and passed along to members through monthly carrying charges.[44] Relatedly, often carrying charges include a pro rata allocation for utilities used within individual units that are not individually metered. For many LECs operating in older buildings, these common utilities include heating, cooling and water. Carrying charges also include property and liability insurance that covers the entire building, which is necessary in addition to individual unit insurance. On the other hand, each LEC member occupies a specific unit that will have its own maintenance and repair problems over time. Whether individual or common, maintenance and repairs range from routine scheduled maintenance or upkeep to emergency repairs and from cosmetic or aesthetic to those necessary for health and safety.

The LEC must decide whether to assign costs and responsibilities for individual unit maintenance and repairs to the LEC as a whole or to individual members. This decision defines the residents' rights and responsibilities as to their homes and highlights the risks and rewards of homeownership as compared to renting in a way that may be more real to residents than even the building purchase itself. LEC residents, most of whom have experience only as renters, are in new roles as members of the cooperative and its Board. They have to determine how to balance possibly conflicting interests—member responsibility against common responsibility; member autonomy against common control; and individual out-of-pocket costs against shared costs paid for through every member's carrying charges.[45]

In deciding who pays for maintenance within units, LECs have a choice between two basic models—one that approximates a rental arrangement or one that approximates a market-rate cooperative. The decisions an LEC makes are reflected in its corporate documents,[46] as shown in the "rental" and "market-rate cooperative" models detailed below.[47] While the market-rate cooperative model seems more consistent with homeownership, the facts that residents are low-income and equity is limited may push an LEC to opt for the rental model, a choice that I believe is ultimately harmful to the LEC, for the reasons discussed in Part IV.

44 Carrying charges also pay for the LEC's other operating expenses, reserves and debt service. Carrying charges are determined annually based on the cooperative's projected budget for the next year.

45 *See* Kennedy, *supra* note 29, at 104-106 (noting choice between a collectivist approach and a tenants' rights approach, and where a Board might merge the two).

46 The LEC's corporate documents include articles of incorporation, cooperative bylaws, member subscription agreement and member occupancy agreement.

47 Both models detailed here are composites of the common types I have seen among existing LECs.

The Rental Model

In some LECs, the cooperative is responsible for virtually all repairs in individual units. This model is similar to the following:[48]

- *Cooperative Responsibilities and Expenses for Repairs.* The cooperative shall provide and pay for all necessary repairs, maintenance, and replacements, except those caused by the member's neglect or misuse, by the member's redecoration, or where items are not furnished by the cooperative. Stove, refrigerator, dishwasher and air conditioners are furnished by the cooperative.
- *Prohibited Activities and Uses of Property.* Without the written consent of the Board, the member shall not make any structural alterations in the unit, permit any additional major appliances or drive any picture or other nails into the woodwork. The member shall not paint, paper, or decorate with adhesive substances, mirrors, cork boards or the like. The member shall not cut, drill or injure any part of the unit. No consent will be given to place a clothes washing machine or dryer in a unit, and any such machine shall be removed at the member's expense immediately upon request of the cooperative.

On its face this regime may seem to be the best way to protect low-income LEC residents who have only limited income or savings that would be available for maintenance and repairs, and are unable to leverage their shares.[49] It is the model that most LEC residents are familiar with. The LEC pays the costs of all regular as well as unusual unit repairs. An LEC resident seemingly avoids the risk that some other low-income homeowners may experience—that such costs could threaten her financial and housing security.[50] In exchange, members are quite constrained in terms of their activities and uses of the property, even within their own units.[51] The LEC has responsibility for repairs to units and takes on a role similar to that of

48 This rental model is more likely to be found in older D.C. LECs from the 1980s and 1990s, which are more likely to have an itemized resale formula and a practice or requirement that the LEC buy back any departing member's share. Even with more recently-formed LECs, some follow a rental model in practice, even where their corporate documents state otherwise. In other words, when individual situations arise, LECs make exceptions to their market-rate cooperative model policies and take responsibility for making and paying for repairs.

49 There is no financial product currently available in the District to LEC members that is equivalent to a home equity line of credit or cash-out refinancing.

50 But *see* discussion *infra* Part IV, Protecting the Financial Health of the LEC.

51 Perhaps some residents hope or expect that in practice these strict use prohibitions will not be monitored or enforced. For example, in one case that I am familiar with, the LEC paid for all repairs but the residents did not follow, and the board of directors did not enforce, the prohibitions with respect to decorating, painting or similar activities.

a landlord (or the landlord's management company) in a rental context. The LEC may have a right or obligation to conduct regular unit inspections. The practical "feel" of this model may be quite similar to what LEC residents experienced as renters.

The Market-Rate Cooperative Model

In contrast, in the market-rate cooperative model, an LEC member is generally responsible for maintenance and repairs within her unit.[52] Some LECs follow a model similar to the following:

- *Maintenance, Repairs and Cleanliness*. The member agrees to keep the unit in good repair, including painting and other upgrades to the unit required from time to time. The member is responsible for all maintenance, repair, redecoration inside the unit, including interior walls, floors, and ceilings; plumbing, gas, heating and cooling fixtures; lighting fixtures; all kitchen equipment and appliances; and all windows, window panes, window frames, sashes, sills, doors, frames and saddles. The term "plumbing, gas, heating and cooling fixtures" shall include exposed gas, steam and water pipes attached to fixtures, appliances and equipment; any special pipes or equipment that the member installs within the wall, ceiling, or floor; but shall not include gas, steam, water or other pipes or conduits within the walls, ceilings or floors or heating equipment that is part of the standard building equipment. The member shall be responsible for the maintenance, repair and replacement of all lighting and electrical fixtures, appliances and equipment, as well as all meters, fuse boxes or circuit breakers and electrical wiring and conduits from the junction box at the riser into and through the unit.
- *Alterations and Redecorating*. The member shall not, without the prior written consent of the cooperative, which shall not be unreasonably withheld, do any of the following: a) make any structural alterations in the unit; in common areas of cooperative property; in property abutting cooperative property; or in water, gas, heating or cooling systems, electrical conduits, plumbing or other fixtures of the unit; b) install clothes washers and dryers, dishwashers, heating or air conditioning equipment, or other appliances in addition to those which are provided for at the time this agreement is signed; and c) attach or place any fixtures, fences, aerials, antennas or other electrical connections, or exterior signs on the building in any common areas.

52 Adopting this model in an LEC's corporate documents does not necessarily mean that it will be followed in practice. *See supra* note 48.

A member is responsible for repair and maintenance of her unit (although certainly there can be disagreement between the member and the LEC about the nature or cause of, and therefore the responsibility to fix, specific problems). The limited constraints on alteration or use within the unit relate to activities or uses that could harm the building's common systems or structures or infringe on other members' uses. This model assumes that a member has the financial means to complete the repairs.[53]

Part III: The Public and Private Goals of the LEC

To determine how an LEC should allocate responsibility for maintenance and repairs, it is necessary to ask the basic question—what is the LEC attempting to achieve? There are two parties essential to the LEC's creation—the LEC, a private corporation that made up of its Board and members, all of whom are residents; and the District, a public entity represented by DHCD. The common endeavor on which the residents and the District embark is affordable homeownership through an LEC, which both parties agree is a positive development for these residents and the District.[54] But what exactly did each party expect to achieve through an LEC as the ownership form? While the District and an LEC's residents may disagree on the relative importance of different aspects of affordable homeownership through an LEC, there is significant commonality of interests and understanding, as shown in their goals and interests set forth below.

The Public (District of Columbia) Goals and Interests

The District, like any public entity, has numerous goals behind its housing programs,[55] an important one of which is providing affordable quality housing

53 A market-rate cooperative model also assumes that members will secure adequate insurance to cover any damage to the cooperative or other members' property for which the member is responsible and to cover the member's personal property. Specifically, the cooperative's corporate documents may specify the required coverage or require cooperative review and approval of members' policies. Its members must also be ready and willing to pay deductibles and increased premiums and negotiate with insurance companies.(In contrast, the strongest language I have seen in LEC corporate documents is recommending and "encouraging" members to secure individual unit insurance.) A market-rate cooperative also may require, for any maintenance or repair work, that members hire only contractors who meet certain licensing, insurance and bonding standards. All of these additional costs would be significant to a low-income LEC member.

54 Consistent with our national housing conversation, particularly prior to the current foreclosure crisis, the desirability of homeownership as a personal and local policy goal was a given in many conversations between the District and the residents.

55 J. Peter Byrne & Michael Diamond, *Affordable Housing, Land Tenure, and Urban Policy: The Matrix Revealed*, 34 FORDHAM URB. L.J. 527, 531 (2008) (outlining

for the District's residents. Through tenant purchase, the District specifically has sought to provide long-term affordability and homeownership for low-income residents. These goals are evident in DHCD's mission—"to create and preserve opportunities for affordable housing and economic development and to revitalize underserved communities in the District of Columbia"[56]—and DHCD's "strategic objectives," which include production and preservation of "quality affordable housing and homeownership" and improving economic opportunities for low-income residents.[57] Tenant purchase as an LEC provides an opportunity for the District to accomplish both.

Affordability in the District is an interesting issue. In many neighborhoods across all four quadrants, affordability means enabling existing low-income households to stay in housing or neighborhoods that otherwise imminently or within the short-term would no longer be affordable. The District considers the long-term, ideally permanent,[58] affordability restrictions discussed above necessary so that the units it subsidizes are preserved as affordable for subsequent purchasers. These assumptions apply across all four quadrants of the District. The restrictions are an essential element of the negotiations between the District and the residents.[59]

---

eight possible objectives of subsidized housing—decent shelter, wealth creation, social integration, urban vitality, civic engagement, training, institution building, and efficient use of public funds). Similarly, shared equity ownership advocates cite a number of potential benefits—affordability, stability, wealth, involvement, improvement, each of which can be viewed from the individual or the community perspective, *see* Davis, *supra* note 3, at 89-114 (evaluating the performance of shared equity housing as to each benefit and both perspectives).

56 DHCD's mission and key objectives are stated on their website at http://dhcd.dc.gov/dhcd/cwp/view,a,3,q,555677,dhcdNav_GID,1575,dhcdNav,%7C32184%7C,.asp ("DHCD focuses on three strategic objectives: preserving and increasing the supply of quality affordable housing; increasing homeownership opportunities; and revitalizing neighborhoods, promoting community development, and providing economic opportunities.").

57 *Id.*

58 A number of earlier tenant purchase projects financed by DHCD did not have durable covenants; some have stayed affordable while others have become market rate properties. *See supra* note 27. The 40-year real covenants that are now standard in DHCD deals in practice may function as permanent affordability given the likelihood of having to refinance for major renovation during the 40-year period, and the factors that make it likely that the LEC would be looking to a public or mission-driven lender for refinancing (e.g., low incomes of the residents, below-market carrying charges, equity restrictions on the property).

59 However, monitoring of the restrictions over time generally is not discussed in any detail. The task of ensuring that the restrictions are not violated is substantial, considering that there are over 2200 LEC units as of 2004. CNHED, *supra* note 5, at 10. LECs are supposed to self-monitor and enforce, which can be problematic for a number of reasons. *See* Rick Jacobus, *Stewardship for Lasting Affordability: Administration and Monitoring of Shared Equity Homeownership*, 5, 7, *available at* http://www.ncbcapitalimpact.org/

In terms of homeownership, the District continues to fund some homeownership projects as crucial to stabilizing and improving communities,[60] notwithstanding drastically reduced local funding.[61] A recent Director of DHCD, commenting on the homeownership concept that DHCD supports, touted familiar meanings and benefits attributed to homeownership:[62] "Homeownership has many benefits—aside from the fulfillment of the 'American Dream.' It provides children with a tangible feeling of 'home,' and adults with the pride of homeownership. It adds a sense of community to neighborhoods—because the residents are invested in the community and there for the duration." [63] She further noted that "[a]lthough rental[s] provide the majority of affordable housing, homeownership stabilizes neighborhoods and families."[64] For the District, homeownership is promoted for its commonly-cited benefits and is a concrete goal that can be measured in numbers of units produced or preserved.

The District's focus is the big-picture goals of homeownership and affordability. Once acquisition financing is closed, the District generally does not have significant ongoing involvement in the operations of the LEC.[65] It does not address a day-to-day issue such as the allocation of responsibility for maintenance and repair. Rather, the covenants binding the LEC for the term of the loan require, in general, timely loan payments, compliance with local and federal law and financial reporting; and in practice, the District has not focused on post-acquisition review or monitoring. Similarly, post-purchase assistance to LECs or residents relating to the challenges of homeownership has been quite limited.

---

uploadedFiles/downloads/Symposium_Tab5_BusinessModel.pdf (proposing that an affordability steward be charged with, inter alia, managing the resale process to assure homes remain affordable).

60 One such example is the District's targeted homeownership efforts in Ivy City, a neighborhood that experienced a number of well-publicized violent crimes in 2006 ("We are making a highly concentrated investment here to transform this six-block area into a safer and healthier community where twice as many residents will own their own homes and have a real stake in the success of this community.") Housing Complex, http://www.washingtoncitypaper.com/blogs/housingcomplex (Dec. 16, 2008).

61 *See supra* note 14 discussing drastic decline in local funding levels.

62 *See infra* Part III, The Private (LEC Resident) Goals and Interests, and notes 70, 71.

63 Leila Finucane Edmonds, *DHCD is Here to Help*, Washington Informer, p. H-5 (2009 Homeownership Supplement), *available at* http://www.washingtoninformer.com/wi-web/images/stories/archives/supplement/09-06homesup.pdf. Ms. Edmonds' tenure as Director ended in 2010.

64 *Id.*

65 To be clear, I think it is appropriate that the District is not involved in the day-to-day affairs of the LECs it finances. Such involvement could be expensive, inefficient and hinder resident autonomy and capacity-building.

The Private (LEC Resident) Goals and Interests

Based on my work with tenant groups, the two concepts discussed above—affordability and homeownership—are essential to residents, but what residents mean by them is somewhat different.[66] For residents, affordability is a threshold concern; they enter the TOPA process with the requirement that they (all or most, depending on the group) need to be able to afford whatever form of housing tenure is the result. Tenant groups approach the District for financing for two key reasons: the District will consider lending to a group consisting of low-income residents with no history of ownership or business operations; and the loan terms it offers translate to the lowest monthly cost per resident, as compared to private lenders.[67] This immediate, individualized understanding of affordability differs from the District's focus on long-term (subsequent purchaser) affordability.[68]

Achieving homeownership surfaces time and again, pre- and post-purchase, as a resident priority. While residents' levels of education about homeownership and engagement with the TOPA process vary widely, within an LEC and across LECs, many residents support the purchase because it presents the opportunity to become homeowners. Residents' strong feelings in favor of homeownership raise the question of what exactly they mean by homeownership. Without a doubt residents see homeownership as a positive and potentially transformative event and expect a sharp departure from their previous experiences as renters. Their priorities resonate with the U.S. cultural context of an "ideology of home" that evokes the values of "family, safety, privacy and community"[69] and attributes emotional or psychological benefits to homeownership.[70] Residents focus on what

66 Each resident brings her unique experiences and perspective to an LEC project, and residents' goals and interests vary between LECs and within each LEC; however, I have found certain priorities are present across projects. There is no research that I am aware of aimed at identifying or ranking what the specific goals of LEC residents in the District might be.

67 *See* CNHED, *supra* note 5, at 16 (comparing annual income necessary for market-rate condominium, market-rate rental and LEC in three gentrifying neighborhoods and finding lowest income necessary for LEC); *see also* Lewis & Higgins, *supra* note 18, at 5 (comparing operating costs and monthly charges of comparable LECs and rental properties and finding lowest monthly charge for LEC).

68 While some residents I have worked with have stated their belief in the principle of long-term affordability for subsequent buyers, my understanding is that most residents agree to it within the context of the limited choices they have.

69 D. Benjamin Barros, *Home as a Legal Concept*, 46 SANTA CLARA L. REV. 255, 255 (2006) (discussing ideology of home, in which "the protection of home and all it stands for is an American virtue"). While the recent subprime lending and foreclosure crises have shown homeownership to be less secure than the cultural narrative assumes, the ideology itself does not seemed to have changed significantly.

70 They resonate with property law theory linking property, especially one's home, to individual identity and development of self. *See* Margaret Jane Radin, *Property and Personhood*, 34 STAN. L. REV. 957, 992 (1982) (characterizing home as "the scene of one's

their everyday experience will be as homeowners.[71] Notably, I have found that most LEC residents do not prioritize the ability to accumulate and cash in on equity at resale.[72]

One key resident priority is stable occupancy, or security. This means that the resident can stay put for as long as she desires, and includes the sense of security, well-being and self-determination[73] that may follow.[74] In general, renting is a less stable

history and future, one's life and growth… The home is affirmatively part of oneself.") Nevertheless, the empirical evidence documenting the benefits of homeownership is somewhat limited. *See* William M. Rohe et al., *The Social Benefits and Costs of Homeownership: A Critical Assessment of the Research*, 22-25 (Joint Ctr. for Hous. Studies of Harvard Univ., Working Paper No. LIHO-01.12, 2001) (finding support for some homeownership social benefits but discussing limitations of existing research). Contra *see* Stephanie Stern, *Residential Protectionism and the Legal Mythology of Home*, 107 MICH. L. REV. 1093 (2009) (arguing that empirical evidence does not support the psychological importance attributed to homeownership). For evaluating shared equity housing models, it would be useful to have empirical analysis comparing benefits, perceived and actual, across the range of ownership forms (single-family home, cooperative and condominium) and equity limitations (LECs, community land trusts, deed-restricted homes and non-restricted homes).

71 Whether residents could meet their goals, equally or even more fully, through another form of housing tenure is an interesting question, but one I do not address here. *Cf.* Byrne & Diamond, *Matrix Revealed*, *supra* note 55, at 69-72 (discussing homeownership versus renting). I suspect that most residents would answer that question in the negative; many groups explicitly consider and reject other forms of tenure when evaluating their tenure and development options related to TOPA.

72 This investment or wealth creation component is a stick in the traditional homeownership bundle that many would consider definitional. While most groups I have worked with want their interests to be structured to allow for the possibility of individual wealth creation through resale, this is not a top priority for those choosing the LEC form. That makes sense given that LEC share resale price is limited, highly LEC-specific and difficult to predict. In addition to the usual factors that a homeowner must consider in attempting to evaluate the likelihood and amount of equity accumulation over time, several factors specific to LECs may have an impact: the LEC's resale formula; the LEC's role in share buy-back; the local acceptance of LECs and market for LEC shares; and the availability of LEC share loans. There is no comprehensive data tracking LEC share resale transactions in the District, so it is impossible to analyze across LECs how much equity departing members realize, how they use it (whether departing residents move to a more traditional form of homeownership or return to renting), and what results when shares are passed to heirs.

73 *See* Lorna Fox, *Re-Possessing "Home": A Re-Analysis of Gender, Homeownership and Debtor Default for Feminist Legal Theory*, 14 WM. & MARY J. WOMEN & L. 423, 451 (2008) (among five "main clusters of value type" that home represent to its occupiers, "home as a territory offering security and control, a locus in space, permanence and continuity, and privacy"); Rohe, *supra* note 70, at 6 (finding some evidence of homeownership leading to increased self-esteem).

74 For example, it was proposed to one longstanding cooperative I worked with that they might use low income housing tax credit financing (and give up ownership) to pay for their much-needed renovations. The LEC's president adamantly refused, stating that

form of tenure.[75] Despite some protections for renters,[76] for the lifelong renter in DC, the rental market can be frighteningly unpredictable. Renters encounter persistent strong demand; a number of permissible grounds for annual and extraordinary rent increases;[77] the possibility of owners converting rental properties to condominiums; and owners' desires to sell buildings as vacant in order to avoid any obstacles to renting at market (often non-affordable) levels. Many times, residents have rented in a building or neighborhood for years, if not decades, and have experienced, as they tell it, the ups and (more often) the downs of their community's recent history. When amenities and improvements begin to arrive, as has happened across many District neighborhoods, residents do not want to be pushed out by the accompanying rising housing costs. Having an assurance of secure, stable occupancy for as long as desired is tremendously valuable to residents.

Another important goal for residents is being able to use and improve one's living space as one chooses, with an assurance of the previously discussed stability of tenure. Making a space into one's home may carry tremendous personal meaning and value for residents.[78] When a resident can use and improve her unit as she desires, it may promote self-expression, personal satisfaction, and pride.[79] Often, I have seen residents cope with long and trying in-place rehabilitations by planning the design and furnishing of their units and keeping in mind the future entertaining of their

---

the residents have been the decision makers for the property for almost twenty years, and there's no way they would give that up. As a result, this LEC has had to work hard to improve its financial health, reduce resident expectations of the scope of rehabilitation and seek alternative public and private financing options in which the residents remain owners. This security and the related psychological benefits are tangible despite the fact that the resale value of the shares of a 20-year resident would be a few thousand dollars at most.

75 *See* Lewis & Higgins, *supra* note 18, at 8 (citing study of affordable cooperatives in New York City finding average length of residency of affordable cooperatives was 13.5 years, as opposed to other forms of affordable rentals which averaged 5.4 to 10.6 years). *See generally* Rohe, *supra* note 70 at 13 (median duration of homeownership of 8.2 years, as compared to median duration of residence for renters of 2.1 years).

76 For an overview of tenant protections in the District, which is considered quite tenant-friendly, *see Washington, D.C. Tenant Survival Guide*, Seventh Edition, Spring 2008, Harrison Institute for Public Law, Georgetown University, *available at* http://ota.dc.gov/ota/frames.asp?doc=/ota/lib/ota/Tenant_Survival_Guide.pdf

77 *Id.* at 17-20 (discussing permissible "automatic" annual rent increases and other allowable rent increases including landlord hardship, capital improvement, substantial rehabilitation and voluntary agreement).

78 *See* Radin, *supra* note 70, 1005 (discussing fungible versus personal object spectrum).

79 Lewis & Higgins, *supra* note 18 at 8 (citing studies showing affordable cooperative residents have higher residential satisfaction than comparable renters); Rohe, *supra* note 70, at 3-4 (finding homeowners' "greater latitude to in customizing units to suit their own tastes…increased their satisfaction with their residence and their life in general").

family and friends in their modern, attractive home.[80] As with the other elements of homeownership emphasized by residents, this ability to use and improve relates closely to the cultural importance[81] and status that attaches to homeownership.[82] Again, this is a marked change from the experience of a life-long renter.

Relatedly, residents value the ability to enjoy one's living space and to exclude, or control the actions of, others who may infringe on one's space. They are very concerned with how, as a cooperative board of directors, they hold the power to determine who their neighbors will be, by accepting or rejecting applicants for membership.[83] They can reject applicants who will not accept the rights and responsibilities of a cooperative member, including the obligations to take care of the property, carry a share of the common responsibilities. and respect others. To that end, it is common for LECs to spend a tremendous amount of time ironing out the details of house rules (for example, pet or noise policies), and what the enforcement mechanisms will be for members who do not comply. Again, this element resonates strongly with residents who have had negative experiences as renters—neighbors who interfered with the residents' enjoyment or even safety—and who were not able to stop the offensive behaviors or to exit without significant costs.

Part IV: The Market-Rate Cooperative Model Best Meets the Public and Private Goals for the LEC

In light of the District and resident goals stated above, I believe that LECs should follow a market-rate cooperative model. This model best secures the goals of affordable homeownership desired by the residents and the District in three ways—by protecting the financial health of the LEC, by maintaining the physical condition of the asset and by delivering the desired experience of homeownership. However, it raises a serious concern that also must be addressed—the possibility of excluding relatively lower-income residents from LEC membership.

---

80 Fox, *supra* note 73, at 451 ("home as a social and cultural unit acting as the locus for relationships with family and friends, and as a center of activities").

81 Barros, *supra* note 69.

82 *See* Fox, *supra* note 73, at 451 (citing "home as a center for self-identity offering a reflection of one's ideas and values, and acting as an indicator of personal status"); *cf.* Nestor Davidson, *Property and Relative Status*, 107 MICH. L. REV. 757, 774-87 (2009) (discussing historical and more recent scholarship on the comparative status-signaling function of property).

83 Given that LEC member selection must be conducted consistent with applicable state and federal fair housing laws, every LEC board of directors needs initial and ongoing training on relevant laws and best practices.

Protecting the Financial Health of the LEC

The market-rate cooperative model reduces and regularizes monthly costs for the LEC,[84] which helps to ensure the financial health, and thereby the long-term viability, of the LEC. The LEC's financial health and survival is the foundation on which all of the other public and private goals tied to affordable homeownership rest. Every LEC must balance minimizing carrying charges with bringing in adequate income to cover expenses and reserves.[85] LECs tend to operate with little if any monthly surplus.[86] Individual unit maintenance and repair costs, in any given month and over time, can amount to a major portion of the LEC's monthly operating expenses, particularly where the Board does not carefully monitor its finances. One small (12-unit) LEC in the District illustrates the point. The Board, looking at a summary of its annual expenses for its first year post-acquisition, was astonished at the amount spent on unit repairs and saw how this expense had a direct negative impact on the LEC's ability to accomplish its goals, including financing repairs to the building's major systems. As one Board member concluded, "We're owners. People need to start fixing things for themselves." Putting this responsibility on individual members through the market-rate cooperative model results in lower LEC monthly costs and enables more accurate LEC budgeting and planning. It also avoids a worst case scenario, not uncommon in my experience, where an LEC's monthly expenses including a substantial amount for maintenance and repairs regularly exceed monthly income;[87] and an LEC cannot meet its financial obligations (e.g., utility payments, debt service), thereby endangering the very existence of the LEC.

The market-rate cooperative model also keeps monthly fixed costs for residents more affordable, and in a practical sense, the financial health of the LEC

84 One could argue that monthly costs may be reduced but the LEC will end of paying for larger, more expensive repairs that affect multiple units or common systems over time resulting from deferred individual unit maintenance. While this may be true in some cases, I posit that with the market-rate cooperative model, assistance for lower-income residents discussed in Part IV and an engaged membership, this degree of unit disrepair and failure of individual responsibility would not be a frequent occurrence.

85 The income side of the balance is complicated by an assumption I have seen among many LEC members, due in large part to income inflexibility and lack of other liquid assets, that any carrying charge increase will not be gradual and small (e.g., 3-5%), and there will not be any large special assessments. In contrast, market rate cooperatives can use either mechanism to maintain optimal operating, reserve and debt levels.

86 Meg Barnette, Pratt Institute Ctr for Comm. and Envir'l Devt, *Creating Multifamily Homeownership at Scale: Affordable Housing Cooperatives in New York City, Washington, D.C., and Chicago*, October 2004, at 9, *available at* http://www.ncbcapitalimpact.org/default.aspx?id=96 ("the size of many of the District's LECs and the limited financial resources of their members result in a limited margin of error in operating these buildings").

87 Solving the problem by dramatically increasing an LEC's income stream often is not a viable solution. Given the low incomes of the residents, LECs tend to avoid large special assessments or carrying charge increases, even when the LEC needs additional income.

is tied to the financial health of its residents. When the LEC does not include unit repair expenses (and any related reserves) in its budget, that means lower monthly carrying charges for all members, which promotes affordability for current and future residents.[88] While LEC carrying charges tend to be lower and increase more slowly than market rents,[89] tenants becoming LEC members through TOPA often are paying more than the rent they paid pre-purchase (albeit for higher-quality housing) and represent a wide range of the affordability spectrum.[90] Even a small dollar-value change in monthly fixed costs can make a big difference to residents, particularly at lower income levels. Lower carrying charges give residents a greater degree of control over how to allocate their income,[91] which may provide more housing stability and security, as well as allowing more flexibility for other housing-related (e.g., self-expression) or non-housing (e.g., education) consumption choices.

Maintaining the Physical Condition of the Asset

Safe, maintained, quality housing is an essential element of long-term affordability and the positive community effects desired by the District and the security, control, and self-expression desired by residents. The market-rate cooperative model has the potential to keep the LEC's property in the best physical condition for several reasons discussed below. In contrast, the rental model, with the costs of individual unit repairs shared by all residents, presents a moral hazard concern. By way of illustration, consider an LEC formed as the result of a tenant purchase. All residents are former renters. Some are very engaged with the purchase and transition to ownership process,

88 Of course, the cost of unit repairs remains on the resident, in addition to monthly carrying charges, as discussed *infra* pp. 178-79, which could have exclusionary implications for lower-income residents and makes saving for repairs a necessity.

89 *See* CNHED, *supra* note 5, at 16; Lewis & Higgins, *supra* note 18, at 5.

90 In D.C. tenant purchase deals, the LEC includes many tenants residing in the building at the time of the notice of sale. Often one of the tenants' goals is to avoid or at least minimize displacement, so the incomes of the initial LEC members are predetermined by who lives in the building. Within an LEC that is 100% affordable (e.g., all households at or below 80% AMI), there can be a broad range of incomes, assets, and financial flexibility. For example, there may be retired seniors with fixed incomes in the range of 30% AMI (in October 2009, $21,567.00 annual income for a one-person household) as well as residents well-established in their careers making close to 80% AMI (in October 2009, $57,512.00 annual income for a one-person household). *See HPTF Limits*, *supra* note 6 (income limits adjusted for Washington, D.C. metropolitan area). It is not unrealistic, especially in gentrifying neighborhoods, to see such an income range within one LEC.

91 Some members' housing costs are at or above the recommended 30% of their income, while others' are below. Some members can and do regularly save, using an LEC's below-market carrying charge to put the money back into their unit, accumulate savings or otherwise build assets, while others struggle each month to meet expenses and do not build savings over time.

while others are not.[92] A management company (not infrequently the same company pre- and post-tenant purchase) continues to complete or manage unit maintenance and repair work. If unit repair costs exceed budgeted costs in a given month, a member does not feel any immediate impact on her carrying charges; if the LEC Board implements a carrying charge increase later on, a member may not know that it is the result, in whole or part, of unit repair costs. In practical terms, little if anything has changed from what the resident experienced as a tenant. While residents are "owners" following the tenant purchase, it may seem to some that more has stayed the same than has changed, a view not unrelated to the resale equity limitation.[93] Some residents continue to act and exercise the same degree of care and attention to maintenance and repairs as they did when they were tenants.[94] Carrying over this level of care to the LEC's long-term operations will not keep the property in the best physical condition.

In contrast, the market-rate cooperative model has the potential to keep the individual units and the property as a whole in the best physical condition because it facilitates a higher level of care by residents. Residents will have direct responsibility for costs, avoiding any "insurance" by the LEC. It makes sense for residents to minimize the repairs needed and to be proactive in maintaining or improving their units where that is less expensive than dealing with negligent or deferred maintenance.[95] For example, one LEC president called an all-members meeting following the completion of the building's substantial renovation, the supervision of which had been a daily responsibility for the president. On the

92 *See* Michael Diamond & Aaron O'Toole, *Leaders, Followers, and Free Riders: The Community Lawyer's Dilemma When Representing Non-Democratic Client Organizations*, 31 Fordham Urb. L.J. 481, 505 (2004) (discussing the free rider theory in context of client organizations).

93 Internalization of "ownership" varies by individual and LEC; the blanket mortgage, uncertain resale market for LEC shares, and the free rider problem are all factors that can affect an LEC member's perspective.

94 *See* Lynne Dearborn, *Homeownership: the Problematics of Ideals and Realities*, 16 J. Affordable Hsg & Cmty. Devt. L. 40, 40 (2006) (renter-occupied housing in worse condition than owner-occupied housing; likely linked to owner's desire to live in house in good repair and potential resale value); Fennell, *supra* note 38, at 1057, n.40 (tenants expected to neglect owner's long-term interests).

95 In the traditional homeownership context, an owner's level of care is based on enjoying and improving their immediate housing consumption and maintaining or improving the asset's long-term (resale) value. *See* Byrne & Diamond, *supra* note 55, at 543. "[t]he owner has significant incentives to take prudent care of her house because she can reap the benefits of expenditures to conserve or improve the value of the home and may suffer consequences of negligent or deferred maintenance" including happiness, cost savings, resale. An LEC's limitations on a departing resident's equity (and the extent to which improvements are allowed or the costs included in the LEC's resale calculation) may affect a resident's choices, *see* Davis, *supra* note 3, at 61-63, but I am not aware of any studies of the effect of that limitation on a resident's level of care.

agenda was the distribution of the warranties for each resident's new in-unit washer/ dryer. As they were distributed, residents were talking among themselves and did not seem particularly interested in the meeting. The president stopped the discussions to remind the other residents that if anything goes wrong with their new appliances, it's the residents' problem now and the residents, not the management company or the president, are the ones who have get it fixed, and they were the ones who would have to pay for it. With that reminder, the residents then wanted to make sure they had the right paperwork and started asking questions about recommended use and maintenance. Assuming that some residents will now take greater care when the responsibility is theirs (and none will take less care), [96] units will be kept in better condition overall and unit maintenance and repair costs will decrease in the aggregate.

As illustrated above, the market-rate cooperative model reinforces the transition from renting to resident ownership, which has other positive effects. Moreover, when the resident has the right to improve the space as she wishes, she may choose to go beyond the minimum standard of maintenance that is an LEC's default. Going beyond a safe, habitable unit to a living space that meets higher functional and aesthetic standards benefits long-term preservation of the asset, the resident's experience of homeownership and perhaps even the District's desired community effects. In addition, common maintenance and repair costs may be reduced as well, through the better care of units (which could affect common areas) and a stronger sense of ownership that would extend to the entire property, thereby further protecting the physical asset and facilitating affordability.

This high degree of care resulting in better-condition units assumes the LEC resident has the desire and the money to do the maintenance and repairs. The risk to the physical property in adopting the model is that individual residents will not maintain their units, which could have negative consequences for the individual, her neighbors and future residents. Facts and circumstances of residents who do not maintain certainly will vary. Accordingly, the LEC may want to take a two-pronged approach: have a mechanism for addressing

96 However, the fact that a resident would like to keep her unit in good condition does not mean that the resident will have the funds available to make all necessary or desired maintenance and repairs. *See* discussion *infra* pp. 178-79.

violation of certain minimal standards[97] and find ways to assist residents in paying for and making the repairs.[98]

Delivering the Desired Experience of Homeownership

The market-rate cooperative model gives residents the fullest opportunity to make their units their home and experience the security, self-expression and control they desire.[99] It creates a more financially stable LEC and reduces residents' fixed monthly costs, both of which contribute to a feeling, and a reality, of more secure tenure. It gives residents freedom to improve and use their units through alteration and decoration to suit their personal interests and tastes.[100] While it may reduce a residents' ability to control exactly how their neighbors maintain their units, overall increased "ownership," and relatedly a stronger, more engaged board and membership may mean fewer repairs, more consistent enforcement and improvement in this aspect of the homeownership experience as well. The market-rate cooperative model also creates the conditions for the individual and community improvement the District is looking for. In contrast, the rental model limits the uses of a unit and a resident's ability to improve or decorate a space as a way to keep the units standardized and control costs for which the LEC is responsible. Residents are limited in the pride, satisfaction and potential for self-expression and individual development in having a place that is their own.[101] They get less than what many understood "affordable homeownership" to mean.[102]

---

97 For example, the LEC's corporate documents could establish minimum standards and fines for violations; after notice and opportunity to cure, the LEC could have the right to make the repairs and charge the resident. Of course, if the resident is not making the repairs because she cannot afford to, it is not realistic to think that she is going to pay fines or the LEC's repair bills. These procedures and repairs would entail costs for the LEC. If the resident does not pay, ultimately the LEC's only alternative is to terminate the member, which entails additional costs for the LEC (including legal fees, likely lost income from that unit for some months and the costs to repair the unit) and could have a significant impact on the LEC community. All remaining members share these costs. That the LEC would not have funds available to make extensive repairs is a possible scenario that LECs should consider and potentially reserve for, but I would predict that the circumstances where failure to maintain would rise to the level of evicting a member would be rare.

98 *See* discussion *infra* Part IV, Excluding Lower-Income Residents?

99 *See* Lewis & Higgins, *supra* note 18 at 9 (citing findings that LECs reduce externalities such as noise, socially disruptive neighbors and residents' wear and tear on housing).

100 Of course, the equity limitation has an impact on what levels of improvement a resident might be able to afford and what a resident might choose to do.

101 *See* discussion *supra* Part III, The Private (LEC Resident) Goals and Interests.

102 For LEC residents who desire wealth creation through resale, see *supra* note 72, the market-rate cooperative model may have the effect of putting residents in the best position to maximize resale value, if the concerns discussed pp. 172-82 can be resolved.

Notably, the recent subprime mortgage and foreclosure crisis have shown that some of these experiential benefits are reduced or erased for low-income residents struggling to maintain homeownership.[103] However, it is important to note that an LEC as created in the District offers a very different scenario from a mortgage an individual low-income household might hold. An LEC mortgage has bargained-for mortgage terms secured by the LEC with the assistance (in most cases) of competent consultants; a mission-based lender offering better-than-market terms; shared mortgage risk; and, historically, low default rates.[104]

The market-rate cooperative model also promotes capacity-building for residents. While the District and the LEC residents may not explicitly state this as a goal, it seems to be an essential component of the experience of homeownership (for the residents) and its ripple effects on the community (for the District) that they do cite, including residents' goals relating to self-determination and control and the District's assertion that homeowners will strengthen communities.[105] In the market-rate cooperative model, individual residents are responsible for matters that the LEC—through its leadership or, often in practice, its management company—otherwise would handle. Where residents are responsible for maintenance and repairs, they must find solutions through their own resources or in conjunction with their fellow LEC members, community partners or other LECs.[106] This model distances LEC residents from the not uncommon "renter's mentality" of deference to and dependence on the LEC's management company, despite the fact that the LEC residents are owners.[107] Tapping into or developing an LEC's internal and

103 *See* Fox, *supra* note 73 at 450 (noting that low-income homeowners are disproportionately exposed to the risk of losing their homes and subject to related financial and psychological stresses that "may outweigh any social and economic value to be gained from having entered the homeowner sector.").

104 *See* NCB Capital Impact, *Shared Equity Ownership: A Foreclosure Solution*, May 2008, at 3, *available at* http://www.ncbcapitalimpact.org/uploadedFiles/downloads/SharedEquityForeclosureSolutionMay08.pdf (discussing lower foreclosure rates on shared equity ownership mortgages than in the general market); but *see* Manna's Response to NCB Capital Impact's Papers on Shared Equity Ownership (SEO) (arguing the low SEO foreclosure rate is misleading, noting, for example, that LEC individual defaults are recorded as evictions not foreclosures). *See generally* CNHED, *supra* note 5 (79% of cooperatives were in stable or excellent financial condition).

105 *See* Davis, *supra* note 3, at 108-111 (discussing evidence of LEC residents' increased interpersonal involvement, social capital and community involvement, as compared to multifamily renters).

106 Such actions could be as simple as LEC residents splitting the cost of a warehouse club membership that would enable cheaper bulk purchasing of maintenance-related items. A similar approach on a larger scale could be coordinating efforts between LECs or community partners to get reduced rates from building contractors or suppliers in exchange for a higher volume of work or materials.

107 Byrne & Diamond, *supra* note 55. *See* Kennedy, *supra* note 29, at 92 (discussing landlord–tenant relationship in low-income rental market where tenants are "without choice in how the building will look, in the level of maintenance versus other uses of rental income,

external resources and relationships can strengthen the LEC by engaging more members and shifting some burdens off of the LEC leadership, which ultimately is crucial to the LEC's survival.[108] At the same time, it may strengthen individuals and the community.

Excluding Lower-Income Residents?

The potential for excluding lower-income residents Over time, using the market-rate cooperative model for maintenance and repairs could shift LEC membership across the District to the upper levels of low-income households in a number of ways.[109] As discussed above, resident monthly carrying charges in the market rate cooperative model are lower than those in a rental model, but residents have to pay for repairs as they arise. These repairs won't arise on a monthly schedule at a cost equal to the average annual maintenance cost divided by twelve. When the need arises, a resident might have to pay a significant amount in a given month. Moreover, residents could be "lucky" or "unlucky" in a given year and end up with higher or lower than average unit repair costs. However, overall average cost would be lower due to the higher degree of care that most residents will put in.

Existing members will have to deal with the shift from a rental model to a market-rate cooperative model. In particular, they will need time to build up savings to pay certain maintenance and repair costs as they arise. For existing members, if they cannot maintain or make repairs, their enjoyment and living conditions, or even health and safety, may be at stake. Ultimately, if an LEC resident does not have the necessary funds for maintenance and repairs, she may choose or be forced to leave the LEC. Prospective residents may find lower carrying charges appealing but choose to not join because of concerns about being able to bear the financial burdens of maintenance and repair. On the other hand, prospective residents may join regardless of ability to bear individual unit repair costs, in which case they will encounter the problems discussed above. LEC leadership selecting or approving new members may reject lower-income applicants, implement a

in decisions about who should fill vacancies, and decisions about who should be evicted or subject to lesser sanctions for anti-social behavior").

108 *See* Diamond & O'Toole, *supra* note 92.

109 It is important to note that LEC membership already does not on average consist of the poorest of the poor. While some tenant purchase LECs have created lower carrying charge levels for very low income original residents, the finances of a D.C. LEC likely would not work with a majority of residents in the lowest levels of AMI. A notable exception is LECs that increase income through additional subsidies (e.g., Section 8 or the District's Local Rent Supplement program). However, it is not clear to me, and there has not been any study of, what degree of demand for LEC membership exists among those in the upper range of affordable incomes. Anecdotally, that question seems to vary based on the LEC and its location. It may be the case that recent tightening in lending, increases in area foreclosures, and continued lack of affordable housing in the District make LECs seem attractive.

higher threshold standard or otherwise favor higher-income applicants (within the prescribed range).[110] Of course, the decision about whether it is necessary or desirable to the LEC to prefer higher-income residents, perhaps at or near an 80% AMI income level (or whatever level is the maximum permissible for the LEC), is the LEC's to make.

This problem is not unique to LECs.[111] Similar to other low-income homeowners, existing LEC members struggle to pay for expected and unexpected maintenance and repairs.[112] However, an LEC member's ability to meet these expenses is challenged in several ways. Income is by definition limited for membership in the LEC, at least at the time of joining.[113] Borrowing against a member's LEC share is generally not available in the District, and many local, federal or private nonprofit programs for low-income homeowners may not be available to LEC members.[114]

Proposals to address potential exclusion of lower-income residents Because, in my view, what an LEC has to offer should be available to the broadest range of low-income residents, the potential for exclusion needs to be minimized, to the

110 This potential effect would be mitigated as to the initial residents who become LEC members in a D.C. tenant purchase. In tenant purchase and conversion to LEC projects, all tenants must be offered the right to buy in. In addition, seniors and disabled residents residing in the building at the time of cooperative conversion have the right to stay on as renters with annual rent increases capped at the lesser of (1) the previous rent charged plus CPI or (2) 5% over the previous rent. Rent Control Reform Amendment Act of 2006, D.C. Law 16-145 (2008). Many low-income seniors elect this statutory tenancy because it protects against the risk of increased housing costs that a cooperative member must accept. There are two major financial implications for the cooperative: (1) seniors rents may start and stay extremely low (e.g., $400-700/month, as low as one-third to one-half of what other members are paying); and (2) the cooperative is a landlord to all renters, with all the requisite maintenance and repair obligations.

111 Kristina Peterson, *Affordable Housing on City's Slate: Recommended Changes Could Increase Homes' Long-Term Value*, Palo Alto Daily News, Oct. 10, 2007 (stating that "[s]ometimes residents are eligible [for affordable housing] but can only barely afford the house and may not have enough savings for 'maintenance or fixing the heater, so over time the unit is not in the best shape,' " quoting Marlene Prendergast, executive director of Palo Alto Housing Corp.).

112 *See, e.g.*, Karen Black, *Issue Brief: Effectively Preserving Philadelphia's Workforce Housing Stock*, Feb. 2009 *available at* http://www.williampennfoundation.org/usr_doc/PreservingHousingBrief.pdf. (1 out of 8 Philadelphia homeowners can not afford to make needed repairs to their homes); Corey Shdaimah, Roland Stahl and Sanford F. Schram, *When You Can See the Sky Through Your Roof: Low-Income Homeownership from the Bottom Up*, *available at* www.brynmawr.edu/Acads/GSSW/schram/shdaimahstahlschram.doc, at 3 (2004) (discussing interviews with low-income homeowners needing financial assistance to repair and maintain their homes and calling for increased support).

113 Whether income qualification is required only at the time of joining the LEC or annually while a resident of the LEC varies depending on the LEC's financing covenants and corporate documents.

114 *See* discussion *infra* pp. 180-82.

extent possible. The practical proposals below are a few starting points that could assist existing or prospective lower-income residents while promoting the goals the District and residents desire.

Focus on pre-purchase and pre-conversion homeownership education, training and counseling The issue of maintenance and repairs informs what residents' actual costs will be and how their experience of homeownership will be defined, their most important goals. It can easily get glossed over, for example, when attempting to structure and finance a tenant purchase under the statutory deadlines. Residents need full and accessible information up front in order to make informed decisions about their responsibilities and costs.[115] Training on the issue of maintenance and repairs is essential at two points—the formation of an LEC[116] and over time as new members join and problems arise.

First, residents need to understand the LEC structure. Not surprisingly, most prospective residents come to the table with a dichotomous rent versus own framework and the common ideological and cultural meanings that attach to each. It is not easy to grasp immediately the legal distinctions and practical implications of how a cooperative differs from a single-family home, a condominium or a rental and how an LEC differs from a market-rate cooperative. Second, the training should focus on the nuts and bolts of maintenance and repairs—what problems they might expect, what they might cost to fix, how to do home repairs and improvements and how to find reputable and well-priced contractors. Third, training should focus on the financial implications of the market-rate cooperative model. For each household, that means budgeting and saving. Residents can consider whether the LEC would play any role in assisting residents, e.g., through creating a limited "emergency fund," establishing a relationship with a community bank or credit union or creating a system of cross-subsidization among LEC members with lower "tiers" of carrying charges for extremely low-income residents. In a broader sense, this practical, specific training relating to maintenance and repairs also could be a useful tool to focus residents' attention on the larger issues of what they are (and are not) getting and what they are taking on by creating or joining an LEC.

Open District resources and programs for funding maintenance and repair to LEC residents As a lender and a policymaker, it is in the District's interest for

115 TOPA rights are group rights, and the related training is group training. Ideally that would be coupled with some form of individual counseling. LEC members may encompass a broad range of incomes, resources, experiences and educational levels; and each potential member has to understand what the burdens and benefits of LEC membership mean for her, particularly at the lower end of the income spectrum.

116 For tenant groups receiving TOPA notices, there is some existing education and training funded or provided by the District and local non-profits. Tenant groups that exercise their TOPA rights receive additional education from the development team they select, which can include lawyers, developers, organizers, contractors and architects.

the LECs it funds to succeed, as a whole and as to the individual residents that make up the LEC. While the District and residents agree that LECs are affordable homeownership, individual LEC residents are not eligible[117] to participate in a number of grant and loan programs that assist low-income homeowners with maintenance and repairs such as housing code violations,[118] accessibility,[119] lead-based paint remediation[120] and energy efficiency,[121] as well as programs for elderly residents.[122] Opening up the District's established single-family residential rehabilitation programs to LEC residents would be an important step in giving LEC residents options to maintain and keep their homes. The exclusion of LECs from these programs highlights again that LECs are a hybrid, difficult-to-categorize form of housing tenure. Working with LEC residents might take additional time on the front end—for example, to understand the building's common and unit-specific systems and structure and what a resident's maintenance and repair

---

117 That individual LEC residents would not be eligible is based on published materials and calls to the respective program offices throughout 2009. Some programs are available to the LEC as the borrower or grantee. While that approach may make sense in certain buildings for certain repairs, it is overly broad and results in excluding many LEC residents who otherwise could benefit and serve the programs goals.

118 DHCD's Single Family Residential Rehabilitation Program provides loans and grants not to exceed $75,000 to income-qualified households for home repairs that "address building code violations; repair roofs; remove threats to health and safety, including lead-based paint hazards; remove barriers to accessibility for persons with mobility or other physical impairments." D.C. Dep't of Hous. and Cmty. Dev., *Single Family Residential Rehabilitation Program Fact Sheet*, http://www.dhcd.dc.gov/dhcd/frames.asp?doc=/dhcd/lib/dhcd/info/pdf/brochures/sfrehabfactsheet.pdf (last visited Apr. 29, 2011).

119 DHCD's "Handicapped Accessibility Improvement Program" (HAIP), provides a grant of up to $30,000 for improvements needed to remove physical barriers within a home for persons with mobility or other physical impairments. *Id.*

120 Lead Safe Washington, administered by DHCD and funded with federal and local matching funds, provides grants to families with children under six years old "to reduce lead based paint hazards and achieve lead-based paint related compliance with local and federal law." D.C. Dep't of Hous. and Cmty. Dev., Lead Safe Washington, D.C., http://www.dhcd.dc.gov/dhcd/cwp/view,a,1243,q,629142.asp (last visited Apr. 29, 2011).

121 The District Department of the Environment provides free assistance to income-qualified households to make homes more energy-efficient, including repair or replacement of windows, doors, refrigerators, heating and cooling systems and weather-stripping. D.C. Dept't of Env't, *Fix Up Your Home and Save Energy For Free*, http://ddoe.dc.gov/ddoe/frames.asp?doc=/ddoe/lib/ddoe/2009.04.08_Weatherization_Flyer.pdf (last visited Apr. 29, 2011).

122 Where the head of household is 60 years or older, the first $10,000 of home repair assistance may be provided as "a permanently deferred loan [and] [d]eferral of additional amounts will be considered on a case-by-case basis." D.C. Dep't of Hous. and Cmty. Dev., Residential and Community Services Division, http://www.dhcd.dc.gov/dhcd/cwp/view,a,1243,q,629884.asp#SFRRP (last visited Apr. 29, 2011).

responsibilities are[123]—but the number of low-income households that could benefit would be worth it.

On the income side, LECs should consider existing programs that could assist residents in keeping their housing burden more manageable, e.g., the District's Local Rent Supplement Program, through which LECs can apply for carrying charge subsidies for extremely low-income residents,[124] or Section 8 homeownership vouchers. District funding could make the difference in allowing a range of low-income residents to remain as homeowners and in keeping an LEC in good financial and physical condition over time.

To the extent that the needs of some LEC residents are not met through existing programs, the District could support its long-term interest in the units and LEC residents by covering a broader range of maintenance and repairs with more options for both loans and grants.[125] It is particularly appropriate for the District to support residents given that it is the equity limitation required by the District to further its policy goals that prevents borrowing against the LEC share to fund repairs.[126] LECs and individual residents also must be proactive in looking for other sources of funding including those available to more traditional single-family low-income homeowners.[127]

---

123 It also may be the case that a resident's problem does not fit within the parameters of a District low-income homeowner program because it actually is a major systems problem—one that the LEC as a whole should be addressing. *See supra* note 118.

124 D.C. Code § 6-226 (2010). The program ties the subsidies to the units, not the residents. If residents exceed the income cap, they can no longer receive the subsidy. If a resident moves out, the unit remains reserved for a household meeting the income cap.

125 It is important to keep in mind that LEC residents are low-income homeowners in a non-traditional form of housing tenure, so particular attention must be paid to any increased borrowing, with a complete evaluation of the risks involved in taking on additional monthly payments and incurring costs that may or may not be recouped at resale.

126 In contrast, there are a limited but sufficient number of commercial lenders in the District who provide home repair or home equity lines of credit (as well as share loans) for market-rate cooperatives.

127 Options to consider include private sector programs that provide free or reduced-cost maintenance and repair services to low-income homeowners. LEC residents may be a good match for the personal and immediate positive impact these organizations seek to have. Some organizations, for example, Rebuilding Together DC (formerly Christmas in April), are dedicated solely to "mak[ing] free home repairs for low-income homeowners, especially elderly, disabled, and families with children in our Nation's capital, Washington, DC," http://rebuildingtogetherdc.org; while other nonprofit or for-profit groups may provide similar services on a more ad hoc basis, e.g., a "community service" initiative for employees.

Conclusion

Allocating costs and responsibilities for maintenance and repairs is not the first issue that residents or the District consider when they are attempting to create or preserve affordable homeownership. Nevertheless, every LEC has to make these decisions and implement them. The decisions arise at the creation of an LEC and often over time when an LEC experiences financial or governance difficulties over time. LEC residents need to examine what they want from the LEC and what they commit to by using District financing. These resident and District goals are the starting point for making the decision about the appropriate model for allocating responsibility for maintenance and repairs. I believe the positive impact of choosing a market-rate cooperative model on these goals is significant and persuasive despite the additional training, resident burdens and potential exclusioniary impact (coupled with efforts to mitigate such impact) discussed above. Shifting responsibility for maintenance to residents is part of a package of decisions and practices through which the residents will determine whether the LEC succeeds or fails as affordable homeownership—in staying affordable, preserving the physical condition of the property and providing the desired experience of homeownership—in the short- and long-term.

Acknowledgement

The author wishes to thank Mark Morelli, Michael Diamond and the participants in the Georgetown Law Fellows Workshop for thoughtful comments on this chapter.

Chapter 8
Preserving Public Peace, Protecting Private Property

Susan S. Kuo

These riots are not only injurious to individuals, but dangerous to the state.[1]

Introduction

When the general public is invited onto private property that serves as a social gathering place, some scholars contend that the private owner's right to exclude is diminished.[2] Thus shopping malls, retail stores, and restaurants may be considered quasi-public space.[3] Because the public lacks a standing invitation to gather at private residences, however, they represent the opposite end of this imagined continuum. Indeed, the argument that certain types of property are infused with public qualities only reinforces the notion that other property is exclusively private.

This chapter uses the example of communal riot responsibility to challenge the notion of a clear continuum running from public property, where the public's interest entirely trumps any private interest, to purely private property—especially the home—where an individual's right to exclude is paramount.[4] In fact, there is a public dimension to all private property. This public dimension is not a question of scarcity and does not implicate the strength of the private owner's right to exclude. It does not alter any property right to possess, use, or dispose because it does not emanate from the property at all. Rather, it stems from the public value of peace embedded in our collective psyche.

---

1 Ratcliffe v. Eden, 98 Eng. Rep. 1200, 1202 (K.B. 1776).

2 Robert E. Pfeffer, *Losing Control: Regulating Situational Crime Prevention in Mass Private Property*, 59 OKLA. L. REV. 759 (2006); James Bernard Murphy, *Equality in Exchange*, 47 AM. J. JURIS. 85, 113 (2002) ("Both Aristotle and Thomas Aquinas understand property ownership as a kind of trust: civil law permits private ownership on the condition that it serve the common good of the community. Each property owner is a kind of trustee who has a duty of justice to ensure that his property meets the needs of his fellow citizens.").

3 Pfeffer, *supra* note 2, at 765 ("To understand what constitutes mass private property, one must realize that the term refers not only to the size of the property, but also to its use: it performs the function of public space.").

4 Although scientific studies use more exacting terms, this chapter employs terms such as "riot," "mob," "disorder," "mayhem," "disturbance," and "hostile outburst" to denote aggressive, violent group behavior.

In England, this value was made concrete by a series of laws, culminating in the Riot Act of 1714, which obligated the public to preserve the peace. If riots formed and mobs damaged private property, the public was held accountable to individual private owners. By requiring communities to pay restitutionary damages for certain harms to private property—specifically, those stemming from a breakdown in public order—England's Riot Act recognized the public's interest in stability and social peace. The public nature of private property was thus reflected in communal responsibility for riot harm. Shared responsibility for failing to maintain order imbues private property with a public aspect.[5]

Although the role of community law enforcement has diminished with the advent of modern police forces, riot acts are more than historical relics. Still in effect in England and abolished only recently in many U.S. jurisdictions, they represent a possible tool for strengthening community involvement in the preservation of property—and, therefore, in maintaining social peace. Action taken in response to an impending riot directly impacts not only the gravity of mob violence, but also opportunities for mobs to form. Perhaps most important, any indecision, delay, or bias in dispensing justice can kindle a riot. In light of the need for a rapid, appropriate response as a mob gathers, a law that recognizes communal responsibility for riot harm could advance the public interest in social peace. If both citizens and police bear responsibility, then there is a greater chance of quelling riots.

The Public Value of Peace

The public interest in social peace and stability rests on a common law foundation. Under the English common law, citizenship was accompanied by communal responsibility for the preservation of private property. In keeping with the English tradition, early state laws in the United States also provided for communal riot responsibility. Although community restitution ensured that individual owners' losses were shared, riot acts served the broader interest of public peace. Thus, compensation was due regardless of the existence of private insurance. Indeed, the private owner victimized would pay for a proportionate share of the damage as a member of the community that failed to prevent the harm.

Hue and Cry Responsibility

Modern notions of collective responsibility for riot harm can be traced back to the tenth century when the Saxons conserved the peace by means of "a well-

5 *See* City of Chicago v. Frank Sturges, 222 U.S. 313, 324 (1911) (noting that private land owners suffering from riot harm "must be compensated by a tax burden which will fall upon all property").

understood principle of social obligation, or collective security."[6] This system was a compulsory one—requiring every adult male to enroll in a group of families referred to as a "tything" or "tithing." Tythings were grouped into "hundreds," which were subdivisions of counties or shires.[7] Each tything was responsible for maintaining order among its members.[8] If a member of a tything committed a crime, "the others had to produce him for trial; if they failed to do so they could be fined or called upon to make compensation."[9]

Canute and the Normans retained this system of collective security. King Canute required all persons to raise a "hue and cry" upon discovering a thief. The failure to raise a hue and cry as well as the failure to respond to the same was penalized:

> [I]f anyone comes upon a thief and of his own accord lets him escape without raising the hue and cry, he shall make compensation ... or clear himself ... [by stating] that he did not know him to be guilty of any crime. And if anyone hears the hue and cry and neglects it, he shall pay the fine for insubordination to the king.[10]

Similarly, the Normans introduced the "frankpledge" system, pursuant to which each adult male member of a tything bore responsibility for the good conduct of the others:

> Every man who wishes to be accounted as free shall be in a pledge, so that the pledge hold him and produce him before the court if he offend. And if anyone of such people escape, let the pledges see that they pay the sum claimed by the plaintiff, and prove that they were privy to no fraud committed by him that has escaped.[11]

The English Parliament codified hue and cry responsibility in the Second Statute of Winchester in 1285.[12] Under the statute, the inhabitants of a locality in which a robbery or other felony was committed had the duty to raise a hue and cry and to pursue the offenders.[13] If the residents failed to apprehend the wrongdoers, the statute imposed civil liability on the local governments for damages sustained from the criminal acts:

---

6 T.A. Critchley, A History of Police in England and Wales 2 (2d ed. 1972).

7 *See* J.H. Baker, An Introduction to English Legal History 7-9 (3d ed. 1990).

8 1 William S. Holdsworth, A History of English Law 14 (7th ed. 1966).

9 Critchley, *supra* note 6, at 2.

10 2 Canute, c. 29 (1027), *reprinted in* A.J. Robertson, Laws of the Kings of England from Edmund to Henry I 175-219 (A.J. Robertson ed., A.J. Robertson trans., 1925).

11 1 Holdsworth, *supra* note 8, at 14 (quoting Will. 1, c. 84, § 8 (Eng.)).

12 Statute of Winchester, 1285, 13 Edw., c. 1, 2 (Engl.).

13 *Id.* c. 1, 4.

> And if the Country will not answer [for the Bodies of such manner of Offenders,] the Pain shall be such, that every Country, that is to wit, the People dwelling in the Country, shall be answerable for the Robberies done, and also the Damages; so that the whole Hundred where the Robbery shall be done, with the Franchises being within the Precinct of the same Hundred, shall be answerable for the Robberies done.[14]

The rationale for this communal liability was to "secure[] the fulfillment of the duty to preserve the peace which is laid upon every citizen."[15] That a loss might have been insured bore no relevance in assessing communal responsibility. The right to recovery was not solely for the purpose of compensating the victim, but also for the purpose of punishing the hundred. As one court explained:

> It is plain that the intent of the legislature in this Act, and others of the like nature, was to make the inhabitants of hundreds vigilant for their own sakes, by making it their interest to prevent the commission of offences, and where that could not be done, to exert themselves to bring the offenders to justice.[16]

In keeping with this rationale, victims, too, were tasked with responsibility. In particular, Parliament observed that victims, presuming to recover their losses from another, were "many tymes negligent and careles" in aiding attempts to apprehend and convict their assailants, and the inequities inherent to the system of compensation provided "great incoragement and [embolding]" to offenders, who very often escaped with impunity, along with their ill-gotten gains. For this reason, the 1735 statute taxed all inhabitants, including any victims and offenders, with losses. And liability did not end at the borders of the hundred: Parliament discerned that the residents of nearby hundreds, to which felons often fled, were less diligent in their response to the hue and cry because they were "not chargeable for any portion of the Goodes robbed." To remedy this, Parliament amended the law and allowed inhabitants of adjacent hundreds to be liable for half the damages if their hundred was negligent in lending assistance.[17]

Thus, the failure of the inhabitants to maintain or restore order to their community resulted in strict vicarious liability for any and all individuals. The law made no exceptions for those unable, due to their ignorance of the ongoing offense or their inability to prevent its occurrence or apprehend the perpetrator, to fulfill its directive. The purpose of the statute was to hold individuals accountable for acts that threatened the safety of others and the public peace by requiring them

---

14 *Id.* c. 2.

15 John Marston, *Riot in the Riot (Damages) Act 1886*, 84 L. Soc'y's Guardian Gazette, June 17, 1987, at 1797 (quoting Professor Heuston).

16 Clark v. Inhabitants of the Hundred of Blything, 107 Eng. Rep. 378-79 (K.B. 1823) (allowing recovery from the hundred for insured loss).

17 27 Eliz., c. 13, §§ 1, 3, 5 (1585) (Eng.) (alteration in original).

to provide redress to victims of injurious acts. Although the hue and cry statutes were repealed in 1827, they demonstrate that the responsibility to keep the peace was a communal one.

The English Riot Act

The Second Statute of Winchester served as a springboard for the Riot Act of 1714, which took communal responsibility to new heights in reaction to challenges to sovereign rule:

> [O]f late many rebellious riots and tumults have been in divers parts of this kingdom, to the disturbance of the publick peace and the endangering of his Majesty's person and government, and the same are yet continued and fomented by persons disaffected to his Majesty, presuming so to do, for that the punishments provided by the laws now in being are not adequate to such heinous offenses; and by such rioters his Majesty and his administration have been most maliciously and falsely traduced, with an intent to raise divisions, and to alienate the affection of the people from his Majesty....[18]

Pursuant to the act, the locality where a riot occurred was strictly liable for property damages.[19] Unlike hue and cry responsibility, this liability was absolute; capturing the perpetrators did not absolve or mitigate a locality's responsibility to make financial amends to victims.[20]

The special dangers presented by riots explain the shift to strict communal liability in the Riot Act. Mobs jeopardize social stability and threaten the rule of law. Accordingly, individuals were responsible not only for bringing wrongdoers to justice, but also for failing to suppress the riot. This reasoning is evident in Lord Mansfield's opinion in *Ratcliffe v. Eden*:

> These riots are not only injurious to individuals, but dangerous to the state.... To encourage people to resist persons thus riotously assembled...by way of inducement to the inhabitants to be active in suppressing such riots, which it is their duty to do; and which being thus made their interest too, they are more likely to execute. This is the great principle of the law, that the inhabitants shall be in the nature of sureties for one another. It is a very ancient principle... whereby the whole neighbourhood or tithing of freemen were mutually pledges for each other's good behaviour.[21]

---

18 1 Geo., c. 5, § 1 (1714).

19 *Id.* § 6.

20 *See* 1 Geo., stat. 2, c. 5 (1714).

21 98 Eng. Rep. 1200, 1202 (K.B. 1776) (charging the hundred with responsibility for the destruction of the furniture and house of a slave trader who attempted to suppress a mob of sailors and who subsequently fell victim to their discontent).

Moreover, a mob represents shared disapproval or rejection of authority. As such, the community "cannot be considered as free from blame."[22]

The English Riot Act remains in force today:

> Where a house, shop or building in a police area has been injured or destroyed, or the property therein has been injured, stolen, or destroyed by any persons riotously and tumultuously assembled together,…compensation…shall be paid out of the police fund of [the area] to any person who has sustained loss by such injury, stealing or destruction….[23]

The statute provides for compensation to be made from the local police fund for damage to real or personal property sustained in a riot. The act also allows for certain insurance claims to be refunded to insurance companies at the expense of the local police unit.[24] Like its sixteenth century forerunner, liability is absolute; good faith attempts by the police to quell disorder will not immunize the locality from liability.

Early Riot Responsibility in the United States

American riot statutes also imposed communal responsibility for riot harm. In passing these statutes, legislatures reaffirmed the principles animating the English tradition of communal liability for riot violence: deterrence of residents from participation in riots; incentive to residents and local law enforcement officials to prevent or suppress unrest; and belief in collective financial responsibility as an evenhanded measure for spreading costs throughout a locality instead of burdening chance victims of mob violence.

By way of example, the legislative history of Maryland's riot statute includes a "revealing statement" by the chairman of the Joint Committee of the Senate and House of Delegates addressing the reasons underlying the passage of act:

> [I]n the judgment of your committee, it is expedient at once to set an example by, and carry out in perspective (*sic*) legislation, provisions that will connect the interest of any tax-payer at least with the support of the laws, and demonstrate to the disorderly and malicious, that those whom they would make victims of lawless

22 Maison v. Sainsbury, 99 Eng. Rep. 538, 540 (K.B. 1782) (allowing suit for recovery for riot damages despite fact that plaintiff had insured the damaged property).

23 Riot (Damages) Act of 1886, 49 & 50 Vict., c. 38 (1886).

24 *Id.* § 2(2). Compensation for riot damages is paid by taxation in the affected districts. D. Bruce La Pierre, *Enforcement of Judgments Against States and Local Governments: Judicial Control Over the Power to Tax*, 61 GEO. WASH. L. REV. 299, 384 (1993).

> wrath, are under the broad shield of indemnity, from which their blows may glance with injury to themselves, or their friends.[25]

As early as 1835, these laws imposed liability on cities and counties for damage meted out by mobs.[26] By 1890 at least 17 states had statutes that spread the loss from destructive mob violence throughout the locality in which the riot took place.[27] By 1936 at least 24 states had enacted mob violence statutes.[28]

Like the English Riot Act and its other English predecessors, American riot statutes required local governments not only to punish rioters, but to prevent riots. Rhode Island, for example, recognized that the primary goal of its riot statute was "to make the citizens of the municipalities law-conscious through apprehension of the penalty that they collectively would have to pay by way of compensation, through the municipality, to an individual whose property was destroyed or injured during a riot."[29] Kansas's statute "was to quicken the public conscience and stimulate a sentiment in favor of law and order by making each citizen and taxpayer responsible for a proportionate share of the loss resulting from mob violence and thus making each a champion of peace and good order."[30] The Pennsylvania act rested on the principle "that every political subdivision of the state should be responsible for the public peace and the preservation of private property" and a finding that "this end could be best subserved by making each individual member of the community surety for the good behavior of his neighbor

---

25 City of Baltimore v. Blibaum, 374 A.2d 1152, 1154 (Md. 1977) (quoting William D. Merrick's statements in the Report of and Testimony Taken Before the Joint Committee of the Senate and House of Delegates, at 6 (1836)).

26 *See* 1835 Md. Laws 137 (originally enacted in 1835).

27 *See* 1835 Md. Laws 137; 1839 Mass. Acts 54; 1841 Pa. Laws 415; 1854 N.H. Laws 1519; 1855 La. Acts 206; 1855 N.Y. Laws 428; 1856 Ky. Acts 594; 1858 Mo. Laws 25; 1862 Kan. Sess. Laws 77; 1863 Wis. Laws 211; 1864 N.J. Laws 237; 1867 Cal. Stat. 418; 1871 Ala. Acts 74; 1871 Me. Laws 207; 1871 S.C. Acts 561; 1875 Ark. Acts 12; 1887 Ill. Laws 573.

28 Cal. Pol. Code §§ 4452-56 (Deering 1931); Conn. Gen. Stat. § 514 (1930); Ill. Rev. Stat. 38, §§ 512-14 (Smith-Hurd 1935); Kan. Rev. Stat. §§ 201-02 (1923); Ky. Stat. § 8 (Carroll 1930); La. Gen. Stat. § 5369 (Dart 1932); Me. Rev. Stat. 130, § 20 (1930); Md. Code Ann. Art. 82, §§ 1-3 (1924); Mass. Gen. Laws ch. 269, § 8 (1932); Minn. Stat. §§ 10036-38 (1927); Mo. Rev. Stat. § 8672 (1919); Mont. Rev. Code § 5086 (1935); Neb. Comp. Stat. §§ 602-06 (1929); N.H. Pub. Laws 42, §§ 41-42 (1926); N.J. Rev. Stat. 979, §§ 5-9 (1877); N.Y. Gen. Mun. Laws 685, § 21 (1892); N.C. Gen. Stat. § 3945 (1939); Ohio Rev. Code Ann. §§ 6280-88 (Baldwin 1934); Pa. Stat. Ann. tit. 16, §§ 3921-25, tit. 18, §§ 339-40 (Purdon 1936); R.I. Gen. Laws § 6055 (1923); S.C. Code §§ 1384-89, 3041 (1932); Utah Rev. Stat. Ann. 104, § 2(26) (1933); W. Va. Code Ann. § 6038 (Michie 1932); Wis. Stat. § 66.07 (1931). By 1977 only 15 states fixed liability for riot losses on local governments. City of Baltimore v. Blibaum, 374 A.2d 1152, 1154 (Md. 1977).

29 Goldman v. Forcier, 27 A.2d 340, 342 (R.I. 1942).

30 Blakeman v. City of Wichita, 144 P. 816, 817-18 (Kan. 1914).

and for that of each stranger temporarily sojourning among them."[31] Accordingly, most of these American statutes held local governments, and thus local residents via taxation, strictly liable for riot damages. No allowances were made for inability or lack of neglect on the part of the city or county.[32]

Courts called upon to enforce state riot acts recognized their deterrent purpose. For example, a Montana court discerned that the purpose of the Montana statute, "and those of similar import, [was] to create municipal liability and tend[ed] to instill in the mind of every person liable to contribute to the public expense a will to discourage violence and to stimulate effort to preserve public safety."[33] Illinois courts held that an object of their statute was "to impose sanctions against the citizens of the community when they participate in or allow [a riot] to arise"[34] and noted the "frequent apathy displayed by ordinarily good citizens at the destructive work of riotous mobs" as a consideration inducing the state legislature to enact a mob violence statute.[35] In considering its own mob violence act, a Louisiana court praised the wisdom of the statute, which, according to the court, "concern[ed] the whole community to prevent the wanton destruction of private property by mobs."[36] Similarly, a New Hampshire court found that the purpose of its statute was "to prevent and suppress riots." To accomplish this, the court noted that the legislature sought to make the statute

> first and chiefly, punitive, in making the loss of property destroyed by mobs, a charge upon the town treasuries, thereby joining the personal interest of tax payers with the official duty of the local authorities, and arraying both against rioters, with a new motive to discover, discourage, overawe, and overpower all riotous proceedings and tendencies; secondly, [the court found the statute to be] remunerative, in encouraging every one to oppose mobs by giving indemnity for property destroyed in consequence of efforts to preserve order.[37]

31 County of Allegheny v. Gibson's Son & Co., 90 Pa. 397, 418 (1879).

32 *See, e.g.*, Palmer v. Concord, 48 N.H. 211, 218 (N.H. 1868) ("The liability imposed by the statute is irrespective of any inability or neglect on the part of the city."); Slaton v. City of Chicago, 130 N.E.2d 205, 210 (Ill. App. Ct. 1955) ("finding that the negligence or inefficiency of local authorities is not the sole basis of the municipality's liability under the statute") (citing Kennedy v. City of Chicago, 91 N.E.2d 138, 142 (Ill. App. Ct. 1950)). *But see, e.g.*, City of Baltimore v. Blibaum, 374 A.2d 1152, 1158 & n.4 (Md. 1977) (disallowing indemnity when civil authorities and citizens have "used all reasonable diligence" to prevent or suppress riotous assemblages) (emphasis omitted) (citing Note, *Riot Insurance*, 77 YALE L.J. 541, 553 (1968)).

33 Butte Miners' Union v. City of Butte, 194 P. 149, 150 (Mont. 1920).

34 Slaton v. City of Chicago, 130 N.E.2d 205, 210 (Ill. App. Ct. 1955).

35 Spring Valley Coal Co. v. City of Spring Valley, 65 Ill. App. 571, 579 (Ill. App. Ct. 1895).

36 Fauvia v. City of New Orleans, 20 La. Ann. 410, 411 (La. 1868).

37 Underhill v. Manchester, 45 N.H. 214, 221 (N.H. 1864).

Courts also observed that riot acts required communities to share the cost of breakdowns in the public order. For example, the New Jersey Supreme Court, in examining the New Jersey riot statute, noted the justness of spreading riot losses among the citizens of a municipality or county.[38] Illinois opined that legislative intent in enacting the state mob violence act was "to impose a penalty upon the community in the form of additional taxes when its members participate[d] in or allow[ed a mob] to arise."[39] The Massachusetts Supreme Judicial Court observed that the communal liability imposed by its statute reflects "the principle of making all members of a territorial or municipal division sureties for each other in criminal matters."[40]

As in the English tradition, because mobs and riots represented risks to society of the gravest nature,[41] statutes imposing communal liability on counties and cities for destruction caused by mobs were "essential to the order and good government of the cities affected by [them]."[42] Furthermore, because they were aimed at stimulating the exertions of the indifferent and law-abiding alike, they "directly operate[ed] on and affect[ed] public opinion," which "tend[ed] strongly to the upholding of the empire of the law."[43]

Repeal of the Riot Laws in the United States

Once commonplace in the United States, strict communal riot liability is a relic of the past. The reasons for the repeal of these statutes and the accompanying trend away from municipal liability are not completely clear. Some states, including California and Kansas, determined that their statutes were no longer necessary because "the risk of property loss from mob or riot activity is now spread through standard provisions of insurance policies."[44] New York's statute, although never formally repealed, has remained inoperative since 1942 when

38 A. & B. Auto Stores of Jones Street, Inc. v. City of Newark, 279 A.2d 693, 698 (N.J. 1971).

39 Slaton v. City of Chicago, 130 N.E.2d 205, 211 (Ill. 1955).

40 Yalenezian v. City of Boston, 131 N.E. 220, 221 (Mass. 1921).

41 A. & B. Auto Stores of Jones St., Inc. v. City of Newark, 248 A.2d 258, 269 (N.J. Super. Ct. Law Div. 1968) (noting that American statutes never sought to encompass the broad reach of the original Statute of Winchester).

42 County of Allegheny v. Gibson's Son & Co., 90 Pa. 397, 410 (Pa. 1879) (discussing riots that had occurred and that would occur in large cities).

43 City of Chicago v. Frank Sturges, 222 U.S. 313, 324 (1911) (upholding the Illinois riot liability statute against constitutional challenge).

44 Cal. Law Revision Comm'n, Recommendations Relating to Sovereign Immunity 818 (1963) *available at* http://www.clrc.ca.gov/pub/Printed-Reports/Pub043.pdf ; Warden v. City of Wichita, 658 P.2d 1043 (Kan. 1983) ("We simply reassert our belief that the mob liability act which emerged in civil war days is obsolete in present day society and should be repealed.") (quoting statement from League of Kansas Municipalities to House Committee on Judiciary (March 20, 1979)).

the state legislature suspended its mandate due to increased demands on the city police to maintain a civil defense network during World War II.[45] These decisions, however, may not have been entirely benign: at least one commentator surmises that Illinois and Louisiana rescinded their statutes in response to the race riots of the 1960s.[46]

At present, only a handful of states appear to retain some type of riot liability statute that allows riot victims to recover for property damage or physical injuries.[47] Moreover, even in states that allow recovery for riot damage, "the circumstances that give rise to this liability are very limited,"[48] and several states cap liability at set amounts.[49] Alternatively, many plaintiffs have sought support in state tort law to combat inadequate policing during riots.[50] A survey of case law, however, reveals a

---

45 *See* Finklestein v. City of New York, 47 N.Y.S.2d 156, 157-58 (N.Y. Supp. 1944).

46 *See* Note, *Compensation for Victims of Urban Riots*, 68 COLUM. L. REV. 57, 75 (1968).

47 *See, e.g.*, Conn. Gen. Stat. § 7-108 (1999); Ky. Rev. Stat. Ann. § 411.100 (Banks-Baldwin 2003); Mass. Gen. Laws Ann. ch. 269, § 8 (2000); N.J. Stat. Ann. § 2A:48-1 (West 2000); Ohio Rev. Code Ann. § 3761.03 (West 2003); R.I. Gen. Laws § 45-15-13 (2002); S.C. Code Ann. § 16-5-70 (Law Co-op 2002); W. Va. Code Ann. § 61-6-12 (Michie 2003); Wis. Stat. Ann. § 893.81 (2003).

48 W. PAGE KEETON ET AL., PROSSER AND KEETON ON THE LAW OF TORTS § 131 (5th ed. 1984); *see, e.g.*, Conn. Gen. Stat. § 7-108 (1999) (allowing liability only when local government fails to exercise reasonable care or diligence in the prevention or suppression of riot).

49 *See, e.g.*, Mass. Gen. Laws Ann. ch. 269, § 8 (2000) (allowing recovery for property damage only and limiting recovery to three-fourths of value of property or amount of injury to property); N.J. Stat. Ann. § 2A:48-1 (West 2000) (allowing recovery for property damage only and capping recovery for aggregated damages at $10,000); Ohio Rev. Code Ann. § 3761.03 (West 2003) (allowing recovery for physical injury only and capping recovery for permanent disability at $5,000, for serious injury not amounting to permanent disability at $1,000, and for minor injury at $500); R.I. Gen. Laws § 45-15-13 (2002) (allowing recovery for property damage only and capping recovery at three-fourths of value of property or three-fourths of amount of injury to property); W. Va. Code Ann. § 61-6-12 (Michie) (capping recovery at $5,000).

50 *See, e.g.*, Fla. Stat. Ann. § 768.28 (2005) (allowing suit against state for negligent or wrongful act of employee acting within scope of office or employment); Iowa Code Ann. § 670.2 (1998) (subjecting municipalities to liability for their torts and those of their officers and employees acting within scope of employment or duties); Miss. Code Ann. § 11-46-9(1)(c) (2002) (exempting governmental entities and employees from liability from claim arising out of act or omission in the performance or execution of duties or activities relating to police protection unless employee acted in reckless disregard of the safety and well-being of any person not engaged in criminal activity at the time of injury); Vt. Stat. Ann. tit. 12, § 5601 (2003) (allowing suit against state for negligent or wrongful act of employee acting within scope of office or employment).

nearly wholesale rejection of governmental tort liability based on a general "failure to provide police protection."[51]

The general repeal of the strict communal liability riot statutes most deeply impacts the urban poor living in riot-wreaked areas.[52] In addition to deterring rioters and providing incentives to citizens and police to prevent and suppress mob violence, riot acts, both English and American, provide redress for injuries when no other manner of compensation may be available.[53] Compared to other sources of loss, which typically occur more equally across socio-economic lines, riot loss has a disproportionate impact on the poor. This loss is "exacerbated by the general inability of potential riot victims to protect themselves against the risk of such loss."[54] As riots have become more common and the damages resulting from them have become more extensive, insurance companies have taken measures to exclude from coverage damages caused by riot and civil commotion, especially in inner-city areas.[55]

If there is a public value to private property, embedded in the idea of social peace, current U.S. law fails to recognize that public interest in our poorest communities. Private insurance has not filled the gap, leaving individual property owners isolated and exposed. The connection between public and private interest

---

51 Keeton et al., *supra* note 48, § 131. While some courts ground rejection of liability in governmental immunity, *see id.*, other courts refuse to find any governmental duty to provide police protection. For example, California's Torts Claims Act provides: "Neither a public entity nor a public employee is liable for failure to establish a police department or . . . for failure to provide sufficient police protection service." Cal. Gov't Code § 845 (West 2008). Thus far, this provision has been an insurmountable hurdle to those seeking a remedy for inadequate police protection. *See, e.g.*, Peterson v. San Francisco Cmty. Coll. Dist., 685 P.2d 1193, 1202 (Cal. 1984); Gates v. Superior Court, 38 Cal. Rptr. 2d 489, 503-04 (Cal. Ct. App. 1995). Courts that acknowledge a duty to protect describe the duty as one owed only to the public at large, leaving individual plaintiffs without legal basis for complaint. *See, e.g.*, Keeton et al., *supra* note 48, § 131. In addition, although most state constitutions contain equal protection and due process clauses, courts generally interpret these provisions in accord with federal constitutional doctrine. As a result, state guarantees of equal protection and due process warrant no greater police protection than federal assurances. *See* Susan S. Kuo, *Bringing in the State: Toward a Constitutional Duty to Protect from Mob Violence*, 79 Ind. L.J. 177, 205-19 (2004).

52 For discussions of the changing demographics in and economic difficulties faced by U.S. cities, see Kathleen J. Tierney, *Property Damage and Violence: A Collective Behavior Analysis*, *in* The Los Angeles Riots: Lessons for the Urban Future 149-70 (Mark Baldassare ed., 1994) and David O. Sears, *Urban Rioting in Los Angeles: A Comparison of 1965 with 1992*, *in* The Los Angeles Riots: Lessons for the Urban Future 237-54 (Mark Baldassare ed., 1994).

53 Abraham v. City of Woburn, 408 N.E.2d 664, 668-69 (Mass. App. Ct. 1980), *rev'd by* 421 N.E.2d 1206 (Mass. 1981).

54 Note, *Municipal Liability for Riot Damages*, 81 Harv. L. Rev. 653, 654-55 (1968).

55 *Abraham*, 408 N.E.2d at 668-69; Note, *supra* note 54, at 655; Note, *Riot Insurance*, 77 Yale L.J. 541 (1968).

seemingly has been severed. One commentator, for example, has argued that while riot statutes have no significant impact on individual behavior, they might discourage any tendency of local governments to contain riots within poor areas without serious efforts to give aid to those in the riot zone.[56] As discussed in the next section of this chapter, inadequate riot responses can make a bad situation much worse.

Public Responsibility for Riot Harm

In modern society, our physical safety depends upon official law enforcement, rather than on groupings of male citizens charged with maintaining public order within their communities. As described in this section, however, something is lost when direct responsibility for protecting private property rests outside the community with public servants who cannot always respond in a timely fashion and whose blunders sometimes cause riots to escalate needlessly.

Scholars of collective disorder have studied the link between law enforcement activities and the development of riots.[57] State action plays a definitive role in not only suppressing, but also constraining mob activity. In particular, policing activities directly impact the initiation and direction of riots.[58] A riot's severity "depend[s] at least as much on the tactics of police and troops as it [does] on the number of people in the streets or the amount of property seized and destroyed."[59]

56 Note, *Municipal Liability for Riot Damage*, 81 Harv. L. Rev. 653, 654 (1968).

57 *See, e.g.*, Gary T. Marx, *External Efforts to Damage or Facilitate Movements: Some Patterns, Explanations, Outcomes, and Complications*, *in* Dynamics of Social Movements (Mayer N. Zald & John D. McCarthy eds., 1979); John D. McCarthy & Clark McPhail, *The Institutionalization of Protest*, *in* A Movement Society? Contentious Politics for a New Century (David Meyer & Sidney Tarrow eds., 1997); Clark McPhail et al., *The Policing of Protest in the United States, 1960-1995*, *in* Policing Protest: The Control of Mass Demonstrations in Western Democracies (Donatella Della Porta & Herbert Reiter eds., 1998); Barbara Salert & John Sprague, The Dynamics of Riots (1980); Albert Bergesen, *Race Riots of 1967: An Analysis of Police Violence in Detroit and Newark*, 12 J. Black Studies 261-74 (1982); Ruud Koopmans, *The Dynamics of Protest Waves: West Germany, 1965 to 1989*, 58 Am. Sociological Rev. 637-58 (1993); Karen Rasler, *Concessions, Repression, and Political Protest in the Iranian Revolution*, 61 Am. Sociological Rev. 132-52 (1996); Marco Giugni & Dominique Wisler, *Political Coalitions, Face-to-Face Interactions, and the Public Sphere: An Examination of the Determinants of Repression with Protest Event Data*, CBSM Working Paper Series 1(4) (1998), *available at* http://www.nd.edu/~ dmyers/cbsm/vol1/berlin98a.pdf (last visited Nov. 9, 2008) (on file with author).

58 Bert Useem, *State and Collective Disorders: The Los Angeles Riot/Protest of April, 1992*, 76 Social Forces 357, 357-58 (Dec. 1997).

59 Charles Tilly, Big Structures, Large Processes, Huge Comparisons 57 (1984).

The Operation of Social Controls

An important determinant of a hostile outbreak is the operation of social control. Social control includes official actions that "prevent, interrupt, deflect, or inhibit" an episode of collective disorder. Two broad types of social controls are (1) controls that minimize societal conditions, such as economic deprivations and inter-ethnic conflicts, that can predispose an area toward riot activity; and (2) controls that are activated to address a particular outbreak of hostilities.[60]

The first type of controls helps prevent the occurrence of riots because they are directed at social and economic conditions that can create a riot-prone environment.[61] Examples of such social tensions and conditions include conflicts of interest, value and cultural clashes, severe economic deprivation, and overcrowding due to inadequate housing, all of which can lead to mob activity. As observed by Professor Luther Lee Bernard:

> Mobs develop with special ease under social conditions in which conflicting interests, ideals and controls are prevalent. The presence in close proximity of two or more races with fairly distinct customs, traditions and standards; of distinct social classes, such as capitalist and labor, rich and poor; of radically distinct religious alignments, each sect or religion holding firmly to its own tenets; of two rival gangs, each intent upon dominating the situation; or of two or more political parties, each with its patronage and graft to protect and candidates to elect, is especially conducive to the appearance of the mob spirit and mob action. Such conditions easily evoke race, class, religious or partisan animosities and hatreds, which become chronic prejudices.[62]

Accordingly, social controls that address and ease these problems can weaken any potential for riots to form. For example, social controls that institutionalize respect for the law and establish orderly means of expressing grievances may assist in alleviating conditions that generate discontent.[63]

The second type of social controls used in response to actual riotous activity "determine how fast, how far, and in what directions the [riot] will develop."[64] These controls are activated after the conflict phase has begun; in particular, this chapter is concerned with the behavior of controlling agencies at the scene of a riot. Relevant agencies include police authorities responsible for deciding whether and how to control the outburst and police officers responsible for implementing those decisions.[65]

---

60 Neil J. Smelser, Theory of Collective Behavior 15-17 (1962).

61 *Id.* at 17.

62 L.L. Bernard, *Mob*, *in* 10 Encyclopaedia of the Social Sciences 553.

63 Smelser, *supra* note 60, at 261.

64 *Id.* at 17.

65 *Id.* at 261-62.

The dominant style of public order policing in the United States is one of negotiated management. This approach, which represents a "softer and more tolerant" style of crowd control, is a departure from the former "uncompromising 'escalated force' model of the 1960s."[66] It emphasizes prevention of confrontation and accommodation of peaceful protest, "while retaining a readiness to deal resolutely with potential or actual disorder (the 'iron fist in the velvet glove')."[67]

Once the conflict phase is under way, however, the preventative policies of negotiated management must give way to tactical intervention; the nature of this intervention "will have crucial implications for the instigation and development of possible confrontation." In other words, police actions can have the unintended effect of contributing to, as opposed to stifling, unrest. For instance, rioters may take advantage of signs of weakness on the part of the police:

> An additional problem may emerge if police lack the power to clear the street or, as in Detroit, to control it once it has been cleared. In Newark after an angry crowd pelted the police station with rocks, bottles, and a few fire bombs, police made several sorties into the crowd using their clubs, and each time withdrew back into the station. Such a seesaw motion, in demonstrating police ineffectiveness and the crowd's parity with control officials, may have emboldened rioters.[68]

Indecisiveness on the part of police authorities with respect to whether to use force also tends to encourage hostilities and may lead to the spread of disorder. Conversely, quick and decisive application of sanctions against mobs may reduce hostilities.[69] (Controlling a mob, however, does not always require the use of force. For example, redirecting the attention of a crowd by throwing people into a state of panic, getting individuals interested in other objects, or engaging them in discussion or argumentation may break up a crowd.[70]) Departments that achieve success in dampening civil unrest have "almost always responded quickly with sufficient manpower and deployed rapidly into troubled areas."[71] "Delay in the use of force, and hesitation to accept responsibility for its employment when the situation clearly demands it, will always be interpreted as weakness, encourage

---

66 David P. Waddington, Policing Public Disorder: Theory and Practice 10-12 (2007).

67 *Id.* at 34.

68 Gary T. Marx, *Civil Disorder and the Agents of Social Control*, 26 J. Soc. Issues 38 (1970).

69 *Id.* at 262 (affirming that vacillation tends to foster the spread of overt hostility).

70 Herbert Blumer, *Collective Behavior*, *in* New Outline of the Principles of Sociology 181-82 (Alfred McClung Lee ed., 1951).

71 1 Richard H. Girgenti, A Report to the Governor on the Disturbances in Crown Heights: An Assessment of the City's Preparedness and Response to Civil Disorder 205 (1993) (quoting Julius Jerico et al., Prevention and Control of Civil Disturbance: Time for Review (U.S. Dep't of Justice ed., 1992)) [hereinafter Girgenti Report].

further disorder and eventually necessitate measures more severe than those which would suffice in the first instance."[72] One expert explanation for this is that:

> Subversive movements, or disorders of any nature, do not break out fully organized. Leaders in the early stages are apt to be more distinguished by their oratorical powers, and perhaps by capacity of political organization, than for military qualities. Given time, leaders who are men of action will assert themselves, and a knowledge of the best means of countering Government measures will be acquired.[73]

For example, in the Chicago Riot of 1919, official hesitation in calling for additional help from the state militia when local police were clearly overwhelmed contributed to a five-day period of lawlessness.[74] In the wake of the riot, 38 people lay dead; hundreds were injured, and over a thousand left homeless.[75] Similarly, during the Detroit Riot of 1943, local authorities vacillated before calling in federal troops to aid police in quelling the disorder that claimed 35 lives, injured nearly seven hundred individuals, and cost two million dollars in property damage.[76] Over 24 hours passed after the initial outbreak of hostilities before Detroit officials finally took steps to attain sorely-needed help.[77]

Intertwined with the general principle requiring the state to adopt an unequivocal position toward riot violence is the need to implement an unambiguous arrest policy and strategy. To make clear their intent and ability to respond to violations of the law, police must affirmatively act when crimes are committed. To refrain from acting effectively excuses lawbreakers and encourages further criminal activity.[78] At a symposium on riot control, commanders of 20 large law enforcement departments agreed that "[t]here should be little tolerance for those who perpetrate riotous activity....[A]nything less will reap increased property loss and injury to citizens and police alike."[79]

Delay in moving law enforcement officers to the riot site may also heavily impact the direction and dimensions of a hostile outburst. For example, police delay was a large factor in the development of a riot in 1949 in Quito, Ecuador,

---

72 Sir Charles W. Gwynn, Imperial Policing 15 (1934).

73 *Id.*

74 Smelser, *supra* note 60, at 264; Chicago Public Library, *Death, Disturbances, Disasters and Disorders in Chicago: 1919 Race Riots*, *at* http://www.chipublib.org/004chicago/disasters/riots_race.html (last modified May 2001) [hereinafter *1919 Race Riots*].

75 *1919 Race Riots*, *supra* note 74.

76 Smelser, *supra* note 60, at 264; PBS website, *Detroit Race Riots 1943*, *at* http://www.pbs.org/wgbh/amex/eleanor/peopleevents/pande10.html (last visited Sept. 27, 2009) (on file with author).

77 *Detroit Race Riots 1943*, *supra* note 76.

78 Girgenti Report, *supra* note 71, at 222-23.

79 *Id.* at 223 (quoting Jerico et al., *supra* note 71, at 21).

when H.G. Wells' "War of the Worlds" was performed by a local radio station. Terrified by the realistic depiction of Martians landing and taking over the city, thousands of people fled their homes, many in their nightclothes.[80] Police were sent to a community nearby Quito where the space ship had presumably landed and were absent when the angry mob discovered that the alien takeover was purely fictional and wreaked its vengeance by burning the radio station, killing fifteen people.[81]

Likewise, actual or apparent bias in dispensing justice can further enflame a riot. When authorities cease to make decisions in an impartial manner, they "enter the conflict itself" and give confidence to the mob.[82] An example of this occurred in the Cicero, Illinois Riot of 1951, when a black man attempted to move into the city of Cicero and the local police arrived to stop him. A white crowd quickly gathered and, fueled by the implicit official acquiescence in the volatility of the situation, soon erupted into a riot.[83] Similarly, police officers encouraged hostilities during the East St. Louis, Illinois Riots of 1917 by "fle[eing] into the safety of cowardly seclusion or listlessly watch[ing] the depredations of the mob, passively and in many instances actively sharing in their work." When the state militia arrived to support the local law enforcement, they also contributed to the riot by "fraterniz[ing] with the mob, jok[ing] with them and ma[king] no serious effort to restrain them."[84] What is more, in the months preceding the culmination of the rioting, city authorities fostered an atmosphere of racism and violence, allowing attacks on African Americans to go unrestrained. Adding further to the anti-African American sentiment, the mayor promised his white constituency to do all he could in his power to drive African Americans from East St. Louis and to prevent them from moving to the city.[85] The riot, which lasted nearly a week, resulted in the deaths of hundreds of black citizens and forced over six thousand African Americans from the city.[86]

---

80 Don Moore, *The Day the Martians Landed*, *available at* http://donmoore.tripod.com/south/ecuador/martians.html (last visited Sept. 27, 2009).

81 *'Mars Raiders' Cause Quito Panic; Mob Burns Radio Plant, Kills* 15, N.Y. Times, Feb. 14, 1949, at 1, 7, *reprinted in* Selected Readings in Social Psychology 304-07 (Stewart Henderson Britt ed., 1950).

82 Smelser, *supra* note 60, at 264-65.

83 W. Gremley, *Social Control in Cicero*, 3 British J. of Sociology 322-23 (1952).

84 Chicago Comm'n on Race Relations, The Negro in Chicago 77 (1922).

85 Marcus Garvey, *Speech regarding the East St. Louis Riots* (July 18, 1917), *in* PBS website, *Primary Sources: The Conspiracy of The East St. Louis Riots*, http://www.pbs.org/wgbh/amex/garvey/filmmore/ps_riots.html (last visited Sept. 27, 2009).

86 PBS website, *People & Events: The East St. Louis Riot*, http://www.pbs.org/wgbh/amex/garvey/peopleevents/e_estlouis.html (last visited Sept. 27, 2009).

The Rodney King Riot

Police response to the Los Angeles Riot of 1992 illustrates the complex dynamic that exists between state action and crowd reaction. The riot, widely recognized as the worst urban riot in United States history, raged for six days, ripping the city asunder.[87] During the riot, the LAPD's inability to elect an effective response strategy led to delays that, in turn, resulted in civil disorder. These problems plagued the LAPD before the riot expanded and engulfed large areas of the city.[88]

The protest began on April 29, 1992, almost immediately after the verdicts of acquittal were read in the trial of the four police officers accused of beating Rodney King.[89] Groups of angry people congregated in South Central Los Angeles to protest the verdicts. At the intersection of Florence and Normandie avenues, dubbed the flashpoint of the riots by numerous commentators, anger swelled into violence and destruction. Demonstrators torched buildings, looted stores, and attacked passing motorists with crowbars, bottles, and rocks. The collective anger over the King decision quickly spilled over into other parts of the city, and lawlessness gained the upper hand for the following six days and five nights.[90]

In his meticulous study of the riot, Professor Burt Useem demonstrates how the failure of social controls impacts riot formation and growth. In particular, he describes the consequences of hesitation in the use of force, vacillation, and delay in moving police officers to the riot site.[91] For example, following the acquittals in the King beating case, the LAPD adopted a strategy of diplomacy, placing officers from its Metropolitan Division ("Metro") on "soft patrol." Although Metro trains its officers for special assignments, including riot control, hostage situations, and high-risk arrests, after the verdicts were announced, its officers were garbed in regular patrol uniforms, instead of riot gear, and drove around the city waving and

---

87 Dennis E. Gale, Understanding Urban Unrest: From Reverend King to Rodney King 7 (1996).

88 Useem, *supra* note 58, at 365-69.

89 William H. Webster & Hubert Williams, The City in Crisis: A Report by the Special Advisor to the Board of Police Commissioners on the Civil Disorder in Los Angeles 11 (1992) [hereinafter The Webster Report]. On March 3, 1991, an individual shot a home video of four white LAPD officers viciously beating a black man, Rodney King. *E.g.*, Gale, *supra* note 87, at 4. The segment showed a non-resistant King lying on the side of the road, enduring a seemingly endless barrage of baton-beatings and kicks delivered by the officers. *Id.* When the jury in the beating case rendered acquittals for three of the officers and a mistrial set the fourth officer free, many Americans were stunned with disbelief. *Id.* at 5.

90 *E.g.*, Gale, *supra* note 87, at 5-7; The Webster Report, *supra* note 89, at 12 & 19.

91 Useem, *supra* note 58.

conversing with residents.[92] (This deployment of Metro was later described as a "giant-assed mistake."[93])

Authorities did not shift toward a strategy of force until several hours after the riot commenced. By this time, the riot's own momentum, coupled with police delay in switching from soft patrol to a riot-ready configuration, had propelled mob activity beyond the immediate reach and control of local law enforcement efforts. What is more, despite orders that a tactical alert be issued when the verdicts were read, which would have allowed commanders to keep officers beyond their shifts, no such alert was broadcast until nearly four hours after the verdicts were read and six hours after the jurors notified the judge that they would be returning a verdict.[94] The delays in recalling officers unquestionably impacted the department's capacity to respond to the riots.

In the initial stages of the riot, the LAPD response was hesitant and uncertain. This official indecisiveness during the first six hours of the disorder spurred riotous activity and "led to situations that spread, intensified, and careened out of control." Law enforcement officials agree that "police must act quickly with strength in response to a potential disorder at the onset." Contrary to traditional riot response protocol as well as sociological findings regarding optimal methods for combating riots, the actions of the LAPD were anything but "quick and decisive."[95] Police response also conflicted with the LAPD's own tactical manual, which espouses traditional riot confrontation philosophy:

> The primary responsibility of the. . .Field Commander during the initial stages of an unlawful assembly or riot is the rapid assembly of sufficient forces to immediately confront the participants. In the case of an unlawful assembly, a dispersal order is ignored, or in the case of riot, law violators must be quickly overwhelmed and arrested.[96]

---

92 Lou Cannon, Official Negligence: How Rodney King and the Riots Changed Los Angeles and the LAPD 268-69, 272-73 (1997).

93 *Id.* at 273.

94 The Webster Report, *supra* note 89, at 19-24. In a study of twenty-four disorders, the Kerner Commission observed that "in one-half of the cases police withdrew from the initial encounter for fear that they might not be able to maintain control. In these cases the violence spread rapidly." *Id.* at 123 (citing Report of the Nat'l Advisory Comm'n on Civil Disorders 20 (1968)). Accordingly, the Webster Commission cites a pivotal error made by law enforcement in failing to return to the Florence and Normandie vicinity after retreating from a confrontation with an angry crowd. Although officers were outnumbered during the initial incident, the failure to return in force was a significant tactical blunder. *Id.* at 121.

95 *Id.* at 24, 104-14, 121.

96 *Id.* (quoting the LAPD tactical manual).

The Crown Heights Riot

A study of official response to the disturbances in Crown Heights yielded similar findings. The event precipitating this riot was a car accident that occurred in August 1991 when a station wagon escorting the Lubavicher Rebbe Menachem Schneerson collided with another vehicle, veered out of control, and accidentally struck two African American children, killing one and seriously injuring the other. The accident "sparked an immediate and violent reaction among certain members of the African-American community, which quickly spread to the streets of Crown Heights." The fiery response was reportedly generated by a general perception that the city bestowed preferential treatment on the Hasidic community and by a false report that an ambulance owned by a private Jewish organization that had arrived at the accident before the city ambulance had failed to aid the child victims, favoring the Hasidic driver and passengers who were less in need of medical help. Scant hours after the accident, a young rabbinical student was attacked by a group of young African American men and stabbed to death. The following three days saw violent unrest throughout the Crown Heights neighborhood.[97]

The report, prepared by the director of criminal justice for the state of New York, noted the correlation between official action and mob activity and identified many of the same social control problems experienced by the LAPD during the 1992 riot. As with the Los Angeles riot, Crown Heights law enforcement struggled with its strategy for addressing the disorder. Officials initially opted for a policy of restraint and non-confrontation, but this plan, which lacked tactical strategy, such as containment and dispersal, was unsuccessful in ending the violence. Nonetheless, despite clear evidence that diplomacy was not only ineffective but also feeding further violence, officials doggedly adhered to this strategy for three days. Among its extensive findings, the study determined that the police should have realized that the policy of restraint, even if initially justifiable, was not achieving the desired outcome and that the official failure to modify this approach until the fourth day of the rioting "allowed the disorder to continue unabated."

In addition, notwithstanding the need for "rapid deployment of sufficient personnel" to keep unstable conditions from escalating into violence, mobilization and deployment of police during the first night of the rioting was slow. The resulting shortage of officers impeded efforts to contain the spread of the disorder. Moreover, the conspicuous absence of law enforcement gave confidence to rioters and exposed the inadequacy of the police response. Specifically, after the catalytic car accident, when roving bands had formed and were moving through the areas surrounding the crash site, destroying property and assaulting individuals, the officers present were not sufficient in number to deal with these groups. Further exacerbating mob conditions, police in the affected areas were primarily assigned to fixed posts and were unable to pursue the roaming clusters of youths. Instead,

97 Estate of Rosenbaum v. City of New York, 975 F. Supp. 206, 209-20 (E.D.N.Y. 1997).

widespread use of mobile patrols was necessary to combat the groups roaming through the neighborhoods causing mayhem.

Analysis also revealed that, despite the obvious mayhem occurring on the streets, police officers were anything but aggressive in making arrests throughout the initial days of the disorder. Only 48 arrests were made during the first three days of the disturbance—30 of these arrests were made on Day Three of the riot. Underlying the low arrest numbers were operational and tactical problems related to the lack of a clear mission and strategy. Not until the fourth day of the disorder did authorities take on a coherent plan to address and contain the rioting, adding mobility and revised tactics to confront the mob and arresting people for unlawful assembly, which likely prevented additional crimes from occurring. The change in strategy extinguished the riot.[98]

The city, itself, accepted responsibility for its equivocal position toward the riot violence in a statement made by then-Mayor Rudolph Giuliani:

> In the spirit of conciliation, the City of New York accepts responsibility for the mistakes that were made in August 1991, and apologizes to the residents of Crown Heights. . . .The City of New York hereby reaffirms that in the future it will not allow several days of rioting without adequate response. There is no excuse for allowing people to victimize others based on their race, religion, ethnicity or for any other reason without a strong and immediate response from City government.[99]

As in the 1992 Los Angeles Riot, the collective failures on the part of city and police officials during the disturbance in Crown Heights not only allowed riot violence to occur, but actually increased the dangers to riot victims. Analyses of these disturbances demonstrate that the size and scope of a riot is inextricably linked to the actions of law enforcement in responding to a mob. Official uncertainty and delay can escalate existing conflict or even incite a riot.

Reviving the Riot Acts?

Given what we now understand about how delayed and misguided official action can contribute to the escalation of collective violence, we should revisit everything from policing methods and policies to zoning decisions and other city-planning choices. I have argued elsewhere that municipal liability for riot harm ought to

---

98 Girgenti Report, *supra* note 71, at 205-06, 216-17, 222, 224-25, 229-31, 235-36, 241-65, 345, 347-55, 361-63.

99 *Statement by Mayor Rudolph W. Giuliani Regarding the Settlement of the Crown Heights Lawsuit*, Archives of the Mayor's Press Office (April 2, 1998) (on file with author).

be part of the equation.[100] We should also consider whether riot acts might help preserve the peace and social order in areas most prone to riot violence.

For the reasons discussed above, communal responsibility for riot harm would help reinforce the public's interest in social peace—an interest that current policing practices cannot satisfy. In order to establish new riot act laws, however, we would have to address a number of serious objections. It may be that the practical impediments outweigh any possible benefits.

First, we would need to establish the parameters of any duty to act pursuant to riot statutes. In particular, to preserve the state's monopoly on the use of force, we would want to be very careful about effectively deputizing local members of the community to use physical violence to suppress a potential riot. This could potentially cause more problems than it would solve. One possible approach would be to combine English riot act and "hue and cry" responsibilities, requiring members of the community to (1) use their influence to discourage those who might participate in riots; and (2) when appropriate, to alert law enforcement to potential trouble. (Notably, local community leaders followed this latter course of action before the Rodney King riots. Unfortunately, their warnings were not heeded.[101]) To fully specify the nature of the legal obligation, we would have to answer difficult questions, such as whether to include a scienter requirement, whether to impose liability on individuals or groups, and, given our reluctance to allow community members to use force, whether we ought to accept that an individual or community could satisfy all legal obligations to preserve the peace even though a riot took place.

Second, we would have to identify the scope of the relevant community. Some commentators argue that federal or state compensation for riot damages is preferable to municipal liability because the larger national or state tax base would reduce the possibility that other important programs would be cut to fund riot costs. Federal- or state-based compensation might also stem migration of people and business to the suburbs.[102] Nevertheless, if we were to sweep too broadly, many of those contributing toward property damages would have no immediate connection to the area where the harm occurred. This would serve the goal of spreading the loss and might also encourage reforms that could alleviate the socioeconomic disparities that can spark riots. On the other hand, those closest to the problem would have less incentive to act (unless a specific duty to act triggered separate liability), especially if wealthier surrounding areas would bear the brunt of the economic losses. But if we were to define the relevant community more

100 *See generally* Kuo, *supra* note 51.

101 *Id.* at 180, 227-33.

102 *See generally* Amos H. Hawley, The Changing Shape of Metropolitan America (1956) (discussing the relocation of people and business from urban to suburban areas); *see also* Raymond Vernon, The Changing Economic Function of the Central City 41-62 (1959) (same).

narrowly, then those in the poorest neighborhoods could suffer a double-loss: the damage caused by the riots and the need to pay for the damage.

Third, as the official indifference to community warnings about the impending Rodney King riot illustrates, it is unclear whether riot acts would have stopped or even ameliorated any recent riots. At most, community action can supplement official responses. Also, the existing social science evidence demonstrates only that inadequate official action will exacerbate riot conditions; the evidence does not prove that enhanced community involvement would fill the gap. Nevertheless, given the proximity of members of the community to the problem, and the likelihood that they will know the individuals who comprise a mob, it seems reasonable to expect that a community—if sufficiently motivated—could help to quell riots.

Conclusion

Perhaps riot acts can be redesigned so as to protect our communities from mob violence. I believe that this is a question that merits further inquiry. The broader point, though, is that individual property ownership should not be understood solely as a right to exclude backed by the power of the state. Property ownership serves other values and is protected in other ways.

Today as much as ever, we depend upon our neighbors to keep an eye out for us, as we do for them. These reciprocal relationships bind us together and link our property interests. Rather than strain to understand ourselves as distinct, private property owners disconnected from the places where we live and the people who surround us, we ought to recall that we are fundamentally social beings. That does not mean that others have the right to claim our property as their own or that private property is an empty concept. Rather, property is a rich concept; our mutual obligations, whether merely social or embodied in law, reveal a deeper sense in which private property exists for the benefit of the individual owner and, at the same time, makes possible the continuation of a stable, peaceful social order.

Acknowledgement

I would like to thank Tommy Crocker, Michael Diamond, Josh Eagle, Benjamin Means, and Jason Richardson for sharing their thoughts on this topic and commenting on earlier drafts of this chapter. Thanks also to the participants at the November 2008 PCSE Workshop at Georgetown University Law School, sponsored by Georgetown Law and the Syracuse University College of Law Center on Property, Citizenship, and Social Entrepreneurism, for their comments at a presentation of a prior draft of this chapter. Finally, I am grateful to Harry Brenner, Alina Dudau, and Julie Moore for their stellar research assistance and to the University of South Carolina School of Law for research funding and support. Portions of this chapter appeared previously in Susan S. Kuo, *Bringing in the State: Toward a Constitutional Duty to Protect from Mob Violence*, 29 IND. L.J. 178 (2004).

Chapter 9

Adult Adoption of Lovers and Spouses to Help Ensure Their Inheritance: Fair or Foul?

Terry L. Turnipseed

Introduction

The public nature of private property is beautifully exemplified by the myriad state controls, both statutory and common-law jury biases, which attempt to keep certain individuals from getting their assets to a desired beneficiary after death. One trendy way around these legal barriers is for one adult—whether heterosexual and homosexual—to adopt his or her lover or spouse, thereby better ensuring the adoptee's inheritance. For some time now adults have been adopting their lovers and spouses all over the country for various reasons: to better guarantee the adoptee's right to inherit directly from the adoptor; to keep collateral relatives from having standing to contest the adoptor's estate plan; or to add a loved one to a class of trust beneficiaries (allowing the adoptee to inherit "through" the adoptor). It appears that, post-*Lawrence v. Texas*,[1] both the academy and the judiciary have completely overlooked this steadily growing, albeit stealthy, development.

State definitions of who can challenge an estate plan post-death are at the heart of the public's involvement in the seemingly-private arena of property transmission at death. The same can be said for the documented jury biases against one same-sex partner attempting to leave property to another. So, state property rules force private individuals to engage in extreme planning to overcome these very high obstacles. Should someone have to go to such extremes to get their assets into the hands of their lover or spouse? In many states the answer is still yes.

In many states, there are indeed some potentially-serious side effects of this technique: like a prosecution for incest (with quite serious jail terms attached) and the irrevocable nature of the adoption itself.

There is, of course, a federal constitutional angle to this behavior. Even if a state agrees that adoption of a lover or spouse is incest, will *Lawrence* now protect this behavior, preventing these people from being successfully prosecuted for this type of incest? Indeed, given its prevalence in modern society, I believe this should be the first post-*Lawrence* individual sexual privacy rights case to which the Court will grant a writ of certiorari.

1 Lawrence v. Texas, 539 U.S. 558, 562 (2003).

In no less than four instances, Justice Scalia in *Lawrence* warned that adult incest can no longer be outlawed by state or federal governments.[2] Others have echoed Justice Scalia's sentiments.[3] Since the Court's decision in *Lawrence*, the median viewpoint among legal scholars seems to be that incest is the next battle.[4] This battle has begun with a whimper, though, and not a bang. It has not started with what is considered "core" incest (sexual relations between biological parents and children or between biological full siblings), but instead with a growing set of behavior classified in many states as incest—sexual relations between an adult who adopts his or her lover or spouse (a subset of "non-core" incest that also includes sexual relations between distant relatives such as cousins). The definition of incest is broad enough in many states to include not only sex between a parent and his or her adult biological child, but also between a parent and his or her adult adopted child.

The ancient scrums over estate property are obviously not new, but there are very few areas of property law where lifetimes of bottled-up intensity spew forth in such a vehement way after the death of a "loved" one. So, the strong public controls over every step of an adult adoption—from the decision on whether to award the adoption itself to the determination of the ultimate property results of the adoption—need to be visited, and visited quickly. Though no one seems to realize it right now, the outcome of these upcoming battles might well impact countless lives and their ability to leave property to whomever they choose.

---

2 *Lawrence*, 539 U.S. at 586, 590, 599 and 600 (Scalia, J., dissenting).

3 Including U.S. Senator Rick Santorum in a statement just before *Lawrence* was issued: "If the Supreme Court says that you have the right to consensual [gay] sex within your home, then you have the right to bigamy . . . you have the right to incest, you have the right to adultery. You have the right to anything." Courtney Megan Cahill, *Same-Sex Marriage, Slippery Slope Rhetoric, and the Politics of Disgust: A Critical Perspective on Contemporary Family Discourse and the Incest Taboo*, 99 Nw. U. L. Rev. 1543, 1544 (2005) (citing Associated Press interview with Senator Rick Santorum (Apr. 7, 2003)). Of course, Senator Santorum and those who espouse his view on this issue have their critics. *See, e.g.*, *id.* at 1544 (citing Dahlia Lithwick, *Slippery Slop: The Maddening Slippery Slope Argument Against Gay Marriage*, Slate, May 19, 2004) ("Since few opponents of homosexual unions are brave enough to admit that gay weddings just freak them out, they hide behind the claim that it's an inexorable slide from legalizing gay marriage to having sex with penguins outside JC Penney's. The problem is it's virtually impossible to debate against a slippery slope. Before you know it you fall down, break your crown, and Rick Santorum comes tumbling after.").

4 *See, e.g.*, Cahill, *supra* note 3, at 1546 (citing Brett McDonnell, *Is Incest Next?*, 10 Cardozo Women's L.J. 337, 337 (2004); Cass Sunstein, *What Did Lawrence Hold?: Of Autonomy, Desuetude, Sexuality, and Marriage*, 2003 Sup. Ct. Rev. 27, 48).

Why Would Someone Choose to Adopt a Spouse or Lover?

In olden times, the notion of adoption was, mostly, to care for orphaned children.[5] But it has also served other very important purposes: to provide an heir for the adoptor and/or to perpetuate a family name by a childless individual;[6] to enable a stepparent to adopt a spouse's children, whether adult or not;[7] or to adopt an adult who was raised by the adoptor (but, for whatever reason, did not get adopted during childhood).[8] In the twentieth and twenty-first centuries, two different and more controversial motives have emerged as well, detailed below.[9]

Some background is important. Without exception in America, if an unmarried individual dies without a will, and is survived by an adopted child but no biological children, the adopted child will take all of the decedent's probate property via intestacy to the exclusion of any other biological relative, including the decedent's siblings and parents.[10] Even if someone has a will (making intestacy irrelevant, assuming the will withstands challenge), adoption generally keeps other relatives from having standing to challenge a will (more on this is going to be discussed later in this chapter). Adoption, then, is an obvious, well-tested technique that helps to ensure that the adoptee takes the adoptor's property.[11]

First, for homosexual people in jurisdictions that do not recognize same-sex marriage (or something close that yields many of the same benefits and burdens), adoption is one darn sure (or darn-close to darn sure) way of ensuring inheritance, albeit drastic (read "irrevocable").[12] There are many contract-based methods that are available to any competent individual of majority—wills, trusts, life insurance,

5 Russell G. Donaldson, Annotation, *Marital or Sexual Relationship Between Parties as Affecting Right to Adopt*, 42 A.L.R.4th 776, § 2[a] (1985).

6 *Id.* (citing Walter Wadlington, *Adoption of Adults: A Family Law Anomaly*, 54 Cornell L. Rev. 566, 567 (1969); *Id.* at § 3[a] (citing In re Adoption of Robert Paul P., 63 N.Y.2d 233, 235 (N.Y. 1984)).

7 Donaldson, *supra* note 5, at § 3[a] (citing *Adoption of Robert Paul P.*, 63 N.Y.2d at 235).

8 *Id.*

9 Unlike tracking the adoption of children, there are no statistics on the number of adults adopted—lovers or otherwise—in the United States. *See e.g.*, Karen Hawkins, *Adoption: Not Just for Children*, The Washington Post, Mar. 14, 2007, *available at* http://www.washingtonpost.com/wp-dyn/content/article/2007/03/14/AR2007031400263.html.

10 Jeffrey G. Sherman, *Undue Influence and the Homosexual Testator*, 42 U. Pitt. L. Rev. 225, 253 (1981).

11 One sure disadvantage, in addition to its obvious irrevocable nature, is that adoption very often cuts off the ability of the adoptee to inherit from his or her own natural parents under intestacy (the natural parents could still provide for the adoptee via a valid will). The law in this area varies dramatically from state to state. *See, e.g.*, Dukeminier, Johanson, Lindgren & Sitkoff, Wills, Trusts, and Estates, 87 n.1 (7th ed. 2005).

12 *See, e.g.*, Mandi Rae Urban, *The History of Adult Adoption in California*, 11 J. Contemp. Legal Issues 612, 615 (2000) (citing Gwendolyn L. Snodgrass, *Creating Family Without Marriage: the Advantages and Disadvantages of Adult Adoption Among Gay and*

retirement plans, powers of attorney for financial and health care matters, etc.—but all are subject to claims by heirs-at-law (those who would take probate property absent a will) of undue influence against the partner-recipient of the assets.[13] These suits are more successful than one might imagine, since anti-gay biases are often quite evident in jury verdicts.[14]

To prevent blood relatives from having standing to sue after the death of the higher-net-worth partner, the lower-net-worth partner is adopted. Then, the decedent has a "child" who is his or her sole heir at law (the sole person who would take probate property absent a will) to the exclusion of siblings, parents, and more remote relatives. Because generally only heirs are given standing to sue to overturn a will or other contract to pass property, this situation would prevent blood relatives from having standing to sue to overturn a will, trust or life insurance policy, on undue influence grounds.[15] How elegant.

Second, lovers or spouses (whether same-sex or not) who have trusts set up for their benefit with remainder to their "children" might desire to adopt their lover or spouse to make them a remainder beneficiary of the trust. Believe it or not, this has been done with a fair amount of regularity.

Finally, there are, sometimes, other lesser advantages—some tax-related and some not—that encourage adult adoptions. In some states, the state inheritance tax rate is lower if property flows to a close relative than if it flows to someone unrelated, an advantage mentioned in at least one reported case.[16] One can also imagine almost countless other possible advantages, including, but certainly not limited to: access to health insurance coverage and other employee benefits of the

---

Lesbian Partners, 36 BRANDEIS J. FAM. L. 75, 83 (1998) ("Unless fraud or undue influence is present, adoption cannot be annulled.")).

13 *See generally* DUKEMINIER ET AL., *supra* note 11, at 158-86; Sherman, *supra* note 10, at 255.

14 Snodgrass, *supra* note 12, at 76 (citing Adam Chase, *Tax Planning for Same-Sex Couples*, 72 DENV. U. L. REV. 359, 386 (1995)).

15 *See, e.g.*, In re Adoption of Brundage, 134 N.Y.S.2d 703 (N.Y. Sup. Ct. 1954), *aff'd* 143 N.Y.S.2d 611 (N.Y. App. Div. 1955), *appeal denied*, 144 N.Y.S.2d 921 (N.Y. App. Div. 1955) (holding that adoptive parent's blood relatives are estopped from questioning validity of adoption order).

16 *See, e.g.*, In re Adoption of Swanson, 623 A.2d 1095, 1096 (Del. 1993). Note that Delaware has since repealed its inheritance tax and replaced it with an estate tax that does not differentiate the rate based on who is receiving the property. 71 Del. Laws, 902 (1999). Eleven states still collect an inheritance tax, including: Connecticut, Indiana, Iowa, Kansas, Kentucky, Maryland, Nebraska, New Jersey, Oregon, Pennsylvania, and Tennessee. *See* Retirement Living Information Center, *Taxes by State*, http://www.retirementliving.com/RLtaxes.html (last visited July 3, 2008). In some of these states, transfers to children are exempt from taxation completely, or have a reduced taxation rate. *Id.* Adult adoption also triggers some income tax considerations, including dependency exemptions and head of household status. Chase, *supra* note 14, at 388.

adoptor; allowing recovery in tort actions and survivor benefits;[17] circumventing housing and zoning restrictions; life insurance beneficiary designation;[18] Social Security payments;[19] consent authorizations or visitation privileges relating to hospitals, jails, and other governmental agencies;[20] attainment of immigration status; obtaining royalty status; taking advantage of rent control;[21] and, something

---

17 *See, e.g.*, Snodgrass, *supra* note 12, at 82-83 ("Because adult adoption creates a legal relationship between two people, it also creates the right to recover damages in tort for actions available only to family members."). Snodgrass also cites the case of a man that witnessed the physical assault of his gay partner, but was unable to recover tort damages. *Id.* at 83 (citing Coon v. Joseph, 237 Cal. Rptr. 873 (Cal. Ct. App. 1987)).

18 As one commentator explained:

Before they will issue life insurance policies, insurance companies often require evidence of a close relationship between the insured and her/his proposed beneficiary. While an individual may designate anyone she/he wishes as beneficiary, and some states prohibit carrier discrimination in the issuance of policies on the basis of sexual orientation, prospective heirs might raise undue influence to attack the deceased policyholder's designation of beneficiary. In such instances, adoption may provide persuasive factual evidence as to the relationship between the beneficiary and the insured thus countering an allegation of undue influence.

Peter N. Fowler, *Adult Adoption: A "New" Legal Tool for Lesbians and Gay Men*, 14 Golden Gate U. L. Rev. 667, 682 (1984) (citation omitted).

19 Angela Chaput Foy, *Adult Adoption and the Elder Population*, 8 Marq. Elder's Advisor 109, 119 (2006).

20 Fowler, *supra* note 18, at 681.

21 Though probably not an adoption of a lover, the following is illustrative of the genius of the human spirit. Some time in 1940, Jerri Blanchard began renting an apartment in Manhattan. 333 East 53rd Street Associates v. Mann, 503 N.Y.S.2d 752 (N.Y. App. Div. 1986). In 1970, Helen Mann moved into the apartment as a co-tenant with Blanchard. *Id.* In 1983, the building was converted to a co-op, but Blanchard and Mann were allowed to continue to rent under a rent-controlled regime, though at all times Blanchard was the only official tenant. *Id.* Five days after the conversion to co-op status, Blanchard's (then age 83) adoption of Mann (then age 67) became final via a New York County Surrogate Court order. *Id.* Blanchard died in 1984, at which time Mann invoked § 56(d) of the New York City Rent, Eviction and Rehabilitation Regulations, 9 NYCRR § 2104.6[d], that provides in part: "No occupant of housing accommodations shall be evicted under this section where the occupant is either the surviving spouse of the deceased tenant or some other member of the deceased tenant's family who has been living with the tenant." *Id.* The co-op association sued to evict Mann arguing that the order of adoption was fraudulent because it was obtained for the sole purpose of allowing Mann to keep the rent-controlled apartment after the death of Blanchard. *Id.* With one dissenter, the majority of the Appellate Division of the New York Supreme Court ruled for Mann saying that the adoption would not have been fraudulent even if the co-op association could prove it had been solely motivated by the desire to protected Mann's rights in the rent-controlled apartment after Blanchard's death. *Id.* at 291. The court cited the A.L.R.3d: "Most of the cases which permit the adoption of an adult have recognized, at least by implication, that the fact that an adult is adopted for the purpose of making him eligible to inherit property or to share in the distribution of a trust

near and dear to my heart, permitting an adopted child of a university employee to enroll in said university, or a reciprocal university, free of charge.[22]

Are Adult Adoptions of Lovers Generally Recognized as Valid?

This chapter addresses two types of non-core family concepts: adult adoption and adoptive incest. Neither is what people typically think of when they think of adoption or incest. In this way, they are related. They are also related in that courts and legislatures have tried to set policy and determine the validity of both, absent the federal constitutional overlay only recently present post-*Lawrence*, by using almost exactly the same set of arguments discussed in detail below. The statutory and common law bottom lines of both, in addition, vary dramatically between jurisdictions. Precisely because they are both non-core, there is something tangibly important to looking at them together in a single piece since adult adoption and adoptive incest have more in common than people might think at first glance.

Adoption "is the common[23] means by which a status or relationship of parent and child is created between persons who are not so related by nature."[24] It is strictly a creature of statute, not common law.[25] Generally, if a jurisdiction's statute does not specifically authorize the particular type of adoption being attempted, then a court will disallow its validity.[26] So far, neither Congress nor the federal courts have recognized a right to adopt.[27] In lieu of the dearth of federal action, many state legislatures have recognized such a right. The Uniform Adoption Act, for example, allows an adult to be adopted.[28] There appear to be only six states—Arizona, Florida, Idaho, Nebraska, New Jersey, and Ohio—plus Puerto Rico, which currently prohibit or place restrictions on adoptions of adults, even in the absence of a sexual or marital relationship.[29] It should be noted that Ohio has a

---

does not necessarily affect the validity of the adoption." *Id.* (citing K.M. Potraker, *Adoption of an Adult*, 21 A.L.R.3d 1012, 1029 (1968)).

22 Urban, *supra* note 12, at 612, 612 n.1.

23 As of the 1980s, an estimated 150,000 children were adopted annually, about 5% of the children born annually in the U.S., and the relationships created affected up to one-third of the citizenry. Jan Ellen Rein, *Relatives by Blood, Adoption, and Association: Who Should Get What and Why*, 37 Vand. L. Rev. 711, 711-12 (1984).

24 Potraker, *supra* note 21, at § 2.

25 Donaldson, *supra* note 5, at § 4[a].

26 *Id.*

27 *See, e.g.*, David D. Meyer, *A Privacy Right to Public Recognition of Family Relationships? The Cases of Marriage and Adoption*, 51 Vill. L. Rev. 891, 894-95 (2006).

28 Unif. Adoption Act § 3 (1994).

29 *See* Ariz. Rev. Stat. Ann. § 14-8101 (2007), *amended by* 2008 Ariz. Legis. Serv. Ch. 162 (2008) (requiring any adult adoptee older than 21 to be a "stepchild, niece, nephew, cousin or grandchild of the adopting person" and allowing a foster parent to adopt an adult

unique statute that allows an individual to designate an heir, which might serve the needs of the couple just as well (and perhaps better in some instances) than adoption if inheritance is the prime motivating factor.[30] Is it possible, by the way, that something as simple as this replicated in other states might appease both sides of this issue? It certainly seems quite sound from a policy perspective.

Once you add a sexual relationship between two adults who desire to enter into a parent/child bond, however, the plot definitely thickens in many states. Despite scholars thinking about this issue as early as the mid-nineteenth century,[31] the situation today is indeed murky.

To start, the official commentary to the Uniform Adoption Act specifically prohibits the adoption of a spouse, though adoption of a non-spousal lover is conspicuously absent from the uniform act's language.[32] As one might expect, reported cases of spousal adoption,[33] are rare (and mostly in Kentucky, for some

---

who was placed in his or her care as a juvenile as long as the foster parent and the adoptee have maintained a familial relationship for at least five years); *see also* Fla. Stat. Ann. § 63.042(3) (2007) (stating that no "person eligible to adopt under this statute may adopt if that person is a homosexual"); William M. McGovern, Jr. & Sheldon F. Kurtz, Wills, Trusts and Estates, 104 n.42 (3d ed. 2004)(citing Matter of Adoption of Chaney, 887 P.2d 1061 (Idaho 1995) (refusing to allow an 18-year-old to be adopted because statutory procedures contemplated only adoption of minors)); Neb. Rev. Stat. § 43-101 (2007) (stating that adoption of an adult by another adult who is not the adoptee's stepparent is only permitted if the two have had a parent–child relationship for a period of at least six months preceding the adoptee's age of majority); N.J. Stat. Ann. § 2A:22-2 (2000) (stating that adoptee must be at least 10 years younger than adopter, but court may waive requirement); Ohio Rev. Code Ann. § 3107.02 (2006) (stating that adult may be adopted only if disabled, mentally retarded, or established a child–parent relationship while still a minor); and P.R. Laws Ann. tit. 31, § 531(4) (2007) (requiring adoptee to be at least 14 years younger than adoptor). Note that two other states require that the adoptor be older than the adoptee, which would not as much hinder an adult adoption as fix who is to be the adoptor and who is to be the adoptee. *See* Mass. Gen. Laws Ann. ch 210, § 1 (2007); Nev. Rev. Stat. § 127.190 (2007). The person who has the shorter life expectancy and the wealthier relatives should be the adoptor. Sherman, *supra* note 10, at 256-57 (noting two relevant issues: first, in some states, the adoptee's blood relatives would have standing to contest the adoptee's will if the adoptee dies first; and second, in most states, an adopted person loses his or her right to inherit from or through his natural parents so the person with the wealthier relatives should be the adoptor).

30 Fowler, *supra* note 18, at 703 (citing Ohio Rev. Code Ann. § 3107.02 (stating that any competent person may file a written declaration that appoints another as an heir at law and will take via intestacy the same as a child born in lawful wedlock)).

31 Naomi Cahn, *Perfect Substitutes or the Real Thing?*, 52 Duke L.J. 1077, 1141-42 (2003).

32 Unif. Adoption Act, § 3(4) (Official Commentary).

33 The advisability of intra-family marriage prohibitions generally have long been disputed, at least since Biblical times. Walter Wadlington, *The Adopted Child and Intra-Family Marriage Prohibitions*, 49 Va. L. Rev. 478, 479 (1963) [hereinafter Wadlington, *Intra-Family Marriage Prohibitions*] (citing 2 Pollock & Maitland, The History of

odd reason). However, as you might not expect, almost all of those rare cases have allowed the validity of these adoptions, although the adopted spouse has not always been allowed to be the beneficiary of a will drafted by an ancestor of the adoptor under principles of will construction.[34]

At first blush, the acceptance of these spousal adoptions is an odd result, is it not? The husband's wife is also his daughter, or vice-versa. Courts have, however, struggled to find any way of stopping these seemingly unnatural multiple legal relationships.

Outside of the instances where one spouse is attempting to bring the other spouse into a class of trust beneficiaries ultimately for pecuniary gain, the remaining controversial adult adoptions do not involve adopting a spouse, but instead adopting a non-spousal lover—either heterosexual adulterers or same-sex lovers.[35] Once you think about it, this makes sense because most heterosexual, unmarried lovers who desire to ensure (or at least to vastly increase the chances) that their partner ultimately becomes their heir and/or beneficiary need only get married.[36] Of course, many same-sex couples may now gain many of these same rights in a large handful of states, at least at the state level.[37] While the list is growing, in the overwhelming majority of jurisdictions same-sex couples cannot marry, and so are not able to gain the state-level privileges of marriage.

Should we really care why one is being adopted? Should adoption be purpose-neutral? Or should we require some sort of true parent–child-type relationship in order to adopt? Commentators and courts are both split, with some jurisdictions judging harshly the morals of a paramour or spousal adoption[38] and some indicating that it is irrelevant absent specific statutory language preventing someone from adopting a lover[39] or spouse.[40]

For courts that reject the right to adopt a lover or spouse, several grounds that provide a basis for this decision consistently arise: (1) non-statutory public policy;[41] (2) very narrow statutory interpretation;[42] (3) fraud on the court by attempting to conceal the sexual relationship;[43] and/or (4) incest-related arguments.[44]

ENGLISH LAW 383-87 (1895); Moore, *A Defense of First-Cousin Marriages*, 10 CLEV.-MARSHALL L. REV. 136, 137 (1961)).

34 *See* Donaldson, *supra* note 5, at §§ 2[a], 7.

35 *Id.* at § 2[a], 8 and 9.

36 *Id.* at § 2[a].

37 Also note that the Defense of Marriage Act (DOMA) disallows all federal rights and privileges to same-sex couples. The DOMA was codified at 1 U.S.C. § 7 (2008) and 28 U.S.C. § 1738C (2008).

38 Donaldson, *supra* note 5, at §§ 2[a], 8[b] and 9.

39 *Id.* at §§ 2[a] and 8[a].

40 *Id.* at §§ 2[a] and 7.

41 *Id.* §§ 2[a] and 3[a].

42 Donaldson, *supra* note 5, at §§ 2[a] and 4[a].

43 *Id.* at §§ 2[a] and 6[a].

44 *See infra* Part IV; *see also* Donaldson, *supra* note 5, at §§ 2[a] and 5[a].

Most courts supporting the right to adopt a lover or spouse make the simple argument that, in essence, adoption is purely a statutory creation and, if the statute says you can adopt anyone, then you can adopt anyone—case closed.[45] Some have gone on to say that concealment of the sexual relationship is not sufficient to stop the adoption,[46] and some have expressly rejected the adoption-creates-incest argument.[47] Keep in mind as well that most state statutes do not require that the parties serve notice of the adoption on either their own biological parents or other blood relatives,[48] which obviously tends to give courts a rather one-sided version of the situation.

New York courts, in particular, have had to struggle with numerous reported cases of adult adoption of lovers. New York's adoption statute gives little in the way of guidance on these issues, stating simply that "an adult unmarried person or an adult husband and his adult wife together may adopt another person"[49] as long as the parties involved obtained consent.[50] New York courts, then, have had to fill in the blanks.

While the first reported New York case found that the adoption of a homosexual lover did not violate public policy,[51] this result has since been overturned.[52] Currently, as a matter of common law in New York state, one may not adopt one's lover—whether homosexual or heterosexual.[53] Besides the hotbed of New York case law, one other court has rejected an adoption based on incest or quasi-incest principles.[54]

By and large, though, most American courts that have been faced with the adoption petitions of lovers have acceded to the petition and not looked at the underlying relationship between the parties.[55] California, in particular, seems to grant petitions for adult adoption of gay and lesbian partners routinely, without a reported court case,[56] although they disallow spousal adoptions by statute.[57]

45 Donaldson, *supra* note 5, at §§ 2[a] and 3[b].

46 *See id.* at §§ 2[a] and 5[b].

47 *See infra* Part IV; *see also* Donaldson, *supra* note 5, at §§ 2[a] and 5[b].

48 Rein, *supra* note 23, at 756 ("How can one respond to something he does not even know has occurred?").

49 N.Y. Dom. Rel. Law § 110 (McKinney 2008).

50 *Id.* at § 111.

51 *See* Matter of Adoption of Adult Anonymous, 435 N.Y.S.2d at 531; *see also* In re Adult Anonymous II, 452 N.Y.S.2d at 200.

52 In re of Robert Paul P., 63 N.Y.2d 233, 233 (N.Y. 1984).

53 *Id.* at 239.

54 In re Jones 411 A.2d 910, 910-11 (R.I. 1980).

55 *See, e.g.*, Donaldson, *supra* note 5, at § 5[b].

56 *See* Lynn D. Wardle, *A Critical Analysis of Interstate Recognition of Lesbigay Adoptions*, 3 Ave Maria L. Rev. 561, 596 (2005) (citing Snodgrass, *supra* note 12, at 75); *see also* Urban, *supra* note 12, at 616 n.23 ("It has been estimated that somewhere between two and three hundred adult adoptions in California are granted each year, and that about 30-40% of these adoptions are lesbian or gay adult adoptions."). Presumably with the passage of Proposition 8, upheld by the state court system, these adoptions will continue.

57 Cal. Fam. Code § 9320(a) (2007).

This does not mean, however, that acceptance of the adoption would foreclose a criminal incest prosecution. Let us now explore that possibility.

What Exactly is the Crime of Incest and Does It Really Cover the Adult Adoption of a Lover?

Since the beginning, almost all cultures (except, most notably, ancient Persia) have outlawed at least some form of sexual relations and/or marriage between family members.[58] Written prohibitions can be traced as far back as the Levitical Codes.[59] While the ecclesiastical courts of England punished incest as an "offense against good morals," at common law incest is not an indictable offense.[60] It is, then, a statutory crime that has been around in America since colonial times,[61] and that varies considerably in definition[62] from state to state.[63]

---

58 *See, e.g.*, Note, *Inbred Obscurity: Improving Incest Laws in the Shadow of the "Sexual Family,"* 119 Harv. L. Rev. 2464, 2464 (2006) [hereinafter *Inbred Obscurity*]. Cleopatra, in fact, "was the issue of at least eleven generations of incest and was herself a sibling partner." Milton C. Regan, Jr., *Reason, Tradition, and Family Law: A Comment on Social Constructionism*, 79 Va. L. Rev. 1515, 1523 (1968) (citing James B. Twitchell, Forbidden Partners: The Incest Taboo in Modern Culture 11, 243-45 (1987)).

59 Michelle Murray, *Problems with California's Definition of Incest*, 11 J. Contemp. Legal Issues 104, 105 (2000) ("The Old Testament's prohibitions, for example, include the consanguineous relationships of parent–child, full siblings and half siblings, aunts/uncles and nephews/nieces, and the relationships-by-affinity of spouse's sibling, spouse's parent, spouse's child, parent's spouse, sibling's spouse, child's spouse, and aunt's or uncle's spouse.") (citing *Leviticus* 18:6-18, 20:11-21). The author goes on to point out one other interesting tidbit:

> Yet the Israelites' incest taboos admitted of exceptions, at least prior to their creation. The Israelites claim to descend from Abraham and Sarah, who were half-siblings; *see Genesis* 20:2-18. And Jacob, contrary to what would become the Levitical prohibitions, married two sisters who together bore him the twelve sons whose progeny became the twelve tribes of Israel; *see Genesis* 29-30.

Id. at 105 n.5.

60 State v. Rogers, 133 S.E.2d 1, 2 (N.C. 1963) (citing Donaldson, *supra* note 5).

61 Naomi Cahn, *Perfect Substitutes or the Real Thing?*, 52 Duke L.J. 1077, 1139 n.299.

62 As one commentator notes: "Surely, an act against nature should not be so dependent on time and place for its definition." Carolyn S. Bratt, *Incest Statutes and the Fundamental Right of Marriage: Is Oedipus Free to Marry?*, 18 Fam. L.Q. 257, 288 (1984). Indeed.

63 1A. Am. Jur. 2d *Incest* § 1 (2007). Incest has been criminalized by virtually "every literate society and many pre literate tribal groups." *See* 3 Encyclopedia of Crime and Justice 880, 881 (Sanford H. Kadish ed., 1983) ("The Code of Hammurabi (c. 1750 b.c.), probably derived from Sumerian law (c. 3500 b.c.), specifies four prohibited acts of incest and establishes different penalties for each.").

The "dark figure" of offenses,[64] incest, is rare in judicially-reported case law, and even those cases reported to law enforcement officials (that do not make it to judicially-reported case law) are likely only a small fraction of the actual incidents that occur.[65] Making things harder is the fact that national crime reports do not separate out incest from other sex offenses. Incest between consenting adults is a subset of these incest cases, and sexual relations between a parent and an adopted adult child is an even smaller set. For all of these reasons, studying this issue is difficult.

For our purposes, though, the key distinction is what motivates a state legislature to outlaw certain sexual relations: are there primarily biological considerations, or is there something greater at play that would include a broader definition of incest even where there is no chance of the parties producing abnormal children?[66] Generally, society has been confused on these issues throughout history and into the present day. Indeed, are we asking the wrong question? Should the inquiry instead be case-by-case whether a true parent–child relationship exists rather than distinguishing between blood or adoption?[67] More to come later on these questions.

To date, there have been relatively few reported cases where an adult adoptor was prosecuted for incest for having sexual relations with his or her (so far exclusively his, to be precise) adopted child. Consistently, incest has received precious little attention from scholars throughout American history, with the non-core incest subcategory of adopted relationships receiving even less.[68] As one commentator noted: incest has "supplanted homosexuality as '[t]he love that dare not speak its name.' There is no incest lobby in the halls of Congress, no incest legal defense fund, and no incest pride parade."[69] Perhaps these sexual relationships have been,

---

64 Graham Hughes, *The Crime of Incest*, 55 J. CRIM. L. CRIMINOLOGY & POLICE SCI. 322, 324 (1964) ("[W]ith incest the 'dark figure' of offenses that never come to the attention of the authorities is incalculable but probably extensive").

65 Leigh B. Bienen, *Defining Incest*, 92 NW. U. L. REV. 1501, 1502 (1998). Summarizing the studies to date, one 1983 book estimated that incest affected the lives of "as many as twenty million Americans," and that "incest is found at all social levels" of society and not just in what some might call the steerage class. GEORGE THORMAN, INCESTUOUS FAMILIES, v (1983).

66 *See generally* Cahill, *supra* note 3, at 1569–77.

67 *See, e.g.*, Cahn, *supra* note 31, at 1139. Cahn notes:

> [T]he history of adoption and incest indicates, once again, the difficulties of applying existing law to emerging families, and of assuming that analogical reasoning is appropriate. Because courts and legislatures have focused on the differences between biological and adoptive families, rather than on the similarities of the parent–child relationships, they have not treated incest within adoptive families as punitively as incest within biological families.

Id.

68 *Id.* at 1142.

69 Brendan J. Hammer, *Tainted Love: What the Seventh Circuit Got Wrong in* Muth v. Frank, 56 DEPAUL L. REV. 1065, 1065-66 (2007). There is an international, internet-based group called CUDDLE ("Cousins United to Defeat Discriminating Laws through Education") that promotes an agenda to remove barriers to cousins being lovers or

in a relative sense, under the radar screen of modern prosecutors, but they will not be for long as adoption of lovers increases in frequency.

Until the 1960s or so, negative eugenics was the underlying basis for incest laws,[70] but something broader runs through many modern statutes. By explicit statutory reference, at least 25 states and territories, representing over 140.8 million people (approximately 46.03% of the total population)[71] in the United States, are subject to statutory or common laws that include the adopted parent/adult child relationship within the definition of incest (which clearly would have no eugenics-type motive). Those states with relevant statutes are: Alabama, Arkansas, Colorado, Connecticut, Delaware, Guam, Illinois, Kansas, Kentucky, Mississippi, Missouri, Montana, New Hampshire, North Carolina, Ohio, Oregon, Pennsylvania, Puerto Rico, Tennessee, Texas, Utah, West Virginia and Wyoming.[72] While other state statutes are silent on whether sexual relations between a parent and an adopted

---

getting married. Nancy J. White, *Kissing Cousins; Stigma Attached to Marriage Between Relatives*, TORONTO STAR (July 3, 2004), *available at* 2004 WLNR 6137363. The CUDDLE website gets about 5,000 hits per month. *Id.* Their website points out that, in addition to the myriad ancient cousin marriages, Albert Einstein, Charles Darwin, and Canada's first prime minister, Sir John A. Macdonald, wed cousins. *Id.* Another website, www.cousincouples.com, gets about 600 hits daily. *27 Million Ways to Live Your Life*, TORONTO STAR (Apr. 6, 2004), *available at* 2004 WLNR 6076618. Am I alone in seeing the Darwin marriage as a tad ironic? Finally: "You can't appeal to Victorian morality; Queen Victoria married her first cousin. You can't appeal to the Bible; in the Bible, God commands marriages between first cousins." William Saletan, *The Love That Dare Not Speak Its Surname*, SLATE, Apr. 10, 2002, http://www.slate.com/id/2064227/.

70 Cahn, *supra* note 31, at 1140-41 (citing Wadlington, *Intra-Family Marriage Prohibitions*, *supra*, note 34, at 483). There has been much written about the terrible misconceptions relating to assertions of a strong correlation between consanguineous matings and genetically defective offspring. *See, e.g.*, Bratt, *supra* note 62, at 267-81 (gathering and summarizing all the scientific statistical evidence, concluding that there is almost no statistically significant increase in the odds of a genetically defective child being born of even a core incestuous relationship, much less non-core).

71 *See* U.S. Census Bureau, Resident Population 2000, *available at* http://www.census.gov/population/www/cen2000/respop.html (last visited July 3, 2008) (describing state and territory population estimates by the United States Census Bureau, using information collected during the year 2000 census).

72 Ala. Code 1975 § 13A-13-3(a)(1) (2007); Ark. Code Ann. § 5-26-202(a)(2) (2007); Colo. Rev. Stat. § 18-6-301(1) (2007); Con. Gen. Stat. 530.020 (2007); Del. Code Ann. 11 § 766(b) (2007); Guam Code Ann. 9 § 31.15 (2007); 720 Ill. Comp. Stat. 5/11-11(2) (2007); Ky. Rev. Stat. Ann. § 530.020(1) (2007); Miss. Code Ann. §§ 97-29-5, 93-1-1 (2007); Mo. Rev. Stat. 568.020.1(1) (2007); Mont. Code Ann. § 45-5-507(1) (2007); N.H. Rev. Stat. Ann. § 639:2(I) (2007); N.C. Gen. Stat. Ann. § 14-178(a) (ii) (2007); Ohio Rev. Code Ann. § 2907.03(5) (2007); Or. Rev. Stat. §§ 163.505(2), 163.505(2) (2007) (*see* State v. Buck, 757 P.2d 861, 862 (Or. Ct. App. 1988) ("[M]arrying the natural or adoptive parent of a child creates the relationship that the statutory proscription against incest is intended to protect."); 18 Pa.Cons. Stat.§ 4302 (2007); Tenn. Code. Ann. § 39-15-302 (2007); Tex. Penal Code Ann. § 25.02(a)(1) (2007); Utah Code Ann. 1953 § 76-7-102(1) (2007); W. Va.

adult child or grandchild is included within the definition of incest,[73] other states, by common law, have decided this issue in the affirmative, including Montana.[74] In Massachusetts and Georgia, strong dicta in related cases indicates that the definition of incest would include relationships by adoption.[75] There have been a few successful prosecutions for incest under these modern statutes.[76] Indiana has had an unusual line of cases relating to whether a man can be convicted of incest with his biological daughter, who had been adopted by another family as a four-year-old child, an issue that goes directly to the heart of the blood relation versus parent–child type relationship dichotomy found in current incest statutes[77] (a notion Cahn refers to as the blood/function distinction[78]).

Other countries have struggled in a similar way with these issues.[79] For example, in 1986 Parliament amended the English Marriage Act to disallow marriages between an adult and his or her adopted child in instances when said child "has lived in the same household [as the parent] and been treated by that person as a child of his family."[80] The English approach, then, would seem to

---

Code § 61-8-12(a) (2007), and Wyo. Stat. Ann. § 6-4-402(a)(i) (2007); *see also* Richard A. Posner & Katharine B. Silbaugh, A Guide to America's Sex Laws, Ch. 10 (1998).

73 Note that one state has no incest statute and another does not outlaw adult incest at all. *Inbred Obscurity*, *supra* note 58, at 2469-71, 2469 n.37, & 2470 n.39. "Rhode Island repealed its criminal incest statute in 1989 [Act of July 5, 1989, ch. 214, 1989 R.I. Acts & Resolves 563] . . . and New Jersey does not punish acts committed when both parties are over eighteen years old [N.J. Stat. Ann. § 2C: 14-2 (West 2005)]." *Id.* at 2469.

74 *See* State v. Leslie McQuiston, 922 P.2d 519, 521 (Mont. 1996), *overruled on other grounds by* State v. Herman, 188 P.3d 978 (Mont. 2008) (upholding conviction of incest between man and adoptive daughter). Some incest statutes include in the definition of incest only sexual relations with an adopted child only when said child is below a certain age. *See, e.g.*, 41 Am Jur. 2d *Incest* § 11. Courts have held that these laws create a defense for one accused of incest with an adult adopted child. *Id.*

75 Edmonson v. State, 464 S.E.2d 839, 842 (Ga. Ct. App. 1995) ("The effect of this adoption was to create 'the relationship of parent and child ... as if the adopted individual were a child of biological issue . . . .'" "Because adopted individuals 'enjoy every right and privilege of a biological child,' they are statutorily protected from incest.") (citing Ga. Code Ann. § 19-8-19(a) (2)). The *Edmonson* case is an imperfect analogy because the adopted child was a minor. *Id.* at 323.

76 State v. George B., 785 A.2d 573, 584 (Conn. 2001) (holding that the incest statute encompasses "adopted as well as blood relatives"); State v. McQuiston, 922 P.2d 519, 521 (Mont. 1996) (upholding a conviction of incest between man and adoptive daughter).

77 Cahn, *supra* note 31, at 1145-46.

78 *Id.* at 1146.

79 *Id.* at 1145.

80 Margaret M. Mahoney, *A Legal Definition of the Stepfamily: the Example of Incest Regulation*, 8 BYU J. Pub. L. 21, 34 (1993) (citing Marriage (Prohibited Degrees of Relationship) Act 1986, § 1, *reprinted in* 27 Halsbury's Statutes of England 562 (4th ed. 1987)).

allow an adoption of an adult lover as long as there had never been a traditional parent–child relationship.

From a policy perspective, whether or not one believes adult adoption of a lover is incest seems to be quite instinctual, something we perhaps think about in an almost subconscious way somewhere in the murky base of our brain.

In sum, the states are currently split on whether someone who adopts a lover can be prosecuted for incest as well as on the related question of whether they would be allowed to adopt in the first instance. There have been no *Lawrence*-based challenges, though, to these proscriptive laws; so the jury is still very much out on whether the statutory and common law impediments to adopting a lover, or adopting a spouse, would withstand a full-on post-*Lawrence* constitutional attack.

Everything this chapter has discussed so far has related to the law of incest at the state level. But what about a federal prosecution of someone who has adopted an adult lover? One of the most famous (or infamous) federal criminal code sections is 18 U.S.C. § 2421, commonly known as the "Mann Act."[81] The Mann Act has been broadened quite a bit since its inception in the first half of the twentieth century, when it targeted exclusively men who carried female prostitutes over state lines. Now, the Mann Act states:

> Whoever knowingly transports any individual in interstate or foreign commerce, or in any Territory or Possession of the United States, with intent that such individual engage in prostitution, or in *any sexual activity for which any person can be charged with a criminal offense*, or attempts to do so, shall be fined under this title or imprisoned not more than 10 years, or both.[82]

While no reported cases of Mann Act prosecutions for incest-related activities appear, it seems clear from the Act's language that, in states where the incest statute covers sexual relations between a parent and an adopted adult, federal prosecutors could utilize the Mann Act (and/or conspiracy to violate the Mann Act) to prosecute the parties involved. This could lead to a federal court *Lawrence* showdown[83] similar to the state court arena showdown described above.[84]

---

81 The Mann Act, 18 U.S.C. § 2421 (2008).

82 18 U.S.C. § 2421 (emphasis added).

83 From its inception, the Mann Act's reach has been the subject of significant speculation given the unspecific nature of the Act's text. *See, e.g.*, Laura Elizabeth Brown, Comment, *Regulating the Marrying Kind: The Constitutionality of Federal Regulation of Polygamy Under the Mann Act*, 39 McGeorge L. Rev. 267 (2008).

84 Note that being married is not a defense to the Mann Act under prior precedent. *See* Pappas v. U.S., 241 F. 665 (9th Cir. 1917); *see also* Whitt v. U.S., 261 F.2d 907 (6th Cir. 1959); Cohen v. U.S., 214 F. 23 (9th Cir. 1914).

After *Lawrence*, are Statutory and Common Laws that Criminalize Sexual Relations between a Parent and His or Her Adult Adopted Child Unconstitutional?

A vast, almost overwhelming, number of law review words have been penned in response to the 2003 Supreme Court decision in *Lawrence*.[85] When put together, from sex toys[86] to gay marriage, these analyses have peered into every conceivable legal and policy nook and cranny, with every conceivable viewpoint on display. I do not, then, plan to attempt to reproduce the sizable body of work relating to the constitutionality of traditional incest laws post-*Lawrence*. The body of work is literally too voluminous to cite.[87] Having read a great deal of it, I can assure the reader that the only thing We (the Royal We, of the Academy) are certain of is the uncertainty of how our post-*Lawrence* individual constitutional privacy rights world will play out.

With regard to incest laws in particular, the median viewpoint seems to me to be represented quite well by a 2004 article simply and relevantly entitled *Is Incest Next*?[88] Using both formalistic and realist inquiries, Professor McDonnell concludes that "it is unlikely that the Court would protect [core] incest any time soon."[89] (Sexual relations involving minors are off the table; there is no chance that a state will be kept from regulating said behavior.) This view is supported by the only post-*Lawrence* federal appellate case testing the constitutionality of core incest: the Seventh Circuit (with the petition for a writ of certiorari denied) did not extend *Lawrence* protection to two adult married siblings who had been successfully prosecuted for incest, though one complicating factor was the fact that the conviction had preceded *Lawrence* and so the case did not directly address the question of whether incest prosecutions are constitutionally permissible post-*Lawrence*.[90] [As one commentator correctly noted: "The *Muth* decision may not

---

85 A Westlaw search revealed 338 law review and journal articles (as of April 15, 2008) with *Lawrence* in the title written after the date of the decision, June 23, 2003.

86 I kid you not. Michael J. Hooi, *Substantive Due Process: Sex Toys After Lawrence*, 60 FLA. L. REV. 1065 (2008).

87 Of the 338 law review and journal articles relating to *Lawrence* cited, *supra* note 85, 107 of those were articles that related in one way or another to incest.

88 McDonnell, *supra* note 4, at 337. This work was produced as part of a symposium entitled "Privacy Rights in a Post *Lawrence* World: Responses to Lawrence v. Texas."

89 *Id.* at 338.

90 Muth v. Frank, 412 F.3d 808 (2005), *cert. denied*, Muth v. Frank, 546 U.S. 988 (2005) (concluding that *Lawrence*, holding that states could not enact laws that criminalized homosexual sodomy between consenting adults, did not announce a new rule proscribing state laws that criminalized incest between consenting adults or announce existence of constitutionally protected fundamental right of adults to engage in all forms of private consensual sexual conduct, including incest, and thus did not entitle petitioner whose state-court conviction for incest preceded Supreme Court's issuance of *Lawrence* decision to writ of habeas corpus).

garner much public sympathy; it is unlikely anyone will recall *Muth* as the *Dred Scott*[91] of the sexual realm."][92] Three post-*Lawrence* state court opinions—two in Ohio—relating to core incest convictions held that *Lawrence* did not apply.[93]

Despite Professor McDonnell's reservations for *Lawrence* protection of core incest, he goes on cogently to argue that there is "some chance" that non-core incest should receive said protection.[94] While none of the articles speak directly to the issue of the current constitutional protection of a parent and an adult-adopted child's right to engage in sexual relations, the clear implication is that the further away from "core" incest the facts of a case get, the more likely that *Lawrence*-type protection will be afforded. Let us think about just how far away from "core" incest this type of activity really lies.

One noted post-*Lawrence* article outlined a large handful of factors that the *Lawrence* majority looked to in protecting the actions of John Geddes Lawrence and Tyron Garner; (1), the sex involved only two people; (2), it was not polyamorous; (3), both were of the age of majority (so no chance of minor–minor sex or adult–minor sex); (4), the sex was consensual and not coercive; (5), the acts occurred in a home, not in public; and (6), there was not an economic exchange as in prostitution.[95] Look at these factors. Each could equally apply to a prosecution for incest for an adult who adopts an adult lover or an adult spouse who adopts the other adult spouse. Perhaps the scenario presented in this chapter fits quite nicely into the protections afforded by *Lawrence*? Or perhaps the fact of the adoption, where the government must give formal recognition to the relationship at issue, is a distinguishing factor here?[96] Let us take a closer look.

In one sense, sexual relations between a parent and an adult-adopted child are quite a distance from the same activities between a parent and his or her biological

---

91 Dred Scott v. Sandford, 60 U.S. 393 (1856).

92 Hammer, *supra* note 69, at 1095-96.

93 *See* State v. Freeman, 801 N.E.2d 906 (Ohio Ct. App. 2003) (rejecting *Lawrence's* application to core incest where there was uncertainty as to the consensual nature of the sexual act); *see also* State v. Lowe, No. 2004 CA00292, 2005 WL 1983964, at *3 (Ohio Ct. App. Aug. 15, 2005) (holding that *Lawrence* does not render core incest laws unconstitutional because of a "legitimate interest in protecting the family unit"); Beard v. State, No. M200402227CCAR3PC, 2005 WL 1334378, at *2 (Tenn. Crim. App. June 7, 2005) (holding that the *Lawrence* decision does not establish a new constitutional right that protects core incest).

94 McDonnell, *supra* note 4, at 338.

95 Ariela R. Dubler, *Immoral Purposes: Marriage and the Genus of Illicit Sex*, 115 Yale L.J. 756, 759 (2006).

96 *Id.* at 760 ("[T]he relationship between Lawrence and Garner did 'not involve whether the government must give formal recognition to any relationship that homosexual persons seek to enter.' Lawrence and Garner, in other words, never sought to formalize their relationship as a marriage." (quoting Lawrence v. Texas, 539 U.S. 558, 578 (2003))).

child. Certainly, concerns relating to abnormal offspring[97] are present in one case, and completely irrelevant in the other. But a closer look is warranted. Two other issues are at play that could bring these two fact patterns closer, rather than farther apart.

The first inquiry might be whether a true parent–child relationship existed while the child was a minor. Assume the parent raised the child as he or she would have raised a biological child, with all the attending attachment and power discrepancy issues present. In this instance, one might query whether consent could truly be obtained—even after the child reached the age of consent—given what might be a very strong authority figure towering over someone with potentially less bargaining power: power being the key word here. This is akin to the undue influence concept in challenging wills and contractual instruments.

Because societal norms and views are still probably relevant to the court's inquiry, the second question might ask whether society really views sexual relations between a parent and a child as equally repugnant if the relation were biological or adoptive. Perhaps society as a whole makes no meaningful distinction between the two. Though it probably goes without saying, there appear to be no empirical studies that might reveal societal views on this point.

So, are there case-by-case differences, then, that might be important here? Might the crucial inquiry be whether or not there ever existed a true parent–child relationship? This speaks directly to consent. If there is not a true parent–child relationship, what are we really worried about? Or does the whole varied lot seem wrong for some reason we cannot really put a finger on: wrong for some reason buried deeply inside our consciousness? And what of adopting one's spouse? Certainly no parent–child relationship ever existed, and there is presumably no blood relation, but is it just too much to be a spouse and a child of someone at the same time? (Or perhaps it is the greedy motive behind the adoption we dislike?)

There are many tough questions, with few easy answers. However, let us get back to the scenario at the core of this chapter: one adult adopting another adult who is a lover or spouse, neither of whom (let us assume) were ever in any sort of parent–child-type relationship, for the main purpose of better ensuring that the adoptee will inherit from or through the adoptor. This scenario allows us to strip out several arguments, including all genetic arguments and all consent-based arguments (because no true parent–child relationship ever existed, which would in turn disallow the consent argument). Thus, the remainder is simply a societal, perhaps subconscious, "ick" factor that is hard to pin down or put into meaningful words. This would seem to be the farthest orbit around "core" incest: farther than sex involving any minor; farther than sex between more distant relations; and certainly farther than sex between stepparents and their adult stepchildren. In

---

97 If a court or legislature addressing adult incest is primarily interested in negative eugenics, then "[i]ronically, adult homosexual incest may be protected because the secular justification for precluding heterosexual incest is not present in regard to homosexual incest." Arnold H. Loewy, *Morals Legislation and the Establishment Clause*, 55 ALA. L. REV. 159, 171 (2003).

each of these latter situations, the parties are either related by blood or they had some sort of parent–child relationship prior to sexual relations, neither of which is present in the scenario at the heart of this chapter. Perhaps the whole analytical process is summarized as follows:

> Once you begin to think about which kinds of incest-like activities lack particular identifiable harmful consequences for particular identifiable participants, you begin to think about the unthinkable and about why some "incest" is harmless incest. As this process continues, the emotional force of the taboo, its force as a general deterrent, is eroded.[98]

Additionally, modern incest statutes are undoubtedly both under and over inclusive.[99] They are underinclusive because often times incest laws do not apply to parent/adopted child relationships, stepparent relationships, to non-family-member caretakers, or to forms of abuse not involving sexual relations: they are arguably overinclusive because they prohibit sexual relations between fully consenting adults and between fully consenting minors engaging in sexual relations (which may not "raise the specter of child exploitation in the way that relations between adults and children do").[100] As one author summarized quite rightly: "[W]hen incest sanctions are applied to private conduct of consenting adults, there is no legitimate state interest at stake and, therefore, no legitimate state interest is furthered."[101] This can only give ammunition to those that would seek to overturn incest laws as unconstitutional because they are a rather "crude form of regulation."[102]

Finally, let us circle back to what might be the best argument against *Lawrence*-based constitutional protection for incest in this case: The fact that the actors have affirmatively asked for, and been granted, affirmative state action in the form of the adoption certificate. Like the marriage certificate very definitely not at issue in *Lawrence*, the state's approval of the adoption perhaps gives the state some say over the actions of the parties. Much has been written about this point vis-à-vis same-sex marriage licenses (and the potential lack of *Lawrence* protection because of the state action involved).[103] This same line of argument will undoubtedly be employed when the sexual actions of adopted parties ripen into a criminal complaint.

---

98 Regan, *supra* note 58, at 1526 (citing Carl E. Schneider, *State-Interest Analysis in Fourteenth Amendment "Privacy" Law: An Essay on the Constitutionalization of Social Issues*, 51 Law & Contemp. Probs. 79, 98 (1988)).

99 Regan, *supra* note 58, at 1525.

100 *Id.*; *see also* Bratt, *supra* note 62, at 290-91.

101 *Id.* at 293.

102 Regan, *supra* note 58, at 1525.

103 *See* Dubler, *supra* note 95, at 760 ("[T]he relationship between Lawrence and Garner did 'not involve whether the government must give formal recognition to any relationship that homosexual persons seek to enter.' Lawrence and Garner, in other words, never sought to formalize their relationship as a marriage." (quoting Lawrence v. Texas,

The counterargument in our very specific case is that the parties are not asking the government for anything because, by definition, the adoption has already been approved if incest charges have been brought. The defendants—post-adoption at this point—are simply asking for what John Geddes Lawrence and Tyron Garner were asking for: the right to be left alone in their own home. The state, in fact, might well be said to have sanctioned the whole deal when it approved the adoption, assuming the entity making the decision knew of the sexual relationship.

Who wins? Who knows? Supreme Court Justices are, in the minds of many, quite uncomfortable and unpredictable when adjudicating cases involving sexual issues. It seems to me that, on balance, the stronger legal arguments favor constitutional protection against criminalization of sexual relations with one's adopted adult lover where no prior parent–child relationship ever existed, i.e., *Lawrence* protection for this non-core behavior. I suspect that with the right set of facts, the right proponents, and a Court that takes *Lawrence* at its word, incest laws as they relate to adult adoption of lovers will fall, and fall relatively soon.

My view is that incest statutes may survive a facial attack under *Lawrence*, but should fall in a challenge as-applied to the non-core incest scenarios addressed in this chapter. States wishing to avoid such a showdown loss ("red" states?) might adopt an Ohio-like statute allowing an individual simply to designate an heir, thereby relieving much of the incentive for adults to adopt other adults.

This whole mess, of course, can be easily remedied by state legislatures through the removal of sexual relations between a parent and his or her adopted adult "child" from the definition of incest if no true parent/child relationship was ever present. From a policy perspective, there is absolutely no rational policy argument—none at all—for criminalizing this category of non-core behavior. I would hope that jurisdictions will revisit their often-ancient incest laws to correct this obvious flaw. No incest: No need for *Lawrence* protection.

Conclusion

The battle between the state, blood relatives of a decedent and a decedent's desire to leave assets to an adopted spouse or lover is a large, ever-increasing property-rights issue that has the potential to boil over at any time. Dead hand control over property is something that individuals have yearned for since ancient times. In general, most Americans are free to leave their property to whomever they desire. In most states, though, same-sex couples are not. The public—through state and federal statutes and through state jury biases—have made the seemingly-simple

539 U.S. 558, 578 (2003))); *see also* Meyer, *supra* note 27, at 891-92 ("[A] privacy claim to formal recognition by the state—in the form of a marriage license, for example—would represent something fundamentally different: a claim on government not to get out of the way, but rather to involve itself by lending its affirmative assistance in fulfilling a couple's relational ambitions.").

act of getting property from the hand of A to the hand of B an extremely difficult task. To me, it is a sad commentary that certain groups in our society believe they must resort to the quite extreme step of adopting their lover to overcome these very real public obstacles to their private right to alienate property.

There is, of course, at least one good way of addressing these issues short of adoption, short of incest, and short of *Lawrence*. Perhaps the simplest and best way is what Ohio has done: allowing an individual to designate an heir. Absent that or widespread adoption of same-sex marriage, this adult adoption technique, with its accompanying property, criminal and constitutional issues, will be with us for the foreseeable future.

Acknowledgement

The author has a J.D. and LL.M. in Taxation from the Georgetown University Law Center, two Master of Science degrees from the Massachusetts Institute of Technology, and a Bachelor of Science degree from Mississippi State University.

The author wishes to thank Dr. Keith J. Bybee of the Maxwell School of Citizenship and Public Affairs and the College of Law at Syracuse University, and The Honorable Morris Sheppard Arnold of the U.S. Court of Appeals for the Eighth Circuit, both of whom provided valuable editorial assistance in the preparation of this chapter. Finally, the author could not have completed this chapter without an incredible team of research assistants over the last couple of years, including Lee Miller, Ryan Tougias, and Jaime Hunsicker.

Table of Cases

333 East 53rd Street Associates v. Mann, 503 N.Y.S.2d 752 (N.Y. App. Div. 1986)
A. & B. Auto Stores of Jones St., Inc. v. City of Newark, 248 A.2d 258(N.J. Super. Ct. Law Div. 1968)
Abraham v. City of Woburn, 408 N.E.2d 664 (Mass. App. Ct. 1980), rev'd by 421 N.E.2d 1206 (Mass. 1981)
Anderson v. Abbott, 321 U.S. 349 (1944)
Associated Provincial Picture Houses v. Wednesbury Corporation [1948] 1 K.B. 223 (Eng.)
Baker v. Raymond Int'l, 656 F.2d 173, 179 (5th Cir. 1981), cert. denied, 456 U.S. 983 (1982)
Beard v. State, No. M200402227CCAR3PC, 2005 WL 1334378, at *2 (Tenn. Crim. App. June 7, 2005)
Berman v. Parker, 348 U.S. 26 (1954)
Blakeman v. City of Wichita, 144 P. 816 (Kan. 1914)
Blecic v. Croatia, App. No. 59532/00, 41 Eur. H.R. Rep. 185 (2004)
Brown v. Bd. of Educ. of Topeka, 347 U.S. 483 (1954)
Buckley v. UK, App. No. 203848/92, 23 Eur. H.R. Rep. 101 (1997)
Butte Miners' Union v. City of Butte, 194 P. 149 (Mont. 1920)
Central Sunderland Housing Company Ltd v. Wilson, [2002] EWCA (Civ) 04 (Eng.)
Century 21 Real Estate Corp. v. LendingTree, Inc., 425 F.3d 211 (3d Cir. 2005)
Champion Spark Plug Co. v. Sanders, 331 U.S. 125 (1947)
Chapman v. U. K., 33 Eur. H.R. Rep. 399, 427 (2001)
City of Baltimore v. Blibaum, 374 A.2d 1152 (Md. 1977)
City of Chicago v. Frank Sturges, 222 U.S. 313 (1911)
Clark v. Inhabitants of the Hundred of Blything, [1823] 107 Eng. Rep. 378 (K.B.)
Clow v. Woods, 5 Serg. & Rawle 275 (Pa. 1819)
Cohen v. U.S., 214 F. 23 (9th Cir. 1914)
Connors v. U.K., App. No 66746/01, Eur. Ct. H.R. (2004), *available at* http://cmiskp.echr.coe.int/tkp197/view.asp?action=html&documentId=699671&portal=hbkm&source=externalbydocnumber&table=F69A27FD8FB86142BF01C1166DEA398649
Coon v. Joseph, 237 Cal. Rptr. 873 (Cal. Ct. App. 1987)
Council of Civil Service Unions v. Minister for the Civil Service, [1985] A.C. 374 (appeal taken from Eng.)
County of Allegheny v. Gibson's Son & Co., 90 Pa. 397 (Pa. 1879)
Davis v. Turner, 45 Va. (4 Gratt.) 422 (Va. 1848)

Di Palma v. U.K., 10 Eur. H.R. Rep. 159 (1986)
District Intown Properties v. District of Columbia, 198 F.3d 874 (D.C. Cir. 1999)
Doherty v. Birmingham City Council, [2008] UKHL 57 (appeal taken from Eng.)
Dred Scott v. Sandford, 60 U.S. 393 (1856)
Edmonson v. State, 464 S.E.2d 839 (Ga. Ct. App. 1995)
Entick v. Carrington, (1765) 95 Eng. Rep. 807 (K.B.)
Estate of Rosenbaum v. City of New York, 975 F. Supp. 206 (E.D.N.Y. 1997)
Ex parte Daly, [2001] 2 W.L.R. 1622 (Eng.)
Fauvia v. City of New Orleans, 20 La. Ann. 410 (La. 1868)
Finklestein v. City of New York, 47 N.Y.S.2d 156 (N.Y. Supp. 1944)
Gates v. Superior Court, 38 Cal. Rptr. 2d 489 (Cal. Ct. App. 1995)
Gerber v. Grabel, 16 Ill. 217 (Ill. 1854)
Gillow v. U.K., 109 Eur. Ct. H.R. (ser. A) §55 (1986)
Goldman v. Forcier, 27 A.2d 340 (R.I. 1942)
Hammersmith and Fulham London Borough Council v. Monk, [1992] 1 A.C. 478 (appeal taken from Eng.)
Hawaii Housing Auth. v. Midkiff, 467 U.S. 229 (1984)
Hoy v. Sterrett, 2 Watts 327 (Pa. 1837)
Huang v. Secretary of State for the Home Department [2007] UKHL 11 (appeal taken from EWCA (Civ)) (U.K.)
In re Adoption of Brundage, 134 N.Y.S.2d 703 (N.Y. Sup. Ct. 1954), aff'd 143 N.Y.S.2d 611 (N.Y. App. Div. 1955), appeal denied, 144 N.Y.S.2d 921 (N.Y. App. Div. 1955)
In re Adoption of Robert Paul P., 63 N.Y.2d 233 (N.Y. 1984)
In re Adoption of Swanson, 623 A.2d 1095 (Del. 1993)
In re Adult Anonymous II, 88 A.D.2d 30 (N.Y. App. Div. 1982)
In re Jones, 411 A.2d 910 (R.I. 1980)
Jacque v. Steenberg Homes, Inc., 563 N.W.2d 154 (Wis. 1997)
James and Others v. U.K., 8 Eur. H.R. Rep. 123 (1986)
Kay v. Lambeth LBC; Price v. Leeds CC, [2006] UKHL 10 (appeal taken from EWCA (Civ))(U.K.)
Keats v. Hugo, 115 Mass. 204 (Mass. 1874)
Kelo v. City of New London, 545 U.S. 469 (2005)
Kennedy v. City of Chicago, 91 N.E.2d 138 (Ill. App. Ct. 1950)
Klein v. Gehrung, 25 Tex. 232 (Tex. 1860)
Lawrence v. Texas, 539 U.S. 558 (2003)
Lochner v. New York, 198 U.S. 45 (1905)
London Borough of Harrow v. Qazi, [2003] UKHL 43 (appeal taken from Eng.)
Lucas v. South Carolina Coastal Council, 505 U.S. 1003 (1992)
Maison v. Sainsbury, 99 Eng. Rep. 538 (K.B. 1782)
Malone v. Commissioner of Police for the Metropolis (no. 2), [1979] 2 All E.R. 620 (Eng.)
Marckx v. Belgium, App. No. 6833/74, 2 Eur. H.R. Rep. 330 (1979)
Marzari v. Italy, App. No. 36448/97, 28 Eur. H.R. Rep. Comm'n Dec. 175 (1999)

Matter of Adoption of Chaney, 887 P.2d 1061 (Idaho 1995)
Matthews v. Bay Head Improvement Ass'n, 471 A.2d 355 (N.J. 1984)
McCann v. U.K., App. No. 19909/04, 21 Eur. Ct. H.R. 97 (2008)
Miller v. Elliot, 17 F. Cas. 315 (C.C.D. D.C. 1839)
Mitchell v. Mayor and City Council of Rome, 49 Ga. 19 (Ga. 1873)
Muth v. Frank, 412 F.3d 808 (2005), cert. denied, Muth v. Frank, 546 U.S. 988 (2005)
O'Rourke v. U. K., App. No. 39022/97, Eur. Ct. H.R. 889 (2001)
P. v. U.K., Application No 14751/89, 67 Eur. Comm'n H.R. Dec. & Rep. 264 (1990)
Palmer v. Concord, 48 N.H. 211 (N.H. 1868)
Pappas v. U.S., 241 F. 665 (9th Cir. 1917)
Parents Involved in Community Schools v. Seattle School Dist. No. 1, 551 U.S. 701 (2007)
Parker & Edgarton v. Foote, 19 Wend. 309, 316 (N.Y. 1838)
Patel v. Pirabakaran, [2006] EWCA (Civ) 685 (Eng.)
Penn Central Transportation Co. v. City of New York, 438 U.S. 104 (1978)
Peterson v. San Francisco Cmty. Coll. Dist., 685 P.2d 1193 (Cal. 1984)
Price & Ors v. Leeds City Council, [2005] EWCA (Civ) 289 (Eng.)
PruneYard Shopping Center v. Robins, 447 U.S. 74 (1980)
Quanta Computer, Inc. v. LG Elecs., Inc., 553 U.S. 617 (2008)
R (McLellan) v. Bracknell Forest Borough Council, [2001] All E.R. 214 (Eng.)
R v. Ministry of Defence, Ex parte Smith, [1996] Q.B. 517 (Eng.)
Raleigh Ave. Beach Ass'n v. Atlantis Beach Club, Inc., 879 A.2d 112 (N.J. 2005)
Ratcliffe v. Eden, (1776) 98 Eng. Rep. 1200 (K.B.)
Regina v. Secretary of State for the Home Department, Ex parte Daly, [2001] 2 W.L.R. 1622
Reigate and Banstead Borough Council v. Benfield, [2001] EWCA (Civ) 1510 (Eng.)
San Remo Hotel, L.P. v. City and County of San Francisco, 41 P.3d 87 (Cal. 2002)
Semayne's Case, (1604) 77 Eng. Rep. 194 (K.B.); 5 Co. Rep. 91a
Sheffield City Council v. Smart, [2002] EWCA (Civ) 04 (Eng.)
Slaton v. City of Chicago, 130 N.E.2d 205 (Ill. App. Ct. 1955)
Southampton Port Health Authority v. Seahawk Marine Foods Ltd., [2002] EWCA (Civ) 54 (Eng.)
Spring Valley Coal Co. v. City of Spring Valley, 65 Ill. App. 571 (Ill. App. Ct. 1895)
State v. Buck, 757 P.2d 861(Or. Ct. App. 1988)
State v. Carothers, 594 N.W.2d 897 (Minn. 1999)
State v. Freeman, 801 N.E.2d 906 (Ohio Ct. App. 2003)
State v. George B., 785 A.2d 573 (Conn. 2001)
State v. Leslie McQuiston, 922 P.2d 519 (Mont. 1996), overruled on other grounds by State v. Herman, 188 P.3d 978 (Mont. 2008)

State v. Lowe, No. 2004 CA00292, 2005 WL 1983964 (Ohio Ct. App. Aug. 15, 2005)
State v. McQuiston, 922 P.2d 519 (Mont. 1996)
State v. Rogers, 133 S.E.2d 1 (N.C. 1963)
State v. Shack, 277 A.2d 369 (N.J. 1971)
Stefan v. General Medical Council, [1999] 1 W.L.R. 1293 (Lord Clyde) (Eng.)
Sturtevant & Keep v. Ballard, 9 Johns. Ch. 337 (N.Y. 1812)
The Queen (on the application of Susan Weaver) v. London & Quadrant Housing Trust, [2008] EWHC (Admin) 1377 (Eng.)
Underhill v. Manchester, 45 N.H. 214 (N.H. 1864)
United States v. Jon-T Chems., Inc., 768 F.2d 686 (5th Cir. 1985)
Ure v. U.K., App. No. 28027/95, Eur. H.R. Rep. (1996) (unreported), *available at* http://cmiskp.echr.coe.int/tkp197/view.asp?action=html&documentId=667561&portal=hbkm&source=externalbydocnumber&table=F69A27FD8FB86142BF01C1166DEA398649
Village of Euclid v. Ambler Realty Co., 272 U.S. 365 (1926)
Warden v. City of Wichita, 658 P.2d 1043 (Kan. 1983)
Washburn v. Pima County, 81 P.3d. 1030 (Ariz. Ct. App. 2003)
Whitt v. U.S., 261 F.2d 907 (6th Cir. 1959)
Wood v. U.K., App. No. 32540/96, 24 Eur. H.R. Rep. CD 69 (1997)
Yalenezian v. City of Boston, 131 N.E. 220 (Mass. 1921)
YL v. Birmingham City Council, [2007] UKHL 27 (appeal taken from Eng.)
Youngstown Sheet & Tube Co. v. Sawyer, 343 U.S. 579 (1952)

Table of Statutes and Legislative Material

1 Geo., c. 5, § 1 (1714)
1 Geo., stat. 2, c. 5 (1714)
1 U.S.C. § 7 (2008)
110 P.L. 289 (2008)
12 C.F.R. pt. 3, app. A (2009)
12 U.S.C.A. §§ 1701, 1709, 1715z-23(m) (2009)
12 U.S.C.A. §§ 1455, 4501–4526, 1719
12 USCS § 2901 (2008)
12 USCS §§ 4701-4718 (2008)
17 U.S.C. § 107 (2010)
17 U.S.C. § 109 (2010)
18 Pa.Cons. Stat.§ 4302 (2007)
18 U.S.C. § 2421
1835 Md. Laws 137
1839 Mass. Acts 54
1841 Pa. Laws 415
1854 N.H. Laws 1519
1855 La. Acts 206
1855 N.Y. Laws 428
1856 Ky. Acts 594
1858 Mo. Laws 25
1862 Kan. Sess. Laws 77
1863 Wis. Laws 211
1864 N.J. Laws 237
1867 Cal. Stat. 418
1871 Ala. Acts 74
1871 Me. Laws 207
1871 S.C. Acts 561
1875 Ark. Acts 12
1879 N.Y. Laws ch. 504, § 3, amended by 1901 N.Y. Laws ch. 334
1887 Ill. Laws 573.
26 USCS § 42 (2009)
27 Eliz., c. 13, §§ 1, 3, 5 (1585) (Eng.)
28 U.S.C. § 1738C (2008)
29 U.S.C. §§ 701 et seq. (2006)
42 U.S.C. §§ 12131-12181 (2006)
42 U.S.C. §§ 12181-12213 (2006)

42 U.S.C. §§ 4151- 4157 (2006)
71 Del. Laws, 902 (1999)
720 Ill. Comp. Stat. 5/11-11(2) (2007)
Act of July 5, 1989, ch. 214, 1989 R.I. Acts & Resolves 563
Ala. Code 1975 § 13A-13-3(a)(1) (2007)
American Recovery and Reinvestment Act of 2009, Pub. L. No. 111-5, 123 Stat. 115 (2009)
Americans with Disabilities Act of 1990
Architectural Barriers Act of 1968
Ariz. Rev. Stat. Ann. § 14-8101 (2007), amended by 2008 Ariz. Legis. Serv. Ch. 162 (2008)
Ark. Code Ann. § 5-26-202(a)(2) (2007)
Cal. Fam. Code § 9320(a) (2007)
Cal. Gov't Code § 845 (West 2008)
Cal. Law Revision Comm'n, Recommendations Relating to Sovereign Immunity 818 (1963) available at http://www.clrc.ca.gov/pub/Printed-Reports/Pub043.pdf
Cal. Pol. Code §§ 4452-56 (Deering 1931)
Caravan Sites Act 1968
Colo. Rev. Stat. § 18-6-301(1) (2007)
Con. Gen. Stat. 530.020 (2007)
Conn. Gen. Stat. § 514 (1930)
Conn. Gen. Stat. § 7-108 (1999)
D.C. Code § 42-3402.02 (2010)
D.C. Code § 6-226 (2010)
D.C. Code §29-901 et seq. (2010)
D.C. Code §29-918
D.C. Code §42-2801 (1C) (2010)
D.C. Code §42-2802 et seq. (2010)
D.C. Code §42-3402.02 et seq. (2010)
D.C. Code §42-3404.02 (2010)
D.C. Code §42-3404.03, §42-3404.08 (2006)
D.C. Code §42-3404.11 (2010)
D.C. Mun. Regs. tit. 14 § 4700 et seq. (2010)
Del. Code Ann. 11 § 766(b) (2007)
Exec. Order. No. 13217, June 18, 2001
Fair Housing Act, 42 U.S.C. § 3601 et seq. (2008)
Fair Housing Amendments Act of 1988
Fla. Stat. Ann. § 63.042(3) (2007)
Fla. Stat. Ann. § 768.28 (2005)
Fla. Stat. Ann. § 776.013(4) (West Supp. 2008)
Ga. Code Ann. § 19-8-19(a) (2)
Guam Code Ann. 9 § 31.15 (2007)

Historic Landmark and Historic District Protection Act, D.C. Code § 6 – 1101, et seq.
Housing and Economic Recovery Act ('HERA') Pub. L. No. 110-289, 122 Stat. 2654 (2008).
Housing Production Trust Fund, D.C. Code § 42-2802 (2001)
Ill. Rev. Stat. 38, §§ 512-14 (Smith-Hurd 1935)
Inclusive Home Design Act of 2007, H.R. 4202, 110th Cong. (2007-08)
Iowa Code Ann. § 670.2 (1998)
Kan. Rev. Stat. §§ 201-02 (1923)
Ky. Rev. Stat. Ann. § 411.100 (Banks-Baldwin 2003)
Ky. Rev. Stat. Ann. § 530.020(1) (2007)
Ky. Stat. § 8 (Carroll 1930)
La. Gen. Stat. § 5369 (Dart 1932)
Marriage (Prohibited Degrees of Relationship) Act 1986, § 1, reprinted in 27 Halsbury's Statutes of England 562 (4th ed. 1987)
Mass. Gen. Laws Ann. ch 210, § 1 (2007)
Mass. Gen. Laws Ann. ch. 269, § 8 (2000)
Mass. Gen. Laws ch. 269, § 8 (1932)
Md. Code Ann. Art. 82, §§ 1-3 (1924)
Me. Rev. Stat. 130, § 20 (1930)
Minn. Stat. §§ 10036-38 (1927)
Miss. Code Ann. § 11-46-9(1)(c) (2002)
Miss. Code Ann. §§ 97-29-5, 93-1-1 (2007)
Mo. Rev. Stat. § 8672 (1919)
Mo. Rev. Stat. 568.020.1(1) (2007)
Mont. Code Ann. § 45-5-507(1) (2007)
Mont. Rev. Code § 5086 (1935)
N.C. Gen. Stat. § 3945 (1939)
N.C. Gen. Stat. Ann. § 14-178(a) (ii) (2007)
N.H. Pub. Laws 42, §§ 41-42 (1926)
N.H. Rev. Stat. Ann. § 639:2(I) (2007)
N.J. Rev. Stat. 979, §§ 5-9 (1877)
N.J. Stat. Ann. § 2A:22-2 (2000)
N.J. Stat. Ann. § 2A:48-1 (West 2000)
N.J. Stat. Ann. § 2C: 14-2 (West 2005)
N.Y. Dom. Rel. Law § 110 (McKinney 2008)
N.Y. Gen. Mun. Laws 685, § 21 (1892)
Neb. Comp. Stat. §§ 602-06 (1929)
Neb. Rev. Stat. § 43-101 (2007)
Nev. Rev. Stat. § 127.190 (2007)
New York City Rent, Eviction and Rehabilitation Regulations, 9 NYCRR § 2104.6[d]
Ohio Rev. Code Ann. § 2907.03(5) (2007)
Ohio Rev. Code Ann. § 3107.02

Ohio Rev. Code Ann. § 3107.02 (2006
Ohio Rev. Code Ann. § 3761.03 (West 2003)
Ohio Rev. Code Ann. §§ 6280-88 (Baldwin 1934)
Or. Rev. Stat. §§ 163.505(2), 163.505(2) (2007)
P.R. Laws Ann. tit. 31, § 531(4) (2007)
Pa. Stat. Ann. tit. 16, §§ 3921-25, tit. 18, §§ 339-40 (Purdon 1936)
R.I. Gen. Laws § 45-15-13 (2002)
R.I. Gen. Laws § 6055 (1923)
Rehabilitation Act of 1973 § 504
Rent Control Reform Amendment Act of 2006, D.C. Law 16-145 (2008)
Rental Housing Conversion and Sale Act of 1980, D.C. Code Ann §42-3404.01 et seq. (2010)
Report of and Testimony Taken Before the Joint Committee of the Senate and House of Delegates (1836)
Report of the Nat'l Advisory Comm'n on Civil Disorders (1968)
Riot (Damages) Act of 1886, 49 & 50 Vict., c. 38 (1886)
S.C. Code §§ 1384-89, 3041 (1932)
S.C. Code Ann. § 16-5-70 (Law Co-op 2002)
Statute of Winchester, 1285, 13 Edw., c. 1, 2 (Engl.)
Tenant Opportunity to Purchase Act D.C. Code §42-3404.02 (2001)
Tenn. Code. Ann. § 39-15-302 (2007)
Tex. Penal Code Ann. § 25.02(a)(1) (2007)
The Code of Hammurabi (c. 1750 B.C.)
The Mann Act, 18 U.S.C. § 2421 (2008)
The Statute of Westminster the Second (*De Donis Conditionalibus*) (1285) (c. 1), *availableat*http://www.statutelaw.gov.uk/content.aspx?activeTextDocId=1517444
Unif. Adoption Act § 3 (1994)
Unif. Adoption Act, § 3(4) (Official Commentary)
Utah Code Ann. 1953 § 76-7-102(1) (2007)
Utah Rev. Stat. Ann. 104, § 2(26) (1933)
Vt. Stat. Ann. tit. 12, § 5601 (2003)
W. Va. Code § 61-8-12(a) (2007)
W. Va. Code Ann. § 6038 (Michie 1932)
W. Va. Code Ann. § 61-6-12 (Michie 2003)
Will. 1, c. 84, § 8 (Eng.)
Wis. Stat. § 66.07 (1931)
Wis. Stat. Ann. § 893.81 (2003)
Wyo. Stat. Ann. § 6-4-402(a)(i) (2007)

Bibliography

1A. Am. Jur. 2d Incest § 1 (2007)

2 Canute, c. 29 (1027), reprinted in A.J. Robertson, Laws of the Kings of England from Edmund to Henry I 175-219 (A.J. Robertson ed., A.J. Robertson trans., 1925)

41 Am Jur. 2d Incest § 11

94 Cornell L. Rev. (2008-09) (Special Issue on Property and Obligations)

A Fourth Way? Privatization, Property, and the Emergence of New Market Economies (Gregory S. Alexander & Graznya Skapska eds., 1994)

Ackerman, Bruce A., Private Property and the Constitution (1977); Ackerman, Bruce, We The People: Foundations (1991); Ackerman, Bruce, We The People: Transformations (1998)

Affordable Housing and Public-Private Partnerships (Nestor M. Davidson & Robin Paul Malloy eds., 2009)

Ahern, Raymond J., Cong. Research Serv., The Global Economic Downturn and Protectionism (2009)

Alexander, Frank S., *Property and Christian Theology*, *in* Christianity and Law (John White & Frank S. Alexander eds., 2008)

Alexander, Gregory S., *The Social-Obligation Norm in American Property Law*, 94 Cornell L. Rev. 745 (2009); Alexander, Gregory S., Commodity & Propriety: Competing Visions of Property in American Legal Thought 1776-1990 (1997)

Alexander, Gregory S., & Eduardo M. Peñalver, *Properties of Community*, 10 Theoretical Inquiries L. 127 (2009)

Alexander, Gregory S. et al., *A Statement of Progressive Property*, 94 Cornell L. Rev. 743, 743–44 (2009)

Anderson, Charles D. et al., *Deconstructing a Mortgage Meltdown: A Methodology for Decomposing Underwriting Quality* (May 29, 2009) (unpublished working paper), available at http://ssrn.com/abstract=1411782

Aquinas, Thomas, The Summa Theologica, II –II Q 55, art. 1, 1476 (1947)

Arai-Takahashi, Y., The Margin of Appreciation Doctrine and the Principle of Proportionality in the Jurisprudence of the European Convention on Human Rights (2002)

Ariely, Dan, Predictably Irrational: The Hidden Forces that Shape our Decisions (2008), (rev. ed. 2009)

Aristotle, The Politics (Ernest Barker trans., 1962)

Armour, John & Whincop, Michael J., *The Proprietary Foundations of Corporate Law*, 27 Oxford J. Legal Stud. 429 (2007)

Arrunada, Benito & Andonova, Veneta, *Common Law and Civil Law as Pro-Market Adaptations*, 26 Wash. U. J.L. & Pub. Pol'y 81 (2008)

Babcock, Linda & Loewenstein, George, *Explaining Bargaining Impasse: Self-Serving Biases*, 11 J. Econ. Perspectives 109 (1997)

Baird, Douglas G. & Jackson, Thomas H., Security Interests in Personal Property (2d ed. 1987)

Baker, J.H., An Introduction to English Legal History (3d ed. 1990)

Balkin, Jack M. & Siegel, Reva B., *Principles, Practices, and Social Movements*, 154 U. Pa. L. Rev. 927 (2006)

Barros, D. Benjamin, *Home as a Legal Concept*, 46 Santa Clara L. Rev. 255 (2006)

Barth, James R., et al., The Rise and Fall of the U.S. Mortgage and Credit Markets: A Comprehensive Analysis of the Market Meltdown (2009)

Beard, Charles A., An Economic Interpretation of the Constitution of the United States (1913)

Bebchuk, Lucian A., *Buying Troubled Ass*ets, 26 Yale J. on Reg. 343 (2009)

Bell, Abraham & Parchomovsky, Gideon, *A Theory of Property*, 90 Cornell L. Rev. 531 (2005)

Bell, Daniel A., *Confucian Constraints on Property Rights*, *in* Confucianism for the Modern World (Daniel A. Bell and Hahm Chaibong eds, 2003)

Bergesen, Albert, *Race Riots of 1967: An Analysis of Police Violence in Detroit and Newark*, 12 J. Black Studies 261-74 (1982)

Bernard, L.L., *Mob*, *in* 10 Encyclopaedia of the Social Sciences 553

Bickford-Smith, Stephen & Francis, Andrew, Rights of Light: the Modern Law (2d ed. 2007)

Bienen, Leigh B., *Defining Incest*, 92 Nw. U. L. Rev. 1501 (1998)

Blackstone, William, Commentaries on the Laws of England (facsimile ed. 1979) (1765-69)

Blumer, Herbert, *Collective Behavior*, *in* New Outline of the Principles of Sociology (Alfred McClung Lee ed., 1951)

Boehm, Thomas, P. et al., *Housing and Wealth Accumulation: Intergenerational Impacts, Low Income Homeownership*, *in* Examining the Unexamined Goal (Nicolas P. Retsinas & Eric S. Belsky eds., 2002)

Brace, Laura, The Politics of Property: Labour, Freedom and Belonging (Palgrave 2004)

Bratt, Carolyn S., *Incest Statutes and the Fundamental Right of Marriage: Is Oedipus Free to Marry?*, 18 Fam. L.Q. 257 (1984)

Brendan J. Hammer, *Tainted Love: What the Seventh Circuit Got Wrong in Muth v. Frank*, 56 DePaul L. Rev. 1065 (2007)

Bronin, Sara C., *Modern Lights*, 80 Colo. L. R. 101 (forthcoming November 2009)

Brosnan, Sara, et al., *Endowment Effects in Chimpanzees*, 17 Current Biology 1704 (2007)

Brown, Laura Elizabeth, *Comment, Regulating the Marrying Kind: The Constitutionality of Federal Regulation of Polygamy Under the Mann Act*, 39 McGeorge L. Rev. 267 (2008)

Bruchey, Stuart, *The Impact of Concern for Security of Property Rights on the Legal System of the Early American Republic*, 1980 Wisc. L. Rev. 1135

Burke, Marcilynn A., *Much Ado About Nothing: Kelo v. City Of New London, Babbit v. Sweet Home, and Other Tales From the Supreme Court*, 75 U. Cin. L. Rev. 663 (2006)

Burnham, Walter Dean, *Constitutional Moments and Punctuated Equilibria: A Political Scientist Confronts Bruce Ackerman's We The People*, 108 Yale L.J. 2237 (1999)

Byrne, J. Peter, *Hallowed Ground: The Gettysburg Battlefield in Historic Preservation Law*, 22 Tul. Envtl. L.J. 203 (2008); Byrne, J. Peter, *Ten Arguments for the Abolition of the Regulatory Takings Doctrine*, 22 Ecology L.Q. 89 (1995)

Byrne, J. Peter & Michael Diamond, *Affordable Housing, Land Tenure, and Urban Policy: The Matrix Revealed*, 34 Fordham Urb. L.J. 527 (2007)

Cahill, Courtney Megan, *Same-Sex Marriage, Slippery Slope Rhetoric, and the Politics of Disgust: A Critical Perspective on Contemporary Family Discourse and the Incest Taboo*, 99 Nw. U. L. Rev. 1543 (2005)

Cahn, Naomi, *Perfect Substitutes or the Real Thing?*, 52 Duke L.J. 1077 (2003)

Cannon, Lou, Official Negligence: How Rodney King and the Riots Changed Los Angeles and the LAPD (1997)

Capoccia, Giovanni & Keleman, R. Daniel, *The Study of Critical Junctures: Theory, Narrative, and Counterfactuals in Historical Institutionalism*, 59 World Pol. 341 (2007)

Carlson, Paul H., The Plains Indians (1998)

Carter, Stephen L., *Does It Matter Whether Intellectual Property Is Property?*, 68 Chi-Kent L. Rev. 715 (1993)

Cass, Ronald A., *Patent Remedy*, Wall St. J., Aug. 28, 2007, *available at* http://online.wsj.com/article/SB118824874547610202.html

Chan, Joseph, *Giving Priority to the Worst Off: A Confucian Perspective on Social Welfare*, *in* Confucianism for the Modern World (Daniel A. Bell & Hahm Chaibong eds., 2003)

Chase, Adam, *Tax Planning for Same-Sex Couples*, 72 Denv. U. L. Rev. 359 (1995)

Chiapetta, Vincent, *The (Practical) Meaning of Property*, 46 Willamette L. Rev. 297 (2010)

Chicago Comm'n on Race Relations, The Negro in Chicago (1922)

Cleere, Scott R., *Intellectual Property: The Capital of the Information Age*, Advocate, June 2005, at 10

Coase, Ronald, *The Problem of Social Cost*, 3 J. L. & Econ. 1 (Oct. 1960)

Cohen, Felix S., *Dialogue on Private Property*, 9 Rutgers L. Rev. 357 (1954)

Cohen, Lizabeth, A Consumers' Republic: The Politics of Mass Consumption in Postwar America (2003)

Cohen, Morris Raphael, *Property and Sovereignty*, 13 Cornell L. Q. 8 (1927)

Cooter, Robert & Ulen, Thomas, Law and Economics (1988)

Craig, P., Administrative Law (6th ed. 2008)

Critchley, T.A., A History of Police in England and Wales (2d ed. 1972)
Cronon, William, Changes in the Land: Indians, Colonists and the Ecology of New England (1983)
Cropsey, Joseph, *Karl Marx, in* Leo Strauss & Joseph Cropsey, History of Political Philosophy (3rd ed. 1987)
Cummings, Scott L. & Deborah L. Rhode, *Public Interest Litigation: Insights from Theory and Practice*, 36 Fordham Urb. L.J. 603 (2009)
Dana, David A., *The Foreclosure Crisis and the Anti-Fragmentation Principle in State Property Law*, U. Chi. L. Rev. (forthcoming 2010), available at http://ssrn.com/abstract=1415006
Dana, David A., & Thomas W. Merrill, Property: Takings 36 (2002)
Davidson, Nestor, *Property and Relative Status*, 107 Mich. L. Rev. 757 (2009)
de Soto, Hernando, The Mystery of Capital: Why Capitalism Triumphs in the West and Fails Everywhere Else (2000)
Dearborn, Lynne, *Homeownership: the Problematics of Ideals and Realities,* 16 J. Affordable Hsg & Cmty. Devt. L. 40 (2006)
Demsetz, Harold, *Toward a Theory of Property Rights*, 79 Am. Econ. Rev. Proc. 347 (1967)
Diamond, Michael, *Affordable Housing and the Conflict of Competing Goods: A Policy Dilemma, in* Affordable Housing and Public Private Partnerships (Nestor M. Davidson & Robin Paul Malloy eds., 2009); Diamond, Michael, *The Meaning and Nature of Property: Homeownership and Shared Equity in the Context of Poverty*, 29 St Louis University Public Law Review 85 (2009)
Diamond, Michael & O'Toole, Aaron, *Leaders, Followers, and Free Riders: The Community Lawyer's Dilemma When Representing Non-Democratic Client Organizations*, 31 Fordham Urb. L.J. 481 (2004)
DiMartino, Danielle & Duca, John V., *The Rise and Fall of Subprime Mortgages*, Econ. Letter (Fed. Reserve Bank of Dallas, Dallas, Tex.), Nov. 2007, at 1
Donaldson, Russell G., *Annotation, Marital or Sexual Relationship Between Parties as Affecting Right to Adopt*, 42 A.L.R.4th 776, § 2[a] (1985)
Downs, Anthony, An Economic Theory of Democracy (1957)
Dubler, Ariela R., *Immoral Purposes: Marriage and the Genus of Illicit Sex*, 115 Yale L.J. 756 (2006)
Dukeminier, Jesse, et al., Property (6th ed.2006)
Dukeminier, Johanson, Lindgren & Sitkoff, Wills, Trusts, and Estates (7th ed. 2005)
Earnest, Leslie, *Pink Slips Litter Loan Industry: The Turmoil in the Sub-Prime Mortgage Sector Hits Some Workers As Hard As Borrowers*, L.A. Times, Apr. 6, 2007, at C1
Edwards, Susan M., Policing 'Domestic' Violence: Women, the Law and the State (1989)
Ehrlich, J.W., Erlich's Blackstone (1959)
Eisen, Richard C., *The Rental Housing Conversion and Sale Act: A Practitioner's Roadmap to Tenant Ownership*, 2 D.C. L. Rev. 1 (1993)

Eisenberg, Melvin A., *The Conception That the Corporation is a Nexus of Contracts, and the Dual Nature of the Firm*, 24 J. Corp. L. 819 (1999)

Eldridge, Niles & Stephen Jay Gould, *Punctuated Equilibria: An Alternative to Phyletic Gradualism, in* Models in Paleobiology (Thomas J.M. Schopf ed., 1972)

Ely Jr., James W., The Guardian of Every Other Right: A Constitutional History of Property Rights (3d ed. 2008)

Encyclopedia of Crime and Justice (Sanford H. Kadish ed., 1983)

Engel, Kathleen C. & McCoy, Patricia A., *A Tale of Three Markets: The Law and Economics of Predatory Lending*, 80 Tex. L. Rev. 1255, 1261 (2002)

Epstein, Richard A., Supreme Neglect: How To Revive Constitutional Protection For Private Property (2008); Epstein, Richard A., *Blind Justices: the Scandal of* Kelo v. New London, Wall St. J., July 3, 2005, at Opinion; Epstein, Richard A., *Intellectual Property: Old Boundaries and New Frontiers*, 76 Ind. L.J. 803 (2001); Epstein, Richard A., Takings: Private Property and the Power of Eminent Domain (1986)

Fagundes, David, *Property Rhetoric and the Public Domain*, 94 Minn. L. Rev. 652 (2010)

Fairfield, Joshua A.T., *Virtual Property*, 85 B.U. L. Rev. 1047 (2005)

Farnsworth, Ward, *Do Parties to Nuisance Cases Bargain After Judgment? A Glimpse Inside the Cathedral*, 66 U. Chi. L. Rev. 373 (1999)

Fennell, Lee Anne, *Homeownership 2.0*, Nw. U. L. Rev. 1047 (2008); Fennell, Lee Anne, *Taking Eminent Domain Apart*, 2004 Mich. St. L. Rev. 957 (2004)

Fenwick, H., & G. Phillipson, Media Freedom under the Human Rights Act (2006)

Findley, Keith, A. & Michael S. Scott, *The Multiple Dimensions of Tunnel Vision in Criminal Cases*, 2006 Wis. L. Rev. 291 (2006)

Finkel, Norman J., Commonsense Justice: Juror's Notions of the Law (1995)

Fisher, III, William Weston, *Stories About Property*, 94 Mich. L. Rev. 1776 (1996); Fisher, III, William Weston, The Law of the Land: An Intellectual History of American Property Doctrine, 1776-1880 (Oct. 1, 1991) (unpublished doctoral thesis, Harvard University)

Florida Legislation—The Controversy Over Florida's New "Stand Your Ground" Law—Fla. Stat. 776.013 (2005), 33 Fla. St. U. L. Rev. 351, 355 (2005)

Foote, Christopher L., et al., *Subprime Facts: What (We Think) We Know about the Subprime Crisis and What We Don't* (Fed. Reserve of Boston: Pub. Policy Discussion Papers, Paper No. 08-2, 2008), *available at* http://ssrn.com/abstract=1153411

Fowler, Peter N., *Adult Adoption: A "New" Legal Tool for Lesbians and Gay Men*, 14 Golden Gate U. L. Rev. 667 (1984)

Fox, Lorna, Conceptualising Home: Theories, Laws and Policies (2006); Fox, Lorna, *Re-Possessing "Home": A Re-Analysis of Gender, Homeownership and Debtor Default for Feminist Legal Theory*, 14 Wm. & Mary J. Women & L. 423 (2008)

Foy, Angela Chaput, *Adult Adoption and the Elder Population*, 8 Marq. Elder's Advisor 109 (2006)

Friedman, Lawrence M., A History of American Law (1985)

Friedman, Milton, Capitalism and Freedom (1962)

Friedman, Ori, *First Possession: An Assumption Guiding Inferences About Who Owns What*, 15 Psychonomic Bull. & Rev. 290 (2008)

Friedman, Ori & Neary, Karen, *First Possession Beyond the Law: Adults' and Young Children's Intuitions About Ownership*, 83 Tul. L. Rev. 679 (2009); Friedman, Ori & Neary, Karen, *Determining Who Owns What: Do Children Infer Ownership from First Possession?* 107 Cognition 829 (2008)

Gale, Dennis E., Understanding Urban Unrest: From Reverend King to Rodney King (1996)

Garnett, Nicole Stelle, *The Neglected Political Economy of Eminent Domain*, 105 Mich. L. Rev. 101 (2006)

Gigerenzer, G. & D.G. *Goldstein, Reasoning the Fast and Frugal Way: Models of Bounded Rationality*, 103 Psychological Review 650 (1996)

Gilbert, Daniel, Stumbling on Happiness (2005)

Gilmore, Grant, Security Interests in Personal Property (1965)

Girgenti, Richard H., A Report to the Governor on the Disturbances in Crown Heights: An Assessment of the City's Preparedness and Response to Civil Disorder (1993)

Godsil, Rachel D. & Simunovich, David V. *Protecting Status: The Mortgage Crisis, Eminent Domain, and the Ethic of Homeownership*, 77 Fordham L. Rev. 949 (2008)

Goodman, Peter S., *Chilly Review From Experts*, N.Y. Times, Sept. 23, 2008, at A1

Gordon, Colin, *Rethinking the New Deal*, 98 Colum. L. Rev. 2029 (1998)

Gordon, Wendy, *Fair Use as Market Failure*, 82 Colum. L. Rev. 1600 (1982)

Gray, Kevin & Gray, Susan Francis, Elements of Land Law (4th ed. 2005)

Green, Richard K. & Wachter, Susan M., *The American Mortgage in Historical and International Context*, 19 J. Econ. Persp. 93 (2005)

Gremley, W., *Social Control in Cicero*, 3 British J. of Sociology 322 (1952)

Grey, Thomas C., *The Disintegration of Property*, *in* Modern Understandings of Liberty and Property (Richard A. Epstein ed., 2000); Grey, Thomas C., *The Disintegration of Property*, in XXII Nomos: Property (J. Roland Pennock & John W. Chapman eds.,1980)

Grow, Brian et al., *The Home Foreclosure Fiasco: How the Banking Industry is Undermining Efforts to Keep People in Their Houses*, Business Week, Feb. 23, 2009, at 34

Gwynn, Sir Charles W., Imperial Policing (1934)

Hale, Robert L., *Bargaining, Duress, and Economic Liberty*, 43 Colum. L. Rev. 603 (1943)

Harcourt, Bernard E., Neoliberal Penality: The Birth of Natural Orders, The Illusion of Free Markets (2008)

Hardin, Garrett, *The Tragedy of the Commons*, 162 Science 1243 (Dec. 13, 1968)

Hathaway, Oona, Path *Dependence in the Law: The Course and Pattern of Legal Change in a Common Law System*, 86 Iowa L. Rev. 101 (2001)

Hawley, Amos H., The Changing Shape of Metropolitan America (1956)

Hayek, F.A., The Constitution of Liberty (1960)

Heilbroner, Robert L., The Worldly Philosophers (4th ed. 1972)

Heller, Michael A., *The Tragedy of the Anticommons: Property in the Transition from Marx to Markets*, 111 Harv. L. Rev. 621, 622–23 (1998)

Holdsworth, William S., A History of English Law (7th ed. 1966); Holdsworth, William S., An Historical Introduction to the Land Law (1927)

Honoré, A.M., Ownership, in Oxford Essays in Jurisprudence (A.G. Guest ed., 1961)

Hooi, Michael J., *Substantive Due Process: Sex Toys After Lawrence*, 60 Fla. L. Rev. 1065 (2008)

Hook, Jay, *Judgments About the Right to Property from Preschool to Adulthood*, 17 L. & Hum. Behav. 135 (2002)

Hovenkamp, Herbert, *Evolutionary Models in Jurisprudence*, 64 Tex. L. Rev. 645 (1985)

Howell, J., *Land and Human Rights*, 63 Conv. & Prop. Law. (N.S.) 287 (1999); Howell, J., The Protection of Rights of Property in Land under the Human Rights Act, in The Human Rights Act 1998—What it Means (L. Betten ed., 1999)

Hughes, Graham, *The Crime of Incest*, 55 J. Crim. L. Criminology & Police Sci. 322 (1964)

Hurst, Willard *The Release of Energy*, *in* American Law and Constitutional Order: Historical Perspectives (Lawrence M. Friedman & Harry N. Scheiber eds., 1988)

Jensen, Michael C. & William H. Meckling, *Theory of the Firm: Managerial Behavior, Agency Costs and Ownership Structure*, 3 J. Fin. Econ. 305 (1976)

Jerico, Julius, et al., Prevention and Control of Civil Disturbance: Time for Review (U.S. Dep't of Justice ed., 1992)

Johnson, D. Bruce, *The Formation and Protection of Property Rights Among the Southern Kwakiutl Indians*, 15 J. Legal Stud. 41 (1986)

Jolls, Christine, Sunstein, Cass, & Thaler, Richard H., *A Behavioral Approach to Law and Economics*, 50 Stan. L. Rev. 1471 (1998)

Jones, Benita, The Property Paradox: Limited Equity Housing Cooperatives and the Challenge of African-American Wealth Creation (Apr., 2007) (unpublished paper, Georgetown Law, on file with author)

Jones, Leonard A., A Treatise on the Law of Easements (1898)

Josephine, Louie, Belsky, Eric S., & McArdle, Nancy, The Housing Needs of Low-Income Homeowners, Joint Center for Housing Studies (1998)

Juergensmeyer, Conrad Julian & Roberts, Thomas E., Land Use Planning and Development Regulation Law (2d ed., Practitioner's Treatise Series 2007)

Kahan, Dan M., *The Cognitively Illiberal State*, 60 Stan. L. Rev. 115 (2007)

Kahnerman, Daniel, Knetsch, Jack L. & Thaler, Richard H., *Experimental Tests of the Endowment Effect and the Coase Theorem*, 98 J. Polit. Econ. 1325 (1990)

Kaplow, Louis, *An Economic Analysis of Legal Transitions*, 99 Harv. L. Rev. 509 (1986)

Karkkainen, Bradley C., *The Police Power Revisited: Phantom Incorporation and the Roots of the Takings "Muddle"*, Minn. L. Rev. 826 (2006)

Keeton, W. Page et al., Prosser and Keeton on the Law of Torts § 131 (5th ed. 1984)

Kenn, Deborah, *Paradise Unfound: The American Dream of Housing Justice for All*, 5 B.U. Pub. Int. L.J. 69 (1995)

Kennedy, Duncan, *The Limited Equity Coop as a Vehicle for Affordable Housing in a Race and Class Divided Society*, 46 How. L.J. 85 (2002)

Kent, James, Commentaries on American Law (1836)

Kindleberger, Charples P. & Aliber, Robert Z., Manias, Panics and Crashes: A History of Financial Crises (5th ed. 2005)

Kittredge, William, Owning It All (1987)

Kolber, Adam J., *How to Improve Empirical Desert*, 75 Brook. L. Rev. 433 (2009)

Koopmans, Ruud, *The Dynamics of Protest Waves: West Germany, 1965 to 1989*, 58 Am. Sociological Rev. 637 (1993)

Kramer, Larry, *What's a Constitution for Anyway? Of History and Theory, Bruce Ackerman and the New Dea*l, 46 Case W. Res. L. Rev. 885 (1996)

Krinsman, Allan S., *Subprime Mortgage Meltdown: How Did It Happen and How Will It End?*, J. Structured Fin., Summer 2007, at 16-17

Kuo, Susan S., *Bringing in the State: Toward a Constitutional Duty to Protect from Mob Violence*, 29 Ind. L.J. 178 (2004)

Kuhn, Thomas, The Structure of Scientific Revolutions (1962)

La Pierre, D. Bruce, *Enforcement of Judgments Against States and Local Governments: Judicial Control Over the Power to Tax*, 61 Geo. Wash. L. Rev. 299 (1993)

Lametti, David, The Objects of Virtue, in Property and Community (Gregory S. Alexander & Eduardo M. Penalver eds., 2009)

Landler, Mark & Bajaj, Vikas, *Some Currencies Plunge as Stocks Sink Worldw*ide, N.Y. Times, Oct. 25, 2008, at A1

Lazo, Alejandro, *A Trying Year, By the Numbers*, Wash. Post, Mar. 28, 2009, at F01

Leigh, I. & Masterman, R., Making Rights Real: The Human Rights Act in its First Decade (2008)

Leiter, Brian & Weisberg, Michael, *Why Evolutionary Biology Is (So Far) Irrelevant to Legal Regulation*, 29 L. & Phil. 31 (2010)

Levine, D.S. & Perlovsky, L.I., *Neuroscientific Insights on Biblical Myths: Simplifying Heuristics versus Careful Thinking: Scientific Analysis of Millennial Spiritual Issues*, 43 Zygon: J. of Sci. & Religion 797 (2008)

Levitin, Adam J., *Resolving the Foreclosure Crisis: Modification of Mortgages in Bankruptcy*, 2009 Wis. L. Rev. 565 (2009)

Locke, John, The Second Treatise of Government: An Essay Concerning the Origin, Extent and End of Civil Government (1690)

Loewy, Arnold H., *Morals Legislation and the Establishment Clause*, 55 Ala. L. Rev. 159 (2003)

Mahoney, Margaret M., *A Legal Definition of the Stepfamily: the Example of Incest Regulation*, 8 BYU J. Pub. L. 21 (1993)

Malloy, Robin Paul, Law in a Market Context: An Introduction to Market Concepts in Legal Reasoning (Cambridge 2004); Malloy, Robin Paul, *Inclusion by Design: Accessible Housing and Mobility Impairment*, 60 Hastings L.J. 699 (2009); Robin P. Malloy, *Mortgage Market Reform and the Fallacy of Self-Correcting Markets*, 30 Pace L. Rev. 79, 80 (2009)

Mandelker, Daniel R., Land Use Law (5th ed. 2003 & Supp. 2008)

Marston, John, *Riot in the Riot (Damages) Act 1886*, 84 L. Soc'y's Guardian Gazette, June 17, 1987, at 1797 (quoting Professor Heuston)

Marx, Gary T., *External Efforts to Damage or Facilitate Movements: Some Patterns, Explanations, Outcomes, and Complications*, *in* Dynamics of Social Movements (M. Zald and J. McCarthy, Winthrop Publishers, 1979); Marx, Gary T., *Civil Disorder and the Agents of Social Control*, 26 J. Soc. Issues 38 (1970)

Marx, Karl, Feuerbachian Criticism of Hegel, in Writings of the Young Marx on Philosophy and Society (Lloyd D. Easton & Kurt H. Guddat eds. & trans., 1967); Marx, Karl, *Critique of the Gotha Program (1875)*, *in* Marx & Engels: Basic Writings on Politics and Philosophy (Lewis S. Feuer ed., 1959);

Marx, Karl & Engels, Frederich, The Communist Manifesto (1998)

Mathiessen, Peter, Indian Country (1994)

McCaffery, Edward J., Kahneman, Daniel J. & Spitzer, Matthew L., *Framing the Jury: Cognitive Perspective on Pain and Suffering Awards*, 81 Va. L. Rev. 1341 (1995)

McCann, Michael A., *It's Not About the Money: The Role of Preferences, Cognitive Biases and Heuristics Among Professional Athletes*, 71 Brook. L. Rev. 1459 (2006)

McCarthy, John D. & McPhail, Clark, *The Institutionalization of Protest*, *in* A Movement Society? Contentious Politics for a New Century (David Meyer & Sidney Tarrow eds., 1997)

McDonnell, Brett, *Is Incest Next?*, 10 Cardozo Women's L.J. 337 (2004)

McGovern, Jr. William M. & Kurtz, Sheldon F., Wills, Trusts and Estates (3d ed. 2004)

McPhail, Clark, et al., *The Policing of Protest in the United States, 1960-1995*, in Policing Protest: The Control of Mass Demonstrations in Western Democracies (Donatella Della Porta & Herbert Reiter eds., 1998)

Mercuro, Nicholas & Medema, Steven G., Economics and the Law: From Posner to Post-Modernism (1997)

Merrill, Thomas W., *Property and the Right to Exclude*, 77 Neb. L. Rev. 730 (1998)

Merrill, Thomas W. & Smith, Henry E., *The Morality of Property*, 48 Wm. & Mary L. Rev. 1849 (2007); Merrill, Thomas W. & Smith, Henry E., *Optimal*

Standardization in the Law of Property: The Numerus Clausus *Principle*, 110 Yale L J. 1 (2000)

Meyer, David D. *A Privacy Right to Public Recognition of Family Relationships? The Cases of Marriage and Adoption*, 51 Vill. L. Rev. 891 (2006)

Meyer, Lee G., *Intellectual Property in Today's Financing Market*, 19 Am. Bankr. Inst. J., Mar. 2000, at 20

Michelman, Frank I., *Ethics, Economics and the Law of Property*, 24 Nomos 3 (1982); Michelman, Frank I., *Property, Utility, and Fairness: Comments on the Ethical Foundations of "Just Compensation" Law*, 80 Harv. L. Rev. 1165 (1967)

Mill, John Stuart, Principles of Political Economy with Some of Their Applications to Social Philosophy, *quoted in* C.B. MacPherson, Property: Mainstream and Critical Positions (1978)

Moore, *A Defense of First-Cousin Marriages*, 10 Clev.-Mar. L. Rev. 136 (1961)

Moran, Eamonn K., *Wall Street Meets Main Street: Understanding the Financial Crisis*, 13 N.C. Banking Inst. 5 (2009)

More, Thomas, Utopia (Edward Surtz, S.J. ed., 1964)

Moskowitz, Stuart S., *Cooperative Apartments: The Enforceability of Transfer Restrictions and the Impact of Bankruptcy*, 18 Real Estate L.J. 142 (1989)

Munzer, Stephen, Property as Social Relations, in New Essays on the Legal and Political Theory of Property (Stephen Munzer, ed., 2001)

Murphy, James Bernard, *Equality in Exchange*, 47 Am. J. Juris. 85 (2002)

Murray, Michelle, *Problems with California's Definition of Incest*, 11 J. Contemp. Legal Issues 104 (2000)

Nadler, Janice & Diamond, Shari Seidman, *Eminent Domain and the Psychology of Property Rights: Proposed Use, Subjective Attachment, and Taker Identity*, 5 J. Empirical Legal Stud. 713 (2008)

Note, *Compensation for Victims of Urban Riots*, 68 Colum. L. Rev. 57 (1968)

Note, *Inbred Obscurity: Improving Incest Laws in the Shadow of the "Sexual Family"*, 119 Harv. L. Rev. 2464 (2006)

Note, *Municipal Liability for Riot Damage*, 81 Harv. L. Rev. 653 (1968)

Note, *Riot Insurance,* 77 Yale L.J. 541 (1968)

O'Mahony, Lorna Fox, *Homeownership, Debt, and Default: The Affective Value of Home and the Challenge of Affordability*, in Affordable Housing and Public-Private Partnerships (2009)

Pelletiere, Danilo, *Preliminary Assessment of American Community Survey Data Shows Housing Affordability Gap Worsened for Lowest Income Households from 2007-2008*, Nov. 30, 2009, National Low Income Housing Coalition

Peñalver, Eduardo M., *Land Virtues*, 94 Cornell L. Rev. 821 (2009); Penalver, Eduardo, *Property as Entrance*, 91 Va. L. Rev. 1889 (2005)

Peterson, Kristina, *Affordable Housing on City's Slate: Recommended Changes Could Increase Homes' Long-Term Value*, Palo Alto Daily News, Oct. 10, 2007

Pfeffer, Robert E., *Losing Control: Regulating Situational Crime Prevention in Mass Private Property*, 59 Okla. L. Rev. 759 (2006)

Phillipson, G., *The Human Rights Act, 'Horizontal Effect' and the Common Law: A Bang or a Whimper*, 62 Mod. L. Rev. 824 (1999)
Pipes, Richard, Property and Freedom (1999)
Plato, Laws (Benjamin Jowett trans., 2008); Plato, The Republic (H.D.P. Lee trans., 1962)
Pollock & Maitland, The History of English Law (1895)
Posner, Richard A. & Silbaugh, Katharine B., A Guide to America's Sex Laws (1998)
Posner, Richard A., Economic Analysis of Law (6th ed. 2003) and (7th ed. 2007); Posner, Richard A., *Killing or Wounding to Protect a Property Interest*, 14 J.L. & Econ. 201 (1971)
Potraker, K.M., *Adoption of an Adult*, 21 A.L.R.3d 1012 (1968)
Prentice, Robert, *Enron: A Brief Behavioral Autopsy*, 40 Am. Bus. L.J. 417 (2003)
Privacy and Human Rights (A.H. Robertson ed., 1973)
Privacy Rights in a Post Lawrence World: Responses to Lawrence v. Texas 10 Cardoza Women's L.J. 337 (2004)
Pynoos, Jon et al., *Aging in Place, Housing, and the Law*, 16 Elder L.J. 77 (2008)
Radin, Margaret J., *Property and Personhood*, 34 Stan. L. Rev. 957 (1982)
Ramesh, Randeep, *Credit is a Basic Human Right*, Guardian Weekly (U.K.), Jan. 5, 2007, at 28
Rasler, Karen, *Concessions, Repression, and Political Protest in the Iranian Revolution*, 61 Am. Sociological Rev. 132 (1996)
Rauf, Muhammad Abdul, *quoted in* Siraj Sait & Hilary Lim, Islamic Land Theories and Its (*sic*) Applications, Paper 1 in UN-Habitat Islam, Land and Property Research Series (2005)
Regan, Jr., Milton C., *Reason, Tradition, and Family Law: A Comment on Social Constructionism,* 79 Va. L. Rev. 1515 (1968)
Reich, Charles A., *The New Property*, 73 Yale L.J. 733 (1963-64)
Rein, Jan Ellen, *Relatives by Blood, Adoption, and Association: Who Should Get What and Why*, 37 Vand. L. Rev. 711 (1984)
Remembering Slavery: Africans-Americans Talk About Their Personal Experiences of Slavery and Emancipation (Iral Berlin, Marc Favreau & Steven Miller eds., 1998)
Restatement (1st) of Property *Introductory Note* (1936)
Roback, Jennifer, Exchange, Sovereignty, and Indian-Anglo Relations, in Property Rights and Indian Economies (Terry L. Anderson ed., 1992)
Robinson, Paul H. & Darley, John, *Intuitions of Justice: Implications for Criminal Law and Justice Policy*, 81 S. Cal. L. Rev. 1 (2007)
Robinson, Paul H. & Kurzban, Robert, *Concordance and Conflict in Intuitions of Justice*, 91 Minn. L. Rev. 1829 (2007)
Rohe, William M., et al., The Social Benefits and Costs of Homeownership: A Critical Assessment of the Research (Joint Ctr. for Hous. Studies of Harvard Univ., Working Paper No. LIHO-01.12, 2001)

Rose, Carol, M., *The Several Futures of Property: Of Cyberspace and Folk Tales, Emission Trades and Ecosystems*, 83 Minn. L. Rev. 129 (1998); Rose, Carol M., *Possession as the Origin of Property*, 52 U. Chi. L. Rev. 73 (1985); Rose, Carol M., *Mahon Reconsidered: Why the Takings Issue is Still Such a Muddle*, 57 S. Cal. L. Rev. 561 (1984)

Rousseau, Jean-Jaques, *Discourse on the Origin and Foundations of Inequality*, in The Social Contract and Discources (G.D.H. Cole trans., 1950)

Ruhl, J.B., *Ecosystem Services and the Common Law of the "Fragile Land System"*, 20 Nat. Resources & Env't. 3 (2005)

Ryan, Alan, Property (1987)

Sait, Siraj & Lim, Hilary, Land, Law & Islam: Property and Human Rights in the Muslim World, *in* UN-Habitat Islam, Land and Property Research Series

Salert, Barbara & Sprague, John, The Dynamics of Riots (1980)

Salsich Jr., Peter W., *Property Law Serves Human Society: A First-Year Course Agenda*, 46 St. Louis U. L.J. 617 (2002)

Samuelson, Williams & Zeckhauser, Richard J., *Status Quo Bias in Decision Making*, 1 J. of Risk & Uncertainty 7 (1988)

Sax, Joseph L., *Takings, Private Property and Public Rights*, 81 Yale L.J. 149 (1971)

Scheiber, Harry N., *Property Law, Expropriation, and Resource Allocation by Government, 1789-1910*, in American Law and Constitutional Order (Lawrence M. Friedman & Harry N. Scheiber eds., 1998)

Schill, Michael H., *The Impact of Capital Markets on Real Estate Law and Practice*, 32 Marshall L. Rev. 269 (1999)

Schrecker, Ellen, Many are the Crimes: McCarthyism in America (1998)

Schwartz, Steven L., *Systemic Risk*, 97 Geo. L.J. 193 (2008)

Sears, David O., *Urban Rioting in Los Angeles: A Comparison of 1965 with 1992*, in The Los Angeles Riots: Lessons for the Urban Future (Mark Baldassare ed., 1994)

Sherman, Jeffrey G., *Undue Influence and the Homosexual Testator*, 42 U. Pitt. L. Rev. 225 (1981)

Shermer, Michael, The Borderlands of Science: Where Sense Meets Nonsense (2001)

Singer, Joseph, Entitlement: The Paradoxes of Property (2000)

Singer, Norman J. & Singer, J.D. Shambie, Sutherland Statutes and Statutory Construction §61 (7th ed. 2008)

Smelser, Neil J., Theory of Collective Behavior (1962)

Smith, Henry E., *Exclusion Versus Governance: Two Strategies for Delineating Property Rights*, 31 J. Legal Stud. 453 (2002)

Smith, James Charles, *Restrictions on Freedom of Expressions Imposed by Servitudes*, 16 Digest 1 (2009)

Snodgrass, Gwendolyn L., *Creating Family Without Marriage: the Advantages and Disadvantages of Adult Adoption Among Gay and Lesbian Partners*, 36 Brandeis J. Fam. L. 75 (1998)

Somin, Ilya, *The Limits of Backlash: Assessing the Response to* Kelo, 93 Minn. L. Rev. 2100 (2009)

Sorkin, Andrew Ross, *Merrill is Sold: Failing to Find Buyer, Lehman Set to File for Bankruptcy*, N.Y. Times, Sept. 15, 2008, at A1

Spellman, Barbara & Schauer, Frederick, *Symposium: A Psychological Perspective on Property Law: Artists' Moral Rights and the Psychology of Ownership*, 83 Tul. L. Rev. 661 (2009)

Stake, Jeffrey Evans, *The Property Instinct*, 359 Phil. Trans. R. Soc. Lond. 1763 (2004)

Starmer, K., European Human Rights Law: The Human Rights Act 1998 and the European Convention on Human Rights (1999)

Stegman Michael A. et al., *The Wealth-Creating Potential of Homeownership: A Preliminary Assessment of Price Appreciation among Low-Income Homebuyers*, *in* Chasing the American Dream, New Perspectives on Affordable Homeownership (William M. Rohe & Harry L. Watson eds., 2007)

Stern, Stephanie, *Residential Protectionism and the Legal Mythology of Home*, 107 Mich. L. Rev. 1093 (2009)

Strahilevitz, Lior, *The Right to Destroy*, 114 Yale L.J. 781 (2005)

Streitfeld, David, *Almost Entire Town Is Drowning in Debt as Home Values Plunge*, N.Y. Times, Nov. 11, 2008, at A1

Suk, Jeannie, *Taking the Home*, 20 L. & Literature 291 (2008)

Sunstein, Cass R., *What Did Lawrence Hold?: Of Autonomy, Desuetude, Sexuality, and Marriage*, 2003 Sup. Ct. Rev. 27; Sunstein, Cass R., *Introduction, in* Behavioral Law & Economics (Cass R. Sunstein ed., 2000); Sunstein, Cass R., *Constitutionalism After the New Deal*, 101 Harv. L. Rev. 421 (1987)

Sunstein, Cass & Thaler, Richard, Nudge: Improving Decisions About Health, Wealth, and Happiness (2008)

Sweeney, James, *Margins of Appreciation: Cultural Relativity and the European Court of Human Rights in the Post-Cold War Era*, 54 ICLQ 459 (2005)

Tamanaha, Brian Z., On the Rule of Law: History, Politics, Theory (2004)

Thaler, Richard, *Toward a Positive Theory of Consumer Choice*, 1 J. Econ. Behav. & Org. 39 (1980)

The Analects of Confucius (Watson trans., 2007)

The New Oxford Annotated Bible (Michael D. Coogan ed.,1991)

Thorman, George, Incestuous Families (1983)

Tierney, Kathleen J., *Property Damage and Violence: A Collective Behavior Analysis*, in The Los Angeles Riots: Lessons for the Urban Future (Mark Baldassare ed., 1994)

Tilly, Charles, Big Structures, Large Processes, Huge Comparisons (1984)

Turner, Patricia A., I Heard It Through the Grapevine: Rumor in African-American Culture (1993)

Twitchell, James B., Forbidden Partners: The Incest Taboo in Modern Culture (1987)

Underkuffler, Laura, The Idea of Property: Its Meaning and Power (2003)

Urban, Mandi Rae, *The History of Adult Adoption in California*, 11 J. Contemp. Legal Issues 612 (2000)

Useem, Bert, *State and Collective Disorders: The Los Angeles Riot/Protest of April, 1992*, 76 Social Forces 357 (Dec. 1997)
Van Dijk, P. & Van Hoof, G.J.H., Theory and Practice of the European Convention on Human Rights (3rd ed. 1998)
Varieties of Capitalism: The Institutional Foundations of Comparative Advantage 6–66 (Peter A. Hall & David Soskice eds., 2001)
Veblen, Thorstein, Absentee Ownership and Business Enterprise in Recent Times: The Case of America (1923)
Vernon, Raymond, The Changing Economic Function of the Central City (1959)
Waddington, David P., Policing Public Disorder: Theory and Practice (2007)
Wadlington, Walter, *Adoption of Adults: A Family Law Anomaly*, 54 Cornell L. Rev. 566 (1969); Wadlington, Walter, *The Adopted Child and Intra-Family Marriage Prohibitions*, 49 Va. L. Rev. 478 (1963)
Waldron, Jeremy, The Right to Private Property (1988)
Wardle, Lynn D., *A Critical Analysis of Interstate Recognition of Lesbigay Adoptions*, 3 Ave Maria L. Rev. 561 (2005)
Wardrip, Keith, et. al., *Out of Reach 2009*, National Low Income Housing Coalition (2009)
Waters, Frank, Brave Are My People, *quoted in* Bruce E. Johansen, The Encyclopedia of Native American Economic History (1999)
Webster, William H. & Williams, Hubert, The City in Crisis: A Report by the Special Advisor to the Board of Police Commissioners on the Civil Disorder in Los Angeles (1992)
Wendy, Gordon, *Fair Use as Market Failure*, 82 Colum. L. Rev. 1600 (1982)
Williams, Joan, *The Rhetoric of Property*, 83 Iowa L. Rev. 277 (1989)
Williams, Sean, *Sticky Expectations: Responses to Persistent Over-Optimism in Marriage, Employment Contracts, and Credit Card Use*, 84 Notre Dame L. Rev. 733 (2009)
Wilmarth, Arthur E. Jr., *The Dark Side of Universal Banking: Financial Conglomerates and the Origins of the Subprime Financial Crisis*, 41 Conn. L. Rev. 963 (2009)
Wolf, Michael Allan, *Hysteria versus History: Public Use in the Public Eye*, *in* Private Property, Community Development, and Eminent Domain (Robin Paul Malloy ed., 2008)
Wood, Gordon S., The Radicalism of the American Revolution (1992)
Wray, L. Randall, *Lessons from the Subprime Meltdown* (The Levy Econ. Inst. Of Bard Coll., Working Paper No. 522, 2007), *available at* http://ssrn.com/abstract=1070833
X v. Germany, 1 Y.B. 202 (1956)
Yourow, Howard Charles, The Margin of appreciation Doctrine in the Dynamics of European Human Rights Jurisprudence (1996)

Miscellaneous

'Mars Raiders' Cause Quito Panic; Mob Burns Radio Plant, Kills 15, N.Y. TIMES, Feb. 14, 1949, at 1, 7, *reprinted in* SELECTED READINGS IN SOCIAL PSYCHOLOGY 304-07 (Stewart Henderson Britt ed., 1950)

27 Million Ways to Live Your Life, TORONTO STAR (Apr. 6, 2004), *available at* 2004 WLNR 6076618

Aguilar, John, *Hard Feelings on Hardscrabble Drive*, DAILY CAMERA, Nov. 19, 2007, *available at* http://www.dailycamera.com/news/2007/nov/19/protest-draws-hundreds-hard-feelings-on-drive/

Associated Press Interview with Senator Rick Santorum (Apr. 7, 2003)

Barnette, Meg, Pratt Institute Ctr for Comm. and Envir'l Devt., *Creating Multifamily Homeownership at Scale: Affordable Housing Cooperatives in New York City, Washington, D.C., and Chicago*, October 2004, at 9, *available at* http://www.ncbcapitalimpact.org/

Black, Karen, *Issue Brief: Effectively Preserving Philadelphia's Workforce Housing Stock*, Feb. 2009, *available at* http://www.williampennfoundation.org/usr_doc/PreservingHousingBrief.pdf

Bureau of Labor Statistics, Labor Force Statistics from the Current Population Survey, *available at* http://data.bls.gov/PDQ/servlet/SurveyOutputServlet?data_tool=latest_numbers&series_id=LNS14000000 (last visited June 1, 2010)

Caplin, Andrew, et al., *Shared-Equity Mortgages, Housing Affordability, and Homeownership, 2007* Fannie Mae Foundation, *available at* http://cess.nyu.edu/caplin/SEM2007.pdf

Castle Coalition Website, http://www.castlecoalition.org/leegislation/states/index.asp

Chicago Public Library, *Death, Disturbances, Disasters and Disorders in Chicago: 1919 Race Riots*, *available at* http://www.chipublib.org/004chicago/disasters/riots_race.html (last modified May 2001)

Coal. for Nonprofit Hous. and Econ. Devt., *A Study of Limited-Equity Cooperatives in the District of Columbia* (2004), *available at* http://www.cnhed.org

Cruickshank, Paula, *Treasury Issues New Restrictions on Executive Compensation Paid by Financial Institutions*, CCH FIN. CRISIS NEWS CTR., Feb. 4, 2009, *available at* http://www.financialcrisisupdate.com/2009/02/treasury-issues-new-restrictions-on-executive-compensation-paid-by-financial-institutions.html

Davis, Emmeus, *Shared Equity Homeownership, The Changing Landscape of Resale-Restricted, Owner-Occupied Housing* (NAT'L HOUS. INST. 2006), *available at* http://www.nhi.org/pdf/SharedEquityHome.pdf

D.C. Dep't of Hous. and Cmty. Dev., *About DHCD*, *available at* http://dhcd.dc.gov/dhcd/cwp/view,a,3,q,555677,dhcdNav_GID,1575,dhcdNav,%7C32184%7C,.asp

D.C. Dep't of Hous. and Cmty. Dev., Lead Safe Washington DC, http://www.dhcd.dc.gov/dhcd/cwp/view,a,1243,q,629142.asp (last visited Apr. 29. 2011)

D.C. Dep't of Hous. and Cmty. Dev., Residential and Community Services Division, http://www.dhcd.dc.gov/dhcd/cwp/view,a,1243,q,629884.asp#SFRRP (last visited Apr. 29, 2011)

D.C. Dep't of Hous. and Cmty. Dev., *Single Family Residential Rehabilitation Program Fact Sheet*, *available at* http://www.dhcd.dc.gov/dhcd/frames.asp?doc=/dhcd/lib/dhcd/info/pdf/brochures/sfrehabfactsheet.pdf (last visited Apr. 29, 2011)

D.C. Dep't of Employment Services, *District of Columbia Jobless Rate 11.9 Percent*, *available at* http://newsroom.dc.gov/show.aspx/agency/does/section/2/release/19560/year/2010/month/3

D.C. Dept't of Env't, *Fix Up Your Home and Save Energy For Free*, *available at* http://ddoe.dc.gov/ddoe/frames.asp?doc=/ddoe/lib/ddoe/2009.04.08_Weatherization_Flyer.pdf (last visited Aug. 24, 2009)

D.C. Home and Condo Prices, *available at* http://www.dchousingprices.com/2009/03/wapo-smackdown-district-sales-full-year.html (last visited Mar. 30, 2009)

Edmonds, Leila Finucane, *DHCD is Here to Help,* WASHINGTON INFORMER (2009 HOMEOWNERSHIP SUPPLEMENT), *available at* http://www.washingtoninformer.com/wi-web/images/stories/archives/supplement/09-06homesup.pdf

Epstein, Richard, "*Blind Justices: The Scandal of* Kelo v. New London," WALL ST. J. ONLINE, July 3, 2005, *available at* http://www.opinionjournal.com/extra/?id=110006904

Federal Reserve Bank of Kansas City, *Financial Industry Perspectives*, Dec. 2009, *Trends in Residential Mortgage Loan Originations and Their Impact on Community Banks*, *available at* http://www.kc.frb.org/banking/bankingpublications/prs09-12.pdf

Garvey, Marcus, *Speech Regarding the East St. Louis Riots* (July 18, 1917), in PBS Website, *Primary Sources: The Conspiracy of The East St. Louis Riots*, *available at* http://www.pbs.org/wgbh/amex/garvey/filmmore/ps_riots.html (last visited Sept. 27, 2009)

Genesis 20:2-18

Genesis 29-30

Giugni, Marco & Wisler Dominique, *Political Coalitions, Face-to-Face Interactions, and the Public Sphere: An Examination of the Determinants of Repression with Protest Event Data*, CBSM Working Paper Series 1 (4) (1998), *available at* http://www.nd.edu/~ dmy

Gorton, Gary B., *The Panic of 2007* (Yale Sch. of Mgmt. and Nat'l Bureau of Econ. Research, Working Paper No. 08-24, 2008), *available at* http://papers.ssrn.com/sol3/papers.cfm?abstract_id=1255362

Gray, Jim, *Shared Equity Gains Acceptance in Affordable Multifamily Development, Commercial Mortgage Insight* (May 2008) at 18, www.cmi-online.com

Harsanyi, David, *Property Right Wrongly Taken*, DENVER POST, Nov. 19, 2007, *available at* . http://www.denverpost.com/harsanyi/ci_7501264

Hawkins, Karen, *Adoption: Not Just for Children*, THE WASHINGTON POST, Mar. 14, 2007, *available at* http://www.washingtonpost.com/wp-dyn/content/article/2007/03/14/AR2007031400263.html

Haynes, V. Dion, *DC Unemployment Rate Increases Overall Number for Washington Metro Area*, WASH. POST., Feb. 3, 2010, *available at* http://www.washingtonpost.com/wp-dyn/content/article/2010/02/02/AR2010020202258.html

Hetzel, Lisa & Smith, Annetta, U.S. Dep't of Commerce, Brief No. C2KBR/01-10, *The 65 Years and Over Population: 2000* (2001), *available at* http://www.cenus.gov/prod/2001pubs/c2kbr01-10.pdf

Housing Complex, *available at* http://www.washingtoncitypaper.com/blogs/housingcomplex

How We Are Housed: Results from the 1999 American Housing Survey, available at http://www.huduser.org/periodicals/ushmc/fall00/summary-2.html (last visited Mar. 23, 2009)

HPTF Limits Effective 3/19/09, *available at* http://dhcd.dc.gov/dhcd/cwp/view,a,1242,q,646929.asp

Jacobine, Kenn, *U.S. Property Rights in Line with Tenets of Communism*, *available at* http://blogcritics.org/politics/article/us-property-rights-in-line-with/ (lamenting estate tax as an offense to property rights) (last visited Aug. 9, 2010)

Jacobus, Rick, *Stewardship for Lasting Affordability: Administration and Monitoring of Shared Equity Homeownership*, *available at* http://www.ncbcapitalimpact.org/uploadedFiles/downloads/Symposium_Tab5_BusinessModel.pdf

Joint Press Release, Bd. of Governors of the Fed. Reserve Sys., Fed. Deposit Ins. Corp. & U.S. Dep't of the Treasury, Joint Statement by Treasury, Federal Reserve, and the FDIC on Citigroup (Nov. 23, 2008), *available at* http://www.federalreserve.gov/newsevents/press/bcreg/20081123a.htm

Kennickell, Arthur B., "A Rolling Tide: Changes in the Distribution of Wealth in the U.S., 1989-2001," U.S. Federal Reserve Board, August 2003, http://www.federalreserve.gov/pubs/oss/oss2/papers/concentration.2001.10.pdf

Knowledge@Wharton, The Subprime Crisis: A Timeline, http://knowledge.wharton.upenn.edu/special_sections/subprime/timeline.cfm# (last visited Feb. 2, 2010)

Lazere, Ed, D.C. Fiscal Policy Inst., and Robert Pohlman, Coal. for Nonprofit Hsg. and Econ. Devt., *Affordable Housing in the District Depends on a Stable Housing Production Trust Fun*d (Oct. 20, 2008), *available at* http://dcfpi.org/wp-content/uploads/2008/

Lazere, Ed, *Nowhere to Go: As Affordable Housing Costs Rise, Residents Are Left with Fewer Affordable Options*, *available at* http://dcfpi.org

Leviticus 18:6-18

Leviticus 20:11-21

Lewis, Terry & Lindley R. Higgins, *The Advantages and Disadvantages of Cooperative Housing as an Affordable Alternative*, *available at* http://www.ncbcapitalimpact.org/documents/Advantagesanddisadvantages.pdf

Limbaugh, Rush, Liberals Like Stephen Breyer have Bastardized the Constitution, Radio Transcript, Oct. 12, 2005, *available at* http://www.freerepublic.com/focus/f-news/1501453/posts (visited Dec. 20, 2006)

Lithwick, Dahlia, *Slippery Slop: The Maddening Slippery Slope Argument Against Gay Marriage*, SLATE, May 19, 2004, *available at* http://www.slate.com/id/2100824/

Maisel, Jordana L., Ctr. For Inclusive Design & Envtl. Access (IDEA), *Visitability as an Approach to Inclusive Housing Design and Community Development: A Look at Its Emergence, Growth and Challenges* (2005), *available at* http://www.udeworld.com/visitability.html

Manna's Response to NCB Capital Impact's Papers on Shared Equity Ownership (SEO) (on file with author)

Mike Industries, *When Your Neighbor Builds a Jackass Home*, *available at* http://www.mikeindustries.com/blog/archive/2008/07/when-your-neighbor-builds-a-jackass-home

Moore, Don, *The Day the Martians Landed*, *available at* http://donmoore.tripod.com/south/ecuador/martians.html (last visited Sept. 27, 2009)

Nader, Ralph, Statement, June 23, 2005, *available at* http://ml.greens.org/pipermail/ctgp-news/2005-June/000507.html (visited Dec. 21, 2006)

NAHB Supports Voluntary "visitability,' NATION'S BUILDING NEWS ONLINE, May 26, 2003, http://www.nbnnews.com/NBN/issues/2003-05-26/Seniors+Housing/2.html

Nat'l Association of Realtors, *Metropolitan Median Prices*, *available at* http://www.realtor.org/research/research/metroprice

NCB Capital Impact, *Shared Equity Ownership: A Foreclosure Solution*, May 2008, at 3, *available at* http://www.ncbcapitalimpact.org/uploadedFiles/downloads/SharedEquityForeclosureSolutionMay08.pdf

Nesvetailova, Anastasia, *The End of a Great Illusion: Credit Crunch and Liquidity Meltdown* (Danish Inst. for Int'l Studies, Working Paper No. 2008/23, 2008), *available at* http://www.diis.dk/graphics/Publications/WP2008/WP2008-23_Credit_Crunch_and_Liquidity_Meltdown.pdf

PBS website, *Detroit Race Riots 1943*, *available at* http://www.pbs.org/wgbh/amex/eleanor/peopleevents/pande10.html (last visited Sept. 27, 2009)

PBS website, People *& Events: The East St. Louis Riot*, *available at* http://www.pbs.org/wgbh/amex/garvey/peopleevents/e_estlouis.html (last visited Sept. 27, 2009)

Pima County Visitability Ordinance (Dec. 23, 2003), *available at* http://www.accessiblesociety.org/topics/housing/pimacoruling.html

Press Release, Bd. of Governors of the Fed. Reserve Sys., Federal Reserve is Prepared to Expand the Term Asset-Backed Securities Loan Facility (TALF) (Feb. 10, 2009), *available at* http://www.federalreserve.gov/newsevents/press/monetary/20090210b.htm

Press Release, U.S. Dep't of the Treasury, Statement by Secretary Henry M. Paulson, Jr. on Actions to Protect the U.S. Economy (Oct. 14, 2008), *available at* http://www.treas.gov/press/releases/hp1205.htm

Press Release, U.S. Dep't of the Treasury, Treasury Announces TARP Investment in GMAC (Dec. 29, 2008), *available at* http://www.treas.gov/press/releases/hp1335.htm

Rebuilding Together Website, http://rebuildingtogether.org

Retirement Living Information Center, *Taxes by State*, *available at* http://www.retirementliving.com/RLtaxes.html (last visited July 3, 2008)

Rode, Steve, *Woman Chains Self to Home to Prevent Foreclosure*, *available at* http://getoutofdebt.org/2533/woman-chains-self-to-home-to-prevent-foreclosure

Saletan, William, *The Love That Dare Not Speak Its Surname*, SLATE, Apr. 10, 2002, *available at* http://www.slate.com/id/2064227/

Schneider, Carl E., *State-Interest Analysis in Fourteenth Amendment "Privacy" Law: An Essay on the Constitutionalization of Social Issues*, 51 LAW & CONTEMP. PROBS. 79, 98 (1988)

Shdaimah, Corey, Stahl, Roland and Schram, Sanford F., *When You Can See the Sky Through Your Roof: Low-Income Homeownership from the Bottom Up*, *available at* www.brynmawr.edu/Acads/GSSW/schram/shdaimahstahlschram.doc

Spegal, Katie & Liebig, Phoebe, *Visitability: Trends, Approaches, and Outcomes* (2003), (unpublished manuscript), *available at* http://www.usc.edu/dept/gero/nrcshhm/.8.te sc.edu/dept/gero/nrcshhm/

Social Trends 39 (2009); Statistics available online at http://www.statistics.gov.uk/downloads/theme_social/Social_Trends39/Social_Trends_39.pdf

Stark, Judy, *And Access for All*, ST. PETERSBURG TIMES (Fla.), June 8, 2002, *available at* http://www.sptimes.com/2002/06/08/Homes/And_access_for_all.shtml

Statement by Mayor Rudolph W. Giuliani Regarding the Settlement of the Crown Heights Lawsuit, Archives of the Mayor's Press Office (April 2, 1998)

Statement from League of Kansas Municipalities to House Committee on Judiciary (March 20, 1979)

Testimony of Jenny Reed, Policy Analyst, D.C. Fiscal Policy Inst., at the Public Hearing on the Fiscal Year 2010 Budget Oversight Hearing for the Dept. of Hsg. and Community Devt., D.C. Committee on Hsg. and Workforce Devt., Apr. 8, 2009, *available at* http://dcfpi.org/?p=390

U.S. Census Bureau, Resident Population 2000, *available at* http://www.census.gov/population/www/cen2000/respop.html (last visited July 3, 2008)

U.S. Census Bureau, State and County Quick Facts, *available at* http://quickfacts.census.gov/qfd/states/11000.html

U.S. Dep't. of Hous. and Urban Dev., Affordable Housing Needs 2005: Report to Congress 36 (2005), *available at* http://www.huduser.org/publications/pdf/Affhsgneeds.pdf

U.S. Dep't of the Treasury, Fact Sheet: Financial Stability Plan, *available at* http://www.financialstability.gov/docs/fact-sheet.pdf

U.S. Dep't of the Treasury, Homeowner Affordability and Stability Plan: Fact Sheet, *available at* http://www.treasury.gov/initiatives/eesa/homeowner-affordability-plan/FactSheet.pdf

United States and States — R1803. Percent of People 65 Years and Over with a Disability (2005), *available at* http://factfinder.census.gov/servlet/GRTSelectServlet?ds_name=ACS_2005_EST_G00_&_lang=en&_ts=254773591968 (follow the link to the right of "R1803" under "Aging")

Wang, Qi, U.S. Dep't of Com., Report No. CENSR-23, *Disability and American Families: 2000*, at 3 tbl.1. (2005), *available at* http://www.census.gov/prod/2005pubs/censr-23.pdf

Washington, D.C. Tenant Survival Guide, (7th ed., Spring 2008) Harrison Institute for Public Law, Georgetown University, *available at* http://ota.dc.gov/ota/frames.asp?doc=/ota/lib/ota/Tenant_Survival_Guide.pdf.

Webel, Baird, Cong. Research Serv., Ongoing Government Assistance for American International Group (AIG) (2009)

White, Nancy J., *Kissing Cousins; Stigma Attached to Marriage Between Relat*ives, Toronto Star (July 3, 2004), *available at* 2004 WLNR 6137363

Wikipdia, *Home Ownership in the United States*, *available at* http://en.wikipedia.org/wiki/Homeownership_in_the_United_States (last visited Aug 10, 2010)

Wikipedia, *Joe the Plumber*, *available at* http://en.wikipedia.org/wiki/Joe_the_Plumber

Wikipedia, *Lost Liberty Hotel*, *available at* http://en.wikipedia.org/wiki/Lost_Liberty_Hotel

World Visitability Legislation, Sample U.S. State and Local Ordinances, http://www.concretechange.org/policy_legislative_local.aspx

Index

absolutism, ix, 13, 15, 19, 21-32, 34-35, 83, 86
accessibility, xi, 56, 133, 137-142, 145-146, 149-150, 181
accessible, xi, 133-135, 137-143, 146-149, 151-152, 180
Ackerman, Bruce, 66
administrative adjudication, 4
adoption, xii, 209-212, 214-222, 224-228
adverse possession, 8, 19
aesthetic, 14, 25, 140-142, 162, 175
affordability gap, 156
affordable housing (affordability), xi, 3, 12, 38-39, 53, 55-57, 59-60, 62, 114, 127, 145, 155-156, 159-160, 166-167
Alexander, Frank, 46
Alexander, Gregory, x
Allah, 42
amenity, 149-150
American International Group (A.I.G.), 74
Americans with Disabilities Act, 143, 151
"ancient lights" doctrine, 6-9
anti-commons, 2, 80
anti-discrimination, 22, 135, 143
appreciation, 38, 72, 91, 96, 101-103, 107, 122, 160
Architectural Barriers Act (ABA), 143 (see also barriers)
Area Median Income (AMI), 58
Aristotle, 45

bankruptcy, 5-6, 65, 73-74
barriers, ix, 9-10, 12, 46, 133, 135, 137, 143, 209 (see also Architectural Barriers Act)
Beard, Charles, 68
behavioral economics, 15
behavioralism, ix, 15
Benthamite utilitarian, 24
bias, 27, 30, 32-33, 86, 200, 209, 212, 227
Blackstone, ix, 15-16, 22, 47, 70
Brown v. Board of Education, 22
bureaucratic management, 6

Center for Inclusive Design and Environmental Access, 150
chattels, 4
Christian-Humanist, 44
Civic Republican, 69-70, 81-82
Civil War, 67-68
Classical Liberal, 44, 47, 69, 79, 86
Coase, Ronald, 24
Cohen, Morris Raphael, 50-52
colonial, x, 218
common law, ix, 1-6, 9-12, 14, 25, 50-51, 66, 111-112, 186, 209, 214, 217-218, 220-223
commons (tragedy of), 59, 134
commons license, 12
communal, 5, 7, 12
communitarian, 21, 70, 76, 82
community, xi, 1-2, 45-46, 55-57, 59, 61, 65, 86, 95, 108, 113-114, 129, 133-134, 137-140, 142, 144, 151, 155, 158-160, 167-168, 170, 173, 175-178, 180, 186, 188, 190-193, 196, 200, 203, 205-206
Community Development Financial Institutions (CDFIs), 55
Community Land Trusts (CLT), 56-57
comprehensive legal systems, 6
Confucius, 40-41
Connors v UK, 96, 106, 114, 117, 119, 122, 124
conservative, x, 66
Constitution, xii, 1, 3, 21, 66-71, 78, 90, 148, 207, 209, 214, 222-224, 226-228
constitutional law, 1, 21
consumer preference, 146

contract, xii, 68, 82, 97-100, 104, 106, 112, 116, 133, 136, 158, 211-212, 225
control, 3, 9, 28, 41, 51-52, 57, 61, 70, 81, 83-85, 127, 142, 150, 162, 171, 173, 176-177, 185, 197-199, 201-203, 209-210, 213, 227
cooperative, 12, 61, 153-156, 158-164, 171-172, 174-178, 180, 183
copyright, 1, 20
cost and benefit, 141
covenant, 14, 17, 57-58, 167
conveyance (fraudulent), 4
creditor, 4-6, 115-117
Cronon, William, 43
culture, x, 37, 39-40, 42, 65, 68, 78-80, 86, 90, 218

Davis, John Emmeus, 61, 159
debtor, 4-6, 117
default, 5, 30, 71, 73, 90, 175, 177
Demsetz, Harold, 24, 80
Department of Housing and Urban Development (HUD), 142
design (buildings), x-xii, 133-151, 170
digital property, 12
disability, 133-134, 137-138, 144-145, 148
discrimination (and anti-discrimination), 22, 135, 143
disasters-Hurricane Katrina, emergency relocation, 134, 136
dominion, 3, 9, 15-16, 19, 42-43, 45-48, 62, 70

easement, 2, 7-9, 14, 17
economic crisis, x, 66, 83, 85
economics, 9, 11, 15, 23-24, 41, 52
efficiency, 2, 6, 9, 11, 14, 24, 29, 52, 181
eminent domain, 13, 17, 19, 23
endowment effect, 27, 31-32
endowment - waft, 42
entitlements, 20, 24-26, 31-32, 35, 71, 86
environment (environmental), 3-4, 23, 28, 46, 51-52, 61-62, 65, 72, 135, 138, 150, 197
equity, x-xi, 12, 37-40, 50, 52-62, 74-75, 82, 85, 153-156, 159-162, 169, 174, 182
essentialism, 15, 29-30, 34
ethnic, 20, 197
ethnicity, 137, 204
European Convention on Human Rights, x, 89, 92
  Article 8, x, 89-94, 96-127, 129-130
European Court of Human Rights, 90-91, 93, 95-96, 106, 108-109, 111, 117-119, 122-123, 125-126, 130-131
evict (eviction), x, 89-90, 94-95, 98-101, 104-107, 109-112, 114, 117, 119-121, 123, 125-127, 129-131
exclude (exclusion)-right to exclude, 1, 16, 52, 137, 171, 185, 206
Executive Order 13217, 143

fair use, 18
Fannie Mae (FHA), 74, 83, 136
Freddie Mac, 74, 83
Federal Reserve, 72, 74-75
FHA, 74, 136
financial crisis, 65
first possession, 28
first sale (doctrine), 18
first-in-time, 8
foreclose (foreclosure), 19, 73, 76-77, 79, 82, 177, 218
free-rider, xi

gentrification, 156
Gillow v UK, 102
Great Depression, 65, 69, 76-77

Hardin, Garrett, The Tragedy of the Commons, 59
Hegel, 51
Heller, Michael, 80
Homeowner Affordability and Stability Plan (HASP), 75
homeownership, 37-40, 52-53, 58-61, 65, 72, 79, 81, 85, 146, 153-155, 157, 159, 162, 165-168, 171-172, 175-177, 180-183
House of Lords, 89-93, 95-99, 107-109, 112, 116-117, 121-126, 128-131
Housing and Economic Recovery Act ("HERA"), 74, 81
housing stock, 38, 115, 127, 135-137, 140, 142, 145-147, 149-150, 160

Human Rights Act of 1998, 90, 92, 96, 107, 111, 115-116, 125-126
Hume, David, 51

immigration, 11, 213
incentivize, 81
incest, 209-210, 214, 216-228
Inclusive Design Housing Act, 143
Incrementalism, 67, 82
Individualism, 18, 70
industrialization, 11
interest rates, 56, 61, 72-73, 76
intestate succession, xii
Invisible Hand, 52, 134
Islam (Islamic conceptions of property), 41-42

Jim Crow era, 22
joint tenancies, 96
judicial review, 118, 120-127, 129-131
jurisprudence, 69, 90, 96, 102, 117, 130

Kant, 51
Kelo v. City of New London, 13-15, 19
Kent, James, 4, 27
kinship, 43

laissez-faire, 86
land use, 4, 9-10, 147
landlord, 52, 90, 92, 98, 100, 105, 108, 110-118, 120, 123, 126-127, 130, 164, 170, 179
law and economics, 9, 11, 15, 23-24, 52
Lawrence v. Texas, xii, 209-210, 214, 222-224, 226-228
lease, 57, 100-101, 161
Leeds City Council v Price (Kay & Price), 95, 108-109
Legal Realism, 22
levy (and execution), 5, 42
Libertarian, 14, 16
Limited Equity Cooperative ("LEC"), xi, 12, 61, 153-154, 156
Lochner, 69-70
Locke, John, 47-48, 50-51, 71, 76
London Borough of Lambeth v Kay, 89-90, 95-96, 99, 108-109
low income (families, buyers, renters), x, xi, 3, 12, 37-40, 53-60, 154-155, 159-161, 163, 166, 168, 177-182
Lucas v. South Carolina Coastal Council, 3

Madoff, Bernie, 80
Marckx v Belgium, 93
Markets
  Market correction, 81
  Market economy, 84
  Market failure, 78-79, 82
  Market imperfections, xi, 134, 149-150
Marx, Karl, 44, 48-51
McCann v UK, 96, 117-121, 124-127, 130
Mensius, 40-41
Mill, John Stuart, 7, 47-48
minimalism, 14
mobility impairment, xi, 133-140, 143-145, 149, 152
mortgage, 4-5, 19, 38, 58, 65, 69, 72-75, 77, 80-82, 90, 114-115, 126-127, 135-136, 146, 161, 177

National Association of Home Builders, 149
New Deal, 67, 69-70, 72, 76
New Property, (The), x, 10, 23, 51, (see also Reich, Charles)
non-profit, 40, 54-56
nonpossessory interests, 5, 17
nuisance, 4, 10

Obama (President of the United States of America), 75-76, 81
ownership, x-xi, 1, 3, 12, 15-18, 20-21, 23-24, 26-31, 34-35, 37-46, 49-55, 58-61, 65, 70-72, 77-85, 97, 127, 145-147, 153-157, 159, 162, 165-168, 171-173, 175-177, 180-183, 185, 206

patent, 1, 20
Pima County, Arizona-Washburn v. Pima County, 147-148, 151
planned unit development, 9
planning, 4, 141, 170, 172, 204, 209
Plato, 44-45
ponzi scheme, 80

positive (law, positivism, positivist), ix, 1, 14, 17-19, 21, 26, 34, 78
possession,
potlatching, 43
price, 25, 49, 57-58, 61, 72, 79, 149, 158, 160-161, 169, 180
privacy, x, 7, 82, 89-91, 93, 99-100, 133, 148, 168, 209, 214, 223
public good, 15, 23, 101, 134, 136, 149
public interest, 3-4, 12, 17, 89, 103-104, 107-108, 110, 113, 119, 131, 134, 147, 155, 186, 195
public land, 17, 42, 105
public use, 14

quasi-public, 134, 136-137, 142, 149, 185

Radin, Margaret, 28, 51-52
Ratcliffe v. Eden, 189
rational choice theory, 30
rational-actor, 24, 29-30
real property, 15, 25, 37, 39, 61
Recovery and Reinvestment Act, 76
Reich, Charles A., 51 (see also New Property, The)
rent control, 52, 213
renter, 38, 61, 76, 145-146, 153, 162, 164, 168, 170-171, 173, 177
right to housing, x
Riot Act of 1714, xi-xii, 186, 189-193, 195, 197, 204-206
Rousseau, 49

same sex marriage, xii, 211, 226, 228
search-and-seizure, 99
secondary mortgage market, 73, 135-136
secured lending, 5
security interest, 4-6, 10, 12
Security Interests in Personal Property, 4, 6
segregation, 22
servitude, 2
shared equity housing, 37-38, 52-54, 59-62, 154-155
Sheffield City Council v Smart, 105
Smith, Adam, 52, 134 (see Invisible Hand)
social change, 11
social cost, 38, 58, 62, 149
social investment, 54-55, 57
social networks, 138, 144-145, 150
social norms, 15, 22, 27-29
spillover, 77, 142
stakeholders, 61
subprime, 72-74, 80-81, 83, 177
subsidy, 58-59, 127, 136
subsistence (right to), 41, 48-50, 82, 84
substantive due process, 69

Takings Clause-regulatory takings doctrine, 3, 6, 11, 13, 19
taxation-federal taxation, 15, 17, 56, 62, 192
technology, 2, 4, 6, 59
Tenant Opportunity to Purchase Act (TOPA), 153, 157, 160, 168, 173
tenants in common, 51
Term Asset-Backed Securities Loan Facility (TALF), 75
toxic debt, 75
tradable pollution permit, 12
Treasury (Dept. of), 74-75, 82-83
Troubled Asset Relief Program (TARP), 75, 82

U.S. Department of Housing and Urban Development, 142, 158
Uniform Commercial Code (U.C.C.), 5
universal design, 139-140, 142
unsecured creditors, 4-6
urban development, urbanization, 9, 142

value, 2, 11, 14, 24-25, 31, 38, 44, 46, 49, 52-53, 57-59, 72-73, 75, 77, 79, 113, 116, 131, 150, 168, 170-171, 173, 185-186, 195, 197, 206
variance (in zoning), 9-10, 141
Village of Euclid v. Ambler Realty Co, 10
visitability, xi, 139-141, 147, 149-151

well-field theory, 41

X v Germany, 93

zero-step (entrance; elevation), 140, 150
zero-sum, 9
zoning, 4, 6, 9-10, 12, 14, 17, 23, 25, 52, 62, 141-142, 151, 204, 213

For Product Safety Concerns and Information please contact our EU representative GPSR@taylorandfrancis.com
Taylor & Francis Verlag GmbH, Kaufingerstraße 24, 80331 München, Germany

www.ingramcontent.com/pod-product-compliance
Ingram Content Group UK Ltd.
Pitfield, Milton Keynes, MK11 3LW, UK
UKHW010957180926
475701UK00004B/425
* 9 7 8 1 1 3 8 2 5 1 9 7 7 *

Chapter 1

Introduction: A Historic Methodology of Military Law and Governance

One of the critical aspects of modern military operations is that the actions of a single service member may have strategic consequences for American foreign policy in a manner in which the individual soldier in World War II could not have imagined. A second lieutenant, for instance, who condones abuses of captured enemy forces or non-combatant civilian populations, can cost the nation the ability to continue military operations to a degree that his or her counterpart who landed at Normandy in 1944 did not come close to possessing. The current 24-hour news cycle and instant dissemination of electronic information may produce unplanned-for difficulties including, potentially, the loss of allied support. Likewise, an errant officer or enlisted member engaged in cyber operations in the United States can place the nation's security at risk. The conduct of civilian government employees and contractors may have a similar impact on military operations and national strategy. Military discipline is important today, and in the future for the same reasons as in the past where the discipline of a regiment of soldiers was essential to battle plans, but the newer reasons make it all the more critical. Yet the importance of a disciplined military establishment should never translate into a diminution of due process in military disciplinary decisions, and with this realization, the federal judiciary has a defined role in the supervision of the military's governance. This book is a study on how the federal judiciary, since 1968, shaped not only the military's internal governance, but also the broader aspects of the military establishment's place in the nation. For reasons further noted below, this book's conclusions and methods differ from other analysis of the judiciary's involvement in military governance.

Prior to World War II, the federal judiciary seldom reviewed the internal decisions of the military establishment. As a result, an officer who believed he was wrongly denied a promotion, or a soldier or sailor challenging the due process of a court-martial finding, could expect little chance of relief in the federal courts. Even when the federal judiciary reviewed appeals stemming from the military's internal decisions, federal judges and justices mostly deferred to the military establishment's reasons. Thus, military law became a system, separate and apart, from the nation's larger legal construct. Following World War II, the federal judiciary began to depart from deferring to the military establishment. The enactment of the Uniform Code of Military Justice in 1950 enabled greater judicial review over the military. But the social upheaval attendant with the Vietnam Conflict and the drive for equal rights had an impact on the judiciary's governance of the military establishment away from deferring to the military establishment's rationale for a variety of administrative and disciplinary programs to a greater judicial oversight.

Among the academic community, there remains a consensus that the federal judiciary remains overly deferential to the military establishment. This study does not concur with this consensus. Although this book focuses on the period beginning with the election of Richard Milhous Nixon and Chief Justice Warren Burger's tenure on the nation's highest court, since 1953, the Supreme Court has taken an active part in the governance of the military, and with it, the federal courts of appeal and district courts. To understand this point, the definition of military law has to considered in its most expansive context.

The governance of the military establishment, or military law, encompasses far more than military discipline. Not surprisingly, most studies on military law focus on courts-martial, in part, because of the public's interest in criminal trials. But, the field of military law begins with the Constitutional foundations of civil and military relations, followed by constitutional criminal law and international law. This body of law also includes the government's liabilities to the nation's citizenry for damages to personal property and health, the authority of federal agencies to regulate their personnel, and martial law. The nation's military law is, in effect, all of the domestic and international law that governs the existence and reliability of the military, as well as the military's place in the United States' democratic society. Military law is also a close relation with national security law, though that field includes federal and state law enforcement, and other police functions, as well as public health and natural disaster policies. Because the period of this study concentrates on the judiciary after the termination of conscription, appeals arising from Vietnam War era challenges to the nation's selective service program are not analyzed except as these appeals applied to the post-conscription registration program. There are, admittedly, dozens of books on the Supreme Court (hereafter the Court) and the governance of the military. That said, a reasonable question arises as to why should there be another examination of the relationship between the federal judiciary and the military? There are at least two reasons why:

a. Current State of Military Legal History Scholarship

Analysis of the judiciary's role in the shaping of military law is important, if for any other reason than if it is true that the nation's judges and justices overly deferred to the military establishment without reasoned thought to the consequences of their deference, then the nation's military establishment might be less than constitutional. Although several studies claim this to be the case, none of the contemporary studies on the Court and the military examine judicial intent with any detailed historic methodology, and are one-sided in their conclusions on the historic and current existence of an overarching judicial deference. For instance, in a recent book, Professor Diane Mazur claims that the modern military is, in part, a reflection of Chief Justice William Rehnquist's intention to create a conservative institution immune from legislative or even public criticism. She is not alone is such claims, but along with her book, contemporary studies provide little analytic context of the Cold War and post-Cold War environment. Any perusal of the bibliographies of the most recent studies evidences that very little primary research—the most important element of originality and accuracy—has been undertaken. Most of the current books carry on themes of older studies, generally calling for a narrowing of judicial deference to the military establishment, with a strong indication that the military establishment (that is, the nation's military's leadership from the President on down) is less than constitutional in the administration or exertion of its lawful authorities.[1]

The efforts of these scholars should not be degraded within an accusation of conducting their scholarship in bad faith, and a continuing scholarly analysis of civil-military relations is a healthy aspect of the military governance. Nonetheless, the lack of historic methodologies in their works gives rise to a reasonable criticism that their conclusions are incomplete. In 1965, legal history scholar, Albert Kelley criticized the Warren Court for using history in an amateurish and selective manner. Kelley claimed the justices had failed to take full cognizance of what has been occasionally labeled "the historians' craft." This "craft," or more appropriately, historic methodology includes the use of primary sources to discern the intentions of the participants. The Executive Branch may at times embark on irresponsible military and foreign policies, and Congress may at times unwisely abrogate their authority to the Executive Branch. The Judicial Branch, including the Court under Warren Burger's and William Rehnquist's chief justice tenures, however, has not failed to govern the military establishmentwithin its constitutional authority.[2]

---

1 See e.g. Diane Mazur, "Rehnquist's Vietnam: Constitutional Separatism and Stealth Advance of Martial Law," 77 Indiana Law Journal (2002): 701–84, 703. Mazur specifically writes, "Broad judicial deference to military discretion is only a creation of the post-Vietnam, all-volunteer military and, more specifically, only a creation of one single Justice of the Supreme Court, William H. Rehnquist." Id. See also, Diane Mazur, A *More Perfect Military, How the Constitution Can Make our Military Stronger* (New York: Oxford University Press, 2010); Steven Lichtman, "The Justices and the Generals: A Critical Examination of the U.S. Supreme Court's Tradition of Deference to the Military, 65 *Maryland Law Review* (2006) 907–50; Jonathan Turley, "Tribunals and Tribulations: The Antithetical Elements of Military Governance in a Madisonian Democracy," 70 *George Washington Law Review* (2002): 649–768; Jonathan Turley, "The Military Pocket Republic," 97 *Northwestern University Law Review* (2002): 1–126; Robert S. Rivkin, *GI Rights and Military Justice: The Draftee's Guide to Military Life and Law* (New York: Grove Press, 1970), 215; Robert Sherrill, *Military Justice is to Justice as Military Music is to Music* (New York: Harper and Row, 1970), 172–7.

2 Alfred H. Kelly, "Clio and the Court: An Illicit Love Affair," *Supreme Court Law Review* (1965), 119.

b. The Full Dimension of Military Legal History and Cold War History

A second reason that a reevaluation of the judiciary's role in military governance is important is because no contemporary study analyzes the judiciary within the context of either military history or Cold War history. Military history is not, of course, simply a recitation of battles and commanders. It is the study of the political, economic, cultural, and environmental effects of armed conflict, or the potential of armed conflict, on society. This arena of historical study not only includes the shaping of national strategy, but also an analysis of the political and military leaders' comprehension of the social and economic forces in their time. This treatise is, therefore, in part, a study on the judiciary's perception of the political, social and cultural environment affecting the military establishment during the time in which the judiciary's decisions were issued. It includes a complimentary analysis on how facets of society viewed the cultural, social, and political issues before it, including equal rights for women, the decriminalization of homosexuality, and the rise of a drug culture, and how these issues were addressed by the military establishment and the judiciary.[3]

1. Military legal history

American military legal history dates before the nation's founding, and while one could traverse to ancient Greece, as some scholars have done, the sources of modern military law, following the Constitution, are legislation such as the Articles of War and the UCMJ, as well as decisions of various courts. The laws governing the Army, titled the Articles of War were adopted from the British in 1775, amended in 1776, and congressionally enacted into law in 1806. In 1874 Congress legislated a new Articles of War which removed antiquated language, and it did so again in 1916, and then again in 1920. Following World War I there was an intense, albeit brief, debate in the War Department and Congress on courts-martial reform. However, the 1920 Articles of War only incorporated a few reforms advocated by critics of the courts-martial system. In 1948, a new Articles of War, which adopted more of the post-World War I criticisms was enacted, but was replaced two years later by the UCMJ.[4]

For much of the nation's history, a significant influence on military law were the scholars of the subject. Prior to the Civil War, the writings of American officers such as Alexander Macomb, John O'Brien, and William Chetwood De

3 There are multiple definitions of "military history," but see e.g. John Keegan, *A History of Warfare* (London: Pimlico, 1993); Jeremy Black, *Rethinking Military History* (London: Routledge, 2004); Robert M. Citino, "Military Histories Old and New: A Reintroduction," *The American Historical Review* Vol. 112 (2007): 1070–90.

4 See e.g. Jonathan Lurie, *Arming Military Justice: The Origins of the United States Court of Military Appeals, 1775–1950* (Princeton, NJ: Princeton University Press, 1992), chs II–III; also, Frederick Bernays Wiener, The Seamy Side of the World War I Court-Martial Controversy, 123 *Military Law Review* (1989) 109–21.

Hart, as well as a number of British authors, such as Alexander Fraser Tytler, (also titled as Lord Woodhouselee), were found in published federal judicial decisions. After the Civil War, a veteran officer named Colonel William Winthrop authored *Military Law*—later expanded to *Military Law and Precedents*—which became the most cited source on military law. Indeed, the Court and the lower federal judiciary still regularly cite to Winthrop's work as of 2013. The federal judiciary has also cited to other scholars such as Generals Guido Norman Lieber and George Breckenridge Davis, who were also Civil War veterans, and Colonel Frederick Wiener a former student and confidant of Justice Felix Frankfurter and World War II veteran.[5]

Winthrop, Davis, Lieber, and Wiener did not author treatises in ignorance of the Court's constitutional and criminal jurisprudence. Importantly, they incorporated the broader civil laws into their works. For instance, while Winthrop noted that a court-martial is an "instrumentality of the executive power" and not a part of the judiciary, it was required to adhere to the principles of civil law. With only a minority within the military establishment disagreeing with Winthrop's assumption that the military establishment could be entrusted to independently apply the nation's laws to its internal construct, through World War II, the military establishment was generally permitted to internally govern itself subject to the Legislative Branch. Davis, Lieber, and Wiener, moreover, advocated for Winthrop's assumption.[6]

What can also be learned from their exhaustive military legal studies is not only an examination of the nation's military laws, but also a contextual analysis of the reasons for a separate system of governance. They believed that the experience of the American War of Independence led the citizens who crafted the Constitution and the nation's early laws, including the Articles of War, to understand the importance of unitary command in wartime, as well as a system of laws in peacetime to ensure that the needed unity was unquestioned within the ranks. However, the nation's legal founders also placed in Congress, the primary responsibility for setting the parameters for maintaining the unity of command. The founders did not envision the United States as a world military power, such as the United Kingdom, Prussia, Russia, or France. Indeed, most of these men only grudgingly conceded the need for a small standing army. That said, Winthrop, Davis, Lieber, and Wiener, all believed that the Constitution was intentionally

5 See e.g., Alexander Tytler, *Essay on Military Law and the Practice of Courts-Martial* (London: T. Edgerton, 1880); Alexander Macomb, *The Practice of Courts-Martial* (New York: S. Coleman, 1840); William Chetwood De Hart, *Observations on Military Law and the Practice of Courts-Martial* (New York: Wiley and Putnam., 1846); John O'Brien, *A Treatise on American Military Law and the Practice of Courts-Martial With Suggestions for their Improvement* (Philadelphia: Lee and Blanchard, 1848); William Winthrop, *Military Law and Precedents* (Washington, DC: GPO, 1895).

6 William Winthrop, *Military Law and Precedents*, 49–61.

flexible enough to enable the Army to have the broadest jurisdictional reach over its service members, if Congress empowered the Executive Branch to this end.

From the nation's founding until 1950, the governance of the Navy was a different matter than that of the Army. The first Congress established the Articles for the Navy. The new nation would, after all, rely on ocean-going commerce for its existence, and in looking at the British, French, and Dutch naval examples, there was no opposition to a standing Navy, or even a wholly federalized Navy, replete with a harsh disciplinary code. Although from time to time naval courts-martial came under criticism, and the Court would issue decisions arising from naval courts-martial, there were fewer calls for reform in the Naval Articles, then calls against the Army.[7]

There are two other severable historic aspects to understanding the federal judiciary's role in influencing the nation's military laws prior to World War II. The first aspect is to analyze the Court's decisions directly affecting military law from the nation's founding through to the attack on Pearl Harbor. The most important military law decisions prior to the Civil War were *Martin v. Mott* decided in 1824, *Luther v. Borden*, decided in 1849, and *Dynes v. Hoover*, decided in 1857. Arising from the War of 1812, *Mott* was essentially a decision involving national security, the nature of federal-state relations regarding the militia, and the President's authority to declare an emergency. In a narrower sense, the Court determined that obedience to orders was a lawful requirement of military service. The decision originated from a court-martial where a militia soldier had been convicted of refusing to obey a call-up order, and the soldier appealed to the Court for redress from the conviction.

In *Luther*, the Court determined that a governor's authority to use forces to defeat an internal insurrection was a "political question," and therefore the Court would not second-guess the governor's authority to imprison a person accused of insurrection. The "political question" doctrine became a means of judicial non-intervention for a variety of challenges to Executive Branch authority. However, in *Luther,* the Court acknowledged the efficacy of military laws as a legal body apart from the nation's other laws. Finally, *Dynes,* was a decision in which the Court determined that the federal judiciary would only intervene in military trials of service-members where the military's jurisdiction over the person on trial was contested. The Court, in *Dynes*, made clear that the procedural fairness of courts-martial was a matter for the Legislative and Executive Branches. Shortly after *Dynes*, the statutory construct of the Court of Claims enabled a narrow venue of collateral attack on courts-martial. That is, the claims court could award back

7 Joshua Kastenberg, "A Sesquicentennial Historic Analysis of *Dynes v. Hoover* and the Supreme Court's Bow to Military Necessity: From its Relationship to *Dred Scott v. Sandford* to its Contemporary Influence," 39 *University of Memphis Law Review* (2009) 595–663.

pay if it concluded that a court-martial conviction was wrongly decided. That court could not, however, directly overturn the conviction.[8]

Two decisions issued during the Civil War, *Ex Parte Vallandigham* and *Ex Parte Milligan* went to the heart of how far military jurisdiction could expand over civilians. In 1863, the Court, in *Vallandigham,* turned to the three pre-Civil War cases listed above to conclude that it would not overturn the Executive Branch's assertion that its military jurisdiction went so far as to extend to citizens in Ohio, a loyal state where the federal courts fully functioned. Clement Vallandigham, however, was not a random civilian. He was a locally powerful former congressman who publicly railed against the war and accused Lincoln of creating a dictatorship. He also encouraged his followers to obstruct the Union's war efforts. In *Milligan,* decided three years later, the Court reached a different result than in *Vallandingham,* and determined that military jurisdiction did not constitutionally extend to citizens in the United States under any circumstances while the civil courts functioned. This decision deprived Congress of the authority to legislate such an extension of military jurisdiction, even though the Legislative Branch had little involvement in the Civil War military trials to begin with. To several justices during and after World War II, *Milligan* was a critical decision in further narrowing military jurisdiction over service-members as well. However, in reality, *Milligan* reinforced the constitutionality of the military's internal disciplinary processes and continued the tradition of the federal judiciary's deference to the military for internal matters.[9]

Between the end of the Civil War and World War I, the Court issued several decisions of importance to the military establishment, but since most of these decisions upheld the prior doctrine of judicial non-intervention in courts-martial, none were influential in evolving the military law, in the sense that the Court did not direct the military to reform courts-martial. The reason for this deference though, was the assumption that the courts-martial had to conform to constitutional and criminal law. After all, in 1884, Winthrop reminded the War Department that courts-martial were bound by the judiciary's broader constitutional and criminal law decisions, and in 1865, the Judge Advocate General likewise informed the Army of this fact. In 1887, Chief Justice Morrison Remick Waite, in *Runkle v. United States* emphatically stated courts-martial "sit to pass upon the most sacred questions of human rights that are ever placed on trial in a court of justice; rights which, in the very nature of things, can neither be exposed to danger nor subjected to the uncontrolled will of any man, but which must be adjudged according to law."[10]

---

8 *Martin v. Mott*, 25 U.S. 19 (1827); *Luther v. Borden*, 48 U.S. 1 (1849); *Dynes v. Hoover*, 61 U.S. 65 (1857).

9 *Ex Parte Vallandigham*, 68 U.S. 243 (1864); *Ex Parte Milligan*, 71 U.S. 2 (1866).

10 *Runkle v. United States*, 122 U.S. 543 (1887); See also *Johnson v. Sayre*, 158 U.S. 109 (1895); and, *Ex Parte Mason*, 159 U.S. 696 (1882).

Almost a decade prior to *Runkle*, the Court, in *Coleman v. Tennessee* opined that Congress had the authority to confer on the Executive Branch exclusive jurisdiction over soldiers. However, Congress had not explicitly done so in Coleman's case. The Army court-martialed Coleman, an enlisted soldier, for the murder of a civilian non-combatant, and the court-martial had sentenced him to death on May 9, 1865. Following Lincoln's assassination, a general amnesty was granted and Coleman's sentence was commuted to imprisonment. In October, 1874, a Tennessee state prosecutor sympathetic to the former confederacy obtained an indictment against Coleman for the same murder he had been court-martialed for. Coleman pled not-guilty but he also challenged the indictment on the basis of double jeopardy to the United States District Court.[11]

Although Justice Stephen A. Field, the author of the decision, and with him the majority, noted that Congress could create exclusivity for military jurisdiction, Field applied international law principles to free Coleman from the indictment. In the nineteenth century, international law recognized that when a friendly sovereign nation permitted a foreign army to traverse its territory, it also waived its jurisdiction over the passing traversing soldiers. Field reasoned that if a friendly state waived jurisdiction, then an enemy or occupied enemy state also implicitly waived its jurisdiction. Hence, as Tennessee in 1865, was largely under occupation with a military governor, then it too lacked jurisdiction over Union soldiers such as Coleman. Ironically, the two twentieth-century justices at opposite ends of the judicial spectrum in regards to military governance, William O. Douglas and William H. Rehnquist would overlook this narrow aspect of the *Coleman*, but it is notable that Field was hardly an adherent of assertions of Executive Branch authority. The other interesting aspect of *Coleman* is that the decision was a compromise between John Marshall Harlan and Nathan Clifford, who feared that southern states would be given license to prosecute former Union soldiers for alleged offenses committed during the war, and the rest of the justices who wanted strong states' rights language in the decision. Clifford would ultimately dissent, arguing that a court-martial served as a double jeopardy bar to a later state prosecution.[12]

With the exception of *Coleman* and its attendant political questions involving Reconstruction, the Court approached most of its military governance decisions with little enthusiasm, at a time when the Army, including its legal apparatus went through a period of internal professionalization. The judiciary's disinterest in military affairs was not unusual. With the exception of the use of the Army in labor unrest, Congress, and even to an extent, the Executive Branch, were also aloof from the military during the "Gilded Age," as well.[13]

---

11 *Coleman v. State of Tennessee*, 97 U.S. 509 (1878).

12 Waite, Conference Assignment Notes, October 26 1978 [MRW/40].

13 See e.g. Robert Utley, *Frontier Regulars: The United States Army and the Indian, 1866–1891* (New York: MacMillan Publishing Co., Inc, 1973), 61–70; and William A. Ganoe, *History of the United States Army* (New York: D. Appleton and Co., 1924), 306.

For instance, in 1890, in *In re Grimley*, a decision upholding the Army's jurisdiction over a soldier who lied about his age at enlistment and then deserted, the issue of jurisdiction was important to the Army, but not the Attorney General. Grimley was not an under-aged youth, which statutorily would have terminated jurisdiction. To the contrary he was 40 years old, but claimed to be only 28. Factually, Grimley was statutorily over the permissible enlistment age. At the time, he was not atypical in lying about his age at enlistment. False statements to recruiters and enlistments under pseudonym were not uncommon features of the post-Civil War frontier Army. The Attorney General deferred to the Judge Advocate General to prepare the arguments to the Court. Chief Justice Melville Weston Fuller assigned Justice David Brewer to the case, because none of the other justices expressed an interest in it.[14]

Similarly, in 1897, in *Swaim v. United States*, a decision which upheld the principle of limited federal judicial *habeas* jurisdiction, Fuller assigned Associate Justice George Shiras to write the majority opinion simply because he was the only willing justice at the time of the assignment to author the decision. In *Swaim*, the Army court-martialed its judge advocate general for taking kick-backs from contractors, then lying about his knowledge of the scheme to Secretary of War Robert Todd Lincoln. President Chester Arthur was upset at the leniency of the sentence and sent the case back three times to the court-martial to reconsider its sentence. Swaim was a corrupt senior officer, but in modern parlance, he was also a victim of unlawful command influence. However, the justices were unconcerned with President Arthur's actions because courts-martial remained outside of the traditional jurisdiction test.[15]

The federal judiciary's deference to the military did not change after World War I, even though the justices were well aware of a congressional investigation into the fairness of military law and an intense public debate which created discord in the Army over the subject. In 1921 the Court in *Kahn v. Anderson* had occasion to further define when the judiciary could review courts-martial. The 1916 revised Articles of War mandated a 13-officer court-martial panel, unless exigent circumstances existed. Without any statement of exigency by their command, the soldiers involved in this case were tried by eight officers. The Court determined that the number of officers was discretionary, and therefore would not consider the lesser number a reason to deprive the court-martial of jurisdiction. Nor was the fact that two of the officers assigned to the court-martial were retired a matter for reversal. Of greater importance, the soldiers in *Kahn* were prosecuted for murder, but under the Articles of War, the crime of murder, if committed

14 Fuller to Brewer, undated 1890, [MWFP]. On conditions in the Army, see, e.g. Don Rickey Jr., *Forty Miles a Day on Beans and Hay* (Norman, OK: University of Oklahoma Press, 1963), 17–32 and 137–84.

15 *United States v. Grimley*, 137 U.S. 147 (1890); *Swaim v. United States*, 165 U.S. 552 (1897). On the conference discussions in these cases see, Fuller to Brewer, undated, assignment on Grimley [MFWP]; and Shiras to Fuller, February 13, 1897 [MFWP].

in the United States, could not be court-martialed in time of peace. The Army conducted the court-martial after the Armistice was signed, but before Congress had signified an end to war. Relying on previous decisions, the Court upheld the Army's court-martial jurisdiction to extend to the point in time in which Congress determined an end to hostilities, and not when an enemy belligerent surrendered. Neither Oliver Wendell Holmes Jr., nor Louis Brandeis, the Court's principle liberals, dissented in the decision.[16]

At the same time the Court decided *Kahn*, it also decided *Givens v. Zerbst*. This decision arose from a court-martial of an officer who killed an enlisted soldier. Givens challenged that the commanding officer who convened the court-martial did not possess the statutory authority to do so, and that the court-martial had been held in time of peace. The Court's holding was similar to *Kahn*, and it further reinforced the traditional notion of limited federal court jurisdiction.[17]

A subtle change in the Court's attitude occurred in the following two decades. In 1938, the Court decided *Johnson v. Zerbst*, a decision which reversed a federal conviction over two Marines, after the United States Attorney and then the federal judge denied them counsel. This decision did not arise from a court-martial, but rather it extended federal *habeas* jurisdiction to include review errors which "amounted to a deprivation of constitutional right." During World War II, and in the following Cold War period, *Johnson v. Zerbst* would provide an avenue to soldiers collaterally attacking courts-martial, but this avenue frequently failed to bring relief. When a federal court reviewed a court-martial appeal, it did so by granting *habeas*, in what was known as a "collateral attack." In authoring the decision, Hugo Black did, in fact, consider its implications in courts-martial, though his belief that the decision would open the door to greater judicial review is not readily apparent in the published decision.[18]

Although this study does not concentrate on the establishment of military trials over enemy combatants, it is helpful to note that during World War II, the Court determined, in *Ex parte Quirin* that captured German saboteurs, or other law of war violators, could be prosecuted in a military commission and the federal judiciary did not possess the jurisdictional authority to review the procedures or fairness of the trial. Implicit in the decision however, was the Court's expectation that the trials afforded to such persons would possess procedures which mirrored the fairness of courts-martial. *Quirin* has come under intense criticism, particularly in the legal academy after September 11, 2001. But even before George W. Bush's presidency, Justice Antonin Scalia called *Quirin*, "not the Court's finest hour," and urged that the decision undermined *Milligan*. To be sure, the Bush administration lawyers cited to the decision as a basis for the detention, prosecution, and denial of *habeas*, to captured combatants including United States citizens. In response, Yale Professor Bruce Ackerman argued that the decision provides "the slam dunk

16 *Kahn v. Anderson*, 255 U.S. 1 (1921).

17 *Givens v. Zerbst*, 255 U.S. 11 (1921).

18 *Johnson v. Zerbst*, 304 U.S. 458 (1938); Black, Conference Memorandum, undated [HLB/254].

argument for apologists of presidential power." On the other hand, *Quirin* does not stretch to citizens at any rate, and those who argued that it does missed the fundamental limitation of the decision.[19]

At the end of the war, the Court once more addressed the limits of jurisdiction over enemy combatants in *In re Yamashita*. This decision arose from the prosecution of a Japanese general convicted in American military tribunals and sentenced to death. In *Yamashita*, and its companion decision *Homma*, the Court retreated from the suggestion that due process applied in some form in such tribunals, but the Court maintained that the judiciary had no oversight authority into the procedures employed by such trials. A similar result occurred in a decision stemming from the military's capture, trial, and transference of German personnel captured in China, but still engaged in the war after the German surrender. In *Johnson v. Eisentrager*, the Court, in a bare majority, determined that it would not review the military's actions, even in regard to the question of whether the Germans had violated the law of war in the first place. *Quirin, Yamashita*, and *Eisentrager* became important for the detention and prosecution of enemy combatants, after a generation of dormancy, following September 11, 2001.[20]

Although the Court did not reverse any court-martial convictions arising from World War II, a process toward limiting deference was underway. In *Burns v. Wilson*, the Court, though it upheld the death sentences of two Air Force enlisted members, noted that if the military appellate courts, created as part of the UCMJ in 1950, failed to "fully and fairly" evaluate appeals, the federal judiciary could then intervene. The Court did not define what "fully and fairly" meant, and even at present, the courts of appeal have not accepted a universal definition as to the term "fully and fairly." Courts of appeal have differing definitions as to that term to this day. In areas outside of courts-martial, the Court continued to mostly defer to the military establishment. The same year the Court issued *Burns*, it also applied the state secrets doctrine to peacetime military operations in *United States v. Reynolds*, effectively shielding the government from liability when it claimed that evidence critical to national security

19 *Ex parte Quirin*, 317 U.S. 1 (1942). See e.g., Bruce Ackerman, *Before the Next Attack: Preserving Civil Liberties in an Age of Terrorism* (New Haven, CT: Yale University Press, 2006), 23; 111–12; James Staab, *The Political Thought of Justice Antonin Scalia: A Hamiltonian on the Supreme Court* (Lanham, MD: Rowman and Littlefield, 2006); Louis Fisher, *Nazi Saboteurs on Trial* (Lawrence, KS: Kansas University Press, 2003), 1–9; Pierce O'Donnell, *In Time of War: Hitler's Terrorist Attack on America* (New York: The New Press, 2009), 1–10.

20 *In re Yamashita*, 327 U.S. 1 (1946); The companion case is, *Application of Homma*, 327 U.S. 759 (1945); See also, A. Frank Reel, *The Case of General Yamashita* (Chicago, IL: University of Chicago Press, 1949), Richard Lael, *The Yamashita Precedent: War Crimes and Command Responsibility* (Wilmington, DE: Scholarly Resources, 1982), and, William O. Douglas, *The Court Years: The Autobiography of William O. Douglas*, (New York: Random House, 1980), 38; John Ferren, *Salt of the Earth, Conscience of the Court* (Chapel Hill, NC: University of North Carolina Press, 2010), 310–12; *Johnson v. Eisentrager*, 339 U.S. 763 (1950).

had to be suppressed. The Court also contemporaneously issued *Orloff v. Willoughby*, in which the majority of the Court determined that the judiciary had to defer to the internal security decisions of the military establishment. The plaintiff in *Orloff* was a medical doctor who was drafted into the Army as an enlisted service-member but the Army refused him a commission because of his prior association with organizations the government had deemed subversive.[21]

During the same period the Court deferred to the military establishment over its internal administrative decisions, it also upheld an expansive immunity from lawsuits raised by service-members against the military in *Feres v. United States*. This decision has an important history and legacy. The Court combined three appeals which had percolated through the federal trial and appellate courts. In the appeal arising from the named claimant, the Court of Appeals for the Second Circuit determined that a claim of wrongful death from a boiler explosion in a barracks was from military service and therefore the government could not be held liable in tort. The second appeal, which arose through the Court of Appeals for the Fourth Circuit involved a claim of medical malpractice. A surgeon had left a towel inside of an active duty patient after an operation, but the appellate court held that lawsuit was likewise precluded. The third appeal originated in the Court of Appeals for the Tenth Circuit where that court determined, similarly to the Fourth Circuit, that the government could not be liable for a wrongful death to an officer caused by a military doctor's negligence during a surgery. Thus, in *Feres*, the Court comprehensively upheld Congress' authority to bar active duty members from suing the United States Government in tort on the basis of negligence.[22]

Feres would, over time, be roundly criticized by the lower courts and in the academic community. In large measure, this has occurred because the Court has ascribed reasons to the Federal Tort Claims Act (FTCA) that are absent from the plain language of either the statute or *Feres* itself. Although recently criticism has tapered off, there have been too many well publicized instances where aggrieved service-members or their families have been left without the full recourse in tort law against the cause of their injury. A male prisoner sexually assaulted at Fort Leavenworth (who actually happened to be innocent) when the prison authorities knew he was targeted by other inmates, the family of a soldier murdered by another soldier who Army officers knew posed a significant danger, the testing of lysergic acid diethylemide (LSD) on unknowing service-members, and the murdered active duty spouse of a naval officer who had scored dangerously close to sociopathic levels on a submarine fitness psychological test, have all resulted in no financial liability

21 *Burns v. Wilson*, 346 U.S. 137 (1953); *United States v. Reynolds*, 345 U.S. 1 (1953); See also, Louis Fisher, *In the Name of National Security: Unchecked Presidential Power and the Reynolds Case* (Lawrence, KS: Kansas University Press, 2006); *Orloff v. Willoughby*, 345 U.S. 82 (1953).

22 See *Feres v. United States*, 177 F.2d 535 (CA 2, 1949) 340 U.S. 135 (1950); *Jefferson v. United States*, 178 F.2d 518 (CA 4, 1950); and, *Griggs v. United States*, 178 F.2d 1 (CA 10, 1950).

to the government in the same manner as a civilian would be entitled to claim. On top of these extreme examples, hundreds, if not thousands, of otherwise meritorious medical malpractice claims provide no relief to the aggrieved service-members.[23]

From 1953 through 1968, the Court would curtail a significant aspect of military jurisdiction. In a series of decisions beginning with *United States ex rel Toth v. Quarles*, through *Reid v. Covert*, and its progeny, the Court determined that civilians, including former service-members who committed crimes while on active duty, could not constitutionally be subject to the military's jurisdiction. On the other hand, the Court did not diminish the military's jurisdiction over its own personnel until 1969, at the height of the Vietnam Conflict.[24]

2. Cold War legal history

Related to military legal history is a legal history of the Cold War. The Court, during the period 1945 to 1968, issued dozens of decisions arising from the federal and state governments' efforts to limit the spread of communism. After World War II, individual rights had been undermined through the extensive application of government loyalty programs. From 1947 through 1953, the Court deferred to governmental claims of national security over individual rights. The justices' Cold War jurisprudence included upholding the contempt findings and disbarment of attorneys affiliated with the Communist Party of the United States (CPUSA), convictions arising from refusals to testify to Congress, limits on free speech, as well as preventing persons listed on the Attorney General's Subversive Organizations List from serving in labor union leadership positions. Cold War historian David Caute assessed the federal judiciary's role during the age of McCarthyism as: "shamefully, as the American Judiciary bowed and bent to the Realpolitik of the 'American Century,' it never completely abdicated its independence and was soon able to stage an admirable recovery of nerve, restoring support to the Bill of Rights." The judiciary's role in its oversight of the military's internal governance and the broader military law must be analyzed in parallel with its Cold War jurisprudence.[25]

In 1957, the Court issued *Harmon v. Brucker*, a decision which arose from the lower courts' giving carte blanche to the military establishment over how to deal with a perceived internal threat of communism in the ranks. The Court, in reversing the lower courts, however, provided protection for service-members accused of prior ties to subversive organizations. *Harmon* involved two servicemen who brought suit against the Secretary of the Army Wilbur Brucker. The Army drafted Howard D. Abramowitz in 1951, and he earned a silver star while fighting in

23 See e.g. *United States v. Stanley*, 483 U.S. 669 (1987); *Dexheimer v. United States*, 608 F.2d 765 (CA 9, 1979); *Yolken v. United States*, 590 F.2d 1303 (CA 4, 1976).

24 *United States ex rel Toth v. Quarles*, 350 U.S. 11 (1955); *Reid v. Covert*, 354 U.S.1 (1957).

25 David Caute, *The Great Fear: Anti Communist Purges* (New York: Simon and Schuster 1978), 17.

the Korean War. In 1953 the Army released him from active duty and transferred him into the reserves. After discovering in 1955 that he had once been a CPUSA member prior to his active military service, Army officials discharged him with an undesirable discharge. Abramowitz unsuccessfully appealed the Army's decision to the District Court for the District of Columbia and then to the Court of Appeals for the District of Columbia.[26]

The government inducted John Henry Harmon III, a Bucknell University graduate, into the Army in October, 1952. Two years later, Harmon's commander ordered him to answer a questionnaire focusing on subversive affiliations. Harmon responded that the Detroit Urban League employed him prior to his military service, he was registered to vote with the American Labor Party, and he solicited funds for the defense of two citizens indicted under the Smith Act. Additionally, the Federal Bureau of Investigation listed his father and step-mother as "subversives." The Army did not initially remove Harmon, and instead transferred him to routine non-sensitive duties. However, shortly after Harmon's transfer to routine military duties, the Defense Department issued a new regulation which, if followed to the letter, required the Army to discharge Harmon. On June 2, 1954, the Army discharged Harmon with an "undesirable discharge." Although an "undesirable discharge," was non-punitive, (that is, not the result of a court-martial), it classified service members as not successfully or honorably completing their enlistment and precluded most veterans' benefits. Additionally, the undesirable discharge would have the effect of negatively labeling a person for civilian employment. The appellate court upheld the Army's action against Harmon.[27]

In a *per curiam* decision, with only Tom Clark dissenting, the Court found that the Army had exceeded its authority in issuing less than fully honorable discharges. *Harmon* did not negate *Orloff*, but the decision showed a trend away from deferring to the military establishment. In conference, all of the justices but Clark accepted Felix Frankfurter's argument that the military establishment was, in fact, punishing individuals for prior political beliefs, and that no statutory or compelling basis existed to do so.[28]

---

26 *Harmon v. Brucker*, 355 U.S. 579 (1958); *Abramowitz v. Bruker*, 253 F.2d 854 (CA DC 1957). There is less information on Abramowitz than on Harmon. After his military service, Abramowitz earned a doctorate in sociology and taught at Skidmore College. He also was employed by the International Ladies Garment Workers Union. See, Obituary, Abramowitz, New York Times, April 10, 1990. On Secretary of the Army Wilbur Brucker, see *Maxwell Taylor, Swords and Plowshares: A Memoir* (New York: Da Capo, 1972), 167. General Taylor wrote "Brucker was too honorable a man to yield to unjustified pressure and developed into a stalwart defender of the Army's role in national security."

27 ACLU Records of Southern California [Box 92/folder 6 UCLA]; See also "GI Discharged as a Red Because of Urban League," *Jet Magazine*, August 12, 1954, pp. 10.

28 Earl Warren, conference notes [EW/634]; Brennan, memorandum, February 6, 1958 {WJB I:11].

One other comment on Cold War legal history bears mention. Extreme right-wing organizations such as the John Birch Society accused the courts of being riddled with communist sympathizers. During Frederick Vinson's tenure as chief justice, Westbrook Pegler a prominent journalist who stoked hatred against Jews, racial minorities, and other peoples he did not approve of, accused Frankfurter of being a Marxist ideologue. In the later 1960s congressional Republicans attempted to smear William O. Douglas of being a communist sympathizer, as well as having ties to organized crime. Nothing could be further from the truth as to any of these claims. Indeed, there has never been a provable instance of a justice, or even a federal judge on a lower court of being a communist, or even having communist ideals. Communism is antithetical to the American judiciary whether a judge is a liberal or conservative, or a strict constructionist or activist.

The attorneys who argued military governance cases before the courts were another matter. A few of these attorneys were communists or affiliated with organizations considered to be subversive. These attorneys influenced the judicial shaping of the national defense. The CPUSA and communist ideologues in the Soviet Union concluded by 1945, that United States citizens would not rise to overthrow their government on the basis of ideology alone. Their party strategy was to weaken the nation's Armed Forces, so that communism could grow elsewhere. Under this strategy, over the long term, an isolated United States would become ineffectual as it lacked overseas markets and international influence, and then capitalism would collapse. Counsel affiliated with the CPUSA and other attorneys believed the judiciary could be used as an instrument to undermine military discipline. While it is certainly wrong to assess an attorney's motive based solely on the client the attorney represents, the military establishment was confronted with a small number attorneys who had publicly stated their goal at undermining "American imperialism," particularly the nation's foreign and military policies. Certainly amongst the conservative justices, and particularly Warren Burger, there was intolerance for attorneys who were deemed to be sympathetic to communism or socialism.[29]

As an example, the issue of attorneys with ties to suspected subversive personnel occurred in *Kauffman v. Secretary of the Air Force*, an appeal which arose from a court-martial of an Air Force captain for espionage. In 1961, an East German defector notified the Federal Bureau of Investigation that East German intelligence had interrogated Captain Joseph Kauffman and released him. What actually had occurred was that Kauffman, while on leave, had taken a train from Hamburg to West Berlin. As the train transited the German Democratic Republic,

29 United States Army Surveillance of Dissidents, Report on Resistance Inside the Military, April 18, 1968 [UPA/17]; Hoover to Truman, January 9, 1946; January 11, 1946, [HST R/21];Robert Ferrell, Harry S. Truman, A Life (Missouri), 227–8. R. Alton Lee, "The Army Mutiny of 1946," *The Journal of American History*, Vol. 53, No. 3 (Dec., 1966), 555–71; John E. Haynes and Harvey Klehr, *Early Cold War Spies* (New York: Cambridge, 2006), 23–66.

the East German police or "Stasi," removed him from the train. Under interrogation he agreed that if he were released, he would return to East Berlin. East German agents unsuccessfully attempted to turn Kauffman into a spy. However, Kauffman never reported his several meetings with the foreign agents, as the law required him to do.[30]

Military authorities searched Kauffman's California home and eavesdropped on his conversations with his trial defense lawyer, Benjamin Dreyfus, who had previously represented persons accused of CPUSA ties. After charging Kauffman at his home station in California, the Air Force transferred him to Germany for court-martial, making it difficult for his civilian attorney to represent him. Prior to his transit through communist Germany, Kauffman had been stationed in Greenland, but he had never been stationed in Germany. Though the UCMJ would have permitted his court-martial to occur anywhere in the world, the decision to hold the court-martial in Germany broke with long-standing military practice, and was clearly designed to affect Kauffman's defense. The court-martial sentenced Kauffman to twenty years in confinement and a dismissal. The Court of Military Appeals reversed his conviction on two of the charges and reduced his sentence from twenty years of imprisonment to two, but the dismissal, a lifetime stigma of dishonorable service, remained.

David Rein and Leonard Boudin represented Kauffman during his appeal the the Court of Appeals for the District of Columbia. The appellate court determined that Kauffman's claims rose to a constitutional level, and determined that it had jurisdiction to decide the merits of the Kauffman's appeal that he had been denied due process. The government argued for a narrow interpretation of the standard of review akin to *Orloff.* But the appellate court disagreed, ruling that the judicial review of the military appellate courts would occur on the same level and against the same standards as federal judicial review of civilian criminal trials. Ironically, having reviewed the Court of Military Appeals' decision, the Court of Appeals for the District of Columbia determined that the military appellate court had "fully and fairly considered [Kauffman's] claims of constitutional error and disposed of them in accordance with Supreme Court standards." Leaders in the military establishment were concerned with Kauffman being represented by attorneys who would not ordinarily be granted access to classified documents, gaining access under the Constitutional principle of the right to counsel in criminal trials.[31]

Other attorneys advocated for courts-martial and command reforms simply because they believed the military had fallen behind in due process of other constitutional values. The traditionally conservative American Bar Association's leadership concluded after World War II that significant reforms in military justice were necessary. Attorneys working with the National Association for the Advancement of Colored People (NAACP) were involved in several important

30 415 F.2d 991 (CA DC 1968).

31 See e.g. House of Representatives, Investigation of Attempts to Subvert the United States Armed Services, Hearings before the House Armed Services Committee, 1969.

cases as well, and the arguments they raised could not legitimately be assessed as designed to undermine the military, though certainly bigoted leaders in the war and naval departments, and later the Department of Defense would accuse them of such. Through their litigation, NAACP attorneys often pointed out glaring inequalities in the treatment of minorities and improved the fairness of military legal practices.

I: Basic Legal Principles of Military Governance

As noted earlier, from the nation's founding until World War II, the federal judiciary had rarely reviewed appeals from courts-martial, or at least the substantive claims within appeals. Such appeals, known as "collateral attacks," were limited in part because of federal judiciary's concept of its own jurisprudence, whether created by statutory limitations or constitutional interpretation. With the exception of *Milligan*, and suits by civilians against the War Department, the judiciary treated courts-martial similar to state criminal trials. The sole question that a court would entertain was whether the court-martial possessed jurisdiction over the person prosecuted. However, this did not simply mean that a soldier in uniform was automatically without legal recourse.

In *McClaughry v. Deming,* the Court, in 1902, reversed a court-martial conviction of a National Guardsman where the Army failed to compose the court-martial with National Guard personnel as required by statute. The Court added to its interpretation an interesting justification for its ruling, finding that regular Army officers would be unduly prejudiced against guardsmen. For much of the twentieth century, the Court of Claims could collaterally decide whether a court-martial was conducted in compliance with the Articles of War, the UCMJ, or binding case-law, and then order the War or Navy Departments (or Department of Defense) to restore pay to a wrongly discharged individual. The judiciary's absence from the military's internal governance was predicated on deference to the Executive Branch, but with the understanding that the military would apply common law principles to courts-martial. No nineteenth-century American military law scholar urged the Army to ignore due process, and to the contrary, Winthrop and the later scholars argued that where courts-martial ignored due process, the Secretary of War, the President, and Congress had a duty to rectify injustices. The post-Civil War records of the Judge Advocate General and the Adjutant General are replete with instances where courts-martial were overturned on this basis.[32]

That said, there are several principles of law important to remember in analyzing the extent to which the post-World War II justices deferred to the military establishment. Three of these principles: Jurisdiction, *Lex Non Scripta* and military custom, Exhaustion Doctrine, are addressed here.

32 *McClaughry v. Deming*, 186 U.S. 49 (1902).

a. The Meaning of Jurisdiction in Military Law

For a court to adjudicate a matter over a person or a contested issue, it must possess the lawful jurisdiction over the person or issue. Broadly, jurisdiction must exist in two manners: *in personam* (Latin for over the person), and *in rem* (subject matter). *In personam* jurisdiction is often easy to discern, because the question is simply, does a court have jurisdiction over a person? A Kansas state court, for example, generally will not have jurisdiction over a contested event which occurred in California that has no bearing on the commerce of Kansas. This is true even in the federal courts. Subject matter jurisdiction is another issue. In the context of criminal law, a court does not possess jurisdiction over a behavior or act that has not been codified into the criminal law. Moreover, subject matter jurisdiction does not exist where the codified crime runs afoul of the Bill of Rights or some other right. This is why, for instance, criticizing the federal government is not an offense, though in 1776, in the United Kingdom public criticism of the King constituted a crime. There was a profound difference between the laws of the two nations in 1789 in regards to individual rights. In the United States, the First Amendment's enumerated right of freedom of speech usually deprives a court of jurisdiction over a codified offense prohibiting public expressions of discontent.

In 1812, the Court, in *United States v. Hudson and Goodwin*, determined that for an offense to exist, Congress must first create a law specifying the illegality of an act, and the act itself cannot abridge the Bill of Rights. This decision originated in the federal prosecution of newspaper editors who maligned President Thomas Jefferson and the Congress. The Court overturned the broad, almost borderless, law under which the editors had been charged because it lacked a specific prohibition. Less evident in *Hudson and Goodwin* was the larger issue of criminalizing speech, but over time, it became increasingly difficult to punish speech. Even during the height of the Cold War, the statutory broadening of the criminalization of speech was short-lived. However, *Hudson and Goodwin* was never thought to apply to the military and not until the later stages of the Vietnam War did some federal judges argue that it did. This view did not ultimately prevail.[33]

There is a third part to jurisdiction, which specifically addresses which court has the authority to determine a contested issue. Not all federal courts have expansive jurisdiction. Congress possesses the constitutional authority to create courts of special jurisdiction. Over the nation's history such courts have included the Court of Claims to adjudicate claims against the government, admiralty courts to adjudicate vessel ownership and maritime tort claims, the patent court, and courts-martial. From the nation's founding through the end of World War II, federal courts were constrained against reviewing courts-martial decisions except through a collateral attack on the basis of *habeas corpus* or through Court of Claims decisions. (*Habeas* is an avenue of redress to the federal courts for matters which might not ordinarily arise within their jurisdiction.) During the Civil War, World

33 *United States v. Hudson and Goodwin*, 11 U.S. 32 (1812).

War II, and following the government's internment and prosecution of captured enemy combatants, *habeas* became a significant feature of military law.

The question of when a federal court could intervene in courts-martial or the enforcement of other military policies was not settled law in 1945. Nor did the UCMJ resolve all questions of jurisdiction, even though Congress, in enacting Article 76 of that code stated that a court-martial was not "final and conclusive" until it was reviewed by the military appellate courts, and that the federal courts should not intervene in courts-martial until such trials were "final and conclusive." This is important language in the sense that customarily the federal courts would not review an issue until the courts of another sovereign, such as a state court, had ruled conclusively on an issue. This doctrine developed out of the concept of federalism. That is, the federal judiciary, like the Congress and the Executive Branch was supposed to respect the sovereignty of the states, unless an act of the state deprived individuals a constitutional right.

Of course federalism is the doctrine defining state and federal relations, and the military is not a state, but an arm of the federal government. Nonetheless, military law was allowed to develop on its own as though it were a separate sovereignty. For 150 years, this relationship was virtually unchallenged in the courts and Congress, much in the same manner that, with the exception of the federal Reconstruction of the post-Civil War south, the federal judiciary remained outside of the sphere of state governments. In the multiple instances where a federal court intervened in a court-martial, than then federal courts certainly did influence military law and take a significant role in the development of that body of law. This is true even in cases where the judiciary ruled in the military's favor.

When in 1950, Congress enacted the UCMJ, it also created the Court of Military Appeals. Initially this court had jurisdiction over courts-martial where a sentence included a punitive discharge or confinement for one year or more. A judge advocate general in any of the three services could also certify an issue for the Court of Military Appeals to determine, such as in instances where a court-martial sentenced a service member to less than the jurisdictional limits noted above. The three judges (and later five judges) appointed to this court statutorily had to be civilians to alleviate concerns of command influence. The Department of Defense, including the Secretary of Defense are bound by the court's decisions, subject to an adverse ruling by the Court. Although the Court of Military Appeals and its successors are an Article I court, and the judges do not possess a life tenured position such as their federal counterpart, Congress intended that the authority of its judges would be similar to that of federal judges within their jurisdiction. In 1968, Congress renamed the court, the United States Court of Military Appeals and in 1994, Congress renamed it to the Court of Appeals for the Armed Forces. In 1983, Congress expanded the Court's *certiorari* jurisdiction over the Court of Military Appeals.[34]

34 For a history of the Court of Military Appeals, see Jonathan Lurie, *Pursuing Military Justice: The History of the United States Court of Appeals for the Armed Forces*

This did not mean that in 1983, for the first time the Court heard issues arising from courts-martial cases. Traditionally, the route that appeals traversed from courts-martial to the Court was through a writ of *habeas* that a lower federal appellate court had granted or denied. This is an important point. Prior to 1983, the majority of courts-martial issues to arise before the Court were first decided by a federal district court and then a federal court of appeals. Before 1953, the majority of Article III federal courts held that *habeas* could only be granted if the court-martial lacked jurisdiction to begin with. Since 1983, when the Court has granted certiorari from a court-martial appeal, it has almost, without exception, been from the highest military appellate court.

b. Lex non Scripta

That the military has its own body of laws, regulations, is repeatedly stressed both in this study, as well as by those who critique the judiciary's alleged overarching deference to the military establishment. The military also has customs, or unwritten rules. A commissioned officer may be prosecuted under Article 133 for conduct unbecoming an officer and gentleman for a behavior which is not specifically prohibited by statute. An officer who disrupts a religious service, publicly disparages an individual legislator, discriminates on the basis of race or religion, or sexually harasses a peer may be convicted in a court-martial. In no other criminal law jurisdiction is this possible. Historically, commissioned officers were thought to be men of honor, and the officer who dishonored his commission could be tried for his conduct. Enlisted service-members do not have the same charging possibilities under Article 134, even though this general article has come under similar criticism. It is true that there is considerable room for prosecutions of non-enumerated offenses. Unlike Article 133 however, the government must prove that the enlisted service-member's behavior eroded "good order and discipline," or was of a nature to bring discredit upon the armed forces. In the Nineteenth Century, Article 134 was called the "Devil's Article," and during the Vietnam War, the federal courts took a heightened interest in both Article 133 and Article 134 as a result of arguments that such articles were vague and failed to place service-members on notice that a certain activity or conduct could constitute a crime. The government would counter that a thorough review of courts-martial since World War II did not evidence that either article had been used for odd or malicious charges. Today, the service-member who collects child pornography,

(New Jersey: Princeton, 1998). To date Lurie's book (a two volume study) is the only detailed analysis of the Court of Military Appeals but it is limited to the first thirty years of the court and it does not center its analysis of that court's relationship to the Supreme Court. Rather, it focuses appropriately on the Court of Military Appeal's influence in shaping the military law and the political battles involved in its creation and the ensuing judicial appointments.

repeatedly lies to ranking personnel, or is intoxicated at a formal event are the common examples of the historic uses of these articles.

c. Exhaustion Doctrine

All federal agencies are empowered to make rules for the administration of their personnel. Some of the agencies, such as the Equal Employment Opportunity Commission possess the authority to establish administrative hearings to determine, for instance, whether a private commercial employer has discriminated against an employee or applicant. The federal courts are charged with deferring to the decisions of agencies unless the agency has "abused its discretion." In other words, unless the agency acts contrary to its own rules or legal constraints, or in disregard of any reasonable interpretation of the facts before it, the federal courts are supposed to defer to the agency. The two-fold reason for this system is that the agency itself is supposed to be staffed by subject matter experts; and, without this doctrine, the federal courts would become clogged with claims. Congress has, over time, created this system, and it has given tacit approval to the doctrine of exhaustion. That is, before the federal courts grant review of an issue, the challenging party must exhaust all administrative avenues of redress within an agency. In *Parisi v. Davidson*, the Court, in an opinion authored by Justice Potter Stewart, held "that the basic purpose of the exhaustion doctrine is to allow an administrative agency to perform functions within its special competence-to make a factual record, to apply its expertise, and to correct its own errors so as to moot judicial controversies."[35]

The Department of Defense has several administrative hearing venues which cover both its civilian and uniformed personnel. Congress has created each of these venues, ranging from the office of the inspector general, to the internal military equal opportunity offices, to the four services discharge processes. There are administrative and statutory avenues for bringing claims against superior officers as well. The difference between the other federal agencies and those of the military establishment is that the Department of Defense's personnel are subject to a greater array of rules and regulations then the employees of any other agency, and non-adherence to the rules and regulations may result in a punitive response. Another difference between the administrative discharge process in the military and any civilian counterpart is that if the uniformed service member receives a less than honorable discharge characterization, the characterization could last for a lifetime, and it does have significant economic and social effects. In 1958, Frankfurter scolded the Solicitor General for arguing otherwise. An engineer fired from employment by NASA, who is never prosecuted in a criminal trial, is simply a fired engineer and not a citizen with a negative military discharge excluding him or her from a variety of government programs. A former service-member

35 *Parisi v. Davidson*, 405 U.S. 34 (1972), citing to *McKart v. United States*, 395 U.S. 185 (1968).

discharged with even a general discharge characterization for minor infractions or homosexual conduct (which, for the most part, is no longer a basis for discharge), is not viewed by society as having honorably served in the military.

III: The Methodologies of Judicial History

Bernard Schwartz, one of the second half of the twentieth century's leading legal historians, suggests in his study on the Burger Court that because the Court's most important work is done in private, studying correspondences from the conference sessions which occur after the cases have been argued are critical to assessing how the majority, concurring, and dissenting opinions were formulated and what the justices intended. I agree with Professor Schwartz, and the same can be said to be true in regard to the lower federal courts. Almost every judicial decision has a record from its first penciled draft to the final copy, often accompanied by the suggestions and disagreements amongst the justices. Of course, only the final published opinions bear weight before the federal and state courts. But a legal history involving the federal courts has to be more than a court's final decision standing alone. The justices and their decisions must be analyzed alongside of the political and social environment of the times in which the decisions are issued, and the personal correspondences of the judges and justices provide fertile evidence to their understandings of the environment. Similar to Schwartz, Professor Lawrence Friedman, another of the late twentieth century's prominent legal historians, aptly observed that legal history is far more than the passage and enforcement of laws; it is also about the people on both ends of the process. This book is also written with Friedman's view of legal history.[36]

Schwartz and Freidman were pioneers in the nation's legal history, but they are by no means alone in monopolizing the subject area. Melvin Urofsky has written, among other works, a two volume constitutional history which effectively weaves social, political, and cultural history into it. Former Douglas clerk, Professor Lucas Powe, in his, *The Warren Court and American Politics* has likewise succeeded in creating a model judicial study. Powe argues though, that in the later 1970s political science departments divorced law from their studies, and commensurately, law schools began to eliminate political science from their curricula. To Powe, this separation of law from political analysis has had the unfortunate result of law becoming a stale study of fixed rules. Powe's study is itself, an outstanding integration of history, political analysis, and the judiciary. Perhaps Powe overstates his argument, but the relationship between the federal judiciary and military law has been lacking in a historic or social-science analysis, particularly in tying the individual justices' and judges' perceptions on national

---

36 Bernard Schwartz, *The Ascent of Pragmatism: The Burger Court in Action* (Reading, MA: Addison-Wesley Publishing Co., 1990), 11. Lawrence Friedman, *Law in America, A Short History* (New York: Random House, 2002), 1–19.

security needs, the cultural, social, economic, and political forces, and the process of deciding controversies.[37]

This book is modeled combining the methodologies of Friedman, Schwartz, Urofsky, and Powe, among others, in analyzing the judiciary's oversight of military governance alongside of the other historic forces in America. This historic approach is not difficult because much of the time the justices' and judges' memoranda, drafts, and correspondences are replete with their perceptions of these forces. As an example, Harry A. Blackmun interposed a sound knowledge of military history, including Russian military history, throughout many of his writings, and he sought to exclude relativism as an influence in the law.

A favored approach used by legal historians is to break the Court into periods divided by the tenures of chief justices. For instance, historians write of the Marshall Court, the Taney Court, the Warren Court or the Rehnquist Court. This approach is sensible to an extent, but since the chief justice is merely a "first among equals," the division can also be conflated. A chief justice certainly influences the Court's character, and presumably a president's nomination of a chief justice embodies the aspirations and hopes of the nominating president to preserve a legacy. Yet, often throughout history, the chief justice is not the powerful intellect on the Court. Joseph Story, John Harlan, Oliver Wendell Holmes Jr., Louis Brandeis, and Hugo Black were never chief justices but arguably each left a more compelling influence in the nation's jurisprudence than the chief justices they served alongside with. One historian has articulated that the Warren Court could justifiably be called the Brennan Court, since Brennan was the Court's foremost liberal consensus builder. In terms of the nation's military law, Rehnquist, as an associate justice, was a far greater influence than Chief Justice Warren Burger.[38]

Another valid approach to studying the Court is to place it in the context of a respective historic era. The Jeffersonian Republic, the so-called "Era of Good Feelings," pre-Civil War Jacksonian America, the Civil War, the Gilded Age, the Progressive Era, the era of total war and the Depression, the Cold War, and our present post-Cold War all provide division points to analyzing how the justices on the Court were attuned the times in which they lived and whether they sided with preserving a status quo or sought change. This study uses both approaches, though it primarily centers on the Cold War, with the post-Cold War concluding the study.

In 1969, the last year of Chief Justice Warren's tenure, the Court, in *O'Callahan v. Parker,* significantly narrowed the military establishment's scope of jurisdiction over its service-members. Authored by William O. Douglas, the justices' reasons for doing so were to curtail what had become to be known as "the Imperial

---

37 Melvin, Urofsky, *A March of Liberty: A Constitutional History of the United States*, Vol. II, From 1877 to the Present (New York: Oxford University Press, 2002); Lucas Powe, *The Warren Court and American Politics* (Cambridge, MA: Harvard-Belknap, 2006), xi–xvi.

38 Mark Tushnet, *A Court Divided: The Rehnquist Court and the Future of Constitutional Law* (New York: W.W. Norton, 2005), 35.

Presidency." The first chapter begins with *O'Callahan* and it concludes with how the decision was interpreted by the lower courts, which in turn shaped the governance of the military establishment. Two of the more important decisions, *Calley v. Callaway*, which arose from a court-martial of perhaps the most heinous war crime in American military history, and *Cortright v. Resor*, which originated in a military administrative decision, are analyzed in detail. Decisions involving the military establishment's policies on homosexuality and religion are likewise analyzed.[39] *O'Callahan* ultimately enabled the lower federal appellate courts and district court judges to diminish the military's authority over individual servicemen to a degree which had never before, or since, occurred. From 1969 through 1987, the military found itself in federal litigation for a variety of matters ranging from an individual's assertion of a right to not receive a haircut to whether the military could ban an underground newspaper. This type of litigation, and its attendant cost, would have been unthinkable prior to 1969.[40]

Warren's successor, Warren Burger, attempted to narrow the Warren Court's criminal law and civil rights decisions, alongside its attempts to preserve a broader executive and legislative authority in national security matters. When Burger, a Richard Nixon appointee, became chief justice, the war in Vietnam remained the prominent aspect of the American political environment, and the nation's social unrest showed no promise of abating. Burger's appointment reflected conservative hopes of diminishing the Warren Court's influence, whether in the field of civil rights or criminal procedure. Burger's tenure is divided into three chapters, one which includes the conservatives' efforts to narrow *O'Callahan*, a second chapter analyzes the Court's free speech jurisprudence in the military governance context, and its efforts to depoliticize the military. This is an important, but often overlooked aspect in the Burger Court's jurisprudence. Generally, the Court's free speech jurisprudence is analyzed as a judicial acceptance of limitations on the individual rights of service-members, without either the historic setting of the rulings, or without the understanding that the military was increasingly becoming a political institution. Senior uniformed leaders were concerned with this issue. So too was the judiciary worried about a politicized military establishment. The third chapter analyzes the Court's adoption of equal protection jurisprudence into the military law. Among the important analytic features to each of these chapters, the Burger Court took an active role in integrating the broader laws into the laws governing the military establishment. This aspect has almost gone unnoted by critics of the judiciary's alleged sweeping deference to the military.

For all of Burger's conservatism, the Court took an active role in shaping the military, both in terms of gender equality and military readiness. It did not permit the military establishment to return to more freely operating as it had prior

---

39 *O'Callahan v. Parker*, 395 U.S. 258 (1969); *Calley v. Callaway*, 519 F.2d 184 (CA 5, 1975); *Cortright v. Resor*, 442 F.2d 245 (CA 2, 1971).

40 See e.g. *Friedman v. Frohlke*, 470 F.2d 1351 (CA 1, 1972); and *Campell v. Beaughler*, 519 F.2d 1307 (CA 9, 1975).

to the "Warren Court." One of the unique features of the Court's military law jurisprudence during Burger's tenure is that for the first time, the Court actively and regularly considered how decisions arising from the military establishment could generally affect the nation's laws, and likewise how the Court's constitutional and criminal law decisions might affect the military.

Beginning with his elevation to chief justice, Rehnquist led the Court to overturn *O'Callahan*. Under his leadership, the Court also provided efficacy to the military's justice system in a decision involving the special status of military judges, as well as a continued integration of the military's legal construct into the broader civil laws. Rehnquist believed that the military should be unencumbered in securing its own discipline as Congress intended it do, but he never believed that the military establishment should be permitted to ignore judicial decisions pertaining to it. Indeed, contrary to allegations that he sought first and foremost to create a conservative military, he believed that the nation had to possess a highly disciplined apolitical force to bolster the nation's allies and keep the spread of communism at bay. His approach to military law is open to criticism because in overturning *O'Callahan* he overturned a decision based on a poor rendition of history with an equally poor rendition, and he disregarded the honored concept of *stare decisis*. Rehnquist's motives in his jurisprudence were never singular, but his primary focus was on enabling a reliable military, flexible to changing political and social conditions so that it could confront the Soviet Union. While in some other matters, a majority of the Court proved unwilling to intrude into the administrative decisions of the military's leadership, even when those decisions collided with religious rights enshrined in the First Amendment, the Court, with only Scalia dissenting, issued a significant military governance decision on equal rights for women.

One area that this study does not cover is whether the Court under Rehnquist or Chief Justice John Roberts, or for that matter, the federal judiciary, has altered its military jurisprudence, as a result of George W. Bush's legal doctrine of Executive Branch supremacy. The papers of the contemporary justices are not readily available, and will not be for a long time to come. Moreover, the judiciary has long since removed itself from considering that it has the competency to decide on the constitutionality of the government committing forces overseas.

This book begins with an analysis of the Court during Earl Warren's last year as chief justice in 1969, and then breaks into three chapters on the Court under his successor Warren Burger. Following these three chapters, the Court's military law jurisprudence is analyzed during the period of Chief Justice Rehnquist's tenure. Finally, the book concludes with an examination of the Court's current military law jurisprudence.

IV: Conclusion

When placed in the context of the Vietnam Conflict, and its aftermath, as well as alongside of the political, social, and cultural forces in the United States since 1968, it becomes clear that although the justices and judges often broke into differing camps regarding national security and military policy, the federal judiciary has taken a prominent role in defining the parameters of military governance. This role has not been premised on a blind deference to the military establishment. Rather, despite conflicting jurisprudential approaches, the Court has addressed the needs of a disciplined military, harmonized to the Constitution.

Chapter 2
O'Callahan v. Parker: The Last Year of the Warren Court

There can be little doubt that the United States' involvement in the Vietnam Conflict resulted in an unparalleled political and social upheaval in twentieth-century American society. The war in Vietnam affected the judiciary, not only in such constitutional issues as freedom of speech and association but also in the arena of military law. While most of the legal challenges to the war arose from of appeals against Selective Service decisions, the Court, during Warren's final year issued *O'Callahan v. Parker*. This decision was a significant curtailment on the military's jurisdiction over its service-members, and it upended the Legislative Branch's grant of authority to the military establishment to provide a disciplined and reliable military force for the national defense. To understand how *O'Callahan* came about, and what its effects were, it is essential to consider William O. Douglas' jurisprudence and extra-court scholarship in the two decades preceding the decision. That is, the judicial motivation behind *O'Callahan* was not simply in rectifying perceived due process problems in courts-martial. It is true that Douglas was one justice, and in 1968 Earl Warren, Hugo Black, Abe Fortas, and Thurgood Marshall would join him in *O'Callahan*, while John Harlan, Potter Stewart, and Byron White opposed the decision. But Douglas did more to shape the Court's almost wholesale abandonment of deference to the military establishment than any other justice. Nonetheless a brief note on the other justices is contextually important to explain *O'Callahan.*

In 1969, Earl Warren served as chief justice. A former state attorney general and governor of California, who had supported the internment of Japanese Americans during World War II, once on the Court he championed civil rights, leading the Court to a unanimous decision in *Brown v. Board of Education* in 1954. The senior justice, Hugo Black, a former Alabama senator appointed to the Court by President Franklin Roosevelt also championed civil rights and freedom of speech. He had also, prior to his election to the Senate in 1926, been a member of the Ku Klux Klan. Following Black was Douglas, and then John Harlan, William J. Brennan, Potter Stewart, Bryon White, Abe Fortas, and Thurgood Marshall. Appointed by President Eisenhower, Harlan was a World War II veteran and the Court's leading conservative. Stewart was also an Eisenhower appointee, but aligned himself as often with Harlan as with the Court's liberals Black, Douglas, and Brennan. During World War II, Stewart, a naval officer, defended sailors in courts-martial. Eisenhower appointed Brennan, but came to regret the appointment as Brennan proved to be one of the more liberal justices. Brennan was likewise a World War II veteran, and on the Court he generally advocated for minority and gender equality. President John F. Kennedy appointed White, who had served in the Navy in World War II, and while White was staunchly in support of civil rights, on military and criminal justice issues he tended to be conservative. Lyndon Johnson appointed Fortas in 1965, but Fortas' brief tenure on the Court was marred by allegations of unethical conduct. Fortas was one of Johnson's trusted advisors, including on the escalation of military forces in Vietnam. Finally, Marshall, a Johnson appointee in 1968, was not only a judicial liberal and the first African American justice in the nation's history, he had also served as solicitor general and an appellate court judge. Marshall and Brennan would generally align with Douglas on most, but not all, appeals arising from military decisions.[1]

I: Douglas, the Court, and the Legality of the War

William O. Douglas was born in Minnesota, raised in Yakima, Washington, served in the Army during World War I, and educated at Columbia University's law school. Following law school graduation he worked at a large law firm and taught at Yale's and Columbia's law schools. He was an intimate advisor to President Franklin Roosevelt who, in turn, appointed Douglas to chair the Securities and Exchange Commission. Douglas was only 39 years old when appointed to the Court, and he was to serve over three decades. While he supported Roosevelt and the New Deal, as well as the wide enforcement of civil rights (he did not

1 *Brown v. Board of Education*, 347 U.S. 483 (1959). On Black see, Howard Ball, *Hugo L. Black: Cold Steel Warrior* (New York: Oxford, 1996), 52–60; and Roger K. Newman, *Hugo Black: A Biography* (New York: Fordham, 1994), 16–124. On Warren see, Bernard Schwartz, *Super Chief: Earl Warren and His Supreme Court*, 2–3; and Lucas Powe, *The Warren Court and American Politics* (Cambridge, MA: Harvard-Belknap, 2006). On Harlan see Harlan's life, see Tinsley Yarborough, *John Marshall Harlan: Great Dissenter of the Warren Court*, 9–38; On Brennan see, Seth Stern and Stephen Wermiel, *Justice Brennan: Liberal Champion* (New York: Houghton-Mifflin, 2010), 75–80; Hunter R. Clark, *Justice Brennan, The Great Conciliator* (New York: Birch-Lane, 1995), 1–18. For Stewart's World War II experience, see, Tinsley Yarborough, "Potter Stewart," in Charles M. Lamb, *The Burger Court: Political and Judicial Profiles*, 375–6; William H. Rehnquist, *The Supreme Court* (New York: Vintage Press, 1987), 199. On Fortas see Laura Kalman, *Abe Fortas: A Biography* (New Haven, CT: Yale University Press, 1990), 8; Bernard Brodie, *War and Politics* (New York: MacMillan, 1973), 140; Robert J. MacMahon, "Ambivalent Partners: The Lyndon Johnson Administration and its Asian Allies," in H.W. Brands, ed: *Beyond Vietnam: The Foreign Policies of Lyndon Johnson*, 160–62. Henry J. Reske, "Pragmatic White Retires,"ABA Journal, May 1993, 16–18; Charles Lamb, *The Burger Court: Political and Judicial Profiles* (Urbana, IL: University of Illinois Press, 1991), 408; On Marshall see, Mark V. Tushnet, *Making Constitutional Law,: Thurgood Marshall and the Supreme Court, 1961–1991* (New York: Oxford, 1997), 6–7; Earl Maltz, *The Chief Justiceship of Warren Burger*, 1969–1986 (Columbia, SC: University of South Carolina Press, 2000), 15.

oppose the internment of American citizens of Japanese descent in World War II), he became disenchanted with the growth of the power of the Executive Branch and he opposed the government's intrusion into people's privacy and limitations on the First Amendment's guarantee of freedom of speech during the Cold War. Moreover, he was adamantly against the United States' military involvement in Vietnam.[2]

At some point after 1949, Douglas developed a relationship with *Look Magazine* and authored a series of articles for the monthly publication, analyzing military and political policies. On March 11, 1952, the magazine published his article, "We Have Become Victims of the Military Mind," in which he criticized President Harry S. Truman for staffing the executive branch with individuals "who look at domestic affairs in terms of giving orders and expecting obedience." Douglas cautioned that as a result of the inundation of retired career officers in government agencies, the government would become monolithically orthodox in its views. He worried that the government's response to political demonstrations would be a police-style crackdown, rather than a thoughtful investigation as to why the protest began in the first place. Drawing a parallel to foreign affairs, he claimed that the military did not know how to "win the affections of a people." His article was not as controversial as may be seemed. He claimed that he did not question Omar Bradley, Dwight Eisenhower, John Marshall, or even Douglas MacArthur's integrity, but rather he criticized the desire to militarily look strong against the Soviet military threat, without emphasizing that the Soviet Union would have to be defeated at the political level "through emissaries who teach freedom and justice and show there is an alternative to war."[3]

Missing from the published article, however, was a visceral criticism of military education, which, in an early draft, Douglas lamented had not produced "a Shakespeare, Voltaire, Tolstoy, Gibbon, Toynbee, Aristotle, Plato, or Jesus, Mohammad, or Buddha." Equally important was Douglas' public recognition of MacArthur's integrity in the published article. By 1952, Douglas believed MacArthur cared little for the constitutional requirement of an apolitical military subservient to the civil government, and fretted over whether the Republican Party would nominate MacArthur. His earliest drafts omitted MacArthur's name from the list of exceptional military leaders, but it is likely that he included MacArthur in the published article to deflate conservative criticism. These drafts included such introductory statements that "the military in American history has been justifiably

2 Bernard Schwartz, *The Ascent of Pragmatism*, 19; Howard Ball, "Loyalty, Treason, and the State, An Examination of Justice William O. Douglas's Style, Substance, and Anguish" in Steven Wasby ed., *He Shall Not Pass This Way Again: The Legacy of William O. Douglas* (Pittsburgh, PA: University of Pittsburgh Press, 1997), 7; Philip J. Cooper, "William O. Douglas: the Conscience of the Court," in Charles M. Lamb, ed., *The Burger Court: Judicial and Political Profiles* 163–5 (2000).

3 William O. Douglas, "We Have Become Victims of the Military Mind," March 11, 1952 [WOD/855].

suspect." With the exception of MacArthur, Douglas did not fear that the military would topple the government, but he predicted that military solutions would increasingly take the place of diplomatic efforts, and in doing so, undermined one of democracy's most distinctive characteristics, tolerating a diversity of opinions.[4]

On December 16, 1952, Douglas predicted, in another *Look Magazine* article, that the French regime in Indo-China would fall to communism. The article was the fourth in a series about Asia. In it, he commented that the French use of American weapons and their mastery of modern warfare were futile against the Viet Minh, and that the only force that could prevent a communist takeover was from within the Vietnamese population. Related to his earlier anti-military article, he worried that the military would push for increased involvement in Vietnam, alienating the local population in the process. Douglas did not write this article from an "ivory tower," he had recently toured Vietnam and witnessed the Bao Dai government's conduct.[5]

In his fifth article on Asia, Douglas analyzed the state of the Korean War. He defended Truman's decision to send forces into Korea, considering it a necessity. "Had the North Koreans been victorious, there would have been a series of violent eruptions which by now might have extended the Communist power over vital areas," he cautioned. Douglas though doubted that an all-out war with China would bring the struggle to an end, but barring a political settlement with China he believed it might become necessary. Absent from the published article was a criticism of MacArthur's conduct in war for baiting China into entering the conflict. Yet again, in his draft articles he wrote disparagingly of MacArthur's conduct.[6]

Douglas' purpose in authoring the articles provides insight into his early efforts to narrow the military's court-martial jurisdiction and his increasing criticisms of the military establishment. From 1952 onward, he sought to weaken the Executive Branch, even when Congress had sanctioned its authority. He was mostly alone in his efforts, though Black, Warren, Brennan, and even Felix Frankfurter might join him in a decision. Their reasons for doing so were hardly to support Douglas' motivations, although by Lyndon Johnson's presidency, Black and Brennan were more willing to favorably consider his motives.

The war in Vietnam was socially different than any of America's prior twentieth-century conflicts. Not since the Civil War did a sizeable and vocal minority allege that the Executive Branch had brought the United States into conflict without following the Constitution. To be sure, several conflicts in American history prior to Vietnam were unpopular. New England Federalists opposed the War of 1812 against Great Britain and made it difficult to establish a unity of national effort.

4 William O. Douglas, "We Have Become Victims of the Military Mind," draft dated December 12, 1951 [WOD/855].

5 William O. Douglas, "Indo-China Near Disaster," *Look Magazine*, December 16, 1952 [WOD/856].

6 William O. Douglas, "The Choice in Korea: Recognize or Crush Red China," *Look Magazine*, December 30, 1962 pp. 12–14; draft, undated, [WOD/856].

Northern anti-slavery forces opposed the Mexican-American War, though the rapid successes of the United States forces may have dampened their hopes for a political surge against that conflict. The anti-war riots and "Copperhead" opposition to Lincoln in the Civil War reflected a deep political division in the Union and gave rise to the belief of "an enemy from within." In the late nineteenth and twentieth century, opposition to involvement in foreign conflicts from religious organizations such as William Jennings Bryan's Anti-Imperialist League in 1897, or socialist and communist organizations were small and ineffective. In both world wars, Congress formally declared war, and whatever opposition existed, it could hardly be argued that the American participation in those conflicts were "illegal." Moreover, even if by the end of the Korean War, that conflict proved unpopular, few called it "illegal." The United Nations had, in fact, sanctioned the use of force against North Korea so long as the use of force was relegated to the Korean peninsula, with the purpose of protecting South Korea's sovereignty.[7]

In 1951, the Court of Appeals for the Second Circuit determined that a refusal to comply with an induction order based on a claim that the induction would result in being shipped off to fight in an undeclared—and hence, illegal—war was not a defense to a criminal charge. But, in a sense, the appellate court avoided the critical question of a citizen's liability to fight in an undeclared war. "Any question as to the legality of an order sending men to Korea to fight in an "undeclared war" should be raised by someone to whom such an order has been directed, not by the appellant, who might never be ordered abroad for military duty, even if he reported for induction," the appellate court concluded.[8]

By 1967, the United States' participation in Vietnam was widely challenged. Service members appealed to the federal courts in the hopes of a judicial determination that an undeclared war exempted them from being forced to deploy to Vietnam. Members of the legal academy had proclaimed that the war was illegal and accused President Johnson of manipulating Congress into agreeing to compulsorily putting citizens into the armed forces and then ordering them in harm's way, without constitutional sanction. Between 1965 and 1974, citizens petitioned to have the Court answer whether the use of American forces in Vietnam was "lawful." With the exception of Douglas, most of the justices consistently were determined not to enter into the political thicket of this question.

---

7 See e.g. for the War of 1812, Donald Hickey, *The War of 1812: The Forgotten Conflict* (Champaign, IL: University of Illinois Press, 2012), 261–84; for the Civil War, see e.g. Jennifer L. Weber, *Copperheads: The Rise and Fall of Lincoln's Opponents in the North* (New York: Oxford, 2006), 215–16; and Joshua Kastenberg, *Law in War, Law as War*, 327–44; for Bryan's anti-imperialism adherents, see Robert W. Cherny, *A Righteous Cause: The Life of William Jennings Bryan* (Norman, OK: University of Oklahoma Press, 1994), 72–91; and Robert Kleidman, *Organizing for Peace: Neutrality, the Test Ban, and the Freeze* (New York: Syracuse, 1993), 14.

8 *United States v. Bolton*, 192 F.2d 805 (CA 2, 1951).

In early 1966, Robert Luftig, an Army private, sued to prevent the Army from shipping him to Vietnam. Luftig did not claim that he was unlawfully conscripted into the Army, and he did not claim conscientious objector status. Rather, he argued that the use of military forces in Vietnam was unconstitutional because no war had been declared, nor had Congress expressly authorized the use of forces in Vietnam. At the district court, Judge Alexander Holtzoff, a long-serving judge and Army veteran of World War I, dismissed Luftig's case with no published decision. In the late 1940s Holtzoff had served on a committee to recommend reforms in courts-martial which culminated in the UCMJ. In a *per curiam* authored by future Chief Justice Burger, the Court of Appeals for the District of Columbia determined that Luftig's claim presented a "political question" to which the judicial branch could not take jurisdiction over. "It is difficult to think of an area less suited for judicial action than that into which Appellant would have us intrude. The fundamental division of authority and power established by the Constitution precludes judges from overseeing the conduct of foreign policy or the use and disposition of military power; these matters are plainly the exclusive province of Congress and the Executive," the *per curiam* concluded.[9]

In a similar instance, David Henry Mitchell, a citizen who refused to submit to an induction order, argued that because Vietnam was "a war of aggression," in violation of the principles set forth in the Treaty of London and the Nuremberg trials, he was faced with the choice of violating international law or the domestic law, and his civilian conviction should be overturned. In early 1967, only Douglas voted for *certiorari*. Douglas' claim that he had not determined the efficacy of Mitchell's argument was hardly believable. Mitchell had been originally convicted in 1965, but the Court of Appeals for the Second Circuit reversed the conviction on the basis that the district court did not provide enough time for Mitchell's counsel to effectively represent Mitchell. However, the government re-prosecuted Mitchell, and on a second appellate review the appellate court sustained the conviction, finding Mitchell's Nuremberg defense baseless.[10]

In 1967, three soldiers who were drafted in 1965 petitioned the federal courts to enjoin the Army from shipping them to Vietnam. The District Court for the District of Columbia and the Court of Appeals for the District of Columbia dismissed their lawsuits. The Court voted to deny *certiorari*, but both Potter Stewart and Douglas dissented from the denial. The soldiers' argument was simply that if they refused to comply with what they believed to be an illegal order, the Army would court-martial them. However, if the federal judiciary determined the war was legal, then their refusal to transfer to Vietnam would also be illegal. Stewart believed that the issue was important for review and agreed to dissent with Douglas, so long as Douglas removed the language in one of his initial drafts that if the view that the war powers contained in the Constitution were non-justiciable, "there has been a

9 *Luftig v. McNamara*, 373 F.2d 644 (CA DC 1967).

10 *Mitchell v. United States*, 386 U.S. 972 (1967); *United States v. Mitchell*, 369 F.2d 323 (CA 2, 1966).

pervasive revision of the Constitution without resort to the amending process." Stewart also insisted on ensuring that the published dissent contained no reference as to how he or Douglas might rule on the merits, but rather, he wanted to make it emphatically clear that the issue itself was of such significance that the Court should decide it.[11]

The three soldiers ultimately refused to embark for Vietnam and were court-martialed. The Army's internal surveillance program concluded that one of the soldiers, Dennis Mora had a sister who was an active CPUSA member, and the Army claimed that Mora was determined to sow dissent in the ranks. Whether the Army's judgment on Mora was accurate or exaggerated was not a concern to Douglas in his dissent. Douglas certainly understood that if the Court ruled that the war was "legal," the Army would have the authority to court-martial the three men. Yet, he may also have held out hope that if Marshall, Warren, Black, and Brennan would join him, it might cause Congress to end the nation's military participation in to the conflict. This hope was illusory, and Douglas, for the most part, reverted to collaterally fighting the conflict on his own. A review of the Army's intelligence files evidence that the military's leadership feared the Court might rule against the government in a critical case which would cause the administration to find it too difficult to continue the conflict, but they did not believe such a decision would arise at the behest of soldiers they considered subversive.[12]

In 1968, Douglas issued several orders preventing the government from calling up Army reservists for service in Vietnam. He hoped to force the Court into deciding whether the Executive Branch possessed the authority, absent a declaration of war, to call up reserves for service in Vietnam. This was a collateral attack on the war to be sure, but Douglas' interpretation of the plain statutory language governing the nation's reserve forces provided some debatable efficacy to his arguments. Nonetheless, Douglas repeatedly angered his peers. In one instance, Douglas' ally Black refused to grant a stay against the Army sending a reservist to Vietnam, but on October 22, 1968, Douglas intervened and ordered the Solicitor General to provide a response to the reservist's arguments on the "invalidity of the conflict" affecting the statutory call-up to active duty so that he could present the arguments to the Court's conference on October 25, to determine whether to grant *certiorari*. On October 24, the Army shipped the reservists to Vietnam infuriating Douglas.

11 *Mora v. McNamara*, Douglas, draft, October 12, 1967 [WOD/1421]; Douglas to Stewart, October 19, 1967 [WOD/1421]; For commentary on the three soldiers, see Telford Taylor, *Nuremberg and Vietnam: An American Tragedy* (Chicago: Quadrangle, 1976), 112. Taylor, the former chief prosecutor at Nuremberg, opposed the United States military involvement in Vietnam, but he believed that Congress had authorized Johnson to send forces there.

12 United States Army Surveillance of Dissidents, "Report on the Fort Hood Three" [UPA/16].

By this point, not even Brennan or Warren sympathized with Douglas, because Black had already denied the stay.[13]

Almost contemporaneously though, Douglas denied a stay to a soldier placed into pretrial confinement while awaiting court-martial. The soldier's term of enlistment would have expired one week after the Army charged him with a sexually assaulting a minor on Fort Sam Houston. However the UCMJ enabled the Army to continue to hold him on active duty for the purpose of court-martialing him. The soldier contested this law to the United States District Court for the Western District of Texas which ruled against him. The soldier then sought to prevent the Army from court-martialing him by appealing to the Court. But even Douglas proved unwilling to order a stay against the court-martial. In light of his conduct in *O'Callahan*, his refusal to order a stay in this instance is perplexing.[14]

On September 15, 1969, Douglas published a dissent from the Court's denial of *certiorari* in *Jones v. LeMond.* Jones had been convicted in a court-martial for absence without leave, but prior to his absence, he had applied for conscientious objector status through his chain of command. The absence for which he was court-martialed was not the first such infraction, but Jones claimed that his conscientious objector application, which had been mired in military bureaucracy, served as a defense against his court-martial since, if granted, the military would not have had jurisdiction over him. No federal court granted Jones a hearing, and Douglas, though he claimed in the published decision that he expressed no opinion on the merits, argued that the judiciary had never considered whether the conscientious objection of a serving service-member was a bar to prosecution, and it was important to do so.[15]

By early 1968, Douglas' opposition to the United States involvement in Vietnam was so well known that a government official in Hanoi sent him a communiqué through a neutral country inquiring whether Clark Clifford, who had recently replaced Robert McNamara as Secretary of Defense, was sincere in his willingness to scale back the conflict. Douglas forwarded Clifford the communiqué without his personal analysis, but noted "it has not apparently been presented as yet to the Department of State." Three weeks earlier Douglas warmly congratulated Clifford on being confirmed and hoped that he could undo some of Johnson's Vietnam policies.[16]

---

13 *Morse v. Boswell*, 393 U.S. 1052 (1969); *Johnson v. Powell*, 393 U.S. 920 (1969). Following the Court's denial of certiorari, the plaintiffs in Powell, 105 members of the Kentucky National Guard brought suit claiming their call-up into the active duty forces was unlawful regardless of where the Army sent them. The Court of Appeals for the Fifth Circuit ruled against them. See *Johnson v. Powell*, 414 F.2d 1060 (CA 5, 1969).

14 See *Roman v. Critz, 291* F.Supp 99 (WD Tx, 1968); *cert denied*, 393 U.S. 921 (1968).

15 *Jones v. LeMond*, 396 U.S. 1227 (1969).

16 Douglas to Clifford, February 25, 1968 [WOD/316]; Clifford to Douglas, February 3, 1968 [WOD/316].

On February 1, 1969, a Marine reservist named Paul V. Winters, appealed to the District Court for the Southern District of New York to prevent his call-up orders to active duty. Judge John Francis Dooling, a Kennedy appointee, decided the claim adversely to Winters. Dooling would, over the later course of the Vietnam conflict, issue other rulings adverse to plaintiffs who alleged the unconstitutionality of the war.[17]

Winters had enlisted in 1965, under a similar contract agreement as had the Army reservists, but with the Department of the Navy. While his contract stated that he could not be involuntarily called into active duty under normal circumstances, if the President declared a national emergency, then all marine reserves could be involuntarily called to active duty for a 24-month period. Additionally, reservists who failed to take part in 90 percent of their drill weekends could also be ordered onto active duty. In 1966, Congress legislated to the President the authority to call reservists to active duty who had not previously served on active duty. In 1967, the Department of the Navy also heightened the drill requirements 100 percent attendance on drill weekends. Winters failed to make the 100 percent requirement. Thus, while Winters' call-up to active duty was statutorily permissible, a question remained as to whether Congress had the authority to alter the enlistment contracts of reservists, since that is what Congress essentially had done. Problematic to Winters' defense was that it appeared that he altered a hospital record to have his command characterize a missed drill as "excused."

The district court determined that the more stringent training requirements were permissible, as well as Winters' call-up. In the language of deference, the district court's published opinion stated that the military's exercise of its discretion was "non-reviewable," and within the ambit of military law, the federal courts were limited to determining whether the military acted within its own jurisdiction. In a very brief *per curiam*, the Court of Appeals for the Second Circuit upheld the district court. Winters' appeal would be decided almost contemporaneously with that of another group of reservists.[18]

On August 6, 1968, the District Court for Maryland, in *Morse v. Boswell*, denied 113 Army reservists an injunction against the Secretary of the Army from transferring them to Vietnam. The reservists pointed out that when they enlisted into the Army, they did so on a contractual basis, and that if Congress declared a national emergency, the reservists could be called into active duty for the duration of the emergency, with an additional six months of service. Likewise, the Army could order them to serve 45 continuous days of active duty per year. Absent these conditions, only in instances of substandard performance could the

---

17 *Winters v. United States*, 281 F.Supp 289 (ED NY, 1968). On Dooling, see Leslie Bennetts, *Judge John Dooling Jr., 72, Dies; Made Ruling on Abortion Funds*, *N.Y. Times*, Jan. 13, 1981.

18 *Winters v. United States*, 390 F.2d 879 (CA 2, 1968). Henry Friendly authored the *per curiam* decision. He was later to author another contentious decision in *Cortright v. Resor*, analyzed in Chapter 10.

reservists be ordered inducted into active duty. Although not in the language of the enlistment contract, following the Korean War, Congress authorized the President to call-up reserve forces if the President declared a national emergency. After the 113 reservists had enlisted, Congress, in response to the Tet Offensive and refusal of the North Vietnamese to negotiate a settlement which guaranteed the sovereignty of South Vietnam, enacted another law which enabled the President to specifically call up reserve forces for a 24-month period. Johnson, with full statutory authority, delegated the duty of determining which units to call-up to the Secretary of Defense and the service secretaries.[19]

Problematic to the reservists' contention of an unlawful call-up to active duty was that the Army had in place an application process for exemption from call-up, and only 19 reservists had made use of this process. On the other hand, because the reservists alleged an unconstitutional act by the Executive Branch, they urged the court that the application procedure was not applicable to the court's decision. And, most of the applications for exemption were rejected by the Army at any rate. The district court adjudicating Morse' claim recognized that the judiciary had already issued conflicting rulings. After all, in *Winters*, the lower courts determined that the President possessed the statutory authority to alter regulations governing the reserve components, and call reservists into duty who failed to adhere to the new rules. But, the District Court for the Central District of California, in an unpublished decision had sided with a group of reservists against the administration, based on similar facts. The Court of Appeals for the Fourth Circuit upheld the district court in *Morse v. Boswell* in August, 1968. The outstanding feature of the appellate court's conduct in this case is not that it acted with blind deference to the military establishment or to the President. Chief Judge Clement Haynsworth of the Court of Appeals for the Fourth Circuit and a future Nixon nominee convened a special session on August 13 to insure that the reservists did not lose their right to an appeal or have their appeal become moot as a result of their transfer to Vietnam.[20]

In his dissent from the denial of *certiorari*, in *Morse*, Douglas argued that the Court had to enforce the plain language of an existing statute at the time of an enlistment contract. But, he also had to concede that Congress had the authority to change laws regardless of the change's effect on the nation's citizenry. Douglas issued his dissent on October 7, 1968. Two weeks later, he issued his dissent in *Winters*, but that case had additional complication. After the Court of Appeals for the Second Circuit decided adversely to Winters, the Marine Corps deactivated and then reactivated Winters and transferred him to California. Winters appealed anew, but without success, to the district court and Court of Appeals for the Ninth Circuit, and Douglas believed that the Court had to address the merits of the Ninth

19 *Morse v. Boswell*, 289 F.Supp 812 (DC MD 1968); *Winters v. United States*, 89 S.Ct 57 (1068).

20 McArthur v. Clifford, 402 F.2d 58 (CA 4, 1968); Haynsworth to Winter and Butzner, August 13, 1968 [CFH/17].

Circuit decision not to remand to the district court. More cuttingly, he accused the military of "secretly cloaking their decisions," and citing to *Milligan*, urged that the Court's duty was to protect people from military discipline. "Civil Liberty and Military Control are irreconcilably antagonistic," he concluded. Finally, on December 16, 1968, Douglas dissented from the Court's denial of *certiorari* to another reservist, arguing that a unique question was raised regarding presidential power to use forces without a declaration of war existed.[21]

Douglas' vehemence provided an outlet to hundreds of service members. By 1968, he received hundreds of letters from service-members and reservists imploring him for help against shipment to Vietnam, citing training deficiencies and claims of retaliation by commanding officers. The *Morse v. Boswell* file alone contains over 100 such letters. Mr. A.R. Morse penned to Douglas, thanking him for his "courageous decision," but also expressing his concerns over the Army's treatment of his son. Morse was convinced that his son's duty assignments were in retaliation for being the named petitioner on the decision, expressing that "S.P. Morse is a Lehigh Graduate with an M.E. Degree, and two MOS (Military Occupational Specialties), one as a computer programmer and another as a radio mechanic, yet the War Machine has assigned him to wash uniforms in Vietnam for 2 years!"[22]

Douglas realized that in most appeals he could not prevail, even amongst his allies, in his quest to terminate the war and weaken the Executive Branch through the issues raised by reservists. On December 5, 1968, he angrily issued a denial of a stay against sending 368 Washington State National Guardsmen to Vietnam. In a published statement, he lamented that the Court had already considered the issue to be non-jusiticably political in nature, and therefore had no choice but to deny the guardsmen's application. On the other hand, he commented that in 1862, while the Court ruled in the *Prize Cases* that Lincoln could use military forces without a declaration of war, the nation was engaged in an insurrection. To Douglas, the Civil War-era Court had courage to enter into a political question, and it was likely if the question had been whether the president had the authority to send militia overseas against a foreign adversary in the absence of a declaration of war, that Court would have ruled in opposite of his peers. Given the 1862 Court's composition, Douglas was likely right in his conclusion as to what that Court would have ruled. Yet, Congress did not, in 1964, preclude President Johnson from using forces in Vietnam, and therein rested untenable element in Douglas' analysis. However, Douglas found a means to collaterally influence foreign and military policy through weakening the military's ability to ensure a full range of discipline over its personnel.

21 "Judicial Shop Around," *Washington Post*, September 16, 1968; *McArthur v. Clifford* 393 U.S. 1002 (1968).

22 Morse to Douglas, September 12, 1968 [WOD/1441].

II: *O'Callahan v. Parker*

The facts which gave rise to *O'Callahan v. Parker* were, in comparison to hundreds of courts-martial appeals, unremarkable, and that Sergeant James F. O'Callahan's case came before the Court was as much a product of happenstance than on the merits of his argument. After all, if the military did not possess jurisdiction over Sergeant O'Callahan, then it did not possess jurisdiction over thousands of other courts-martial. Notably, O'Callahan was not the first court-martialed service-member to argue to the judiciary that the military did not possess jurisdiction over him; he was only the first to succeed in this argument. The Court's grant of review of *O'Callahan* has more to do, however, with O'Callahan's counsel, as well as Douglas belief that the issue presented an opportunity to weaken the military's discipline and, in turn, serve as a bulwark against the growth of Executive Branch power.

While on an evening pass from Fort Shafter, Hawaii, O'Callahan and another soldier named Charles Redden rented a hotel room. According to Redden's testimony, O'Callahan hatched a plan for the two soldiers to rape a teen-aged girl, but Redden refused to be a part of the plan and warned O'Callahan against it. Sometime later, a hotel security guard heard the girl's screams, and chased a shirtless O'Callahan out of her room, eventually apprehending him. The civilian police arrested and interrogated O'Callahan and shortly after, he confessed to attempting to rape the young girl. Ultimately the Army charged O'Callahan with housebreaking, assault with intent to commit rape, and attempted rape. Six witnesses including the victim, Redden, and the hotel guard testified against him. There was little doubt of O'Callahan's guilt. The ensuing court-martial convicted him and sentenced him to 10 years in confinement and a dishonorable discharge. The court-martial was not controversial when it occurred, and perhaps reflecting the mundane aspect of the trial, it was not reported outside of a local Honolulu newspaper. The offenses occurred in July 1956, a time of national peace.[23]

O'Callahan's appeals through the military appellate system were unsuccessful, in all likelihood, because of the strength of the evidence against him. The Army transferred O'Callahan to its prison at Fort Leavenworth in 1958, but shortly after, as a result of the finality of his appeals, he was transferred to United States Penitentiary in Lewisberg, Pennsylvania. In 1960, he succeeded in obtaining parole. The conditions of his parole were such that if he committed any criminal misconduct, he would be returned to prison to serve out the remainder of his sentence. In 1962, after O'Callahan violated his parole terms by travelling to Arkansas and committing a civilian offense, the Department of Justice's Board of Parole concluded that he would have to serve out the remainder of his prison term. The board ordered him re-incarcerated in a federal prison in Massachusetts. Had O'Callahan not violated his parole by committing criminal offenses in Arkansas,

23 "The Law: Curbing Courts-Martial," *Time Magazine*, June 13, 1969.

it is unlikely that he would have ever appealed to another federal court, let alone the Court.

In 1964, O'Callahan unsuccessfully appealed to the District Court for the District of Massachusetts and then to the Court of Appeals for the First Circuit, claiming that his military sentence had already run its course, because had he remained in military custody he would have been credited with 10 "good time days" per month, and therefore would have been released in 1962. The military's early release program was historically more favorable than the federal prison parole program, but military prisoners who were transferred into the federal prisons become subject to the federal rules. However, O'Callahan was unlikely to prevail on the issue of parole because other courts had already decided similar claims lacked merit.[24]

O'Callahan secondarily challenged his confinement on the basis that only the military parole board possessed jurisdiction to set parole conditions on him, since he was still technically subject to the UCMJ. Given his later challenge of the military's jurisdiction to court-martial him in the first place, this was an ironic argument. The First Circuit found both arguments meritless and upheld his incarceration. The Court denied *certiorari,* and no justice, not even Douglas, appears to have given O'Callahan's appeal any more than scant attention. It is true that O'Callahan represented himself in these proceedings and did not raise the ultimate jurisdictional issue he later succeeded on, but it is also true that he had become something of an accomplished prisoner-lawyer.[25]

O'Callahan next appealed via a writ of *coram nobis* to the Court of Military Appeals in 1967. *Corman Nobis* appeals are a unique basis for bringing an otherwise already exhausted claim before the court. In essence, when a new condition of law arises, or newly discovered evidence of a substantial exculpatory nature is discovered, the doctrine of *Coram Nobis* enables a federal court to reconsider earlier decisions. However, this jurisdictional avenue is seldom granted. O'Callahan's principal argument was not that the military lacked jurisdiction to prosecute him in a court-martial, but rather that the admission of deposition testimony over his objections had deprived him of due process. Three years after O'Callahan's court-martial, the Court of Military Appeals ruled, in another case, that deposition testimony in lieu of actual witness presence deprived an accused of the Sixth Amendment's guarantee of the right of confrontation. Until the early 1960s depositions and interrogatories had normally been acceptable in

24 *Koyce v. United States Board of Parole*, 306 F.2d 759 (CA DC, 1962).

25 *O'Callahan v. Attorney General*, 230 F.Supp. 766 (DC MA, 1964) and *O'Callahan v. Attorney General*, 338 F.2d 989 (CA 1, 1964). The judges deciding O'Callahan's challenge were Bailey Aldrich, an Eisenhower appointee, Peter Woodbury, a World War I veteran and Roosevelt appointee, and John Patrick Hartigan, a Truman appointee and World War I veteran. The denial of *certiorari* is found at 381 U.S. 926 (1965).

federal and state criminal trials. At issue then, was whether the later decision could be retroactively applied to O'Callahan's case.[26]

O'Callahan had earlier created a second line of appeals. In 1966, he petitioned via *habeas* to the United States District Court for the District of Massachusetts where, for the first time, he argued his court-martial did not possess jurisdiction to prosecute him. In an unpublished decision, that court denied relief. While the Court of Military Appeals was in the process of deciding O'Callahan's claims that depositions rendered his court-martial as less than fair, he also appealed to the United States District Court for Pennsylvania. In a decision authored by Judge Patrick Follmer, a Truman appointee with no military background, the district court noted that the First Circuit had adopted a standard of courts-martial review mirroring the language in *Burns*. In essence, the district court issued two determinations. First, the Army had possessed jurisdiction over O'Callahan, and second, the military courts had given full consideration to his constitutional challenges. O'Callahan also urged the court to give *Miranda v. Arizona* a retroactive application in the hopes that if the district court ordered a remand, his confession would be suppressed in any subsequent court-martial. But, in 1966, the Court had already determined that *Miranda* was prospective application and therefore the district court ruled against O'Callahan. Likewise, again O'Callahan argued that the use of interrogatories violated his right to confront witnesses, but once more, the laws on this matter were prospective rather than retroactive.[27]

Because of the confusion resulting from two district courts reviewing O'Callahan's claims, as well as the Court of Military Appeals granting a third appeal to O'Callahan, when O'Callahan first appealed to the Court of Appeals for the Third Circuit, that court, in a *per curiam* decision determined that his appeal was untimely. However, because the Court of Military Appeals once more determined that O'Callahan's appeals were without merit, the Third Circuit would now, for the first time, review his claims.[28]

In a decision authored by William Hastie, a Truman appointee, and joined by Collins Seitz, a Johnson appointee, and James Ganey, a Kennedy appointee, the Court of Appeals for the Third Circuit determined that O'Callahan's claims that the court-martial was unfair were meritless. The three judges agreed with the military appellate court that the evidence against O'Callahan was substantial, and even if the interrogatories had not been permitted into evidence, he would

---

26 *United States v. O'Callahan*, 16 U.S.M.A. 568, 37 C.M.R. 188 (1967). The particular case on which O'Callahan sought relief was *United States v. Jacoby*, 11 USCMA 428, 29 CMR 244 (CMA 1960). In *Jacoby*, the Court of Military Appeals determined that the Sixth Amendment right of confrontation applied to courts-martial.

27 *O'Callahan v. Chief U.S. Marshall and Dept. of Army*, Misc.Civil 66–8-W (1966); The District Court denied release without ruling on the merits of the case. See *O'Callahan v. Parker*, 256 F. Supp. 679 (M.D. Pa. 1966). Miranda was ruled prospective in *Johnson v. State of New Jersey*, 384 U.S. 436 (1966).

28 *O'Callahan v. Parker*, 372 F.2d 136 (CA 3, 1967).

have been convicted nonetheless. In rather strident language, the court concluded, "no rational trier of fact could have acquitted the accused in the light of the above outlined undisputed testimony of witnesses in open court and the confession of the accused." O'Callahan also raised, for the first time, a claim of ineffective assistance of counsel. This was a relatively new claim in the law, making O'Callahan's appeal somewhat novel. The Court, in *Gideon v. Wainright,* determined that all persons have the right to counsel in felony trials, and therefore the state and federal governments owed indigent and poor persons at least an appointed counsel. But the judiciary had not added the caveat that this right included the right to a competent and effective counsel, and not until 1984, would the Court do so. On the other hand, there was no evidence that O'Callahan's military defense counsel had been difficient, and, as the appellate court noted, this issue had to be first addressed through the military appeals courts.[29]

O'Callahan also urged the appellate court that the military lacked jurisdiction to court-martial him in the first place. Repeatedly, the federal courts had disagreed with this position in other cases. In 1963, in *Thompson v. Willingham*, the Third Circuit determined that not only did the military possess jurisdiction over offenses committed in a time of peace in the Continental United States, but also, the fact that Oklahoma had prosecuted the soldier for the same offense as the court-martial did not deprive the military of jurisdiction. In the last sentence of its *O'Callahan* decision, Hastie noted that O'Callahan's counsel had "ably briefed a detailed and well-documented argument to support the proposition that the military courts lack jurisdiction over such a crime as is charged in this case." But, despite the argument of counsel, the law was not in O'Callahan's favor.[30]

A note on both Hastie and O'Callahan's counsel is important to the context of the Court's deliberations and ultimate decision. President Kennedy had considered nominating Hastie to the Court, but Warren and Douglas warned Kennedy that Hastie would turn out to be "another Frankfurter," and the president nominated White instead. In 1961, Hastie published a *per curiam* decision which upheld a 30-year sentence of imprisonment adjudged by a court-martial for a soldier convicted of taking part in a group rape of a German national. Seven African American soldiers were convicted for the rape and each received lengthy sentences of confinement, in an environment where German newspapers compared the conduct of the soldiers to that of the Soviet Army. The local sentiment had become, in the opinion of the local commanders, decidedly anti-American, and the American commanders made public pronouncements promising "swift justice." The soldiers appealed on the basis of a trial conducted in a mob atmosphere. The Court of Appeals for the Fourth Circuit upheld the convictions and sentences of

---

29 *Gideon v, Wainwright*, 372 U.S. 339 (1963). For the right to effective counsel see *Strickland v. Washington*, 466 U.S. 688 (1984).

30 *Thompson v. Willingham*, 318 F.2d 657 (CA 3, 1963).

one of the seven soldiers. Hastie's *per curiam*, issued two months, later, upheld the sentence and convictions of two others.[31]

Hastie was a prominent African American attorney, and in large measure an individual whose fortitude forced the bar and the judiciary to open to minority membership. Born in Tennessee in 1904, he attended Amherst and after graduating at the top of his class, attended Harvard's law school where he became part of Felix Frankfurter's "inner circle." In 1937, at Frankfurter's urging, Roosevelt appointed Hastie to a federal judgeship for the United States Virgin Islands Territory. Two years later he was appointed Howard University's law school dean, and after the United States entry into World War II, he became a special advisor to Secretary of War Henry Stimson. Hastie's work contributed to the lowering of racial barriers, including the establishment of the first African American fighter squadron and reforms to reduce institutionalized racism in military medicine. On several occasions Hastie studied the records of courts-martial which led him to argue to Stimson that racism continually undermined due process in military trials. By 1943, Hastie became convinced that the War Department had moved too slowly and he resigned. In 1949, Truman appointed him to the Court of Appeals for the Third Circuit making him the first African American to serve on a federal appellate court.[32]

Prior to serving on the appellate court, Hastie served in another national defense role. In 1946 Truman convened a special advisory group to study the possibility of Universal Military Training. Co-headed by Joseph Edward Davies, a former controversial ambassador to the Soviet Union who advised Truman during the Potsdam Conference, as well as Nobel Laureate Arthur Compton, a physicist who participated in the development of the first atomic bomb and was serving as the chancellor of Washington University in Saint Louis, the group analyzed "all known features of universal military service." Hastie focused on the military's seeming inability to fully integrate and equitably treat all of its members. "I regret to say that whatever its statements of policy from the top may be, the military establishment is not going to carry out a policy of desegregation in its actual functioning," he concluded before urging that mandatory universal service be avoided unless deemed absolutely imperative for the nation's survival. While Hastie's jurisprudence generally mirrored that of Frankfurter's, he had fully understood the shortcomings of courts-martial, particularly in racial disparities.

31 See William E. Nelson, "Byron White: A Liberal of 1960," in Mark Tushnet, ed., *The Warren Court in Historical and Political Perspective* (Charlottesville, VA: University of Virginia Press, 1993), 14; *Gordon v. Willingham*, 294 F.2d 515 (CA 3, 1961); *Kassey v. Goodwyn*, (CA 4, 1961).

32 On Hastie's life, see Gilbert Ware, William Hastie: Grace Under Pressure (New York: Oxford, 1984), 31–115; and Phillip McGuire, *He Too Spoke for Democracy: Judge Hastie, World War II, and the Black Soldier* (New York: Greenwood Press, 1988).

And, Hastie did not support the United States' military involvement in Vietnam. Thus, Hastie did not let his political beliefs infect his adherence to precedent.[33]

Victor Rabinowitz represented O'Callahan. An admitted one-time communist who had, at one time, also been a member of the International Labor Defense, an organization created by the Communist Party of the United States (CPUSA), Rabinowitz had made a legal career of defending people accused of subversive un-American activity as well as labor unions. In 1948, he represented labor unions in *American Communications Association v. Douds* and later memorialized his admiration for Black as a result of his dissent. He defended Alger Hiss, and his reputation was such, that in 1950, Ethel Rosenberg sought his counsel. In 1964, Rabinowitz was a named petitioner in a Court decision. He unsuccessfully challenged the government's requirement of having to list himself under Foreign Agents Registration Act as a result of representing the Cuban government in United States courts. He also represented the Cuban national bank before the Court.

Along with several other attorneys, Rabinowtiz had represented Julian Bond who the Georgia legislature attempted to dislodge from his rightfully elected seat after Bond spoke against the United States involvement in Vietnam, as well as one of the petitioners in *Harmon v. Brucker*, persons challenging the Subversive Activities Control Board, conscientious objectors, and organized labor officers and unions. He had also initiated a suit against Attorney General Robert Kennedy. Owing to an unpopular war and an increasingly less trusted Executive Branch, the climate of the second half of the 1960s was far more favorable to the CPUSA and other anti-government groups as well as their attorneys.

Rabinowitz's motivation for representing O'Callahan stemmed from his experience in *Harmon v. Brucker*, where he believed the Court, even though it sided with the two petitioners, decided the issue on statutory rather than constitutional grounds. "It was shocking that the government plucked a young man from civilian life, inducted him into the army, sent him abroad where he risked his life in military service, returned him to civilian life with an honorable discharge, then years later sought to stigmatize him for life, for lawful activities he had engaged in years before induction," he wrote.[34]

How Rabinowtiz came to represent O'Callahan, however, was not by any design on Rabinowitz's part. Former Teamsters' Union president, James R. Hoffa introduced Rabinowtiz to O'Callahan, his cell mate at the Lewisburg Federal Prison. "He had no money for legal fees, but [Hoffa], very generous with my time, quickly talked me into taking the case," he later recorded Rabinowtiz believed that O'Callahan was guilty of the attempted rape but thought the time was appropriate

33 Report of the First Meeting of the President's Advisory Commission on Universal Military Training: January 24–25, 1947, pp 672–3 [Joseph Edward Davies Papers].

34 Victor Rabinowitz, *Unrepentant Leftist: A Lawyer's Memoir* (Champaign, IL: University of Illinois, 1996), 50, 152–3 291–2; Ronald Radosh and Joyce Milton, *The Rosenberg File* (New Haven, CT: Yale University Press, 1997), 90; *Rabinowitz v. Kennedy*, 376 U.S. 605 (1964), *Banco National de Cuba v. Sabbatino*, 376 U.S. 398 (1964).

to challenge the military's jurisdiction over all common law offenses. He did not develop a personal affinity for O'Callahan as he had with many other clients, later writing, he "disliked O'Callahan and wasn't emotionally involved in his case." O'Callahan was not a political activist. He was an intelligent prisoner, self-taught in the law. In his memoirs, Rabinowitz penned, "I never saw O'Callahan again—not even a thank you did I get for my pains. A year later I did hear from him—he was in trouble in Massachusetts and asked for my help. This time I declined."[35]

The *O'Callahan* judicial conference was contentious from the start. Douglas, who assumed he was in the minority, penned what can only be described as a tirade against what he termed, "military injustice." He railed against the "military industrial complex," and claimed that "the Pentagon had usurped the government from the people." While it is true that the term "military industrial complex," had been used by President Dwight D. Eisenhower, by the Vietnam era the term came into use by the war's opponents. Harlan challenged Douglas with the fact that only three years earlier, he lauded the military justice system as being fairer than many of the states. On June 13, 1966, the Court issued *Miranda v. Arizona*, which ranks among the most important and well known decisions in the nation's history. *Miranda* had nothing to do with military justice, as it arose from a state criminal conviction, but it had everything to do with the fairness of criminal trials and police conduct. The Court placed upon arresting law enforcement officers a constitutional duty to inform suspected persons of their respective Fifth Amendment rights before any interrogation. In authoring the majority decision, Warren lauded an aspect of the military justice system, penning "the Uniform Code of Military Justice has long provided that no suspect may be interrogated without first being warned of his right not to make a statement and that any statement he makes may be used against him. Denial of the right to consult counsel during interrogation has also been proscribed by military tribunals. There appears to have been no marked detrimental effect on criminal law enforcement in these jurisdictions as a result of these rules."[36]

It is true that the Court noted that several foreign jurisdictions, notably the British and other common law legal systems, required law enforcement to notify suspects of rights before questioning commenced. How the language of the UCMJ and military tribunals appears in the decision, is, however, instructive. Telford Taylor, a World War II veteran who had graduated from Harvard's law school in 1928, argued as an amicus attorney for the New York state attorney general urged this inclusion. In 1946, after Robert Jackson left the Nuremberg Trials, Taylor succeeded him as chief prosecutor. He prosecuted several German Army generals accused of war crimes and argued for criminal accountability for German industrialists. Taylor had also opposed the House Un-American Activities Committee, publicly accused Senator Joseph McCarthy of undermining

35 Victor Rabinowitz, *Unrepentant Leftist*, 291–3.

36 *Miranda v. Arizona*, 384 U.S. 436 (1966).

democracy, and later was fervently against the United States' military involvement in Vietnam.[37]

On May 5, 1966, Warren prepared his first *Miranda* draft for circulation, though he did not circulate it until two weeks later, sharing it only with Brennan, Black, and Douglas, in the interim. The draft contained the language lauding the military justice system. But two weeks earlier, in his first draft for his own consumption, the language is absent. Indeed, Section IV of the *Miranda* draft, where the language occurs is a brief four paragraphs, but in the published opinion Section IV is 12 pages. In between Warren's personal draft and the circulation, Douglas surprisingly suggested that the decision incorporate Taylor's brief referencing the UCMJ, while Brennan suggested adding the information about military tribunals.[38]

On April 8, 1969, Harlan circulated his first draft opinion in O'Callahan, believing that he had White, Fortas, Stewart, and Marshall on his side. Warren was non-committal in conference. Harlan's draft essentially conformed with post-World War II case law on courts-martial, iterating that the Executive Branch was limited to what Congress had statutorily empowered it to do, but that the Executive Branch had not exceeded its authority. As to O'Callahan's argument that the historic interpretation of military jurisdiction made courts-martial held in the United States for common law or non-military crimes unconstitutional, Harlan responded that the martial law of seventeenth- and eighteenth-century Britain was far more arbitrary and alien to the legal principles of that time then courts-martial were to the legal principles of 1969. To that end, Harlan noted there was an absence of discussion of subject matter jurisdiction regarding military trials in the constitutional debates at the nation's founding. He also reminded the Court that Alexander Hamilton argued, that congressional authority to prescribe rules for the government of the armed forces "ought to exist without limitation." The final point of importance to Harlan was that the Constitution was created at a time when the Army numbered 718 soldiers and the nation relied on militia for its defense. In 1969, the armed forces numbered over three million and the possibility of conflict with a foreign power was much higher, requiring a consistently disciplined force.[39]

Immediately after circulating his draft opinion, Stewart, White, and Fortas informed Harlan that they would join. White had, earlier, pointed Harlan to a quote from George Washington which read "all improper treatment of an inhabitant by an officer or soldier being destructive of good order and discipline as well as subversive of the rights of society is as much a breach of military, as civil law and is punishable by the one as the other." White also provided to Harlan a more

---

37 See e.g., Telford Taylor, *Nuremberg and Vietnam: An American Tragedy*, 107; and generally Telford Taylor: *Grand Inquest: The Story of Congressional Investigations* (New York: DaCapo, 1974).

38 Warren, Uncirculated draft, May 9, 1966 [EW/616]; Warren, Memorandum to the Conference, May 18, 1966 [BW/88]; Warren, Circulated Draft, May 18, 1966 with Douglas' notation [EW/616]; Brennan notation on Circulated Draft, June 11, 1966 [EW/617].

39 Harlan, draft opinion, April 8, 1969 [TM/55].

contemporary context for the quote, writing "the soldier who acts the part of a Mr. Hyde while on leave is, at best, a precarious Dr. Jekyll when back on duty."[40]

Three days after reading Harlan's draft, however, Fortas switched his position from supporting Harlan's proposed decision, to authoring a dissent. Fortas claimed to take exception to the principle that the military could prosecute ever person on active duty "for every offense, whatever, wherever, committed, merely because he is in the military." He admitted that he had initially voted to affirm the lower court at the conference, but claimed he did so only on "narrow grounds." His narrow grounds, which were to later influence a limitation on Douglas' majority decision, were that the military would have to prove that the offenses had "a sufficiently direct and immediate impact upon the performance of the Armed Forces military mission." To Fortas, the fact that O'Callahan's offense had occurred in Honolulu, a city with a large military population, might have been fact enough to establish such an impact, but this would require a remand.[41]

Harlan disagreed with Fortas on a remand for two reasons. To Harlan, Fortas advocated a more limited jurisdiction than simply "status," which encroached into Congress' powers. Moreover, Fortas' suggested standard would create a case-by-case analysis and by fiat, limit the military's jurisdiction to purely military crimes, even if this was not Fortas' intent. (Fortas had, in fact, disavowed any intent to limit the military's jurisdiction to purely military offenses such as desertion or sleeping on post, but ultimately he joined an opinion when tended toward that direction.) Secondly, a remand would require both O'Callahan and the military establishment to prove an impact on the military mission either occurred or did not occur, 10 years after the original trial. For either side, this requirement would be an exercise in speculation, with an impossible standard.[42]

On May 15, Fortas authored a draft dissent in which he described the structural differences between courts-martial and civil trials. At the time the Army court-martialed O'Callahan, military trials were led by a presiding officer rather than a judge, and courts-martial were not staffed by random juries, but rather panels of officers or a mixture of officers and enlisted members, all of whom outranked the service-member on trial. In 1968, Congress established the position of military judges with authorities somewhat commensurate to federal judges, but O'Callahan was prosecuted several years prior to this change. Nonetheless, Fortas couched his dissent, not in his views on the unfairness of courts-martial, but on the greater principle of whether the Constitution tolerated an expanded military jurisdiction. Fortas concluded, not surprisingly, that the Constitution did not permit unlimited subject matter jurisdiction over active duty personnel. He relied on *Toth* and *Reid* to argue he was not articulating a new principle. Yet, both of these decisions involved jurisdiction over civilians, and not service-members at all, and Fortas did

---

40 White's notes on Harlan's draft opinion, April 8, 1969 [BW/147].

41 Stewart to Harlan, April 8, 1969 [TM/55]; White to Harlan, April 8, 1969 [TM/55]; Fortas to Harlan, April 11, 1969 [TM/55].

42 Harlan to Fortas, April 15, 1969 [TM/55].

admit that the Court never before addressed whether courts-martial jurisdiction over common crimes was constitutional. He turned to the historic practice of early American and British military law. Ironically, both Fortas and Harlan cited to Winthrop's *Military Law and Precedents* for their respective arguments. To Harlan, Winthrop's treatise showed that the military had prosecuted soldiers for a variety of common offenses, and thus an extended jurisdiction was well known to the federal judiciary. Fortas responded that Winthrop urged such prosecutions should only occur when the crime affected "good order and discipline."

Fortas did not disagree with Harlan that the military's interest in deterrence and the maintenance of a disciplined force were important to the military, but he countered there were non-judicial means for addressing malfeasant service members, such as administrative discharges. There were significant weaknesses to Fortas' draft dissent, which later were incorporated into Douglas' majority. Although Fortas cited to *Milligan* for the proposition that since courts-martial supported the "discipline necessary to the efficiency of the army and navy," the jurisdiction of such trials had to be narrowly construed whoever the accused person on trial. But this is precisely not what the Court in *Milligan* intended. To the contrary, in *Milligan*, the Court intended to give Congress full latitude in regards to the military's disciplinary construct. Fortas made a similar mistake in citing to *Coleman v. Tennessee* in which the Court recognized Congress' authority to legislate exclusive jurisdiction of courts-martial over soldiers thereby preventing the civil courts from prosecuting soldiers. The Court did not limit this jurisdiction to times of peace or proof of a nexus to a military operation.[43]

Perhaps Fortas', and commensurately Douglas', glaring deficiency in scholarship was their bare recognition, if not outright dismissal, of *Ex parte Mason*, a late nineteenth-century decision arising from a court-martial. In 1881, the Army court-martialed Sergeant John Mason, who was assigned as a prison guard, after Mason attempted to murder Charles J. Guiteau, who had recently been convicted of assassinating President James A. Garfield. Mason in a similar manner as O'Callahan, argued that his crimes were of a common law nature and not directly related to military discipline. In a brief decision without any dissent, Chief Justice Morrison Waite implied that even in instances where the civil law proscribed behavior, even in the case of an attempted murder of a civilian, Congress possessed the authority to enable military jurisdiction.

Both the victim in O'Callahan's case and Mason's case were civilians. There were, however, two differences between Mason and O'Callahan. Mason was on duty at the time he committed his offense and O'Callahan was not, though an understanding that an active duty service-member is technically always on duty minimizes this difference. The other difference was that Congress had not specifically codified Mason's offense, there were no specific orders prohibiting his conduct, and the Army court-martialed him under the Articles of War's general article. O'Callahan was prosecuted under an enumerated codification, prohibiting

43 Fortas, draft dissent, May 15, 1969.

rape. In short, O'Callahan had specific notice that the UCMJ prohibited his conduct, while arguably Mason was without notice because the 1874 Articles of War under which he was court-martialed stated nothing about murdering a prisoner, even one as notorious as Charles Guiteau. Given that several of the justices serving during Waite's tenure were equally, if not more suspicious of the military, than the justices in 1969, Fortas' brief mention of *Mason* in a footnote presents a glaring deficiency in his analysis.[44]

There was another problem with Fortas. He was facing a possible impeachment. Having lied to the Senate Judiciary Committee about the depth of his advice to Johnson and his financial relationship to a benefactor, his switch in *O'Callahan* could be seen as a means to distance himself from Johnson. Harlan believed this to be the reason for his switch, but he would not articulate his beliefs to the conference.[45]

The same day that Harlan circulated his draft majority decision, Douglas did the same with his draft dissent, which mirrored much of the anti-war rhetoric found on university campuses, as well as his criticism of military influence in the civil government found in his *Look Magazine* article, over 15 years earlier. Douglas used terms such as "military industrial complex," which had become the norm amongst anti-war protest groups. "The Court's opinion leaves me aghast," he began before penning that the Pentagon's authority had, in too many instances, superseded the nation's civil authority. The issue, to Douglas, was not whether O'Callahan had received a fair trial, and Douglas more or less conceded that O'Callahan's court-martial was fair, even in comparison to civil trials, though he did argue that "courts-martial as an institution are singularly inept in dealing with the nice subtleties of constitutional law." But this language was buried in the final third of the draft dissent. His second, and longest, argument in the draft dissent began: "We have at stake the civil liberties of the citizen, not the image of the Pentagon which is made, or re-made by the financial adventures of the military-industrial complex," reflected a language which the anti-war movement frequently utilized. Whether Johnson, McNamara, and the military chiefs had honestly believed that the war was necessary was unimportant to many anti-war Americans, and Douglas intended to add a judicial imperatur to the anti-war position.[46]

Douglas was not, however, altogether realistic about how much support he had, either for his dissent or his majority draft. He assumed that Black, Brennan, and Marshall would willingly join him, but only Black truly would. Warren, Brennan, and Marshall were more inclined to join with Fortas' dissent than Douglas,' if they were to dissent at all. As another indicator of Douglas' misjudgment on the strength of his position was in his final draft paragraph which concluded he "would put this case down for re-argument and designate Frederick B. Wiener, our foremost military law expert to present the case as

44 *Ex parte Mason*, 105 U.S. 696 (1882).

45 Harlan, Conference Notes, undated [JMH/357].

46 Douglas, Draft dissent, issued April 8, 1969 [WOD/1449].

amicus curiae of the Court." Wiener did not support Douglas on his *O'Callahan* position, and to Wiener it was one thing to oppose military jurisdiction over civilians, but another to have the judiciary obliquely undermine the Executive Branch's foreign policy and war powers authorities on a specious constitutional argument. On several occasions after Douglas' majority decision was issued, Wiener criticized the Court for *O'Callahan.*

Of the justices who ultimately joined in the majority, Marshall was the most unenthusiastic with Douglas' dissent and the same held true with Douglas initial draft majority decision. He favored Fortas' May 15 dissent, particularly the passages which noted that courts-martial had significantly improved in terms of fairness, but still fell short of civil trials. Fortas had also shied away from Douglas' inflammatory rhetoric about the military industrial establishment. Marshall urged that Fortas' approach was a reasonable compromise between Douglas and Harlan, but, he also determined not to author a concurrence. Thus, when Douglas, on May 26 circulated a third draft majority opinion, Marshall's clerk noted to the agreeing justice that it had "improved about as much as it is going to improve and I suppose it's time to join up."[47]

O'Callahan has to rank as one of the more poorly historically researched decisions in the second half of the twentieth century. In previous decisions Douglas had lauded the civilian staffed Court of Military Appeals, but in the published *O'Callahan* decision, that court was given scant credence. Relying on *Toth,* he reiterated some of the criticisms that courts-martial fell short of the due process standards of criminal trials, but he paid little credence to improvements in courts-martial procedures since *Toth.* It is true that at the time O'Callahan was court-martialed, no military judge adjudicated the proceedings and there was no requirement of a unanimous jury. Moreover, the majority reiterated that courts-martial are not trials of one's own peers in a traditional sense. But Douglas and the majority also claimed that significant differences in the rules of evidence existed between civil trials and courts-martial. This was simply not correct. By the time O'Callahan was court-martialed, and certainly at the time the Court issued its decision, the military's evidentiary rules mostly mirrored that of their federal counterparts. Douglas concluded this part of the decision with a gratuitous comment that claimed that while civilian trials were conducted in "at atmosphere conducive to the protection of individual rights," courts martial were purely retributive. Then Douglas followed by quoting to a highly critical law review article supporting Captain Howard Levy, one of the more controversial courts-martial of the Vietnam conflict.

None of Douglas' prefatory comments on the fairness or lack of fairness of courts-martial were necessary to the decision. In order to divest the military of as much jurisdiction as possible, Douglas relied on historic precedent dating to pre-Revolutionary War Britain. British Whigs, who remembered the "Bloody Assizes" and other abuses of the Crown, believed that standing armies were a menace to

47 RJG to Marshall, May 26, 1969 [TM/55]; Marshall to RJG, undated [TM/55].

individual liberties. As a result, British soldiers were tried in civil courts for ordinary crimes, when the trials occurred in Britain. Of course, by the time this British practice came into being, much of the British Army was scattered across their vast empire, and very few soldiers were stationed in Britain.

This British practice carried into early American jurisprudence. For instance, on the eve of the American War for Independence, John Adams defended British soldiers tried in civil courts. Following independence, very few courts-martial were adjudicated at all, and almost all appear to have had a direct military nexus. This much of *O'Callahan* was accurate, but from early American experience, Douglas and the majority then determined that constitutionally, courts-martial could only try service-members for offenses of a purely military nature, or for common law type offenses committed outside of the United States. Never before had a federal court determined that this limitation was constitutionally required.

Absent, of course, from the published decision was Douglas' highly critical comments about the on-going war in Vietnam and Johnson's abuse of authority, all found in his earlier drafts when he believed he was authoring a dissent. But, what Douglas accomplished was a dramatic alteration in the Executive Branch's relationship to the individual service-member. Under *O'Callahan,* Courts-martial would cease to be the guarantor of a disciplined force that had previously existed.

Harlan's draft majority decision became the published dissent with very little modification. It pointed out the weaknesses in Douglas' jurisprudence. English legal history regarding military courts was far more complex than Douglas and the majority presented, and Harlan took the majority to task on this point. Neither the Constitutional Convention, nor the writings of the framers indicated what jurisdictional constraints, if any, ought to apply to courts-martial. Early American court-martial practice, Harlan pointed out, varied in the quantum of subject matter for which soldiers were tried. Moreover, Harlan relied on some of the leading military history scholars, such as Russell Weigley while Douglas relied on contemporary law reviews.

White and Stewart remained supportive of Harlan's position, providing Harlan their historic research in the hopes that the dissent would effectively counter the majority's claim as to what the Constitution's drafters intended, regarding the extension of military jurisdiction over its own uniformed service members. Stewart additionally saw *O'Callahan* for what Douglas intended, and simply concluded that he could not take part in it. Harlan would not live to witness the reversal of the decision, but White and Stewart ultimately took part in reversing the decision.[48]

48 White to Harlan, May 24, 1969 [BW/147]; Stewart to Harlan, May 26, 1969 [BW/147].

III: *O'Callahan*'s Aftermath

In analyzing the conference deliberations and the efficacy of both the decision and the dissent, it must be understood that customarily there is an absence of acknowledgement by the legal academy as to what actually occurred in both the court-martial and the wide-ranging traverse of O'Callahan's appeals. *O'Callahan* was a unique decision which upended deference to Congress with the purpose of curbing the Executive Branch's war powers and foreign policy authorities. And it had a greater impact than narrowing the military's jurisdiction.

In 1970 Douglas published, *Points of Rebellion*, a short book in which he accused the government of operating in secrecy all the while questionably claiming that Soviet and Chinese plans required an aggressive military policy. He called for removing Central Intelligence Agency and Department of Defense contracts and personnel from universities and significantly diminishing military budgets. "An American GI in Vietnam wrote me in early 1969, stating that bald truth: somewhere in our history, though not intentionally, we slowly moved from a government of the people to a government of a chosen few," Douglas cautioned. Failing a significant reform in government, he urged that a right to rebel against the three branches of government existed.[49]

That same year, American Civil Liberties Union attorney Robert Rivkin claimed that *O'Callahan* "has thrown the military establishment into considerable panic—and with some justification, since no one knows anymore what the limits are of its power to punish." Robert Sherrill, an investigative journalist authored Military *Justice is to Justice as Military Music is to Music*, lauded *O'Callahan*. In opposite, incoming Secretary of Defense Melvin Laird complained that *O'Callahan*, "deals a cruel blow to law enforcement in the armed forces." Laird had a strong point. How the military was supposed to exercise its full discipline from the moment a citizen was brought into its ranks through their exit to civilian life became a critical concern to the military establishment after *O'Callahan*.[50]

This military establishment's concern was best encapsulated in the court-martial and judicial review of Lieutenant William Laws Calley, who was prosecuted for his conduct in what has become known as the My Lai massacre. Although human rights violations are endemic to warfare, reported war crimes from Vietnam exceeded those from any conflict in twentieth-century American military history. The gravest of these occurred on March 16, 1968, when an Army platoon commanded by Calley, murdered between 340 and 500 civilians in the small hamlet of My Lai, Vietnam.

---

49 William O. Douglas, *Points of Rebellion* (New York: Random House, 1970), 53–94.

50 Robert S. Rivkin, *GI Rights and Military Justice: The Draftee's Guide to Military Life and Law* (New York: Grove Press, 1970), 215; Robert Sherrill, *Military Justice is to Justice as Military Music is to Music* (New York: Harper and Row, 1970), 172–7.

The massacre was initially reported through command channels as a successful military operation. Calley's chain of command reported that incidental civilian casualties occurred, and then a formal investigation headed by a future Chairman of the Joint Chiefs of Staff, Major Colin Powell found that no massacre had occurred. The view of an exaggerated massacre would not last through the year. One of the soldiers accompanying Calley's platoon was an Army photographer who provided pictures to the *Cleveland Plain Dealer* in November 1969, after his honorable discharge. On November 12, 1969 journalist Seymour Hersh gave the public their first view of what had occurred. By the end of the month all of the major television networks and print publications had shown pictures and relayed interviews of the participants. A higher level investigation concluded that Calley's chain of command had colluded in a cover-up of the massacre and 14 officers, including the major general commanding the division which Calley served were charged under the UCMJ. Only Calley was convicted and sentenced in a court-martial.[51]

On March 31, 1971, Calley was sentenced to 20 years in prison and a dismissal, the equivalent of a dishonorable discharge. The court-martial was surrounded by media, and on appeal Calley not only challenged the fairness of his court-martial and pretrial publicity, he also alleged that unlawful command influence undermined the efficacy of the trial. Both the Army's appellate court and the Court of Military Appeals upheld Calley's conviction.[52]

The Court of Appeals for the Fifth Circuit likewise sustained the conviction and sentence, although to do so it overturned a district court which had sided with Calley. Absent from the Fifth Circuit's published decision was any citation to *O'Callahan* and it could easily be the presumption that the decision was deemed irrelevant to Calley's court-martial, since the charged offenses had occurred overseas in a theatre of war, and the offenses were clearly military in nature. But a presumption of *O'Callahan's* irrelevance to the appellate court would be false, because, in fact, both Calley and the government argued the decision extensively in their briefs. Calley cited to *O'Callahan* as proof that the military was inept in complex cases of a constitutional magnitude such as his, and that his trial should have occurred in a district court, or in the alternative O'Callahan mandated increased judicial review. The government, for its part, argued in opposite urging "the entire thrust of *O'Callahan* is that the jurisdiction of courts-martial should be limited to those cases which they are equipped to handle." Both Robert Ainsworth writing for the majority and Griffin Bell, writing for the dissent, had originally placed commentary on *O'Callahan*, in their draft decisions, distancing their

---

51 Guenther Lewy, *America in Vietnam* (New York: Oxford University Press, 1978), 356–61; William Thomas Allison, *Military Justice in Vietnam: The Rule of Law in an American War* (Lawrence, KS: University of Kansas Press, 2007), 93–7.

52 *United States v. Calley*, 46 CMR 1131 (ACMR 1973); *United States v. Calley*, 48 CMR 19 (CMA 1973).

analysis from that Douglas' statements on the fairness of military trials, but in the end, both judges deleted their commentary on *O'Callahan.*[53]

Nixon was involved in Calley's court-martial and appeals process. The President permitted Calley to remain under house arrest during the appeals rather than being transferred to Fort Leavenworth. After the Secretary of the Army reduced Calley's sentence to 10 years, Nixon ensured Calley would be freed on parole, and as a result, Calley ended up serving only six months in prison at Fort Leavenworth. That Calley's court martial was sustained by an appellate court should not, in retrospect, be of any surprise. But *O'Callahan's* impact stretched far beyond courts-martial.

In Cortright v. Resor, the Court of Appeals for the Second Circuit reversed a district court which prevented the Army from transferring a band member from New York to Texas. The band member had taken part in anti-war and anti-military demonstrations. The district court relied on *O'Callahan* as proof that the military establishment violated its personnel's constitutional rights of free speech. In *Culver v. Secretary of the Air Force*, the Court of Appeals for the District of Columbia in a fractured decision upheld the court-martial conviction of an officer who encouraged enlisted personnel to violate a regulation prohibiting political activity in a friendly foreign country. Following *O'Callahan*, lower courts began to consider challenges to military regulations ranging from the prohibition of political activities on installations to hair lengths. And, with the service-connected test created as a result of *O'Callahan*, it was likely that the military would be unable to prosecute a narcotics user who happened to only use illicit narcotics off-post.[54] While it is critical to acknowledge what impact that *O'Callahan* had on the military establishment, it is also critical to acknowledge what *O'Callahan* wasn't. That is, the decision was not the cause of the lapse in the military's reliability and indiscipline in the late Vietnam era, but rather a restraint on the military establishment to rebuild discipline and reliability contrary to the intent of the Legislative Branch and the customary means of the military to internally do so.

---

53 General Counsel, USA to Clerk of Court, June 24, 1975 [LRMP-UGA/33]; Brant to Douglas, June 17, 1972 [Brant 13]; Telford Taylor: *Nuremberg and Vietnam: An American Tragedy, 138.*

54 *Cortright v. Resor*, 447F.2d 245 (CA 2 1971); *Culver v. Secretary of the Air Force*, 559 F.2d 622 (CA DC, 1977)

Chapter 3

The Burger Court, Military Governance, and the Vietnam Conflict

In several respects, the Burger Court became a Court of President Richard Nixon's creation. Nixon, after all, appointed four justices in his first presidential term, and his judicial appointments were made with a broad purpose of restoring judicial conservatism. In 1968, he ran for the presidency on a "law and order" platform which appealed to "middle America." Anti-war demonstrations, campus and race riots, and a spike in crime alienated enough traditional Democrats to vote against Nixon's opponent Hubert Humphrey. By innuendo, if not outright allegation, Nixon claimed that the alleged excesses of the Court under Warren's leadership contributed to the rise in crime and disrespect for national institutions, and he pledged to create a conservative court which would undo the previous decade's decisions. More than Nixon disliked Warren, who was soon to depart the Court he despised William O. Douglas, and would use Douglas' excesses as a further reason for his judicial appointments. Nixon and the nation's conservatives knew that with Warren's retirement and Fortas' unfortunate failure to truthfully testify before Congress, two Court vacancies would open in the first months of Nixon's or Humphrey's presidency. Perhaps for the first time in history, Court nominations became one of the major features of a presidential campaign with no incumbents.[1]

Judicial vacancies were only one of Nixon's concerns on taking office. The United States had 536,000 service-members in Vietnam and over 200,000 more in the Pacific and Asia supporting the war efforts. Over 30,000 service-members had already been killed, and the cost of the war exceeded 30 billion dollars per year. Adjusting for inflation, in 2010, this number was close to 200 billion dollars per year. In further comparison, the cost of operations in Iraq between 2003 and 2011 totaled over 800 billion dollars. Nixon wanted to reduce military expenditures by at least five billion dollars annually by 1970, and he reduced the defense budget from 44 percent of the federal budget in 1969, to 30 percent in 1970.[2]

---

1 .John Ehrlichman, *Witness to Power: The Nixon Years* (New York: Simon and Schuster, 1982), 113–18; David G. Savage, *Turning Point: The Making of the Rehnquist Court* (New York: John Wiley and Sons, 1992), 45; Allan J. Matusow, *Nixon's Economy: Booms, Busts, Dollars, and Votes* (Lawrence, KS: Kansas University Press, 1998), 2–3; Sue Davies, *Justice Rehnquist and the Constitution* (Princeton, NJ: Princeton University Press, 1989), 3.

2 Allan Matusow, *Nixon's Economy*, 219.

Nixon came to the presidency convinced that the United States could no longer win the war in a traditional sense. Along with his national security advisor, Henry Kissinger, the administration began to try to withdraw from Vietnam while maintaining international credibility. They believed that to succeed, the withdrawal would require not only a negotiated settlement between North and South Vietnam, but also a strengthened military, and eventually a reunified public. Nixon's administration placed less emphasis on human rights abroad and civil rights domestically then the five previous administrations. Instead, the principle of "peace through strength," existed at the forefront of the administration's international policies, but under the idea that democracy could follow any pushback of communism. Nixon believed that the federal judiciary stood as a barrier to his international strategy.[3]

To reshape the Court, Nixon selected Warren Burger as Warren's replacement, but neither Nixon nor Burger succeeded in radically reversing the Warren Court. Legal scholar Vincent Blasi has labeled the Burger Court, "the counter-revolution that wasn't." On the other hand, if the Burger Court was unable to significantly reduce the import of the Warren Court's constitutional and criminal law decisions, it succeeded in holding the line against further diminishing the military's ability to police itself. The Court, as Tinsley Yarbrough noted, broadly construed the term "service connected," though this is an oversimplification because the justices approached the definition only once directly. The broader issues of jurisdiction, retroactivity, and when the judiciary could collaterally review courts-martial, consumed the Court's energies. On the other hand, it can be fairly characterized that while Douglas tried to collaterally curtail the Executive Branch's foreign policy and war powers authorities, the Burger Court collaterally tried to curtail *O'Callahan*.[4]

Importantly, related to the Court's narrowing of *O'Callahan*, for the first time in American legal history the Court's military law decisions were arrived at with the recognition of the larger context of how the decisions affected the nation's laws on the whole. Thus, equal rights and discrimination, the death penalty, religious accommodation, criminal law and constitutional issues arising from military decisions were decided not merely on the basis of military governance, but rather society as a whole. This phenomenon may have had its roots in the "second" Warren Court, but it did not come to fruition until Burger was at the helm. This is not to state that Burger had a major role of integrating military decisions into

3 Walter Isaacson, *Kissinger: A Biography* (New York: Simon & Schuster, 1992), 159; Herbert Parmet, *Richard Nixon and his America* (Boston: Little, Brown and Co., 1990), 611–26; Amy Belasco, *The Cost of Iraq, Afghanistan, and other Global War on Terror Operations Since 9/11*, Congressional research Service, March 29, 2011 (Washington, DC: CRS, 2011), 1.

4 Tinsley Yarbrough, *The Rehnquist Court and the Constitution* (New York: Oxford, 2000), 75; Vincent Blasi, *The Burger Court: The Counter-Revolution That Wasn't* (New Haven, CT: Yale, 1986).

broader criminal law jurisprudence. He did not, and it was primarily to Blackmun, Powell, and Brennan that this occurred.

Also, for the first time since the Civil War, the federal judiciary was truly confronted with the relationship between the First Amendment and the military. There had been other occasions in which the military's actions impacted on First Amendment rights, particularly during the Civil War. But, prior to 1968, the judiciary had never delved into the extent to which the military could limit freedom of speech amongst its personnel, nor since the end of the Reconstruction era did it address the military's authority or coercive powers over the nation's citizenry. The Vietnam Conflict and its attendant social upheaval changed the judiciary's role in not only military affairs, but also the military's relationship to the nation. Clearly, there had never been a time in American history that service-members had an unfettered free speech right. On the other hand, the societal upheaval during the Vietnam conflict caused the Department of Defense's leadership to worry that external pressures on the military could undermine military discipline and reliability, as well as endanger internal safety to the point that the military establishment conducted broad surveillance programs.

The Burger Court extended over four presidencies beginning with Richard Nixon, and followed by Gerald Ford, James Carter, and Ronald Reagan. However, this chapter covers the military policies of the first three presidents, even though Burger's tenure lasted through the first five years of Reagan's presidency and several important decisions, analyzed in this chapter occurred during that time.

I: Burger Court and the Military Establishment

Nixon believed that the reversal of the Warren Court's landmark decisions in criminal law would constitute a signature conservative achievement. This did not occur. Nixon's nominations to the Court did not reverse *Gideon*, *Miranda*, the Red Monday decisions, or the other civil rights decisions the conservatives had railed against. Moreover, the Court, under Burger only narrowed the scope of *O'Callahan* rather than overturn it, though the majority of justices would repeatedly reaffirm the traditional congressional role of regulating the military. From a conservative perspective, this was at best a modest achievement, and only partially answerable by Nixon's nominees.

In 1969, Nixon nominated Burger who, while serving as a judge on the Court of Appeals for the District of Columbia had been one of the Warren Court's foremost critics. Burger lobbied for the position and he advised Nixon's incoming chief of staff H.R. Haldeman and incoming White House counsel John Ehrlichman on a variety of matters. Although it was well known that Burger would try to undo the Warren Court's rulings, he was confirmed with little opposition. Unlike Rehnquist's leadership which was seen as effective and forceful, Burger's tenure as chief justice has been derided for weaknesses in his leadership abilities, which some of his fellow justices relayed to Court historians such as Bernard Schwartz.

Burger was not, in all respects, a conservative. On one occasion he sided with the majority in determining that women in military service had to be accorded the same benefits in pay and allowances as men of like rank.[5]

Burger was born in 1907, to working-class parents in Minnesota. He was admitted to Princeton University, but could not afford its tuition. He attended Saint Paul College and later its law school at night, while working as an insurance salesman during the day. This was the type of non-Ivy League background that Nixon championed. Burger's political background included a pre-judicial stint as a Minnesota Republican Party organizer. In 1952, at the Republican Convention, he shepherded the state's delegates away from Robert Taft to Eisenhower, when Minnesota's "favorite son" Governor Harold Stassen could not receive enough votes to remain in contention for the party's nomination. In 1953, Burger became an assistant attorney general in charge of the Department of Justice's Claims Division where he represented the Executive Branch in civil suits. Three years later Eisenhower nominated him to the United States Court of Appeals for the District of Columbia.[6]

Despite his poor leadership on the Court, Burger was qualified to serve as chief justice. Yet, his confirmation is surprising because his earlier appellate rulings were at odds with the Warren Court's internal security, military law, and criminal law decisions. Earlier, while working in the Department of Justice, he argued before the Court in a case that Solicitor General Simon Sobeloff refused to participate in. The issue was whether a citizen denied government employment on the basis of a loyalty suspicion had a right to confront his accusers in the same manner that a criminal defendant would in court. Sobeloff was concerned that innocent citizens could be tarred with the stigma of communist beliefs without a Constitutional check in place which might bring to light the ulterior motives of the accusers. Burger, moreover, was convinced that the federal courts had gone too far in securing citizen's privacy under the Fourth Amendment.[7]

Burger was a traditional conservative who articulated deference to the military establishment on most matters. He actively advised presidents on how the judiciary might react to matters of national security. Early in his tenure, he advised the Carter administration on drafting a bill to establish the Foreign Intelligence Surveillance Court. He also personally discussed with Carter the potential for the Soviet invasion of Afghanistan to result in a broader conflict.

---

5 John Robert Greene, *The Limits of Power: The Nixon and Ford Administrations* (Bloomington, IN: Indiana University Press, 1992), 38; John Ehrlichman, *Witness to Power: The Nixon Years*, 113–18; Melvin Urofsky, *A March of Liberty*, Vol. II, 897–8.

6 Bernard Schwartz, *The Ascent of Pragmatism*, 3–4.

7 Earl M. Maltz, *The Chief Justiceship of Warren Burger: 1969–1986* (Columbia, SC: University of South Carolina Press, 2000), 9–12; Charles Lamb, "Warren E. Burger: A Conservative Chief for Conservative Times," in Charles Lamb and Stephen Halpern eds, *The Burger Court: Political and Judicial Profiles* (Champaign, IL: University of Illinois, 1991), 130; Archibald Cox, *The Court and the Constitution*, 300.

When Reagan initiated a policy of combating communism in Central America using covert forces, he sought Burger's assurance that the clandestine programs would withstand judicial scrutiny.[8]

To replace Fortas, Nixon first nominated Clement Haynsworth from the Court of Appeals for the Fourth Circuit, but a combination of liberal Democrats and northeastern Republicans aligned to defeat the nomination on the basis of Haynsworth's animus to labor unions. Nixon next nominated George H. Carswell, another southern judge, but while Haynsworth was clearly qualified, Carswell was not. Carswell had expressed pro-segregationist positions and had one of the highest reversal rates of any sitting district court judge. After the failure to appoint Haynsworth and Carswell, Nixon appointed another Minnesota Republican, Harry A. Blackmun, who was panned by the media alongside Burger as the "Minnesota Twins." The two men were boyhood friends and Burger took part in Blackmun's wedding. A Harvard law graduate, Blackmun had served as the Mayo Clinic's general counsel, as well as on the Court of Appeals for the Eighth Circuit. Frankfurter had been one of his professors and though he was not part of Frankfurter's "inner circle," Blackmun claimed at his confirmation hearings to adhere to Frankfurter's judicial restraint philosophy. Blackmun also served in the Minnesota National Guard, but he avoided a call-up to active service in World War II.[9]

Blackmun's volumes of correspondences, housed at the Library of Congress, detail not only the Court's internal compromises in the issuance of majority and minority decisions, but also his own legal analysis and insights into pending issues to a depth not found in other justices' collections. While serving as an appellate court judge, Blackmun's military law jurisprudence evidenced deference to the military. In 1964 he authored a *per curiam* decision, *Burns v. Harris* which upheld a court-martial conviction for unpremeditated murder. The accused had been in pretrial confinement for eight days before being formally charged, and the UCMJ's statutory rule on speedy trials mandated an accused be charged within two days after placement in pretrial confinement, unless there were extraordinary circumstances.

There was such a reason for the delay in formal charging. On November 26, 1953, a German national was found in a coma, brought on by having been stabbed by a large knife, in Wiesbaden, Germany. On December 8 of that year, Army investigators arrested Private John F. Burns, and placed him in pretrial confinement where he confessed to trying to murder the German national. During this time, it appeared that the German national might survive. Eight days later, the Army formally charged Burns with attempted murder, but on December 26, the victim died. In between the charge and death, the Army conducted one Article 32 pretrial

8 Griffin Bell, *Taking Care of the Law* (New York: William Morrow and Co., 1982), 104–5.

9 Linda Greenhouse, *Becoming Justice Blackmun: Harry Blackmun's Supreme Court Journey* (New York: Henry Holt, 2005), 2–8; Tinsley E. Yarbrough, *Harry A. Blackmun: The Outsider Justice* (New York: Oxford, 2008), 53, 126.

investigation, but after the death, a second pretrial investigation was conducted, this time recommending a charge of premeditated murder. A court-martial found Burns guilty and sentenced him life imprisonment. Blackmun stressed that the Army had informed Burns of the accusations against him, and that the distinction between being informed and formally charged was not a basis for granting jurisdiction to launch a collateral attack, particularly where Burns had not brought up the issue during his military appeals. In short memoranda to his fellow judges, Martin D. van Oosterhaut, and Harvey M. Johnson, Blackmun stressed that the federal courts should not easily enter into military trials.[10]

In 1969, he authored *Harris v. Ciccione*, a decision originating from a court-martial for murder which took place in 1950. During the pretrial investigation, two officers with no law training represented the accused, but at trial a military lawyer represented the accused, and he also retained the services of a civilian counsel. The court-martial sentenced the accused to 25 years imprisonment and a dishonorable discharge. Blackmun's decision noted that *O'Callahan* had been recently been issued and the language that courts-martial were singularly inept at matters of constitutional law was included in that decision, but the court-martial in question before the appellate court nonetheless had been conducted according to the UCMJ and therefore would be upheld.[11]

Hugo Black announced his retirement in late 1971, and in his place Nixon nominated Lewis Powell. Born in 1907, Powell served as an intelligence officer in the Army Air Forces in World War II. His military experience included graduating as a distinguished graduate from the Army Air Force's intelligence school, having a role in the intelligence preparations for the Operation Torch landings in North Africa in 1942, and later assisting in deciphering German codes through the Allies' top secret ULTRA program at Bletchley Park in the United Kingdom. During the conflict Powell was promoted to colonel within two years of being commissioned a lieutenant. He reported directly to General Carl Spaatz and routinely briefed the allied supreme commander, General Dwight Eisenhower. The antithesis of William O. Douglas, Powell liked his military service and he was not opposed to secrecy, intelligence, or advocating for a disciplined military. Until the end of his life, he also defended the allied aerial bombing of Dresden, Hamburg, Hiroshima, Nagasaki, and Tokyo. These World War II air raids resulted in unprecedented destruction, but Powell insisted that each was conducted within the parameters of the laws of war. However, privately he called the raid on Dresden a "dreadful mistake," because of that city's historic importance. Powell would be the sole justice to encourage *certiorari* for Calley's conviction, and he took exception to

---

10 *Burns v. Harris*, 340 F.2d 383 (CA 8, 1965); Blackmun to Johnson and van Oosterhaut, January 18, 1965 [HAB/34].

11 *Harris v. Ciccone*, 417 F.2d 479 (CA 8, 1969).

the district court's treatment of the law of war. To Powell, Calley had violated the law of war, and he wanted to make a clear statement to this effect.[12]

Powell earned both his undergraduate and law degrees from Washington and Lee University in Virginia. After his admission to the Virginia Bar in 1930, he pursued a one year advanced course of study at Harvard's law school where he studied under Frankfurter. Between his admission to the Virginia Bar and his commission into the military, he worked in private practice, and became a prominent member of the Virginia Bar. Though Powell was not pro-integration, he never campaigned for segregation and following *Brown,* he worked for a non-violent transition of Virginia schools to integrate. His legal interests were primarily focused on business law and deregulation. His representation of the state tobacco industries and his service on a school board which governed segregated schools were the only aspects of his career likely to cause difficulties in the nomination process. However, the National Association for the Advancement of Colored People did not contest his nomination, focusing on Rehnquist, who had been nominated on the same day instead. Several prominent African American's endorsed his nomination to the Court.[13]

Following his discharge from active duty Powell returned to his law practice, but he remained associated with the military establishment. In October, 1948, Attorney General Tom Clark invited Powell to serve as a selective service commissioner on the Virginia appeals board. Powell accepted with the caveat that his firm represented several corporate clients who conducted business with the Department of Defense and he remained in the reserves. "Our firm has occasion from time to time to represent clients in litigation and in negotiation with the government and its agencies ... and I served in the Air Force during the war and now hold a reserve commission as a colonel in the Air Force," Powell responded. Clark did not believe this presented any ethical dilemmas for the appointment, and Powell was sworn in at the end of the month.[14]

Powell believed that the Court, and in particular, *O'Callahan,* had undermined military discipline, and like Nixon's other appointees, he also felt that the Court's activism contributed to the erosion of social cohesiveness. He treated all of his fellow justices kindly, but he privately complained about Douglas' rudeness and intolerance for the opinions of others. When the opportunity arose to directly overturn *O'Callahan* directly, instead of by implication, Powell enthusiastically

12 John Calvin Jeffries, *Justice Lewis F. Powell Jr.*, (New York: Fordham University Press, 2001), 61–71; For the destruction of Hamburg and Dresden, see Jeffrey M. Diefendorf, *In the Wake of War: The Reconstruction of German Cities After World War II* (New York: Oxford, 1999), 3–11; For the Tokyo Air Raids, see Michael S. Sherry, *The Rise of American Air Power: The Creation of Armageddon* (New Haven, CT: Yale University Press, 1989), 275–80.

13 John C. Jeffries, *Lewis F. Powell*, 29–50.

14 Powell to Clark, October 18, 1948 [LP/box 88]; Clark to Powell on October 25, 1948 [LP/1948].

joined with Rehnquist. Perhaps, because of Powell's calm demeanor, historians have missed his role in shaping military law. He often drove Rehnquist to write cutting, conservative opinions, sometimes complaining that Rehnquist's first circulated drafts were "milquetoast."[15]

But, for all of Powell's belief that the Warren Court had undermined the military, he was not a cheerleader for war. Writing to historian Daniel Boorstin in 1980, Powell complained that the congressional and military rhetoric against the Soviet Union was ill-advised. "All of this talk about war disturbs me more than a little," he penned. "Apart from other reasons, it is little short of madness to talk about fighting the Soviet Union on the Eurasian land-mass 8,000 to 10,000 miles away without adequate bases, means of transport or indeed anything like adequate forces." Included in Powell's objections were the nation's dependence on Middle East oil and a lack of discipline in the armed forces. He concluded his criticism with the observation that he "would have thought any sixth-grade child—after the 1973 embargo—would have known this."[16]

Like Blackmun, Powell recorded his views prior to conferences and after oral arguments, as well as the other justices' impressions. He labeled his personal memorandum, "my tentative view," and he also did not hesitate to write on his clerk's memoranda his disagreement or acceptance with his clerk's position, as well as directions to further research issues. His collections, housed at Washington and Lee's law school, are impressive but seldom cited, and this may be a reason why Rehnquist is often solely credited with achieving a proper constitutional balance in the judiciary's governance of the military (or reviled, with trying to restore expansive deference, thereby turning the military establishment into an unquestioned conservative bastion and endangering civil–military relations).

Nixon's fourth appointment, William Hubbs Rehnquist was born in 1924 in Milwaukee Wisconsin, the home city of Douglas MacArthur. He attended Kenyon College in Ohio for one year, but following the United States' entry into the war he enlisted in the Army Air Forces, serving in North Africa as a meteorologist. After the war, he completed his bachelors' degree at Stanford, a masters' degree in political science at Harvard, and then graduated Stanford's law school where he graduated first in his class. Rehnquist had a connection to the Nixon administration in that was a classmate of John Ehrlichman at Stanford University.[17]

His first legal position was as a clerk to Justice Robert Jackson. In June 1953, after his clerkship ended he moved to Arizona and worked in private practice. He gave speeches to the state bar association, criticizing the Warren Court for enabling communism in the United States, and in 1964, he campaigned for Barry Goldwater. That same year, he engaged in voter registration oversight, where he was accused of

15 John C. Jeffries, *Lewis F. Powell,* 196, and 255–7.

16 Powell to Boorstin, February 7, 1980 [Boorstin/139].

17 John P. Greene, *The Limits of Power: The Nixon and Ford Administrations* (Bloomington, IN: Indiana University Press, 1992), 66–7; David L. Hudson, *The Rehnquist Court: Understanding its Impact and Legacy* (Westport, CT: Greenwood Press, 2007), 2.

intimidating Hispanic voters. On the Court, on one occasion, Rehnquist referred to illegal immigrants as "wetbacks," infuriating Brennan and Marshall. Rehnquist's conduct as Jackson's clerk was particularly troubling to Senate liberals after his nomination. Prior to the *Brown* re-argument, he prepared a brief for Jackson which supported *Plessy*. During his confirmation hearings, he testified that Jackson had wanted two briefs, one in support of overturning *Plessy* and the other, a dissent from the majority's *Brown* decision. Rehnquist's explanation has, as a result of the evidentiary record, been in doubt, but he ascended to the Court and then the chief justiceship after Burger's retirement nonetheless. He also authored an article in U.S. News and World Report in 1957 attacking law clerks for "extreme solicitude for claims of communists and other criminal defendants."[18]

As a foreshadowing of Rehnquist's national security jurisprudence, in 1953 he conveyed to Robert Jackson his approval of Jackson's stance in the Rosenberg trial. After stating that capital punishment is solely a legislative decision (though he conceded that there were sound arguments against its use and that every accused person has a right to a fair trial), he accused the Court of behaving like "a bunch of old women." More importantly, he was convinced the "Rosenberg case had dragged on too long as it did," and that Jackson had saved the Court's public reputation. Although subsequent evidence had conclusively shown that the Rosenbergs conveyed highly classified information to Soviet Agents, there remains the question as to whether their trial was fairly conducted, or the death penalty appropriate. Jackson never stated that he believed either to be the case, but rather, it was not for the Court to conclude that, absent constitutional violations in the trial, the death penalty was improper. Rehnquist believed that the trial was fair and the death penalty deserved.[19]

On November 24, Professor John Frank, a leading constitutional law scholar, wrote to Elizabeth Black, Hugo Black's widow, "the facts are that Mr. Rehnquist is a man of character and ability who will do all in his power to reverse much of what you and I believe in." Rehnquist would immediately undertake to do so, and unlike Burger, he assumed the leading role in first narrowing, and then reversing *O'Callahan*, believing the decision detrimental to national security. On occasion, for reasons shown through the next two chapters, Rehnquist's efforts were stymied because of his display of what can best be described as arrogance toward women and religious minorities serving in the ranks (an arrogance he was accused of having consistent with his views on minorities in general). However, any characterization of his decisions as an attempt in create a conservative military culture in which servicemen had a monolithic allegiance to the Republican party is simply untrue.[20]

18 Sue Davies, *Justice Rehnquist and the Constitution*, 5–13; Mark Tushnet, *A Court Divided: The Rehnquist Court and the Future of Constitutional Law* (New York: W.W. Norton, 2005), 22.

19 Jackson to Rehnquist, undated, 1953 [RHJ/19].

20 Frank to Elizabeth Black, November 24, 971 [JPFP/1].

Rather, Rehnquist believed that Congress, as the Constitution mandates, was the primary vehicle for regulating and guiding the military establishment, rather than the courts, and only in the instance of failures to adhere to due process or statutory violations should the Court intervene. This is not to state that Rehnquist always sided with the military courts of appeal or the civilian Court of Military Appeals, because there were notable instances where he did not. But, Rehnquist trusted the military's civilian and uniformed leadership far more than Warren or the Court's liberals. He also believed it was essential to display to the Soviet Union as well as its erstwhile allies that while the United States military lacked in numbers, its technology and discipline made it a reliable symbol of democratic might. In this respect, Rehnquist was a continuation of Frankfurter and Harlan.

Two other changes on the Court occurred during Burger's tenure. Douglas retired in 1975 and was replaced by John Paul Stevens. From that point forward, the Court has lacked a justice who penned fiery language toward the military in dissenting opinions. Ford was more constrained than Nixon in selecting a justice, and Stevens' moderation on the appellate bench made him likely to be confirmed. However, Stevens initially maintained Douglas's jurisprudence, at least toward *O'Callahan*, though not in all instances toward the military law as a whole. To Irving Brant, Brennan penned "we are all missing Bill very much, but his successor is a delight both as Justice and person."[21]

A native Chicagoan born in 1920, Stevens attended the University of Chicago and then served in the Navy in World War II. Following the war, he enrolled in the Northwestern University School of Law where he earned the highest grade point average in the school's history. After admission to the bar, he clerked for Wiley Rutledge. When Stevens retired, he would be the last justice to have served on active duty in the military. He would also be the last serving justice to have not matriculated an Ivy League law school.

Stevens' early legal interests were not in national defense or military law, and instead he concentrated in antitrust law, publishing several treatises and teaching courses in the subject at the University of Chicago. An Illinois judicial commission appointed Stevens to investigate corruption, leading to the prosecution of two state supreme court justices in 1969. In 1970, Nixon appointed Stevens as a judge on the Court of Appeals for the Seventh Circuit.[22]

While on the appellate court, Stevens authored *Wimberly v. Laird*, in which a judge panel concluded that *O'Callahan* had no extraterritorial application. As a result, service-members court-martialed overseas for common law offenses would obtain no relief based on a jurisdictional deficiency claim through the Seventh Circuit. In *Champagne v. Schlesinger*, he also evidenced his belief that homosexuals were not a protected class within the military, and as a three judge panel the court permitted less than honorable discharges to be given to otherwise

21 Brennan to Brant, January 23, 1976 [Brant/4].

22 Kenneth A. Manaster, *Illinois Justice: The Scandal of 1969 and the Rise of John Paul Stevens* (Chicago: University of Chicago Press, 2001).

superbly performing sailors stationed at Great Lakes Naval Base who happened to have engaged in consensual homosexual acts while off-duty. In 1972, he authored *American Civil Liberties Union v. Laird*, where he concluded that the Seventh Circuit had to defer to the Court of Appeals for the District of Columbia regarding the Army's domestic surveillance program. Analyzed in the next chapter, the Court ultimately considered the military's domestic intelligence operations a political question, without ruling on the constitutionality of the military establishment collecting data on United States citizens. However, in *American Civil Liberties Union*, Stevens and his two peers, Chief Judge John Simpson Hastings and Robert Arthur Sprecher, another Nixon appointee, assumed the Army's surveillance program was illegal and when taken to excess, would dissuade free speech by frightening citizens.[23]

Prior to his retirement, Stevens was called "a lone ranger in a black robe." Like Douglas, his idiosyncratic predecessor, Stevens did not seek consensus in opinion writing. Stevens would not support overturning *O'Callahan,* not because he believed it was good law, but because of a respect for precedent. Nonetheless, he would as easily side with Rehnquist on other aspects of the judicial governance of the military, as he would with Brennan and Marshall. After his retirement, Stevens wrote that he had little respect for Rehnquist's jurisprudence, but this was not always evident during their time together on the bench.[24]

The last change at the Court under Burger was Reagan's appointment of Sandra Day O'Connor in late 1981. O'Connor was the Court's first female justice. She had an impact on the Court's military law jurisprudence during Burger's tenure, in the sense that she sided with Rehnquist and Powell on most issues. On the other hand, her criminal law jurisprudence often ensured the Court compromised on issues such as the right to effective defense counsel in *Strickland v. Washington*, which limited state prisoner's *habeas* access to the federal courts, or the government's right to limit what activities could occur on military installations. O'Connor would also be instrumental in the judicial evolution of blending military law decisions into the broader law.[25]

Born in 1930, in El Paso, Texas, O'Connor grew up on an Arizona ranch as well as in Texas. She attended Stanford University as well as its law school

---

23 *Wimberly v. Laird*, 472 U.S. 923 (CA 7, 1973). Thomas Edward Fairchild, a Johnson appointee and Wilbur Frank Pell joined in the decision. Neither judge was a military veteran, though Pell served in the Federal Bureau of Investigations during World War II and Fairchild in the Office of Price Administration. On Steven's role in the judicial review of the Navy's treatment of homosexuality, see *Champagne v. Schlesinger*, 506 F.2d 979 (CA 7, 1974); *American Civil Liberties Union v. Laird*, 463 F.2d 499 (CA 7, 1972). Like Stevens, Sprecher was also a Nixon appointee.

24 John Paul Stevens, *Five Chiefs: A Supreme Court Memoir* (New York: Little Brown and Co., 2011), 184; Bradley C. Cannon, "Justice John Paul Stevens: Lone Ranger in a Black Robe," in Charles Lamb, ed., *The Burger Court*, 343.

25 *Strickland v. Washington*, 466 U.S. 668 (1984).

graduating with high honors alongside of Rehnquist. Unlike Rehnquist, O'Connor faced gender discrimination, and no law firm offered her an associate position. She had a familiarity with military law in the sense that her husband served as a judge advocate in the Army between 1952 and 1954. Following his active duty service, he was employed as a civilian attorney with the Department of the Army. Between 1952 and 1954, O'Connor was a deputy district attorney for San Mateo, California, and between 1965 and 1969, she served as a deputy state attorney general for Arizona. In 1969 she was elected to the state senate, and became its majority leader in 1974. The following year, the state governor named her to the state superior court, and then in 1979, the Arizona Court of Appeals.[26]

In addition to Nixon's Court appointees, there was a change at the Justice Department which further influenced the shaping of the nation's military law. In 1973, Erwin Griswold, who had served as solicitor general under both Johnson and Nixon, stepped down, and in his place, Nixon appointed Robert Bork, a University of Chicago Law School graduate and Yale Law School professor. In Bork, the Executive Branch found an ardent advocate for national security and military discipline. Very little, if any of the positions he undertook regarding the military have been repudiated by the judiciary or Congress. Bork, moreover, was not a stranger to the military's needs or to national security. Born in 1927, he enlisted in the Marine Corps in the closing days of World War II. He served in China for a ninth-month period and qualified as a sharpshooter. He received an honorable discharge, but was commissioned as a reserve officer in 1952. Promoted to Captain in July, 1953, Bork was medically discharged shortly after.[27]

Between January 14, 1974, and January 22, 1975, Bork argued several significant military law cases before the Court, which resulted in the Court reaffirming the Legislative Branch as the definer of military governance. The appeals brought before the Court included the two subject matter cases which went to the essence of military discipline, but were challenged on the First Amendment and Due Process claims. He also successfully argued to narrow when the judiciary could step into the disciplinary and administrative processes. Like the Court's conservatives, Bork ardently believed that Soviet foreign aggression had to be countered by an effective disciplined military.

II: Department of Defense Leadership, Military Reform, and Watergate

Dozens of published decisions bear the name Melvin Laird, who served as Secretary of Defense during Nixon's first term in office. Laird was not a "Nixon man," and he quickly became appalled at Nixon and his national security advisor Henry Kissinger's secrecy. A naval veteran of World War II, he had served in

26 See Joan Biskupic, *Sandra Day O'Connor: How the First Woman on the Supreme Court became its Most Influential Justice* (New York: ECCO, 2005).

27 Bork's military records are found in his papers [Bork/21].

Congress for 16 years prior to his appointment as Secretary of Defense. Before his congressional tenure, he served six years in the Wisconsin State Senate, beginning at the age of 23, where, as a Republican, he surprisingly criticized McCarthy and managed to politically survive. He survived a typhoon in the Philippine Sea in late 1944, as well as a kamikaze attack in which he was wounded. When, in 1956, Eisenhower considered replacing Nixon with another vice presidential running mate, Laird lobbied against replacing Nixon. In 1964, Laird backed Barry Goldwater against Johnson claiming that Johnson had not confronted the communist leadership in North Vietnam strongly enough. That Nixon sought him to serve as the Secretary of Defense during the withdrawal from Vietnam as well as the transition to the All Volunteer Force (AVF) is unsurprising. Moreover, Laird supported maximizing military jurisdiction over service-members. However, he ultimately opposed Nixon's interference in the Calley court-martial.[28]

Laird's tenure in the Department of Defense was complicated not only by the twin goals of transition to the AVF and withdrawal from Vietnam, but also because of an unusual division of power between Kissinger and the Department of Defense. According to General William Westmoreland, Laird also had difficulties with the Joint Chiefs of Staff because he was unable to accept that the military's senior leaders strove, for the most part, to be apolitical. "Military discipline in the nation's headquarters broke down under Laird and Nixon in Nixon's first term because with the focus on reelection and secrecy, the administration went to extremes to avoid negative publicity," Westmoreland claimed. There is a good deal of evidence that the justices were attuned to the infighting between Laird and Kissinger as well as the senior officers serving on the joint staff.[29]

In Laird's last year as Secretary of Defense, he commissioned a study group to examine whether racism pervaded military justice. In November, 1973, the group, co-chaired by Lieutenant General C.E. Hutchins, the commander of the First Army, and Nathaniel R. Jones, the general counsel for the NAACP, also consisted of the four service Judge Advocates General, as well as W. Haywood Burns, the chair of the National Conference of Black Lawyers, Charles Stanley Blair, a United States District Court Judge for the District of Maryland, and John Carro, a state criminal court judge in New York City. Blair had served in the Army from 1953 to 1956, and went on to a political career which culminated in a position as Vice President Spiro Agnew's chief of staff. In 1971, Nixon appointed Blair to the bench. Carro, a judge of Puerto Rican descent, was a rising star who was recommended for a federal judgeship in 1988, but never achieved that position. Burns graduated from Yale Law School in 1966, served as general counsel to Martin Luther King, and in 1969 founded the National Conference of Black Lawyers "to serve as the legal arm of the Black Revolution." He publicly opposed Nixon's failed judicial

28 Dale Van Atta, *With Honor: Melvin Laird in War, Peace, and Politics* (Madison, WI: University of Wisconsin Press, 2008), 3–100; Walter Isaacson, *Kissinger: A Biography*, 198–202.

29 William Westmoreland, *A Soldier Reports* (New York: Doubleday, 1972), 388.

nominees, Clement Haynsworth and G. Harold Carswell. In 1974, he defended inmates charged in the Attica prison riots and in 1987, he was named dean of the New York Law School. In all, the study group was balanced in its composition between liberals and conservatives.[30]

The group concluded that discrimination existed in the Armed Forces, including in the entry level test, known as the Armed Forces Qualifying Test (AFQT) used to assign persons to various jobs, in violation of *Griggs v. Duke Power Company*. African American and Hispanic service-members were disproportionately assigned in the less technical military fields, and had a higher rate of disciplinary actions than whites. The Court, in *Griggs*, held that if a corporation's employment tests adversely impacted minorities, then the corporation must prove that the tests are "reasonably related to the employment." The Duke Power Company required intelligence quotient tests for prospective employees, and high school diploma requirements for positions which had little, if anything, to do with specific jobs. In writing for the majority, Burger acknowledged that the corporation failed to account for the fact that for decades African Americans had received an inferior education in segregated schools, and even if the corporation did not intend to discriminate, the judiciary could find unlawful discrimination if the conditions of employment evidenced a disparate impact on minorities. Applying this model, the military study group concluded that because enlisted personnel in the lower qualifying positions such as military police or motor transport had a higher rate of courts-martial and other adverse disciplinary actions, then the higher qualifying positions such as aviation maintenance or intelligence, the AFQT was biased. The military ultimately modified the AFQT without judicial intervention, though the relationship between the test and discipline rates was likely tenuous and the doctrine of selective prosecution already governed courts-martial.[31]

Analyzed later, *Parker v. Levy* and *Avrech v. Secretary of the Navy* had yet to be decided, but the study urged that Article 134 be abolished and replaced with a specifically enumerated set of offenses which incorporated federal and state crimes. The study conceded that Article 134 had "its historic uses" but it enabled commanders another vehicle to create racially disparate conditions in the administration of military justice. The Court would ultimately uphold the article, as well as Article 133, conduct unbecoming an officer and gentleman.[32]

---

30 See Report of the Task Force on the Administration of Military Justice in the Armed Forces, November 30, 1972. For a detailed analysis of the Report see Robinson O. Everett, *The New Look in Military Justice*, 3: Duke Law Journal, 1973, 649–70. On Burns see, Obituary, *New York Times*, April 4, 1996. Burns was killed in South Africa in a vehicle accident at the age of 55. On Carro, see "Public Lives: Son Won't Walk in Father's Footsteps", *New York Times*, June 5, 1998.

31 *Griggs v. Duke Power*, 401 U.S. 424 (1971).

32 *Parker v. Levy*, 417 U.S. 733 (1974); *Avrech v. Secretary of the Navy*, 418 U.S. 676 (1974). See Report of the Task Force on the Administration of Military Justice in the Armed Forces, November 30, 1972.

More important, the study group determined that summary courts-martial should either be terminated or significantly altered. The group found that minorities were more likely to be prosecuted in summary courts-martial for infractions than whites, who were more likely to be punished through non-judicial (Article 15) punishment, for similar conduct. This troubled the group because a summary court-martial created a permanent conviction record. If the Department of Defense or Congress were unwilling to end the use of summary courts-martial, as a secondary reform, they recommended that only judge advocates serve as summary court officers and all enlisted personnel be afforded a defense counsel. Additionally, the group recommended that upon reenlistment or discharge, the conviction be expunged from all military records. On that point, the group noted that only two percent of the judge advocates in the four service branches were minority members, while minorities made up one third of the military.[33]

After Laird resigned in 1973, Nixon replaced him with Elliot Richardson who was expected to have a full tenure. A former lieutenant governor of Massachusetts, Richardson's stay as Secretary of Defense would be a brief four months. Nixon nominated him to become Attorney General, after John Mitchell resigned in disgrace in 1973. (Nixon determined not to nominate the deputy attorney general, Richard Kleindeist.) Richardson was an Army veteran of the Normandy invasion and European campaign in World War II, and his later conduct in the Watergate affair marked him as one of the more ethical cabinet officers in Nixon's administration.

Richardson was a talented attorney who had served as a clerk to Felix Frankfurter, and earlier to Judge Learned Hand on the United States Court of Appeals for the Second Circuit. Although Hand had championed the protection of free speech early in his judicial career, he departed from Oliver Wendell Holmes Jr.'s "clear and present danger test" jurisprudence following World War II. This test enabled criminal prosecutions for speech that intended for a crime to immediately occur or inciting a crime. Under the extension, a person could be prosecuted for advocating the overthrow of the government through violence at some future time. Richardson lauded Hand's extension of the clear and present danger test to include predictions of future dangerousness in *Dennis v. United States*, writing to Hand, "I have frequent occasion to return to your *Dennis* opinion and I come away from it each time with increased admiration. I knew it was a great opinion when I first read it—now I really know it." He also praised the Court's opinion in *American Communications Association, C.I.O v. Douds*. "Someone, I think, deserves great credit for the Chief's [Frederick Vinson's] opinion in *Douds*. It seems to me a very able analysis of the relevant issues," he wrote to Frankfurter.[34]

Richardson was expected to be a conservative Secretary of Defense who would complete the Vietnamization program and then strengthen forces in NATO. He also was expected to fight to limit *O'Callahan* to the maximum extent possible.

33 Id.

34 Richardson to Hand, August 9, 1951 [Elliot Richardson Papers/51]; Richardson to Frankfurter, August 9, 1951 [Elliot Richardson Papers/51].

As an attorney and Frankfurter acolyte he had the credentials to be successful in this goal, but was never able to act on it since he quickly moved to the Justice Department. Also, he would not be blindly loyal to Nixon. He refused to fire the special Watergate prosecutor and resigned from office. Nixon appointed James Schlesinger as Secretary of Defense following Richardson's move to the Justice Department, and several judicial decisions also carry his name.[35]

On July 24, 1974, the Court issued *United States v. Nixon*, in which it determined that while executive privilege existed, it did not exist to the extent to shield the President from criminal prosecution. Nixon had, in fact, directed a criminal enterprise including unlawful wiretapping and the distribution of questionable funds for political gain. Although the decisions arising from the Watergate scandal and eventual impeachment were not directly related to the military, the fact that the President is commander in chief of the Armed Forces meant that any judicially imposed limitations on presidential authority might impact military affairs and national security policies. Nixon's Secretary of the Treasury, John Connally, a former Kennedy supporter, supposedly claimed that the President, as commander in chief, was at liberty to ignore the Court. As result, all of the justices agreed that the Court had to issue a unified decision. Certainly, the specter of Nixon trying to seize power through a *coup d' état* was rumored, though since he had little support from within his own party, even if he had attempted one, it was doubtful it would have succeeded. Additionally, the military's leadership would not have backed him. Yet, Schlesinger claimed to have placed military forces on alert in case Nixon tried to seize power. President Ford removed Schlesinger after forcing him to recant the statement as untrue. Even though Schlesinger's statement proved to be a fabrication, Douglas, Brennan, and Marshall believed the possibility to be real so that the military's power had to be further checked.[36]

After Schlesinger's departure, Ford turned to his former chief of staff and ambassador to NATO, Donald Rumsfeld to be Secretary of Defense. Had Rumsfeld's tenure with the Department of Defense ended with Ford's presidency, little controversy today would be attached to his name. He served between November 1975, after the Mayaguez incident with Cambodia, and to the end of Ford's term in 1977. However, having served in the same cabinet position under George W. Bush, he has become perhaps the most controversial civilian head of the military since Edwin Stanton. As a student at Princeton, Rumsfeld's senior thesis, "the steel seizure case," might have been thought to portend an adherence to the laws of the nation. In his second term as defense secretary, the employment of "enhanced interrogation techniques," the expansive use of civilian contractors, coupled with the neoconservative belief in expanded executive authority, has made a dispassionate analysis of his leadership during his term under Ford difficult.

35 Christopher Matthews, *Kennedy and Nixon: The Rivalry that Shaped Postwar America* (New York: Simon & Schuster, 1996), 326.

36 See, Brennan, Memorandum for the Conference, June 14, 1974 [WJB/I:332]; For Schlesinger's conduct, see, Dale Herspring, *The Pentagon and the Presidency*, 233.

From 1954 to 1975, he served in the Navy as an aviator, though in a reserve capacity after 1957. In 1962, he was elected to Congress as a Republican at the age of 30, and served through 1969. As Secretary of Defense, he worked to increase the military budget and remove Kissinger's influence from military policy.[37]

In 1977, President James Carter appointed Harold Brown as Secretary of Defense. A former physics professor who worked on modernizing the Navy's nuclear submarine missile programs, Brown was not a stranger to the military establishment. He served as Secretary of the Air Force between 1965 and 1968, and supported Johnson's Vietnam policies. He also supported the continuation of containment and lobbied for new weapons systems. Both Carter and Brown believed that Nixon's pursuit of détente had permitted the Soviet Union to increase their dominance in Europe. Brown would become instrumental in shaping the Rapid Deployment Joint Task Force, a forerunner of United States Central Command, as well as the means for placing United States forces into the Persian Gulf in 1990. Yet, under Carter, the United States did not militarily intervene in the Cambodian genocide, fearing the nation would not support sending forces to Southeast Asia. Carter and Brown both supported maximizing the military jurisdiction over service-members, though neither would argue to undo *O'Callahan*. On the other hand, Brown would unsuccessfully try to weaken the civilian Court of Military Appeals by placing it under the Court of Appeals for the Fourth Circuit, the nation's most conservative appeals court.[38]

At a time where the national strategy needed a disciplined reliable military force to a degree not needed since the end of World War II, it simply did not possess one. The United States' involvement in Vietnam was a windfall for the Soviet Union. Not only did the United States military budget grow to enormous levels, world opinion turned against the United States, and the war brought Johnson's presidency to an end. Ironically, by the time the last United States forces left Vietnam, the populations of the developing nations in sub-Saharan Africa, Central and South America, and Southeast Asia leaned toward allying with the Soviet Union, or any government that would support strong socialist reforms. It might have surprised United States government officials, but for the two decades between 1968 and 1988, a large swath of the world was more interested in the promise of socialism than that of American style liberty. This was a change from the two decades following World War II. Led by the General Secretary of the Communist Party of the Soviet Union, Leonid Brezhnev, the Soviet leadership

---

37 Raymond L. Garthoff, *Détente and Confrontation: American–Soviet Relations from Nixon to Reagan* (Washington, DC: Brookings Institution, 1992), 492; Walter Isaacson, *Kissinger: A Biography*, 669–71; and, Sean Wilentz, *The Age of Reagan: A History, 1974–2008* (New York: Harper and Row, 2009), 62.

38 Robert K. Brigham, *Iraq, Vietnam and the Limits of American Power* (New York: Public Affairs Journal, 2006), 156–77; also Zbignew Brzezinski, *Power and Principle: Memoirs of the National Security Advisor,* 1977–1981 (New York: Farrar, Strass, and Giroux, 1983), 444. On Brown's efforts see Clement Haynsworth to Diane Siemer, May 15, 1978 [CHP/163] and accompanying papers.

intended to take advantage of this change in events, and the Soviet military had modernized where it could play a substantial role in world affairs. In the Arab states, the combination of United States support to Israel and the Soviet Union's backing of Arab nationalism increased the popularity of the Soviet Union, despite the inevitable clash between Islam and a theory of political governance which minimized religion.[39]

In 1968, Brezhnev not only announced a doctrine promising Soviet aid to communist political groups in other countries, but also Soviet intervention in socialist countries where the local government was threatened with pro-capitalist movements. Brezhnev's doctrine reflected a return to Stalin's foreign and military policy, but unlike Stalin, Brezhnev, felt more comfortable militarily opposing the United States and its allies. There were sound reasons for confidence in Brezhnev's strategy.[40]

In the Cuban missile crisis' aftermath, the Soviet Union established a military policy of seeking parity against the combined strength of all NATO forces. This parity goal did not include Warsaw Pact militaries which Soviet military strategists worried might not be reliable in a full-scale war against the west. Nor did Soviet military policy look to China as a potential ally in a war with the west. In short, by 1965 the Soviet military strategy was premised on a "go it alone" force even though their geopolitical strategy still espoused communism as a unifier of peoples. Part of their military strategy had to do with the lack of unity between the People's Republic of China and the Soviet Union, and partly because of the recognition of nascent discontent in the Eastern Bloc. On the other hand, the numbers of Soviet military advisors increased throughout the world. During the Six Day War as well as the 1973 war between Israel and the Arab League allies, Soviet advisors took a direct role in assisting in the Syrian and Egyptian armed forces. In 1975, a large Soviet military exercise along the Dnieper River proved that a large force was capable of invading Western Europe. Les Aspin, an anti-Vietnam War critic who later became Secretary of Defense under President William J. Clinton, conceded that the Soviet preponderance of forces could force Western European governments into accommodations with the Soviet Union such as had occurred with Finland.[41]

---

39 Robin Edmonds, *Soviet Foreign Policy, 1962–1973*; Paul L. Savage and Richard A. Gabriel, "Cohesion and Disintegration in the American Army: An Alternative Perspective," in Paul Karsten ed. *The Military in America: From the Colonial Era to the Present* (New York: Free Press, 1980), 403; David Cortright, *Soldiers in Revolt: GI Resistance During the Vietnam War* (Chicago: Haymarket Books, 1975), 23; Luther C. West, *They Call it Justice: Command Influence and the Court-Martial System* (New York: Viking Press, 1977), 278.

40 Alexander Haig, *Caveat: Realism, Reagan, and Foreign Policy* (New York: MacMillan, 1984), 26.

41 Jack Kemp, Realities of Soviet Power: Two Views, *AEI Defense Review*, Vol. II, No.3, 22; Les Aspin, "Putting Soviet Power Into Perspective: Two Views," *AEI Defense Review*, Vol. II, No.3, 22.

Between 1958 and 1960, Nikita Khrushchev had forced out over 250,000 older officers and promoted 454 new generals, but this did not stop a trend in the aging of the senior officer ranks. In response, in 1965, the Soviet government conducted a survey of the efficiency of all of its officers and discovered that its officers were the oldest among the world's modern militaries. In 1967, mandatory retirement laws were put into effect and a new generation of military leadership took command. By 1970, the Soviet Army fielded two million soldiers for its ground forces and its air force and undersea naval force exceeded those of the United States. Only the United States surface naval forces were larger than the strength of the comparable Soviet naval forces. In an era where the United States' conventional forces were thought of as a hollow shell, the Soviet Union was militarily at its most formidable.[42]

In 1968, Soviet forces entered into Czechoslovakia as that country's government had made attempts to liberalize relations with the west and reduce autocratic control over its population. Brezhnev claimed that the Soviet Union had the right to secure Eastern Europe's borders against the west. Mired in Vietnam, Lyndon Johnson could only express outrage at the invasion of Czechoslovakia, and the North Atlantic Treaty Organization idled its forces without responding with a show of force. Western inaction emboldened further military aggression by the Soviet government, and increased numbers of their military advisors were found across the globe. In particular, Soviet military advisors were sent to the southern Mediterranean nations in larger numbers. This led to Israeli lobbying as well as that of the American petroleum industry to increase American presence in that region.[43]

When Carter became president in 1977, he reduced covert operations, but enlarged the nation's conventional forces. Carter believed in minimizing government while still maintaining a sizeable deterrent. He did not, as his detractors have alleged, attempt to downsize the nation's military forces to appease the Soviet Union. Nonetheless, there were troubling aspects to the nation's conventional and nuclear forces. In 1979, Lawrence Korb, a future assistant secretary of defense, noted that even the nation's nuclear forces—the triad of B-52 bombers, land-based missiles, and nuclear missile capable submarines, were in decay. Moreover, Korb argued that Nixon's return to a "Europe First strategy," had weakened United States influence in Asia, the Middle East, and the Pacific. In January 1980, Carter initiated the development of the Rapid Deployment Task Force (RDTF), a joint military force eventually numbering approximately 200,000 troops with the capability of deploying to the Persian Gulf. With the support of congressional Republicans, Carter maintained

42 John Erickson, Soviet Military Power, United States Strategic Studies Institute, Report 73-1 (Washington, DC, USSI, 1973).

43 Matthew Ouimet, *The Rise and Fall of the Brezhnev Doctrine in Soviet Foreign Policy* (Chapel Hill, NC: University of North Carolina Press, 2003), 30–39; Clark Clifford, *The 1970 Defense Budget and Defense Program for the Fiscal Years, 1970–1974*, 6–10.

the possibility of conscription through selective service registration, but no effort was made to reinstate the draft. He attempted to engage the Soviet Union to reduce both nations' nuclear stockpiles, but after the Soviet invasion of Afghanistan in late 1979, tensions between the two nations rose.[44]

Diminished United States pressure on the Soviet Union was, to be sure, problematic. By 1980, the Soviet Union had invaded Afghanistan and appeared to be making significant gains there. Ethiopia and Yemen had become governed by communist party members backed by the Soviet Union. Cuban soldiers advised African militaries. Libyan leader, Moammar al-Qaddafi provided weapons to European pro-communist terror organizations such as Bader Meinhoff and the "Red Brigades" with tacit Soviet approval. Although not related to Soviet foreign policy, Ayatollah Khomeini's Iranian forces had not only deposed a pro-western ruler, but also held American non-combatant personnel hostage for over a year. The United States appeared to be at its weakest point in influencing world affairs since World War II, and the state of its armed forces certainly contributed to this weakness.[45]

III: Military Justice in the Aftermath of *O'Callahan*

Even when considered outside of its encroachment into Congressional authority and its other ramifications *O'Callahan* was a dramatic decision, in part, because of the questions the decision did not answer. Foremost among the unresolved issues was whether the decision was to be retroactively (or as some justices interchangeably termed it "retrospectively") applied. There was an argument, reasonable or otherwise, that if the military was so singularly inept at protecting the due process rights of servicemen, then prior courts-martial convictions of non-unique military offenses conducted on American soil adjudicated under the UCMJ, or perhaps even those adjudicated under the earlier Articles of War should be overturned. Why this did not occur is partly answerable by the Court's criminal law decisions between 1954 and 1965. These included the exclusion of evidence seized in violation of the Fourth Amendment in *Mapp v. Ohio* (1961), the absolute right to counsel in criminal trials in *Gideon v. Wainright* (1963), and the right against self-incrimination in *Miranda v. Arizona* (1966). These three decisions led Chief Justice Warren to create a retroactivity test. After all, if law enforcement authorities had violated the constitutional rights of citizens, the Court had to address the issue of whether a ruling was to be retroactively applied.

---

44 Allan R. Millet and Peter Maslowski, *For the Common Defense: A Military History of the United States* (New York: Free Press, 1994), 609–14; Lawrence Korb, "The Policy Impacts of the Carter Defense Program," in Sam C. Sarkesian, *Defense Policy and the Presidency: Carter's First Years* (Boulder, CO: Westview Press, 1979), 179.

45 Alexander Haig, *Caveat: Realism, Reagan, and Foreign Policy* (New York: MacMillan, 1984), 30.

In *Linkletter v. Walker*, the Court accomplished just that, but the standard this decision created was not helpful to determining *O'Callahan*'s retroactive application. Several district courts concluded *O'Callahan* was retroactive, while others found in opposite. Decided before *O'Callahan,* and certainly not with the military in mind, *Linkletter* originated in a Louisiana state burglary conviction. The police obtained evidence in the defendant's residence without a warrant. The police already had the defendant in custody and had taken his house keys from him. Moreover, there were no exigent circumstances to justify the intrusion under post-*Mapp* decision. Linkletter, however, was convicted in 1959, and the Louisiana Supreme Court upheld the conviction the following year. So too did the Court of Appeals for the Fifth Circuit on *habeas* review. Linkletter argued that *Mapp* had to be applied to his case. The Court rightly understood that if it followed the traditional common law approach to retroactivity, thousands of convicted persons would be set free. (Under this same argument, if retroactivity applied to *O'Callahan*, then thousands of courts-martial would be invalidated.) To answer fears of sweeping retroactive application to its criminal law jurisprudence, the Court created a three-part test in which retroactivity would not apply when the decision created a rule which constituted a "new" principle of law; the rule's operation would be retarded by retroactive application; and the equities of the case favored non-retroactivity. In addition to the "*Linkletter*" being unhelpful to solving the question of *O'Callahan's* retroactivity, Black and Douglas dissented in *Linkletter*.[46]

O'Callahan presented other problems. It required offenses to be service-connected, but the decision never defined with any specificity what that term meant. Some offenses would be self-evident in terms of service connection such as disobedience to orders or desertion, but other offenses, such as narcotics use, would not, at least to a judiciary bent on limiting the military's jurisdiction. Finally, in addition to the retroactive application and lack of specificity problems inherent in *O'Callahan,* there remained a question of the constitutionality of certain offenses unique to the military. Douglas, in authoring *O'Callahan* had penned into the decision a doubt on the constitutional efficacy of the general article as well as Article 133, the article reserved for governing the behavior of officers.

a. Relford v. Commandant*: The Parameters of Service-Connection*

In 1971, the Court issued *Relford v. Commandant,* a decision that the justices believed would bring greater clarity to *O'Callahan.* In conference, all of the justices agreed that some definition of "service connection" had to be issued. Burger assigned Blackmun to author the decision. But the case did not originate solely as a service-connection challenge. Rather, it arose under a claim of *O'Callahan's*

46 *Linklatter v. Walker*, 381 U.S. 618 (1965). Jill E. Fisch, "Retroactivity and Legal Change: An Equilibrium Approach," *110 Harvard Law Review* (March 1997) 1055–123, 1059; Black to Douglas, on draft dated May 28, 1965 [HLB/383].

retroactive application. Oddly, the justices agreed in conference not to consider the issue of retroactivity. Argued on December 15 and 16, 1970, the Court decided the appeal on February 24, 1971. There were still over 50,000 troops in Vietnam at this time, but their numbers were steadily decreasing.[47]

The facts underlying *Relford* were little different than in *O'Callahan*, although in *O'Callahan* the offenses were committed outside of a military installation, and in *Relford* the offenses occurred within the confines of Fort Dix, New Jersey. In 1961, a court-martial convicted Corporal Isiah Relford of kidnapping and raping two civilian women on a "military reservation." Both women had a connection to the military in the sense that one was married to a serviceman and the other was visiting her hospitalized brother who was a serviceman stationed on the post. In each instance, Relford wore civilian clothes. He was convicted, and sentenced to death, but the Army Board of Military Review commuted the sentence to a term of 30 years imprisonment.

Similar to Sergeant O'Callahan, Corporal Relford did not initially challenge the military's jurisdiction over him. His appeal to the United States District Court for the District of Kansas was a based on a claim of ineffective assistance of counsel. The district court denied relief, and Relford appealed to the Court of Appeals for the Tenth Circuit, raising additional claims regarding the admissibility of his confession, the results of a line-up, and the fairness of his court-martial. In a very brief decision, the appellate court dismissed Relford's ineffective assistance of counsel claim. Like the lower court, the appellate court noted that since the military appellate courts had given "full and fair consideration" to Relford's claims, they would not overturn the lower court. For the first time on appeal, Relford also claimed that his confession was involuntary and he had been subjected to an illegal lineup. Because his confession occurred prior to *Miranda*, the appellate court determined to assess his claim on the basis of whether the totality of the circumstances dictated that the confession was involuntary. There were, simply no facts in the record to substantiate Relford's claim on either this point or the matter of the line-up. The one issue Relford did not raise was whether the military possessed the jurisdiction to court-martial him in the first place. This would unanimously be decided by the Court nonetheless.[48]

The Court's decision to grant *certiorari* stemmed from Relford's claim that since *O'Callahan* was decided on a constitutional issue, it applied retroactively. If *O'Callahan* rested on sound historic evidence, Relford's retroactivity argument was timely. Interestingly, Solicitor General Erwin Griswold agreed that the Court should decide whether *O'Callahan* had a retroactive effect, but for the reason that he argued *O'Callahan* articulated a new rule than a preexisting right. Despite the apparent agreement between Relford's attorney and the Justice and Defense

47 *Relford v. Commandant,* 401 U.S. 355 (1971).

48 *Relford v. Commandant*. 409 F.2d 824 (CA 10, 1969). The Court went so far as to note that it would address the two contentions raised for the first time instead of remanding to avoid a habeas repetition.

Departments on the importance of retroactive application, the Court did not address the issue. Instead, as Blackmun wrote, the Court determined its only task was to further define the service-connected test. This decision was not a deliberate indifference to the importance of the retroactivity issue. Indeed, in conference, Blackmun concluded that the facts arising in *Relford* precluded *O'Callahan's* retroactivity under the "three part test: as enumerated in *Linkletter,*" but the justices differed in their opinions on this subject.

In conference, Blackmun acknowledged that both Relford and the Solicitor General urged the Court to determine retroactivity as well as establish wide-ranging guidelines for courts-martial jurisdiction. Rehnquist, Douglas, and Marshall argued for retroactivity, but Brennan indicated a preference not to entertain the issue. Burger, Powell, Blackmun, and Stewart argued against retroactivity. The one agreement amongst the justices was to formulate a unified decision. In his first draft, Blackmun drew attention to his avoidance of creating guidelines by *dicta*. "I am personally entirely content to stay with the *ad hoc* approach here," he urged. "Incidentally there are many cases, particularly at the [Court of Military Appeals] in which these factual variations are being presented. I think it is well they percolate there for a time." Thus, Blackmun at least wanted the military courts to define for themselves the parameters of "service connection." On the other hand, he noted that although the Court could not "cure everything or give answers to all questions," it also could not dodge "the retrospectivity issue" and would have to decide it in the near future.[49]

After circulating his first draft but before receiving any comments, Blackmun issued a second draft opinion to explain why he did not address retroactivity. He also presented a 12-part test for determining courts-martial jurisdiction under the service connected test. He claimed to prefer the Solicitor General's argument that any offense which jeopardized the security of a military installation or military personnel was *per se* service-connected. As to the retroactive application issue, he switched positions and became convinced that if *Linkletter* were properly applied, *O'Callahan* would have retroactive application. Problematic to this assumption was the conservative justices' dislike of *Linkletter*, which, like *O'Callahan*, would eventually be replaced. Nonetheless, the justices accepted Blackmun's second draft and it became the published decision with no dissents.[50]

Focusing on defining the meaning of service-connected, the Court accepted Blackmun's 12-factor test. The test did not require the military to satisfy each part. The Court did not, in any manner, undermine *O'Callahan*, but it added a level of complexity to determining when court-martial jurisdiction began. The 12 factors the Court found pertinent were as follows: (1) The Serviceman's proper absence from the base at the time of the offense; (2) The crime's commission away from the base; (3) Its commission at a place not under military control;

49 Blackmun, Conference Memorandum, February 11, 1971 [HAB/124]; Harlan to Marshall, February 11, 1971 [TM/69].

50 Blackmun, Second Conference Memorandum, February undated, 1971 [HAB/124].

(4) Its commission within [United States'] territorial limits and in an occupied zone of a foreign country; (5) Its commission in peacetime, and its being unrelated to authority stemming from the war power; (6) The absence of any connection between the defendant's military duties and the crime; (7) The victim not being engaged in the performance of any duty relating to the military; (8) The presence and availability of a civilian court in which the case can be prosecuted; (9) The absence of any flouting of military authority; (10) The absence of any threat to a military post; (11) The absence of any violation of military property; and (12) The offense's being among those traditionally prosecuted in civilian courts.

Relford's offense occurred in an area under military control, and the second victim was a government employee whose employment related to the military. These facts satisfied the "service connected" test. On the other hand, the justices understood that at best this decision only provided limited clarity to *O'Callahan.* After recognizing that the "service connected" test was an *ad hoc* approach, the Court concluded: "we take some comfort in the hope that the present decision should eliminate at least some of the confusion that the parties and commentators say has emerged from *O'Callahan.*"

Because *O'Callahan* was ultimately overturned, *Relford* is today of minimal utility. But it cannot be argued that *Relford* was a step in diminishing *O'Callahan.* To the contrary, the Court did not divorce *Relford* from the judicial activism inherent in *O'Callahan*, and instead, the justices issued a decision barely addressing original issue raised before it. In doing so, Blackmun gained Douglas' approval who wrote "you have written a splendid opinion in No. 98—*Relford v. Commandant.*" From the author of *O'Callahan*, this was, to say, an interesting compliment.[51]

b. Gosa v. Mayden *and* O'Callahan*'s Lack of Retroactivity*

The Court finally decided whether *O'Callahan* had retroactive applicability in 1973, in *Gosa v. Mayden.* This decision was based on two disparate courts-martial, consolidated into a single appeal. The first court-martial had origins similar to that in *O'Callahan.* In 1966, the Air Force court-martialed Airman Third Class James Gosa for a rape which took place off-base in Wyoming. He was lawfully off-base and not in uniform, and the civilian victim had no connection to the military. Sentenced to 10 years confinement, the Air Force Board of Review confirmed the findings and sentence and the Court of Military Appeals declined Gosa's petition for review. As a result, his conviction was final within the meaning of UCMJ Article 76. Gosa unsuccessfully challenged the military's authority to court-martial him before the Court of Military Appeals, the District Court for the Northern District of Florida, and the Court of Appeals for the Fifth Circuit. Applying *Linkletter*, both District Court Judge, Winston Arnow, a Johnson appointee who served as a judge advocate during World War II and a two-judge majority who

51 Douglas to Blackmun, February 18, 1971 [HAB/124, f. 1].

were both World War II veterans on the Fifth Circuit held that *O'Callahan* was not a retroactive decision.[52]

The second, and more important challenge stemmed from a World War II Navy court-martial. In 1944, John Flemings, a sailor assigned to a navy ammunition depot in New Jersey pled guilty to unauthorized absence from duty and stealing a civilian's automobile. A Navy court-martial held at the Brooklyn Navy Yard sentenced him to three years confinement and a dishonorable discharge. In 1970, Michael Meltsner a civil rights attorney who sometimes worked for the NAACP and later the dean of the Northeastern University Law School, represented Flemings in the United States District Court for the Southern District of New York.

In addition to relying on the *Relford* factors in determining that Flemings' auto-theft offense was not service-connected, the district court found it significant that Navy court-martialed Flemings at a different location than the base to which Flemings was assigned. In overturning a quarter century-old court-martial, the district court acknowledged that Flemings' unauthorized absence was service-connected, and directed the Naval Board to upgrade the discharge to no worse than a bad conduct discharge. A three judge panel of the Court of Appeals for the Second Circuit agreed with the district court.[53]

Unlike the unanimity in *Relford*, *Gosa* was a fractured opinion. Burger again assigned Blackmun to write for the majority, but only Burger, Powell, and White joined him. Brennan and Marshall dissented together, Douglas dissented on his own, Rehnquist concurred, and Stewart authored a concurring and dissenting opinion. The plurality determined that *O'Callahan* was not retroactive to the hundreds of courts-martial convictions poised to be reversed. But, the plurality decision was not as clear on the issue of retroactivity as hoped.[54]

Blackmun acknowledged that the appellate courts and legal scholars were divided on *O'Callahan's* retroactivity, providing several examples of each. He also stated that *O'Callahan* was a "clear break with the past." But, rather than indulge in a detailed historic analysis to either buttress or minimize *O'Callahan*, Blackmun turned to the Constitution's plain language to establish that while the Bill of Rights might be expanded to its maximum extent over service-members, nothing in the Constitution prevented Congress from legislating new offenses and affixing punishments to the offenses. To the plurality, it was notable that in

---

52 *Gosa v. Mayden*, 450 F.2d 753 (CA 5, 1971). Both Charles Clark, a Nixon appointee who served in the Navy in World War II, and John M. Simpson, a Truman appointee to the District Court and Johnson appointee to the Fifth Circuit who served as an Army officer provided an exhausting analysis of not only why *O'Callahan* did not require retroactive application, but also the difficulty with the Court's guidance on retroactivity in light of *Linkletter*.

53 *Flemings v. Chafee*, 330 F.Supp. 193 (EDNY, 1971); *United States ex rel Flemings v. Chafee*, 458 F.2d 544 (CA 2, 1972); See Jeffrey B. Morris, *Leadership on the Federal Bench, The Craft and Activism of Jack Weinstein* (New York: Oxford, 2011), 37–9.

54 *Gosa v. Mayden*, 413 U.S. 665 (1973).

Relford the Court concluded that courts-martial were not inherently unfair. The plurality then determined that because *O'Callahan* did not void all courts-martial jurisdiction, and instead limited jurisdiction to instances where the civil courts were not available or when offenses were service-connected, retroactivity was not required.

Stewart's brief dissent was a clear statement of disagreement with *O'Callahan.* "I dissented in [that case] and continue to believe that that case was wrongly decided," Stewart wrote. However, he also believed that the basis on which *O'Callahan* was decided required retroactive application for Gosa's case. As to Flemings' court-martial, Stewart took a different view stating, "I believe that a serviceman who deserts his post during a time of congressionally declared war and steals an automobile is guilty of a service-connected offense." Stewart circulated a draft opinion arguing for *O'Callahan's* retroactive application, but because he criticized the case, Marshall and Brennan were not inclined to join him.[55]

Rehnquist's opinion was likewise brief. In a conference memorandum he argued that any serviceman's offense committed in a time of war was unrebuttably service connected. Rehnquist also endorsed Harlan's dissent in *O'Callahan.* Rather than adopt the plurality's decision, Rehnquist too criticized *O'Callahan* as "wrongly decided." Nonetheless, because of *O'Callahan*'s basis—a court lacking in jurisdiction—Rehnquist argued that it had to be applied retroactively. Notably, Rehnquist did not approve of *Linkletter*, believing the case and its progeny encouraged judicial activism. In criticizing *Linkletter*, Rehnquist turned to, *Robinson v. O'Neil*, a more recent decision he authored to buttress his argument that *O'Callahan* had to be overturned. In *Robinson*, Rehnquist penned a statement that *Linkletter*, had, in fact, announced a new exception to the rule of traditional rule of retroactivity, and no other justice disagreed with this point.[56]

Douglas, in his dissent, agreed with Stewart that Flemings had committed a service-connected crime. But Gosa presented a different issue. Because that case, in Douglas' words, was "on all fours" with *O'Callahan*, it should have been remanded to the lower court to determine whether Gosa's offense was service-connected, and whether Gosa raised a jurisdictional challenge at the time of his court-martial. If Gosa's offense were ruled to be not service-connected then retroactivity should apply, unless another doctrine of law such as *res judicata* (a matter that should have been initially raised bars a subsequent challenge) prevented him from doing so. Douglas was mostly displeased though, with the Court's characterization of *O'Callahan.* In conference Douglas compared Gosa's claims to *Miranda*, noting that *Miranda* did not upend the thousands of cases before it. But nowhere in his published dissent did Douglas mention *Miranda*, and, in reality *Miranda* was a procedure based opinion. *O'Callahan,* after all, decided a jurisdictional principle that courts-martial did not possess the constitutional competency to adjudicate

55 Stewart, draft opinion and memorandum, June 19, 1973 [TM/114].

56 Rehnquist, conference memorandum, June 20, 1973 [TM/114]; *Robinson v. O'Neil*, 409 U.S. 505 (1973) .

common law offenses with no connection to the military. The rights involved in *O'Callahan*, in Douglas' judgment, were far more sweeping than in *Miranda*.[57]

Marshall, joined by Brennan in his dissent, differed from Douglas in two fundamental areas. Marshall and Brennan did not believe that Gosa required a remand to determine whether Gosa had raised a jurisdictional challenge at the time of his court-martial. Indeed Marshall criticized Douglas on this point more than he did the plurality. Ironically, in his dissent Marshall defended *O'Callahan's* importance more than the aging Douglas. "I am unable to agree with the plurality's characterization of *O'Callahan,*" Marshall argued. "In my view, it can only be understood as a decision dealing with the constitutional limits of the military's adjudicatory power over offenses committed by servicemen. No decision could more plainly involve the limits of a tribunal's power to exercise jurisdiction over particular offenses and thus more clearly demand retroactive application."

Shortly after its issuance, the legal community criticized *Gosa* for several reasons. As the Burger Court reached its fifth year, legal scholars lamented the increasing number of plurality decisions. It was one thing for a single justice to issue a concurring opinion. Moreover, a plurality in the nature of *Youngstown*—which allowed subsequent justices to favor Jackson's opinion over Frankfurter's, Black's, Douglas' or Burton's—had stood out as an exceptional case. Now such events were commonplace. In 1985, the editors of the *Harvard Law Review* concluded that despite its other merits, *Gosa* was an "illegitimate plurality." The editors correctly guessed a fundamental point on Rehnquist's motives, even though research into the justices' intents would not have been available to them. Unlike in *Relford*, and several other decisions, to Rehnquist, *Gosa* was a deliberate step in overturning *O'Callahan*, and *Linkletter*.[58]

A 1980 Columbia University Law Review note stressed, "*Gosa* has caused considerable confusion among the lower courts. Some courts have recognized that it does not provide a determinative ruling on the retroactivity issue, and have looked to other precedents in the area or have simply adopted the rationale deemed most convincing." The author went on to presciently argue that any clarity for *O'Callahan's* retroactive application could not be achieved until the Court established once and for all whether the case was soundly decided. This would not occur with the *Gosa* plurality.[59]

57 Douglas, *Gosa v. Mayden* Conference Memorandum undated [WOD/1608]. See *Youngstown Sheet & Tube Co. v. Sawyer*, 343 U.S. 579 (1952).

58 Anon, *Plurality Decisions and Judicial Decision Making* 94 Harvard law Review 1127–46 (1981), 1134.

59 Linda Noval, The Precedential Value of Supreme Court Plurality Decisions, 80 *Columbia Law Review* 756–81 (1980) 772–3.

c. The Limits of Judicial Intervention in Courts-Martial: McLucas v. DeChamplain *and* Schlesinger v. Councilman

Article 134 contains a clause enabling the military to prosecute non-capital state and federal offenses through the Assimilative Crimes Act. Article 134 requires that when a state or federal offense is assimilated, the military must prove, in addition to the offense itself, that the violation resulted in a detriment to good order and discipline or that its act was a discredit to the armed forces. In a court-martial for espionage, the accused, Sergeant Raymond DeChamplain, challenged the constitutionality of Article 134's third clause.[60]

The Air Force prosecuted Sergeant DeChamplain in 1971, after federal agents discovered he had provided classified documents to a Soviet agent in Thailand. The proof of DeChamplain's guilt was compelling. In addition to photographic evidence and witness testimony, DeChamplain admitted to military intelligence agents his guilt. In addition to charging him with failing to report his contacts with a foreign agent in violation of Article 92, and conspiring to communicate classified information to an agent of foreign government in violation of Article 81, the Air Force also charged him with violating Article 134, incorporating into that statute a federal prohibition against copying classified documents without authority and then transferring the documents to an unauthorized person. The general court-martial convicted DeChamplain of all charges and sentenced him to 15 years imprisonment. However, the Air Force Court of Appeals determined that DeChamplain's statements of confession were improperly admitted into evidence and reversed the conviction. The Air Force appealed to the Court of Military Appeals, but that court sided with the Air Force appellate court.[61]

Air Force authorities determined to retry DeChamplain, though on amended charges which comported with the appellate court's ruling. Additionally, Air Force officials decided to remove allegations involving three of the documents found in DeChamplain's possession. In his second court-martial, DeChamplain hired Leonard Boudin as his lead counsel, likely, knowing that the Defense Department would resist providing Boudin, who like Rabinowitz had ties to organizations believed to be subversive, access to classified evidence.[62]

Air Force commanders placed restrictions on DeChamplain access to evidence, but none of those restrictions prevented DeChamplain's military defense counsel

---

60 *McLucas v. DeChamplain*, 421 U.S. 21 (1975). Known as the Assimilative Crimes Act, 18 USC 13 permits the federal government to incorporate state crimes committed on federal enclaves such as national parks. Civilians too may be charged under this act.

61 *United States v. DeChamplain*, 46 CMR 784 (AFCMR 1972); affirmed in, *United States v. DeChamplain*, 46 CMR 150 (1973). Although ignored by contemporary critics of the military justice system, the fact that a service court composed of uniformed officers reversed a significant conviction is noteworthy evidence that neither the service courts nor the Court of Military Appeals were "rubber stamping" convictions.

62 Blackmun, conference notes, December 9, 1974 [HAB/200].

from reviewing the classified documents. The military judge permitted Boudin access to some classified material, but not fully so. After exhausting pre-trial appeals, DeChamplain appealed to the District Court for the District of Columbia, arguing that Article 134 was unconstitutionally vague and that his civilian counsel should be given complete access to all classified evidence. DeChamplain finally urged the District Court to order the Air Force to open his court-martial to the public during all portions of it. This was a form of what became known as "graymail," because if the military were forced to provide access to Boudin, it might decide it was in the interests of national security to drop all charges. (Congress had yet to address the issue of "graymail," and it would not do so until 1980.) To try to obtain this result, DeChamplain not only retained Boudin, he also hired Eric Lieberman, and David Rein to represent him before the federal judiciary. Notwithstanding the access to evidence issue, a three judge district court panel determined "the status of Article 134 is not uncertain at this time-it is unconstitutional." The district court also criticized the military for pursuing prosecutions worldwide despite the three appellate decisions. "The military, however, has refused to accept this ruling, and, as evidenced by this suit, persists in prosecuting under the outlawed provision."[63]

The government's initial argument was that the district court should not have intervened until the military had decided "fully and fairly," the service-connected issue. But then their argument transited to the issue of whether Article 134 could be sustained at all. In the conference, Burger assigned Powell to write the majority opinion. Argued on December 9, 1974, and decided on April 15, 1975, this was the last military law case the Court issued before Saigon fell to the North Vietnamese Army on April 30, 1975. Though there was no discussion that Powell's military intelligence background provided him a unique insight into case, his assignment gave the impression that the case was a national security issue as well as a straight military law case. After dismissing DeChamplain's contention that the Court did not have the jurisdiction to take a direct appeal, Powell turned to the contention that Article 134 was unconstitutionally vague. This was an important point because the test of whether a district court should intervene in a subject matter jurisdiction case (e.g. a challenge to an act of Congress) is whether the issue presents a substantial claim. In conference, Burger articulated the most evident flaw in DeChamplain's argument. Because the Air Force had merely assimilated a federal crime into Article 134, it "strained credulity" to claim that the principle of notice was at play. After all, unlike the free speech issues inherent in *Avrech* and *Levy,* every

63 *DeChamplain v. McLucas*, 367 F.Supp 1291 (DC DC 1973); *Hooper v. Laird*, 482 F.2d 784 (CA DC, 1973). Hooper, a Navy flag officer, had been recalled from retirement and court-martialed for homosexual conduct. As noted in Chapter VII, Victor Rabinowitz represented Hooper throughout his appeals. Initially, the Court of Appeals for the District of Columbia upheld the military's jurisdiction. In an appeal beginning in 1971, Hooper successfully challenged his convictions under Article 133 and Article 134 as being unconstitutionally vague. However, he remained convicted of violating Article 125, a prohibition against sodomy.

American service-member knew of the criminality of espionage. On this point, Douglas, Brennan, and Marshall concurred.

Because the Court had already decided *Levy* and *Avrech*, discussed in the following chapter, it found DeChamplain's claim insubstantial and ruled that the third clause in the article met due process. More importantly, Powell inferentially conveyed to the lower courts his view that interfering in the court-martial before it had run full course was not proper. He arrived at this not only through upholding Article 134 but also in regards to the issue of access to classified evidence.

Powell did not deny that DeChamplain had a due process right to have his attorneys gain access to classified evidence. However, he acknowledged that there were limitations as to this right. On the basis of *Schlesinger v. Councilman* argued one day after arguments in *DeChamplain* (but decided one month earlier), the Court determined that the federal courts should not intervene to stop the military from proceeding a court-martial and would have to wait until after the court-martial concluded to determine whether to grant *habeas*. Unlike in *Avrech* and *Levy*, no justice dissented in *DeChamplain*. Rather, in a brief concurrence, Brennan, Douglas, and Marshall agreed that the federal courts had to wait until the military courts had fully ruled on the issue of access to classified evidence.

If *DeChamplain* had an obvious result, the question of when a federal court could interpose in a court-martial was hardly settled. *O'Callahan* did not answer the question as to whether or when the federal judiciary could terminate a court-martial based on an accused's claim that his or her offenses were not service-connected, and therefore the military was without jurisdiction. In *Schlesinger v. Councilman* the Court provided some limitations on the judiciary to review a court-martial before it occurred. On June 27, 1972, the Army attempted to court-martial Captain Bruce R. Councilman at Fort Sill, Oklahoma for using marijuana off-post and distributing a small quantity of the illegal narcotic to a person he assumed was an enlisted soldier. The recipient of Councilman's marijuana was, in fact, a military undercover law enforcement agent. While *Schlesinger* is part of a line of decisions governing when the federal judiciary can intervene in courts-martial, its importance extends beyond this issue. The decision goes to the heart of the discipline of the Armed Forces while at the same time it established a further limitation on *O'Callahan*.[64]

Although charged under Article 134, Councilman did not argue the general article's unconstitutionality. Rather, he argued that there was no *nexus* between his alleged private narcotics use and distribution, and the military's need for good order and discipline. As a result, he urged the Army did not meet the 12-part jurisdictional test articulated in *Relford*. When the court-martial did not dismiss charges, Councilman filed a *habea*s writ in the United States District Court for the Western District of Oklahoma. That court determined that an officer's off-duty sale of narcotics to an enlisted man did not confer jurisdiction to the military, because the conduct was not "service-connected." As a result, the Army was

64 *Schlesinger v. Councilman*, 420 U.S. 738 (1975).

prevented from proceeding with the court-martial. Significantly, Councilman did not hire attorneys who publicly criticized the military or who were involved in representing citizens alleged as subversives, or who represented anti-war, socialist or communist causes. Instead, locally well respected criminal defense attorneys took his case through the entire appellate process.[65]

The government appealed the district court's ruling to the Court of Appeals for the Tenth Circuit. The appellate court in upholding the district court opined, "it appears that 'service connection' based on this theory is so remote as to be not at all within the meaning of that term as used by the Supreme Court in *O'Callahan* and *Relford*." To the Department of Defense General Counsel and the Judge Advocate General, this decision constituted an illogical absurdity. The military depends on obedience to orders issued by its officers and non-commissioned officers, and an officer who visibly breaks the law degrades not only his status, but the status of other officers. Put another way, an officer who knowingly engages an enlisted member in an illegal activity inherently undermines discipline.

During the conference, Burger assigned Powell to write for the majority. To Powell, the issue presented would result in an easy decision, but it required lengthy exposition, in part, because at the time the lower appellate court decided *Councilman*, the Court had not issued its decisions in *Avrech* or *Levy*. Powell, Burger, Rehnquist, Stewart, and Blackmun agreed that the service-connection in this case was obvious and the lower courts had erred. But Powell reminded the conference that a conflict on the extent of "service-connection" existed between the Tenth Circuit and a number of military appellate court decisions regarding narcotics and instances which solely involved servicemen. Rehnquist then pushed for the Court to decide the case on a wholly separate issue: at what point should the federal judiciary be permitted to decide whether a court-martial possessed jurisdiction over a service-member?[66]

Thus, instead of deciding on the service-connection issue, the Court requested supplemental briefs on the jurisdiction of the District Court; Councilman's exhaustion of remedies; and, the propriety of a federal district court enjoining a pending court-martial proceeding. Powell and Rehnquist were concerned with the increased intervention of the federal judiciary in military matters after *O'Callahan*. In a second memorandum to the conference Rehnquist requested that the parties be asked to supplement their briefs "on (1) the jurisdiction of the district court, (2) exhaustion of remedies, and (3) the propriety of a federal district court enjoining a court-martial proceeding." As a result, the Court ignored the issue of service-connection as well as the Solicitor General's initial argument and in place, decided a jurisdictional issue not raised by either side.[67]

The majority's reasoning for taking this approach had to do with the district court's assertion of jurisdiction before the court-martial began. "In effect,

65 *Councilman v. Laird*, 418 F.2d 416 (CA 10, 1975).

66 Rehnquist, Memorandum to the Conference, February 21, 1974 [TM/142].

67 Rehnquist, Conference Memorandum, March 27, 1974 [HAB/195].

Councilman is attempting to attack collaterally the military authorities' decision to convene the court-martial and the refusal of the military judge to dismiss the charges." Bork argued that in enacting UCMJ Article 76. Congress intended to preclude this type of jurisdiction. Powell did not completely agree with Bork's argument, and instead decided that each assertion of a jurisdictional defect raised before a court-martial commenced had to be considered within the normal *habeas* test, albeit in a hypothetical examination. But, based on *Burns*, Powell also argued that the federal courts had to at least permit the military courts of appeal to determine all jurisdictional challenges first.[68]

Nonetheless, Powell and the majority did not conclude that the district court, simply because it lawfully asserted jurisdiction, correctly decided the merits of Councilman's service-connected claims (the majority believed the district court's ultimate decision finding no service connection was in error), or even should have made a decision at all. To Powell, there was an equally important issue of equitable jurisdiction, which both the district and lower appellate courts failed to consider. That is, because the service-connected rule had to be determined on a case by case basis, the district court failed to allow the military courts the opportunity to review the matter. Powell conceded that Councilman could have been convicted in a court-martial, but this was a matter of conjecture because the court-martial did not proceed. The court-martial could have also found Councilman not guilty on the facts, or not-guilty based on a "service-connected" defense. "It therefore appears that Councilman was 'threatened with (no) injury other than that incidental to every criminal proceeding brought lawfully and in good faith," Powell concluded.

To arrive at this decision, Powell compared courts-martial with state criminal proceedings. The federal judiciary traditionally, on the basis of federalism, only reluctantly intruded into state criminal proceedings, until the decisions of those proceedings became final. Of course, courts-martial were a different matter because such trials, although temporal in nature, were federal trials. Nonetheless, to Powell, the equity test demanded a similar caution, but for a different reason.

He accepted that the military was a society apart from the civilian population with the specialized needs of good order and discipline. Citing to *Noyd v. Bond*, he also lauded the military justice system's evolution since the UCMJ's enactment. "Implicit in the congressional scheme embodied in the Code is the view that the military court system generally is adequate to and responsibly will perform its assigned task," Powell wrote. "We think this congressional judgment must be respected and that it must be assumed that the military court system will vindicate servicemen's constitutional rights."

Burger concurred in the result, but he did so arguing that the majority's decision still took to expansive a view on federal court jurisdiction. Burger made clear that he believed that federal courts could grant review, only in instances where a court-martial had run its entire course. That is, the federal judiciary was

68 Burger to Powell, March 21, 1975 [TM/142]. Although Burger ultimately concurred in the result, he pushed for the inclusion of Burns into the decision.

limited to review only through a *habeas* writ and not as a matter of equity. Burger's conservatism in this instance was more doctrinaire than either Powell or Rehnquist would agree to.

Brennan, Marshall, and Douglas concurred with the majority's determination that UCMJ Article 76 did not limit *habeas* jurisdiction to court-martial conviction. But the three justices dissented against the principle that a serviceman charged by the military with an offense had to exhaust all remedies within the military justice system when arguing to a district court for dismissal on service-connected grounds. Writing for the dissenters, Brennan disregarded the majority's argument that the Court of Military Appeals—a court of civilian judges free from command influence—were the final step in the exhaustion of remedies. Brennan also emphasized that the majority's opinion ignored such past precedent as and *Reid v. Covert*. But Powell countered correctly that Brennan's reliance on these cases was misplaced because *Reid* involved civilian citizens who argued that the military could not constitutionally assert jurisdiction in the first place.

Skeptical of the ability of military courts to determine service-connected issues, Brennan urged that *Reid* was applicable. In a penned draft, he wrote, that "because it is a constitutional tenet to restrict courts-martial to the narrowest jurisdiction deemed essential to military discipline among troops," on the federal judiciary could honestly rule what that narrow jurisdiction was. In his published dissent, he accused the majority of providing "no reasoned justification" for its departure from *Noyd* but derided this "failure" as not surprising since plainly there is wholly lacking in military tribunals the qualification ordinarily relied on to justify the exhaustion requirement, namely, the know-how or 'expertise' of an agency particularly knowledgeable in the determination of the same or like questions." Brennan also likened Powell's decision as an analogue to judicial review of administrative agency rules when in fact, jurisdiction is a constitutional issue.[69]

Turning to *O'Callahan* to justify his criticism, Brenan restated "it is virtually hornbook law that courts-martial are singularly inept in dealing with the subtleties of constitutional law." Brenan also argued that since the Court of Military Appeals had found service-connection lacking in cases similar to Councilman's, Councilman should not have to wait for a similar result. As to the ultimate issue which Powell did not address—service connection in this particular case—Brenan's dissent concluded that service connection did not exist. He derided the government's argument that an officer selling illegal drugs to an enlisted member off-post directly affected good order and discipline. Instead, he concluded that Councilman's offense was commonly found in civilian courts and as a result, could not have been service-connected.

Brennan's dissent echoed a debate over the harm that illicit drugs caused to society, which at the time perhaps was a legitimate debate, but in retrospect often

69 Brennan, pen draft, undated [WJB/I:345]; Marshall to Brennan, February 27, 1975 [WJB/I:345]; Douglas to Brennan, February 27, 1975 [WJB/I:345]; *Drug Abuse in the Armed Forces,* 95th Cong., 2d Sess. 26 (1978).

argued in ignorance of the damaging addictive and other long-term effects of narcotics. In 1970, Congress passed the Comprehensive Drug Abuse Prevention and Control Act which eliminated mandatory minimum sentences for certain drug offenses and established a drug classification process. The next year, Congress specifically found that drug usage in the armed forces had degraded discipline and reliability. In 1978 Congress reaffirmed its findings and directed the Department of Defense to establish programs to reduce drug usage. Within a decade Congress after studying the harm illicit drugs caused to society, enacted a number of mandatory minimum sentences for drugs such as cocaine. Brennan seems to have ignored Congress and not appreciated that all illicit drug usage by service members was likely to have a service connection of some degree.[70]

Indeed, in terms of the applying the drug debate to the military, Brennan's dissent ignored the evident damage of the widespread use of illicit and dangerous drugs in the military's ranks. "The petitioners introduced no evidence that respondent's actions in any way impaired or threatened to impair the discipline and effectiveness of military personnel at Fort Sill," Brennan claimed. "Similarly, and related, the record is devoid of any evidence whatever that use of marihuana in any amounts under any circumstances adversely affects a serviceman's performance of his duties." Although Brennan also noted that the prosecution could have introduced evidence that marijuana damaged military readiness into evidence, this ignored the fact that Congress had already made a determination of its harmfulness by outlawing it in the first place.[71]

The military establishment was pleased with the decision. It enabled the reassertion of jurisdiction over service-members using illegal narcotics. Given the high drug usage rates in the military at the time, this was an important step toward re-instilling discipline. Former Army Chief of Staff Maxwell Taylor lauded the majority in *Councilman* for once more differentiating between civilian and military life. Often missed in the analysis of Schlesinger was the fact that there exists a counterpart decision regarding federal judicial interference into state criminal trials. In *Younger, District Attorney of Los Angeles v. Harris*, the Court, in 1971 in a decision authored by Black, held that absent highly unusual circumstances, such as the inability to challenge the constitutionality of a judicial procedure, the federal courts should not stop state criminal trials from progressing. In point of fact, *Councilman* and *Younger* should be viewed as companion cases: one for the military and one for the states.[72]

---

70 Lawrence Friedman, *American Law in the Twentieth Century* (New Haven, CT: Yale, 2002), 257.

71 For a synopsis of the widely reported drug problem in the military in the 1970s and '80s, see e.g. Christopher Bassford, *The Spit-Shine Syndrome*, 27; and William Thomas Allison, *Military Justice in Vietnam: The Rule of Law in an American War*, 117–39.

72 Maxwell Taylor, *Precious Security*, 63; *Younger, District Attorney of Los Angeles County v. Harris*, 401 U.S. 107 (1971).

d. Other Due Process Aspects: Eighth Amendment and Summary Courts-Martial

In 1974, the Court issued *Schick v. Reed*, a decision whose genesis began during the Eisenhower administration. In 1954 the Army court-martialed Master Sergeant Maurice Schick for the murder of an eight-year-old girl. Schick had confessed to committing the crime, but claimed he was insane at the time of the murder. His insanity defense did not prevail and the court-martial sentenced him to death. However, President Eisenhower commuted the death sentence to life imprisonment with no possibility of parole. Part of the commutation required Schick to agree to never apply for parole, a provision which had questionable enforcement abilities, but which Schick agreed to nonetheless. Had the court-martial sentenced Schick to life imprisonment, he would have been eligible for parole in 1969, because the UCMJ did not, at the time, have a provision for sentencing service members to life without parole. The president, however, did have the authority to grant clemency to persons sentenced to death.

In 1972, the Court, in *Furman v. Georgia*, struck down a common state statutory mechanism for sentencing defendants to death as a violation of the Eighth Amendment's prohibition against cruel and unusual punishment. *Furman* arose from a Georgia imposed death penalty, but *Schick*, provided the Court an avenue to examine the military applicability of the Court's death penalty ruling in the civil courts. Schick claimed that because he could not have anticipated *Furman*, he made an ill-advised choice in accepting Eisenhower's offer. Initially, only Douglas, Marshall, and Brennan voted to grant *certiorari*, but Douglas persuaded White to vote to grant review. In a proposed dissent against the denial of *certiorari*, Douglas commented that the punishment of life without the possibility of parole "was at odds with the penal goal of rehabilitation," and claimed that Eisenhower had usurped the Legislative Branch in a manner reminiscent of Truman during the steel seizure. Douglas' dissent was never published as a result of White's intervention.[73]

Burger assigned Blackmun to write for the majority, but then inexplicably assigned the opinion to himself. In conference, Burger conceded that Schick had argued in the district and appellate courts that pretrial publicity had marred his court-martial, as well as that the court-martial did not require a unanimous vote for sentencing a service-members to death, and that the no-parole condition was a denial of due process, but he urged that the Court merely concentrate on whether the no-parole provision was a denial of due process. This presented an easy response from the Court, because in *Ex parte Wells*, decided in 1855, the Court upheld the constitutionality of a no-parole limitation in the exercise of executive clemency.

73 *Schick v. Reed*, 419 U.S. 256 (1974); *Furman v. Georgia*, 408 U.S. 238 (1972); Douglas, Draft dissent containing White's response, April 17, 1973 [BW/301]; White to Douglas, April 18, 1974 [BW/301].

Douglas, Brennan, and Marshall dissented from Burger's position, arguing that *Furman* was entirely retroactive under the *Linkletter* doctrine.[74]

Blackmun, Rehnquist, and Powell wanted the decision to emphasize the military as a separate society with unique disciplinary requirements. Concerned that the Court's holding in *Furman* might reach into the military, Blackmun drafted a proposed decision which turned to *Parker v. Levy* to argue why *Furman* did not apply to the military. In *Furman*, both Blackmun and Powell had dissented partly on the basis that the Court's decision abolishing the death penalty was written so broadly it could be construed to prohibit capital punishment for terrorism, espionage, or in military trials. "The Court in the recent case of *Parker v. Levy* indicated that military law is something different," Blackmun penned to the Court. "Further, military personnel live with deadly weapons, and in these circumstances capital punishment may be necessary and is far more appropriate than in civilian ones."[75]

It may have been a result of Blackmun's stridency to focus the decision on the military that led Burger to simplify the published decision into a straight-forward analysis of whether *Furman* applied to prisoners whose sentences had been commuted to life without the possibility of parole, rather than have *Schick* become another referendum on military law. In this instance, Burger's caution was well founded. The grant of *certiorari* arose from the Court of Appeals for the District of Columbia, where a judge had criticized the fairness of the court-martial, noting that four Army psychiatrists had diagnosed Schick as being in control of his faculties, but two Japanese psychiatrists had found in opposite. While Schick was in confinement, but prior to Eisenhower's commutation, Doctor Karl Menninger who was known as one of the world's leading psychiatrists, concluded that Schick suffered from a lifelong mental illness which had been exacerbated during combat service in World War II.[76]

When Congress enacted the UCMJ it provided the military branches with four judicial means of ensuring discipline. The most severe of the judicial means were general courts-martial, akin to felony trials where the ceiling on a maximum sentence was governed by the type of offense. Thus, the death penalty could be adjudged for premeditated murder, and the maximum sentence for larceny of

74 Burger, Memorandum to the Conference, January 7, 1945. *Ex parte Wells*, 55 U.S. 307 (1855). Wells has been followed since that time; Marshall, Memorandum to the Conference, December 5, 1974 [WJB/I:363].

75 Blackmun, circulated memorandum, September 9, 1974 [Blackmun/205]. Blackmun recognized that *Furman* arose in an era where the Court, at least the liberal bloc, was concerned that economic and social inequities affected not only education and environmental quality, but also the fairness of the criminal justice system. In this vein, he concluded that *Furman* need not apply at all to the military because "the discriminatory application of the death penalty is far less likely in the military system." While this point was true at the time, and remains so, he conceded that the issue was best not raised and accepted Rehnquist's urging to "bypass the Furman issue."

76 *Schick v. Reed*, 483 F.2d 1266 (CA DC, 1973).

property over $100 in value could result in five years in confinement. Special courts-martial, akin to misdemeanor trials, could not sentence an accused to more than six months in confinement. Both general and special courts-martial possessed the authority to adjudge punitive discharges, and officers could only be tried by general courts-martial. At the low end of the disciplinary spectrum was a non-judicial forum codified under UCMJ, Article 15. This article enabled a commanding officer or commissioned supervisor to punish an enlisted service-member with reductions in rank, fines, and various short-term restrictions on liberty. Officers as well could be punished through this article, and be fined and restricted, but not reduced in rank. Article 15 is titled "non-judicial punishment," and under most circumstances a service-member may refuse to accept the Article 15, and demand a trial by court-martial.

Summary courts-martial are a judicial forum between the Article 15 and the two types of courts-martial. Such courts could only be used to prosecute enlisted service-members below the non-commissioned ranks, and these trials do not possess the authority to punitively discharge the service members. Moreover, the jurisdictional limits of this type of court are capped at 30 days of confinement. A service member was not statutorily entitled to a defense counsel, though the Air Force and Army often provided such counsel, and the trial itself was conducted by a single commissioned officer, rather than a jury. The statute governing summary courts-martial entitled an accused service-member to refuse trial in this forum, but such a refusal would likely lead to trial in a special court-martial. The summary court-martial's civilian analog was a municipal violation. Summary court martial was designed to ensure the "exercise of justice for relatively minor offenses under a simple form of procedure."[77]

After the Court established the Sixth Amendment's right to defense counsel in *Gideon v. Wainright* extended to the state and federal government providing indigent defendants counsel, the Court, in several decisions, extended *Gideon* to cover misdemeanor and juvenile trials. Unlike the Army and the Air Force, the Navy did not provide defense counsel for summary courts-martial, and five Marines who had been prosecuted in such courts appealed their convictions. The five marine defendants were consolidated into a single suit by the United States District Court for Hawaii, which then issued a world-wide injunction against the military from prosecuting any service members in summary-courts-martial. The Court of Appeals for the Ninth Circuit reversed the lower court, in a decision captioned, *Daigle v. Warner*, holding both that the district court did not possess the broad jurisdiction to issue such an injunction, and the Sixth Amendment did not require defense counsel at summary courts-martial.[78]

77 *Middendorf v. Henry*, 425 U.S. 25 (1975).

78 *Daigle v. Warner*, 490 F.2d 358 (CA 9, 1974). For *Gideon's* extension to misdemeanor trials see, *Argersinger v. Hamlin*, 407 U.S. 25 (1972); and for juvenile trials see, *In re Gault*, 387 U.S. 1 (1967).

In *Middendorf v. Henry*, the Court determined that the summary court-martial construct was constitutionally sound and *Gideon* did not extend this far. Writing for the majority, Rehnquist conceded that the Court, in *Argersinger v. Hamlin* extended the right to counsel to misdemeanor trials, and in *In re Gault* this right was extended to juvenile courts as well. In 1973, the Court held that the right to counsel did not apply to probation and parole revocation hearings. In *Middendorf*, Rehnquist and the majority concluded that summary courts-martial were not adversarial proceedings akin to criminal trials. More tellingly on Rehnquist's jurisprudence, was his argument that *Toth v. Quarles'* statement that "it is the primary business of armies and navies to fight or be ready to fight wars," actually bolstered the efficacy of summary courts-martial. Perhaps most surprisingly was White's support of this position.[79]

Blackmun and Powell agreed with Rehnquist but determined to concur because they felt he did not go far enough in explaining why the military's "separate society" requirements included trials by summary courts-martial. Additionally, Blackmun argued "nothing supports the thought that the framers intended the Sixth Amendment to extend to courts-martial." A leading scholar on military law, Frederick Wiener had articulated this point in a 1957 *Harvard Law Review* article, but Wiener, in fact, went on to argue that Congress should extend the right because notions of due process had evolved since 1806. Blackmun had another reason for concurring, stating to his clerks, "on the balance I think we can go too far in some of these areas. Just how important are the consequences of an SCM? That type of proceeding is for minor infractions and it is fairly informal." Wiener had served as a judge advocate in World War II and with the Solicitor General's office both before and after the conflict.[80]

Powell went so far as to question the importance of the issue before the Court, wondering why it ought to grant *certiorari* in the first place, beyond giving the military back control over their internal judicial processes. He had discerned that Congress was likely to abolish the summary court-martial in the near future, and that the Army was on the verge of discontinuing such trials in any event. Of course, Powell recognized that the issue arose from the Department of the Navy, but felt that the Army set the example in the practice of military justice. Congress did not abolish the summary court-martial and the Army continued its use. However, since 1975, by regulation, service members tried in summary courts-martial are represented by defense counsel except in narrow exemptions.[81]

In conference Brennan and Marshall argued that the majority undermined *Argersinger*, especially after the Court of Military Appeals and the Judge Advocates General of the Army and Navy explicitly concluded that *Argersinger*

79 *Argersinger v. Hamlin*, 407 U.S. 25 (1972); White to Rehnquist, March 4, 1976 [TM/161].

80 Blackmun, conference notes, January 1, 1975 [HAB/213]; Blackmun to Rehnquist, February 17, 1976 [WJB/I:375]. Reflecting a common aspect of his early Court tenure, Blackmun's clerks advised him to join in Marshall's dissent, but he would not do so.

81 Blackmun, conference notes, undated [HAB/213].

applied to the military. The military appellate court's decision on this matter might have mooted the issue before the Court, but neither the dissenting justices nor Rehnquist believed it did, because the military appellate court did not statutorily have jurisdiction over summary courts-martial. Moreover, Marshall believed the absence of a jury alone made such trial less than constitutional. When he circulated his draft dissent, he ensured that it contained a statement as to the choice facing service-members: a choice of trial by jury with the risk of lengthy imprisonment, or the acceptance of a less than constitutional forum. Marshall's argument resulted in Rehnquist placing into the published decision the fact that an accused possessed the right to refuse this forum and demand trial by court-martial. Brennan pointed out that Rehnquist had opposed the majority in extending the right to counsel to misdemeanor trials in which no confinement was adjudged, and saw the majority in *Middendorf* as adopting his position that *Argersinger* was wrongly decided. Likewise, Stewart urged that the majority undermined the military appellate court, and this could have devastating consequences on military justice. Stewart's prediction has not come to be, and the summary court-martial has been noticeably absent from the federal judiciary.[82]

IV: Conclusion

The Court under Burger grappled with the confusion caused by *O'Callahan* not only in terms of the application the service-connected test, but also in terms of when and how the federal judiciary could delve into courts-martial. If studied in a vacuum, and without considering the Executive Branch's conduct during Nixon's presidency, analysis of the Burger Court's military law decisions could result in conclusion that the judiciary had, in fact, attempted to reassert a jurisprudence marked by deference. However, when coupled with a further contextual linking of the military's disciplinary problems and the political and social environment, as covered in the following chapters, it can be readily concluded that the Court was, in fact, harmonizing the military establishment to the Constitution as well as considering the needs of national security.

82 Marshall, draft dissent, February 4, 1976 [TM/161]; Rehnquist to Marshall, February 6, 1976 [TM/161]; Stewart to Rehnquist, March 16, 1976 [WJB/I:375].

Chapter 4
Restoring Military Discipline and Maintaining the Military's Subordination to the Civil Government

By the time Burger had become Chief Justice, military discipline had eroded and the open speech activities of service-members reached a historic twentieth-century apogee. During this time, the size and strength of the Soviet military and its Warsaw Pact allies increased in comparison to those of the United States and NATO, and more worrisome was that Soviet foreign policy became increasingly aggressive and confrontational. In 1974, the Court determined two significant cases involving the First Amendment's free speech parameters in the military context. The two decisions, *Parker v. Levy* and *Secretary of the Navy v. Avrech* are generally analyzed apart from other military law decisions and most of the scholarly analysis both avoids the Cold War context of the Court's reasoning and ignores the realities of the decline of military discipline in the latter half of the Vietnam Conflict. *Levy* was, to be sure, a controversial decision, but the Court's majority and concurring opinion can only fully be analyzed in light of the state of military discipline as well as the social forces in the nation's population at the time.

Between 1967 and 1971, approximately 130 "underground newspapers" were published within the military both in Vietnam and in the United States. Almost all of these newspapers criticized, and in many instances scathed the President, the Department of Defense's leadership, generals, and U.S. foreign policy. A military-sociological study published in 2003 concluded that there were several reasons for the rise in underground newspapers, including distrust in the two sanctioned media, *Stars and Stripes* and Armed Forces Radio. The military's rank and file had become highly politicized as a result of an imbalanced selective service program, an unpopular conflict in Vietnam, and a distrust of the government. Underground newspapers reflected this phenomena as much as they contributed to it. The majority of the underground newspapers were anonymously published, though in one notable instance, Roger Priest, a sailor stationed at the Pentagon used his real name. In authoring *OM: The Serviceman's Newsletter*, Priest provided information on how to seek asylum in Canada and how to avoid prosecution for desertion. He also derided Secretary of Defense Melvin Laird, Federal Bureau of Investigations Director J. Edgar Hoover, and compared House Armed Services Chair, Congressman Mendel Rivers to "a pig pissing and shitting on the country." Rivers, a "defense hawk," had certainly opened himself to criticism. Although a Democrat, he opposed integration in the Armed Forces, backed pro-segregationist

Strom Thurmond in 1948, and then Eisenhower in 1952. In 1968, George Wallace asked Rivers to run as Vice President on his ticket. In 1972, Rivers openly praised Lieutenant Calley and denied the My Lai massacre had taken place. Rivers was so incensed with *OM*, that he demanded the Navy court-martial Priest, which likely would have occurred without his demands. Nonetheless, Rivers' demands lent to a allegation of unlawful command influence.[1]

Thousands of servicemen in Vietnam and Thailand read Priest's newsletter. In April 1970, the Navy court-martialed Priest, charging him with violating two specifications under Article 134, and one charge of soliciting others to desert in violation of Article 82. Priest's attorney, David Rein who had been accused of CPUSA ties, attempted to have former Douglas clerk, Vern Countryman, testify as to the illegality of the military's constraints on free speech, as well as retired Marine General David Shoup, testify as to his outspoken criticism of the Vietnam Conflict and the right of service-members to "speak their minds." Rein also tried to introduce 20 books critical of the military establishment to prove that Priest's writings were not inflammatory. At the top of these books was Douglas' *Points of Rebellion*. In concert with the rules of evidence, the trial judge did not permit either Countryman's testimony or the books to come into evidence. On the other hand, the judge permitted an expert military witness to testify that in the expert's opinion, newsletters such as Priest's did not undermine discipline any more than a crowd at a baseball game shouting "kill the umpire" undermined the game of baseball. The court-martial found Priest guilty of two of the three charges and sentenced him to a bad conduct discharge. After exhausting his military appeals, he appealed to the federal courts. In 1977, the Court of Appeals for the District of Columbia upheld his conviction, finding that the Navy did not violate his First and Fifth Amendment rights. Rein represented Priest on appeal as well. Though Priest was not alone in being court-martialed for similar activity, his case represented an extreme example of conduct which, if permitted, would significantly undermine military discipline. (The military convened over a dozen courts-martial of servicemen who edited and published these papers.)[2]

The Department of Defense's leadership worried that external organizations such as the CPUSA and the Socialist Workers Party had stoked dissension, particularly inside of the Army. As a result, the Army created counter-resistance programs overseen by its Military Intelligence leadership which concluded

1 James Lewes, *Protest and Survive: Underground GI Newspapers During the Vietnam War* (Westport: Praeger, 2003), 51–82. See also "The Law: Priest's Progress," *Time Magazine*, May 11, 1970. David Rein defended Priest at his court-martial as well as on appeal.

2 The Court of Military Appeals decision is *United States v. Priest*, 46 C.M.R. 368. The federal court appeal is *Priest v. Secretary of the Navy*, 570 F. 1013 (CA DC, 1977). Tom Clark was assigned to the panel reviewing the decision, but died before the opinion was published. See also, "Defense Rests Case in Sailor's Trial," *Washington Post*, April 22, 1970; and OM, April 30, 1970.

that the CPUSA had made inroads into over 20 stateside installations. "With the introduction of US troops in Vietnam, the Communist apparatus in the US began increasing their efforts to harass and effect a reduction of the US effort, both militarily and politically," the program director advised the Secretary of Defense, Attorney General, and Department of Defense General Counsel. The program director also advised that the CPUSA supported religious opponents of military service as well as advocates of reform of military governance. Whether accurate or not, the military's leadership was convinced that several underground newspapers had CPUSA support, the CPUSA intended to foment racial divisiveness in the ranks, and the party's leaders believed that judicial decisions favorable to conscientious objectors and war protesters would undermine the nation's armed forces in the same manner hoped for in 1946, with the post-war demobilization demonstrations.[3]

Perhaps the Department of Defense's leaders exaggerated the danger from the CPUSA. On the other hand, there were clear signs that the military's conventional reliability was at its lowest since World War II. In 1976, former Army Chief of Staff, Maxwell Taylor warned that the military's ranks were just as polarized as the nation. Fractures along racial and ethnic lines undermined the cohesiveness required of a disciplined force. Taylor's view on why this occurred aligned with the Court's conservatives. "In the domestic turmoil of the Vietnam war period, radical elements often tried and sometimes succeeded in infiltrating military posts with political propaganda and inducing soldiers to join political demonstrations against the policies of their commander in chief, the President," Taylor warned. He was by no means alone in worrying that the federal judiciary was in the process of enabling the erosion of discipline, and certainly, a number of decisions beginning with *O'Callahan* permitted external influences to undermine the military's readiness and reliability.[4]

There was no single cause of military indiscipline, but it has to be acknowledged that from the end of the conscripted forces through the first term of Reagan's presidency, there were worrisome trends in military readiness, particularly when assessed against the Soviet's military arsenal. By 1969, the Army's discipline had begun to disintegrate. High desertion rates, increased drug addiction, mutinies and the "fragging," or assassination of officers, had become a reality of military service, particularly in Vietnam. In 1970 alone, the Army prosecuted 382 courts-martial for insubordination in Vietnam. Regardless of their party affiliation, Nixon, Ford, and Carter believed that the nation's military forces were instrumental in preventing Soviet expansion, but the military's effectiveness to accomplish this was in jeopardy.

There were troubling aspects of military discipline which existed at the highest levels of command as well. Dissension amongst senior officers in the later

3 United States Army Surveillance of Dissidents, Report on Resistance Inside the Military, April 18, 1968 [UPA/17].

4 Maxwell Taylor, *Precarious Security* (New York: Norton, 1976), 65.

stages of the Vietnam War was largely stoked by the unique governing style of Nixon and his national security advisor, Henry Kissinger. Prior to his political appointment, Kissinger, while at Harvard, presciently argued that the Soviet Union and Communist China welcomed American involvement in limited wars because such conflicts were of long duration and would lose the approval of the American citizenry. Instead, he believed in strengthening the nation's nuclear forces as well as building conventional forces for the singular purpose of deterring (or entering into) a full-scale war with the Soviet Union. Nixon largely adopted to Kissinger's national defense views. There should have been a natural alliance between the military's senior leaders and a Republican president who promised to maintain a strong military. But there was no such alliance because of Nixon's closeted leadership. In addition to Nixon's treatment of the Calley court-martial, a number of other instances formed the basis for the distrust.[5]

In June, 1969, an Army Special Forces unit under the command of a Colonel Robert Rheault killed a Vietnamese national they suspected had become a double agent. Rheault's soldiers operated alongside the Central Intelligence Agency in missions designed to find intelligence leaks within the Army of the Republic of Vietnam. Rheault's statements to military investigators were contradicted by other soldiers, and Rheault initially claimed that the Vietnamese national was killed in the line of duty. In fact, the Vietnamese national was killed under Rheault's orders. General Creighton Abrams, Westmoreland's successor in Vietnam preferred murder charges against Rheault, after concluding that the colonel had lied to his staff. On July 21, 1969, Rheault was formally charged, but the Central Intelligence Agency leadership refused to assist the prosecution and provide witnesses and evidence which may have either been exculpatory or damaging to Rheault. Although Abrams and Secretary of the Army Stanley Resor opposed the dismissal of charges, Rheault was freed, because under the UCMJ, as well as constitutionally, an accused citizen is entitled to favorable evidence, as well as full access to the government's evidence, but the story on Rheault did not simply end with the right to a fair trial being made an impossibility because of the agency. At Nixon's direction, Laird interfered with Resor to forgo a court-martial. For a brief time the episode captured the nation's attention as media giants such as *Life Magazine* headlined the story.[6]

In 1970, Nixon approved of a secret bombing campaign in Cambodia, a neutral country. It was true that communist sanctuaries existed in both Cambodia and Laos, and neither government was able, or willing, to remove armed Vietnamese, but the large-scale aerial bombing incursion into a neutral country was contrary to international law. The planning for the operation was done without Secretary of

5 Henry A. Kissinger, *Nuclear Weapons and Foreign Policy* (New York: Doubleday, 1958), 69–70.

6 Lewis Sorley, *Thunderbolt: General Creighton Abrams and the Army of His Times* (Bloomington, IN: Indiana University Press, 1992), 269–77; also, Dale Van Atta, *With Honor: Melvin Laird*, 238; William Westmoreland, *A Soldier Reports*, 368.

Defense Laird's knowledge, and he protested that any attempt to keep a large-scale operation secret would prove both disastrous to foreign relations, and had a significant question of legality. Moreover, the bombing of Cambodia resulted in widespread protests on college campuses, leading to the use of National Guard troops to police universities.[7]

Nixon and Kissinger also intentionally excluded Laird from decisions on the employment of military forces. During the Indo-Pakistani War, the placement of United States naval vessels off Pakistan as a show of force to the Indian government that the United States supported Pakistan came to a surprise to Laird. There were significant leaks to the press, some of which originated from the Joint Chiefs of Staff. In 1974 a senior naval non-commissioned officer named Charles Radford assigned to Kissinger's office, provided the Joint Chiefs of Staff information Kissinger intended to keep internal to his national security staff, Nixon, and a few civilian advisors. Radford retrieved discarded files from Kissinger's "burn basket" and passed these on to senior naval officers. Admiral Elmo Zumwalt, who later called Nixon, "the most immoral participant," wanted Radford court-martialed, but because a public trial would have further exposed Nixon's more secretive foreign policy and military use decisions, Nixon refused to permit the trial to proceed.[8]

Nixon's secretive leadership over military affairs extended to the judiciary. He believed that directly lobbying the Supreme Court to defend the government's wiretapping of Muhammad Ali, was not an impropriety, and his back-channel efforts during Burger's tenure did not abate. Indeed, at one point, Burger felt he had to rebuff Nixon's efforts to collect intelligence on William O. Douglas when Douglas was threatened with impeachment. This is not to argue that Burger and the other judicial conservatives approved of Douglas' conduct. To the contrary, much of their expressed conservatism in military law jurisprudence was in reaction to Douglas.[9]

I: Douglas' Efforts to Curb the War and his Waning Influence

The conservative judiciary's reaction to the nation's diminished military reliability has to also be analyzed in response to Douglas and other outspoken judicial liberals. Douglas' push for the most expansive judicial governance of the military in the nation's legal history, extended to areas that even Brennan and Marshall found difficult to accept. Douglas nonetheless had an impact on military readiness.

---

7 Walter Issacson, *Kissinger*, 174; Klenton Clymer, "Cambodia and Laos in the Vietnam War," in David L. Anderson ed., *The Columbia History of the Vietnam War* (New York: Columbia University Press, 2011), 370–75; Herbert Parmet, *Richard Nixon and His America*, 5.

8 Stanley Kutler, *The Wars of Watergate*, 116–17; Elmo Zumwalt Jr., *On Watch: A Memoir* (New York: Quadrangle, 1976), 401–11; Walter Isaacson, *Kissinger*, 380–85.

9 John Ehrlichman, *Witness to Power*, 130; Steven Wermiel, *Justice Brennan*, 312.

Hundreds of service-members and thousands of citizens wrote to Douglas, viewing him as either able to stop the Johnson and Nixon Administrations from sending American service-members into foreign conflicts, or at least as a conscience against the Executive Branch's foreign and military policies. Douglas saw himself as having the stature to curb presidential excesses. If he were to have prevailed, the traditional constitutional separation of powers construct would have been significantly altered.

By 1968, Douglas' congressional critics alleged he engaged in unethical activity and compared him to Fortas. Soon after, Nixon joined this group. While Nixon believed Warren had undermined national security, he despised Douglas and attempted to have him impeached through surrogates. In Congress, Mendel Rivers and F. Edward Hebert accused Douglas of subverting national security by weakening the military. Hebert's statements were not likely to frighten Douglas and because Hebert had mistreated minority members of Congress, Douglas likely welcomed any challenge from the congressman. Along with Gerald Ford, Hebert formally moved to impeach Douglas. Ford, at Nixon's behest, went so far as to allege Douglas had ties to organized crime, even though he knew the allegations were baseless. The impeachment hearings never occurred, in part, because more reasoned congressman understood that this action threatened the judiciary's independence, and with it, the constitutional structure which enabled a full democracy, even though a conservative consensus agreed with Hebert's conclusions. The legal academy and American Bar Association largely defended Douglas. For instance, Irving Brant came to Douglas' aid. Brant wrote an article defending Douglas and *O'Callahan* and before submitting it, he gave Brennan a draft, who called it "persuasive." From his retirement, Black promised to defend Douglas as well. Nonetheless, and perhaps in response to Nixon, Douglas had become increasingly erratic, stretching the theory of judicial intervention beyond that of any modern justice.[10]

In 1970, the Massachusetts state attorney general brought suit to enjoin Secretary of Defense Laird from ordering its state residents into military service in Vietnam. This suit was the first time in the twentieth century that a state governor or attorney general challenged the federal government on the use and assignment of military forces. During the War of 1812, the New England states placed restrictions on the use of their militia, but the federal courts had not taken part in adjudicating state and federal relations. In 1970, the Court denied Massachusetts standing to sue the federal government. Unsurprisingly Douglas dissented, arguing that Massachusetts had a sufficient interest in the lives and liberties of its citizens to overcome both the doctrine of standing as well as the political question of the war. Harlan and Stewart dissented without stating their reasons for doing so.[11]

---

10 Brant to Brennan, October 14, 1970 [Brant/4] ; John Ehrlichman, *Witness to Power: The Nixon Years*, 116.

11 *Massachusetts v. Laird*, 400 U.S. 886 (1970).

In 1971, in *Reservists Committee to Stop the War v. Laird*, Judge Gerhard Gesell of the District Court for the District of Columbia, determined that because the Constitution, in Article I stated that no member of congress could be appointed to a civil office under the "authority of the United States," congressmen who held reserve commissions in the military could not be called to duty. The problem with Gesell's decision was twofold. One hundred and seventeen congressmen held reserve military commissions, and since the nation's founding, dozens of congressmen also served in uniform in wartime. This list included James A. Garfield during the Civil War and Lyndon Johnson in World War II. Secondly the parties which brought the suit in the first place did not include any member of congress.[12]

It is true that citizens holding a reserve commission, whether in the ready or retired reserves, may be recalled to active duty without their consent. It is also true that the Constitution's framers worried about preserving the separation of powers to the point that they prohibited congressmen from serving as ambassadors or in cabinet positions, simultaneous with their legislative duties. The Constitution uses the language "civil office," and does not expressly state "military duties," or similar terms. The reason for this is that there were no reserves, such as existed in 1970, at the time of the nation's founding, and the state militia commissions were not seen to be incompatible with congressional duties. In 1916, Congress concluded that a National Guard commission was incompatible with congressional service. On the other hand, in 1930, Congress appeared to have reversed its conclusions.

Whatever the constitutional answer to the issue was, however, Gesell had to determine whether the particular plaintiffs had standing to sue. Standing was an issue of concern to the Burger and Rehnquist Courts since, in the final years of Warren's tenure the Court had expanded the test of standing beyond those parties who were likely to suffer a significant demonstrable injury. The reservist plaintiffs included a large number of veterans who were opposed to the Vietnam conflict, but Gesell viewed them more as responsible citizens seeking to maintain the separation of powers, rather than persons with a potential for active military service. The reservists claimed that the over 100 congressmen with reserve affiliation, who had the potential to be called to active duty, were more likely to defer to the military establishment then to represent the desires of their constituents. They also claimed that because of their military affiliation, the congressmen were subjected to the Executive Branch's undue influence and this worked as a detriment not only to veterans as well as reserve officers and enlisted personnel, but to the nation on the whole. In countering the reservists' arguments, the Executive Branch argued that the issue raised was against the individual members of Congress, not the Secretary of Defense, and therefore the congressmen were the real party to the suit. Gesell dismissed this argument and issued a judgment stating that the plain text of the Constitution prohibited congressmen from holding military commissions of any

12 *Laird v. Reservist Committee to Stop the War*, 323 F.Supp. 833 (CA DC 1971).

sort. But, Gesell stopped short of issuing an injunction against the Secretary of Defense on this matter because he did not believe that he had the authority to do so. Gesell's decision was not likely to survive appellate scrutiny. Although he rejected the plaintiff's standing based on their military status as well as based on their taxpayer status, he granted standing based on their status as citizens.

The Court of Appeals for the District of Columbia affirmed Gesell's decision, but without publishing a decision. The Court granted *certiorari*, and in a decision re-captioned as *Schlesinger v. Reservists Committee to Stop the War*, a majority of justices overturned Gesell on the matter of standing. In conference, Douglas urged that every citizen should have standing on any Constitutional question and called the issue of justiciability—whether the question was one that the Court could competently address—"frivolous." Brennan believed there was standing in this particular issue, but not in all constitutional issues. Marshall sided with Brennan. Burger and Stewart urged that Gesell's decision usurped the election process. Although White called it "a close case," he ultimately sided with Burger. Unsurprisingly, Rehnquist claimed Gesell's decision "turned *Marbury v. Madison* on its head." Powell, for his part, joined with Rehnquist, but he wanted to add into the decision that Gesell's accusation of the Court abandoning the concept of standing in prior decisions was driven by his own anti-war positions "and not embedded in any legal reality."[13]

In conference, Blackmun, argued that taxpayer status alone was not enough to establish standing in this particular case, but he did not want to shut the door to similar suits. He added that he "would have a whale of a time convincing himself otherwise." In private he wondered whether with the war coming to an end, the issues raised "were obsolete," and penned that the case "was largely a matter of emotion." Yet, he also acknowledged that if the Court were to take up the issue on its merits, the Reservists' Committee would likely prevail because the Constitution's incompatibility clause and the statutes governing reserve military duties were both clearly drafted in such a way, whether by design or not, as make it likely that the Court would have to invalidate the commissions of the reservists. This was because, Blackmun believed, the Court possessed no power to unseat a congressman. Even so, he found it "amusing to contemplate the effect in certain sectors in Congress, if [Gesell's] decision were affirmed."[14]

Burger had argued that at best, the plaintiffs could only point to "an injury in the abstract" in which Congress failed to do its legislative duties free from executive coercion. Interestingly, the Court had only once in its history confronted the issue of constitutional ineligibility to serve in an office when a citizen sued to prevent Hugo Black from becoming a justice. Because Black remained a sitting senator at the time of his nomination, the citizen urged that Black was,

13 Powell, Conference Notes: 1/16/74; Douglas, Conference Notes, January 18, 1974 [WOD/1647].

14 Blackmun, Conference Notes, January 16, 1974 [HAB/179]; Blackmun, notes on Schlesinger v. Reservists Committee, January 9, 1974 [HAB/179].

in effect, serving in two coordinate branches of government at the same time. In that instance, the Court quickly brushed aside the citizen's standing and found the contention meritless. In *Reservists Committee*, Burger and the majority concluded that even where a constitutional issue is alleged, there must be a cognizable injury. Burger and the majority also sustained Gesell's opinion that taxpayer standing did not exist in relation to the issue raised.[15]

Stewart concurred with the majority, but simply to reiterate that no injury existed to provide the reservists standing to sue. Douglas dissented on the basis of a disagreement with Burger's view on standing, though he countered that the majority also enabled the Pentagon to be increasingly immune from citizen protests. He centered on the Constitution's purpose of prohibiting members of congress from falling under the Executive Branch's sway. Marshall dissented as well, accepting Douglas' position, but adding that because the plaintiffs possessed a First Amendment right to convince Congress to end the Vietnam conflict, implicit in that right was another right to petition congressmen free from the oversight of the Executive Branch. In *Reservists' Committee*, Douglas had allies, but on other matters, he remained alone.

In 1973, Congresswoman Elizabeth Holtzman brought suit in the United States District Court for the Eastern District of New York both as a citizen and an elected representative, to stop the Nixon Administration from expanding the conflict beyond Vietnam into Cambodia. On July 1, 1973, Congress passed two laws prohibiting the expenditure of funds for military operations in Cambodia, including aerial operations. Despite this law, and the fact that the governments of North Vietnam and the United States agreed to cease military operations in Cambodia and Laos, both sides continued to do so.

The use of the United States' military forces was in reaction to the Northern Vietnamese continuation of carrying the conflict beyond their borders. Communist forces moved through Cambodia and Laos, and the Air Force and Navy conducted aerial interdiction missions to stop this movement. Hundreds of civilians were killed in the process and it was clear that Nixon had defied Congress. Holtzman, a first term legislator, had already planned to introduce an article of impeachment against Nixon, but the lawsuit brought another avenue to raise the issue as to whether the judiciary could determine the Nixon's ordered military activity in Cambodia and Laos unconstitutional. Holtzman's selection as a plaintiff is an important feature of the decision. New York University law professor Burt Neuborne recruited her because her Brooklyn legislative district was part of Judge Orrin G. Judd's jurisdiction. Judd had previously determined that because Congress appropriated monies for military operations in Vietnam, the Legislative Branch had lawfully enabled the President to send service-members into that

15 *Schlesinger v. Reservist Committee to Stop the War*, 418 U.S. 208 (1974).

nation. Neuborne and Holtzman concluded that an opposite ruling would be required regarding Cambodia and Laos.[16]

The Executive Branch appealed to the District Court to grant summary judgment but stressed that both Secretary of State Kissinger and Secretary of Defense Laird would be able to testify as to the necessity for continuing interdiction operations in both Cambodia and Laos. The fundamental issues before the District Court were at the heart of the separation of powers doctrine. There are two noteworthy questions that the judiciary had to address. First, could a federal court limit the commander in chief from conducting military operations? Second, does the congressional act of defunding part of a conflict prohibit the Executive Branch from continuing operations?

Judd sided with Holtzman and her co-plaintiffs, including three Air Force officers assigned to fly missions over Cambodia. One of the officers, Captain Donald E. Dawson was facing a court-martial for refusing to conduct missions in a B-52 over Cambodia, while the other two officers were grounded from flying. Judd, a Johnson appointee who had served as a special hearing officer in conscientious objector appeals between 1953 and 1958, issued an injunction against the continuance of military operations. The decision was published on July 25, 1973, but the effective date of the injunction was extended to July 27 in order to allow the government time to appeal. The Court of Appeals for the Second Circuit, heard argument on July 27, in the morning, and prior to issuing its decision, it temporarily stayed (or "lifted") the injunction, until August 13. This temporary suspension of the injunction was done to provide more time for both parties to prepare for argument. As a result, the government was free to continue military operations in Cambodia, and Captain Dawson's hoped for declaration of "an illegal" or unconstitutional operation, in order to provide him a defense to his refusal to obey orders in a potential court-martial, did not occur.[17]

On August 1, 1973, Holtzman directly appealed to Marshall in his individual capacity to remove the appellate court's stay. Marshall denied Holtzman's appeal to lift the stay, and this should have been conclusive, unless the Court acted to reverse Marshall's refusal. Nothing in Marshall's refusal should have been analyzed as a binding decision as to whether the Cambodian operations were lawful or not. Rather, Marshall had determined that the proper course of action

---

16 Elizabeth Holtzman, *Who Said It Would Be Easy: One Woman's Life in the Political Arena* (New York: Arcade Publishing, 1996), 70–72; See also, Telford Taylor, *Nuremberg and Vietnam: An American Tragedy,* 107. Taylor wrote that while he believed Congress had authorized the conflict in Vietnam, Nixon's ordered aerial campaign over Cambodia had also been forbidden.

17 *Holtzman v. Schlesinger*, 361 F.Supp. 553 (DC ED NY 1973). Little is known on the pilots, but Holtzman stated that all were removed from their duties. See Elizabeth Holtzman, *Who Said it Would Be Easy*, 77. Holtzman mistakenly wrote that Judd was a Nixon appointee, but this is incorrect. Johnson appointed Judd in the final year of his presidency. See also, David Cortright, *Soldiers in Revolt*, 137.

was to permit the lower appellate court to fully consider Holtzman's claims and issue a ruling. Marshall's decision, however, was not to remain intact, because the following day Holtzman appealed to Douglas, who apparently believed he possessed the authority to override Marshall, ironically pitting one liberal against another. Douglas issued his ruling on the morning of August 4, 1973, though he claimed reluctance to do so. Marshall issued a counter-ruling that afternoon, but not before he had the full backing of the other justices including Brennan. This infuriated Douglas who countered that none of the other justices could have taken the time to read his decision. He then accused Marshall and his fellow justices of undermining the Court in the public's esteem, an interesting argument to be sure, because Douglas had been repeatedly accused of doing just this.

A Supreme Court in upheaval, and a district court siding with a member of Congress against the Nixon administration, was the environment in which the Second Circuit had to decide, Holtzman's claims. Composed of Judges William H. Mulligan, a World War II veteran and Nixon appointee, James Lowell Oakes, a Nixon appointee, and William Timbers, an Eisenhower appointee, the appellate court determined that Holtzman's claim presented a non-jusiticable political question to the judiciary. The three judges had, in fact, decided consistent with several other courts of appeal on this point. Obviously Congress could impeach the president, or pass a law specifically defunding the military, and either action would have settled the matter. Moreover, the populace could exercise their disagreement with the Executive Branch and vote to recall legislators, or wait until the next presidential election. The courts, however, were not the constitutional forum to address the challenge to the Nixon administration. Oakes dissented, but this was not enough for the Court to grant *certiorari*.[18]

On August 8, 1973, the day the appellate court issued its decision, Douglas forwarded Marshall a dissent from the Court overturning his August 4 order. Douglas accused Marshall of misstating facts, and included a comment that he had issued several draft orders. Marshall was able to show that Douglas had issued a single order on August 3, restoring the district court's injunction. Douglas' conduct is inexplicable. In the midst of a conflict which both he and Marshall believed to be immoral, he turned on his most likely allies, for no discernable result. Although the Court's conservatives could have benefited from a contentious argument amongst the liberals, Burger intervened to head off a fight he believed would prove detrimental to the Court in the long run. On August 13, 1973, he denied Holtzman's third request for a stay and this ended the issue. Within two years, the United States would have no further forces engaged in Vietnam, Cambodia, and Laos, and Nixon would be out of office.[19]

---

18 *Holtzman v. Schlesinger*, 484 F.2d 1037 (CA 2, 1973); *Holtzman v. Schlesinger*, 414 U.S. 1304 (1973) [Marshall's order against removing the stay of the injunction]; 414 U.S. 1316 (1973) [Douglas counter to Marshall]; 414 U.S. 1321 (1973) [Marshall's final order].

19 Marshall to the Conference, August 8, 1973 [WOD/1639].

II: Free Speech, Due Process, and Military Discipline: *Parker v. Levy* and *Secretary of the Navy v. Avrech*

Just how far the military establishment or Congress could regulate free speech in the military had become an open question by the time Burger became Chief Justice. From the time of the Continental Army in the War for Independence, through the present, the Articles of War and the UCMJ have contained two general articles which do not enumerate specified offenses, but rather allow the military to prosecute service members for "disorders and neglects to the prejudice of good order and discipline in the armed forces," and "conduct unbecoming an officer and gentleman." The two articles appear at odds with a basic rule of civilian criminal law. In 1812, the Court, in *United States v. Hudson and Goodwin* struck down the concept of a federal common law of crimes. In essence, the Court ruled that for conduct to be considered a crime, Congress had to specifically codify the specific conduct into a crime, and then clearly state that the courts have jurisdiction over the offense. *Hudson and Goodwin* originated in the conviction of newsmen prosecuted under the Alien and Sedition Acts after accusing President Jefferson of negotiating with Napoleon Bonaparte. The Court found that this type of political crime was repugnant to freedom.[20]

Put another way, the Court in *Hudson and Goodwin* recognized through recent British and European history that if the requirement of notice did not exist, then trials for nefarious reasons would be all the more easily accomplished. Because the Fourteenth Amendment did not exist at the time of *Hudson and Goodwin*, the individual states could still prosecute citizens for non-enumerated offenses such as public immorality. But even in state prosecutions, this type of charging was on the decline after 1865 because a fundamental tenet of due process is notice. That is, an individual has to reasonably know that certain conduct is prohibited by the express language of law, and criminal statutes are supposed to be as specific in their prohibiting language as possible and the states began to incorporate this aspect of the Bill of Rights into their criminal law jurisprudence. By 1970, state statutes had been largely cleansed of such offenses.[21]

Although the Articles of War and its succeeding UCMJ are federal law, *Hudson and Goodwin* was never thought to apply to the military. Critics after the Civil War derided the general article (the predecessor to Article 134) as "the Devil's

---

20 11 U.S. 32 (1812). The Court specifically held that for a crime to exist in law, "[the] legislative authority of the Union must first make an act a crime, affix a punishment to it, and declare the Court that shall have jurisdiction of the offence." See, also, G. Edward White, *The Marshall Court and Cultural Change, 1815–1835* (London: Cambridge, 1988), 865–6; and, Gary D. Rowe "The Sound of Silence: *United States v. Hudson & Goodwin*, the Jeffersonian Ascendancy and the Abolition of the Federal Common Law of Crimes," 101 *Yale Law Journal* 919.

21 Herbert A. Johnson, *The Chief Justiceship of John Marshall: 1801–1835* (Columbia, SC: University of South Carolina Press, 1997), 141–3.

Article." But the federal courts and the nation's leading legal scholars believed the articles were important to military governance. Moreover, in 1857, the Court in *Dynes v. Hoover* enabled the Army and Navy to court-martial soldiers, sailors, and marines for offenses which did not expressly appear in the two services' respective codes.[22]

It was not until the Vietnam War where Article 133 and Article 134 came under attack in the federal judiciary, not only for failing to enumerate prohibited conduct, but also for potentially criminalizing conduct otherwise protected by the First Amendment. The UCMJ and its predecessor Articles of War in specified articles already prohibited some speech such as fostering a mutiny or deriding the president, Congress, or a state governor. Other acts, such as openly deriding government policies were prosecutable under Article 134 and Article 133. Few legal scholars could sincerely doubt the constitutionality of such prohibitions. But a blanket grant of authority to design crimes without direct congressional involvement troubled a number of judges and the legal academy.[23]

a. Parker v. Levy

Parker v. Levy, was singularly the most contentious military law decision arising from a court-martial to come before the Burger Court and it rivaled *Laird v. Tatum*, a decision involving the use of the military to collect information on the public issued three years earlier, in terms of public and academic disagreement. *Levy* was, as one scholar called it, "the Vietnam War on Trial," and this characterization was true not only in a judicial sense, but also within the broader scope of a public trial. Anti-war leaders such as Dr. Benjamin Spock, and a large number of prominent entertainment industry personalities, including Jane Fonda and Edward Asner supported Captain Howard Levy. Amnesty International's British Section campaigned for Levy and that organization's German counterpart, the Deutsche Section e.V, adopted Levy as "a prisoner of conscience." Major news journals headlined Levy's court-martial, and it was amply covered on television network news stations. Walter Cronkite, the respected CBS news anchor, began his evening news program with features on the court-martial. In opposite of the thousands of courts-martial arising from the conflict, Levy's trial likely was second in popular coverage only to that of Lieutenant William Calley's. Unlike Calley, Levy's case did not involve a heinous war crime, but it would traverse through several federal courts—more so than Calley's appeals—and thrice be heard by the justices on the Court. By its second and most important hearing before the Court, Levy's case

22 Joshua Kastenberg, *The Blackstone of Military Law*, 128.

23 See e.g. Major General Keithe E. Nelson, "Conduct Expected of an Officer and a Gentleman: Ambiguity," 12 USAF Law Review (1970), 124–36.

became symbolic of not only the military disciplinary system on trial, but also, in some measure, its existence.[24]

The underlying facts in Levy's appeal had similarities to Dr. Orloff's appeals in the early 1950s. Levy was a medical doctor—in this case a dermatologist—whose military service had been deferred while he attended medical school. Like Orloff, Levy was from New York City. In 1965, Levy reported for active duty at Fort Jackson, South Carolina, despite being staunchly opposed to the military's involvement in Vietnam. Prior to his military service, Levy attended Militant Labor Forum meetings, an organization not listed on the Attorney General's subversive list, but affiliated with the Socialist Worker's Party. While on active duty, Levy participated in African American voter registration programs, volunteering his time with the Southern Christian Leadership Conference. Neither activity was prohibited, and Levy's voter registration work was an important fulfillment of both the Fifteenth Amendment and the Voting Rights Act of 1965. Making no attempt to disguise his activities, he freely indicated his involvement in both groups. Levy had also expressed admiration for Che Guevara, a communist insurgent who assisted revolutionary groups in Cuba, Bolivia, and the then Belgian Congo. Army intelligence officers questioned Levy prior to being charged with violating the UCMJ.[25]

The lack of discipline at Fort Jackson, as on many military bases, was, by 1967, endemic. By the time of Levy's court-martial, 20 enlisted soldiers had been punitively disciplined for circulating anti-war petitions and anti-military underground newsletters. One enlisted soldier attempted to organize a union, and obtained over 100 signatures. By 1969, the union organization, self-titled "G.I.s United Against the War in Vietnam" had become a fixture on base post, and there were "sit-ins" in the base mess halls. By 1969, an anti-war coffee house had been established off-post, and on-post, Malcolm-X literature chastising the government abounded. Levy himself informed the *Washington Post* and *New York Times* that his activity had paved the way for this conduct to occur."[26]

24 Robert N. Strassfield, The Vietnam War on Trial: The Court-Martial of Dr. Howard B. Levy, 1994 Wisconsin Law Review, (1994), 839. Strassfield's article is the most comprehensive study on the court-martial, though he clearly sympathized with Levy over the military in this article. Nonetheless, the article is meticulously researched into both Levy's motives, the impact of his conduct, and the conduct of the court-martial. See also "Nation: Guilty as Charged," Time Magazine, June 9, 1967; and *New York Times*, June 3, 1967, p. 1; and, Douglas, Levy File [WOD/1468].

25 Strassfield, The Vietnam War on Trial," 839; "Army's Dr. Levy Says Politics Led to Verdict," *Washington Star*, December 11, 1969.

26 "Jackson Eight: Tiny Group Causing Army Big Concern," *Washington Post*, April 27, 1969; Martin Oppenheimer, "The American Military: What it Does," in Martin Oppenheimer, *The American Military* (New Brunswick, NJ: Transaction, 1971), 96–8; "War Foe Levy Unchanged by Imprisonment," *Washington Post*, August 21, 1969; "Levy Now Presses Heath Care Shift," *Washington Post*, December 7, 1969.

Levy's commanding officer decided that despite his extra-military activity, there was no evidence of subversive conduct, and he recommended retention on active duty. Nonetheless, the Army had maintained a special file on Levy and this fueled suspicion that the intelligence reports contributed to the decision to ultimately court-martial him. In perhaps the most detailed study on the case, Professor Richard Strassfield concluded that although the Army's prosecution ultimately deprived Levy of due process, it was likely nothing more than coincidence that an intelligence investigation into Levy's background occurred near the time of the trial, and the Army likely would have court-martialed him at any rate. It is true that Levy's commanding officer initially decided to offer him non-judicial punishment under Article 15, but after reading the intelligence files decided to pursue a court-martial. And, the intelligence reports evidence that Levy was not simply a disgruntled conscientious objector. Nonetheless, to some of the federal judges who later passed judgment on the court-martial, and certainly to Douglas, this became a significant issue.[27]

Levy's duty at Fort Jackson was to train Army Special Forces soldiers for medical service in Vietnam. Specifically, he was supposed to teach the students how to identify and treat skin diseases endemic to the unusual environment which they were ultimately being sent. By mid 1966, Levy initiated conversations with his students and other patients on the wrongness of the war, and he repeatedly missed teaching appointments. His commander, in response, ordered him to conduct the required training but Levy refused to do so, claiming that the order conflicted with his medical ethics. Levy's refusal ultimately formed the basis of one charge accusing him of violating Article 90, a statute prohibiting a service-member violating lawful orders.

A more significant set of charges had to do with Levy's discussions with enlisted personnel. Levy's statements were encapsulated in a charge under the general disorders provision of Article 134. In this charge, the Army accused Levy of making statements such as "I would refuse to go to Viet Nam if ordered to do so," "I don't see why any colored soldier would go to Viet Nam" and that African American soldiers "should refuse to go to Viet Nam, and if sent, should refuse to fight because they are discriminated against and denied their freedom in the United States, and they are sacrificed and discriminated against in Viet Nam by being given all the hazardous duty and they are suffering the majority of casualties." He also expressed to enlisted men that "Special Forces personnel are liars and thieves and killers of peasants and murderers of women and children." In addition to other offenses, the Army also charged Levy with conduct unbecoming an officer and gentleman under Article 133 for similar conduct, as well as for boasting that he would refuse to follow his commander's orders. Levy would later claim that the First Amendment shielded him from prosecution because this was a matter of

27 Id, at 869.

freedom of speech. But history was not on his side. In the Civil War and during both world wars, such boasts were routinely prosecuted in courts-martial.[28]

Levy was not an ordinary accused represented by ordinary military counsel. Charles Morgan, a talented attorney who had recently successfully argued to the Court that state legislative districts had to be equal in population, agreed to represent Levy alongside Levy's military defense counsel. Morgan had worked for the NAACP on numerous civil rights issues, including the unfair apportionment of state election districts. He represented both Muhammad Ali and Cleveland Sellers in their appeals of their convictions for refusing induction into the Army. In 1966, Morgan successfully represented Julian Bond, the African American Georgia legislator who the state legislature refused to seat after he voiced anti-war views. The Court determined that the state legislature could not deny Bond his elected position for asserting his First Amendment rights. Morgan was not as successful in defending Levy. He urged the court-martial to acquit based on a Nuremburg defense, which if valid, would justify refusing an order. After a 15-day trial, on June 2, 1967, the court-martial found Levy guilty of each of the charges albeit with some alterations.[29]

Before the court-martial commenced, however, Morgan also unsuccessfully petitioned Judge Howard Corcoran of the District Court for the District of Columbia to convene a three-judge panel so that he could argue that the charges against Levy were unconstitutionally vague, and then if he were unsuccessful, he could appeal directly to the Court. After the failure to convince the district court, Morgan appealed to the Court of Appeals for the District of Columbia to stop the Army from proceeding with the court-martial. That court did not grant Levy relief. However, the dynamics in the three judge proceeding reflected the political and social environment of the country and presaged the ultimate Court decision six years later. The decision, captioned as *Levy v. Corcoran*, resulted in a split between David Lionel Bazelon a confidant of Douglas and Brennan on the one side, and Harold Leventhal and Edward Tamm on the other. An activist judge, Bazelon, like Douglas, had sought to judicially curb the Executive Branch's assertions of immunity in national security matters including nuclear testing. Bazelon also frequently clashed with Burger when Bruger sat on the Court of Appeals for the District of Columbia. In his correspondences to Blackmun before both sat on the Court, Burger derided Bazelon over his position on judicial interference in nuclear testing.[30]

---

28 *United States v. Levy*, 39 CMR 672 (CMA, 1968); See Joshua Kastenberg, *Law in War: Law As War*, 218–25; and Steven J. Ramold, *Baring the iron Hand: Discipline in the Union Army* (DeKalb, IL: Northern Illinois University Press, 2010).

29 The apportionment case is *Reynolds v. Sims*, 377 U.S. 533 (1964); the Georgia legislative decision is *Bond v. Floyd*, 385 U.S. 116 (1965); On Morgan's role in Ali and Sellers, see Anne Emmanuel, *Elbert Parr Tuttle*, 300.

30 See e.g. *Pauling v. McElroy*, 278 F.2d 252 (CA DC 1960); *Pauling v. McNamara*, 331 F.2d 796 (CA DC 1963); Burger to Blackmun, September 8, 1960 [HAB/26].

Leventhal was a liberal judge, who, like Bazelon had been part of the New Deal, and Tamm generally had a conservative jurisprudence. While Leventhal did not support the United States involvement in Vietnam, he did not believe that a judicial departure from not interfering in courts-martial was warranted in Levy's appeal to prevent the court-martial from occurring in the first place. On July 11, 1967, Leventhal delivered a speech at the Pentagon, urging that the right of "orderly" dissent be preserved in wartime. In the judicial conference he stated that he did not believe that Levy had engaged in orderly dissent. Tamm agreed with Leventhal, but went further in conference, stating that the federal appellate court was without jurisdiction until Levy was convicted and had essentially exhausted all available other remedies.[31]

After Levy's court-martial conviction, Morgan unsuccessfully argued to the Army Court of Appeals for bail. That court, in denying Levy's petition, determined that Congress had not empowered military judges to grant bail, and bail was generally reserved for pre-conviction imprisonment. Levy then appealed to the United States District Court for South Carolina to order release with bail, but that court also concluded that bail only applied to pre-conviction appellants and did not include military trials. Likewise, the Court of Appeals for the Fourth Circuit, in a *per curiam* decision, upheld the Army and district courts shortly after. Ultimately Levy was freed from prison prior to the Court taking up the merits of his appeal. On his release from confinement, Levy expressed no change in his position on the war, concluding that his stand resulted in hundreds of other service-members expressing their opposition to the war, and the Army deciding that future courts-martial for similar conduct ought to be avoided, but this was five years after the issue of bail was addressed by the courts.[32]

Shortly after his conviction, the Army moved Levy from Fort Leavenworth to its penitentiary in Pennsylvania. This move provided the Court of Appeals for the Third Circuit jurisdiction over Levy's claims. By the time that court heard argument on Levy's case, the District Court for the District of South Carolina, the Court of Appeals for the Fourth Circuit and the Court had reviewed the issue of bail; and the District Court for the District of Columbia, the Court of Appeals for the District of Columbia, and the Court had indirectly addressed the constitutionality of the charges against Levy prior to the court-martial adversely to Levy. It is true that the Third Circuit was the first federal court to directly decide the constitutionality of Article 133 and Article 134, but given that six federal courts had not viewed this

31 Leventhal's speech is contained in Leventhal's letter to Danaher, July 11, 1967 [Leventhal/4]. *Levy v. Corcoran*, 389 F.2d. 929 (CA DC 1967); and, 387 U.S. 915 (1967). Leventhal's view on Bazelon's dissent was that it was a protest against the war cloaked in a legal statement." Notes, May 22, 1967, [Leventhal/45]; Bazelon, notes *Levy v. Corcoran:* Box 7.

32 *Levy v. Resor*, Civ. No. 67–442 (D.S.C. July 5, 1967), aff'd per curiam, 384 F.2d 689 (CA 4, 1967), *cert. denied*, 389 U.S. 1049 (1968); "War Foe Levy Unchanged by Imprisonment," *Washington Post*, August 21, 1969.

question as compelling enough to force the military to forgo the court-martial, or release Levy on bail, it might have been predicted that the Third Circuit would rule against Levy. This did not occur.

By the time of Levy's appeal before the appellate court, his defense team had been enlarged to include not only Charles Morgan, but also Norman Siegel, a member of the New York Civil Liberties Union, Professor Anthony Amsterdam of Stanford University who, had recently prevailed before the Court in *Furman v. Georgia* arguing that under contemporary sentencing standards the death penalty was unconstitutional, Melvin Wulf of the American Civil Liberties Union, and Professor Emily Carssow as well as several others. This was a formidable array of civil rights attorneys who convinced the Third Circuit that both Article 133 and Article 134 were unconstitutionally vague because such charges failed to specifically place a service-member on notice as to the criminality of a behavior.

The appellate court presented a brief history of both articles as well as an acknowledgement that the Court of Military Appeals, in *United States v. Howe*, had determined that Article 133 was constitutional and did not violate the First Amendment. The judges on the court, moreover, conceded that Levy's conduct actually fell within the ambit of itemized examples described in both Article 133 and 134. These examples included "praising the enemy," and "attacking the war aims of the United States," as well as "denouncing our form of Government." But, strangely, the judges reasoned that even if Levy had notice that his conduct was prohibited, others might not. Therefore they concluded that because the two articles were generally "void for vagueness," it did not matter whether Levy knew his conduct was unlawful.

Two of the three judges though sought to effectuate a change in the military's disciplinary construct by circumventing Congress. He acknowledged the federal judiciary's long standing deference to the two articles, but he also noted that "concepts of justice change." And it was on this issue where he pointed to *O'Callahan* for proof, because in that decision Douglas had "expressed doubts as to the constitutionality of [Article 134]," even though *O'Callahan* had nothing to do with Article 134. When Douglas granted Levy bail, he also expressed a doubt that the court-martial conviction would survive scrutiny on the vagueness issue, a matter Aldisert considered important. In addition to deferring to Douglas, the court incorporated Bazelon's dissent from the Court of Appeals for the District of Columbia's refusal to enjoin for Levy's court-martial. "Our conclusion that Articles 133 and 134 fail to set forth satisfactory standards of conduct leads to the inescapable corollary that enforcement of these articles is to varying degrees arbitrary and discriminatory," the appellate court concluded.[33]

The Third Circuit issued *Parker* on April 18, 1973, one month after the Court of Appeals for the District of Columbia issued *Avrech v. Secretary of the Navy*. Analyzed in greater detail below, the six judges on the two appellate courts

33 On Douglas' grant of bail to Levy see, Anthony D'Amato, *International Law and Political Reality* (Amsterdam, Netherlands: Kluwer Law International, 1995), 4–5.

communicated with each other to harmonize *Parker* and *Avrech* with the goal of giving greater strength to *O'Callahan*, and further weakening the military's ability to discipline its forces. All of the judges were certainly aware that their decisions were likely to reach the Court, and not only were these two decisions urged on the Court. In July 1973, the Court of Appeals for the Tenth Circuit, in *Councilman v. Laird*, determined a jurisdictional issue adverse to the military. The Department of Defense's leadership and Attorney General John Mitchell agreed to appeal to the Court to review all three decisions. However, *Parker* was to be the most important decision among the three, and in retrospect, while each of the three decisions would form a basis for eventually overcoming *O'Callahan*, it was *Levy* which drew the most interest.

Once before the Court, Levy's defense team was pitted against Solicitor General Bork who proved more formidable than the government's attorneys who argued to the lower courts. In preparing for argument, Bork conferred with the Army Judge Advocate General as well as Frederick Wiener, a former judge advocate who had frequently testified before Congress on a variety of national security law matters. The three men, and presumably the defense establishment's leadership agreed that Article 133 was essential to military discipline. "Although it has a slightly quaint ring, there is no doubt of its meaning," Bork observed to Wiener. For his part, Wiener agreed, noting that the higher standards of conduct expected of officers existed because officers had to have the authority to issue orders that might ultimately determine the life or death of men under their command. He encouraged Bork to argue that Levy's conduct was more damaging to good order and discipline then if an enlisted man had committed the same conduct. "In Levy's court-martial, Article 133 was not used out of the clear blue sky," Wiener argued. "Tradition, history, context, function, common knowledge of what an officer's job is, constituted the basis for the charge." In turn Bork prepared to argue, "if Capt Levy can lawfully do what he did, why cannot the Joint Chiefs of Staff publicly condemn the President and his policies."[34]

Initially Burger wanted Stewart to write the majority opinion believing that because Stewart had dissented in *O'Callahan*, he would vote to reverse the Third Circuit. But Stewart informed Burger that he could not do so. "My conference notes indicate that five of the brethren are of the view that Articles 133 and 134 are constitutionally valid; I am not one of them," he answered. In conference, Stewart stated he opposed the government based on his belief that the First Amendment's protections were more important than the survival of an un-enumerated offense others thought important to military discipline.[35]

Burger then assigned Rehnquist to write the majority decision, though the Chief Justice ultimately joined a more stinging concurrence against the predictable dissents. Surprisingly, in his draft, Rehnquist barely acknowledged the two dissenting opinions and initially authored a bland decision. He began with a bare

34 Notes, *Parker v. Levy* File [Bork/28].

35 Stewart to Burger, March 4, 1974 [WOD/1654]; also found in [HAB/195].

recitation of the facts in the case, none of which contradicted the lower court's exposition of Levy's court-martial. His main criticism of the Third Circuit had to do with the appellate court measuring Article 133 and Article 134 against civilian standards. He avoided discussing the jurisdictional holding of the appellate court as well, simply commenting that while the district court earlier determined military tribunals had given "full and fair consideration" making the role of federal courts reviewing courts-martial limited, the appellate court disagreed, and claimed a broader scope of appeal. Rehnquist also quickly dismissed Levy's argument that the Solicitor General's appeal was defective and therefore the Court could not decide on the case. This part of Rehnquist's draft decision drew no criticism from the dissenting justices.

The central question before the Court in *Levy*, Rehnquist pointed out, was to what extent federal courts could oversee the military's specialized society. There was ample case law dating from 1827, through the Warren Court which recognized the role of the military as an arm of the Executive Branch, with disciplinary requirements not existing in civilian society, and that military officers had a unique position of responsibility within a specialized military society. Rehnquist traced the historic lineage of the law governing officer behavior from its seventeenth-century British antecedents to the present time. He pointed out that the post-Civil War nineteenth-century cases *Smith v. Whitney*, *United States v. Fletcher*, and *Swaim v. United States* supported the constitutionality of Article 133. But, he also had to acknowledge that in the twentieth century, the Court had produced no support for either the Third Circuit's decision or his own opinion, and in reality there was no modern case law on the subject. Other UCMJ articles prohibited conduct, which in civilian life would not be considered criminal, and few people could honestly believe that a military offense such as malingering which had no civilian analogue was unconstitutional. Moreover, Congress had, he explained, in enacting Article 137, required the military to carefully explain the UCMJ to each enlisted member, and presumably officers with college educations would also understand both the code and the unique requirements of military service. The requirement to educate military personnel on the law, in fact, dated to the 1806 Articles of War, if not before.

Rehnquist's exposition of a specialized military society and its respective jurisprudence then set the stage for reversing the lower court. He criticized the court of appeals for acknowledging that while Levy's conduct clearly matched the example of "praising the enemy, attacking the war aims of the United States, or denouncing our form of government," listed under Article 134, they nonetheless accepted Levy's argument of unconstitutional vagueness. Since, Rehnquist reasoned, Levy himself had no doubt that his conduct constituted prohibited conduct, his challenge against the articles for being unconstitutionally vague had to fail. Additionally, Rehnquist acknowledged that while enforcement of the articles could become arbitrary or "while there may lurk at the fringes of the articles a court-martial for conduct which is protected by the First Amendment," the articles themselves were not overbroad or vague.[36]

After Rehnquist circulated his draft on May 10, 1974, White, Powell, and Blackmun quickly joined him. Within two days, Douglas informed the Court he intended to dissent, as did Stewart. On June 11, Stewart circulated his dissent and temporarily gained Brennan's support for it. Blackmun, after reconsidering Rehnquist's draft decision in light of the dissents decided that while he agreed with Rehnquist, his draft did not go far enough to counter the dissents. "In addition to tradition, there may be something more fundamental involved here," he argued. "It is the old fashioned concept of honor and the old fashioned idea that there is a difference between *malum in se* and *malum prohibitum*." This was not all. Blackmun asserted that character and discipline were required of officers if the nation were to possess a reliable fighting force. If the two articles were found unconstitutional, he believed the military would face the "danger of decimation as a fighting force." Blackmun, in his conference memorandum, derided Stewart's dissent as a "judicial flight of fancy."[37]

On June 14, Blackmun circulated his draft concurrence, but would have retracted it had Rehnquist adopted some of its criticism of Stewart's dissent. Rehnquist refused to do so, believing it unnecessary to the appealed issues. Burger, also angry at Stewart's dissent, decided to join with Blackmun instead of Rehnquist's majority.[38]

Douglas predictably dissented, but was unable to have any other justice join him. By this stage in Douglas' tenure he did not seem to mind that he stood alone. Yet, in this case he was perplexed at Stewart's refusal to agree with his reasons for dissenting. Instead, Douglas also joined in Stewart's dissent, as did Brennan. Marshall would have likely dissented as well, but did not participate in the case. The reasons for Douglas' separate dissent had to do with his application of the First Amendment to service-members and his initial attempts to have the Court rule that the Solicitor General had not timely filed an opinion. Douglas' clerk urged him to avoid this issue because the rest of the Court would rule for the Justice Department and Congress might step into the fray. Besides, his clerk noted, the timeliness issue was not central to the decision.[39]

Douglas then centered on the First Amendment, arguing that since Congress never possessed the constitutional authority to limit the reading of books "or prohibit barroom discussions," it could not create a law so broad as to enable prosecution for such conduct in the military, and certainly both Article 133 and 134 could be used for to this effect. Levy's statements, Douglas noted, affronted his superiors. "The military, of course, tends to produce homogenized individuals

36 Rehnquist, First Draft, undated [BW/].

37 Blackmun, memorandum to the conference, undated [HAB/186].

38 Parker v. Levy, conference notes, [Brennan/I: 327].

39 R.B. to Douglas, undated 1973 [WOD/1633]; Douglas to Stewart, June 14, 1974 [HAB/195].

who think as well as march in unison," he caustically argued. Yet, he conceded that non-First Amendment acts could be punishable under the general articles such as excessive debts or alcoholism. As a result, while he did not find Article 133 or 134 unconstitutionally vague, he did find that Levy's speech was unconstitutionally prosecuted on First Amendment grounds by bootstrapping it under the two articles.

Stewart, who had dissented in *O'Callahan*, also dissented in *Levy*, which would, at first glance, seem to be odd. But *O'Callahan* was an *in personam* jurisdiction case, and Stewart's First Amendment jurisprudence tended to be liberal. Yet, he dissented not as a matter of opposition based on the curtailment of free speech. Instead, he argued, "I find it hard to imagine criminal statutes more patently unconstitutional than these vague and uncertain general articles." He urged the majority to consider the room for abuse in charging service-members under this offense, claiming that the protection from such abuse was limited only by a commander's creativity. Why Stewart chose the "void for vagueness" position was simple. He believed, unlike Douglas, that the military still had the authority to curtail some speech because the hierarchical nature of military discipline required this authority, if used reasonably. On the other hand, if Congress wanted to provide this authority, it had to do so expressly through a specific statute and not through a generic antique "catch-all."[40]

Stewart's dissent was notable for another reason. He attacked the intellectual underpinnings of the military's justice system which had been unquestioned long before Colonel Winthrop had published *Military Law* in 1886. His position was difficult because of the historic use of the two articles. "It might well have been true in 1858 or even 1902 that those in the Armed Forces knew, through a combination of military custom and instinct, what sorts of acts fell within the purview of the general articles," he argued, before adding that times "have surely changed." In Stewart's view, the continuing influence of Winthrop and the "old Army," had to give way to the more modern scholarship of those urging an increasingly narrowed military jurisdiction.

In his brief, but stinging concurrence, Blackmun, joined by Burger, derided Stewart's dissent, labeling Stewart's views of changing times rendering articles vague and uncertain, a "judicial fantasy." Countering the argument that the modern service-member could not know right from wrong, Blackmun wrote that the concepts of right and wrong were the same in 1974 as these concepts were under the American Articles of War in 1775. Utilizing the historic example of the weakness of the Soviet Army in the early days of the Russian Revolution, Blackmun pointed that "command indulgence of an undisciplined rank and file can decimate a fighting force."

Blackmun had a valid argument. From 1918 through 1922, the Soviet Union possessed a sizeable military force, but because of a weak command structure and

---

40 Richard Benha to Douglas, May 11, 1973 [WOD/1654]. Benha explained to Douglas that he understood the void for vagueness was all that Stewart would agree to from Stewart's clerks.

poor discipline, it barely defeated its Tsarist opponents. Moreover, during that period, the Soviet military lost a war against the new Polish state, which hardly had an effective military of its own. One study of the Soviet military during this period explained "soldiers henceforth would enjoy the rights of an ordinary citizen, and saluting off-duty was abolished. Officers would no longer enjoy their previous exalted form of address, and rudeness to soldiers was prohibited."[41]

But it was Blackmun's conclusion that touched on a social issue which increasingly perturbed conservatives. "Relativistic notions of right and wrong, or situation ethics, as some call it, have achieved in recent times, a disturbingly high level of prominence in this country, both in the guise of law reform, and as a justification of conduct that persons would normally eschew as immoral and even illegal," he noted. To Blackmun, as to many citizens, the domestic social upheaval which grew during the Vietnam conflict weakened the nation's social structure and its institutions. Clearly, by 1973, many citizens had moved away from believing in absolutes and embraced relativism. Academic institutions had been teaching the merits of relativism during the 1960s, though this was not always popular. One law school dean who appreciated Blackmun's concurrence wrote: "your Honor's last paragraph says it so beautifully, giving wonderfully inspiring leadership to those of us who have been tempted to enter into the disgusting futile quagmire of relativistic thinking in recent years." The erosion of support for relativism was precisely what Blackmun had hoped to accomplish.[42]

b. Secretary of the Navy v. Avrech

At roughly the same time *Parker v. Levy* traversed the federal courts, a Marine private first class named Mark Avrech challenged his court-martial conviction to the District Court for the District of Columbia and the Court of Appeals for the District of Columbia. While stationed in Vietnam in 1969, Avrech drafted a newsletter criticizing the role of American combat forces and deriding the willingness of the Vietnamese to fight communism. Avrech concluded his letter with the question, "do we dare express our feelings and opinions with the threat of court-martial perpetually hanging over our heads? Are your opinions worth risking a court-martial? We must strive for peace and if not peace then a complete

---

41 While Blackmun did not leave what sources he consulted on this point, he was accurate, and it matched the a prevailing opinion among military historians. For studies on the Soviet military published before *Levy*, see, John Erickson, *The Soviet High Command: A Military-Political History*, 1918–1941 (London: St Martin's Press, 1962), 1–83; see also John Coffey, *Deterrence in the 1970s* (Denver: University of Denver Press, 1970); and Raymond Garthoff, *Soviet Military Policy: A Historical Analysis* (London: Faber and Faber, 1966). From 1975 to 1977, Garthoff served as the United States Ambassador to the Soviet Union.

42 Daniel D. Smith, dean of the International School of Law (now George Mason University, School of Law) to Blackmun, June 22, 1974 [HAB/186].

U.S. withdrawal. We've been sitting ducks for too long." The letter was not widely disseminated and the impact of it on the morale of the armed forces in Vietnam was certainly minor. Nonetheless, as Avrech's acts were precisely the type which undermined military discipline in Vietnam, his commander believed a court-martial necessary. A special court-martial sentenced him to 30 days confinement, a sentence too minimal to grant him review in the military appellate courts. As a result, he appealed to the District Court for the District of Columbia claiming that Article 134 was void for vagueness and it violated his right of free speech.[43]

After the district court denied Avrech relief and ruled that Article 134 was constitutionally sound, he successfully appealed to the Court of Appeals for the District of Columbia. Interestingly, retired justice, Tom Clark, who had been a judicial conservative served as the lead judge by special designation and led the appellate court to rule against the military.

In authoring the decision, Clark acknowledged the longevity of Article 134 in both British and American military law. He recognized that both William Hough, a leading early nineteenth-century British military law scholar, and Colonel Winthrop argued that the predecessor article to Article 134 fitted the special needs of the military. But he then called these scholars "old authorities [who] bear little weight." Instead, he turned to the more modern arguments of Frederick Wiener, and a former Army judge advocate general, Kenneth Hodson. Hodson had recently advocated abolishing the general article as antiquated and replacing it with a more comprehensive code. Wiener did not advocate anything of the sort, but he had conceded that the general articles could lead to abuses. Clark quipped "the Manual is not exhaustive of Article 134 misconduct; its crazy quilt of offenses does not cover Article 134's bed." He concluded, however, that the appellate court had already addressed the particular issue in Avrech's favor five years earlier in *Kauffman v. Secretary of the Air Force.* In retrospect, this conclusion was problematic because *Kauffman* was a jurisdictional decision, not an issue which involved the First Amendment.[44]

43 The facts of Avrech are found in *Avrech v. Secretary of the Navy*, 477 F.2d 1247 (CA DC 1973). Avrech was convicted in a second court-martial for stealing a camera from the Navy Exchange store, though no errors claimed in this second court-martial were raised to either the appellate or Supreme Court. However, the prosecution in his second court-martial, argued that the first court-martial proved Avrech had no rehabilitation potential and should be punitively discharged from the military, which is what occurred.

44 Id. *Kauffman v. Secretary of the Air Force*, 415 F.2d 991 (CA DC 1969), *cert denied* 396 U.S. 1013 (1969). J. Skelley Wright, [File 82]: Wiener, Are the General Military Articles Unconstitutionally Vague? 54 ABA Journal 357, 363 (1968). Kenneth J. Hodson (Chief Judge, United States Army Court of Military Review), "Perspective, The Manual for Courts-Martial, 1984," 57 Military Law Review 1, 12 (1972). Hodson argued that Article 134 should be replaced with Article 92, which prohibits violations of lawful orders.

The Department of Defense general counsel, service judge advocates and Attorney General John Mitchell were unsure how the Court would rule in *Levy*, but as *Avrech* presented a similar issue, there was a clear consensus to appeal this decision in concert with *Levy*. In essence, the Department of Defense's leadership saw the two cases as a final defense for a beleaguered military justice system. As with *Levy*, Secretary Richardson insisted to the Justice Department that the appellate court's ruling be challenged. The Justice Department agreed and Bork took the case before the Court.[45]

Worried that Avrech's comments were mild in comparison to some of the literature found at the Post Exchange, Bork wanted to ensure he could differentiate between the sale of lawful newspapers and magazines and the acts of an individual. And, military libraries, Bork noted, carried Douglas' *Points of Rebellion*. Bork consulted with the Army Judge Advocate General who provided a study on court-martial statistics of accused service members charged under the Article, arguing that not one of the convictions resulted from vagueness. As a result of his research, Bork was able to conclusively argue to the Court, "millions and tens of millions of men have served under the General Article and their predecessors through every war in our history and the appellee cites not one case of injustice, a conviction for conduct that could not have been foreseen to be illegal." Bork additionally wanted to prepare to answer the inevitable question about how the military viewed Avrech's appeal in terms of importance, because even though Avrech's offenses were considered serious, the Marine Corps prosecuted him in a special court-martial. To this end, he focused his arguments on the principle of the general article, rather than Avrech's specific offense.[46]

Bork was also concerned with the appellate court's use of Wiener's article and he consulted with Wiener for advice on whether the government should appeal the ruling to begin with. Interestingly, Wiener, for his part, assured Bork that the appellate court had misused his article and assisted the Solicitor General's preparation of arguments to take before the Court. Wiener and Bork differed on the extent to which federal courts could rule on military policies. He disagreed with Bork's position that *habeas* was the only jurisdictional remedy available for testing a military conviction in the federal courts, because the Court of Claims still offered an alternative, and individuals could challenge court-martial jurisdiction based on their non-military status prior to a court-martial convening. Bork rested his view on *Augenblick*, but Wiener pointed out, "all that *Augenblick* can be fairly held to hold is that merely evidentiary issues are not jurisdictional."

Nonetheless Wiener believed that the erosion of military discipline would be accelerated if Avrech won on the constitutional issues raised against Article 134. He was especially disturbed that the courts had misused his law review article, because he never urged that Article 134 was unconstitutionally vague, but rather, it ought to be updated. "I do very much hope that you will win out on the general

45 Preparation Memoranda, undated, *Avrech* [Bork Papers/29].

46 Preparation Memoranda, undated, *Avrech* [Bork Papers/29].

articles, because it would be a hard and completely unwarranted blow at the country's armed forces if provisions of such ancient lineage were now suddenly held unconstitutional," he informed Bork.[47]

Unlike *Levy*, *Avrech* was to be a short decision, in part, because *Levy* answered several of the questions raised in *Avrech*. As a result of Rehnquist's authorship in *Levy*, Burger assigned Rehnquist to write the decision, though it is listed as *per curiam*. Both Rehnquist and Blackmun urged Burger to make the case a *per curiam* decision because they believed that it would heighten the importance of the decision. Blackmun and Rehnquist were not alone in pushing for a *per curiam* decision either. Surprisingly, Stewart independently favored this approach as well, particularly because Douglas had decided to dissent and he feared that with Douglas' dissent would come the idea that *O'Callahan* remained settled law.[48]

In conference, Rehnquist conceded that the Court could vacate the lower court and remand for reconsideration in light of *Levy* but he opposed this course of action because, "it suggests *sub silentio* that the lower court did have jurisdiction, and by our order vacating to reconsider the merits have approved the proposition that there was jurisdiction in the courts below." Instead, he argued to reverse the lower court outright without a remand. In other words, he did not want to further empower *O'Callahan*. His determination not to give further credence to *O'Callahan* could have been problematic because both Avrech's counsel and Solicitor General Bork had briefed extensively on jurisdiction as an issue. But as Avrech's substantive claim was that Article 134 was unconstitutionally vague and therefore violated the notice requirement inherent to due process, Rehnquist focused his efforts on this issue.[49]

Marshall argued inapposite of Rehnquist. Four months before Rehnquist lobbied the conference to avoid including a jurisdictional analysis in the decision, Marshall insisted that the Court do so, even though he concluded that the court-martial had jurisdiction over Avrech. As for much of Burger's tenure, the Court remained divided into two camps over *O'Callahan* and even in instances where the military clearly possessed jurisdiction to prosecute an accused, one camp insisted on creating a legacy strengthening *O'Callahan*, while the other camp, led by Rehnquist, sought to diminish *O'Callahan* by omitting it in opinions in which it was not directly pertinent to the issues raised.[50]

The resulting opinion was brief, and in relying on *Levy*, the majority dismissed Avrech's argument that Article 134 was unconstitutionally vague. The majority also took verbatim from Rehnquist's memorandum an argument that because of *Levy*, "the most zealous advocate would find his ardor somewhat dampened in arguing

47 Frederick B. Wiener to Bork, April 2, 1974 [Bork Papers/29].

48 Blackmun to Rehnquist, July 1, 1974 [HAB/183]; also Rehnquist, Memorandum to the Conference, June 28, 1974 [HAB/183].

49 Rehnquist, Memorandum to the Conference, June 19, 1974 [HAB/183]; also found in [WOD/1652].

50 Marshall, Memorandum to the Conference, February 21, 1974 [WOD/1652].

a jurisdictional issue where the decision on the merits is thus foreordained," and determined not to address jurisdiction as an issue. Rehnquist had another reason for not wanting to touch on the issue of jurisdiction. Several of the lower courts had concluded that writs of *mandamus* (a means for obtaining a hearing without the claim of a constraint of liberty) were a proper mechanism for judicial review of military decisions. The Court of Appeals for the Second Circuit, in 1971, concluded that *mandamus* presented a broad jurisdictional grant as did the Court of Appeals for the Sixth Circuit in the prior year. Rehnquist did not want to make a definitive statement on *mandamus* in *Avrech* because doing so would result in a fractured decision. Instead, he wanted to wait for one of the lower court decisions regarding whether the military could require grooming standards of its reservists to attack the increase of *mandamus* grants. Powell initially called Rehnquist's avoidance of jurisdictional analysis "nonsense," but Burger convinced him to retract a threatened concurrence.[51]

Stewart concurred with the majority in *Avrech* but he did not retract from his belief that Article 134 was void for vagueness. Instead, he conceded that because he did not "prevail," in *Levy*, he agreed that it would be wrong to require further argument of the jurisdictional issues, as well as the challenge to Article 134. Recognizing his dissent in *O'Callahan*, Stewart appeared to believe that while Congress had the constitutional authority to expand to military's jurisdiction over its servicemen to include all offenses, it was required to codify criminal conduct in a manner no different than the federal criminal law. But, unlike Douglas, he was unwilling to propound his decision into multiple dissents.

Douglas predictably dissented, and unsurprisingly much of his published dissent contained language critical of the military's justice system. His initial draft contained harsher language than the published dissent. He argued that in the First World War soldiers made far more damning statements about commanders or the purpose of the war than had Avrech, and "the doughboys of 1917" did so with no impact as to the discipline or willingness of the soldiers to fight. "We heard lurid tales about Gen. Black Jack Pershing that may have been false; but we were ready believers," Douglas claimed, "that it was a bankers' war and a munition makers' war, and at least we thought so and groused about it." Douglas added that "no one went AWOL by reason of our complaints; we shaped up when on duty." As in *Levy*, Douglas assailed the military's court-martial of Avrech as proof that it stood against the notion of an open society.[52]

Douglas added that since in World War I, just as in the Vietnam conflict, soldiers were free to write their congressmen and senators about their views on military command, there was no reason that they could not petition each other over grievances. However, in the published dissent, he omitted the words "lurid tales," and instead claimed that soldiers lambasted Pershing for being "distant,

---

51 Powell to Rehnquist, June 19, 1974 [LP/]. See, *Feliciano v. Laird*, 426 F.2d 424 (CA 2, 1971); and Schatten *v. United States*, 419 F.2d 187 (CA 6, 1969).

52 Douglas, draft dissent, July 3, 1974 [WOD 1652].

remote, and mythical." Douglas in this instance cribbed from contemporary histories which had increasingly found fault with military commanders throughout American history. He did not serve on the front lines and it is doubtful that he took part in the conduct he had claimed he undertook, given his commander's recommendation to have him attend commissioning school. Brennan and Marshall also dissented, but the two justices did not join Douglas. Both justices argued for a remand to the appellate court to determine whether the particular offenses Avrech was found to have committed violated the First Amendment right of free speech.[53]

III. *Levy*, *Avrech*, and the Legal Academy

There are hundreds of law review articles and books on free speech in the military which center on *Levy*, (and to a much lesser extent, *Avrech*), perhaps, because *Levy* was the Burger Court's most visible military law decision. Legal scholars have mainly analyzed *Levy* as a free speech, or anti-free speech, ruling within the military. For instance, David Cortright, who as a soldier, lost in his appeal to the Court of Appeals for the Second Circuit, challenging an order to transfer from New York to Texas, wrote a book in 1974 criticizing the Court for diluting free speech rights in the military and reversing the appellate courts in *Levy* and *Avrech.* Like Cortright, the majority of treatises on the decisions are critical of the Court, at least in regards to the treatises written prior to 2000. However, over time, *Levy*'s doctrine has become accepted as an important part of military discipline, and the abuses its critics feared simply have not materialized.[54]

Analyzing *Levy* to discern the intent of the justices, in light of other decisions and their correspondences is another matter. Peter Irons, a legal history scholar who earlier credibly established that in World War the Solicitor General had knowingly conflated the threat of Japanese espionage to the Supreme Court, criticized the Burger Court for sidestepping the fact that the conflict in Vietnam was an undeclared war and therefore Levy was not subject to wartime laws. This criticism is misplaced and not even Douglas viewed *Levy* in this manner because Captain Levy would have been subject to Article 133 and Article 134 regardless of whether the nation was at war. One study titled *The Burger Court: Political and*

53 For Douglas' military experience see, Military Discharge Certificate, William O. Douglas, dated December 20, 1918 [WOD/1771].

54 David Cortright, *Soldiers in Revolt: GI Resistance During the Vietnam War* (New York: Haymarket Books, 1975), 234. Cortight's analysis is questionable for several reasons. He believed that the 1946 demonstrations consisted of a public rebuke of military discipline. He also stressed that *Hagopian v. Knowlton* was a decision of great importance. For this case cite, see 436 F.Supp. 27 (DC NY 1972), aff'd 470 F.2d 201 (CA 2, 1972). This case applied to the United States Military Academy's processes for administratively separating cadets who received more demerits than permitted. Victor Rabinowtiz represented Hagopian.

Judicial Profiles concluded that *Levy* showed Blackmun's negative view towards relativism, and believed it had no place in the military, while Douglas saw the case as a referendum on Nixon and Vietnam. This is an accurate, but overly simplistic conclusion. More recently Professor Diane Mazur, posited that Rehnquist used *Levy* as "a springboard for introducing a new brand of civil-military relations under the Constitution." Far more convincingly, New York University law professor, James Jacobs in his 1986 study on civil-military relations noted that *Levy* made it clear that judicial activism under the Burger Court would no longer penetrate into military affairs. The simple fact is that Rehnquist worried, as did Blackmun, White, Powell, and Burger, that the Armed Forces were being undermined by weak discipline, and they sought to protect Congressional authority to reverse this trend. This is all the historic record evidences.[55]

Rehnquist, of course, had made it his goal to reverse *O'Callahan*, and *Levy* (and *Avrech*), evidence this aspect of his jurisprudence. When analyzed from a distance of over three decades, *Levy* and *Avrech* were only nominal step-stones to overturning *O'Callahan*. Even if *O'Callahan* were allowed to stand, at best, *Levy* and *Avrech*, the two subject-matter decisions would have buttressed the separate society principle in reminding service-members that the military's legitimate expectations of individual behavior were of a higher standard than society writ large.

One historic aspect of the two decisions which no scholar has appeared to analyze is the Court's view of the Nixon impeachment hearings in relation to *Levy* and *Avrech*. Rehnquist, a student of Civil War history, was acutely aware that throughout that war, anti-Lincoln elements in the military were problematic to the Union's war efforts, as well as undermining the hierarchal placement of the civil government above that of the military. He feared that Nixon might stoke anti-Congressional sentiment in the military's ranks, and he wanted to ensure that military leaders would be able to quash any mutiny, however small. For this reason he lobbied the conference to announce the results of Levy and Avrech "on July 8, before the argument in *United States v. Nixon*." All of the justices readily agreed to do so.[56]

---

55 Peter Irons, *Brennan v. Rehnquist: The Battle for the Constitution* (New York: Alfred A. Knopf, 1994), 158; Charles Lamb and Stephen Halpern, *The Burger Court, Political and Judicial Profiles* (Champaign, IL: Illinois, 1991), 81; Dianne Mazur, *A More Perfect Military*, 58; and, James Jacobs, *Socio-Legal Foundations of Civil Military Relations* (New Jersey: Transaction Books, 1986), 19. Surprisingly, *Parker v. Levy* is absent from Bernard Schwartz's study on the Burger Court.

56 Rehnquist to Brennan, June 24, 1974 [WJB/I:325]; Douglas to Burger, June 24, 1974 [WJB/I:325]; Blackmun to Burger, June 24, 1974; [WJB/I:325].

IV: The Judicial Response to the Kent State University Massacre and Military Surveillance of Civilians

As the conflict in Vietnam became increasingly unpopular, the Department of Defense's internal surveillance activities extended to collecting information on public persons. Problematic to these activities was the fact that a large number of officers in the intelligence community did not approve the military's role in collecting information on citizens. They hoped that Nixon, on becoming president would curtail the program, but instead the he expanded it. In 1970, and Army captain named Christopher Pye exposed the program to the press. What also emerged was that Rehnquist had advised on the program's legality.[57]

Clearly the political elites involved in the nation's founding opposed the Army operating as an executive police force or domestic spy agency, for the sound reason that the military would be used for nefarious ends to undermine freedom. When anti-war groups, the popular media, and several elected officials discovered the Executive Branch's use of the Army to collect intelligence on anti-war groups, a public uproar ensued. Not surprisingly, an upsurge in First Amendment litigation occurred. The judiciary was placed in a quandary. The military establishment had a legitimate reason for an expanded intelligence network. Not only were fears of internal subversion based on real data, the security of Army posts and personnel were heightened as ROTC offices were bombed and other threats against military installations discovered. Nonetheless, why the Federal Bureau of Investigation could not expand its operations to protect the military also remained an open question. More tellingly, mainstream media outlets alleged that military intelligence officers had collected information on politicians, including congressmen, a charge that was later substantiated. Moreover, none of the Army's domestic intelligence program was statutorily authorized. Beginning in early 1971, Senator Samuel Ervin, a conservative North Carolina Democrat who ordinarily would have been Nixon's ally in terms of "law and order" issues, conducted a congressional investigation to determine the extent of the Army's surveillance program. Ervin would prove a formidable opponent to Nixon not simply because as a conservative he had opposed civil rights legislation and taken a tough stance on crime, but also because of his authority over the Senate's premier investigative committee. Even Nixon's public promise to terminate the program would not satisfy Ervin, who ultimately would argue the unconstitutionality of the program to the Court.[58]

On the initial challenge and first appeal, the American Civil Liberties Union represented the plaintiffs. Both before the district court and the Court of Appeals for the District of Columbia, the American Civil Liberties Union's attorneys conceded that the military establishment had some authority to conduct internal surveillance activities. However, they argued that the wide ranging nature of the

57 Stanley Kutler, *The Wars of Watergate*, 119–22.

58 Joan Jensen, *Army Surveillance in America* (New Haven, CT: Yale University Press, 1991), 249–52.

intelligence program, which included placing clandestine active duty agents in war protest groups and keeping secretive records of civilians in over a dozen national records centers far exceeded any constitutionally enumerated or implied authority granted to the Executive Branch. Moreover, the civil liberties attorneys pointed out that the effect of the surveillance programs was to intimidate political discourse, a matter protected by the First Amendment.

The Justice Department counter-argued to both the district and appellate courts that the intelligence program was non-justiciable (a matter outside of the courts' jurisdiction), and failing this argument, the injury alleged was not quantifiable to the $10,000 threshold required for federal court jurisdiction. Essentially, the Justice Department's leadership concluded that it could be disastrous for the federal judiciary to look into the Army's intelligence activities for reasons outside of military governance, and tried to convince the courts not to accept jurisdiction over the issue at all. This attitude would arise in the aftermath of the September 11, 2001 attacks once more.

The government's contention did not impress a three judge panel of the Court of Appeals for the District of Columbia. In a decision authored by Malcolm Wilkey, and joined by Edgar Tamm, a former Federal Bureau of Investigations agent and Johnson appointee, the appellate court recognized that the Army had a legitimate interest in protecting itself. The judges also conceded that the Court of Appeals for the District of Columbia had only recently determined that Congressional committees, and in particular the House Un-American Activities Committee, were not required to provide investigative files to concerned citizens. Nonetheless, Wilkey and Tamm differentiated *Tatum* from its prior decision involving the Legislative Branch committee, on the basis that it was the Army conducting surveillance and maintaining records on citizens, rather than Congress. To this end, the two ordinarily conservative judges determined that the use of the Army to conduct intelligence activities against American citizens was too great of a threat to civil liberties to dismiss the appeal on the basis of a lack of jurisdiction or pronounce to be lawful.[59]

With the exception of Blackmun, the Court voted to grant *certiorari*, but the justices were divided into three camps on how to decide the issue. On one side, Rehnquist and Powell wanted to confront the First Amendment issue head on, and rule that the surveillance program was constitutional. In opposite, Douglas and Marshall were determined to argue that the Executive Branch had exceeded its constitutional authority. Brennan and Stewart also agreed with Douglas and Marshall that the surveillance program was unconstitutional, but they did so without the fiery anger displayed by Douglas. Burger, Blackmun, and White wanted to avoid the controversy altogether and determine the issues were either moot, or too distantly subjective for the Court to rule at all. In other words, Burger

59 *Laird v. Tatum*, 408 U.S. 1 (1972); *Tatum v. Laird*, 444 F.2d 947 (CA DC 1971). The case involving congressional record keeping is *Davis v. Ichord*, 412 F.2d 1207 (CA DC 1969).

leaned toward denying the petitioners' assertion that the federal judiciary had any jurisdiction over the particular issue at all.[60]

Prior to the grant of *certiorari*, the Department of Defense ordered the Army to scale back its domestic intelligence operations to internal military investigations only. Army officials also destroyed records on citizens in an attempt to win public confidence back for the military, and prove that the military was not acting lawlessly. This action had the opposite effect, and Ervin claimed the destruction of records proved that the Department of Defense intended to conceal the extent of its unlawful actions. While the destruction of records was unlikely to satisfy civil rights leaders, it provided a vehicle for the Court's conservatives to avoid deciding on the ultimate issue as to whether the Executive Branch exceeded its constitutional powers. Burger possessed a degree of legal acumen to be sure, but in authoring the majority decision, he was unnecessarily dismissive of a critical constitutional issue by finding the issue moot.[61]

To Burger, even if the issue were not moot, the question of whether the Army's domestic intelligence program "chilled" the First Amendment rights of citizens by scaring them away from public demonstration, was at best a subjective standard in which no proof of harm existed. It is true that the petitioners could not point to the loss of a job or the denial of a professional license as a result of political activities, but the central issue, and one that Burger minimized, was whether the presence of the military frightened citizens from exercising their First Amendment rights. This, to the Court's conservatives, was too attenuated for the courts, though they conceded that it was a proper matter for the legislative branch. It is true that Congress had held hearings into the Army's intelligence program, but it is equally true that the Court in the past had clearly spoken on matters involving the Constitution's limitations on governmental authority. Had the majority taken the same approach in *Youngstown*, Congress might have ended up doing nothing, or it might have impeached the president. But *Youngstown* has definitively provided to the presidency the constitutional parameters of its authority in a way that Congress could have never accomplished. Thus, Burger and the majority could have determined that the Department of Defense's requirements of maintaining a disciplined reliable force, reasonably included its domestic surveillance program, or the majority could have determined the program unconstitutional. Instead, the majority avoided making any substantive constitutional decision at all.

In conference it became apparent that while Burger was clearly influenced by the Department of Defense's termination of its surveillance program, Blackmun was not. He believed that the Army had overstepped its position, but Congress was the proper branch of government to terminate the surveillance program. "This is a terribly hard case with which to grapple," Blackmun concluded. Initially, Blackmun had not wanted to grant *certiorari* on the basis that the controversy constituted a "political question." Even his clerks were split on whether to join

60 White to Burger, June 9, 1972 [BW/221].

61 Joan Jensen, *Army Surveillance in America,* 253.

Burger or Brennan, but there was unanimity amongst his, White's and Powell's clerks that Rehnquist should have recused himself. Powell disagreed with his clerks over Rehnquist's recusal, reminding them that Justice Black had set a standard for recusal in *Jewell Ridge*,[62] a labor decision issued in 1945 in which one of the litigants was represented by Black's former law partner. Black did not recuse himself.

Like Burger, Powell believed the whole issue was mooted by the Department of Defense's discontinuing the surveillance program. But he was more adamant that any ruling on the constitutionality of the program would place the Court in the political arena. In his "tentative impression" that he wrote to himself, he penned: "It is doubtful whether a court could fashion a decree that would accommodate the admitted need of the military to collect intelligence data, and at the same time protect in a class action suit rather than a case involving specific injury to a particular individual, the First Amendment Rights of millions of people. This can best be handled by legislation." Powell then concluded that Congress had "to prescribe appropriate limits on military intelligence activities; and to police such activities in the future." On the other hand, he did not believe that the Department of Defense had overstepped its authority, because there were legitimate fears of internal subversion and even terrorism. To this end, he thought Burger's decision was "tepid," "confusing," and to his clerk, he added the word "disingenuous."[63]

In such a unique issue, it should be unsurprising that there were several unusual aspects. Senator Ervin, representing the Unitarian Universalist Association, filed an *amicus* brief to the Court and argued in a manner which apparently frightened Burger. Ervin indeed convinced Blackmun that the Army had acted egregiously. "As a practical matter, I think the Army's program probably does have a potential for great harm (at least before being cut back), and that should be justiciable," Blackmun concluded. Yet, the force of the senator's argument also caused Blackmun to reassess whether the issues before the Court were, in reality, a "political question." Burger worried that if the Court proceeded, Blackmun would side with Douglas, Marshall, Brennan, and Stewart, and the chief justice had good reason to worry about Blackmun. In conference Blackmun informed his fellow justices that he, like Douglas and Brennan, feared the growth of the military establishment's domination.[64]

In order to maintain a majority opinion without worrying about Rehnquist and Powell authoring a concurrence, and therefore creating a plurality, Burger, Blackmun, and White lobbied Rehnquist, bringing up the issue that his decision not to recuse himself would create significant complications if he were to author a concurrence. Burger went so far as to threaten to dissent from any position

---

62 Burger, Bench memorandum, undated [HAB/146]; Blackmun, Bench memorandum, March 24, 1972 [HAB/146]; Powell, Conference Notes, June 6, 1972 [LP/71-288].

63 Powell, Conference Notes, June 6, 1972 [LP/71-288].

64 Burger, Conference Memo, undated [HAB/146]; Douglas, conference notes, March 31, 1972 [WOD/1563-fol. 2].

affirming the legality of the surveillance program if Rehnquist proceeded with a concurrence. On the other hand, Burger needed Rehnquist's participation, because without him, then the lower court would have likely been upheld. In the end, the majority, with Rehnquist in agreement, concluded their opinion with a clear statement that no judicial endorsement of the program could be interpreted by the Court's decision, and that should any "military intrusion" occur, the public could have confidence that the federal courts were able to fashion a remedy. This passage did not occur in Burger's first draft, but on June 1, 1972, when he circulated his second draft he noted it gave "more pointed emphasis to the limited scope of the proposed disposition."[65]

In his dissent Douglas chastised the majority for not deciding the true issue of whether the Constitution permitted the Executive Branch the authority to use the Army to collect intelligence on citizens. He reminded his fellow justices that in *Youngstown*, the Court scolded Truman for seizing private property. He also lectured that just as the disciplined legions of Republican Rome ultimately destroyed the republic, the Department of Defense's claims of necessity of their surveillance to ensure military discipline would come at a high cost. Douglas concluded his dissent by scoffing at the Court's avoidance of the constitutional question and calling the surveillance program a cancer on the body politic. Finally, Douglas attached three appendices to his dissent. The second of the three concluded with a criticism of subordination of civil government and common sense to the military establishment. Brennan, with Stewart joining him, authored a more subdued dissent which argued that the issue was, in fact, jusitciable, not moot, and that the petitioners did have standing to sue.

In January 1973, Secretary of Defense Laird informed Congress that the program had been ended. In doing so he reminded Congress that the program originated with Attorney General Robert Kennedy. "When I became Secretary of Defense in 1969 I learned of the dimensions of the extra-curricular involvement of various elements of the Department of Defense in what has been described as snooping on civilians. I learned that virtually all of this surveillance had been initiated by former civilian authorities including the then Attorney General. I ordered action taken to terminate these practices and comprehensive testimony was presented to Congressional Committees." By this time, Nixon had to retreat from claiming necessity.[66]

Tatum bought to the fore a different issue of greater constitutional implications than *O'Callahan*. The almost contemporaneous "Pentagon Papers" fiasco heightened the public's distrust of the Army surveillance program. In that scandal,

---

65 Burger to White, undated on draft Bench Memorandum [BW/221]. Burger wrote, "Byron. I will not circulate until you give me your comments;" Burger, Bench memorandum, undated [HAB/146]; Burger, Conference Memorandum, June 1, 1972 [TM/88]; Powell, Conference Notes, June 6, 1972 [LP/71-288]; Douglas, notes, undated [WOD/1563].

66 Laird, Final Report to the Congress of the Secretary of Defense, January 1969 to January 1973 (draft) [Elliot Richardson Papers/].

in which the administration had pillaged through the private psychological records of a civilian without a court authorization, not only did the Executive Branch attempt to convince the judiciary to support an injunction against the *New York Times*, it also attempted to indict a senator's aide after the senator caused official information critical of the United States' involvement in Vietnam to be published.[67]

Certainly *Tatum* had nothing directly to do with military discipline, though one could perhaps argue that an officer or soldier who collected information on citizens was less likely to respect individual rights, and this in turn could manifest itself in the military's disciplinary functions. The main focus in this appeal, however, was to what degree the military could be used to augment the president's political power. The United States was founded on the principle that dissent was so important to democracy's survival that the use of the military to collect information on dissenters chilled the very dissent undergirding democracy. This was Douglas' point in his dissent and it was certainly the basis for Senator Ervin's argument. The decision had everything to do with whether the military's role went beyond self-protection and into frightening the citizenry from expressing opposition to government policies. Yet, the Court's conservatives and for that matter, the Nixon administration did not view the issue in this light. To them, the military was the last line of defense to hold a society together that was socially and politically falling apart because of radical influences. The conservative's beliefs on this point had earlier manifested in their response to the Kent State University shootings.[68]

On May 4, 1970, Ohio National Guardsmen fired on student demonstrators at Kent State University in Ohio, killing four students and wounding nine. The guardsmen were not on active duty orders at the time and had been directed by Governor James Rhodes to maintain order on the campus. The mayor of Kent, Ohio had already declared a state of emergency on May 1, and for a three-day period guardsmen patrolled the campus, arresting hundreds of students for violating several state laws and local ordnance prohibitions. Unlike the active duty Army, the state guard possessed the inherent authority to act as a police arm of the governor, but what occurred on May 4 was reminiscent of the use of the guard in late nineteenth-century strike-breaking operations. In response to an order to disperse, students pelted guardsmen with rocks, who in turn opened fire on the students.

Student organizations sued Governor Rhodes seeking an injunction against the further use of the Ohio National Guard to restrain student demonstrations, or in the alternative permit a judicial supervision of the guard. This was a highly unusual petition with little historic equivalent. As earlier noted, in 1930, the governor of Texas limited oil production and when small-scale oil drillers refused to comply, he declared several counties in a state of insurrection. Texas National Guardsmen seized oil wells and prohibited the production of oil. The governor refused to

---

67 See *Gravel v. United States*, 408 U.S. 606 (1972).

68 Joan M. Jensen, *Army Surveillance in America: 1775–1980* (New Haven, CT: Yale, 1991), 251–5.

comply with the United States District Court, after that court's judge ordered him to desist. In a 1931 decision authored by the conservative Chief Justice Charles Evan Hughes, the Court, in upholding the District Court, reaffirmed that the Constitution, and not the state militia, governor, or military, was the supreme law of the land.[69]

When the students' petition came before the Court of Appeals for the Sixth Circuit, in a decision captioned as *Morgan v. Rhodes*, in 1971, two of the judges relied, in part, on the 1931 decision. While the appellate court's majority was unwilling to enjoin the governor from calling out the guard in the future, it ruled that the Judicial Branch had the jurisdiction to inquire into the training of the guard. This was an unusual determination since the federal judiciary had never previously held that the courts could oversee the military, a point the dissenting judge argued. And, in *Orloff*, the Court had stated that judges "are not tasked with running the military." What should have appeared clear to the appeals court was hardly transparent to the Court. In *Orloff*, the petitioner was the injured party, and there was little doubt of his standing to sue. In *Morgan*, none of the appellants had been injured in the shootings, nor were they under the threat of violence. Thus a significant issue regarding standing was sidestepped by the appellate court.[70]

Following the Court's vote to grant *certiorari* in what became captioned as *Gilligan v. Morgan*, solely on the question as to whether the judiciary possessed the jurisdictional authority to review the National Guard's training and regulations, Burger determined to assign the decision to himself. He initially hoped to declare the issue moot, and remand the remainder of the decision to determine whether the plaintiffs had standing to sue. After all, the Ohio governor had been replaced, and none of the students in the initial suit remained at Kent State University. Moreover, the state's brief to the Court focused on the issue of mootness. Powell and Blackmun derided Burger for this approach, because the appellate decision would remain intact. This had an effect on Burger. Although he ultimately placed facts suggesting mootness into the decision, he did not declare the issue moot. Instead, he focused on the Article I provision which granted to Congress the power to organize, arm, and discipline the militia, ignoring the First or Fourteenth Amendment arguments the plaintiffs' raised. In this respect, Burger clearly wanted to settle the issue on the basis of separation of powers and the "political question doctrine," coupled with standing. On June 5, 1973, Burger penned to the conference, "I am unwilling to allow the CA 6 opinion to stand because it ignores the most elementary standards of what this Court has said—and repeated—that it takes to make a justiciable issue." White and Rehnquist agreed with Burger on issuing a decision limited to standing and the political question, and although Blackmun and Powell concurred, the two justices wanted a more direct review of the question of judicial competency to supervise the military, with the purpose of reaffirming *Orloff*.[71]

---

69 See *Sterling v. Constantin*, 287 U.S. 378 (1932).

70 *Morgan v. Rhodes*, 456 F.2d 608 (CA 6, 1972).

71 *Gilligan v. Morgan*, 413 U.S. 1 (1973); Powell to Burger, February 23, 1973

Burger's reason for not claiming the issue moot was to avoid a partial dissent from Blackmun, Powell, and White. The three justices concluded that a declaration of mootness was tantamount to timidity. White, for his part, called Burger's draft comments regarding mootness as "calculated ambiguity," a point which Burger ultimately agreed with. On the other hand, Douglas, Brennan, Stewart, and Marshall wanted the issue declared moot, in part, because this declaration would enable the appellate court's decision to remain persuasive. Initially, Marshall had determined to remand the decision to the lower court to determine the issue of mootness, but this drew a rebuke from Douglas and Stewart.[72]

Another issue arose creating a needless complexity to the decision. The Ohio Attorney General had authored a slovenly brief which failed to comport with the Court's rules. Burger determined to give the state another opportunity to supplement their brief, drawing a rebuke from the dissenters. Marshall complained, "in the first place, I do not think we should establish the policy of passing on the merits of the briefs duly filed which comply with the technicalities of our rules. Secondly, I do not think that the State of Ohio should be given a second chance to do its job." Powell too, expressed that he "would be happy to reject the Ohio brief," believing it would remind state attorneys general to "become more conscious of the generally inadequate representation on behalf of the states." In response Stewart conceded that the state filed a short, and "not very good" brief, but the Court should nonetheless consider it. Brennan sided with Stewart on this point, as did Douglas.[73]

In the end, the majority's decision addressed the Judicial Branch's inability to supervise the training of the military, because to do so would violate the separation of powers. Citing to *Flast v. Cohen*, a decision which defined standing to sue the government by creating a three part test, Burger opined that the student organizations could not meet any of the three parts. "It is difficult to conceive of an area of governmental activity in which the courts have less competence. The complex, subtle, and professional decisions as to the composition, training, equipping, and control of a military force are essentially professional military judgments, subject *always* to civilian control of the Legislative and Executive Branches," he concluded. Remarkably, it was only at the end of the decision where Burger cited to *Orloff*, a decision that should have remained front and center to *Gilligan*. The dissenters held fast to their belief that the appeal had become moot.[74]

[HAB/162]; Burger to the Conference, June 5, 1973 [HAB/162]; Burger to the conference, June 20, 1973 [HAB/162].

72 Burger to White, Blackmun, Powell, and Rehnquist, June 8, 1973 [HAB/162]; Stewart to Burger, June 14, 1973; Marshall, Memorandum to the Conference, March 20, 1973 [HAB/162]; Stewart to Marshall, March 20, 1973 [WJB/I:299]; Douglas to Marshall, March 21, 1973 [HAB/162].

73 Stewart to Burger, February 28, 1973 [WJB/I:299]; Douglas to Burger, February 28, 1973 [WJB/I:299]; Brennan to Burger, February 28, 1973 [WJB/I:299]; Marshall to Burger, March 1, 1973 [HAB/162]; Powell to Burger, February 27, 1973 [HAB/162].

74 *Flast v. Cohen*, 392 U.S. 83 (1968).

The majority's decision can be further understood when analyzed alongside of another decision, *Gravel v. United States*. That decision arose from Senator Mike Gravel's act of reading aloud portions of what had become known as "the Pentagon Papers," during a public works subcommittee hearing on June 29, 1971. At the very time Gravel read from classified papers and placed these, in their entirety, into the congressional record, Nixon administration officials attempted to quash their publication in the *New York Times*. Gravel's conduct was protected in the plain text of the Constitution in what is known as "the Speech and Debate Clause," but he went beyond Congress and arranged for the papers to be published by the Beacon Press, a commercial publishing firm in Boston. In response, the Justice Department sought indictments for "gathering and transmitting defense information" as well as the unauthorized conversion of public records against Gravel's aides who participated in the transaction. Both of these offenses were codified in the United States criminal code. The lower courts ruled that the Constitution protected only what had occurred in a committee, but not the republication of documents in a commercial press. The lower courts disagreed with the administration that a senator's aide and the senator were different entities, even when in committee. In a decision authored by White, the Court's majority found that Gravel's conduct in committee was constitutionally protected, as was that of his aide. However, the transference of government documents to a commercial printing house was not protected.[75]

Douglas dissented, but found that he had no other justice willing to join him in his argument that the Executive Branch routinely over-classified thousands of documents and "when a publisher obtained a classified document, he should be free to publish it without fear of retribution." To Douglas, without unfettered congressional oversight, immune from prosecution for divulging classified information, the Executive Branch's power would grow to lengths the nation's founders believed was untenable for the Republic's existence. Brennan dissented and he was joined by both Marshall and Douglas on the basis that the Court had too narrowly focused on the plain text of the Speech and Debate Clause. Brennan had a point, because for several decades Congress relied on commercial printing houses to publish committee hearing transcripts from hearings into organized crime and automobile safety. Stewart dissented as well, but on the basis that the majority extended their decision into areas which were not raised in the grant of *certiorari*.

Both the majority and the dissenters understood that the decision would directly impact the national defense. In conference Burger claimed that Gravel attempted to terminate the conflict in Vietnam by swaying public opinion against continued military operations instead of cutting funding for the war. To Burger, White, and Blackmun, Gravel's conduct was problematic in that that he wanted to divulge secret information with impunity. Moreover, Gravel's aide, Dr. Louis

75 *Gravel v. United States*, 408 U.S. 606 (1972). Senator Ervin also argued before the Court in this decision in a position which Douglas ultimately adopted.

Rodberg, was a physicist who belonged to the same group of scientists such as Linus Pauling who Burger despised. Neither White nor Blackmun agreed with Burger that Rodberg's affiliation, even if true, was necessary to the decision, and to place it into the decision would politicize the Court.[76]

V: Balancing the Public's Access to the Military with the Need for an Non-Political Force

After World War II Congress empowered commanders of military installations with the authority to bar individuals from access to installations. In essence, any commander may determine the conditions of trespass not only by fencing off an area, but also by individualizing barment decisions on specific people. Neither military regulations nor Congress permitted such decisions to be made on the basis of race, gender, of for reasons restricting constitutionally based access. The public's access to military installations was always believed to be within the military's authority to restrict on the basis of national security. Even Douglas would not have likely considered that the public had a right to access nuclear stockpiles or submarines. On the other hand, most military installations do not possess nuclear arsenals or engage in secret missions. Indeed, a considerable amount of military hardware such as naval vessels, armor and artillery, and aircraft had long been open to public viewing, as a means for maintaining a connection between civilian populations and the Armed Forces. The rise of public demonstrations at and near military installations against the conflict in Vietnam and the nation's nuclear arsenal brought the issue of civilian free speech and the military's need for discipline to the Court.[77]

The Court appeared to fashion a reasonable balance between the public's rights of access and military necessity in 1972, in *Flower v. United States*, a short *per curiam* decision. In late October 1969, the commanding general at Fort Sam Houston, Texas barred John Flower, a civilian, from the installation. Flower, a leader of the American Friends Service Committee intended to convince soldiers to avoid service in Vietnam. Two months after receiving the order, he entered Fort Sam Houston once more, but was arrested for trespassing, convicted, and sentenced to six months' imprisonment. He unsuccessfully appealed to the Court of Appeals for the Fifth Circuit. The appellate court relied on a 1966 decision involving the government's authority to restrict speech on its property.

In 1966, Black, authored a decision upholding a prohibition against prison demonstrations, and the Fifth Circuit likened the military installation, a base

76 Blackmun, conference notes [HAB/147].

77 Congress' authorization is found in 18 U.S.C. sec 1382. The Court of Appeals for the Fourth Circuit held, in 1973 that when a military installation is generally open to the public, a commander does not have the authority to prohibit "leafleting." See *Burnett v. Tolson*, 475 F.2d 877 (CA 4, 1973).

dedicated to military training, to a prison rather than an open public square. The Fifth Circuit judges also pointed out that in 1960, Blackmun, while on the Court of Appeals for the Eighth Circuit, had authored *Holdridge v. United States*, a decision similar to the challenge Flower raised.[78]

In *Holdridge*, three young men, one of whom was a Quaker seminary student and another the son of a Methodist minister, trespassed onto an Air Force ordnance depot in Nebraska, to issue leaflets protesting nuclear weapons. None of the three men were violent, but after being ordered to leave the depot, the three men refused, and were arrested and convicted of trespassing. On appeal, the men argued that public roads had traversed the ordnance depot leaving it open and available for public use, even though the federal government condemned the area. The appellants' arguments were not as specious as might be initially thought, because in a series of decisions unrelated to national security or the military, the federal courts had held that a federal condemnation of land did not necessarily prohibit public entry. However, in this case, the government had not only condemned the roads, but also claimed exclusive ownership over it. Blackmun, in writing for the three judge majority, pointed this out though he had to do some of his own research in order to conclude the decision.[79]

The United States Attorney had largely neglected these facts in both the trial court and on appeal, a matter that Blackmun believed evidenced the prosecutor's laziness. On his own, Blackmun wrote to the Register of Plats in Saint Louis to gain information on the property's historic boundaries, and the specific features of the condemnation. When Blackmun presented his draft opinion to Judges John Brown and Marion Matthes, he assured them that one of his primary motives in avoiding commentary on the intent of the three men in their trespass was to ensure the decision was "immune" from a grant of *certiorari*.[80]

Another informative point was in his correspondence with Burger on the decision. Blackmun forwarded his opinion to Burger, calling it "feeble," yet at the same time lauding *Pauling v. McElroy*, a decision that despite being published *per curiam*, he assumed Burger was the author. Burger responded that he had not authored the decision, but labeled Pauling and Bertrand Russell both fools. "I'm fed up with letting crackpots use the courts to propagandize their 'ban the bomb

---

78 *Flower v. United States*, 452 F.2d 80 (CA 5, 1972), reversed, 407 U.S. 97 (1972). James Plemon Coleman, a former Mississippi Governor authored the majority opinion and was joined by Paul Hitch Roney. John Milton Bryan Simpson dissented. The 1966 decision is *Adderley v. Florida*, 385 U.S. 39 (1966).

79 *Holdridge United States,* 282 F.2d 302 (CA 8, 1960).

80 Blackmun to Robert Tucker, May 23, 1960 [HAB/26]; Blackmun to Robert Tucker, August 1, 1960 [HAB/26]; Blackmun to Robert Tucker, August 5, 1960 [HAB/26]; Blackmun to Snaborn and Matthes, August 17, 1960 [HAB/26].

and rely on Russia' doctrine. Happily the public is too bright to take these boys seriously," Burger concluded.[81]

The Court summarily reversed the Fifth Circuit in *Flower*, without granting argument, and emphasizing that the area which Flower entered was not controlled by the military in the sense that no gates or sentry personnel prevented the general public from entering. Moreover, over 17,000 private vehicles per day drove on the street that Flower intended to demonstrate on, and many of the vehicles' occupants had no connection to the military. Under these circumstances, the Court determined that a commander had no authority to order a citizen to desist from passing out leaflets. In other words, had the area been cordoned, or used for training, the commander might have possessed the authority to issue an order. This decision was unsatisfactory to Burger, Rehnquist, and Blackmun who disagreed at the Court arriving at a decision without granting oral argument.

Four years after *Flower*, the Court reached a different result in *Greer v. Spock*, a decision originating at Fort Dix, New Jersey. Most of the Fort Dix military installation was unrestricted to civilian visitors, and the installation's commanders had permitted public speakers to discuss religion, alcoholism, drug abuse, and business management. Civilian bands and acting troupes performed on the base as well. The commanding general had, however, prohibited political activities of any type, and the rule had been rigidly enforced. In 1972, Benjamin Spock, Julius Hobson, and other candidates of a "third party," organization known as "The Peoples' Party," applied for entry onto the post to distribute literature, but the installation commander denied their request.

Spock and Hobson unsuccessfully appealed to the United States District Court for the District of New Jersey to enjoin the commander from preventing their campaigning and distributing literature on-post. The government argued that the prohibition against political activity was rooted in the need for an apolitical military which is subordinate to the civil government, both in fact and in appearance. Judge Clarkson S. Fisher, a World War II veteran and Nixon appointee, found the prohibition reasonable and distinguished the suit from *Flower*, which did not involve a political campaign. The Court of Appeals for the Second Circuit reversed and remanded the case to Fisher for greater specificity on the First Amendment implications to the base's policy. This time Fisher issued a permanent injunction against the commander from prohibiting Spock and Hobson from campaigning.[82]

In conference, Burger assigned Stewart to write for the majority, but then authored his own concurrence. Stewart recognized that the Army regulations permitted some political activity but left it to the installation commander's discretion to prohibit political activity designed to undermine discipline or foment disloyalty. Political speeches and demonstrations of all types were prohibited at

81 Blackmun to Burger, September 6, 1960 [HAB/26]; Burger to Blackmun, September 8, 1960 [HAB/26].

82 *Spock v. David*, 349 F.Supp, 179 (DC NJ 1972); *Spock v. David*, 505 F.2d 953 (CA 2, 1974); *Greer v. Spock*, 424 U.S. 828 (1976).

Fort Dix. Stewart distinguished *Flower*, which arose from an installation that permitted the public unfettered access, to the limitations at Fort Dix. Moreover, Stewart made clear that *Flower* could not be read expansively as creating a new principle of constitutional law, and found it reasonable to enable commanders to decide whether a pamphlet posed a danger to loyalty or discipline. Blackmun was not as sure as Stewart as to *Flower's* inapplicability to Fort Dix. "My normal and inherent reaction is in favor of the Government. I feel this way because I think an army must be trained to fight and the military command should have control over what is essentially a military enclave," Blackmun began. Indeed, Blackmun wanted to overturn *Flower*, rather than distinguish *Spock* from it but he was alone in wanting to overturn *Flower*.[83]

Burger concurred for no other reason to espouse a history lesson. He claimed that for over two centuries, the nation had intentionally kept the military from the political process in order to ensure the military's subordination to the civil government. He reminded the Court that the election of 1864, during the height of the Civil War, was conducted in such a manner as to bring the result of military ballots in doubt. Burger's concurrence might have been derided at the time, but no less than President Kennedy had this same concern with the Army prior to appointing White to the Court. Powell concurred as well, stressing that the issues involved were directly related to *Levy*, in that the military, as a separate society, had to have the ability to reasonably curtail some speech.

Brennan and Marshall dissented, urging that there were minor differences between the facts in *Flower* and Spock's activities, and the Court's decision undermined the very principle of a non-political military, it claimed to be protecting. Marshall separately dissented as well, coupling *Middendorf v. Henry*—a decision finding that the right to counsel did not extend to summary courts-martial—to *Spock* in concluding that the Court enabled the military to deny fundamental constitutional rights whenever military leaders believed that the military's functions would be enhanced by the denial. Brennan did not join Marshall, however, in a dissent that mirrored Douglas' past stridency, in part, because he believed this type of language in a decision would result in a lost position over a long-term.[84]

In 1985, the Court visited the issue of access to military installations once more in *United States v. Albertini*. In 1972, James Vincent Albertini gained access

83 Blackmun, conference notes, November 7, 1975 [HAB/216]. Blackmun also took issue with the government's refusal to distinguish areas of military importance such as training grounds, from the common use areas of an installation. "Clearly the public may be totally excluded, and therefore political campaigners and their camp followers may be excluded from restricted areas in which purely military functions are performed," he wrote, before discussing a "twilight zone for other areas" such as residential sections and public roads.

84 Marshall to Brennan, February 4, 1976 [TM/163]; Brennan to Marshall, January 7, 1976 [TM/163].

to Hickam Air Force Base and destroyed documents classified as secret and top secret, by pouring animal blood over them. In addition to being convicted in federal court, the commander issued Albertini a barment order prohibiting him from entering onto the installation. In 1981, Albertini accessed Hickam Air Force Base once more and was arrested, though this time it was during an event open to the public. He and several companions posed in front of a B-52 Bomber with a sign which read "carnival of death." In reality, Albertini's act fell somewhere in between *Flower* and *Greer*, because as in the case of *Flower*, Hickam Air Force Base was open to the public; and similar to the facts in *Greer*, Albertini had lawfully been placed on notice that he was, in effect, trespassing if he entered onto the installation.

In conference Burger claimed he wanted to avoid a discussion over whether the 1972 barment order was stale nine years after its issuance. Brennan scoffed at Burger's position, pointing out that Albertini had accessed the base with permission in 1976 to teach a literacy class. Blackmun retorted that Albertini was barred from several military installations in 1981 after being caught and prosecuted for defacing government property, and, moreover, the Hawaiian installations, as a matter of reciprocity, honored all barment issuances, regardless of which installation the barment originated from. To Blackmun, Albertini's conduct on base was what mattered, and clearly Albertini had come onto base with the purpose of making a political statement. White sought a middle ground to remand the case to the lower court to determine whether the original order was valid. Rehnquist and Powell wanted the Court to reverse the Court of Appeals for the Ninth Circuit's decision reversing the conviction. White's "middle ground" ultimately prevailed, though not in the exact form he lobbied.[85]

The Court, in a decision authored by O'Connor, found that the use of the base as an open ground for the public did not undermine the statutory authority of the installation commander to prohibit a specific individual from entering the installation. Stevens, Brennan, and Marshall dissented, arguing that *Flower*, rather than *Greer* governed, as well as the fact that nine years had elapsed between the original barment order and the second trespass. As a result of the decision, Albertini's First Amendment rights were limited because of his earlier conduct, but both *Flower* and *Spock* remained sound parameters governing public access to the military.[86]

Brennan's hopes for a reversal of *Spock* and *Albertini* have never materialized, in part, because the curtailment of political activity is essential to military governance. For instance, during the repeal of the Don't Ask Don't Tell policy, religious and political organizations wanted to conduct their own studies on the repeal's impact, and in the process likely undermine the repeal. That these groups were prohibited from doing so enabled the repeal to occur without significant difficulty. More recently, Army officials determined that singer-entertainer Ted

85 Blackmun, Conference Notes, April 17, 1985 [HAB/421].

86 *United States v. Albertini* 472 U.S. 675 (1985).

Nugent, who publicly disparaged President Barack Obama at a National Rifle Association event, could not perform in a planned concert at an installation, because of the likelihood that Nugent's appearance would undermine military discipline. Perhaps Burger and Rehnquist could not have foreseen that the Court's decisions would apply to people who possessed similar political views to theirs, but it must be more likely the case, that they intended to permit the military to shield its personnel from undermining influences across the spectrum.

VI: Regulating the Political Activity of Service Members: Jurisdictional Parameters and Limitations on Service-Members

In 1971 in *Schlanger v. Seamans*, the Court held that the District Court for Arizona did not possess jurisdiction over the Air Force to determine whether its actions in reassigning a non-commissioned officer from Arizona State University to Moody Air Force Base, Georgia. The non-commissioned officer had participated in anti-war protest activities contrary to regulations in Arizona, but his supervisors and records were stationed at Wright Patterson Air Force Base, Ohio, and his commander at Moody Air Force Base, Georgia. The Court did not rule on the merits of the Air Force's actions, but instead determined that statutorily the courts in Ohio and Georgia possessed jurisdiction, because absent incarceration, the location of a custodian of personal records, rather than that of a service-member dictated which district court had jurisdiction.[87]

Douglas authored the majority opinion, and only Stewart dissented but did not explain his reasons for doing so. Blackmun in his notes and in conference called the issue "a nuisance case, however, there is obviously a feeling that the military is basically unfair in all respects" and in conference went on to deride the petitioner, Herbert Schlanger, accusing him of "playing games." Despite Blackmun's belief that the Court would side with Schlanger, it did not, in part echoing his argument that had Schlanger prevailed, it "would open up many possibilities of disruption of the military command and mission."[88]

The Court modified *Schlanger* somewhat the following year in *Strait v. Laird.* This decision arose from a reserve officer, Joseph Strait, who had resided in California while attending law school and had passed the state bar examination. Strait applied for conscientious objector status at Fort Ord in California and officials at the base recommended its approval. However, as Strait's records were housed at Fort Benjamin Harrison, Indiana, Army officials appealed the Fort Ord recommendation to senior officers at Fort Benjamin Harrison, which in turn disapproved the conscientious objector application. Strait filed a *habeas* petition in California, but the Court of Appeals for the Ninth Circuit, relying on *Schlanger* dismissed the appeal on jurisdictional grounds. Because Strait had no connection

87 *Schlanger v. Seamans*, 401 U.S. 487 (1971).

88 Blackmun, Case Notes, February 19, 1971 [HAB/131].

to Indiana, other than the Army housing his records in that state, the Court held that the federal courts in California had jurisdiction over his *habeas* petition. Again, the Court did not rule on the merits of the petition, but it differentiated Strait's case from Schlanger's in that Schlanger was already on active duty and had not permanently domiciled in Arizona.[89]

Rehnquist, Burger, Brennan, and Powell dissented, arguing that *Strait* undermined *Schlanger.* However Rehnquist also dissented on another basis, arguing that since currently serving service members do not possess a statutory right to conscientious objection, the scope of *habeas* review was significantly narrowed. In this respect Rehnquist considered *Burns* and *Orloff* to be dispositive in keeping the federal courts out of conscientious objector claims from currently serving service members not facing court-martial. Likewise, Powell concurred with Rehnquist's position. "Subject to discussion at the Conference, I think the judgment below should be affirmed. The *habeas corpus* statute already has been stretched very considerably to embrace military people within the concept of 'custody'. I would leave this matter to Congress, if the statute needs to be enlarged," he recorded in his "tentative view." Blackmun's observations of Rehnquist's position were highly critical. "In addition to the fact that, insofar as appears, no federal judge has ever endorsed the theory put forth by Justice Rehnquist, there are some very serious holes in his position, logically, constitutionally, or otherwise."[90]

In 1976, the Court issued *Department of the Air Force v. Rose*, a decision that could be placed in a section on government transparency—it arose from a denial of information pursuant to a Freedom of Information Act request—as easily as it could be placed in a section on free speech or political activity. Analysis of the Court's internal deliberations, however, reasonably places the decision into the category of political activity. Lieutenant Michael T. Rose, a commissioned Air Force Academy graduate attending law school, filed a request for the disciplinary records of academy cadets. The academy had an internal system of administrative hearings to determine whether cadets had violated the internal honor and ethics code, and published summaries of the hearings' boards' findings and penalties. Rose, a student at New York University's law school attending on an Air Force program was in the process of writing a book on the military academies' disciplinary systems and the constitutional infirmities in each. It was clear that Rose wanted to publish a book to effectuate a change in the service academies' policies of internal discipline. It is also clear that Congress enacted the Freedom of Information Act to maximize government transparency.[91]

---

89 *Strait v. Laird*, 406 U.S. 341 (1972).

90 Powell, "My tentative view" March 22, 1972 [LP/71-83]: Blackmun, Bench Memorandum, April 25, 1972 [HAB/145]; Powell did not fully explain his reasons to Rehnquist for not joining fully in the dissent, writing only, "As I concur in Part I of your dissenting opinion, and think it dispositive of the case as I view it, I do not reach a consideration of the issues in parts II and III of your opinion." April 29, 1972, [LP/71-83].

91 *Department of the Air Force v. Rose*, 425 U.S. 352 (1976).

Nonetheless, Congress created various exemptions from mandatory disclosure of information, including "personnel and medical files and similar files, the disclosure of which would constitute a clearly unwarranted invasion of personal privacy." The Air Force Academy and ultimately the Secretary of the Air Force relied on this exemption, as well as an exemption for internal agency rules, but Rose had only sought summaries of disciplinary hearings where the names of disciplined cadets and witnesses were deleted. The academy had routinely posted similar summaries, but, Air Force personnel claimed that enough information existed on the summaries to constitute an invasion of privacy. The Air Force prevailed in the District Court for the District of New York, but not the Court of Appeals for the Second Circuit. That court ordered the Air Force to supply the sought-after summaries to the district court for an *in camera* (private) review by the district court judge. The Court, in a decision authored by Brennan adopted the reasoning of the lower appellate court, and did not hint that unique features to military governance were questioned in their decision.

In conference, Douglas, who ultimately did not participate in the decision, argued that Rose's request could be another step to maximizing the military's accountability to the public. Brennan likewise felt that upholding the Second Circuit would achieve this end, but according to Blackmun, Brennan also believed the judiciary should encourage the very type of quasi-political activity that Rose engaged in. Marshall and Stewart were instrumental in convincing Brennan to issue a decision which blandly adhered to a Freedom of Information Act analysis, however, and much of the language Brennan and Douglas would have wanted in the decision disappeared. Powell too, was willing to join the majority insofar as the release of information occurred at the behest of the district court following an *in camera* review.

Burger, however, was incensed with Brennan's conclusions, and believed Brennan and the majority undermined the military's ability to self-govern. He went so far as to accuse Brennan of trying to diminish *Levy* and contribute to a further erosion of military discipline. Blackmun's draft dissent, more forceful than his published dissent, was prefaced with an accusation against Rose. "There is something mildly distasteful for me, and unseemly, when the beneficiary of a system attacks it after he has reaped its substantial benefits and enjoyed an undergraduate education at great publish expense," Blackmun began his draft. Contained within the draft also is an accusation that Rose sought to effectuate a public demand for a change in the academies' honor codes by publishing his book. In Blackmun's personal analysis he penned that Rose "had wangled his way into law school at NYU and, of course, made a pretty fair nuisance of himself." He also accused Rose of "stirring up trouble for destructive purposes," and trying to make the Air Force officer corps less accountable to traditional military standards. Most tellingly, he compared Rose's book with Douglas' inflammatory *Points of Rebellion*. Echoing his concurrence in *Levy*, Blackmun concluded, "our military forces require discipline, and they require complete interdependence among those who make up, particularly the officer corps."[92]

Rehnquist's dissent is bland in comparison to Burger's and Blackmun's. The importance in Rehnquist's conduct in this decision was that he convinced Blackmun to remove his accusation against Rose in Blackmun's published dissent. Indeed, Blackmun wanted to place into his dissent that if Rose prevailed, the honor codes were "headed for destruction," and that the abandonment of rigorous standards would degrade the military to its lowest levels of reliability. Rehnquist did not believe the majority's decision constituted as great a danger as Blackmun espoused, but he dissented because he believed the academy cadets had to have some degree of autonomy for developing their leadership qualities. In retrospect, Blackmun was wrong about Rose being a William O. Douglas adherent. Elected to the South Carolina state legislature as a conservative Republican, he also retired honorably from the Air Force reserves.[93]

While there is nothing in either Blackmun's or Rehnquist's papers to that suggest either justice read Rose's book, *A Prayer for Relief: The Constitutional Infirmities of the Military Academies Conduct, Honor and Ethics Systems*, a review of the text does not show any controversial attack on the military. Instead, Rose presented an academic study on where the various student boards and administrative hearings do not favorably compare to civilian administrative hearings, and suggests improvements to do so. At worst, he posited that if "the *O'Callahan* rationale is given its full sweep and applied to administrative as well as criminal proceedings in the military academy, officials lack jurisdiction to punish cadets for offenses which are not service connected." But, Rose did not advocate for the termination of administrative boards, nor did he claim the military's leadership at the academies intentionally trammeled on the Constitutional rights of cadets.[94]

Limiting political activity of any sort on a military installation is certainly sound if the intended reason is to enforce an apolitical military. But, service-members do not abandon their political ideologies simply because they don a uniform and become subject to the UCMJ. From the nineteenth-century experience when two serving generals sought the presidency and campaigned in uniform, through Douglas MacArthur's attempt to gain the Republican nomination, the military establishment issued various regulations prohibiting its members from seeking political office while in uniform, or even appearing at political events in uniform. Indeed, in 1939, Congress passed the "Hatch Act" which prohibited all civil servants from engaging in partisan activity, and although the act itself does not

92 Blackmun, Analysis, September 9, 1975 [HAB/214].

93 Blackmun, conference notes, October 10, 1975 [HAB/214].

94 Michael T. Rose: *A Prayer for Relief: The Constitutional Infirmities of the Military Academies' Conduct, Honor, and Ethics Systems* (New York: New York University Press, 1973).

solely apply to uniformed service members, the Department of Defense issued regulations mirroring the act in the 1950s.[95]

One of the rights of every citizen, including service members, is to petition Congress to address a grievance against the government. Thus, a soldier may write to his or her congressman about the quality of food, or protective body armor in a deployed combat zone, protest an environment that promotes sexism, or the promotion of a general officer who committed undocumented misconduct earlier in his career. In 1951, Congress enacted a statute that prohibited the military establishment from restricting an individual service-member's right to communicate with Congress. This occurred in response to a naval regulation which prohibited individual communications to Congress without command approval.

In 1971, the Secretary of the Air Force issued regulations prohibiting its personnel from soliciting signatures to send a petition to Congress, without first seeking a commander's approval. Under the Air Force regulation, commanders possessed the authority to deny airmen the ability solicit other airmen to join in a group petition, if the commander believed that it would "be a clear danger to the loyalty, discipline, or morale of members of the Air Force." The regulation's language was reminiscent of Judge Learned Hand's expansion of the clear and present danger test earlier noted in *Dennis*, and it reflected the Department of Defense's concern of CPUSA infiltration into the military.

A captain named Albert Glines determined to test the regulation and drafted several petitions to the Secretary of Defense and members of Congress complaining about the military's grooming standards. After Glines solicited a non-commissioned officer to obtain further signatures, his commander determined that he had violated the regulation and therefore failed to meet the standards expected of officers. As a result, the Air Force transferred Glines to the standby reserves. In turn, Glines brought suit against the Air Force, claiming that the regulations violated his First Amendment right of free speech. Both the District Court for the Northern District of California and the Court of Appeals for the Ninth Circuit agreed with Glines. After all, Glines' conduct was nowhere near to being similar to Captain Howard Levy's or Private Mark Avrech's. Instead of sowing dissension, Glines simply wanted to lobby Congress to permit service members to grow their hair longer than the military permitted, and the restriction on communications with Congress, at least to the appellate court, was overbroad.

Relying on *Orloff*, *Spock*, and *Levy*, the Court reversed the lower courts and determined that the regulation governing petitions was not overbroad. In a decision authored by Powell, the Court's majority found that commanders were prohibited from restricting the distribution of publications and mails, but could reasonably decide that a petition could result in the undermining of discipline. Nothing prevented hundreds of airmen from independently writing to their congressmen, and the regulations required a commander to justify to his or her superiors why a prohibition order occurred in the first place. In this context, *Glines*

95 *Brown v. Glines*, 444 U.S. 248 (1980).

represents deference to the military's necessity of maintaining discipline, but not unreasonably so.

Not surprisingly, Burger, White, Blackmun, and Rehnquist joined with Powell. Brennan, Stewart, and Stevens dissented, albeit for somewhat different reasons. In his dissent, Brennan argued that the regulations violated the First Amendment in three ways. The requirement for command approval constituted a "prior restraint" on speech that would dissuade airmen from petitioning Congress at all. The regulatory scheme also enabled censorship of speech. And, finally in Brennan's opinion, the regulations could not be said to truly further a military interest, unlike in *Spock*. In conference, Stewart argued that the restriction could "pass muster," but only if Congress legislated it. Thus, he believed that the regulation was an encroachment into legislative authority under the separation of powers doctrine. Stevens agreed with Stewart on this point as well, but added that the regulation had a "veneer" of an unnecessary restraint on otherwise free speech. Although Marshall did not take part in the decision, he agreed with Stewart's and Brennan's dissent.[96]

In conference, Burger had argued that the regulation did not restrict channels of communication with Congress, but Powell and Blackmun found this argument "silly," pointing out that it made it more difficult for a group of airmen to petition Congress because each of them would have to do so singly, and officers were not likely going to be permitted to hold a meeting urging enlisted personnel to take up a cause without running afoul of some other rule. White called it "not much of a case," and Rehnquist indicated that he "could see both sides." Nonetheless, what the decision truly enabled is the authority of the Department of Defense from a superior officer forcing or coercing subordinates to sign petitions.[97]

In *Secretary of the Navy v. Huff*, the Court determined that the Department of the Navy could require sailors and marines to seek command permission before circulating petitions designed to be presented to members of Congress. Two enlisted marines sought permission to circulate petitions regarding the use of service-members in Japanese labor disputes, support for granting amnesty for deserters and draft resisters who refused to serve in Vietnam, and United States support for South Korea. Both marines also wanted to distribute a leaflet containing the language of the Declaration of Independence and First Amendment, along with a criticism of the policy requiring command permission. The critical language stated "we hold these truths to be self-evident, (but do the brass?)" Not surprisingly, the men were denied permission to distribute most of their requested petitions and the leaflet. One of the marines, Frank L. Huff, decided to violate his commander's order and was court-martialed, sentenced to confinement, and reduced in grade. Like Avrech, his sentence was not severe enough for mandatory appellate review in the military appellate courts. The other marine, Robert A. Falatine did not face

96 Blackmun, conference notes, November 9, 1979 [HAB/303]; Bill Murphy to Blackmun, December 19, 1979 [HAB/120].

97 Blackmun, conference notes, November 9, 1979 [HAB/303]; Marshall to Powell, January 17, 1980 [TM/248].

a court-martial. Both men brought suit in the United States in the hopes that a federal judge would order the enforcement of the regulation to cease. Huff did not challenge his court-martial before the district court, though it may be assumed that had the court found the regulation an unconstitutional restraint against free speech, he would have had a sound basis for challenging his conviction.[98]

The District Court for the District of Columbia found that the regulation pertaining to the on-base distribution of literature was unconstitutional. However, the court found the prohibition regarding off-base distribution withstood the heightened scrutiny of the First Amendment, because of the existence of an agreement between Japan and the United States prohibiting political activities by service-members. The Court of Appeals for the District of Columbia essentially upheld the district court, also finding that the requirement to seek permission to circulate petitions to Congress violated a statute barring the military from restraining individuals access to their legislators. The Court, in a decision authored by Powell, issued *Huff* on the same day as *Glines*, and it was a short *per curiam* decision. Stewart and Stevens dissented for the same reason as in *Glines*. Again, Marshall did not take part in the decision at all. Brennan intended to publish a separate dissent, but did not get around to doing so. However, it was, in all likelihood, to be a recitation of his dissent in *Glines*.[99]

VII: Conclusion

Decisions impacting the intersection of military discipline, the First Amendment, and the military establishment's attempt to assure an apolitical military, do not evidence a judiciary blindly deferring to the military establishment. Rather, the Court, during Burger's tenure, succeeded in preserving the constitutional rights of service-members to a broad extent, while enabling the basic requirements for a disciplined military, as well as a basis for public confidence in an apolitical, civilian controlled the military establishment. The Court particularly maintained the Legislative Branch's primacy in the governance of the military. In the aftermath of *O'Callahan*, with the military suffering degradation in discipline and confronting an aggressive Soviet foreign and military policy, the Court did not readily adopt all, or even the majority of the government's arguments to defer to the disciplinary requirements of the military.

---

98 *Secretary of the Navy v. Huff*, 444 U.S. 453 (1980).

99 *Huff v. Secretary of the Navy*, 413 F.Supp 1976 (DC DC 1976); Brennan to Powell, December 20, 1979 [BW/465].

Chapter 5
Judicial Supervision of the Military in the Era of Equal Protection

Perhaps surprisingly, the Warren Court never addressed discrimination based on race or national origin within the Department of Defense. Certainly, the Warren Court justices believed that racism had infected particular courts-martial, and undoubtedly, the justices were not so naïve to believe that racial equality reached all corners of the military before 1969. Arguably, prior to Burger's ascension to the chief justiceship, the only time the Court entertained racial discrimination in the military, was in its selective service jurisprudence. So, it might appear odd that it was not until his tenure that discrimination in the context of actual military service was first analyzed, and even then, the first discrimination decision involved gender based discrimination rather than race. The Court generally undertook a progressive approach to gender discrimination in the military establishment but the justices were not willing to open the courts to service-members seeking monetary relief in other matters. This was particularly true where male service-members claimed that the military's affirmative action policies denied them the same chances of success as female service-members. Additionally, the Court would continue to expand *Feres* to its maximum extent, even where the military establishment had clearly mistreated its uniformed personnel.

I: Gender, Race, Religion, and Discrimination in the Military

In 1967, President Johnson signed Public Law 90-130, "to remove restrictions on the careers of female officers [in the armed services]." While signing the legislation, Johnson stated that the law should be seen as a precursor to the day when the chief of staff of one of the services or the Chairman of the Joint Chiefs of Staff would be a female. Not all of the armed forces' leadership embraced the idea of women serving in the highest military positions, and nothing was stated on opening up combat positions to women. But, Johnson might have had a better understanding of modern warfare than his conservative opponents, particularly in conducting electronic and intelligence operations from afar.[1]

---

1 Jeanne Holm, *Women in the Military: An Unfinished Revolution* (Novato, CA: Presidio Press, 1982), 192–3. General Holm, in 1982, was the highest ranking, albeit retired, female officer in the Armed Forces of the United States.

There were visible racial inequities in the military. For instance, even as late as 1985, almost a quarter of the Army was composed of African American soldiers, but only eight percent of all officers were African American. At the same time, African Americans composed less than one percent of naval flag officers, and less than three percent of all naval officers. These numbers reflected the effects of past discrimination, but the Department of Defense had made efforts to make promotion boards color-blind. The status of women in the military establishment was a different matter, and the judiciary's approach to discrimination can only be analyzed in its equal treatment jurisprudence.[2]

The Burger Court's uneven approach to affirmative action in the 1970s is evidenced through a number of non-military decisions, beginning with *Griggs*, through *Bakke v. Regents of the University of California,* where, in 1978, the Court, in a plurality decision held that racial preferences for minority graduate school applicants could be sustained if the preferences were one factor among several in the admissions process. Moreover, if the reason for the racial preference was "rationally based," such as a desire to promote diversity, the Court would be likely to sustain a race-based preference. Thus, under some instances, if the government could articulate a rational basis for a discriminatory policy, the courts would sustain the policy. For the most part, the Court's military law jurisprudence on discrimination mirrored its broader discrimination rulings.[3]

In 1973, the Court confronted discrimination against active duty married women and issued a decision adverse to the Department of Defense in *Frontiero v. Richardson.* Prior to *Frontiero*, Congress left to the military departments a discretionary allocation of monies for housing and other benefits as well as cost of living determinations. Thus, the Department of Defense could determine that service members stationed in New York City were entitled to a higher housing allowance than service members stationed in the less expensive city of Montgomery Alabama. Congress also exempted the military from Title VII as well as the Equal Pay Act.[4]

With Congress' tacit approval, the Department of Defense established a scheme which denied many married women the same medical and housing benefits that married men received. In order for a married active duty woman to receive additional benefits, she would have to prove that her husband was reliant on her income and indeed had an income of no more than half of hers. No such burden of proof was placed on married male service members. The Department of Defense's theory behind the difference was that because the preponderance of the active duty military consisted of males, the acceptance of all wives as dependants saved the costs of administrative investigations, and to the extent that married active duty males received an unplanned windfall, this was acceptable.

2 James Coates and Michael Kilian, *Heavy Losses: The Dangerous Decline of American Defense*, 182.

3 *Bakke v. Regents of the University of California*, 438 U.S. 265 (1978).

4 Melvin Urofsky, *A March of Liberty, Vol. II*, 897–9.

As a result, a lieutenant named Shannon Frontiero and her civilian husband were placed at a significant economic disadvantage to her fellow male officers. In reality, the Department of Defense's denial of benefits to married women which were routinely provided to married men could not have been classified as anything but baseless discrimination. In a decision authored by Brennan, the Court held that such discrimination could not withstand scrutiny, but it would not issue a clear decision on where gender discrimination was permissible, though the Court certainly left open the possibility to some level of gender discrimination.[5]

Brennan found the government's argument of "administrative convenience" appalling and Douglas was disgusted at the discrimination, writing to Brennan, "for the purpose of employment I think the discrimination is as invidious and purposeful as that directed against Blacks and Aliens. I always thought our 1874 decision which gave rise to the 19th Amendment was invidious discrimination against women which should have been invalidated under the Equal Protection Clause." The decision Douglas referenced, *Bradwell v. Illinois*, upheld Illinois' exclusion of women from admission to the practice of law.[6]

Brennan's first draft avoided analyzing the appeal under a "strict scrutiny" standard. The "strict scrutiny" standard had become applicable to race and national origin discrimination and required the government to both prove that it had a compelling governmental interest, and that the statute or policy drafted to ensure the interest was narrowly tailored as the least restrictive means to accomplish the ends. In other words, the interest had to be crucial to the government, and the means to accomplish the interest had to have the smallest discriminatory impact. Very few government programs which discriminate, either by design or effect, will meet this test, and clearly the government's argument in *Frontiero* failed as well. Brennan's first draft incorporated the language of "rational basis," a lower standard of review than "strict scrutiny," though the Court still found the military's separate treatment of women unconstitutional.

Essentially, the lower "rational basis" standard would have enabled the military to discriminate based on gender across a broad spectrum of duties, including the combat readiness considerations of males working in nuclear missile launch facilities. This lesser standard was intolerable for White, who essentially wanted stronger language mirroring the language of the Equal Rights Amendment, and Douglas who echoed White's position. Stewart replied to White, Douglas, and Brennan that he saw "no need to decide whether sex is a suspect criterion," and instead urged a finding that the statute was "invidiously discriminatory."[7]

---

5 *Frontiero v. Richardson*, 411 U.S. 677 (1973). A superb analysis of this decision is found in Bernard Schwartz, *The Ascent of Pragmatism: The Burger Court in Action*, 220–26.

6 Douglas to Brennan and Powell, March 3, 1973 [TM/109]; *Bradwell v. Illinois*, 83 U.S. 130 (1872).

7 Brennan, conference memorandum, February 14, 1973 [TM/109] Brennan wrote, "I have structured this opinion along lines which reflect what I understood was out agreement at conference. That is, without reaching the question whether sex constitutes

Brennan's second draft incorporated the higher "strict scrutiny" language, but this led to a plurality decision, in which Douglas, White, and Marshall joined with Brennan. White, for his part, urged that although even under the lowest "rational basis" standard, Frontiero would prevail, he leaned toward finding the discrimination specifically unconstitutional. Burger, Powell, and Blackmun refused to equate gender to race, and determined instead to concur. Had the government argued that women were inferior in performing the military's generic mission, perhaps Stewart or Blackmun might have joined with Brennan. After all, the focus on this decision was not whether women could fly fighter aircraft, serve as riflemen, or control nuclear weapons. Much of the military, (and certainly most of the Air Force), did not directly serve in combat, a point Douglas had made in 1946, in *Girouard v. United States*, a decision linking citizenship with military service.[8]

Stewart concurred, citing to *Reed v. Reed*, in which the Court overturned a state statute that gave a preference to males in the administration of decedents' estates. In conference, Burger who had authored that decision, urged that it "had nothing to do with [Frontiero's case]." Burger, Powell, and Blackmun agreed that the military establishment had engaged in unconstitutional discrimination against Lieutenant Frontiero and more so, women in general. However, the three justices were unwilling to agree that gender could be equated alongside of race, national origin, or religion. Certainly, part of their reticence was based on deference to the military. In Powell's conference notes, it is clear that he did not want to bind the military to the "strict scrutiny" standard in reviewing gender discrimination claims. But, as Frontiero's case arose to the Court during the period of state legislative ratification of the Equal Rights Amendment, Burger, Powell, Stewart, and Blackmun were also reluctant to create a judicial standard which would preempt the ratification of the amendment. Thus, on March 2, 1973, Powell penned into his "initial impression" his desire to keep the Court "out of the amendatory process."[9]

Early on, Powell was concerned that the majority's ruling would preempt the Equal Rights Amendment. He cautioned Brennan on February 15, 1973, "I see no reason to consider whether sex is a suspect classification in this case. Perhaps we can avoid confronting the issue until we know the outcome of the Equal Rights Amendment." But, Powell should have foreseen that the Equal Rights Amendment was doomed. So too should have Blackmun who joined with Powell in urging the

---

a 'suspect criterion' calling for 'strict scrutiny,' the challenged provisions must fall for the reasons stated in *Reed*." White to Brennan, February 15, 1973 [TM/109].

8 White to Brennan, February 15, 1973 [WJB/I:299]. White argued, "the more of this we do on the basis of suspect classifications not rooted in the Constitution, the more we approximate the old substantive due process approach." See also, White to Brennan, March 1, 1973 [TM/109], Marshall to Brennan, March 1, 1973 [TM/109].

9 *Reed v. Reed*, 404 U.S. 71 (1971); Stewart to Brennan, March 5, 1973 [TM/109]; *Giroud v. United States*, 328 US 61 (1946).

Court not preempt the amendatory process, writing to Brennan "we should not, by this case, enter the arena of the proposed Equal Rights Amendment."[10]

Brennan responded to Powell and Blackmun that he had concerns over the amendment's passage. He supported the amendment, but he doubted it would become embedded into the Constitution. Moreover, he did not believe the military should be exempted from the any law prohibiting gender discrimination. "Assuming the ERA is not ratified, the result in this case is probably the right result because a holding that sex is a suspect classification would substantially foreclose further consideration of statutory schemes based on sex under any new approach adopted by the Court in dealing with Equal Protection claims," he argued. Following a brief mention of exceptions based on medical differences between men and women, he concluded "although I think a holding that sex is a suspect classification would seriously dampen the enthusiasm for the ERA, I now wonder whether the Court should put itself in a straight-jacket for the sake of heading off the Amendment."[11]

Powell countered by objecting to the Court preempting the amendment through the judicial process. "The point of this letter is not to debate the merits of the ERA as to which reasonable persons obviously may differ," he urged. "Rather, it is to question the desirability of this Court reaching out to anticipate a major political process of resolution by the duly prescribed constitutional process." Brennan was as unyielding as Powell. Echoing the conservatives, Powell believed that if Brennan and the plurality's opinion were to become a majority decision, the Court would be seen as judicially forcing the ERA on the military, without it having been incorporated into the Constitution. He was further worried that once done, the Court would be further criticized for political activity. To his clerk, Powell wrote, "As you know, I feel quite strongly that the Court is acting unnecessarily and unwisely. It is this sort of action which subjects the Court to criticism which even its friends have difficulty in rebutting. I sincerely think that our democratic institutions are weakened—and the ultimate position of this Court also weakened—by unnecessary action of this kind." [12]

Rehnquist's dissent, along with his conduct in *Goldman v. Weinberger* analyzed further below, provides some evidence, (though not dispositive by any means), to support Professor Mazur's conclusions on Rehnquist's intention to develop the military as a conservative bastion immune from public criticism. But, only so if studied in isolation. In 1971, while serving as an Assistant Attorney General,

---

10 Powell to Brennan, February 15, 1973 [HAB/163]; Powell to Brennan, March 2, 1973 [TM/109]; Blackmun to Brennan, March 5, 1973 [TM/109].

11 Brennan, Conference Memorandum, February 18, 1973 [HAB/163]; Brennan to Powell, March 6, 1973 [TM/109]. On Brennan's support for the ERA, see Seth Stern and Stephen Wermiel, *Justice Brennan: Liberal Champion*, 395–403. However, Brennan ironically was resistant to hiring a female clerk.

12 Powell to Brennan, March 2, 1973 [HAB/163]; Powell to William F. Kelly, March 8, 1973 [LP].

Rehnquist testified to Congress that the Equal Rights Amendment, if enacted, would require the military to open combat positions to women, and moreover, might require the military to draft women along with men. Rehnquist's dissent, to the extent it could be called one, was a brief statement agreeing with the lower court's decision. Captioned as *Frontiero v. Laird,* the decision was issued by a three judge panel district court panel from District Court for the District of Alabama. The panel was composed of Richard Taylor Rives, a judge appointed to the Court of Appeals for the Fifth Circuit by Truman in 1951, and district court judges Frank Hampton McFadden who was appointed by Nixon in 1969, and Frank Minis Johnson who was appointed by Eisenhower in 1956. All three men were veterans. Rives served in the Army in World War I, McFadden in the Navy in World War II, and Johnson in the Army in World War II. Johnson, a pro-civil rights judge ultimately dissented, but found some common ground with Rives and McFadden. Neither Rives nor Johnson quickly concluded which party was in the right, and indeed the two judges struggled over Frontiero's claims.[13]

In their published decision, the three judge panel chastised the government, but upheld its discriminatory policies, on the basis that the policies had a "rational basis" for the discrimination. The government had originally argued that because Frontiero's husband was in receipt of GI Bill benefits, thereby obtaining the benefits of the Educational Assistance Act, she could not claim him as a dependant. But, as the district court countered, this position was never applied to married male service-members, and therefore the government's argument was meritless. On the other hand, Rives and McFadden chose to view the government's statutory scheme as one of a difference of relationships between service members and dependants, rather than as a gender classification difference. The two judges concluded on this point, that even if the distribution of entitlements was discriminatory, the military had a rational basis for making it so. Johnson disagreed in his dissent, arguing instead that the issue was solely related to gender.

Rives and McFadden also reasoned that Frontiero and similarly situated females were not, in fact, denied statutorily based benefits, but rather were being denied monies to which undeserving males were in receipt of. That is, tens of thousands of married male service members collected monies they were not entitled to collect. "All dependency benefits are unquestionably valuable, windfalls are not, but we are of the opinion that the incidental bestowal of some undeserved benefits on male members of the uniformed services does not so unreasonably burden female members that the administrative classification should be ruled unconstitutional," the court concluded. The lower court's decision was clearly illogical, and the fact that the Justice Department would raise such an argument in an era of spiraling defense costs, (a surprising admission of failing to perform a competent stewardship of public monies, to say the least), is strange if one considers that the government is supposed to be a good steward of the public's monies. If taken to its

13 Jeanne Holm, *Women in the Military*, 263, *Frontiero v. Laird*, 351 F. Supp. 201 (DC AL, 1972).

logical extension, the court's ruling would permit the Internal Revenue Service to file civil tax suits solely against women, ignoring all male tax cheats in the process.

Whether Rehnquist knew of the difficulties in negotiations among the three judges is an unknown, but, how the three judge panel arrived at its decision is noteworthy because it clearly evidenced three judges struggling to balance judicial deference to the military against the application of equal treatment under the law to the military establishment. Initially, the government had wanted to argue for a dismissal on the basis of a lack of standing and in the alternative to be permitted to argue the merits of the decision in front of a single judge. Implicit in the government's position was that Frontiero's claim did not constitute a significant constitutional issue and simply was an argument for equity. Johnson, McFadden, and Rives agreed that the government's position was meritless and the issue before the judiciary was of a significant constitutional dimension.[14]

After the court denied the government's motion to hear the case with a single judge, the court received the parties' briefs. Again, the government's arguments appalled the three judges. Rives noted to Johnson and McFadden, "having read the briefs of the parties, I must say that the [government's] brief is very sorry in my opinion." Rives specifically singled out L. Patrick Gray III, then serving as the Assistant Attorney General in charge of the Department of Justice's Civil Division for a "paltry and stupid" brief. Gray, a graduate of the Naval Academy and World War II veteran who served on submarine duty, later became a sometimes acting judge advocate. After retiring from the Navy, he went into private practice, and then joined the Justice Department under Nixon. After J. Edgar Hoover's death, Nixon appointed Gray acting director of the Federal Bureau of Investigation, where he later became implicated in an attempt to provide cover for the Nixon administration over the Watergate break-in. What troubled Rives most about *Frontiero* appears to have been the possibility of the court writing too broad of an opinion that ultimately would create a universal definition of husband and wife, as well as creating a secondary constitutional challenge against the military of favoring married service members over single service members. "Would not this result give rise to another serious constitutional question based on discrimination against single members of the Armed Forces?" he queried Johnson and McFadden.[15]

Initially, Johnson was inclined to side with Rives and McFadden arguing that even though there clearly was unequal treatment to the detriment of female officers, deference to the military was an important factor. But, on October 28, 1971, he informed Rives and McFadden that he would dissent, arguing that ultimately the argument to permit such a wholesale discrimination would undermine the very discipline that the Department of Justice and Department of Defense had argued

14 Johnson to John R. Brown, December 28, 1970 [FMJ/68]; Rives to Johnson and McFadden, May 21, 1971 [FMJ/64], McFadden to Johnson, June 9, 1971 [FMJ/64]; Issued on June 14, 1971, the court's denial of the government's motion to dissolve the three judge panel is captioned as *Frontiero v. Laird*, 327 F.Supp 580 (MD AL, 1971).

15 Rives to Johnson and McFadden, July 8, 1971 [FMJ/64].

was critical to the military. Rives then entertained joining Johnson, until one month later, when McFadden authored a draft dissent. This draft became the majority decision. There is an irony to Rives' and McFadden's reasoning which became apparent only after the Court overturned their decision. Rives congratulated Johnson on the Court adopting his dissent, but also admitted that all along he harbored doubts about the government's position, and his earlier argument that the government's discrimination was based on relationships rather than gender as means to defer to the military establishment.[16]

Frontiero is an important decision in several respects, including the fact that it informed the military establishment that in terms of pay, allowances, and general treatment, women must be considered on an equal plane as men. The Court did not issue a broad decision which would have forced the military establishment to prove its reasons for excluding women from submarine duty, missile officer assignments, and other various combat positions. On the other hand, since much of the military served in combat support roles, it was clear that the Department of Defense would, in the future, have to answer for disparate promotion rates, retention decisions, and a host of other discrepancies between the treatment of women and men. *Frontiero* also opened the doors for further litigation in unpredictable issues. In her study on the judiciary, Professor Mazur notes that the decision is almost always analyzed for its Constitutional reasoning and not its effects on the military establishment, implicitly suggesting that there is a shortcoming to this limitation. Yet, if she had researched through the papers of Douglas, Marshall, Brennan, Powell, White, and Judge Johnson, she might be surprised that there is no evidence any of the justices considered the decision's impact on the military and were almost solely focused on the potential Constitutional alteration of law if the Equal Rights Amendment succeeded. Moreover, one of Frontiero's attorneys, Morris Dees who had been a leading civil rights advocate, urged that the three-judge court view the case as a means for breaking two millennia of discrimination against women, and specifically asked that court to avoid speculating on their decision's effects on the military.[17]

In *Schlesinger v. Ballard*, the Court had to confront what essentially became a claim of reverse discrimination, more akin the issue of preferences in *Bakke*, then what was raised in *Frontiero*. As a result of the court's upholding affirmative

16 Johnson to Rives and McFadden, October 28, 1971 [FMJ/62]; Rives to Johnson and McFadden, October 29, 1971 [FMJ/62]; Rives to McFadden and Johnson, March 27, 1972 [FMJ/62]; McFadden to Rives and Johnson, March 28, 1972 [FMJ/62]; Johnson to Rives and McFadden, March 29, 1972 [FMJ/62]; Rives to Johnson, June 18, 1987 [FMJ/64].

17 Dianne Mazur, *A More Perfect Military*, 48; Morris Dees to Rives, January 4, 1972 [FMJ/64]. Dees provided to Rives a brief he authored for another pending case, and in his cover letter wrote: "The Court no doubt, has followed the woman's right movement. The success of this movement is crucial in America's long tradition of equal rights to all her citizens. Plaintiff's have utmost faith in this Court that this case will be given due consideration in light of its historical significance."

action programs, a necessary question was whether discrimination against white males was constitutional if done to redress the wrongs of race, national origin, or gender discrimination, both in society and the military. One of the differences in the Court's approach to *Ballard* than in *Frontiero*, is that in *Ballard*, the justices actually did visibly consider a potentially discriminatory policy for its impact on the military.[18]

Following *Frontiero*, the Department of the Navy initiated an administrative discharge process which differed considerably between men and women. Commissioned officers holding the rank of captain (or in the case of the Navy, lieutenant) were historically given two board selection opportunities for promotion to major (or in the Navy, lieutenant commander). Those officers who failed to achieve promotion were honorably discharged from active duty. Generally, in the 1970s, the first time that an officer met such a board in the Navy was in their eighth year of service. Thus, officers failing to be selected for promotion to major or its equivalent were administrative discharged from the military in the ninth or tenth year of their service, depending on when the secretary of a military department scheduled future promotion boards. However, Congress initiated a regulation which permitted female officers who were twice passed over to remain on duty until their thirteenth year, giving females at least three further promotion opportunities not available to males. The Navy and Marine Corps purpose in this program was to enable female officers the ability to overcome the handicap of being excluded from combat positions such as service in submarines and aircraft. Ballard, a passed-over male officer challenged this program as an unlawful discrimination against males.

A three judge panel of the United States District Court for the District of Southern California held that the Department of the Navy's discharge scheme was unconstitutionally discriminatory in light of *Frontiero* because it differentiated between the sexes without reason. The court recognized that when separated in his tenth year, Ballard was entitled to $15,000 in separation pay, but if permitted to remain on duty until his thirteenth year, he would receive over $200,000 in pay and benefits. Applying the Fifth Amendment, the court found that the government's reasoning could not overcome the discriminatory feature of the separate promotion rules.

In reviewing the district court's decision Powell called it "a weak and almost juvenile opinion in terms of analysis." Yet, he also urged that "the rational basis for the legislation held unconstitutional by the three-judge court below is substantial, legitimate, and in the best interests of the armed services in terms of their efficiency and combat readiness." To an agreeing Rehnquist, Powell concluded that if the military determined that the advancement of women benefitted readiness, he could support the difference in discharge dates, even under *Frontiero's* constraints. Likewise, when Blackmun's clerk, James Kincely urged him to invalidate the statute, pointing out that what was not in the record was

18 *Schlesinger v. Ballard*, 419 U.S. 498 (1975).

that Ballard had actually served a total of 19 years because he previously had been an enlisted sailor, Blackmun determined not to follow his clerk's advice. In conference, he urged deference to the military and Congress. "We are, first of all dealing with the military and not with some civilian set-up, and I suspect that this adds a protective factor to the government's position," Blackmun noted before addressing the legislative role to which he asked. "This is a Congressional judgment. Are we to restrict the war-making powers of Congress?"[19]

In a decision authored by Stewart, the Court reversed the district court. Stewart, one of the Court's two World War II naval veterans, recognized that prior to 1967, the Navy had placed a large number of duty restrictions on female officers, and these restrictions hampered their promotion chances. Even while the issue was being argued before the Court, there were very few combat duties available to women. In contrast to *Frontiero*, the fact that women were unable to obtain comparable "seagoing service" records similar to men justified the difference in treatment at the promotion boards. Brennan dissented with Douglas, White, and Marshall joining him. Interestingly, in conference, Douglas voted to side with Stewart and the majority, but only dissented after Brennan and Marshall lobbied him to do so. Brennan's dissent focused on the majority's continuing refusal to apply "strict scrutiny" to gender-based discrimination. If this higher standard were applied with equal force to women and men alike, the Court would likely have had to rule in favor of Ballard's arguments. Brennan also cited to Mendel Rivers' and Strom Thurmond's statements on the promotion statute, pointing out that the legislative intent behind the statute was to provide parity with male officers. There was no statutorily set date for the discharge of male officers, the difference occurred, in Brennan's opinion, because the Navy artificially failed to align men to the statutorily set date for the discharge of female twice-passed over officers.[20]

After *Ballard*, the Court developed in *Craig v. Boren*, a non-military decision, an intermediate level of scrutiny for reviewing gender discrimination. This intermediate standard requires the government to prove more than a rational basis, but less than the heightened strict scrutiny standard in order to sustain a statute. In plain words, "the government must prove the existence of specific important governmental objectives, and the law must be substantially related to the achievement of those objectives." Rehnquist dissented from the majority, criticizing the creation of an intermediate scrutiny level.[21]

Following *Boren*, the Court reviewed gender discrimination in the context of the 1976 Military Selective Service Act and the Soviet invasion of Afghanistan in 1979. With the nation relying on an all-volunteer force, Congress left open the

19 *Ballard v. Laird*, 360 F.Supp 643 (DC Cal 1973); Powell, *Summer Memorandum* August 29, 1974 [LP/21]; James Kincely to Blackmun, January 22, 1974 [HAB/196]; Blackmun, conference notes, October19, 1974 [HAB/196].

20 *Schlesinger v. Ballard*, 419 U.S. 498 (1975); Douglas to Stewart, December 4, 1974 [HAB/196].

21 *Craig v. Boren*, 429 U.S. 190 (1976).

option for a re-initiation of conscription if a national emergency arose. The new law required all males between the ages of 18 and 35 to register for the draft in the event that conscription became necessary. President Carter and the director of the Selective Service, Dr. Bernard Rostker had recommended that women as well as men be required to register, but the final statutory amendment providing funds for the registration process, only required the registration of males. A group of males sued in the federal courts, arguing that the failure to register women made males solely amenable military service and its attendant loss of individual rights, and to criminal laws for the failure to register. There was no doubt that the program was discriminatory to the detriment of males, and interestingly the Department of Defense and Carter urged universal gender-blind registration, but congressional conservatives balked, and the statutory requirement was restricted to males. Nonetheless, as enacted, the law had strong bipartisan support, and Reagan, after succeeding Carter, intended it to continue.[22]

Prior to the law coming into effect, a three judge panel from the District Court for the Eastern District of Pennsylvania found that the act violated the Due Process clause and enjoined the government from requiring registration. The government argued, as a first line of defense, the issue of ripeness. None of the males who challenged the law had yet been subjected to it, and indeed, the law had not yet gone into effect. However, the court countered that the director of the Selective Service Agency, Dr. Bernard Rostker testified that it would be more disruptive to the military for a court to decide the issue after the law went into effect. As to the substantive question of discrimination, the court found that while the registration of persons for selective service was undoubtedly compelling, the singling out of males for registration was not.

Consistent with *Frontiero* and later decisions, the lower court refused to apply the strict scrutiny test to the statutory exclusion of women, but it nonetheless found the exclusion unconstitutional. The government had argued that females were excluded from combat roles and therefore were not required in the same numbers as males, but even in recognizing this fact, the court countered that this argument would not prevail against the exclusion of individuals from registration on the basis of race or national origin. The three judges carefully sidestepped the issue of the military limiting women from combat duties, clearly stating that it would not take that matter into consideration because to do so would be a judicial interference with military operations, but then ruled that the exclusion of women did not serve an important government objective. In arriving at this decision, the judges noted that on the one hand Congress, in other matters had determined that the expansion in the numbers of women serving in the military would significantly benefit the national defense, but in the selective statute, it took the opposite position.[23]

22 John W. Chambers, *To Raise an Army: The Draft Comes to Modern America* (New York: The Free Press, 1987), 258–9; Bernard Rostker, *I Want You: The Evolution of the All Volunteer Force*, 417–42.

23 *Goldberg v. Rostker*, 509 F.Supp 586 (DC Pa. 1980).

Within two weeks of the district court's decision, the Court determined it possessed jurisdiction and took up the government's appeal, eventually overturning the lower court. The rapid acceptance of jurisdiction occurred as a result of Brennan ordering a stay of the district court's injunction. Brennan believed that the situation in Afghanistan could lead to a greater conflagration, requiring a quick call-up of forces and a prolonged military conflict. He was not alone in this. Powell shared his fears of war with historian Daniel Boorstin, wondering whether the Carter administration would be able to achieve a Soviet withdrawal by diplomacy.[24]

In conference Burger turned to Rehnquist to write for the majority. Rehnquist began by providing the context for the decision, reinforcing that the judiciary must give to Congress the maximum deference in matters of national defense. While he did not criticize the lower court for applying an intermediate level of scrutiny, he turned to *Ballard*, *Orloff*, and *Levy* to support the difference. Perhaps, to the Court's remaining liberals, the most troubling aspect of Rehnquist's scholarship was his use of *O'Brien*—the Warren Court's upholding of a criminal prohibition against burning draft cards—to link selective service registration to military operations. Yet, Rehnquist's link between these two aspects was not tenuous. If Congress determines that the national security situation is such that the military requires conscripts, then it may set the health, education, and age limits of inductees. After all, a healthy and disciplined fighting force is often an essential ingredient to a successful military strategy.

Rehnquist was reluctant to agree with the Solicitor General that the intermediate standard of scrutiny should not apply to issues of national defense, however. Though he pointed out that even under *Boren*, the interest involved in selective service could be considered an important government interest, he personally believed that the "rational basis" test ought to be applied. In that light, he also defended Congress against the assertion that it had "acted unthinkingly." It has been alleged that Congress ignored the Executive Branch and, more specifically, the military, in exempting women. This view of Congress is true, but in allocating public monies Congress determined that the registration of women did not reflect the needs of the military, and therefore spending monies on the registration program would be wasteful. Of course, historically, Congress has been highly selective on wasteful spending issues. And, admittedly conservatives in Congress succumbed to an outdated and—in looking at the record of women in the military since—a nonsensically insulting stereotype. Yet, no justice, including Brennan and Marshall, in 1981, believed it their duty to advance women in the military, and Rehnquist's position was simply that of upholding Congress. Thus, Rehnquist sided with Congress, but in this instance, there is little evidence that he did so to insulate the military as a conservative bastion.[25]

---

24 *Rostker v. Goldberg* 448 U.S. 1306 [Brennan's stay]; Powell to Boorstin, February 17, 1980 [Boorstin/139].

25 Dianne Mazur, *A More Perfect Military*, 68. Mazur argues that *Rostker* cemented a sweeping doctrine of deference on military issues that would lead courts to withdraw

White dissented, with Brennan joining him, pointing out to a weakness in Rehnquist's and Congress' explanation of the statutory exemption. The majority rested its analysis on the military's immediate combat requirements. If a large scale conflict requiring the renewal of conscription occurred, then males in non-combat positions could be moved into combat positions, while females would be required in larger numbers to fill in for the transferred males. "Common sense and experience in recent wars, where women volunteers were employed in substantial numbers, belie this view of reality," White chastised the majority. Yet, White caveated his dissent with the challenge that if the Department of Defense could prove that it was able to "obtain through volunteers" all of the women it needed in wartime, he would support the majority's decision.[26]

Marshall's dissent, also joined in by Brennan, was purely based in the concept of equal protection of the laws. In both the conference and in his dissent, they accused the majority of succumbing to "ancient canards about the proper role of women." Because the military's leadership had, on other matters, repeatedly testified that including greater numbers of women into the ranks benefitted readiness, the government's justification for the discrimination could not meet any level of heightened scrutiny. (White did not initially set out to write a separate dissent, but he could not agree to Marshall's absolutes regarding equal protection in the context of conscription.) Again, both dissents are meritorious and the military's recent experiences in Iraq and Afghanistan show the lie to the belief that women are unable to serve in combat as equal to the earlier lie that African Americans were less suited to military service than whites. But neither dissent provides any indication as to Rehnquist's motives.[27]

A closer examination of Rehnquist's role in authoring the decision is merited, if in fact, the claim that he intended to create a conservative military immune from public or political criticism. On the one hand, Blackmun's clerk, Susan G. Lahne, pushed for him to join with the dissent, calling Rehnquist's deference to Congress "novel and disturbing for future discrimination cases." Rehnquist's first draft did, in fact, contain language to the effect that the judiciary had to give the broadest deference to military legislation. But, Rehnquist in his redrafted opinion had removed much of this language, and Lahne informed Blackmun that she believed the draft was more acceptable to which Blackmun agreed. Blackmun, for his part, recorded the conference discussions as both he and Stevens urging that while the Solicitor General had overreached by resting on the exclusion of women from combat duties as justifying the exemption, there was enough of a rational

---

from any serious role in ensuring that military personnel policies respected Constitutional principles. This is simply unfounded.

26 Brennan to White, June 18, 1981 [WJB/I:545].

27 White to Rehnquist, May 29, 1981 [TM/276].

basis to uphold the government. Burger too, believed that the exemption served a rational basis.[28]

It was Powell who pushed Rehnquist to author a cutting opinion. When Rehnquist circulated his first draft, Powell recorded that he believed it was "timid and self-conscious, repetitive." On May 6, he penned to Rehnquist, that although he had written "a weak and almost apologetic opinion," he would join. Powell did not mean that Rehnquist's logic was weak, but rather that he did not "go all out" in overturning the lower court. The following day, Powell evidenced more stridency, writing, "Congress would have been irresponsible to have included women in the registration/draft law. We already have an army that probably cannot fight." But he did not end on this note, and provided an analysis of his views on modern warfare. "In recent wars there have rarely been stabilized front lines. With modern mobility on land and in the air, no one can predict when and where fighting may occur. In my view, there are relatively few places in the armed services for personnel—male or female—who cannot fight. In sum, I think the opinion would be strengthened by greater emphasis on the facts that prompted Congress to reject the President's novel view that military needs should be subordinated to 'equitable' considerations." [29]

As a result, while Blackmun and Stevens wanted Rehnquist to temper his decision, and Burger and the soon to depart Stewart remained on the sidelines, Powell pushed for maximum deference to the military's claims as well as why social change ought not to occur in the military before it does in society. Rehnquist countered to Powell that "a possibly divisive discussion of societal consideration," was irrelevant to the issues raised, and he therefore did not want to present a debate about the role of women in the military. Nonetheless, in an effort to keep Blackmun and Stevens from writing a concurrence, he re-circulated a more tempered second draft. Perhaps, ironically missed, was Rostker's opinion of the majority's decision. "If the facts were lost on Rehnquist and the majority, they were appreciated by Justices White and Marshall," Rostker later wrote.[30]

Somewhat related to *Rostker v. Goldberg* was a question as to whether commissioned military officers are federal officials amenable to lawsuit for discrimination in violation of Title VII, or whether military officers remain immune by virtue of *Feres*. The Court addressed this issue in *Chappell v. Wallace*, in 1983. Five enlisted sailors assigned to the USS *Decatur*, brought suit against their commanding officer and seven other officers and non-commissioned officers. The enlisted sailors alleged that they were assigned undesirable duties

---

28 SGL to Blackmun, May 5, 1981 [HAB/333]; Rehnquist, first circulated draft, undated [HAB/333]; SGL to Blackmun, May 11, 1981 [HAB/333]; Blackmun, conference notes [HAB/333].

29 Powell, impressions, May 1, 1981 [LP/79]; Powell to Rehnquist, May 6, 1981 [LP/79]; Powell to Rehnquist, May 7, 1981 [LP/79].

30 Rehnquist to Powell, May 11, 1981 [LP/79]; Rehnquist to Burger, Stewart, Blackmun, Powell, and Stevens, June 12, 1981 [HAB/333]; Bernard Rostker, *I Want You: The Evolution of the All Volunteer Force*, 446.

and threatened, and penalized on the basis of their race. The United States District Court for the Northern District of California dismissed the suit against the five enlisted members ruling that *Feres* barred such suits, and internal military decisions were generally non-reviewable. Moreover, the court pointed out that the five sailors had not exhausted their administrative remedies. The Court of Appeals for the Ninth Circuit reversed, essentially holding that *Harmon v. Brucker* enabled the judiciary to review the plaintiff's contentions, although the appellate court conceded that the specific issue—discrimination suits against commissioned officers—had never been brought before the judiciary for a jurisdictional determination. The appellate court also held that *Feres* did not apply to constitutional violations, and although that decision prevented suits under the FTCA, the law was silent on whether it prevented suits under *Bivens*-type actions. (*Bivens* was an avenue of jurisdiction in suing the federal government for discrimination.)[31]

Emphasizing *Rostker*, *Levy*, and *Orloff*, the Court, in a decision authored by Burger, reversed the Ninth Circuit. Burger pointed out that the Department of the Navy had several administrative avenues of redress for sailors who believed they were victimized by discrimination. Moreover, Congress had specifically authorized the Navy's administrative mechanisms for redress. If the Court, with no dissenters appeared to exempt the commissioned officers from liability for discrimination, greater analysis of the decision proves otherwise. Burger emphasized that the unique disciplinary structure of the military—the only jurisdiction in the United States which can criminalize acts of employment discrimination—serves as more than a bulwark against a would-be discriminator's financial liability found in civil suits. The second footnote in the opinion is perhaps the most important aspect of the decision regarding military law. In their brief the five sailors relied on *Wilkes v. Dinsman*, a pre-Civil War decision in which the Court had permitted a marine to sue his commander for administering punishment which the commander had no authority to administer. But, on Marshall's urging, Burger placed into the opinion that because *Wilkes* predated *Feres*, the common law tort permissible in 1849 was no longer permissible in 1983.[32]

Importantly, no justice dissented from this decision. Brennan merely inquired whether the Court's analysis in footnote two was correct, and after some discussion agreed that it was. Marshall concluded that the lower court's decision was "no way to run an Army." Stevens agreed to join with no reservations as did O'Connor. In O'Connor's case, she emphasized to Burger the importance of extending *Feres* over *Bivens* claims. What is missing from both the appellate and Court decisions is the actual conduct of the plaintiffs. Blackmun's conference notes indicate that the justices were aware that all five sailors were administratively punished for a series of transgressions. Discipline and drug use on the *Decatur* had undermined the vessel's reliability. On the other hand, one of the sailors was a trained electrician who was subjected to menial tasks and then denied a favorable evaluation.

31 *Chappell v. Wallace*, 661 F.2d 729 (CA 9, 1981); 426 U.S. 296 (1983).

32 Marshall to Burger, May 26, 1983 [HAB/383]; *Wilkes v. Dinsman*, 48 U.S. 89 (1849).

The sailor was fined 50 dollars for keeping his clothes in his workspace instead of his berth, while a white sailor was adjudged a suspended fine for seven days of being absent without leave, a UCMJ offense. The other four sailors were treated poorly and denied the opportunity to attend various naval schools, ensuring little opportunity for advancement. Thus there was evidence of discrimination.[33]

In the last year of Burger's tenure, the Court issued *Goldman v. Weinberger*, in which Rehnquist led a majority to uphold the principle of military necessity over the Constitution's guarantee of freedom of religion. The history of freedom of religion in the military can be characterized as one where the military establishment has generally tolerated this freedom, but has been permitted to consider the practice of religion an accommodation of beliefs. Thus, the military establishment has not considered the freedom as an absolute. There can be little doubt that the facts which gave rise to *Goldman* are troubling. Captain Simcha Goldman, an Air Force medical officer and ordained Orthodox Jewish rabbi freely wore a yarmulke, the religious headgear accoutrement of his faith, without objection from his superiors. Only after he testified favorably on behalf of an accused airman in a court-martial was he ordered not to wear the yarmulke while on duty. The day following the order, Goldman disobeyed it, and was administered a letter of reprimand. While far short of a court-martial, or even non-judicial punishment, the letter of reprimand had the potential to end Goldman's career because a promotion board would be entitled to know that he had been so disciplined. While his commander acted arbitrarily and in apparent retaliation for Goldman's testimony, service regulations prohibited the wearing of unauthorized or non-uniform items in lieu of sanctioned items.

Goldman sued his chain of command through to the Secretary of Defense, arguing that the regulations violated his freedom of religion. He had an even stronger argument regarding selective enforcement of the regulation. For years, the Air Force's leadership had tolerated the displaying of ashen crosses on foreheads during Ash Wednesday, giving more than a veneer that the selectivity in enforcement was directed at a religious minority. Religious freedom, like freedom of speech is a cornerstone of the Bill of Rights, and the United States District Court for the District of Columbia, conducted its jurisprudence in this regard. That court, distinguished *Rostker* in which Congress had specifically acted to exclude women from registration, from the Air Force's denial of religious wear via regulation, and held that the regulation violated Goldman's religious rights. Two judicial orders came from this decision. The first court order was an injunction against the Air Force from prohibiting Goldman's yarmulke wear, and the second, an order to rescind the letter of reprimand. The Air Force appealed both orders to the Court of Appeals for the District of Columbia.[34]

33 O'Connor to Burger, May 23, 1983 [HAB/383]; Marshall to Burger, May 26, 1983 [HAB/383]; Brennan to Burger, May 27, 1983 [HAB/383]; Blackmun, Bench Memorandum, [April 10, 1983].

34 *Goldman v. Secretary of Defense,* 530 F.Supp 12 (DC DC 1981). See, *Goldman v. Weinberger*, 475 U.S. 503 (1986).

That court, in a decision composed by Judges Luther Swygert, a Roosevelt appointee serving on the Court of Appeals for the Seventh Circuit by special designation to the Court of Appeals for the District of Columbia, Harry Thomas Edwards, a Carter appointee who replaced David Bazelon, and Abner Mikva, a World War II veteran, former congressman, and Carter appointee, reversed the district court. The appellate court recognized that Goldman had "received outstanding evaluations," and freely had worn the yarmulke without objection. The court also noted that Goldman had been given legal advice that his Air Force superiors had infringed on his religious rights, an important recognition of the principle that government officers relying on legal advice in good faith are generally immune from liability. Because the Court had never addressed religious rights in a military context, there was a difference between the parties as to the level of scrutiny the court should apply to the regulation. Goldman argued for strict scrutiny while the government urged a rational basis test. The court determined that it could not review the regulation in light of either test, but rather "whether the restrictions on Goldman's right to exercise his religion were authorized and justified by the power of the military to regulate itself, giving due weight to each of the conflicting interests."

In that context, the government argued, citing to selective treatises on Jewish law, that Goldman's faith did not require him to wear a yarmulke at all. But the appellate court was not willing to entertain the government's position because there already existed a body of selective service case law that focused the government not on a particular religion, but rather the sincerity of the applicant's faith. This was, after all, a central part of the selective service decisions. The Air Force's other argument was far stronger, because it focused on military discipline. The court encapsulated this argument as the enablement of laxity in one area of uniformity making it likely to undermine discipline in other, more critical, areas of the military. It was for this reason, that the three judges were willing to reverse the district court.

Goldman appealed to the appellate court to reconsider its ruling, *en banc*, but the judicial vote went against him. Interestingly two of the court's more conservative judges, Kenneth Starr, and Anthony Scalia, along with Ruth Bader Ginsburg dissented from the denial of reconsideration. Starr conceded that there exists a tension between the Bill of Rights and the demands of military service, but urged that the court had wrongly sided against the free exercise of religion in the context of this case. Indeed, Starr found the Air Force's actions against Goldman "patently unconscionable." As to the Air Force's response regarding flexibility in the enforcement of uniform regulations, Starr concluded that flexibility and arbitrariness in this instance were essentially the same thing. Ginsburg, with Scalia joining, issued a brief dissent, accepting Starr's reasoning, but adding that at a minimum, Goldman's commander had shown "callous indifference" to Goldman's faith.[35]

35 *Goldman v. Secretary of Defense*, 739 F.2d 657 (CA DC 1987).

In between the appellate court and the Court's scheduling oral argument, it became clear that Congress was likely to interpose in this issue. The Secretary of Defense created a study group to review religious accommodation in the military. Ultimately, none of the eventual dissenting justices were swayed by the prospect of the study group as had occurred with the military's suspension of its domestic intelligence program in *Tatum*, and Blackmun went so far as to call the military's posture "outrageous." Nor would Congress ultimately accept the military's findings, though it waited until after the Court issued its decision.

One other notable matter was that the Court, on Burger's suggestion, temporarily held two other "Free Exercise" appeals which he believed were related to Goldman's even though neither arose from the military. The first of the cases involved a Nebraska resident who refused, on religious grounds rooted in the Second Commandment, to have her color picture taken for a driver's license. In *Quaring v. Peterson*, the Court of Appeals for the Fifth Circuit determined that Nebraska did not have a sufficient enough of an interest to require the color picture. The appellate court, interestingly, partly relied on *Seeger*, in arriving at this decision. The Court, in a *per curiam* decision, split four to four, which resulted in upholding the appellate court's decision. The second case held for review involved a state prison regulation on hair length. In *Wilson v. Schillinger*, the Court of Appeals for the Third Circuit held that the prison requirement for short hair to minimize smuggling was enough of a state interest to overcome the religious exercise of Rastafarian inmates. The Court ultimately denied *certiorari*, but Rehnquist wanted couple, or at least align, *Schillinger* with *Goldman*, placing service members more akin to prisoners than civilians seeking a driver's license.[36]

In conference, Burger articulated his unhappiness with the Air Force's arbitrary enforcement against Goldman, but made clear his unshakable belief that Congress and not the courts were the sole body to address the regulation. This is not to argue that Burger questioned the sincerity of Goldman's beliefs. To the contrary, he believed that Goldman's religiosity was unquestionably sincere. White agreed with Burger on these points. Brennan conceded that the military had a compelling interest in requiring uniformity, but he agreed with Judge Starr, and argued that a yarmulke hardly interfered with the efficiency or discipline of the military. "I agree with Starr that Dr. Goldman has been required to render to Caesar far too much for far too little reason," Brennan concluded. He favored a narrow ruling which permitted uniform regulations to exist, with the caveat that all non-obtrusive religious accoutrements were either banned or permitted. Marshall too, urged that a "yarmulke hurts nothing," and observant Orthodox Jewish service members had openly worn them in the Korean War. Stevens sided with Burger, adding that as a case of retaliation, the Air Force had no defense, but uniformity was essential for the service. O'Connor, the newest justice found the decision "very hard," admitting

36 *Quaring v. Peterson,* 728 F.2d 1121 (CA 8, 1984) affirmed by *Jensen v. Quaring*, 472 U.S. 478 (1985); *Wilson v. Schillinger*, 761 F.2d 921 (1985); Rehnquist, Memorandum to the Conference, March 26, 1986 [HAB/439].

that the judiciary owed "great deference" to the military, but Starr's dissent was nonetheless correct. Rehnquist and Powell were adamant that the military had done nothing wrong to Goldman, and perhaps because of their stridency, Burger assigned Rehnquist to author the majority decision.[37]

What followed was a not only a callous display of Rehnquist's insensitivity to non-Christian faiths at the least, or worse, open anti-Semitism, but also an extreme minimization of the First Amendment's application to service-members. This is how both Blackmun, who dissented, and White who concurred, perceived Rehnquist's first two drafts which essentially derided an orthodox Jewish tenet. There can be no defense of his belittling of religious minorities. Rehnquist described the wear of the yarmulke "an idiosyncrasy," which, if permitted would "simply make [Goldman's] military service pleasant for him and others with similar beliefs." While Blackmun's clerk opined that Rehnquist's draft was "needlessly offensive," Blackmun wondered how Rehnquist could stoop to a level of intolerance. Brennan admonished Rehnquist for using language which would "deeply offend our Jewish friends." Powell came to Rehnquist's defense by pointing out that Rehnquist was merely following Judge Abner Mikva's position, and as a practicing Jew, Mikva could hardly be called bigoted in this case.[38]

In Rehnquist's first circulated draft, he expressed that so long as military regulations "reasonably and even-handedly regulate dress in the interest of the military's perceived need for uniformity," the courts should not interfere. There was little mention of how the rational basis test applied in such instances, and this lent to Blackmun's later criticism that Rehnquist appeared more willing to defer to military regulations than legislatively enacted statutes such as drivers' license requirements. White was the first to join with Rehnquist, followed by Powell. But after rereading Rehnquist's draft, both White and Powell agreed that the Air Force had acted arbitrarily, and decided to join in a concurrence with Stevens which both upheld the military's authority to regulate uniformity, and scolded the retaliatory conduct of Goldman's commanders.[39]

Blackmun, Brennan, Marshall, and O'Connor early on indicated their intention to dissent. All three believed it was irresponsible for the Court to condone the Air Force's conduct. Blackmun challenged that Rehnquist's published decision would lead to discrimination in the military in favor of majoritarian faiths, a

---

37 Blackmun, conference notes, January 17, 1986 [HAB/439]; Brennan conference notes, January 17 [WJB/I:701]; Powell, Conference notes January 17, 1986 [LP/124].

38 Brennan to Rehnquist, February 14, 1986 [WJB/I:701]; Powell, Conference notes January 17, 1986 [LP/124]; Rehnquist's reasoning for the use of the term "idiosyncrasies" was that in one of the briefs, the yarmulke was described as "slightly idiosyncratic apparel." Rehnquist to Brennan, February 18, 1986 [WJB/I:701].

39 Rehnquist, first circulated draft, February 11, 1986 [HAB/439]; Blackmun, conference notes, [HAB/439]; David Sklansky to Blackmun, February 14, 1986 [HAB/439]; White to Rehnquist, February 17, 1986 [HAB/439]; Powell to Rehnquist, February 18, 1986 [HAB/439]; White to Stevens, February 27, 1986 [HAB/439].

notion that Rehnquist disavowed as unfounded. Yet, in the military's treatment of homosexuality, analyzed in chapter X, it is clear that this discrimination is precisely what occurred. In his published dissent, Brennan, joined by Marshall, called Rehnquist's decision "sub-rational," and creating a standard of absolute, uncritical deference to the professional judgment of military authorities.[40]

II: The Endurance of *Feres* and Other Matters of Government Obligations

In 1946, the Court, in *United States v. Causby*, a decision authored by Douglas, determined that low flying military aircraft which caused the degradation of value of a private chicken farm (including chickens killed as a result of flying into structures), was not a compensable "taking" within the Fifth Amendment's definition. Black dissented from Douglas' position, arguing that the Court's interpretation of a "taking" was construed too narrowly, and the low altitude traversing of large numbers of aircraft over private property could constitute a taking. In *Causby*, property owners were compensated for their loss through a tort action, though perhaps not nearly as much had the Court found an unconstitutional seizure of property instead of negligence. It might have been thought that *Causby* was "the final word" on government liability over military aircraft causing damage to private property, but this was not the case. In 1947, the Armed Forces formally entered into the supersonic age when test pilot Captain Chuck Yeager exceeded the sound barrier in a test flight. Unlike propeller aircraft and early jet models which were simply noisy, the military's newer jets created sonic booms which sometimes blew apart windows and rooftops, and caused livestock to react in panic.[41]

In 1972, the Court essentially reaffirmed *Causby* in *Laird v. Nelms* a decision authored by Rehnquist. *Nelms* is an interesting decision on federal-state relations because the Federal Tort Claims Act applies a state's tort law in causes of action against the federal government. *Nelms* arose from a claim of a sonic boom damaging a homeowner's property in North Carolina. A district court, relying on *Dalehite*, issued a summary judgment in favor of the government, but the Court of Appeals for the Fourth Circuit reversed the district court. The appellate court, in a decision authored by Clement Haynsworth, did not erode *Causby* in the sense that the judges concluded a sonic boom did not constitute a "taking," but they found that the FTCA simply placed the Department of Defense in the same position of a private citizen in North Carolina. Applying North Carolina tort law, the appellate court concluded that the government could be found liable on the basis of trespass alone. North Carolina law only required the plaintiffs to prove that the Air Force caused a sonic boom to occur, thereby creating damage, rather than proving the Air Force's negligence. Interestingly, the government relied almost exclusively on

40 Brennan to Marshall and O'Connor, January 27, 1986 [TM/385]; O'Connor to Rehnquist, February 18, 1986 [TM/385].

41 *United States v. Causby*, 328 U.S. 256 (1946).

Dalehite, but the appellate court found that the Executive Branch's discretionary functions were narrowed by a specific Air Force regulation on low flights and sonic booms, which not only limited agency discretion, but established some degree of liability. Although it also does not appear in the appellate court's published decision, Haynsworth referred in conference to the government's reliance on *Dalehite*, "stupid."[42]

On appeal, the Court, in a decision authored by Rehnquist, reversed the appellate court and held that under the FTCA, *Dalehite* remained the law of the land. The Air Force could not, to the majority, have been found to have trespassed over Nelms' private property, and the Court reaffirmed that the judiciary could not hold the military strictly accountable for damages to private property, even when a jet caused sonic boom caved in the roof of a private residence. In essence, the homeowners (or their insurance) would have to prove that the aircraft caused the damage and the operation of the aircraft constituted negligence. Stewart and Brennan dissented on the basis that the federal tort act incorporated state law, and North Carolina law—where the sonic boom damage occurred—held the owners of aircraft strictly liable for damages. (The state law was directed against commercial airlines and not the military.) The problematic distinction with *Dalehite* that Rehnquist and the majority did not squarely address was that in Nelms' claim, the cause of the damage was the government's aircraft, but in *Dalehite*, the commercial vessels and various company employees were at the genesis of the explosion.[43]

Nelms was not a contentious issue in conference, although Douglas surprised the other justices when he determined not to take part in the decision. He had originally intended to dissent with Stewart and Brennan, but this would have required him to distinguish his dissent from his *Causby* decision. In conference Blackmun pointed out that while it was true North Carolina law had a strict liability provision, the FTCA did not, in its language, subject the government to liability without fault. Blackmun's clerk encouraged him to join in Stewart's dissent, but the justice was convinced that *Dalehite's* prohibition against strict liability remained "good law."Although Marshall and Powell joined with Rehnquist, they initially had given notice of their intent to author a concurrence, arguing that *Dalehite* was wrongly decided based on the facts presented before the Court in that case, but the principles involved remained the correct law. However, due to a large workload, but justices ultimately voted with Rehnquist.[44]

Feres continued to be challenged throughout Burger's chief justice tenure, much as it had during Warren's. In 1977, the Court, in *Stencel Aero Engineering v. United States* held that the government was not only immune from negligence suits from service-members for injuries incident to service, it is also immune from

42 *Nelms v. Laird*, 442 F.2d 1163 (CA 4, 1971); Sobeloff, conference notes, May 15, 1970 [SES/206]; Boreman to Sobeloff and Bryan, May 15, 1970 [SES/206].

43 *Laird v. Nelms*, 406 U.S. 797 (1972).

44 Blackmun, Conference notes, undated [HAB/146]; Powell, Conference Notes, undated [LP/].

being brought into a suit as a third party defendant. The issue originated from a defective ejection seat in a fighter aircraft. An ejecting pilot was injured and sued the Stencel Aero Engineering Corporation, who in turn cross-claimed the United States as a defendant. In products liability and other corporate negligence cases, cross-pleading is commonplace. For instance, following a bus accident in which the passengers sue the carrier, the carrier in turn may sue the manufacturer, alleging a design defect as the cause of the injury rather than the distracted bus driver. The Stencel Corporation claimed that because the government required narrow specifications to the ejection seat's design and the aircraft was continually under the control of the government, Stencel's negligence, if any, was passive in comparison to the governments'. This was a reasonable argument, except that *Feres* and the FTCA precluded such suits against the government since the pilot's injuries arose from his military service.[45]

Stencel had another argument. The pilot was the beneficiary of a military compensation scheme from his injuries, but Stencel might still be required to pay damages to the pilot. The Court, however, found that this argument was unpersuasive, because one of the principles underlying the *Feres* doctrine was to reinforce military discipline. The Court's decision made sense for two reasons. Defense contractors are on notice that they may be forced to pay compensation for negligence and do not have an exemption from tort liability. This, in turn, serves as deterrent against shoddy workmanship, and the liability doctrine then, for example, enables the dependants of service-members who were fatally electrocuted due to faulty wiring in portable showers in Iraq and Afghanistan to bring suit against the contractor.[46]

Marshall and Brennan dissented, though not to protect defense contractors. Both justices foresaw commonplace situations where a contractor could become a victim of government negligence. Moreover, they believed Burger's reliance on the needs of military discipline misplaced in unique circumstances in Stencel's claim.[47]

In *United States v. Shearer* the Court held that the government was immune from suit under the FTCA in a situation where one service member murders another, and the murder occurs while off duty. Added to this scenario was the fact that the murderer, a Private Andrew Heard, had been convicted of manslaughter in a German court for a previous offense, spent four years in a German jail, and after leaving jail was assigned to Fort Bliss, Texas, ostensibly to be retained on duty. While at Fort Bliss, Texas, the Army did not place Heard under any restriction. Private Vernon Shearer's mother, acting as his administratrix, sued the Army alleging negligence, but the United States District Court for the Eastern District of Pennsylvania granted the government summary judgment holding that *Feres* barred this type of suit. The Court of Appeals for the Third Circuit reversed the

45 *Stencel Aero Engineering v. United States*, 431 U.S. 666 (1977).

46 *Harris v. Kellogg, Brown, and Root Services, Inc.*, 618 F.Supp.2d 400 (WD Pa 2009)

47 Brennan, Conference notes, undated [WJB/I:424]

district court, finding the case more akin to *Brown* (off duty injuries) than *Feres*. The court pointed out that Shearer was murdered while on leave in New Mexico, several miles from Fort Bliss.[48]

The Third Circuit brought to light the appalling negligence underlying the suit. Heard had raped and murdered a German woman, and several of his superiors, including a brigadier general, urged his discharge because he constituted a threat to safety. Despite the entreaties of ranking officers, no medical personnel performed a psychiatric or mental evaluation of Heard which would have been a requirement for pursuing a discharge. In addition to finding that the off-duty injury was not precluded by *Feres*, the appellate court also found that the government's argument that the FTCA exempted intentional tort suits from service-members was meritless because the allegation was simply that the Army was negligent in permitting Heard to wander freely.

The Court, in a decision authored by Burger, reversed the Third Circuit under the claim that "the *Feres* doctrine cannot be reduced to a few bright line rules; each case must be examined in light of the statute as it has been construed in *Feres* and subsequent cases." In that vein, Burger rested the majority's decision on the requirements of military discipline, citing to *Stencel* and *Chappell*. He also stressed that Heard's absence from base was "a command decision." Burger had a point in the sense that leaves are approved through command channels. A service-member cannot sue the military for ordering an ill-advised assault, or unsafe exercise conditions. In theory, accountability for superiors under the UCMJ would prevent such occurrences. But accountability alone has not been a wholly dependable deterrent. The majority also determined to reverse for reasons outside of *Feres*. Shearer's murder occurred as a result of an assault and battery, and the FTCA exempted the government from liability for injuries arising when one of its agents commits this intentional act.

Brennan, Marshall, Blackmun, and Stevens concurred, but not to Burger's contention that the government is immune from suits arising from intentional torts such as assault. Stevens informed Burger that his discussion of *Feres,* was "sufficient to support the disposition," and the issue of intentional torts unwise to write into the decision. Marshall, in his concurrence, articulated that he wanted to make it clear that he was "not a firm supporter of *Feres*," but would respect *stare decisis* and concur in the result. Brennan informed his clerks that "though he was not entirely satisfied with the way in which the *Feres* doctrine had been applied in the past," he would affirm.[49]

---

48 *United States v. Shearer*, 473 U.S. 52 (1985). The lower court decision is found at *Shearer v. United States*, 723 F.2d 1102 (CA 3, 1989). Garth dissented from the Third Circuit's decision, arguing that Feres barred this type of suit.

49 Brennan to Burger, June 24, 1985 [TM/37]; Blackmun to Burger, May 17, 1985 [TM/370]; Stevens to Burger, May 15, 1985 [WJB/I:682]; Brennan to Burger, May 16, 1985 [WJB/I:682]; Blackmun to Burger, May 17, 1985 [WJB/I:682]; Brennan, Memorandum to the Conference, undated [WJB/I:682].

One matter outside of *Feres*, but reflective of the judiciary's narrowing of governmental obligations to service-members arose within the context of re-enlistment bonuses in *United States v. Larionoff.* Following the post-Vietnam drawdown, the Department of the Navy elected to pay higher bonuses to sailors manning critical occupational specialties. The higher bonuses were not statutorily directed, but rather, made permissible by the Secretary of the Navy. This meant that the Department of the Navy could rescind the bonuses at any time. A sailor who voluntarily underwent a retraining program into one of the special fields accrued a six year service commitment. However, during his training, the Navy rescinded the additional reenlistment bonus. The sailor sued the Navy under a theory of contract breach for not paying him the additional bonus, or in the alternative, releasing him from his commitment. In a decision authored by Brennan, the Court determined that judiciary could only enforce statutorily obligated pay and bonuses. Rehnquist dissented from this decision.[50]

III: Conclusion

If a study of the judiciary's military law jurisprudence were to only extend to analysis of appeals arising from courts-martial, one might conclude, with facial reasonableness, that the judiciary has been deferential to the military establishment. Of course, once placed in a cold war context, a conclusion of judicial deference is somewhat lessened without analysis of the judiciary's approach to questions as to how equal protection under the law applies to the military. Following *Frontiero*, it became clear that the Court intended the military establishment to not only require a strong measure of equal treatment for women, but also to permit programs designed to redress the effects of past discrimination. On the other hand, the Court's approach to *Feres* suits evidenced a continuing deference to the military establishment, and, in point of fact, shielding the military establishment from costly lawsuits where other government agencies would not enjoy such protection.

50 *United States v. Larionoff*, 431 U.S. 864 (1977).

Chapter 6
Rehnquist Court: From *Solorio v. United States* to the War on Terror

In 1987, Yale professor Paul Kennedy published *The Rise and Fall of the Great Powers: Economic Change and Military Conflict from 1500 to 2000*. Kennedy posited that the United States was, as a result of its large military expenditures and seeming inability to modernize its economy, in a state of declining international power. This was a transition similar to what other former powers such as Great Britain, Spain, and France had experienced. Yet, the likelihood of military conflict remained a constant, and therefore a high level of defense spending would continue to occur. One lesson that might have been taken from Kennedy's influential treatise was that military conflict was likely because rising nations would become more assertive. Kennedy was wrong in identifying Japan as a rising nation constituting a threat to international stability or United States hegemony, but his overall thesis was, and is, sound. Government officials and the military establishment's leadership read Kennedy's book. His thesis was taught at the military's senior service war colleges. Rehnquist and Powell read Kennedy's book, as well. Problematic to implementing policies based on Kennedy's thesis such as reducing defense expenditures, was that the Soviet Union had continued to center its expansive foreign policies on its military arsenal.[1]

Soviet foreign and military policy was predicated on a belief that the United States' conventional forces did not constitute a threat outside of Western Europe, and that displays of Soviet power could undermine the west. To Soviet leadership, the image of the disjointed Vietnam evacuation operation in 1975, the Mayaguez incident and failed rescue attempt, and the Iranian hostage crisis of 1979–1980 with its failed rescue operation, were proof of the deterioration of American military readiness. Soviet officials interpreted Nixon's resignation as evidence as a weakened American resolve.

There were, to be sure, weaknesses in the United States' conventional forces. In 1980, the Research and Development Corporation of America (RAND) concluded that the quality of the All Volunteer Forces were below that of the drafted Army five years earlier. One third of enlistees scored below average on the Army's

1 Paul Kennedy, *The Rise and Fall of the Great Powers: Economic Change and Military Conflict from 1500 to 2000* (New York: Random House, 1987); Powell to Boorstin, n.d. 1988 [Boorstin/139].

entry test and lacked high school diplomas. Disciplinary problems increased as did the number of courts-martial for desertion and other military unique infractions. One published study on the failed Iranian hostage rescue mission, Operation Eagle Claw, concluded that the failure occurred as a result of poor training among the nation's elite forces, leaving the public to wonder (along with the Soviet Union's military and political leadership) if the two million service-members in the conventional forces were in an even poorer state.[2]

In 1980, only 27 percent of recruits scored above average on military intelligence and aptitude tests, there were large numbers of high school dropouts in the ranks and roughly one third of all soldiers could not read above the fifth grade level. Perhaps most troubling of all was that in NATO competitions, the Army frequently finished behind Germany, Britain, and Italy, and in armor exercises, the Army finished last among all NATO allies in 1980 and 1981. That Belgium and Denmark showed greater prowess in armored warfare, signaled how poor United States forces had become.[3]

The June 9, 1980, cover of *Time Magazine* displayed an empty Army uniform with the words, "Who Will Serve?" above the image. This question was increasingly pondered within Congress and in the military establishment for a variety of reasons. In 1980, former Secretary of Defense Melvin Laird warned that at most, NATO could rapidly field a 732,000 strong military force against the Warsaw Pact forces which numbered 935,000. More importantly, the Warsaw Pact's armor forces outnumbered NATO by a margin of three to one, and a similar ratio existed with tactical missiles. Laird argued to Congress that NATO could not survive a conventional conflict beyond 30 days, and the Army National Guard could not be considered reliable for any foreign conflict. The Adjutant General of the National Guard had, in May of 1980, testified the state reserve forces "couldn't mobilize enough firepower to stop Snow White and the Seven Dwarfs." More troubling to Laird was that of all enlistees in the Army, 45 percent were classified in the lowest acceptable intelligence level. In short, for the first time since 1945, the military could not make up in discipline what it lacked in numbers.[4]

In 1981, Steven L. Canby in conducting a study for the military establishment advised that the Army had become "an empty shell" and noted that the morale and discipline of many units were low, and the quality of recruits poor. The previous

2 Bernard Rostker, *I Want You: The Evolution of the All Volunteer Force* (Santa Monica, CA: RAND, 2006), 508; Collins, *United States—Soviet Military Balance*, 2–25; for the ramifications of the failed rescue operation in Iran, see Geoffrey Wawro, *Quicksand, America's Pursuit of Power in the Middle East* (New York: Penguin Press, 2010). Wawro, a gifted military historian has published books on the Prussian-Austrian War of 1866 and the Franco-Prussian War of 1870.

3 James Coates and Michael Kilian, *Heavy Losses: The Dangerous Decline of American Defense*, 177–9.

4 Melvin Laird, *The Problem of Military Readiness* (Washington, DC: American Enterprise Institute, 1980), 13–29.

year, the Army reported to Congress that half of its new enlistees had scored in the lowest acceptable category on the Armed Forces Qualifying Test. Two years earlier, political scientist Doris Graber argued that one of the lessons from Vietnam was that soldiers, including those who joined the All Volunteer Force, would likely refuse to fight in foreign conflicts they did not fully approve of. Internal surveys showed that the military's rank and file distrusted senior military and political leadership.[5]

In 1985, Zbigniew Brzezinski, President Carter's former national security advisor, urged an increase in the nation's conventional forces to make up for a lack of reliability. He warned that the Soviet Union had opened a "fourth front," in Central and South America and the Caribbean which, if unchecked, would cause a loss of the United States' ability to stop the expansionism of communism anywhere. While Brzezinski acknowledged that the effects of the Vietnam War made it unlikely that bipartisan support could exist for conventional military operations in South and Central America, he urged that at a strong show of force, coupled with military assistance and covert operations could prevent the spread of communism, which he predicted could even consume Mexico.[6]

At the same time of Brzezinski's warning, Professor Christopher Bassford, a former Army officer now instructing at the National War College analyzed the Army's discipline in relation to how the Army selected its leaders. He correctly surmised that the UCMJ was no longer used for prosecuting military offenses such as cowardice because of the bad publicity such trials would bring. Additionally, by the mid 1980s, officers were seldom court-martialed at all. Enlisted offenders who undermined discipline, and would have been court-martialed in earlier times, were administratively discharged instead. Professor Bassford did not analyze the federal judiciary's role in this change, but his conclusions were otherwise sound.[7]

To conservative jurists, the reasons underlying the military's weakened and undependable condition were not simply sociological, or based on low pay. Historically, the military had received low pay, yet emerged from the nation's modern wars as a highly disciplined force. The Vietnam conflict was different. After the withdrawal of forces from Vietnam and in the aftermath of *O'Callahan*, the military, and particularly the Army, was undisciplined and unreliable. As a result, the nation hardly possessed the military deterrent that all four post-*O'Callahan*

5 Doris A. Graber, "Intervention Policies of the Carter Administration: Political and Military Dimensions," in Sam C. Sarkesian, *Defense Policy and the Presidency: Carter's First Years* (Boulder, CO: Westview Press, 1979), 218–19.

6 Zbignew Brzezinski, *In Quest of National Security* (Boulder, CO: Westview, 1988), 188. Brzezinski originally argued this point in 1985. The book referenced here, incorporates a public speech he made to this effect in 1985.

7 Michael Shafer, "The Vietnam Era Draft," in Shafer ed., *The Legacy: The Vietnam War*, 72; Steven L. Canby, "The Army" in *Reforming the Military* (New York: Heritage, 1981), 29; Christopher Bassford, *The Spit-Shine Syndrome*, 83–125. Interestingly Bassford, lauded the UCMJ as an essential protection against arbitrary actions by senior leaders.

presidents believed it needed. As noted in the prior analysis of the appellate and district courts, there was a belief amongst the conservative judges that the federal judiciary had undermined the military's ability to discipline itself to such a degree that unless *O'Callahan* were overturned, the military would not be a dependable deterrent to Soviet aggression. Rehnquist and Powell certainly believed this to be the case. So too did a number of military legal scholars. Simply, an increase in the size of the nation's conventional forces was seen as being only part of the answer, because the United States could not match the Soviet military in raw numbers.

I: The Reagan Administration and its Foreign and Military Policy

No full understanding of *Solorio* or the Rehnquist Court's other military law jurisprudence can be understood without some background on the Reagan administration's policies which ultimately accelerated the Soviet Union's collapse. On January 20, 1981, Reagan became president, and appointed Caspar Weinberger as Secretary of Defense. The two men had known each other since 1965 and were longtime friends. Weinberger was a Harvard law graduate, World War II veteran, California state legislator, and then Governor Reagan's state director of finance beginning in 1968. He had also served as Director of the Office of Management and Budget and then Secretary of Health, Education, and Welfare under Nixon and Ford. During Carter's presidency, after he left public service, Weinberger was the general counsel of the Bechtel Corporation.

Reagan and Weinberger shared an identical philosophy in matters of national defense, namely, that the underlying strength of the Soviet Union's international influence rested on its military arsenal. The two men also believed that in the aftermath of the Vietnam Conflict, the nation would not support a large-scale military conflict of any duration. Both sought to maximize military deterrence. Deterrence policies were not new to the nation, but Reagan and Weinberger were more assertive in using American forces overseas than Carter or Ford. Reagan did not intend to wage a conflict, but he wanted to make clear to the Soviet Union and its communist bloc allies that the economic might of the United States would be harnessed to build a stronger and more reliable conventional force, as well as nuclear forces. When he appointed Weinberger to head the Department of Defense, he intended Weinberger to rebuild discipline and morale throughout the armed forces. Through Weinberger's efforts, the government instituted military pay improvements, and by 1983, of the new recruits, over 90 percent were high school graduates. None of these improvements, however, could undo the military laws governing discipline. Reagan did factor military policy and national security into his judicial nominations.[8]

8 Caspar Weinberger, *Fighting for Peace: Seven Critical Years in the Pentagon* (New York: Time-Warner, 1990), 51–7.

Ultimately, Weinberger was enmeshed in an illicit operation involving the transfer of weapons from the United States to Iran, and providing monies from this sale to fund anti-communist forces in Central America. This operation also, strangely, involved Israel as an intermediary for the Reagan administration. The administration's actions violated several United States laws, but particularly the Boland Amendment which specifically prohibited financially supporting the anti-Nicaraguan "Contra" guerilla forces. Known as the "Iran-Contra Scandal," Weinberger, along with 11 other Reagan administration officials were indicted, but later pardoned by President George H.W. Bush.[9]

The first four years of Reagan's presidency would be spent increasing the nation's conventional forces, to include a "600 ship Navy," and a military space orbital program to detect and destroy a Soviet missile strike against the United States and its allies. Known as the Strategic Defense Initiative, this expensive program, dubbed "Star Wars" never came to fruition. But, economically it exhausted the Soviet Union, which tried to develop its own system. Reagan's and Weinberger's defense policies also were a source of vibrant political debate within Congress and in the general population as well. Although their detractors accused them of tempting war, Weinberger's military doctrine was not geared to that end. In fact, the three tenets of Weinberger's doctrine were that the United States should only commit its combat forces if a vital national interest, or that of an allied vital national interest were at stake, and only with the clear intention of winning a conflict. Finally, the use of American forces had to be a last resort. This is why, when Great Britain went to war with Argentina over the Falkland Islands in 1982, the United States did not become militarily involved, and had not truly developed plans to do so. The Falklands were important to British prestige, but not to United States strategic interests, nor, arguably, those of Britain.

There were significant tensions which did not result in war, but often appeared to make war a possibility. On September 1, 1983, the Soviet Air Force shot down a Korean Airlines 747 jetliner, killing 269 passengers and crew after the aircraft accidentally strayed into Soviet airspace. For many years the Soviet Union and United States had shot or forced down each other's intruding military aircraft, but the Korean aircraft was clearly a commercial passenger liner. Although the navies of both countries were on high alert as they raced to find the aircraft wreckage, the United States did not militarily respond. Nonetheless, the Soviet Union's actions evidenced the possibility of armed conflict.[10]

---

9 Bob Woodward, *Shadow: Five Presidents and the Legacy of Watergate* (New York: Simon and Schuster, 1999), 200–255; James M. Scott, "Inter-branch Rivalry and the Reagan Doctrine in Nicaragua," in Lorie Bogle ed., *National Security Policy Planning from Truman to Reagan and from Stalin to Gorbachev, Vol. II* (London: Routledge, 2004), 323–4.

10 Robert K. Brigham, *Iraq, Vietnam, and the Limits of American Power* (New York: Public Affairs Publishing, 2006), 159.

a. Military Involvement in the Middle East and Africa

As previously noted, in December, 1979, the Soviet Union invaded Afghanistan in what initially appeared to be a successful military operation. Carter's response was to condemn the invasion, approve covert Central Intelligence Agency-led operations in Afghanistan, and boycott the 1980 Moscow Summer Olympic Games. While it was unlikely that any president, to include Reagan, would have confronted the Soviet Union militarily in Afghanistan, at the same time, a build-up of United States forces elsewhere did not occur under Carter to the point where the Soviet government believed itself pressured. Reagan wanted Soviet leadership to believe that the United States not only possessed an effective conventional force, but would also be willing to employ it if another invasion occurred elsewhere.[11]

By the time Reagan became president in 1981, new political and social forces emerged on the periphery of the East-West conflict, particularly in the Middle East and Iran. Following the Camp David Peace Accords, American forces were stationed in the Sinai as a guarantee to both Egypt and Israel. In 1979, Iran had fallen under the control of Ayatollah Khomeini's theological regime in what can only be described as a revolution whose leaders considered both the United States and Soviet Union to be enemies of Shiite Islam. While both the United States and Soviet Union sought allies in the region, what occurred in Iran had little to do with the United States–Soviet conflict. Yet, the new Iranian government exported terrorism, primarily in the western countries, which could have the effect of weakening the appearance of American resolve in general.

Elsewhere in Africa and the Middle East, there were other threats to security. Ethiopia and Yemen were ruled by communist governments, and both countries existed in a state of civil war. Sizeable Cuban military forces were in three African countries, and Muammar al-Qaddafi, the leader of Libya and nominal Soviet ally, was in the process of arming terrorists in Europe with Soviet made weapons. Qaddafi had gone so far as to provide training for elements of the Irish Republican Army as well. On August 19, 1981, United States naval units engaged in Libyan forces in the Gulf of Sidra. In the first five years of his presidency, Reagan concentrated significant attention on Libya and Syria as well as in Central America.[12]

On August 8, 1983, Reagan directed the placement of two surveillance aircraft and eight fighter aircraft south of Libya to assist the Chadian Army in their efforts to drive pro-Qaddafi forces fighting in Chad, back into Libya. While it was unclear if the Soviet Union or their allies placed advisors alongside of the Libyan forces, by this time, the Soviet government had given nominal support to Qaddafi's efforts in Chad, and supplied almost all Libya's military arsenal. Additionally, the two nations had signed a treaty of friendship. The treaty did not obligate the

---

11 Anthony Arnold, *Afghanistan: The Soviet Invasion in Perspective* (Stanford, CA: Hoover Institution Press, 1985); Beth A. Fischer, *The Reagan Reversal: Foreign Policy and the End of the Cold War* (Columbia, MO: University of Missouri Press, 1997), 20.

12 Alexander Haig, *Caveat: Realism, Reagan, and Foreign Policy*, 30.

Soviet Union to militarily come to Libya's defense, but it brought the two nations into closer alignment, similar to the Soviet alignment with Syria.[13]

On June 3, 1982, the Israeli Defense Forces invaded Lebanon and trapped Palestinian Liberation Organization Forces in Beirut. American foreign policy favored Israel and Yasser Arafat's PLO forces had killed not only Israeli citizens, but Americans as well. Nonetheless, the Israeli response appeared to Reagan to be disproportionate to the terrorist attacks, and the Israeli invasion of Lebanon, a sovereign state whose increasing instability threatened to give to Syria and Iran greater leverage in the Middle East, unwise. Additionally, a Syrian controlled Lebanon would enable further Soviet expansion in the Middle East. A multi-national force of French and British soldiers, and United States Marines landed in Beirut to oversee the evacuation of Palestinian forces to Tunisia, as well as attempt to create stability. The operation ended in a fiasco when a terrorist attack resulted in the death of 241 Marines and 58 French soldiers.[14]

In 1986, United States military forces engaged Libya once more. Pro-Qaddafi terrorists bombed a discotheque in West Berlin frequented by American service-members. The terrorists had operated out of East Germany, with the clear help of the communist government there. In response, in Operation El Dorado Canyon, several Air Force and Naval aircraft bombed Libyan military installations, as well as Qaddafi's residence. Qaddafi was not deterred by the attack, and within two years, his agents orchestrated the destruction of a Pan American 747 airliner over Scotland. Until 2011, Qaddafi remained in power, though in the aftermath of September 11, 2001, he attempted a rapprochement with the United States.[15]

During the entirety of Reagan's administration, and indeed through the present, American forces ensured the flow of oil through the Straits of Hormuz and prevented Iranian and Iraqi expansion into Kuwait and other Gulf states. On September 22, 1980, Iraqi forces launched a surprise attack against Iranian military targets. This began a war which lasted between the two countries until 1988. American naval forces remained in the Straits of Hormuz to protect the flow of oil from the Gulf States to the west, and as a result were on a constant heightened alert. Neither the United States nor Soviet Union provided support to Iran, though Iranian relations with Syria brought Soviet military equipment into Iran. Yet, the Soviet Union also supplied Iraq with military hardware. In 1987, American naval forces fired on Iranian oil platforms after Iranian naval units fired

---

13 Robert O. Friedman, *Moscow and the Middle East: Soviet Policy Since the Invasion of Afghanistan* (London: Cambridge University Press, 1991), 161–4; Beth Fischer, *The Reagan Reversal*, 29.

14 Gail Yoshitani, *Reagan on War: A Reappraisal of the Weinberger Doctrine, 1980–1984* (College Station, TX: Texas A&M Press, 2012), 114–15; Steven F. Hayward, *The Age of Reagan: The Conservative Counter-Revolution* (New York: Random House, 2009), 269.

15 Joseph T. Stanik, *El Dorado: Reagan's Undeclared War with Qaddafi* (Annapolis, MD: Naval Institute Press, 2003), 141–5.

on a Kuwaiti flagged oil tanker. In 1988, an American naval vessel shot down an Iranian passenger jet, killing 290 civilians on board.[16]

b. Military Involvement in Central and South America

By 1975, the Soviet Union, with Cuban involvement, opened a fourth front in Central America. In 1979, the Cuban-backed Sandinista government replaced Nicaraguan president Anastasia Samoza. El Salvador, one of Nicaragua's neighboring countries appeared to be following suit. Reagan determined that a communist presence near the Panama Canal was intolerable, and the Soviet opening of a fourth front in Central America had to be curbed. To Reagan, the military was central to confronting the Soviet Union in this area. However, Weinberger believed that the nation's conventional forces were too weak, and the American public sufficiently anti-war, to confront the Soviet threat even in Central America. The administration settled on the use of clandestine and special forces to undermine communism in Central America. American military forces trained the Honduran military and within three years both Honduran and American forces patrolled the Nicaraguan border, leading to speculation that an invasion of communist led Nicaragua was a possibility.[17] Working in concert with internal opposition to Nicaragua's government, as well as with the El Salvadoran government, American covert operatives mined the Nicaraguan port of Managua and engaged in other covert activities.[18]

On June 27, 1986, the International Court of Justice (ICJ), an international judicial body established in 1945 as a result of the United States' government's insistence of its necessity, determined that the United States covert mining operations against Nicaragua were in violation of international law. The ICJ's decisions are not binding in the sense that the court possesses enforcement authority against nations. The Reagan administration had argued that the ICJ possessed no jurisdiction over the United States over the issue challenged, and secondly that the United States had acted in collective self defense. Nonetheless, the ICJ ruled against the United States and a large majority of nations voted in the United Nations to call on the United States to adhere to the ICJ decision. Perhaps troubling to the legal academy was that in *Reid v. Covert*, the Court specifically cited to the ICJ. And, in *Hamdan v. Rumsfeld*, analyzed later, the Court would cite to the ICJ decision regarding its decision against the United States. The ICJ would, however, never become a viable means for citizens challenging the constitutionality of military operations.[19]

---

16 Bryan R. Gibson, *Covert Relationship: American Foreign Policy and the Iran-Iraq War, 1980–1988* (Santa Barbara, CA: ABC-CLIO), 212–27.

17 Edward A. Lynch, *The Cold War's Last Battlefield: Reagan, the Soviets, and Central America* (Albany, NT: State University of New York Press, 2011), 15–19.

18 Gail Yoshitani, *Reagan on War: A Reappraisal of the Weinberger Doctrine*, 38–6.

19 *Nicaragua v. United States*, 1986 ICJ 14; *Hamdan v. Rumsfeld*, 548 U.S. 557 (2006).

In the Caribbean, Cuban-aligned communist forces in Grenada overthrew the island nation's president, Maurice Bishop. Bishop was not a Reagan ally, and indeed had come to power in a Cuban supported coup. Bishop was reticent to allow Soviet and Cuban forces onto Grenada despite their construction of an airfield. In early October, 1983, a Cuban backed coup captured and assassinated Bishop, despite the island's population supporting him. With its population of 110,000, Grenada hardly constituted a direct threat to the United States, but Reagan administration officials rightly feared that Soviet forces would transit onto the island, giving impetus to other Marxist movements in the Caribbean and Central America.[20]

On October 25, 1983, in what became captioned as Operation Urgent Fury, a force of roughly 8,000 service-members invaded Grenada, overwhelming Grenadian and Cuban opposition in a short period of time. From a public perspective, the invasion was successful, but internally, American military leadership discovered that communications between the service branches were appalling, and the discipline of the armed forces was not to the level as hoped. Had the Cuban government placed more of its forces in Grenada, or if the Grenadian population had been anti-American, the Department of Defense concluded the invasion would not have been successful. For the most part, Reagan's decision to invade Grenada initially received popular domestic support, but not so internationally. Even the United Kingdom publicly criticized the invasion. Shortcomings in military preparedness led to the Goldwater-Nichols Act, realigning command responsibilities within the military. Military discipline also came under review.[21]

Other uses of the military in South and Central America came in the form in trying to curb the importation of narcotics into the United States. In late 1981, the Medellin Cartel in Columbia created a virtual insurgency to protect their cocaine manufacturing and export operations against the Columbian government. In 1984, United States military forces engaged in covert operations in Columbia. In 1985, the cartel murdered the Columbian minister of justice, Rodrigo Lara Bonilla as well as the chiefs of the national police. In 1986, a joint United States and Bolivian operation titled Operation Blast Furnace organized to destroy cocaine networks in Bolivia. A larger operation titled as Snowcap followed in 1987. While most of the anti-drug operations targeted criminal syndicates, on occasion former allies against communism were pitted against the United States. By 1984, it was well known that Panamanian general, Manuel Noriega, who had helped the Central Intelligence Agency fight communism, also assisted the Medellin Cartel.[22]

---

20 David Locke Hall, *The Reagan Wars: A Constitutional* Perspective (Boulder, CO: Westview Press, 1991), 167.

21 Gail Yoshitani, *Reagan on War*, 115.

22 William O. Walker, *Drug Control in the Americas* (Albuquerque, NM: University of New Mexico Press, 1989), 207–16.

II: *Solorio v. United States*: The Court and the Quick Death of O'Callahan

Shortly after Rehnquist became chief justice, the Court overturned *O'Callahan*. It cannot be said, however, that it was "the Rehnquist Court," which accomplished this unique event. After all, Rehnquist had just replaced Burger and Antonin Scalia had joined the Court as Rehnquist's replacement. The Court's jurisprudential balance did not change as a result of either Rehnquist's ascension to the chief justiceship, or Scalia's appointment.

Legal scholar Mark Tushnet has pointed out that there were two "Rehnquist Courts," and the demarcation point between the two occurred during Clinton's presidency. When Blackmun retired in 1994 and was replaced by Stephen Breyer, there were no more appointments made until 2005. This has been the longest period since 1823 in which the Court remained unchanged in composition, and because in 1823, the Court numbered only seven justices, the continuity of the Court from 1994 to 2005 stands as a record. Of the justices appointed after Rehnquist's appointment as chief justice, only three had military experience and none, with the exception of Rehnquist, had ever served on active duty in wartime.[23]

Like the Burger Court, the Rehnquist Court was largely a Republican creation. Reagan, like Nixon, sought to nominate justices who would work to overturn the Warren Court's decisions, and he certainly believed that the Court had a role in enabling a strong disciplined military. During Burger's last year as chief justice, the Department of Defense issued an assessment of the military's capability to defend the United States and its allies. The report noted that as of 1980, the Soviet Union fielded a military strength of 4,368,000 which was double that of the United States' 2,024,000. Moreover, the Soviet Army numbered 2,440,000 soldiers compared to the 758,000 in the active duty United States Army. While the chances of the two militaries engaging in open conflict were low, clearly the Soviet Union could influence the expansion of communism through its military without much fear of American military opposition. There were other troubling aspects to Soviet military strength. Part of Soviet strategy included denying the United States access to critical resources by concentrating on foreign governments which exported raw materials. This strategy was not simply conducted through a force of arms. Typically the Soviet Union supplied armaments to critical countries. For instance, in 1980, India was the largest supporter of mica to the United States, and Zaire the largest exporter of cobalt. The governments of both nations signed agreements of friendship with the Soviet Union, and their military forces became equipped with Soviet aircraft, armor, and other weaponry. The year following the Soviet-Indian agreement saw India invade East Pakistan (now Bangladesh), albeit the conditions in that region called for an intervention of some kind.[24]

---

23 Mark Tushnet, *A Court Divided: The Rehnquist Court and the Future of Constitutional Law*, 67.

24 John M. Collins, *United States—Soviet Military Balance, 1980–1985* (London: Pergamon-Brassey's, 1985), 2–25.

Although the Soviet Union's arsenal strongly influenced American military policy and every president since Roosevelt had to contend with the Soviet threat, Rehnquist, like Reagan, believed that the United States had to outpace the Soviet Union in terms of technology and reconstruct a disciplined force. To fully analyze Rehnquist's military legal jurisprudence, it is not only essential to consider his experiences in Nixon's administration, but also the fact that he understood the quality of the United States' conventional forces when Reagan became president was at a historic nadir.

On September 26, 1986, Burger informed Reagan that he intended to retire from the Court and lead a campaign to honor the Constitution's bicentennial. Reagan quickly settled on nominating Rehnquist as his replacement, in part believing that Rehnquist's difficulties in his earlier nomination were already addressed. This was not the case, and although the Senate confirmed Rehnquist as chief justice, it only did so by a vote of 65 to 33, the closest Senate vote for a chief justice in history. Senators once more questioned Rehnquist on his draft memorandum in *Brown* where he endorsed "separate but equal," as well as his 1957 article in *U.S. News and World Report* where he claimed that a number of clerks sympathized with communism. In addition to the past allegations, his detractors added that his purchase of homes which contained restrictive covenant clauses against renting to minorities, and his refusal to recuse himself in *Tatum* evidenced a lack of judicial ethics. Nonetheless, as a known quantity, Rehnquist's confirmation was likely to occur. Once confirmed, Rehnquist set out to overturn *O'Callahan*. He would do so within a year of Douglas' death, in *Solorio v. United States*.[25]

Much like *O'Callahan*, *Solorio v. United States* did not originate in a contentious or well-known court-martial. Unlike Sergeant O'Callahan's challenges in the federal courts, however, Richard Solorio's first foray into the Article III federal judiciary was with the Court's grant of *certiorari* from the Court of Military Appeals. Solorio, a Coast Guardsman, was accused of sexually abusing the two daughters of other Coast Guardsmen while stationed in Alaska. After being transferred to Governor's Island, New York, the Coast Guard command in Alaska discovered Solorio's criminal activity. The offenses did not occur on a military base, or even on federal property, but rather in Solorio's off-base residence in Juneau. Solorio was also found to have committed similar offenses while stationed in New York, again while off-post. The commander of the Coast Guard's Eastern Regional Command at Governor's Island, New York, convened a general court-martial, charging Solorio under the UCMJ for both the Alaska and New York offenses.

Relying on *O'Callahan*, Solorio successfully motioned the military trial judge to dismiss the charges against him on the basis of a lack of "service-connection."

---

25 *Solorio v. United States*, 483 U.S. 435 (1987); Thomas R. Hensley, *The Rehnquist Court: Justices, Rulings, and Legacy* (Santa Barbara, CA: ABC-CLIO, 2006), 12; Tinsley Yarbrough, *The Rehnquist Court and the Constitution* (New York: Oxford University Press, 2000), 1–2; Bernard Schwartz, *A History of the Supreme Court* (New York: Oxford Universoyt Press, 1993), 363–5.

The Coast Guard appealed first to its service appellate court, and then to the Court of Military Appeals. Both of those appellate courts determined that the crimes of sexually abusing the children of fellow service-members was sufficiently "service connected," because of the possibility of a continuing effect on the service-members, their families, and the potential detriment to the morale of the unit to which both Solorio and the other service members belonged. After the Court of Military Appeals ruled adversely to him, Solorio unsuccessfully petitioned Burger for a stay against the Coast Guard proceeding with his court-martial. The court-martial ultimately found Solorio guilty and sentenced him to several years in confinement and a punitive discharge. He appealed to the Court on the basis of a lack of service-connection. It is clear, as Stevens would ultimately point out, that facially there was enough of a service connection under the *Relford* principles to sustain the court-martial's jurisdiction. Nonetheless, Rehnquist used the case an opportunity to overturn *O'Callahan*.

Represented by his Coast Guard appellate counsel as well as by Eugene Fidell, a former Coast Guard Judge Advocate acting on behalf of the American Civil Liberties Union, Solorio was only one of four petitioners challenging a service connection finding to the Court. Like Solorio, none of the other petitioners were controversial or had attempted to become a cause célèbre. Moreover, there was an absence of counsel who could be accused of ties to subversive groups by judicial or and conservatives. The Air Force had court-martialed two of its service-members for conduct similar to that of Solorio, but unlike in Solorio's court-martial, the military trial judges determined that the offenses had a direct connection to military discipline. Likewise, the Army court-martialed one of its soldiers for sexual misconduct with a child. Again, the Court of Military Appeals affirmed the courts-martial convictions and sentences in each case. Rehnquist initially had wanted to couple all four cases together in a single decision. But Powell, for unknown reasons, urged him to quickly move Solorio's appeal through the Court without consolidating the other potential petitioners.[26]

The government, in its brief, did not initially urge the Court to overturn *O'Callahan*, resting most of its argument on the existence of a service connection. The Solicitor General secondarily argued that if, under the service connected test, the Court were to find that a service-connection did not exist between Solorio's offense and the *Relford* factors, then the Court should consider overturning *O'Callahan*. In opposition to the government, the Vietnam Veterans of America, a large veterans' organization urged the Court to uphold *O'Callahan*, as did the appellate defense divisions of the service branches.

Rehnquist acknowledged that *O'Callahan* had already been narrowed and that the Burger Court's military law decisions solidified the view that Congress has the primary responsibility for creating the parameters of the military justice system,

26 See e.g. *United States v. Puscarik*, 22 M.J. 96 (CMA 1985); and *United States v. Jenkins*, 21 M.J. 154 (CMA 1985); Rehnquist to the Conference, June 22, 1987 [WJB/I:736].

rather than the courts. Nonetheless, even under Burger, the appellate courts were divided on defining service-connection, and to the judicial conservatives, had engaged in overseeing military affairs in an overly extensive manner. There also remains Professor Mazur's accusation that Rehnquist used Solorio's appeal to enable a conservative military immune from social and political pressures. To agree with Mazur, one would have ignore Rehnquist's deference to Congress in his jurisprudence or his concern over the readiness of the military to fight as a disciplined force or maintain its deterrence mission against the Soviet Union. Moreover, one would also have to refuse to delve into the conference discussions.

In conference, Rehnquist called *O'Callahan* an aberrant decision with a poor historic analysis, and he championed Harlan's *O'Callahan* dissent. He also accused *O'Callahan* of enabling the erosion of military readiness. White backed Rehnquist on both points, questioning how the military could serve as a reliable deterrent without the full expanse of discipline over its forces. White also urged that the Court had intruded into the Legislative Branch's constitutional prerogative in *O'Callahan.* Rehnquist agreed with White on this point. O'Connor, wanted Rehnquist to adopt Harlan's dissent almost verbatim, which again stressed that the Court had intruded into legislative authority. Scalia, the newest justice who had advocated the religious rights of Captain Simcha Goldman, agreed with Rehnquist, White, and O'Connor, adding that "Congress had spoken clearly when it drafted the UCMJ." Thus, four justices viewed military discipline in the light of deterring Soviet aggression as well as separation of powers as the two overriding factors. Powell was absent from this conference, but Rehnquist scheduled a second discussion.[27]

In the second conference, Rehnquist conceded that while Solorio's court-martial could be upheld within the framework established by *Relford, O'Callahan* was "an aberration" and had to be overruled. After Brennan expressed his support for *O'Callahan,* White stridently called that decision a "fiction," and expressed that it should "have never come down as it did," adding that Fortas was the cause of it. To this conversation, Blackmun, who ultimately dissented from the majority in *Solorio,* added that when he authored *Relford,* he was constrained by *O'Callahan,* and that he would have voted alongside of Harlan had he been on the Court in 1969. Blackmun returned to his view of military history from *Levy,* and also conceded that *O'Callahan* had a detrimental effect on the military's reliability, but believed that *stare decisis* had to be respected. Stevens disagreed with overturning *O'Callahan,* but urged the Court to extend *Relford* to cover most courts-martial. Marshall's role in the conference appears to be that of a quiet observer, even though he would author the dissent. If Rehnquist had acted in the manner that Mazur urges the legal community to consider that he did, this point was not discovered by two of the dissenters, or by Stevens.[28]

27 Blackmun, Conference Notes, February 27, 1987.

28 Powell, Conference notes, February 27, 1987 [LP/].

The conference discussions had occurred out of order of seniority. Powell, speaking last, argued that the Court in issuing *O'Callahan*, "ignored a century of history and numerous prior decisions." Having earlier scolded Rehnquist for being too tepid in *Rostker* and *Avrech*, Powell now urged that *O'Callahan* created "a vague test for establishing jurisdiction." Interestingly he too initially considered concurring because he was concerned that overturning *O'Callahan* could upend the principle of *stare decisis*. But, in his personal memoranda he stressed that Harlan's dissent was the correct view of jurisdiction, though he conceded he understood why, in 1969, Douglas prevailed.[29]

Powell acknowledged that the state courts were competent to prosecute common law offenses such as Solorio's, and there was nothing inherently wrong in a state doing so, despite the lack of rapidity ion state trials. He assigned Andrew Leipold, his clerk, and now a professor at the University of Illinois' Law School, to "thoroughly research the jurisdictional issue." Leipold responded to Powell that as "an original matter, *O'Callahan* was not constitutionally compelled and its rationale has been so fully undermined but as a matter of *stare decisis*, it should not be overruled." Powell accepted Leipold's analysis as to the first point, but not as to *stare decisis*. Like many of the justices, Powell would, on occasion, depart from his clerk's advice and in this instance he appears to have considered national defense as an overriding concern. Powell incorporated the constitutional analysis of the dissent in *O'Callahan* into his memoranda. O'Connor would later refer to Powell's discussion and Rehnquist's draft decision as "a superb history lesson." But, it was Powell's contribution to the decision that provided the Court its historical analysis into courts-martial jurisdiction.[30]

Unsurprisingly, Brennan and Marshall remained wedded to *O'Callahan*. Brennan noted that he "would not overrule *O'Callahan* or *Relford*," because he believed each "was correctly decided." It was true, Brennan conceded, that *Relford* did not expressly permit the military to consider the impact of an offense on individual service-members victimized by a military accused, such as what had occurred in Solorio's molestation of the children of other service-members. But, this simply meant that *Relford* could be improved and expanded, rather than discarded. Equally tellingly, Brennan believed it was "most significant that the trial court found no evidence to support the government's claim that Solorio's crimes had an impact on military discipline." Despite Brennan's adamancy that

29 Powell, *Memo to File*, February 4, 1987 [LP/] "It is true, as Harlan emphasized, that the Constitution vests open-end authority on Congress to make rules for the "government and regulation" of our military forces," Powell penned to himself. "This authority prompted Harlan to argue and conclude that the jurisdiction conferred on military courts by Congress is not limited to "service-connected" offenses, and that this Court should leave it to Congress to determine the jurisdiction of military courts.

30 Andrew Liepold to Powell, February 11, 1986 [LP/]; O'Connor to Rehnquist, February [HAB/].

O'Callahan remained the correct statement of law, he asked Marshall to write the dissent.[31]

Despite O'Connor's compliments to Rehnquist and Powell, *Solorio*, like *O'Callahan*, is not a compelling historic analysis. This is because there is little in the historic record which supports either the belief that military subject matter jurisdiction was narrowly construed for reasons of constitutionality in early America or Britain, or that the Constitution's signatories believed that Congress could enable an expansive jurisdiction. (Rehnquist did, with Powell's assistance, accurately point out the flaws in *O'Callahan's* historic analysis.) But, *Solorio* is constitutionally sound when adjudged against the Constitution's plain text, in a manner in which *O'Callahan* is not. *Solorio* established an almost universal court-martial jurisdiction over service-members, and no longer would the "service-connected" test be a matter for concern. More importantly, it enabled a fully disciplined military.

When the Court overturned *O'Callahan* in 1987, the Soviet Union remained a potent adversary and it was by no means clear that it would internally collapse. *Solorio* was argued on February 24, 1987 and decided on June 25 of the same year. In between the argument and the issuance of the decision, an Iraqi aircraft fired a missile into a United States naval vessel, the USS *Stark*. It is probable that the Iraqi pilot mistook the *Stark* for an Iranian naval vessel, but the loss of 37 American sailors was a reminder that a long-term American involvement in the Persian Gulf was likely. On October 19, 1987, United States naval forces attacked two Iranian oil platforms in the Persian Gulf in response to Iranian attacks on Kuwaiti flagged oil tankers. The next year, an American naval vessel shot down an Iranian airliner, killing 290 civilians. The commander of the vessel believed that the airliner was a military aircraft and presented a danger to his vessel. Nonetheless, the incident was compared to the Soviet shooting down of the Korean airliner four years earlier. The Iranian government vowed to retaliate. The Soviet Union remained militarily strong, even though its retreat from Afghanistan provided an appearance of a defeated superpower. Between the United States' involvement in South and Central America, and the potential for war in the Persian Gulf, the year of *Solorio* hardly promised peace.

Since the Soviet Union's dissolution, the United States military has almost continuously been employed around the world in disaster assistance, advisory roles, human rights interventions, and in active hostile kinetic as well as electronic and cyber-space operations. Even with Rehnquist's belief that *Solorio* enabled Congress to permit the military establishment to reassert jurisdiction to the point of a complete control over disciplinary functions, the Court as a whole did not intend the military establishment to revert to an insulated, separate system. Its decisions arising from courts-martial often integrated into the nation's broader constitutional and criminal law, continuing the trend which began, or at least accelerated during Burger's tenure.

31 Brennan, Conference notes, undated [WJB/I:736].

III: The Rehnquist Court

Although conservatives hoped the Court under Rehnquist would reverse the Warren Court's equal protection jurisprudence, this did not entirely occur. The government maintains affirmative action programs, including in contract bidding processes, state universities may still consider race as a factor in admissions, abortion in the majority of states remains legal and there is no prohibition on interstate travel for abortions. Employers remain liable for the sexual and racial harassment of their personnel. Indeed, Rehnquist drafted *Meritor Savings Bank v. Vinson* in the last term of the Burger Court in which the Court held that sexual harassment is a form of discrimination. In terms of the Court's military law jurisprudence, following *Solorio*, the Court would not exempt the military from broader constitutional and statutory principles.[32]

Perhaps, because the Senate was once more focused on Rehnquist, Antonin Scalia's nomination to succeed Rehnquist as associate justice occurred without much legislative opposition. Born to immigrant Sicilian parents in 1936, in Trenton, New Jersey, Scalia was a standout student who attended Jesuit schools in Manhattan. His father, an immigrant to the United States, became a professor of Romance languages at Brooklyn College, and his mother an elementary school teacher. In 1957, he graduated from Georgetown University as his class's valedictorian, and from Harvard's law school, cum laude, in 1960. From 1961 to 1967, Scalia worked in a Cleveland law firm, and then became a professor at the University of Virginia's law school. In Nixon's last year, Scalia was appointed as general counsel to the Office of Telecommunications Policy, and then in 1974, to the Department of Justice. After Carter's election, he left government service and joined the American Enterprise Institute. From 1977 to 1982, he served on the University of Chicago's law school faculty, and in 1982, Reagan appointed him to the Court of Appeals for the District of Columbia. While on the appellate court, Scalia evidenced that he would not defer to the military in all matters, particularly where the First Amendment was involved. His dissent in *Goldman* was perhaps the most poignant example of his application of rights jurisprudence in the military context.[33]

In 1986, he and Judge Kenneth Starr in *Bois v. Marsh*, acknowledged that a superior officer's sexual harassment when directed against a subordinate could hamper the subordinate's promotion prospects and career advancement. The two judges also accepted that the quantum of harassment directed against Captain Joyce L. Bois, the aggrieved officer, was intolerable. However, problematic to Bois'

32 *Meritor Savings Bank v. Vinson*, 477 U.S. 77 (1986); *Oncale v. Sundowner Offshore Services*, 523 U.S. 75 (1998).

33 Richard Brsibin Jr., *Justice Anotnin Scalia and the Conservative Revival* (Baltimore, MD: Johns Hopkins Unviersity Press, 1997), 10–28; Bernard Schwartz, *A History of the Supreme Court* (New York: Oxford University Press, 1993), 367–9; Melvin Urofsky, *A March of Liberty*, 947.

appeal was that because she had voluntarily resigned her commission, her appeal was moot in regards to her generalized lawsuit which claimed the Department of the Army's internal procedures did not afford her due process. As to her specific argument for the military to purge her records, the appellate court determined that she had not yet exhausted her administrative remedies. While the decision was certainly not a victory for Bois, it showed that Scalia would not automatically defer to the military establishment in regards to its policies on women.[34]

Scalia showed little interest in expanding the concept of privacy rights, particularly for homosexual service-members or civilian Department of Defense employees. In *Dronenberg v. Zech*, he joined Robert Bork and Glen Morgan Williams, a district court judge sitting by special designation, in limiting privacy rights. The three judges acknowledged that based on *Matlovich v. Secretary of the Air Force*, a 1974 decision in which the Court of Appeals for the District of Columbia determined that at a minimum the Secretary of the Air Force would have to reasonably determine that a decorated service-member's private consensual homosexuality was incompatible with military service, the appellate court now had to take jurisdiction over claims of service-members discharged on grounds of homosexuality. In *Zech*, an honorably discharged sailor sued the Navy alleging that the right to privacy protected consensual homosexual conduct. The three judges concluded that the right to privacy did not extend to homosexual conduct, but then added that within the unique requirements of military discipline, privacy rights are further narrowed. Moreover, the three judges concluded that the Secretary of the Navy was free to implement regulations to enforce morality. Morality is, of course, a loose term which is often defined in a non-universal manner. *Zech* made clear that while Scalia would hold the military establishment to account when its policies conflicted with the Constitution's plain text, he would not do so in other matters.[35]

In 1987, the Department of Defense issued a new regulation requiring "key federal employees," including federal judges, to transfer from the active reserves to the "Standby Reserves," or be discharged. The Standby Reserves is a non-paid category with a nominal reporting requirement, but still with the possibility of a call-up in times of national emergency. The purpose underlying the regulation had to do with personnel holding key positions being unable to fulfill their reserve obligations, and in the case of federal judges, there was also a separation of powers question. The appellant in this case, Allen Sharp, a Nixon appointee, who served as Chief Judge for the Northern District of Illinois, was also a lieutenant colonel in the Air Force Reserves. Both the District Court for the District of Columbia and the Court of Appeals for the District of Columbia sided with the government. Sharp had urged that the Court of Appeals for the Seventh Circuit should have taken jurisdiction. Scalia captioned Sharps suit, "[i]f there is a less profitable expenditure

34 *Bois v. Marsh*, 801 F.2d 462 (CA DC, 1986).

35 *Dronenberg v. Zech*, 741 F.2d 1388 (CA DC 1984). See also, *Matlovich v. Secretary of the Air Force*, 591 F.2d 852 (CA DC 1978).

of the time and resources of federal courts and federal litigants than resolving a threshold issue of which particular federal court should have jurisdiction, it does not come readily to mind."[36]

Much has been written about Scalia's devout Catholic faith and his conservatism, as well as his cutting wit on the Court. Although he is a conservative justice who Reagan had hoped would uphold tough restrictions on criminal defendants, his textual jurisprudence has not been a boon to prosecutors by any means. In Sixth Amendment matters, he has forced prosecutors to produce witnesses and narrowed hearsay exceptions. He has also held the government strictly accountable in instances where law enforcement has gone beyond the parameters of search warrants. Yet, he has also refused to narrow the application of the death penalty or harsh sentencing codes. It is not difficult to see why Scalia would vote to overturn *O'Callahan*, but one has to wonder, given his protection of free speech, whether he would have sided with Rehnquist in *Levy*, *Avrech*, or drafted a concurrence.[37]

Reagan's second nomination, Anthony McLeod Kennedy was born in Sacramento, California in 1936. His father was a prominent local attorney. Kennedy's academic resume includes Stanford, the London School of Economics, and Harvard Law School. He graduated Phi Beta Kappa from Stanford, and with distinction from Harvard. In between his entry into the legal profession and appointment to the Court, he worked in private practice, taught constitutional law at the McGeorge School of Law, and served on the Court of Appeals for the Ninth Circuit. Prior to his appellate court appointment, Kennedy assisted Governor Reagan on state tax issues. He also served in the California National Guard as a private. In 1975, Reagan recommended Kennedy to President Ford for the appellate court. Kennedy also befriended Edwin Meese who would later become Reagan's attorney general, and Meese would later recommend Kennedy to Reagan for the Court.[38]

In 1987, when Powell informed Reagan that he intended to retire from the Court, Reagan first nominated Robert Bork. Unlike the failed nomination of Carswell, none of Bork's opponents could claim he lacked the intellectual wherewithal to serve on the Court. Bork's scholarly resume could match any of the serving justices. But, his conservative jurisprudence on the Court of Appeals for the District of Columbia, as well as his states' rights, anti-*Roe v. Wade*, and strong Executive Branch positions were used to derail his nomination. Reagan's second choice, Douglas Ginsburg, admitted to using marijuana and withdrew his nomination. In turn, Reagan nominated Kennedy who was approved by a 97 to nothing vote in the Senate.[39]

---

36 *Sharp v. Weinberger*, 798 F.2d 1521 (CA DC, 1986).

37 See e.g. *Crawford v. Washington*, 541 U.S. 36 (2004); and most recently, *United States v. Jones*, 132 S.Ct 945 (2012); *Maryland v. Craig*, 497 U.S. 836 (1990) [Scalia dissenting]; and *Bullcoming v. New Mexico* 564 U.S. __ (2011).

38 Timothy Hall, *Supreme Court Justices*: A Biography, 412–13.

39 Thomas R. Hensley, *The Rehnquist Court*, 75–89.

Unlike Scalia, Kennedy left little indication as to what his military law jurisprudence would be. In *Denton v. Schlesinger*, he took part in a decision that determined male officers who claimed that their discharge from the navy was unconstitutional on the basis of gender discrimination, even in light of *Schlesinger v. Ballard*, had to seek redress though the Court of Claims, rather than the district court. This decision was the sole military governance issue to come before Kennedy prior to his ascension to the Court. Kennedy has been a "swing vote" on the Court, and he has evidenced a dislike of Executive Branch primacy. He has mostly sided with the majority on military law decisions.[40]

When Brennan retired in 1990, liberals feared that his replacement would be a conservative justice who would work with Rehnquist to undo the Warren Court's landmark decisions. This did not occur. Born in Melrose, Massachusetts and raised in New Hampshire, David Hackett Souter, the first of George H.W. Bush's appointments to the bench, like his peers, possessed stellar academic credentials. He graduated from Harvard's undergraduate and law schools, and in-between, he received a Rhodes Scholarship to study at Oxford University. While at Oxford in the early 1960s, he openly voiced his disagreement with President Kennedy's policies. Souter never served in the military as a result of being classified 1-Y by the Selective Service for a minor leg deformity. He has become known as a stealth candidate, who has not lived up to the expectations of conservatives. Yet, his resume evidenced a conservative jurisprudence, including a stated admiration of Judge Learned Hand and respect for *stare decisis*.

After a two-year stint in private practice, he joined the New Hampshire attorney general's office working for future senator Warren Rudman. When Rudman left the state attorney general's position, Souter advanced behind him. In 1978, he was named an associate justice of the state superior court, and then, in 1983, the New Hampshire Supreme Court. In 1989, Bush nominated Souter for the Court of Appeals for the First Circuit, but three months after confirmation, Souter was nominated to the Court. His nomination was troublesome in the sense that he did not leave a record of scholarship or judicial decisions to provide the Senate with a full view into his jurisprudence. Nonetheless, the Senate confirmed him by a vote of 90 to nine. Legal scholar Mark Tushnet has convincingly argued that Souter is, in fact, conservative, but he had never dealt with issues of national security, military law, or other Executive Branch matters prior to coming to the Court.[41]

If Souter has failed to live up to the hopes of conservatives, Bush's second appointment, Clarence Thomas, exceeded their expectations. Thomas was born into an impoverished family in segregated Georgia in 1948. He was raised by his mother, and then maternal grandmother and grandfather who worked to ensure he received a Catholic school education. He attended a previously all-white seminary,

40 *Denton v. Schlesinger*, 605 F.2d 484 (CA 9, 1979).

41 Thomas R. Hensley, *The Rehnquist Court*, 80–81; Mark Tushnet, *A Court Divided*, 57; Tinsley Yarbrough, *David Hackett Souter: Traditional Republican on the Rehnquist Court* (New York: Oxford University Press, 2005), 1–24.

and then Holy Cross College, graduating with honors. Like Souter, Thomas received deferments from military service and was ultimately classified 1-A, but he failed a physical examination for a curvature of the spine. After Holy Cross, Thomas attended Yale's law school, graduating in 1974.[42]

For the first three years after his graduation, Thomas worked in the Missouri Attorney General's office under John Danforth, and following Danforth's election to the Senate, Thomas worked in the general counsel's office for the Monsanto Corporation. In 1981, Reagan appointed him Assistant Secretary of Education for Civil Rights, and then in 1982, to the chairmanship of the Equal Employment Opportunity Commission (EEOC). In this position he steered the EEOC away from large class-action lawsuits against employers. In October 1989, Bush nominated Thomas to the Court of Appeals for the District of Columbia where he served a brief 19 months.[43]

While on the appellate court, Thomas dissented in *Doe v. Sullivan*, an appeal from a suit in which a soldier and his wife challenged the authority of the Food and Drug Administration to grant waivers to the Department of Defense, thereby permitting the military establishment during wartime conditions to employ experimental non-approved drugs for protection against biological and chemical warfare. This issue is important to the military establishment. It is also important to individual service-members, many of whom worry about the safety of vaccines, manufactured by companies who have been cited for violations of FDA standards that are manufactured in processes which bypass otherwise mandatory FDA safeguards. The majority decision, authored by future justice Ruth Bader Ginsburg, determined that the challenge remained within the court's jurisdiction, even though the conflict against Iraq had ended. But the appellate court determined that it would defer to the FDA, and by implication the military establishment, in its rule-making. Thomas counteredthat the appeal was moot because the conditions under which the Department of Defense could obtain a waiver were over. Thomas did not state an objection to the use of non-approved, experimental drugs on service-members, nor did he voice an opinion on judicial deference to the military in the decision.[44]

When Bush nominated Thomas after Thurgood Marshall submitted his retirement, the nomination process was one of the most contentious in history. He was accused of sexual harassment, and subjected to a level of scrutiny unlike any prior justice in the modern era about his personal life. Thomas' detractors have accused him of being unqualified for judicial service, or worse, being a clone of Scalia. Neither is true, and such comparisons are reminiscent of those who believed that Frankfurter and Jackson constituted a single vote. Thomas' originalism and

42 Melvin Urofsky, *A March of Liberty: A Constitutional History of the United States, Vol. II*, 1015–17.

43 Thomas R. Hensley, *The Rehnquist Court*, 85–90; Mark Tushnet, *A Court Divided*, 72–4.

44 *Doe v. Sullivan*, 938 F.2d 1370 (CA DC 1991).

textual interpretation of the Constitution have occasionally placed him at odds with Scalia, including in First Amendment decisions. In matters of military law, Thomas would side with the Executive Branch on almost all matters, where Scalia would refuse to do so.

In 1993, Byron White informed President Clinton of his intention to retire from the Court, and in his place Clinton nominated Ruth Bader Ginsburg, a judge on the Court of Appeals for the District of Columbia. Carter appointed Ginsburg to that court in 1980. Ginsburg had, earlier in her career, fought for equal treatment of women and played a critical role in *Frontiero v. Richardson*. She also joined with Scalia in dissenting in *Goldman v. Weinberger*.[45]

Born in 1933, in Brooklyn, New York, she attended Cornell University in 1954, earning a degree in government and graduating Phi Beta Kappa. Following graduation she enrolled at Harvard Law School, but transferred to Columbia University's law school. Although she possessed stellar academic credentials, Frankfurter turned her down for a clerkship, solely based on her gender. From 1963 to 1972, she taught at Rutgers University's law school, and then from 1972 to 1980, she taught at Columbia's law school. Her familiarity with the military included residing at Fort Sill, Oklahoma, where her husband trained as an artillery officer.[46]

Despite Ginsburg's 13 years on the appellate court, her involvement with decisions arising from military governance appeals was minimal, and there appear to be no decisions she took part in that originated in courts-martial. In *Antoine v. United States*, a brief *per curiam* decision, she evidenced adherence to *Feres*. If conservatives had any fears of her military law jurisprudence, these would partly be allayed in 2006, after Rehnquist's death, when she sided with a unanimous Court that the government could withhold funds from universities which refused to permit equal access to military recruiters as with organizations and corporations.[47]

Following Blackmun's notification of his intent to retire, Clinton nominated David Breyer. Breyer was born in San Francisco in 1939, to parents active in the local Democrat Party. He attended Stanford University, graduating Phi Beta Kappa in 1959. In 1961, he also graduated from Oxford University with a second bachelor's degree, and then from Harvard Law School in 1964. Following his law school graduation, he clerked for Arthur Goldberg, and then worked at the Department of Justice until 1967. He also served in the Army Reserves as a corporal after his graduation from Stanford.

Prior to his judicial appointment, Breyer taught at Harvard, and was an assistant special prosecutor in the Watergate break-in trials. He also served as a counsel to the Senate Judiciary Committee, which brought him in close contact with senators from both parties. In 1980, Carter nominated Breyer to the Court of

45 On Ginsburg's role in *Frontiero*, see Seth Sterns and Stephen Wermiel, *Justice Brennan: Liberal Champion*, 393–7.

46 Thomas R. Hensley, *The Rehnquist Court*, 90–92; Timothy R. Hall, *Supreme Court Justices: A Biographical Dictionary*, 424–7.

47 *Antoine v. United States*, 990 F.2d 1377 (CA DC 1993).

Appeals for the First Circuit. Breyer's military law jurisprudence on the appellate court evidenced a balance between deference to the military establishment and forcing the military to strictly adhere to its regulations. In *Chilcot v. Orr*, he took part in an appeal arising from an administrative discharge of an airman. Chilcot, had been arrested by civilian police while selling LSD to an undercover officer. At the time of his arrest, Air Force regulations provided for a discharge board hearing in which a service-member could contest the government's evidence, much in the same manner as a court-martial, but with the lower burden of "proof by a preponderance of the evidence" on the government. The administrative right to a board included first term airmen recommended for a general discharge. However, at the time the Air Force discharged Chilcot, first-term airmen such as Chilcot, had been exempted from the right to a board if the Air Force sought a general or honorable discharge. Chilcot retained the administrative right to present appeal through his chain of command, with the assistance of a military defense counsel, but the discharge decision rested with a single officer rather than a panel.

Chilcot obtained an injunction against the Air Force in the District Court for New Hampshire. However the appellate court reversed, citing to *Orloff* for the principle that "judges are not given the task of running the [military]." The appellate court further determined that a change in regulations does not confer any constitutional rights on a person in the same manner that changes in laws do. In 1969, in a public housing decision, the Court had determined that regulations in place at the time of a hearing governed challenges to governmental decisions, "rather than regulations existing at the time when events giving rise to the action occur." Breyer was in full concurrence with this decision.[48]

In *Hager v. Secretary of the Air Force*, Breyer evidenced a jurisprudence comporting with *Harmon*, even though the appellate decision did not cite to *Harmon*. The appeal arose from the Air Force's denial of conscientious objector status to a medical doctor that the government had sent through medical school on a taxpayer funded government program. Captain Gilbert Hager, as a result of the program, owed little in the way of a student loan debt, but he was obligated to military service. Shortly before hostilities with Iraq in the first Gulf War, Hager claimed conscientious objection. Not surprisingly the military authorities doubted the depth of his beliefs and denied him an exemption. Hager's self-described faith was a meld of Christian and Buddhist pacifism, and while the determination process did not question his sincerity, it denied him conscientious objection on the basis of not possessing a sufficiently deep or profound conviction. This was enough for the Court of Appeals for the First Circuit to remand the issue to the district court which had denied review in the first place, but not for Breyer who authored a concurrence. Breyer added that there was nothing in the record to support the military's denial.[49]

48 *Chilcot v. Orr*, 747 F.2d 29 (CA 1, 1984).

49 *Hager v. Secretary of the Air Force*, 938 F.2d 1449 (CA 1, 1991).

IV: Post-*Solorio* Conflicts: 1988–2002

Leonid Brezhnev died in late 1982 and in his place the Soviet government selected Yuri Andropov as General Secretary. Andropov's foreign policy was as confrontational as Brezhnev's, and it was during his leadership that the Soviet Air Force shot down the Korean airliner. Both Andropov and his successor, Konstantin Chernenko were elderly and in poor health, and in March, 1985, a youthful Mikhail Gorbachev assumed power. Gorbachev inherited a Soviet economy strained by the fact that over one fourth of its gross domestic product was spent on the military. He intended to open the Soviet economy and diffuse tensions with the west, but the unintended consequences of his actions included increased pressures to retreat from Eastern Europe. By 1990, Germany had unified and communists were removed from the government. Communism collapsed in Poland, Bulgaria, Czechoslovakia, Hungary, and Romania. Even the Baltic states of Estonia, Latvia, and Lithuania moved away from Soviet influence. By the end of 1991, the Soviet Union itself began to dissolve as the republics of the Ukraine and Georgia asserted independence, an event unimaginable only five years earlier. Reagan's and Weinberger's policies then had contributed to causing the Soviets to collapse. However successful these policies were, the potential for world peace was low.

In 1992, future Secretary of Defense Les Aspin argued, "in the new world of present and future, we must contemplate an action that only the political right has previously considered: the possibility of conducting a preemptive attack to prevent countries from gaining nuclear arsenals." To ensure that the United States possessed a disciplined visible deterrent, Aspin did not favor significant reductions or a liberalizing of UCMJ jurisdiction. No defense secretary or attorney general since has argued differently. Thus, during Clinton's presidency, and since, there has been no political effort undertaken to return to *O'Callahan*. There is a good reason for this. The military has been almost continuously engaged in operations since *Solorio*. It is true that the focus of military operations shifted away from containing communism, to unconventional warfare in the Middle East, as well as deterring Iran and North Korea, and counter terrorism missions. Added to these two focus areas was the use of the military to reduce international drug trafficking, anti-piracy operations, cyberspace operations, and an incremental increase of forces in the Pacific region to assure allies, as well as humanitarian missions.[50]

---

50 Les Aspin, *Congress and the Future of the United States Military: Text of a Speech Delivered at the University of California Irvine, January 23, 1992* (Irvine, CA: Center for Global Peace and Conflict Studies, 1992), 11. Aspin also noted that such an attack "will have to be done cooperatively with the support and approval of the United Nations or the international community in some organized body, but chances are that it will be the United States military forces who would do the job." Executive Branch advisors during George W. Bush's administration would disagree with Aspin's caveat.

In March 1988, Reagan directed over 1,000 military personnel to augment the over 10,000 already stationed in the Panama Canal Zone and called on Panamanian President Manuel Noriega to resign. Noriega resisted Reagan and ignored the results of an election which clearly indicated he no longer had the support of the Panamanian citizenry. On May 11, 1989, President Bush ordered a further increase in American forces in the canal-zone. Later in that year, American naval aviation confronted Libyan fighter aircraft in the Gulf of Sidra. American forces were also sent to Colombia, Bolivia, and Peru to assist in anti-drug operations. Toward the end of 1989, it became clear that Philippine President Corazón Aquino's government was endangered by a coup. Although her dictatorial predecessor, Ferdinand Marcos had been ousted from power, a small contingent of the Philippine military remained loyal to him. Bush administration officials believed that it would be strategically disastrous to lose the United States' military bases in the Philippines. Ultimately, these bases were ceded back to the Philippines without much incident, but at the time, there were worries of a communist takeover of the Philippine government.[51]

In 1989, Bush ordered an invasion of Panama in what became captioned as Operation Just Cause. Noriega had ties to the Bush administration and the Central Intelligence Agency, but he had also engaged in international narcotics smuggling and his government's human rights record was appalling. Within a six-week period, almost 30,000 American service-members defeated Noriega's questionably loyal forces. While the United States possessed far greater technologic superiority over the Panamanian military, much of the disorganization which characterized the Grenadian invasion was avoided in Panama.[52]

On August 2, 1990, the Iraqi Army invaded Kuwait. United States and Iraqi relations were tenuous since Saddam Hussein had allied with the Soviet Union and supported anti-Israeli groups. Hussein had also funded terrorism against western interests. Nonetheless, following the earlier Iraqi invasion of Iran in 1983, Reagan established nominal relations with Hussein. In response to the Iraqi invasion of Kuwait, and Hussein's refusal to accede to international pressure, Bush obtained from the United Nations Security Council a demand for an Iraqi withdrawal. Shortly after, at the request of the Saudi Arabian government, United States and allied forces moved into Saudi Arabia. Following Hussein's refusal to comply with the Security Council's order that his forces leave Kuwait, allied forces invaded Iraq, beginning with an aerial campaign on January 16, 1991. Within two months, Hussein's military was pushed from Kuwait and no longer able to defend Iraq. Over 20,000 Iraqi soldiers were killed, and 75,000 injured. Allied coalition forces lost less than 500 killed. This one-sided casualty count was largely a result of the

51 Ted Galen Carpenter, *A Search for Enemies: America's Alliances After the Cold War* (Washington, DC: Cato Institute, 1992), 101–4.

52 Lawrence J. Korb, "The United States," in Douglas J. Murray, *The Defense Policies of Nations: A Comparative Study* 3rd ed. (Baltimore, MD: Johns Hopkins University Press, 1994), 19–57.

coalition's command of the air, and the technological superiority of their forces. Nonetheless, the United States military comprised the majority of the coalition, and with few exceptions, its discipline was not in question.

More than any other post-Vietnam conflict prior to 2003, the size and scope of what became known as Operation Desert Storm was a political gamble. That an international coalition, to include both Egyptian and Syrian forces, sided with the United States leant to the legality of the United States' participation in the conflict. Nonetheless, the transfer of over one half of a million service-members to the Middle East was a scale of military operations not seen since Vietnam. There were a number of smallish protests against the United States taking part in the conflict at all, but these were muted by the short duration of the conflict. A few service-members, namely reservists and National Guard troops, refused to transit to the Middle East, or applied for conscientious objection. But, nothing close to the scale of conscientious objection or disciplinary failures in Vietnam occurred during Desert Storm. It is difficult to predict if there would have been lapses in discipline had the conflict continued for any length of time, or if conscription had returned, would it have succeeded. On the other hand, from the end of the Kuwaiti liberation until the present, United States service-members have been deployed in sizeable numbers to the Middle East, and there while there have been disciplinary lapses, prior to 2003 these do not appear to have occurred on the scale of what occurred during the Vietnam conflict. By all reasonable accounts, *Solorio* has accomplished what Rehnquist, Powell, and the other judicial conservatives intended.[53]

In 1992, a United States-led multi-national force, landed in Somalia with the United Nations' sanction. Its purpose of providing humanitarian aid in the midst of a murderous civil war was hardly objectionable. The civil war did not end, even though over 35,000 multi-national service-members were stationed in and around Mogadishu, Somalia. After a Somali attack on Pakistani soldiers, United States forces transitioned into combat operations. However, in 1994, President Clinton ordered the withdrawal of all military units from Somalia, after several Americans were killed in an ambush. Between 1990 and 2000, United States service-members were also deployed to Sierra Leone, Liberia, Haiti, East Timor, Cambodia, and Thailand. Surprisingly, the largest deployment of personnel outside of the Middle East occurred in Southern Europe.[54]

Although following World War II, it seemed unlikely that, absent a full scale war between east and west, conflict between modern states could occur, this is what happened in the former nation of Yugoslavia. A creation of Wilsonian internationalism, Yugoslavia emerged from World War II governed by a pro-communist central government led by strongman Josip Broz Tito. Despite

53 On military discipline during Operation Desert Storm, see Frederic Borch, *Judge Advocates in Combat: Military Operations from Vietnam to Haiti* (Washington, DC: GPO, 2001), 121–94.

54 David Halberstam, *War in a Time of Peace: Clinton, Bush, and the Generals* (New York: Touchstone, 2002), 250–65.

Tito's "iron rule," internal ethnic tensions between the majority Serb population and the Croats, Slovenes, and smaller Muslim populations remained a constant source of instability. Tito died in 1980, and following his death, Slobodan Milošević, a Serbian communist leader became the leader of a Serbian movement to centralize the state governments under his authority. In late 1990, elections in Croatia and Slovenia resulted in declarations of independence from Yugoslavia. The following year, the Serbian-led Yugoslavian military fired on Slovenian forces, and a 10-day long conflict ensued. Ultimately, the Yugoslavian government bowed to European pressure and Slovenia achieved independence. What occurred in Croatia was neither quick nor light in casualties. Serbian led Yugoslavian forces and Croat forces warred for months. Then, in March 1992, Bosnia and Herzegovina declared its independence from Yugoslavia, and a three year long war began which involved United States' military forces.[55]

In 1994, the United Nations Secretary General requested NATO intervention. United States military forces took part in coalition airstrikes against Serbian positions in an effort to terminate the Serbian government's sanction of systematic war crimes. Although Bosnia achieved independence in 1996, in 1999, Serbian military and government forces committed widespread crimes against humanity on a large scale in its Kosovo province, leading to NATO involvement once more. United States casualties were low, but the fact that the majority of Republicans in the House and Senate opposed involvement in the conflict might have provided a means for service-members to challenge the legality of the United States involvement.[56]

While there were courts-martial for refusals to obey orders arising from overseas operations, none of the appeals to the federal judiciary were successful. In *New v. Cohen*, the Court of Appeals for the District of Columbia in 1997, determined that Michael New, a service-member who challenged the legality of serving under United Nations command in Macedonia could not challenge the military's assertion of jurisdiction over him until all his military remedies were exhausted. The Army had already court-martialed New and he was sentenced to a Bad Conduct Discharge. However, his military appeals had not been completed at the time his appeal to the federal judiciary. The federal appellate court relied on *Councilman* and *Parisi* in denying New relief. In *Campbell v. Clinton*, the Court of Appeals for the District of Columbia determined that congressmen challenging the legality of the use of American forces in the conflict lacked standing to bring suit.[57]

55 Ryan C. Hendrickson, *The Clinton Wars: The Constitution, Congress, and the War Powers* (Nashville, TN: Vanderbilt University Press, 2002), 117–38.

56 Andrew J. Bacevich, *American Empire: The Realities and Consequences of U.S. Diplomacy* (Boston, MA: Harvard University Press, 2002), 99–104.

57 *New v. Cohen*, 129 F.3d 639 (CA DC 1997); *Campbell v. Clinton*, 203 F.3d 19 (CA DC 2000).

V: The Court and Courts-Martial

In 1996, the Court of Military Appeals was renamed the Court of Appeals for the Armed Forces. Commensurately the intermediate service appellate courts underwent name changes. The Air Force Court of Review was renamed the Air Force Court of Criminal Appeals; the Army Court of Review was renamed the Army Court of Criminal Appeals; and the Navy–Marine Corps Court of Review was renamed the Navy–Marine Corps Court of Criminal Appeals. The jurisdiction of the courts remained the same as before, and the name changes were largely undertaken to provide a concise title to the narrow subject area of the courts. That is, the military appellate courts were not simply reviewing appeals, but rather accomplishing what the other federal courts of appeal do.

Solorio did not settle all challenges to courts-martial jurisdiction or the construct of courts-martial. All persons tried in criminal courts are entitled to a judiciary which adheres to the laws, and is immune from external influences. After all, this is one principle of ensuring fair trials. In 1968, Congress established the position of military judges for courts-martial, empowering military judges with authorities similar to those of federal district court judges in criminal trials. Federal district court judges and their appellate brethren, with the exception of specified limited jurisdiction courts, enjoy life tenure as a constitutional mandate. In theory, life tenure insulates judges from political or corruptive influences. More importantly, the Constitution, in its "appointments clause," specifically mandates life tenure for the Court and other lesser general jurisdiction courts. Civilian judges on the limited jurisdiction Court of Appeals for the Armed Forces serve for a fixed term of years. Military judges, however, do not hold life tenure or fixed terms, and are subject to chains of command, internal to the service Judge Advocates General. Serving military judges are amenable to be transferred to non-judicial postings. Thus while there is considerable protection from command influence, there is no complete insulation from it. Congress set statutory requirements for military judges, including being a commissioned officer, holding a law degree, and an appointment to practice in the federal courts or admitted to the bar of a state's highest court.

In 1994, the Court determined that the unique conditions of military judges did not violate the "appointments clause," and was therefore constitutional. In 1992, the Court of Military Appeals determined, in two decisions, that the lack of a fixed term of office for military judges is constitutional. That court, however, was divided over whether the requirements of military judges, that is, holding a presidential commission required for all officers satisfied the appointments clause, or whether this clause applied to the military at all. The Court consolidated the two military decisions into a singular decision titled *Weiss v. United States*. A special court-martial convicted Private Eric Weiss of stealing sporting goods from the base exchange and sentenced him to three months confinement and a bad conduct discharge. A general court-martial convicted the other petitioner, a sailor named Ronald D. Graff, of stealing and then selling military property, and the more serious offense of attempted espionage, and then sentenced him to a dishonorable discharge and five years in confinement.[58]

In conference, no justice articulated that the appointment of military judges violated the Constitution, and Rehnquist assigned himself to write the majority decision. In his circulated draft, he concluded that since military judges were already commissioned officers appointed by the President and approved by the Senate, the appointments clause was satisfied. However, he noted that a second question had to be answered, which involved whether Congress intended for a second "appointment" in the creation of the military judge position. The plain language of the 1968 statute establishing the military judge position did not contain "advise and consent" language. Rehnquist conceded that an argument existed that even if Congress had failed to add clear language, the judicial nature of the position differed considerably from the general commissioning of military officers. To diminish this argument, he turned to *Levy* and the broader concept of the separate society. That is, military officers are commissioned once in their career, and the Senate does not individually approve each and every commission every time an officer is promoted to a new rank. The Senate approves promotions below the rank of general officer in bulk.

For the most part, all of the justices agreed with the result of Rehnquist's draft, which he circulated on December 9, 1993. O'Connor agreed to join the following day, Stevens three days later, and Blackmun, Ginsburg and Kennedy after Stevens. Scalia was willing to agree with the result but had reservations with Rehnquist's analysis on the Constitution's appointments clause, because Rehnquist had indicated that he believed the presidential appointment power could be diminished through non-life tenured appointments. On the other hand, he assured Rehnquist that he was "on record in support of the proposition that any process which was around at the beginning of the Republic, and has continued to be used ever since is *ipso facto* due process."[59]

Rehnquist's circulated draft basically became the published decision. Souter concurred, but added that military judges were "inferior officers" within the Constitution, and not "principal officers," requiring a separate confirmation process. Ginsburg's concurrence lauded the present fairness of the military justice system. Scalia and Thomas likewise concurred, but criticized the majority for overanalyzing the applicability of the appointments clause to the issue. Scalia wanted to ensure that the decision was unique to the military and did not intrude

58 *Weiss v. United States*, 510 U.S. 163 (1994); The two Court of Military Appeals decision are *United States v. Graf*, 25 M.J. 450 (CMA, 1992), and *United States v. Weiss*, 36 M.J. 224 (CMA, 1992).

59 O'Connor to Rehnquist, December 10, 1993 [HAB/638]; Stevens to Rehnquist, December 13, 1993 [HAB/638]; Blackmun to Rehnquist, December 13, 1993 [HAB/638]; Ginsburg to Rehnquist, December 13, 1993 [HAB/638]; Kennedy to Rehnquist, December 14, 1993 [HAB/638]; Scalia to Rehnquist, December 14, 1993 [HAB/638].

into the prerogatives of the Legislative Branch. In reality, all of the justices intended not to have the decision apply outside of the military's governance.

In *Davis v. United States*, the Court utilized a court-martial appeal to clarify the point at which law enforcement officers must cease questioning a suspect, when the suspect asserts his or her right to have counsel present during an interrogation. In 1981, in *Edwards v. Arizona*, the Court determined that law enforcement officers had to immediately cease questioning when a suspect asserts his rights, but that decision was predicated on an unambiguous, clear assertion of rights. *Edwards* did not necessarily include a category of suspect who wonders aloud whether he or she should have an attorney. In *Davis*, the accused service member was suspected of murdering a fellow sailor after a dispute in a pool hall on base. The Naval Criminal Investigative Service questioned the accused, who, as in the example above, merely wondered aloud whether he should have a lawyer present. The Court of Military Appeals affirmed Davis' court-martial conviction and sentence to life imprisonment.[60]

In writing for the majority, O'Connor sidestepped the differences between how the Sixth Amendment's right to counsel and the Fifth Amendment's right against self-incrimination applied to the military versus civilians, or how UCMJ Article 31 rights might stand in comparison to the two amendments. Article 31 is similar to *Miranda*, but the military right to remain silent predated *Miranda* by over a decade. Instead, O'Connor, along with the majority, determined that the clear assertion of a desire for counsel governs when questioning must cease. Scalia concurred, but used his concurrence to scold the government for not arguing the confession's admissibility on a statutory basis, which would have been another grounds for admissibility. Souter, Blackmun, Stevens, and Ginsburg concurred as well, but the four justices did not agree with O'Connor's point that the law enforcement officers were under no obligation to clarify statements such as "maybe I should speak with a lawyer." One noteworthy part of this case is that originally, O'Connor was in agreement with Blackmun, Souter, Stevens, and Ginsburg, but after a discussion with Rehnquist, she changed her mind and was assigned the majority decision.[61]

What is striking about *Davis*, is not that it is a visible win for the military, but in opposite, how it avoids any unique military issues altogether. Unlike *Weiss*, in *Davis*, the Court intended to issue a decision applicable to all law enforcement. On the other hand, *Davis* was a win for the military justice system in an indirect way. Six other cases were held over for the Court's decision in *Davis* and each of these arose from state criminal trials. Indeed, only Rehnquist appeared concerned on this point in conference. He wondered whether *Davis* was a sound case to take up at all, simply because it originated in an Article 31 rights advisement challenge. O'Connor was convinced that the public had greater trust in the efficacy of military law enforcement procedures and courts-martial than

---

60 *Davis v. United States*, 512 U.S. 452 (1994).

61 Blackmun, conference notes [HAB/640]; Scalia to O'Connor, May 17, 1994 [HAB/640]; and O'Connor to Rehnquist, May 11, 1994 [HAB/640].

Texas, Florida, or North Carolina police and criminal trials, a development which William O. Douglas would have found disconcerting had he lived to take part in the decision. No longer was the judiciary casting aspersions on the military justice system, or, in any significant manner, questioning the need for the continuance of a separate society.[62]

In 1996, the Court upheld the constitutionality of the military's death sentencing processes in *Loving v. United States*. Rehnquist assigned Kennedy to write the majority decision. On a single day in 1988, Private Dwight Loving murdered two taxi-cab drivers and attempted to murder a third cab driver in Killeen, Texas. Loving confessed to the murders, and a general court-martial sentenced him to death. After exhausting his military appeals through several appellate decisions, he petitioned the Court for *certiorari*, arguing that Congress, although it had legislated capital punishment into the UCMJ, had neither explicitly enumerated the aggravating factors listed in the Rules for Courts-Martial, nor properly delegated to the Executive Branch the responsibility for doing so. Loving secondarily argued that even if Congress had implicitly delegated the responsibility to the President, there was a failure to provide constitutionally adequate standards within the sentencing rules. Thus, Loving did not seek to give rebirth to *O'Callahan* or directly narrow *Solorio*, but rather he argued that Congress could not delegate due process to the Executive Branch. Finally, he challenged his sentence on the basis of the Eighth Amendment's prohibition against cruel and unusual punishment. Loving's Eighth Amendment argument was as likely to fail had he been a civilian in light of the Rehnquist Court's criminal law jurisprudence, and one of the similarities between Loving's trial and civilian trials, is that under the UCMJ, any sentence extending over 10 years imprisonment, including the death penalty, requires a unanimous vote.[63]

The majority acknowledged that for much of the nation's history, the military could not adjudge a death penalty during peace-time. It was not until 1950 that Congress empowered courts-martial to consider such sentences for a limited number of offenses where the prosecution proved various aggravating factors. In one significant respect, courts-martial were more advanced than many state criminal trials. In courts-martial, only a panel, rather than a sitting judge, possesses the discretion to capitally sentence an accused. The panel must find beyond a reasonable doubt that an offense possesses an aggravating factor and this factor "substantially outweighs" any mitigating aspects of the accused. Many states had

62 O'Connor to Rehnquist, June 24, 1994 [HAB/640]. The decisions held over included *Barber v. North Carolina*, 436 S.E.2d 106 (1993), where a suspect asked whether she needed a lawyer, and a police officer responded that he did not know but would read her, her rights as required; *Slawson v. Florida*, 619 So.2d 255 (Fl 1993), where a suspect stated, "what about an attorney?" before agreeing to confess; and, *Dean v. Kentucky*, 844 S.W.2d 417 (Ky 1992), where a suspect asked "should I have someone here," and a police officer responded, "that's up to you."

63 *Loving v. United States*, 517 U.S. 748 (1996).

enabled judges, rather than juries, to sentence a defendant to death, a practice which the Court has only recently, post-*Loving*, found unconstitutional.[64]

The government had not unreasonably argued that *Furman* was inapplicable to military trials, since, Blackmun and Burger had ensured that this was the state of the law as early as *Levy* and *Schick.* Kennedy, with Rehnquist's agreement, now concluded that *Furman* did apply to courts-martial. Although the Court had restored the death penalty in 1976, in *Gregg v. Georgia*, the basic holding of *Furman* remained intact. That is, the Court in *Furman* mandated that a death penalty sentencing process had to permit the finder of fact to consider the character and record of a defendant, and the sentencing process must limit the discretion to sentence a defendant to death. The Court in *Gregg* found that the standards set forth in *Furman* were met by the challenged Georgia statute.[65]

Kennedy based the initial part of his decision on applying *Furman* and *Gregg* into a separation of powers context. Loving had argued that Congress had unconstitutionally "forsook" its duties in permitting the President to develop a scheme which might, or might not, otherwise comport with *Gregg*. In other words, Loving urged that even if the scheme was lawful, the fact that the President initiated it, rather than Congress, rendered the scheme unconstitutional.

Loving had also premised his challenge on an argument that since the nation's founders feared military authority, Congress could not have given the military jurisdiction over capital crimes in peace time. To answer this part of Loving's contention, Kennedy partly turned to the same strand of English and Early American legal history that Black, Frankfurter, Douglas, Harlan, and ultimately Rehnquist, had fought over since *Toth.* Kennedy, in relying on the English historian George Macaulay—who Frankfurter had once termed during the *Toth* conference discussions as "a great historian but not the most accurate"—acknowledged that early English legal history presents a decisive view that the military ought to be permitted to be disciplined through a far more rigid code than the civilian criminal laws. This was because wayward soldiers were a menace to liberty, much as the Executive Branch's abuse of power could be. But he also conceded, in relying on Winthrop's *Military Law and Precedents* treatise, that for most of the nation's history, Congress prevented the military from prosecuting capital offenses in peacetime. The fundamental question before the Court then, was whether the there was a constitutional prohibition which could be inferred from the early practice of courts-martial, or whether the absence of the death penalty was merely a historic preference. Kennedy and the majority deduced that the later conclusion was accurate. What Kennedy neglected was that three decades following the Civil War there were anti-capital punishment bills presented in Congress, by Congressman Newton Martin Curtis, a Congressional Medal of Honor recipient and veteran Civil War general. When Curtis called for the abolition of the military's death penalty, Winthrop along with the Army's Judge Advocate General, G. Norman

64 See e.g. *Ring v. Arizona*, 536 U.S. 548 (2002).

65 *Gregg v. Georgia*, 428 U.S. 153 (1976).

Lieber testified that they did not oppose these bills because of the historic reticence to capital punishment. However, none the post-Civil War bills' advocates or Winthrop or Lieber stated that they believed the death penalty unconstitutional in peacetime.[66]

Deferring to Congress then, the majority concluded that the extension of the death penalty to courts-martial during peacetime for common law offenses was not, in and of itself, constitutionally repugnant. Scalia, in his concurrence, chided the majority for delving into what he believed an unnecessary history lesson. While Rehnquist and the other justices appeared eager to consign *O'Callahan* to a permanent graveyard, Scalia believed this had already been accomplished. Moreover, because Loving had not challenged *Solorio*, Scalia had good reason for concurring. But his optimism of *O'Callahan's* demise might have been premature. In a separate concurrence, Stevens, Souter, Ginsberg, and Breyer opined that capital courts-martial might require a "service-connection" in death penalty cases, because *Solorio* was not a death penalty decision.

Thomas concurred along similar lines as Scalia, adding that while the history lesson of the majority was interesting, the eighteenth-century division of power between Parliament and the British Crown did not provide insight into the division authority between the Legislative and Executive Branches, and therefore the historic inquiry was unnecessary to the decision. Thomas also noted that the applicability of *Furman* to courts-martial remained "an open question," not only because *Schick* had not addressed the question, but also because the government "surprisingly [made] no argument that the military is exempt from the byzantine rules we have imposed on the States in the administration of the death penalty." It would seem that while the Executive Branch was willing to concede that *Furman* applied to courts-martial, at least Thomas had doubts that it did. With over six service-members on death row as of 2012, the judiciary has yet to specifically, in plain language, answer this question. If there is any criticism to made on the Court, it is applicable both the majority and the dissent. Neither side examined the deep well of military legal history in arriving at their respective positions.

In 1999, the Court, in *Clinton v. Goldsmith*, confined the Court of Appeals for the Armed Forces' jurisdiction, in light of a strict reading of the All Writs Act. That Act enables the federal courts to extend their jurisdiction over claims which are necessary or appropriate "in aid of their respective jurisdictions." That is, a federal court may issue an order outside of its geographic or subject matter jurisdiction, if it is necessary to assist in determining an issue within the court's jurisdiction. The Air Force court-martialed Major James Goldsmith for violating a lawful order to inform all sexual partners that he had tested positive for the Human Immunodeficiency Virus (HIV). Goldsmith had failed to do so on at least two

66 Frankfurter to Harlan, October 26, 1954 [JMH/Box 5]; Newton Martin Curtis, *To Define the Crime of Murder, Provide Penalty Therefor, and to Abolish the Penalty of Death: Speech of General Newton Martin Curtis of New York in the House of Representatives, Thursday June 9, 1892* (GPO, 1892), 25–6.

occasions, and in 1994, a court-martial sentenced him to confinement for six years and a substantial forfeiture in pay and allowances. Goldsmith was not punitively discharged from the military and, in theory he could become retirement eligible, either through the military's medical review process, or simply by achieving 20 years of creditable service. The administrative discharge of officers requires an additional board hearing followed by the Secretary of the Air Force's review. This is a process which could have consumed a year or more of time.[67]

Rather than use this process, President Clinton, "dropped" Goldsmith "from the rolls." The term "dropped from the rolls," denotes a historic capability of the President to remove an officer from the military under certain circumstances, without the officer having the right to challenge the decision. An officer dropped from the rolls loses pay, allowances, and the chance for receipt of retired pay. At the time Clinton acted, the Executive Branch possessed the authority to drop an officer from the rolls who had served six months of a sentence adjudged by a state or federal criminal court.

Goldsmith appealed to the Air Force Court of Criminal Appeals, arguing that the All Writs Act gave the military courts jurisdiction to review the President's actions, and then argued that the "dropping from the rolls" in his case violated the Constitution's prohibition against the *ex post facto* application of law, as well as the prohibition against double jeopardy. He additionally claimed that military prison officials had interfered with his receipt of HIV medication. The intermediate service court of appeal denied his appeal, but the Court of Appeals for the Armed Forces reversed, finding that it had jurisdiction to adjudge Goldsmith's claim.

The Court reversed the appellate court, though it conceded that the All Writs Act established a broad base for the federal courts to review claims "in aid of" a court's jurisdiction. Because the Court of Appeals for the Armed Forces possessed a narrower jurisdiction than the federal courts of appeal, to the Court, it was illogical to assume that the military appellate court possessed jurisdiction to review an administrative decision which occurred after a court-martial appeal had already been decided upon. Moreover, Goldsmith had not exhausted his administrative remedies, and the Secretary of the Air Force had not acted on Goldsmith's administrative appeal. The Court also noted that the federal judiciary could possess jurisdiction after Goldsmith had exhausted his administrative appeals. Concededly, Goldsmith's illness could have led to his death prior to initiating a suit in federal court. Nonetheless, the Court of Appeals for the Armed Forces' extension of its jurisdiction beyond its statutory construction was not the appropriate answer to Goldsmith's claims. In recalling the odd alliance between Senator Strom Thurmond and the Department of Defense General Counsel, Diane Siemer, the Court's decision is logical.

In 1998, the Court, in *United States v. Scheffer*, once more granted *certiorari* of an appeal containing an issue applicable to all criminal courts, rather than simply

67 *Clinton v. Goldsmith*, 526 U.S. 529 (1999).

military trials. *Scheffer* originated in an Air Force court-martial where a military judge suppressed polygraph information favorable to an accused. Both the military and federal rules of evidence prohibited the use of polygraph data in criminal trials. Polygraph data had long been understood as being less than accurate in determining whether an individual had honestly answered a question, but because of the expanding nature of admissibility of expert evidence, polygraph results had, on occasion, in various state jurisdictions, been admitted into evidence. Most polygraph results introduced in criminal trials will not be in a defendant's favor. Thus Scheffer's appeal was unusual in that he wanted the polygraph result to be used as exculpatory evidence against a charge of using methamphetamines. The Air Force Court of Criminal Appeals upheld Scheffer's conviction and sentence, but the Court of Appeals for the Armed Forces reversed, determining that a blanket prohibition on polygraph data violated the Sixth Amendment.[68]

In writing for the majority Thomas concluded that since the Court had, long-ago established that the right to present evidence is not unlimited, but rather subject to the reasonable restrictions of relevancy and reliability, the blanket prohibition on polygraph evidence was not unconstitutional, unless it rested on unsound reasons. Thomas pointed out that the problem with polygraph data is three-fold. First, no consensus exists within the scientific community that polygraph data is reliable. Secondly, polygraph data by its very nature, usurps the fact finding role of juries. Finally, Thomas concluded that because of the unreliability of polygraph testing, the introduction of such data would cause trials within trials. The most notable feature of the majority decision is its universal applicability to criminal trials in all jurisdictions.

Kennedy, O'Connor, Ginsburg, and Breyer, concurred, in large part, because the decision foreclosed the possibility that polygraph methods and technology could, at a future time, become reliable, and therefore admissible. Additionally, the four justices urged that Thomas overstated the fact-finding role of juries. Stevens dissented, surprisingly lauding the intelligence and educational levels of service-members serving on courts-martial in comparison to civilian juries. Black and Douglas likely would have taken exception to Stevens' supposition that military juries were, in fact, of a higher caliber than their civilian counterparts.

Steven Lichtman labels *Scheffer* as a victory for the military, but given the decision's universal applicability, it is more reasonable to laud the decision as a victory for the majority of people brought to trial. It is true that Scheffer's polygraph was exculpatory in nature, but it is equally true that most polygraphs will have the opposite result of recording a person's deceptions. This was why the National Association of Criminal Defense Lawyers conceded in their support of Scheffer, that the admission of polygraph data could undermine the defenses of hundreds of persons accused of crimes. Scheffer has little to do with military discipline. It has everything to do with preserving the traditional criminal trial requirements of limiting the government's evidence to eyewitnesses and scientifically reliable data.

68 *United States v. Scheffer*, 523 U.S. 303 (1998).

VI: Civil Military Relations

In 1990, the Court determined that Congress possessed the authority to authorize the President to order the National Guard to train outside of the United States during peacetime, even without the consent of a state governor or the declaration of a national emergency. In early 1987, the Department of Defense ordered various National Guard units to train for their annual two week-long drills in Central America. That year, Congress, in what became captioned as "the Montgomery Amendment," gave the President this authority. The foreign policy purposes underlying the training was to give confidence to pro-United States Central American governments and undermine the Nicaraguan Government as well as communist guerilla forces in El Salvador and Honduras. A broader strategic reason was to show South American governments, as well as the Soviet Union and drug cartels that the United States possessed the capability to put military units in a short period anywhere in the Western Hemisphere. The legitimate training purposes included acclimatizing reserve and National Guard troops to conditions likely to be found in equatorial countries should the a conflict arise in such areas. By 1987, in the event the United States had to conduct a rapid mobilization, 18 of the 24 Army divisions would have been largely comprised of National Guard and reserve forces. Over half of the Air Force's domestic air defense aircraft, and one third of all tanker refueling aircraft were manned by state air guardsmen as well.[69]

Minnesota Governor Rudy Perpich sued the Department of Defense seeking a stay against the transference of Minnesota National Guard units to Central America. Whatever his political motivations, as the commander in chief of the state guard he had standing to sue, because the removal of guardsmen under state control could undermine the state's ability to confront a natural disaster or a large-scale civil disturbance. However, the federal government was, as a matter of statute, responsible for directing the training of National Guard forces because of possibility that such forces could be federalized in the event of a national emergency. The United States District Court for Minnesota rejected Governor Perpich's suit, and though a three judge panel of the Court of Appeals for the Eighth Circuit reversed, *en banc*, that court upheld the district court.[70]

Perpich appealed to the Court for a grant of *certiorari*, and once in conference, it was apparent that no single justice sided with the governor. Rehnquist originally intended to assign the decision to himself, but after Stevens vigorously argued that the history of the Militia Clause and the historic reasons for the formation of the National Guard after the Spanish American War undermined Perpich, Rehnquist assigned him to author the decision. Stevens' draft opinion did not cause any dissension amongst the justices, though Scalia pointed out that Stevens had to ensure that the decision was clearly written to articulate that in

69 *Perpich v. United States*, 469 U.S. 334 (1990).

70 *Perpich v. United States Department of Defense*, 666 F.Supp. 1319 (DC Minn. 1987); *Perpich v. United States Department of Defense*, 880 U.S. 11 (CA 8, 1989).

order to send National Guard forces to Central America for training purposes, the guardsmen had to be brought under federal orders. Marshall likewise insisted that the distinction be made that when the Guardsmen were in Central America the decision must not refer to them as "state guard," but rather as the National Guard of the United States.[71]

Stevens did, in fact, author a non-controversial narrow decision which did not alter the federal-state relation construct. Several state attorneys' general authored amicus briefs urging the Court to upheld the Eighth Circuit's *en banc* decision. For instance, Marc Racicot, the Montana Attorney General wrote to Blackmun, asking the Court to affirm the *en banc* decision because for several years Montana had been used as a training ground for other state guard units and he, along with Montana's legislature, feared a financial loss should state governors become empowered to prevent such training. In light of the United States' conflicts in Iraq and Afghanistan, in which tens of thousands of National Guardsmen have been federalized, *Perpich* was wisely decided. On the other hand, one could wonder how Douglas or even Stewart might have dissented from this decision.[72]

Perpich has little mention among the academic community, and generally only in analyzing the extent to which the National Guard may be used by the Executive Branch, or occasionally in a Second Amendment analysis. The decision though stands for more than an analysis of federal and state relations. During the conference, White recalled how the Massachusetts Attorney General sought to prevent the conscription of Massachusetts residents for service in Vietnam and how in the Civil War and in the War of 1812 state governments challenged federal supremacy. White's recitation had no detractors, and therefore in addition to the federal supremacy aspects of the decision, *Perpich* should also be considered as a part of a military readiness line of decisions.[73]

VII: Equal Protection

In 1996, the Court forced the Virginia Military Institute (VMI), a historic state military institution, to open its admissions to women. The institute was founded in 1839 and modeled partly after the United States Military Academy, but for the purpose of training militia officers. Its faculty and graduates served in large numbers in the Confederate Army during the Civil War. Its most famous alumnus, General George C. Marshall not only served as Chief of Staff of Army in World War II, but also as Secretary of Defense and Secretary of State during Truman's presidency. Although VMI had a storied part of the nation's military history, it also, like many institutions of higher learning, had a past which included overt

71 Scalia to Stevens, May 31, 1990 [HAB/559]; Marshall to Blackmun, May 30, 1990 [TM/509].

72 Marc Racicot to Blackmun, December 14, 1989 [HAB/559].

73 HAB, Notes.

discrimination. Only after being threatened with the withdrawal of federal funds in 1967, 13 years after *Brown v. Board of Education*, did it open admission to African Americans.[74]

In 1989, the Justice Department inquired to the Virginia legislature whether the institution's "males only" admission policy violated equal protection. Virginia Governor Gerald Baliles also lobbied the state legislature to open VMI to women. The state legislature, with a Republican majority, refused to alter VMI's admissions policy. The following year Governor Douglas Wilder, who had succeeded Baliles, called VMI's policies unconstitutional.

In 1991, the District Court for the District of Virginia ruled that the institute's exclusion of women did not violate equal protection within the meaning of the Fourteenth Amendment. Appointed to the court by Reagan in 1981, Judge Jackson L. Kiser, had previously served in the Army's Judge Advocate General's Corps and the Department of Justice. Kiser noted that the Court had previously, during the Cold War, determined that a university must have the freedom to determine who may be admitted to study in its classrooms. He additionally utilized *Rostker* for the proposition that not only do the courts owe to the military deference, but also that the military may treat women differently than men. Moreover, he pointed out, that when the United States Military Academy admitted women, male cadets were distracted from their studies. To Kiser, VMI's reasons for an all-male policy, including the need for hazing (known as the adversative method), an absence of privacy, and rigid *esprit de corps*, survived the intermediate scrutiny test established after *Frontiero*. Kiser's decision was, in fact, the triumph of *Rostker* over *Frontiero*. Counsel for VMI included former Attorney General, and Fifth Circuit judge Griffin Bell, and arguing alongside of the Justice Department was counsel for Virginia's governor. In essence, not only was Kiser called upon to decide a constitutional issue, he also refereed a dispute between Virginia's executive and legislative branches.[75]

The Court of Appeals for the Fourth Circuit accepted Kiser's factual basis for his ruling, but remanded because he failed to state why the exclusion of women was related to "an important policy or objective of Virginia." This would seemingly be a difficult task, because unlike when *Rostker* was decided, the United States military had emerged victorious in a one-sided war against Iraq in which female officers had taken a substantial part. Moreover, women were already successfully attending the nation's service academies. Thus, Virginia could not argue that it was preparing men for a type of military leadership which excluded women, or that women were unsuited for military leadership. Instead, the state legislature argued the more nuanced point that the institution's unique education stressors were only suited for male education in training future officers. In response to the appellate

74 *United States v. Virginia*, 518 U.S. 515 (1996); On VMI's history, see Philippa Strum, *Women in the Barracks: The VMI Case and Equal Rights* (Lawrence, KS: University of Kansas Press, 2002), 7–35.

75 *United States v. Commonwealth of Virginia*, 766 F.Supp. 1407 (WD VA 1991).

court, Virginia established the Virginia Women's Institute for Leadership, an alternative college for women, in a model somewhat reminiscent of the separate schools created for African American students four decades earlier, following *Sweatt v. Painter.*[76]

The Virginia legislature appealed for a writ of *certiorari*, but the Court refused to grant it in light of the appellate court's remand. In a published opinion, Scalia respected the denial, but added that the question of the constitutionality of a same sex institution, particularly one "as venerable as Virginia Military Institution," should receive the Court's attention. On remand, the Virginia legislature and VMI argued that the alternative program created for women satisfied the Fourteenth Amendment's Equal Protection Clause. Although the alternative institution could not compare in terms of faculty, library space, and opportunities with VMI, Kiser found that the state's plan comported with the Fourteenth Amendment. So too did the Fourth Circuit, which concluded that while the alternative college did not possess the rigors of the adversative model of education, it nonetheless comported with equal protection. There was an irony to the appellate court's use of precedent. Absent from the decision was any mention of deference to the military, or a citation to a military law decision. VMI could not rely on deference, because the President had determined not to side with the state. In all likelihood, VMI could also not rely on deference because while it contributes personnel to the military establishment it is not technically part of the military establishment.[77]

The Court, as noted, overturned the Fourth Circuit. In *United States v. Virginia*, Ginsburg in authoring the decision pointed out the clear error in the lower courts' decisions. VMI's mission was to produce citizen soldiers through its unique model of education. The end state of the mission was not its adversative education model, but the education of future officers. Women had already proven themselves as military leaders, and there could be no rational justification for the exclusion. In the one full length study of the decision, Philippa Strum pointed out that in World War I, 21,000 women served in the Army, and Navy Nurse Corps, and in World War II, over 220,000 women served in a variety of positions. Ironically, VMI's most illustrious alum, General George C. Marshall, pushed to make women a permanent part of the uniformed military establishment after the war. With military deference not an issue, the decision should have been obvious. Equal protection in

---

76 *United States v. Commonwealth of Virginia*, 976 F.2d 890 (CA 4, 1992). The Judges sitting on this case were, Paul V. Niemeyer, appointed by George H.W. Bush; James Dickson Phillips, a World War II veteran appointed by Carter; and, Hiram Hamilton Ward, a district court judge from the Middle District of North Carolina sitting by special designation and a World War II veteran, appointed by Nixon. See *Sweatt v. Painter*, 339 U.S. 629 (1950).

77 *Virginia Military Institution v. United States*, 508 U.S. 946 (1993); *United States v. Commonwealth of Virginia*, 852 F.Supp 471 (WD VA 1994); *United States v. Commonwealth of Virginia*, 44 F.3d 90 (CA 4, 1990).

the military context, as well as in any government program, should triumph over historical relics of prejudice.[78]

The most striking part of the decision, however, was not the majority's approach to the issue, but rather, it was Rehnquist's concurrence. To be sure, Rehnquist opined that if the alternative institution was truly equal (though not in the number of Ph.d holding faculty or national reputation on a department by department basis), he might have dissented. He accepted that intermediate scrutiny had become the law of the land, but he criticized the term "exceedingly persuasive justification," that the majority used. More tellingly, he backtracked from his position in *Rostker* that women could not serve in the military with the same distinction as men. "VMI was founded in 1839, and, as the Court notes, admission was limited to men because under the then-prevailing view men, not women, were destined for higher education. However misguided this point of view may be by present-day standards, it surely was not unconstitutional in 1839," he concluded. One cannot imagine Rehnquist issuing his concurrence a decade earlier. Thomas concluded that a conflict of interest existed and did not take part in the decision. Scalia dissented, yet he focused his dissent against Rehnquist, who had, apparently originally intended to dissent, but then concurred.

At almost the same time the Court debated overturning *O'Callahan*, it upheld the principle that there is no right to possess a security clearance in *Department of the Navy v. Egan*. The Navy hired Thomas Egan, a veteran, to work at its Trident Nuclear Submarine facilities, but then concluded he was not eligible to hold a clearance. Following his military service, Egan was convicted in both Washington and California for assault and unlawful possession of a firearm. Egan had only informed the Navy of his Washington state conviction on his application. As part of the administrative scheme in the denial of his clearance, he was given the opportunity to respond to the basis for the denial. In his appeal, he acknowledged his California conviction and conceded that he had overcome an alcohol addiction. He also presented several letters attesting to his reliability and good character. Nonetheless, the Navy did not reverse its denial of a clearance, and removed Egan from his job.[79]

A Merit Systems Protection Act administrative judge determined that the Navy had not sufficiently justified its reasons for the denial in compliance with the applicable law, but the Merit Systems Protection Board reversed the administrative law judge. The Court of Appeals for the Federal Circuit reversed the administrative board, and on the motion of the government, the Court granted *certiorari*. The Court reaffirmed that no person possesses the right to a clearance, but clearance denials could not be arbitrary, or in violation of a statute. In this instance, the relevant statute was drafted broadly in terms of Executive Branch discretion. To the majority, this meant that *Orloff* governed and the judiciary had give deference to the military establishment. Egan had also argued that the Navy

78 Philppa Strum, *Women in the Barracks: The VMI Case and Equal Rights*, 111.

79 *Department of the Navy v. Egan*, 484 U.S. 518 (1988).

had essentially chose the easiest, but incorrect, path in removing him. It is true that he would have been entitled to greater administrative and legal protection had the Navy attempted to terminate his employment based on misconduct, and that the denial of a clearance provided broader discretion than a misconduct hearing. The majority dismissed this contention because the law permitted the chiefs of federal agencies to make such choices.

Brennan, White, and Marshall disagreed with the majority. White did not approve of the legislative delegation that enabled a federal agency to selectively choose the easiest means for terminating federal employment. Brennan agreed with White, but added that the statutory "national security" language as a basis for non-reviewable firing had opened the door to considerable abuses. Egan's criminal background may have been a clear basis for a clearance denial, but the selection of statutory means to discharge him may create venues for arbitrary clearance denials.[80]

The following year, the Court, in *Carlucci v. Doe*, a decision authored by White, permitted the National Security Agency to again select the least difficult means of removing one of its employees. The National Security Agency (NSA) is the Department of Defense's electronic intelligence and cryptographic agency. Its director reports directly to the Secretary of Defense. The NSA director is a general officer and military personnel partly staff the agency. The agency also employs thousands of civilians.

Had the NSA removed Doe for misconduct, he would have been entitled to a hearing, with the right to appeal directly to the Secretary of Defense. The agency did not do so, and instead removed Doe's access to classified data. Because Doe no longer held a clearance, he was ineligible to remain employed at the agency. Problematic to the agency's decision was that Doe had been suspected of engaging in homosexual relationships with foreign nationals. But the agency only discovered this after Doe notified security personnel, and as a result, there was no basis for challenging his truthfulness.

When the agency terminated Doe's employment, it relied on the statutes creating the agency itself rather than the Merit Systems Protection Act. The Court of Appeals for the District of Columbia determined that the agency had acted unlawfully and ordered Doe's reinstatement. However, the majority of the Court determined that Congress had empowered the NSA to select which statute to use in employment decisions. The Court remanded the issue to the appellate court to determine whether the agency had complied with the statute establishing the agency. Clearly Doe had done nothing illegal or attempted to cover up his personal lifestyle. But, the Court, during Rehnquist's chief justice tenure was unsurprisingly not inclined to lift any barriers to homosexuals, including civilians employed by the Department of Defense, and it would not second guess the government's contention of a relationship between homosexuality and personal reliability. Indeed, Congress would not do so for over two decades. Only until

80 Brennan to White, December 4, 1987 [WJB/I:775].

Clinton prohibited discrimination against homosexuals in federal employment through an executive order, would homosexuality begin to cease to be a barrier to federal service. But, it is equally significant to note that neither Brennan nor Marshall concluded that homosexuals were entitled to equal protection.[81]

VIII: Endurance and Expansion of *Feres*

Despite evidence of occasionally reprehensible and unethical treatment of service members, the Court remained wedded to a maximum extension of *Feres* in barring service-members from suing the government under the FTCA. However, at times, Rehnquist and the older justices split from the newer conservative justices, particularly Scalia, who was appalled at what they believed to be a judicial usurpation of Congress in maximizing *Feres*' reach.

Shortly after Scalia's appointment, the Court decided *United States v. Johnson*, addressing the government's immunity from suit in cases where a wrongful death was caused by a civilian agency other than the Department of Defense. A Coast Guard helicopter pilot and his crew were killed while guided by Federal Aviation Administration (FAA) controllers on a search and rescue mission. The pilot's widow received statutory compensation under the Veterans Benefits Act, but sued the FAA, claiming the controllers' negligence contributed to her husband's death. A district court dismissed her case citing to *Feres*, but the Court of Appeals for the Eleventh Circuit reversed, finding that the FAA was not covered by *Feres*. In a decision authored by Powell, the Court reversed the appellate court on the basis that the pilot's death arose in the course of his military service. Scalia, joined by Brennan, Marshall, and Stevens, took exception to the majority's expansive reading of the FTCA's exceptions and *Feres*, and dissented.[82]

In his dissent, Scalia rejected the majority's claim of a relationship between *Feres* and the needs of military uniformity, because the FTCA only contained exemptions stemming from injuries or deaths arising from military service. The FTCA codified no exemptions for civilian Department of Defense employees. "It is strange that Congress' obvious intention to preclude *Feres* suits because of their effect on military discipline was discerned neither by the *Feres* Court nor by the Congress that enacted the FTCA," Scalia challenged. Scalia had several accurate observations on the lack of consistency between the FTCA and the judiciary's expansion of it in *Feres*, and its progeny. If, Scalia reasoned, Congress intended to preclude government liability, it had to do so statutorily. After all, the Court under Rehnquist's leadership had argued in military justice cases that deference to the legislative branch had all but been abandoned in the national defense cases during Warren's tenure as chief justice.

---

81 *Doe v. Carlucci*, 488 U.S. 93 (1988).

82 *United States v. Johnson*, 481 U.S. 681 (1987).

In conference, Rehnquist, White, Powell, Blackmun, and O'Connor sided with the government, and Rehnquist assigned Powell to write for the majority. He circulated his first draft on March 24, 1987, and in response Scalia circulated a dissent two weeks later. Brennan and Marshall had asked Scalia to write the dissent because of his vehemence. (Marshall initially planned on separately dissenting. However, after reading the draft dissent, Marshall concluded Scalia's stridency satisfied him that he had an ally on the Court to narrow *Feres*.) Brennan likewise concurred, writing "the only justification for the *Feres* doctrine is to preserve military discipline by insulating military decision making from judicial review. When an FTCA case brought by a serviceman does not imperil military discipline, it should go forward." As to the government's contention that the Department of Defense would be implicated if the government raised an affirmative defense of contributory negligence, Brennan urged that the government would then make a conscious decision to waive its immunity.[83]

A significant judicial review of the unethical treatment of service-members occurred shortly after issuing *Johnson*. In *United States v. Stanley*, the Court held that although service-members had unknowingly been administered LSD as part of a medical testing program conducted jointly between the Department of Defense and the University of Maryland, and the long-term effects of the testing included mood alterations and hallucinations leading to administrative discharge and hospitalization, suits for recovery of damages under the FTCA were barred by *Feres*. To the majority, the suits were also barred under *Bivens*, an avenue for suit against the government separate from the FTCA, because however disgraceful the testing, it occurred "incident to military service." The fact was that in *Chappell v. Wallace*, the Court had virtually precluded all *Bivens* type suits against the military by its service-members.

Scalia, who had earlier argued that the extension of *Feres* was a fiction, authored the majority decision, while O'Connor concurred, and Brennan and Marshall dissented. O'Connor believed that the unknowing testing could not be covered by the term "incident to service." However, the FTCA nonetheless foreclosed the lawsuit. It troubled the dissenters that the majority adopted the government's argument that the combination of national security and the needs of military discipline precluded suit. Brennan noted that in *Chappell*, the Court had merely determined that *Bivens* did not present an avenue for suit against superior commissioned officers, and in *Stanley*, the doctors who administered LSD were not Stanley's supervisors.[84]

---

83 Brennan to Scalia, March 9, 1987 [TM/421]; Scalia to Brennan, March 9, 1987 [TM/421]; Marshall to Powell, March 24 [TM/421]; Scalia to the Conference, March 24, 1987 [TM/421]; Stevens to Scalia, May 5, 1987 [TM/421]; Marshall to Scalia, May 12, 1987 [TM/421]; Brennan, Memorandum for the Conference, undated [WJB/I:738].

84 *United States v. Stanley*, 483 U.S. 669 (1987); Brennan, conference memoranda, n.d. [WJB/I:742].

The decision was controversial in part, because the United States had shaped international law to prosecute Nazi doctors who conducted medical experimentation on prisoners of war as well as on innocent civilians. No less a figure than Elie Wiesel urged Blackmun to reconsider his vote with the majority. Hundreds of letters protesting the Court's decision were written to the justices and in newspapers. The decision served, albeit for a brief time, as a basis for arguing that once more, the judiciary had extended *Feres* well beyond what the FTCA intended.[85]

IX: Conclusion

A nation's strength in the international community is based on far more than its military capabilities. This is true whether the nation is a democracy or an authoritarian regime. A nation's moral standing is perhaps more important, but moral standing alone will not protect and defend the interests and ideals of democracy. Rehnquist may have failed throughout his career to fully understand this later point to a degree that some of his detractors have claimed, but he certainly understood more than many of his predecessors on the Court that without a disciplined military, a democracy is weakened nonetheless. He keenly knew that the Soviet Union did not intend on a direct confrontation with the United States, but Soviet leadership pursued the spread of communism which would isolate and then bankrupt the United States and with it, world-wide democracy.

Rehnquist's detractors rightly point to *Frontiero*, *Goldman* and *Rostker*, as evidence of his conservatism, willingness to embrace outdated stereotypes, and perhaps antiquated bigotry. But these decisions occurred early in his tenure as an associate justice. None of the decisions he took part in, either as an associate justice or chief justice come close to proving that he intended to create a conservative military free from public scrutiny. To the contrary, whether one reviews *Levy*, *Spock*, *Albertini*, *Solorio*, or *Weiss*, or any of the other decisions, what is clear is that the conservative judges had an honest fear of the Soviet Union, and worried that the United States military was unable to conventionally serve as both a deterrent or a reliable force to counter Soviet aggression should the need arise. The Court's liberals, whether one studies Brennan, Marshall, and later Stevens did not share fully in the conservatives' fears. In other words, if Rehnquist's intentions are clear to the modern scholars who believe that he sought to construct a conservative bastion within the military, those conclusions were lost on Rehnquist's contemporaries. In reality Rehnquist, along with Powell in particular, but also White, and O'Connor, and the justices appointed after, succeeded in enabling a depoliticized military establishment which could withstand public pressures, including, an act that would have

85 Timothy Dyas to Blackmun, July 15, 1987.

surprised him, the successful repeal of the Don't Ask Don't Tell law, as well as in barring conservative entertainers who disparaged the nation's first African American president.

Chapter 7
Conclusion

As noted in the introduction, one of the critical aspects of military law and modern warfare is that the actions of a single service member today may have strategic consequences for American foreign policy in a manner in which a soldier at Normandy, a Marine at Guadalcanal, an airman over Germany, or a sailor on convoy duty in World War II could not have imagined. Lieutenant William Calley's role in massacring over 200 innocent civilians in Vietnam was a critical element in tipping American opinion away from supporting the war in Vietnam. But, it took months for the American public to learn of My Lai, and today it takes only minutes for the world to learn of an offense in violation of international law. Pictures and accounts of the Abu Ghraib scandal in which detainees were violently assaulted and humiliated resulted in worldwide protests, congressional hearings, and an increase in anti-American violence in Iraq. Not only did the Abu Ghraib scandal directly result an increase of American citizens having a negative view of the nation's participation in the conflict, American service-members and those of the nation's allies were killed as a result of an escalation in violence in Iraq. The appalling conduct at Abu Ghraib served as a powerful recruiting message for anti-coalition recruiting groups.

On the other hand, because American service-members are subject to the full jurisdiction of the UCMJ, the discipline of the armed forces today has served as a crucial barrier against devolution into Vietnam-type atrocities. Military discipline is, to be sure, only one aspect of military law, but the majority of federal judiciary, from *Parker v. Levy*, through *Solorio v. United States*, and to the present has understood its broader importance to the foreign policy and national strategy. In and of itself, a fair military judicial system is critical to the ideal of a constitutional military, and the modern military establishment, despite criticism to the contrary, has generally embraced this view. Moreover, the military establishment has understood that military reliability is not only based on discipline, it is also based on morale, and that morale is reflective of a military disciplinary system which incorporates due process.[1]

---

1 For criticism on the military justice system, see, e.g. The Honorable Walter T. Cox, Chair, *Report of the Commission on the Fiftieth Anniversary of the Uniform Code of Military Justice* (Washington, DC: National Institute of Military Justice, 2001). From 1984 to 1999, Cox served as a judge on the Court of Appeals for the Armed Forces. See also, John F. O'Connor, *Foolish Inconsistencies and the Appellate Review of Courts-Martial, 41 Akron Law Review* (2008) 175–230; and Edward T. Pound, "Unequal Justice," *U.S. News & World Report*, December 16, 2002.

In 2002, Lawrence Friedman, in his *American Law in the Twentieth Century* treatise, argued that while aspects of military jurisprudence operate with no civilian equivalent, courts-martial have converged with civilian criminal justice and incorporated much of the civil rights revolution. To Friedman, military justice has become a fair system, and though he does not expressly credit the judiciary with this fairness, he implicitly states that without the judiciary, this would not have likely occurred. The Court under Burger and Rehnquist were part of this process. And it is, to be sure, an ongoing process.[2]

Rather than analyze the Roberts Court's and the current federal judiciary's military governance jurisprudence as to whether its decisions are correctly decided, and thereby add to the large body of legal literature on the Bush and Obama administration's assertions of Executive Branch authority, a brief analysis of how the judiciary, since Rehnquist's death, has interpreted the intents of the prior justices and judges and incorporated these into decisions is appropriate to the thesis of this book. To be sure, appeals arising from the "War on Terror," and the Iraqi and Afghani campaigns continue to come before the judiciary and these decisions will have tremendous significance in the future judicial governance of the military as well in the military's internal governance.

Nothing has occurred in the past five years which would alter the basic thesis of this study. That is, the Judicial Branch has, across the spectrum of its jurisprudential approach to military governance, harmonized the needs of a disciplined and reliable military to the Constitution. This is evident, not only in the judiciary's review of cases arising from the War on Terror, but also in appeals from courts-martial, conscientious objection, and decisions involving the right to privacy in the military establishment.

I: The Roberts Court

When President George W. Bush appointed John Roberts to replace Rehnquist as chief justice, national security had taken on a heightened importance once more in a manner not seen since the end of the Cold War. Certainly national security, and by implication, military governance, was a significant consideration in the appointment of justices both in the Bush and Obama administrations. In addition to Roberts, Bush also nominated Samuel Alito to replace Justice O'Connor. In the first two years of President Barak Obama's presidency, Sonia Sotomayor and Elena Kagan joined the Court after David Souter and John Paul Stevens retired. While only Alito has prior military experience, none of the four appointments to the Court altered its jurisprudential balance in military governance.

John Roberts was born in 1955, in Buffalo, New York, raised in Indiana, attended Harvard, and then Harvard's law school where he graduated magna cum laude in 1979. Following graduation, he clerked for Henry Friendly on the Court

2 Lawrence Friedman, *American Law in the Twentieth Century*, 317.

of Appeals for the Second Circuit, and then for Rehnquist. He served in the Justice Department as well as worked in private practice. George H.W. Bush nominated Roberts to the Court of Appeals for the District of Columbia in 1992, but no Senate vote took place. In 2001, George W. Bush nominated Roberts once more, and it appeared that he would not be confirmed as the Democrats in control of the Senate refused to hold a hearing. Then, in 2003, Bush resubmitted Roberts to the appellate court, and this time he received Senate confirmation. Roberts served on the appellate for three years and no courts-martial appeals, or appeals based on *Feres* were issued.

Roberts took part in the appellate court's decision, *Hamdan v. Rumsfeld*, before it traversed to the Court. The government had urged the appellate court that *Councilman* established a principle of non-review of military trials prior to completion, and went so far as to claim that that decision considerably narrowed *Quirin*. In *Quirin* the Court had at least decided on the merits of the German petitioners' appeals. The appellate court disagreed with the government, correctly pointing out that *Councilman* applied to courts-martial, and the needs of a disciplined military was not applicable to trials of foreign belligerents. However, the appellate court also found that the Geneva Conventions did not confer individual rights on Hamdan and even if it did, as he was a member of al-Qaeda, the convention only entitled him to a trial with certain guaranteed procedures. Initially Bush nominated Roberts to replace O'Connor after she announced her retirement. But following Rehnquist's death, Bush nominated Robert for the chief justiceship. The Senate confirmed Roberts by a vote of 78 to 22.

Samuel Alito, Bush's nomination to succeed O'Connor, is the last nominee to have had some modicum of military service. Born in New Jersey, Alito attended Princeton University and then Yale's law school. Alito was subject to the draft, though in 1970, he enrolled in Princeton's ROTC program. He trained as a signals officer and served four months on active duty, and spent his remaining obligation in the inactive reserve.

Prior to his judicial nomination, Alito had considerable experience in federal government. He clerked for Judge Leonard Garth on the Court of Appeals for the Third Circuit, and then served as an Assistant United States Attorney for New Jersey, as well as in the Solicitor General's office. In 1990, Bush nominated Alito to the Court of Appeals for the Third Circuit. In *Brosius v. Warden, United States Penitentiary*, Alito summarized the ambiguities inherent in *Burns*. However, he missed an important point regarding Frankfurter's dissent in the case. Frankfurter issued two dissents, and in *Brosius*, Alito only credited Frankfurter with his initial opposition to the majority, in which he urged the majority to give more time to read the record of trial. Later, Frankfurter would argue that the Court produced an inherently flawed decision in its analysis of the court-martial. *Brosius* arose from a challenge to the admission of a soldier's confession which was given after law enforcement officers read the soldier his rights against self-incrimination. However, prior to the interrogation, other law enforcement officials and one judge advocate questioned Brosius without providing a rights advisement. After determining that courts-martial were, absent a challenge to a statute's constitutionality, in the same category of *habeas* review as state criminal trials, Alito applied a well-founded body of judicial precedent to uphold the military appellate courts' determinations that the confession was voluntarily given.[3]

On May 26, 2009, President Obama nominated Sonia Sotomayor to the Court. At the time of her nomination, she was a judge on the Court of Appeals for the Second Circuit. Although appointed to the appellate court by Clinton, she had previously served as a judge on the District Court for the Southern District of New York. Bush had appointed her to that position. Born in 1954, in the Bronx, New York to working-class Puerto Rican immigrant parents, Sotomayor attended Princeton University and graduated summa cum laude. She graduated from Yale Law School in 1979, and was an editor on the law journal. Forgoing lucrative law firm offers, Sotomayor began her legal career in the New York County District Attorney's office, then entered into private practice specializing in intellectual property law. She also served on several city and state commissions as well as the Puerto Rican Legal Defense and Education Fund. In 1991, Senators Daniel Moynihan and Alfonse D'Amato forwarded her name to Bush. In 1997, Clinton nominated her to the appellate court. As in the case of the other nominees, there was not a substantial record of military law jurisprudence or other indicators as to how she viewed the extent of the judiciary's oversight of the military establishment.

One published decision which Sotomayor took part in upheld the Executive Branch's regulatory processes for fining a citizen who violated the Iraqi Sanctions Control Act, even when the citizen travelled to Iraq to act as a human shield in protest of the allied invasion of that nation. In *Karpova v. Snow*, the Court of Appeals for the Second Circuit upheld the regulatory requirement that United States citizens had to first obtain a liscense to engage in "travel related transactions" in Iraq Judith Karpova was clearly not engaged in commerce and her reasons for going to Iraq was to bring to the attention of the American public, the death and damage that the war caused on Iraqis. The Treasury Department levied a fine against her, and she appealed. The appellate court found that the administrative procedures in place afforded Karpova due process and the fine did not constitute a restriction on speech. It is interesting that the government was able to convince the appellate court that Karpova's action was a "transaction" of a commercial nature, even if her presence near an oil refinery prevented coalition forces from destroying the refinery. Nonetheless, restrictions from travelling to adversarial nations are constitutional, even when the purpose for doing so is to advance a cause. The decision, narrowly tailored, is another means by which the government may shield the military establishment from political activity, but to a much lesser degree than *Albertini* or *Spock*.[4]

Obama's second nomination, Elena Kagan, was the first nominee since Rehnquist not to have served as a judge on a lower federal court or state court.

3 *Brosius v. Warden*, 278 F.3d 239 (CA 3, 2002).

4 *Karpova v. Snow*, 497 F.2d 262 (CA 2, 2007).

Born in 1960, in New York, Kagan attended Princeton University where she studied under noted historian Sean Wilentz, and graduated with highest honors in 1981. Following Princeton, she attended Oxford University in Britain, and then Harvard Law School. She clerked for Abner Mikva on the Court of Appeals for the District of Columbia, and then for Thurgood Marshall. Like Scalia, she taught at the University of Chicago, and then served as an advisor to President Clinton. Clinton nominated her to the Court of Appeals for the District of Columbia, but the Senate did not act on the appointment. In 2003, she became the dean of Harvard Law School.

Prior to her appointment, Kagan did not possess an easily discernable military law jurisprudence. As a law school dean, she opposed military recruitment on campus because of the discriminatory effect of the Don't Ask Don't Tell law. Although she joined with an impressive array of the law school deans and faculty in challenging the federal government's ability to withhold funding to institutions that deny access to military recruiters, the Court determined that the law was not an unconstitutional infringement on free speech. The decision was a predictable result. There is no constitutional right for a university to receive taxpayer subsidies. The military's prohibition against open homosexual conduct, however, has been fully repealed and most of the universities have not created new barriers to military recruitment. In 2009, Obama appointed Kagan as Solicitor General. With one exception, no military law cases of significance came before her, prior to her nomination to the Court on May 10, 2010, following Steven's announcement of his retirement. The exception arose from a district court's adverse ruling to the military regarding its jurisdiction to retry an officer who refused to deploy to Iraq, publicly called the war illegal, and questioned Bush's compliance with the Constitution and international law. She decided to terminate the government's appeal to reinstate a court-martial.[5]

II: The Survival of the *Burns v. Wilson* Ambiguous Standard

In 2002, Alito, while on the Court of Appeals for the Third Circuit, noted that *Burns* is a problematic decision. Whatever Vinson and the plurality intended, and in retrospect he likely intended to maintain the status quo of jurisdiction with full deference to Congress, it is unlikely that the traditional test of jurisdiction could ever return. In point of fact, it should not return and Minton's concurrence in *Burns* ought to be considered an interesting relic of the early Cold War. That said, the Court has had at least two opportunities since 2005 to address the ambiguities in *Burns*, but it has not done so.

In 2008, the Court of Appeals for the Third Circuit, in *Arman v. McKean*, reiterated that court's prior discussion from its reversed decision, *Levy v. Parker*

5 See, "Army to discharge officer who refused to go to Iraq," *Los Angeles Times*, September 29, 2009.

that the *Burns* standard is easy to state but harder to define. Understanding the military law jurisprudence of Vinson, Jackson, Reed, Clark, and Burton ought to clarify that what the Court intended, was at best, a narrow avenue of collateral review. "Fully and fairly," implies great trust and deference in the military's appellate review processes. The problem with *Burns* is not only that the Court failed to define "fully and fairly," but that it was a slovenly decision in which the military review process that predated the UCMJ was barely what could be called a review process in any modern sense, and the decision ended with a likely unjust result for the particular petitioners who appealed. Nonetheless, "fully and fairly" is not an untenable standard, and indeed, its' essential quality, without so clearly stating, is that wide deference is not for the benefit of the military alone, it exists out of a healthy respect for Legislative Branch as well as a trust in the military establishment. Perhaps there will be a time when the Court clearly articulates this point, but there is no indication that it will. Perhaps further clarification of *Augenblick*, particularly that the federal judiciary should only review appeals of constitutional dimension under the "clearly erroneous" standard should be the guidepost for *habeas* grants.[6]

A second opportunity to clarify *Burns* arose in 2009. That year, the Court, in *United States v. Denedo*, modified *Goldsmith*, in determining that the All Writs Act empowered the intermediate service courts as well as the Court of Appeals for the Armed Forces to entertain petitions for *coram nobis*. This rarely used type of appeal is a unique basis for bringing an otherwise already exhausted claim before the court. When a new condition of law arises, or newly discovered evidence of a substantial exculpatory nature is discovered, the doctrine of *coram nobis* enables a federal court to reconsider earlier decisions. However, this jurisdictional avenue is seldom granted. It should be recalled that Sergeant O'Callahan had kept his appeals alive through this avenue. Jacob Denedo, a former sailor, attempted to do likewise. Denedo had pled guilty to conspiracy, larceny and forgery, after naval investigators discovered that he and others defrauded a community college. In 1998, a special court-martial sentenced him to a bad conduct discharge and three months confinement. Normally, there would be little basis of appeal and indeed, Denedo elected to voluntarily terminate his appeals by 2000.

However, when Denedo enlisted, he was a Nigerian citizen who hoped to become a United States citizen, and the court-martial conviction eliminated this possibility. After his court-martial, he remained in the United States as a resident with a work-permit. In 2006, the Department of Homeland Security sought to remove him from the United States. Denedo tried to appeal again to the intermediate service appellate court and then the Court of Appeals for the Armed Forces, claiming that had he known of the potential for deportation at the time of his guilty plea, he would not have pled guilty. Because his defense counsel did not inform him of this collateral possibility, he claimed that he had been ineffectively represented in violation of the Sixth Amendment. The Navy's appellate court determined that

6 *Arman v. McKeon*, 549 F.3d 279 (CA 3, 2008).

it did not possess the statutory authority to review Denedo's belated claim, but the Court of Appeals for the Armed Forces reversed. The military appellate courts did not decide that issue of ineffectiveness of counsel, and instead only concluded that the service courts of appeal possessed *coram nobis* jurisdiction.

Writing for the majority, Kennedy conceded that the merits of Denedo's claim were questionable, but the government's argument that the military appellate courts, under the All Writs Act, did not possess the authority to grant *coram nobis* would place the military appellate process on a different stature than the federal judiciary. The majority added that even if the act did not expressly state that the federal courts possessed jurisdiction over *coram nobis* appeals, because such appeals were part of an original case, the act's silence would not deprive the appellate courts of jurisdiction. This, to the majority, included the military courts of appeal. One of the silent features of the majority's decision was that it incorporated Hugo Black's belief in the existence of a strong nexus between military service and citizenship. Perhaps the majority did not do so by design or with knowledge of Black's strongly held views, but it is evident nonetheless. The majority did not cite to *Burns* at all.

Joined by Scalia, Thomas, and Alito, Roberts authored a dissent, and a brief discussion on *Burns* appears in the dissent for the proposition that the military has a defined system of appeals. Roberts pointed out a flaw in the majority's reasoning which could be applied to appellate jurisdiction in general. *Coram nobis* was only thought of as an extension of an original trial in a single footnote in a 1954 decision. But that decision did not specifically apply to military courts, and without a jurisdictional grant from Congress, could the Court of Appeals for the Armed Forces be said to possess *coram nobis* jurisdiction? The dissent never suggested that appeals such as Denedo's were foreclosed to any court, but the majority appeared to be abandoning *Goldsmith*. There is an irony in the dissent's use of *Burns*. If the majority is correct, then the military's judicial system will retain a greater span of review over its service-members, which is partly what the judicial conservatives had been urging since before *Burns*, and certainly through *Solorio*.

III: The Judiciary, the Right to Privacy, and Homosexuality

Perhaps the most interesting non-terrorist decision that the Court under Roberts has issued, involved the authority of the Executive Branch to influence universities to permit military recruiters on campus. In 1996, Congress enacted the "Solomon Amendment" in which it authorized the Secretary of Defense to deny grants or other taxpayer funds to universities that prevent ROTC or other military recruitment on campus. Several law schools refused to allow the Judge Advocate Generals' Corps to recruit from the law school body on campus. Many law schools have non-discrimination policies which block law firms and other employers from recruiting unless they agree to non-discrimination policies against homosexuals. In an almost unanimous decision, the Court, in *Rumsfeld v. Forum for Academic and Institutional Rights, Inc*, determined that the Solomon Amendment was constitutional. As long as homosexuals are not statutorily placed in a protected class alongside of race, religion, or gender, this issue should have never come into question. It may be well past the time when homosexuals should fall under a protected category equal to race or gender, but until this occurs, the Court correctly decided the issue. No institution of higher learning has a right to taxpayer funds, free of lawful government conditions. Interestingly, the issue should be considered mooted as Congress has since repealed the statutory prohibitions against open homosexuality in the military with the repeal of the "Don't Ask, Don't Tell" law.[7]

Prior to the repeal of 10 U.S.C. 654, the judiciary had almost universally upheld the military's prohibition against homosexual conduct. There were, however, two notable exceptions. In *Witt v. Department of the Air Force*, the United States District Court for the Western District of Washington held that because its higher court, the Court of Appeals for the Ninth Circuit, had determined that the prohibition was constitutional in 1997, the Court's 2003 decision, *Lawrence v. Texas,* which struck down state laws criminalizing consensual sodomy, did not bring 10 U.S.C 654 into question. That is, *Lawrence* did not overturn Congress' findings that homosexuality was incompatible with military service. But the Ninth Circuit reversed after determining that *Lawrence* applied to discharges under the Don't Ask, Don't Tell law. This meant, to the Ninth Circuit, that the Don't Ask Don't Tell statute had to survive an intermediate scrutiny test as it applied to Witt's challenge. On remand, the district court determined that the military could not meet the intermediate scrutiny test. This was a logical determination since the command in Witt's unit supported her retention in the reserves, and Witt had never intended for a third party to become aware of her conduct. Had Frankfurter's draft dissent in *Beard* been published, the appellate and district courts could have used it verbatim and coupled it to *Frontier,* to arrive at the same result.

Witt was a logical decision, and in point it was what Frankfurter had earlier advocated. The district court applied intermediate scrutiny to a single challenge and arrived at a decision consistent with its standard. At the same time, the District Court for the Central District of California issued a decision titled *Log Cabin Republicans v. United States*. In October 2010, Judge Virginia Anne Phillips, a Clinton appointee, ruled that the Don't Ask Don't Tell law violated due process and the First Amendment, and then enjoined the government from enforcing the law over any service-member. Problematic to this decision was that other courts, including courts of appeal, had upheld the law, and there was a reasonable argument that Phillips had overstepped her authority. Nonetheless, because Congress repealed 10 U.S.C. 654, any appeal from her decision became moot.[8]

The Court of Appeals for the Ninth Circuit reasoned that there remained no basis from which it should hear an appeal of *Log Cabin Republicans*, since, the

7 *Rumsfeld v. Forum for Academic and Institutional Rights, Inc.*, 547 U.S. 47 (2006).

8 *Log Cabin Republicans v. United States*, 716 F.Supp.2d 884 (2010); also, *Log Cabin Republicans v. United States*, 658 F.3d 1162 (CA 9, 2011).

legislative repeal of the prohibition on sexual conduct was consistent with the district court's decision. However, one of the appellate judges, Diarmuid O'Scannlain, a Regan appointee and retired reserve Army judge advocate who served from the end of the Korean War until 1978, pointed out a flaw in Phillips' ruling. Phillips had disregarded the precedent set by the appellate court and emphasized her preferences. This abandonment of restraint could have greater implications, such as Frankfurter had frequently cautioned of. After arguing that the constitutional system demands greater respect than that shown by the district court, O'Scannlain warned, "When judges sacrifice the rule of law to find rights they favor, I fear the people may one day find that their new rights, once proclaimed so boldly, have disappeared because there is no longer a rule of law to protect them." One can see a continuation of William O. Douglas' jurisprudence in the district court, and a "Rehnquist oriented" analysis in the concurring opinion.

IV: Conscientious Objection and Free Speech in the Age of an All Volunteer Force

No conscientious objector appeals have been granted *certiorari*, but a vibrant judiciary has, in at least two instances, shown little deference to the military establishment. In 2008, the Court of Appeals for the First Circuit issued *Hanna v. Secretary of the Army*, a decision that originated in the Army's appeal from a district court decision which determined a reserve officer had been wrongly denied conscientious objector status. The district court placed an injunction on the Army from ordering the officer to duty. Louis P. Font, a West Point commissioned officer who had achieved conscientious objector exemption from military service in 1971 represented Mary Hanna. In a fact pattern commonplace to the post-draft military in times of war, Mary Hanna had attended medical school partly financed by taxpayers though a competitive Department of Defense program. In return for the Department of Defense's contributions, Hanna promised that she would serve on active duty. In all, taxpayers paid $180,000 for Hanna's medical school and the Army had based its manpower planning on her service. Following an order to report to active duty in 2005, Hanna applied for conscientious objector exemption, claiming that her Christian faith forbade her to take part in any killing. Hanna had grown up in a religious family and taught Sunday school, but much of her religious activities occurred prior to signing an agreement with the Army. In other words, her religious exposure and beliefs were not an impediment to military service when she agreed to accept the terms of the government program. Several Coptic Christian priests attested to Hanna's sincerity in her faith, but the Coptic Church to which she belonged was not opposed to participating in war. The church accepted and supported conscientious objectors. On the other hand, as a doctor, Hanna would not directly take part in any killing, and she had performed anesthesiology duties at a hospital that treated police officers, gang members, and provided abortions. An investigating officer recommended approving Hanna's application for exemption, and the reviewing staff judge advocate supported the report. Nonetheless, at the Army's conscientious objection review board, the board's president, a colonel, and a chaplain both voted to disapprove Hanna's application. The district court determined the Army in the wrong and placed an injunction against Hanna's being ordered into military service.[9]

The appellate court decision was a two to one split. Writing for the majority, William W. Schwarzer, a district court judge on the Northern District for California, without citing to *Harmon*, noted that the Army, in denying Hanna's application for discharge, had "misread its own regulation." Schwarzer, a World War II veteran appointed by Ford and on senior status, was joined by Juan R. Tourella, who was appointed to the district court by Ford, and the appellate court by Reagan. After determining that the Army had failed to follow its own rules, they turned to a number of Vietnam era conscientious objector decisions, beginning with *Seeger*, and including *Clay*, *Ehlert*, and *Welsh* to dimsiss the Army's conclusion that Hanna's claim of conscientious objection had only conveniently crystallized after she had completed medical school. None of the majority's decision should have surprised the Army to this point, if for any reason, then the Army's legal officers supported granting Hanna's conscientious objector status. But, the Army had also urged the court to remand the issue back to its conscientious objector board, and the court denied the remand because the Army had failed to raise the issue in its initial brief.

Writing a dissent, Michael Boudin, a Bush appointee and the son of Leonard Boudin who, along with his law partner Victor Rabinowitz, had opposed the military on numerous cases, pointed out that the majority had failed to give the military establishment the deference it was entitled to. Judge Boudin did not argue that the Army was right in its decision, but rather, the court had the legal duty to remand to an agency, the opportunity to cure any errors in its legal analysis or evidentiary conclusions. Because the Army's legal officers had sided with Hanna, the end result would likely have been to sustain Hanna's application, but then the Army would have been enabled to recoup Hanna's debt without further judicial action. "Often, the problem in a hard case is a tension between existing law and what the judge feels is the 'right' result," Boudin concluded. "Here, doctrine gives the close calls to the army. If a judge disregards that doctrine, it is the judge and not the case that has made bad law. This decision, alas, is such an instance." There is more than a small irony to the appellate court's decision and dissent. Two judges appointed by conservative presidents ruled against the military, and the dissenting judge's father had campaigned against the military establishment during the Cold War with the purpose of undermining military discipline. Irony aside, *Hanna* is yet one more example of the flawed argument of a judiciary overly deferential to the military establishment.

This too can be said of another of Mr. Font's successes in federal court. In *Kanai v. Geren*, Font achieved a similar result before the District Court for the District of

9 *Hanna v. Secretary of the Army*, 513 F.3d 4 (CA 1, 2008).

Maryland, including convincing the district court not to grant the Army a remand. Again, deference to the military establishment would have entailed a remand to the Army's administrative processes. It may be the case that the judiciary is not any less deferential to the military in conscientious objector applicant challenges in the era of the All Volunteer Force, than in the prior eras of a conscripted military.[10]

A troubling abandonment of deference occurred in a district court's involvement in a court-martial of an Army lieutenant, named Ehren Watada, whose conduct was reminiscent of Captain Howard Levy's. (Some of Watada's supporters had also stood by Levy.) There were differences between Watada's relationship to the military and Levy's. Watada was voluntarily commissioned through Officers Candidate School, and he owed no statutory obligation to serve. He also joined after September 11, 2001, one month before the invasion of Iraq. After almost four years of service, and after being notified that his unit would be transferred to Iraq, he attempted to resign his commission. Like Levy and many others from the Vietnam Conflict, Watada claimed the United States' involvement in Iraq violated the Constitution as well as international law and was therefore illegal. Moreover, he argued that the basis for the war, the Bush administration's claim of Hussein's possession of weapons of mass destruction, was proved to be false. Watada then attempted to bring his actions to the public's attention through media interviews and spoke at public rallies criticizing the war. He did not use the same type of inflammatory language as did Levy, but he accused Bush of misleading the country, and accused the military of war crimes in Iraq. Like Levy, he encouraged other service-members to refuse to deploy.[11]

The Army charged Watada with missing a movement under Article 87 of the UCMJ and two specifications of conduct unbecoming an officer and gentleman for his public comments. Initially, the Army levied seven charges, but after the pretrial investigation, four of the charges were dropped. Although many of Watada's supporters argued that his comments were protected speech, *Avrech, Levy, Culver, Cortright,* and *Priest*, at least stood for the proposition that, on a fact by fact basis, speech could violate the UCMJ. Thus, even in a vacuum, Watada's public comments could be found to have undermined discipline. But this question would never come before a court-martial to determine.

Watada's court-martial began in February 2007. He had attempted to place the American involvement in the war on trial by raising a Nuremburg defense. Just as Levy had not been permitted to raise the defense of justification for refusing orders, neither would the court-martial permit Watada to do so. Watada and the government entered into a stipulation of fact—an instrument where both parties agree that certain facts are true and cannot be contradicted—that would seem to admit to the elements of the offense of missing a movement. A court-martial was empanelled and the stipulation was presented to the panel as evidence. Prior to the close of the court-martial, it appeared to the military judge that Watada intended to

10 *Kanai v. Green*, 671 F.Supp.2d 713(D. MD, 2009).

11 *Watada v. Head*, 530 F.Supp.2d 1136 (WD WA, 2007).

contradict the stipulation and after a brief discussion, the judge declared a mistrial. There were three substantial questions involved in the mistrial. The first was whether Watada's mistaken belief in the right to refuse to deploy contradicted the stipulation and therefore necessitated a mistrial. A similar question was whether the stipulation had essentially taken the part of a confession. The third question was whether jeopardy attached. Under the rules for courts-martial, a mistrial is to be rarely granted, and then only to prevent a manifest injustice.

Watada unsuccessfully appealed to the Army Court of Criminal Appeals, and then to the Court of Appeals for the Armed Forces, arguing that double jeopardy was a bar to his retrial. The District Court for the Western District of Washington ruled otherwise. Judge Benjamin Settle, who ruled against the Army, was appointed to the bench by Bush in 2007, and had served in the Army as a judge advocate between 1973 and 1976. There is nothing in his resume that evidences any personal bias against the military or the United States' involvement in the conflict in Iraq. On the other hand, Settle appears to have believed that the military trial judge goaded the prosecution into motioning the court-martial for a mistrial.

After acknowledging the basic principle of comity set in *Councilman* and *Noyd*, the district court determined that if the Army were permitted to court-martial Watada once more, double jeopardy—a trial for the same offense—would be violated. Normally, a mistrial does not cause jeopardy to attach, unless government misconduct occurs to cause the mistrial. This basic rule also applies to "hung juries" in criminal trials of civilians. Before Settle could decide this issue, however, he addressed the judicial scope of review over the military by analyzing the applicability of *Burns*. Settle's view of *Burns*, much like several other judges, is that the meaning of "full and fair" has been "anything but clear."

It is clear that the intermediate service appellate court and the civilian Court of Appeals for the Armed Forces considered Watada's jeopardy challenge against proceeding to a new trial. But, both courts failed to provide any findings of fact or legal analysis as to why each ruled against Watada. It is likely, that the reasons which were obvious to the military courts, were not obvious to the district court. Interestingly, Settle turned to *Wade v. Hunter* to buttress his findings that jeopardy had already attached. But, had *Wade* been applied to Watada's case, the opposite result should have been achieved. Moreover, it might have been the case that the military judge "abused his discretion," or "failed to consider possible alternatives" to a mistrial, as Settle concluded, but the proper ruling, would have been to remand back to the Court of Appeals for the Armed Forces to determine why, in its view, jeopardy had not attached.

Again, the bright-line rules for the attachment of jeopardy fully applies after a court, or court-martial, has rendered a verdict. For instance, the Court, in both *Illinois v. Somerville*, and *Arizona v. Washington*, held that a retrial after a mistrial does not necessarily violate the prohibition against double jeopardy. Settle, to be sure, cited to both of these decisions, but it would appear that Watada's statements to the trial court and his desire to continue with a Nuremberg defense undermined the efficacy of the stipulation. A trial judge cannot, by law, permit a stipulation to stand where a defendant's testimony or counsel's arguments contradict it.[12]

There is no evidence that the district court in *Watada* was politically motivated, such as had occurred in *O'Callahan*. On the other hand, the district court's decision provides another instance of the judiciary not overly deferring to the military. The Department of Justice, determined, over the Army General Counsel's and Judge Advocate General's objection not to appeal to the Court of Appeals for the Ninth Circuit. How that court, or for that matter, the Court would have ruled on the appeal is difficult to predict. Yet, if either were to follow the Court's intent in *Councilman,* it would have likely overturned the lower court.

V: Future Challenges to the Efficacy of Military Law

There will certainly be future challenges to the efficacy of military law raised before the judiciary. Appeals against broad assertions of Executive Branch authority will continue at least as long as the nation remains on a war or deterrence footing. In any given judicial term, court-martialed service-members will raise dozens of *habeas* appeals to the judiciary. With the demise of Don't Ask Don't Tell, there will be appeals from both those who believe the military establishment continues to discriminate against homosexuals, as well as those who, for reasons of faith, opposed the repeal and now believe that their religious rights have been trammeled. Likewise, modifications to the military retirement and benefits structure as well as dependant access to medical care will result in lawsuits. Finally, *Feres* will remain a contested issue.

a. The Judiciary and the Confrontation Between Neoconservatives and Liberals

Future appeals are likely to arise from the continuance of military operations in Afghanistan as well as in other areas of the world. The military will also continue to be a central part in the nation's worldwide anti-terrorism operations. Jurisprudential theory may underlie some of the broader challenges, particularly when challenges arise from either of the two ends of a spectrum. Unfortunately a common denominator of both ends of the spectrum is a deficient historic analysis. The other common denominator will be an assertive Executive Branch claiming the necessity of national security.

At one end of this spectrum is an academic population that yearns for judicial activism in the form of expansive oversight over military governance. Only a handful of judges or justices have historically agreed with adopting such a jurisprudence. Even when a justice or judge tends toward this position, with the exception of Douglas or a few others, those who do so, do so with significant

12 *Illinois v. Somerville*, 410 U.S. 458 (1973); *Arizona v. Washington*, 434 US 497 (1978). See also Rules for Court Martial, rule 915(c)(2); and UCMJ, Article 44.

caveats. A case in point is Thurgood Marshall. Former congresswoman Elizabeth Holtzman who sued to stop military operations in Cambodia and Laos, lamented Marshall's unwillingness to assert the judiciary into a political question, even where, a majority of the Legislative Branch and public appeared to view the Nixon administration as immoral. In discussing her role in the suit against Nixon she recalled her disappointment in Marshall who she recalled as, "a justice deeply attuned to the needs of the disempowered, unwilling to take on the president." In contrast, Holtzman stressed her admiration for Douglas who "courageously" used his power to prevent abuses.[13]

Holtzman is wrong on Marshall. Marshall did not shirk from his judicial responsibilities. He was often able divorce what he wished the Executive Branch would do, or refrain from doing, from the role of the judiciary in the military's governance. Marshall disappointed liberals by his refusal to join with Douglas in attempting to judicially end the war in Vietnam. His input into *Chappell v. Wallace* probably also disappointed liberals. On the other hand, his positions in *Frontiero v. Richardson* and *Goldman v. Weinberger* are a reminder that deference is not unlimited. But so too is a study of Frankfurter, Harlan, Stewart, White, Powell, O'Connor, Scalia, and even Rehnquist. For that matter, the Court's jurisprudence towards the military establishment remains mostly what Frankfurter envisioned was the correct approach, and this involves a balance of deference and oversight.

At the other end of the spectrum are a group of legal scholars that has come to be labeled "neoconservative." Neoconservative lawyers serving in leading policy positions in the Bush administration argued that in periods of national crisis, the Executive Branch is the preeminent branch of government. This is nothing new. Roosevelt's attorneys certainly approached Executive Branch authority in a similar manner. But, Bush and his administration were less inclusive of the Legislative and Judicial Branches than Roosevelt. Two of the Bush administration's attorneys went so far as to advocate the termination of the Foreign Intelligence Surveillance Court, ironically a judicial body shaped by conservatives such as Warren Burger. Another Department of Defense attorney publicly called for major defense industries to boycott law firms that provided defense counsel to Guantanamo detainees. However, a progressive American Bar Association and appalled government attorneys provided an additional bulwark against an Executive Branch power diminishing civil liberties, or, for that matter, undermining military discipline. While neither end of the spectrum has been particularly adept in their historic analysis of military law, current neoconservative jurisprudence poses a threat to the traditional civil-military construct, such that if their jurisprudential school were to ever become embedded in the military establishment, the judiciary might well lose confidence in the Executive Branch's governance of the military.[14]

---

13 Elizabeth Holtzman, *Who Said It Would Be Easy*, 69–77.

14 See e.g. James P. Piffner, *Power Play: The Bush Presidency and the Constituion* (Washington, DC: Bookings Institution, 2008), 184; Christopher S. Yoo, Steven Calabresi, and, Laurence D. Nee, "The Unitary Executive During the Third Half Century, 1889–1945,"

b. Fairness of Courts-Martial

The judiciary will likely be called upon to decide the fairness of courts-martial should certain congressional proposals to alter the statutory laws on sexual assault occur. To be sure, the military must curb sexual assault, and commanders must be held accountable for failing to minimize the prevalence of sexual assault as well as the diminution of good order and discipline. After all, the military is not a university policing its fraternity row. Its personnel are charged with the defense of the nation and the prosecution of persons legitimately accused of offenses must occur without fail. Nonetheless, some of the congressional proposals are staggering in undermining the fairness of courts-martial and will certainly have the effect of subjecting courts-martial to warranted public criticism. These proposals include eliminating the defense of mistake of fact in terms of statutory rape, and shifting the burden of proving consent onto an accused service-member. Such proposals will create a kangaroo court as Douglas envisioned. One of the more well known proposals is to eliminate the authority of commanders to charge service-members with offenses, and place this responsibility in the service Judge Advocate Generals. If this proposal were to become law, serious consideration must be given to the question as to whether this weakens the doctrine of command responsibility that was established after the Civil War and brought into full effect following World War II with the Nuremberg and Tokyo trials, as well as by the Court in *Yamashita*. The proposal also would have to take into account the fact that the prosecution, defense, and judicial roles, as well as finance aspects would all be supervised by the same official, and perhaps the establishment of a truly independent judiciary would be required.[15]

In 2009, the Cox Commission, a private entity established by the National Institute of Military Justice concluded that the UCMJ "has weathered the test of time in impressive fashion." Nonetheless, the commission recommended seven substantive reforms. Of these there are at least two that are worthy considerations. The first is to extend appellate jurisdiction to all courts-martial resulting in a conviction, rather than simply those which result in a punitive discharge or a year or more in confinement. This would, in turn, require verbatim trial transcripts. It is true that under the current system, not all meritorious objections or motions to suppress evidence, or dismiss charges, will result in appellate review. Alongside of expanded

80 *Notre Dame Law Review* (2004), 1–107; Glenn M. Sulmasy and John Yoo, *Challenges to Civilian Control of the Military: A Rational Choice Approach to the War on Terror*, 54 UCLA Law Review (2007), 1815–1845. On describing some of the criticism of Yoo, see Neal Kumar Kaytal, "Internal Separation of Powers: Checking Today's Most Dangerous Branch from Within," 115 *Yale Law Review* (2006): 2314–49; Glenn M. Sulmasy, *The National Security Court System: A Natural Evolution of Justice in an Age of Terror* (New York: Oxford University Press, 2009).

15 See e.g. Two Democrats Split on Tactics To Fight Military Sex Assaults, *New York Times*, November 1, 2013.

appeals, the Cox Commission also recommended permitting service-members the right to waive appeals as part of a pretrial agreement. Somewhat related to this proposal is to permit service-members to appeal to the Court regardless of whether the Court of Appeals for the Armed forces has granted review of an appeal. Another recommendation is a prohibition against the government impeaching an expert witness' credentials when the witness was provided by the government in the first place. Again, this is a sound recommendation for reform. The commission also urged that Article 125, the statute prohibiting sodomy, be repealed. In light of *Lawrence v. Texas*, this is an important consideration. Although the Article was revised in 2012, it remains theoretically possible to prosecute consensual conduct and this article does not require proof of a nexus to "good order and discipline."

An important issue not addressed by the commission is ensuring equity in prosecutions. The UCMJ's construct applies to service members of all ranks. There is room for abuse in the discretion in charging service members and referring charges for courts-martial. For instance, during the Senate Armed Service Committee's investigation in the prisoner abuse scandal, Senator Lindsay Graham rightly admonished the service branch chiefs that he, and by implication the Senate, might increase their oversight into military justice if only privates and sergeants were court-martialed. But this is what occurred, and the Senate focused its attentions on other matters. There was little command responsibility guided upward, despite the armed forces doctrine embracing the laws of war regarding command responsibility. Disciplinary lapses were found throughout the command responsible for the prison. No generals, civil servants, or political appointees were held accountable under the UCMJ, except for one brigadier general who received a letter of reprimand. The abandonment of the principle of command authority in the abu-Ghraib and interrogation abuses cases, as well as in unprosecuted contractor malfeasance cases could result in the Executive Branch undermining the efficacy of the military's legal construct by lowering the public's confidence.[16]

There are pending courts-martial of national interest, such as the prosecution of Major Nidal Hasan, who is accused of murdering 13 people and injuring 18 others at a pre-deployment readiness center. Twelve of the dead victims were active duty soldiers. When, in 2012, Major Hasan refused to conform to military standards and shave his facial hair prior to trial, he challenged the order based

---

16 See e.g. *Article 15–6 Investigation of the 800th Military Police Brigade* (Department of the Army, 2004), 34–9 is also known as "the Taguba Report" after its lead investigator, Major General Antonio Taguba. See also, Victor R. Hansen, "What's Good for the Goose is Good for the Gander," 42 *Gonzaga Law Review* (2007): 335–414; and James W. Smith, "A Few Good Scapegoats: The Abu Ghraib Courts-Martial and the Failure of the Military Justice System," 27 *Whittier Law Review* (2006): 672–708. Although Smith is correct in his assertion that too many senior leaders escaped accountability, he makes the same mistakes that Professor Turley does in concluding that the judiciary's overarching deference to the military establishment has enabled an uneven system of justice which favors the higher ranks.

on the Religious Freedom Restoration Act. Congress passed this act shortly after *Goldman*. The act did not expressly override *Goldman,* but the Air Force's actions against Captain Goldman would have failed to pass legal muster in light of the act. The Army Court of Criminal Appeals, in an unpublished decision, upheld the trial judge's order and contempt findings against Hasan. In the unpublished opinion, two of Army's appellate court's judges noted that the relationship between Hasan's attorneys and the trial judge was contentious.

In addition to Hasan's pending court-martial, there is also the ongoing court-martial of Private First Class Chelsea (née Bradley) Manning who is accused of providing classified materials to the Wikileaks website. Whether Manning is guilty of intentionally trying to subvert the military, or she violated regulations while acting as a whistleblower, undoubtedly appeals rooted in the First Amendment will traverse the military appellate courts, and then be brought into the federal judiciary. She will not be alone in this. Service-members have been disciplined for posting derogatory statements about elected officials and commanders on social websites. Traditionally such actions are punishable under the UCMJ, but in a physical sense, it is easy to discern the intent of a Captain Levy or an Ehren Watada. It is not as easy to discern the intent of a frustrated, but less than savvy, junior troop. At some point, an appeal is likely to rise to the federal judiciary in which the appealing party will argue that griping is a time honored tradition in the ranks, protected by the First Amendment, and not a UCMJ violation, much as William O. Douglas claimed in his dissent in *Avrech.*

c. The End of Don't Ask Don't Tell and the Issue of Service-member Benefits

That there has been no rebellion against the repeal of the repeal of Don't Ask Don't Tell is partly an unintended testament to the conservative efforts to rebuild military discipline after *O'Callahan.* Rehnquist would certainly not have supported the repeal, but given the framework of judicial oversight in the governance of the military that he advocated, he would not have created a judicial means to oppose the repeal either. Rehnquist rebuilt the precedence of deference to the Legislative Branch, and no amount of judicial activism is likely to succeed in undoing congressional action in this arena. More importantly, he led a conservative effort to restore the military establishment's full disciplinary range over service-members which has enabled the repeal's implementation to effectively occur. Most tellingly, when, in 2011, Secretary of Defense Robert Gates acknowledged that while homosexuality does not statutorily fall under a protected class, he nonetheless ordered the military establishment to treat uniformed service-members equally without regard to sexual preference. Those orders are enforceable through the UCMJ, much in the same way that overt discrimination or sexual harassment may be prosecuted in a court-martial.

There will be, nonetheless, judicial review over military policies in this arena. Because of the existence of military offenses that have no parallel to the federal and state criminal codes, there undoubtedly will be disciplinary actions undertaken against individual service-members who have engaged in consensual homosexual activity, such as those arising from fraternization. Additionally, the judiciary may be called upon to review challenges to the government assertion of a *nexus* between an individual's consensual activity and that activity's undermining "good order and discipline," or being of a "service discrediting" nature. Although it is unlikely that discrimination against homosexuals will be overt or widespread, the judiciary will likely be called upon to ensure that selective prosecution does not occur. More likely will be challenges to military policies, not only from homosexuals claiming discrimination, but also from heterosexual service-members who claim that their religious rights are being infringed on. When the repeal took effect, a minority of service-members voiced opposition to serving alongside of known homosexuals. Questions were raised as to whether medical or legal ethics enabled judge advocates or doctors from opting out from providing a full range of professional services to homosexual service-members and their dependents. The Secretary of Defense's policy of equal treatment should have stifled those questions since the military is an all volunteer force and there is no absolute right to serve within one's preferred conditions. Nonetheless, one can imagine a judge advocate who, owing to religious beliefs, claims that they need not provide legal advice on adoptions. Ironically, it is the conservative justices' shaping of military governance that enables the military establishment to discipline that individual judge advocate who would refuse to do so.

Since the Vietnam conflict, there have been calls to "reform" the military's retirement and benefits structure. Secretary of Defense Clark Clifford, in 1969, suggested delaying the receipt of retired pay until veterans reached the age of 60, rather than an immediate receipt on retirement. His successors, Melvin Laird, Caspar Weinberger, and Les Aspin, three secretaries whose political affiliation ranged across the spectrum, believed that such a move would not only immorally backtrack on a promised governmental obligation, but would also erode discipline. Retirement reform is once more a possibility. On August 2, 2011, the President signed into law, the Budget Control Act of 2011. That law creates uncertainty to the future Department of Defense budgets, including military pay and benefits, as well as the military pension system. At the same time, a Department of Defense study group publicly called for a conversion of the military retirement system into a 401(k)-type retirement mirroring the federal workforce, without grandfathering in any of the current service-members. If the board's proposals were to go into effect, it would undermine morale and potentially erode discipline. One of the disciplinary features of courts-martial is the potential loss of retirement pay. Because service-members do not contribute personal monies into retirements, the retirement itself is the property of the government. Under the board's proposal, a retirement eligible officer, for instance, could be guilty of a horrendous offense, but there would be no legal vehicle preventing that officer from retaining his or her pension. More troubling is that military retirements for commissioned officers are premised on the government's ability to recall them into service if a national emergency occurs. Under the board's plan, a recall would have to occur through a reinvigoration of selective service. It is true that the Court of Appeals for the Federal Circuit has upheld the conversion of veterans health care into Medicare, but only because there existed no statutory or contractual obligation to keep veterans within the Veterans' Administration system. However, retirements are statutorily governed separate and apart from medical care, and when weighed against the civilian rights and lifestyle that service-members voluntarily relinquish, retirements may well be considered a property interest, protected by the Fifth Amendment.[17]

VI: Conclusion

In 2009, the Court issued *Porter v. McCollum*, a decision whose origins are rooted in the Korean War. George Porter enlisted in the Army at the age of 17 and found himself fighting against the North Koreans and Chinese on the Korean peninsula. Porter earned two purple hearts after being severely wounded in the leg and for another injury. He was also court-martialed for being absent without leave, but received no imprisonment, served for several months after the court, and was honorably discharged. Porter's court-martial was not unusual for the World War II and Korean War era. The type of combat that Porter experienced caused thousands of soldiers—one might recall the lieutenant that Harold Burton came to the aid of—to go absent without leave as a result of a combination of alcohol, combat fatigue, and other nervous disorders that are today recognized as legitimate psychological conditions.

Porter likely never recovered from his war trauma. In 1986, he murdered his former girlfriend and her boyfriend. The state of Florida prosecuted Porter and after his conviction for premeditated murder, the state then sought the death penalty and, in fact, convinced a jury to sentence Porter to death. For much of the trial, Porter represented himself, declining his right to an attorney. After his conviction, but before his sentence, he obtained defense counsel. Nonetheless, the trial court sentenced Porter to death. None of his military record was presented to the jury, and on appeal, the Florida Supreme Court and then the Court of Appeals for the Eleventh Circuit determined that the defense counsel was not ineffective, and therefore the trial comported with due process. A district court in between determined otherwise. The Court overturned the sentence in a rare *per curiam*, with no dissents. After analyzing the deficiency in representation, the justices

17 *Schism v. United States*, 316 F.3d 1259 (CA Fed, 2002); Pub. L. 112-25125 Stat. 240, 259 (2011). Information on the board is found at http://dbb.defense.gov/members.shtml. It is notable that the board is composed primarily of males who serve in senior management positions in corporations. See Joshua E. Kastenberg, "Recent Proposals to Change the Tradition Military Retirement System to Mirror the Federal Service retirement: Eroding Discipline and Civil-Military Relations through Potential Unlawful and Certainly Questionable Acts," *Creighton Law Review* [forthcoming]; and Andrew Bacevich, "Retirement Shouldn't Mimic Corporate America," *Washington Post*, August 21, 2011.

concluded that the failure to produce a military record such as Porter's, even with his prior court-martial, was ineffective to the point of denying him a fair trial. Toward the end of the decision, the Court noted, "our Nation has a long tradition of according leniency to veterans in recognition of their service, especially for those who fought on the front lines as Porter did."[18]

Undoubtedly Douglas, Brennan, and Marshall would have approved of the *per curiam*. But so too would have Rehnquist, Powell, Blackmun, Stewart, and White. Whether the strong language in *Porter* remains limited to criminal trials or translates into the judiciary taking another review of veterans' appeals, challenges to retirement alteration efforts, and even claims supposedly precluded by *Feres,* is another question. However, it is not the case that the judiciary will blindly defer to the military establishment or the Executive Branch in deciding appeals. The level of deference which existed prior to *Burns* in 1953 will not likely ever return. None of the justices has sought to undermine or alter the military establishment's subservience to the civil government. Since the Vietnam Conflict what has occurred is a judiciary which has, with both its conservative and liberal jurists participating, harmonized the nation's need of a disciplined and reliable military to the Constitution.

18 *Porter v. McCollum*, 558 U.S. 30 (2009).

Bibliography

Primary Sources

Manuscript Collections and Personal Papers of:

Chicago Historical Society
Justice

Melville Weston Fuller
Morrison Remick Waite

George Mason University
Other

Herbert Feis
Francis J. McNamara

Harvard
Justice

Felix Frankfurter

Library of Congress
Justices

Hugo Lafayette Black
Harry A. Blackmun
William Brennan
William O. Douglas
Felix Frankfurter
Thurgood Marshall
Earl Warren
Byron White

Judges

Robert Bork
Robert Carter

Charles Fahy
Gerhard Gessell
Clement Haynsworth
Frank Minis Johnson
J. Skelly Wright

Other

Daniel Boorstin
Irving Brant
Clark Clifford
Herbert Feis
John Paul Frank
Frank Kameny
John F. Kennedy
Franklin Libby
National Association for the Advancement of Colored People Records
Richard M. Nixon
Herbert Philbrick
Elliot Richardson

Princeton University
Justice

John Marshall Harlan III

University of Georgia
Judge

Lewis Render Morgan

University of Mississippi
Judge

James Plemon Coleman

University of Virginia—United States Army Judge Advocate General's School

Frederick Bernays Wiener

University of Pennsylvania Law School, Biddle Law Library
Judge

David Lionel Bazelon

Washington and Lee, School of Law
Justice

Lewis Powell

Books

American Bar Association, *Resolutions and Report of the Special Committee on Communist Tactics, Strategy, and Objectives*. Chicago, IL: American Bar Association, 1959.

Article 15–6 Investigation of the 800th Military Police Brigade. Department of the Army, 2004.

Aspin, Les, *Congress and the Future of the United States Military: Text of a Speech Delivered at the University of California Irvine, January 23, 1992*. Irvine, CA: Center for Global Peace and Conflict Studies, 1992.

Brzezinski, Zbignew, *Power and Principle: Memoirs of the National Security Advisor, 1977–1981*. New York: Farrar, Strauss, and Giroux, 1983.

Brzezinski, Zbigniew, *Political Controls in the Soviet Army*. New York: Harvard Russian Research Center, 1954.

Carter, Robert L., *A Matter of Law: A Memoir of Struggle in the Course of Civil Rights*. London: New Press, 2005.

Clifford, Clark, *The 1970 Defense Budget and Defense Program for the Fiscal Years, 1970–1974: A Statement by Secretary of Defense Clark M. Clifford*. Washington, DC: 1969.

Collins, J. Lawton, *War in Peacetime: The History and Lessons of Korea*. New York: Houghton-Mifflin, 1969.

Douglas, William O., *The Court Years: The Autobiography of William O. Douglas*. New York: Vintage, 1981.

Douglas, William O., *Points of Rebellion*. New York: Random House, 1970.

Douglas, William O., *The French are Facing Disaster in Morocco Again*. New York: Cowles, 1954.

Douglas, William O., *Strange Lands and Friendly People*. New York: Harper and Row, 1951.

Ehrlichman, John, *Witness to Power: The Nixon Years*. New York: Simon and Schuster, 1982.

Green, Thomas H., *Martial Law in Hawaii, December 7, 1941—April 4, 1943*. Washington, DC: Judge Advocate General's Department, 1947.

Haig, Alexander, *Caveat: Realism, Reagan, and Foreign Policy*. New York: MacMillan, 1984.

Holtzman, Elizabeth, *Who Said It Would Be Easy: One Woman's Life in the Political Arena*, New York: Arcade Publishing, 1996.

In Pursuit of Equity: Who Serves, When Not All Serve? Report of the National Advisory Commission on Selective Service. Washington, DC: GPO, 1967.

Kissinger, Henry A., *Nuclear Weapons and Foreign Policy*. New York: Doubleday, 1958.
Laird, Melvin, *The Problem of Military Readiness*. Washington, DC: American Enterprise Institute, 1980.
McNamara, Robert S., *In Retrospect: The Tradegy and Lessons of Vietnam*. New York: Vintage, 1995.
Nitze, Paul H., *From Hiroshima to Glastnost: At the Center of Decision, a Memoir*. New York: Grove Press, 1989.
O'Connor, Sandra Day, *The Majesty of the Law: Reflections of a Supreme Court Justice*. New York: Random House, 2003.
Rabinowitz, Victor, *Unrepentant Leftist: A Lawyer's Memoir.* Champaign, IL: University of Illinois, 1996.
Rehnquist, William H., *The Supreme Court: Revised and Updated*. New York: Vintage, 2001.
Rehnquist, William H., *The Supreme Court: How it Was, How It Is*. New York: William Morrow and Co., 1987.
Rose, Michael T., *A Prayer for Relief: The Constitutional Infirmities of the Military Academies' Conduct, Honor, and Ethics Systems*. New York: New York University Press, 1973.
Rostker, Bernard, I Want You*: The Evolution of the All Volunteer Force*. Santa Monica, CA: RAND, 2000.
Stevens, John Paul, *Five Chiefs: A Supreme Court Memoir*. New York: Little Brown and Co., 2011.
Taylor, Maxwell, *Precious Security*, New York: Norton, 1976.
Taylor, Maxwell, *Swords and Plowshares*. New York: Da Capo, 1972.
Weinberger, Caspar, *Fighting for Peace: Seven Critical Years in the Pentagon*. New York: Time-Warner, 1990.
Westmoreland, William, *A Soldier Reports*, New York: Doubleday, 1972.
Whitney, Courtney, "*The Case of General Yamashita:* Memorandum." Washington, DC: US Army, 1949.
Zumwalt, Elmo, *On Watch: A Memoir*. New York: Quadrangle, 1976.

Articles

Harmon, Reginald, "The UCMJ," *Army Navy Journal*, (September 26, 1953).
Warren, Earl, "The Bill of Rights and the Military," 37 *New York University Law Review* (1962) 181.

Secondary Sources

Books

Abraham, Henry Julian, *Justices Presidents, and Senators: A History of the Supreme Court Appointments from Washington to Bush II*. Lanham, MD: Rowman and Littlefield, 2008.

Acacia, John, *Clark Clifford: The Wise Man of Washington*. Lexington, KY: University of Kentucky, 2009.

Ackerman, Bruce, *Before the Next Attack: Preserving Civil Liberties in an Age of Terrorism*. New Haven, CT: Yale University Press, 2006.

Allison, William Thomas, *Military Justice in Vietnam: The Rule of Law in an American War*. Lawrence, KS: University of Kansas Press, 2007.

Altschuler Glenn, and Blumin, Stuart M., *The GI Bill: A New Deal for Veterans*. New York: Oxford University Press, 2009.

Ambrose, Stephen, *Nixon: The Education of a Politician, 1913–1962*. New York: Simon & Schuster, 1988.

Anderson David L., ed., *The Columbia History of the Vietnam War*. New York: Columbia University Press, 2011.

Bacevich, Andrew J., *American Empire: The Realities and Consequences of U.S. Diplomacy*. Boston, MA: Harvard University Press, 2002.

Ball, Howard, *Hugo L. Black: Cold Steel Warrior*. New York: Oxford University Press, 1996.

Barrow Deborah J., and Walker, Thomas, *A Court Divided: The Fifth Circuit and the Politics of Judicial Reform*. New Haven, CT: Yale University Press, 1988.

Bassiouni, Cherif, *International Criminal Law: Criminal Enforcement, Vol. III*. Leiden, Netherlands: Martinus Nijhoff, 2008.

Belknap, Michal R., *The Vietnam War on Trial: The My Lai Massacre and the Court Martial of Lieutenant Calley*. Lawrence, KS: University Press of Kansas, 2002.

Belknap, Michal R., *The Vinson Court: Justices, Rulings, and Legacy*. Santa Barbara, CA: ABC-CLIO, 2004.

Bell, Griffin, *Taking Care of the Law*. New York: William Morrow and Co., 1982.

Berry, Mary Francis, *Stability, Security, and Continuity: Mr. Justice Burton and Decision Making on the Supreme Court*. Westport, CT: Greenwood Press, 1978.

Bickel, Alexander M., *The Least Dangerous Branch: The Supreme Court at the Bar of Politics,* 2nd ed. New Haven, CT: Yale University Press, 1986.

Bickel, Alexander M., *Politics and the Warren Court* (New York: Harper and Row, 1965.

Billings-Yan, Melanie, *Decision against War: Eisenhower and Dien Bien Phu*. New York: Columbia University Press, 1988.

Biskupic, Joan, *Sandra Day O'Connor: How the First Woman on the Supreme Court became its Most Influential Justice*. New York: ECCO, 2005.

Black, Jeremy, *Rethinking Military History*. London: Routledge, 2004.

Blasi, Vincent, *The Burger Court: The Counter-Revolution that Wasn't.* New Haven, CT: Yale University Press, 1986.

Blum, John Norton, *Years of Discord: American Politics and Society*. New York: W.W. Norton, 1991.

Blumenson, Martin, *The Duel for France, 1944: The Men and Battles that Changed the Fate of Europe*. New York: DaCapo reprint, 2000.

Bogle Lori L., *National Security Policy Planning from Truman to Reagan and from Stalin to Gorbachev, Vol. II.* London: Routledge, 2004.

Boorstin, Daniel J., *The Americans: The Colonial Experience*. New York: Vintage, 1958.

Borch, Frederic, *Judge Advocates in Combat: Military Operations from Vietnam to Haiti.* Washington, DC: GPO, 2001.

Botsdorf, Denise M., *Proclaiming the Truman Doctrine: The Cold War and the Call to Arms*. College Station, TX: Texas A&M University Press, 2008.

Brigham, Robin K., *Iraq, Vietnam, and the Limits of American Power*. New York: Public Affairs Journal, 2006.

Brodie, Bernard, *War and Politics*. New York: MacMillan, 1973.

Brsibin, Richard, Jr., *Justice Anotnin Scalia and the Conservative Revival.* Baltimore, MD: Johns Hopkins University Press, 1997.

Caro, Robert, *The Years of Lyndon Johnson, Master of the Senate*. New York: Knopf: 2002.

Carpenter, Ted Galen, *A Search for Enemies: America's Alliances After the Cold War*. Washington, DC: Cato Institute, 1992.

Caute, David, *The Great Fear: Anti-Communist Purges*. New York: Simon and Schuster, 1978.

Caute, David, *The Fellow Travelers: Intellectual Friends of Communism*. New Haven, CT: Yale University Press, 1981.

Chambers, John W., "Conscientious Objectors and the American State from Colonial Times to the Present," in Charles C. Moskos, ed., *The New Conscientious Objection: From Sacred to Secular Resistance*. New York: Oxford University Press, 1993.

Chambers, John W., *To Raise an Army: The Draft Comes to Modern America*. New York: The Free Press, 1987.

Cherny, Robert W., *A Righteous Cause: The Life of William Jennings Bryan.* Norman, OK: University of Oklahoma Press, 1994.

Clark, Hunter R., *Justice Brennan, The Great Conciliator*. New York: Birch-Lane, 1995.

Coates James, and Kilian, Michael, *Heavy Losses: The Dangerous Decline of American Defense*. New York: Viking Press, 1985.

Coffey, John, *Deterrence in the 1970s*. Denver, CO: University of Denver Press, 1970.

Cox, Archibald, *The Court and the Constitution*. Boston, MA: Houghton Mifflin, 1987.

Dallek, Robert, *Flawed Giant: Lyndon Johnson and His Times, 1961–1973*. New York: Oxford University Press, 1998.

Dallek, Robert, *Franklin D. Roosevelt and American Foreign Policy, 1932–1945*. New York: Oxford University Press, 1995.

Dallek, Robert, *Lone Star Rising: Lyndon Johnson and his Times, 1908–1960*. New York: Oxford University Press, 1991.

D'Amato, Anthony, *International Law and Political Reality*. Amsterdam, Netherlands: Kluwer Law International, 1995.

Davies, Richard O., *Defender of the Old Guard: John Bricker and American Politics*. Columbus, OH: Ohio State University Press, 1993.

Davies, Sue, *Justice Rehnquist and the Constitution*. Princeton, NJ: Princeton University Press, 1989.

Delbruck, Hans, *The Dawn of Modern Warfare: History of the Art of War, Vol. IV*. Lincoln, NE: University of Nebraska Press, 1985.

Dunne, Gerald T., *Hugo Black and the Judicial Revolution*. New York: Simon & Schuster, 1977.

Edmonds, Robin, *Soviet Foreign Policy, 1962–1973: The Paradox of a Super Power.* London: Oxford University Press, 1975.

Erickson, John, *The Soviet High Command: A Military-Political History, 1918–1941*. London: St Martin's Press, 1962.

Feis, Herbert, *From Trust to Terror: The Onset of the Cold War, 1945–1950*. New York: W.W. Norton, 1970.

Feldman, Noah, *Scorpions: The Battles and Triumphs of FDR's Great Supreme Court Justices*. New York: Twelve, 2010.

Felton, Peter, "Yankee Go Home and Take Me With You: Lyndon Johnson and the Dominican Republic," in H.W. Brands, ed., *Beyond Vietnam: The Foreign Policies of Lyndon Johnson*. College Station, TX: Texas A&M Press, 1997.

Ferren, John, *Salt of the Earth, Conscience of the Court*. Chapel Hill, NC: University of North Carolina Press, 2004.

Fischer, Beth A., *The Reagan Reversal: Foreign Policy and the End of the Cold War.* Columbia, MO: University of Missouri Press, 1997.

Fisher, Louis, *In the Name of National Security: Unchecked Presidential Power and the Reynolds Case*. Lawrence, KS: Kansas University, 2006.

Fisher, Louis, *Nazi Saboteurs on Trial*. Lawrence, KS: Kansas University Press, 2003.

Foley, Michael S., *Confronting the War Machine: Draft Resistance During the Vietnam War*. Chapel Hill, NC: University of North Carolina Press, 2003.

Friedman, Lawrence, *American Law in the Twentieth Century*. New Haven, CT: Yale University Press, 2002.

Friedman, Robert O., *Moscow and the Middle East: Soviet Policy Since the Invasion of Afghanistan*. London: Cambridge University Press, 1991.

Gaddis, John, *We Now Know: Rethinking Cold War History*. New York: Oxford University Press, 1997.

Garrison, Arthur H., *Supreme Court Jurisprudence in Times of National Crisis, Terrorism, and War*. Lanham, MD: Lexington Books, 2011.

Garthoff, Raymond L., *Détente and Confrontation: American-Soviet Relations from Nixon to Reagan*. Washington, DC: Brookings Institution, 1991.

Garthoff, Raymond L., *Soviet Military Policy: A Historical Analysis*. London: Faber and Faber, 1966.

Gibson, Bryan R., *Covert Relationship: American Foreign Policy and the Iran-Iraq War, 1980–1988*. Santa Barbara, CA: ABC-CLIO.

Graber, Doris A., "Intervention Policies of the Carter Administration: Political and Military Dimensions," in Sarkesian, Sam C., *Defense Policy and the Presidency: Carter's First Years*. Boulder, CO: Westview Press, 1979.

Greene, John P., *The Limits of Power: The Nixon and Ford Administrations*. Bloomington, IN: Indiana University Press, 1992.

Greenhouse, Linda, *Becoming Justice Blackmun: Harry Blackmun's Supreme Court Journey*. New York: Henry Holt, 2005.

Griffith, Robert, *The Politics of Fear: Joseph R. McCarthy and the Senate*. Amherst, MA: University of Massachusetts Press, 1987.

Halberstam, David, *War in a Time of Peace: Clinton, Bush, and the Generals*. New York: Touchstone, 2002.

Hall, David Locke, *The Reagan Wars: A Constitutional Perspective*. Boulder, CO: Westview Press, 1991.

Hall, Simon, *Peace and Freedom: The Civil Rights and Anti-War Movements in the 1960s*. Philadelphia, PA: University of Pennsylvania Press, 2005.

Hall, Timothy, *Supreme Court Justices: A Biographical Directory*. New York: Facts on File, 2001.

Hayward, Steven F., *The Age of Reagan: The Conservative Counter-Revolution*. New York: Random House, 2009.

Hendrickson, Ryan C., *The Clinton Wars: The Constitution, Congress, and the War Powers*. Nashville, TN: Vanderbilt University Press, 2002.

Hensley, Thomas R., *The Rehnquist Court: Justices, Rulings, and Legacy*. Santa Barbara, CA: ABC-CLIO, 2006.

Herring, George C., *America's Longest War: The United States and Vietnam, 1950–1975*. New York: McGraw-Hill, 4th 2001.

Herspring, Dale, *The Pentagon and the Presidency: Civil-Military Relations from FDR to George Bush*. Lawrence, KS: Kansas University Press, 2005.

Hickey, Donald, *The War of 1812: The Forgotten Conflict*. Champaign, IL: University of Illinois Press, 2012.

Hogan, Michael F., *A Cross of Iron: Harry S. Truman and the Origins of the Modern Security State, 1945–1950*. London: Cambridge University Press, 1998.

Holm, Jeanne, *Women in the Military: An Unfinished Revolution*. Novato, CA: Presidio Press, 1982.

Hudson, David L., *The Rehnquist Court: Understanding its Impact and Legacy*. Westport, CT: Greenwood Press, 2007.

Hutchinson, Dennis J., *The Man Who Once Was Whizzer White*. New York: Free Press, 1988.

Irons, Peters, *War Powers: How the Imperial Presidency Hijacked the Constitution*. New York: Metropolitan Books, 2005.

Irons, Peter, *Brennan v. Rehnquist: The Battle for the Constitution*. New York: Alfred A. Knopf, 1994.

Isaacson, Walter, *Kissinger: A Biography*. New York: Simon & Schuster, 1992.

Jensen, Joan, *Army Surveillance in America*. New Haven, CT: Yale University Press, 1991.

Johnson, Herbert A., *The Chief Justiceship of John Marshall: 1801–1835*. Columbia, SC: University of South Carolina Press, 1997.

Kalman, Laura, *Abe Fortas: A Biography*. New Haven, CT: Yale University Press, 1990.

Karnow, Stanley, *Vietnam: A History*. New York: Viking Press, 1953.

Karsten, Paul, *The Military in America: From the Colonial Era to the Present*. New York: Free Press, 1980.

Kastenberg, Joshua, *The Blackstone of Military Law: Colonel William Winthrop, 1831–1899*. Lanham, MD: Scarecrow Press, 2009.

Kastenberg, Joshua, *Law in War, Law as War: Brigadier General Joseph Holt and the Judge Advocate General's Department in the Civil War and Early Reconstruction, 1861–1866*. Durham, NC: Carolina Academic Press, 2011.

Keegan, John, *A History of Warfare*. London: Pimlico Press, 1993.

Kennedy, Paul, *The Rise and Fall of Great Powers: Economic Change and Military Conflict from 1500 to 2000*. New York: Random House, 1987.

Korb, Lawrence J., "The United States," in Douglas J. Murray, *The Defense Policies of Nations: A Comparative Study*, 3rd ed. Baltimore, MD: Johns Hopkins University Press, 1994.

Korb, Lawrence J., "The Policy Impacts of the Carter Defense Program," in Sarkesian, Sam C., *Defense Policy and the Presidency: Carter's First Years*. Boulder, CO: Westview Press, 1979.

Kutler, Stanley, *The Wars of Watergate: The Last Crisis of Richard Nixon*. New York: W.W. Norton, 1990.

Lamb, Charles, and Halpern, Stephen, *The Burger Court: Political and Judicial Profiles*. Urbana, IL: University of Illinois Press, 1991.

Lee Richard T. and Starr, Richard F., *Soviet Military Policy Since World War II*. San Francisco, CA: Stanford University Press, 1983.

Lewy, Gunther, *America in Vietnam*. New York: Oxford University Press, 1978.

Luban, David, *Legal Modernism: Law, Meaning, and Violence*. Ann Arbor, MI: University of Michigan Press, 2000.

Lynch, Edward A., *The Cold War's Last Battlefield: Reagan, the Soviets, and Central America*. Albany, NY: State University of New York Press, 2011.

Lurie, Jonathan, *Arming Military Justice: The Origins of the United States Court of Military Appeals, 1775–1950*. Princeton, NJ: Princeton University Press, 1992.

Lurie, Jonathan, *Pursuing Military Justice: The Origins of the United States Court of Military Appeals, 1950–1980*. Princeton, NJ: Princeton University Press, 1998.

Maltz, Earl, *The Chief Justiceship of Warren Burger, 1969–1986*. Columbia, SC: University of South Carolina Press, 2000.

Manaster, Kenneth A., *Illinois Justice: The Scandal of 1969 and the Rise of John Paul Stevens*. Chicago, IL: University of Chicago Press, 2001.

Mason, Robert, *Richard Nixon and the Quest for a New Majority*. Chapel Hill, NC: University of North Carolina Press, 2004.

Matthews, Christopher, *Kennedy and Nixon: The Rivalry that Shaped Postwar America*. New York: Simon & Schuster, 1996.

Matusow, Allen J., *The Unraveling of America: A History of Liberalism in the 1960s*. Athens, GA: University of Georgia Press, 1990.

Matusow, Allen J., *Nixon's Economy: Booms, Busts, Dollars, and Votes*. Lawrence, KS: Kansas University Press, 1998.

Mazur, Diane, *A More Perfect Military, How the Constitution Can Make our Military Stronger*. New York: Oxford University Press, 2010.

McGuire, Phillip, *He Too Spoke for Democracy: Judge Hastie, World War II, and the Black Soldier*. New York: Greenwood Press, 1988.

McNeill, William H., *The Pursuit of Power*. Chicago, IL: University of Chicago Press, 1982.

Melnik, R. Shep., "The Courts, Jurisprudence, and the Executive Branch," in Aberbach, Joel, and Peterson, Mark A., *The Executive Branch*, New York: Oxford University Press, 2005.

Millet Allan R., and Maslowski, Peter, *For the Common Defense: A Military History of the United States*. New York: Free Press, 1994.

Moskos, Charles and Chambers, John W., *The New Conscientious Objection: From Sacred to Secular Resistance*. New York: Oxford University Press, 1993.

Newman, Roger K., *Hugo Black: A Biography*. New York: Fordham, 1994.

Newman, Roger K., *Owen Lattimore and the Loss of China*. San Francisco, CA: University of California Press, 1992.

Newton, Jim, *Justice For All: Earl Warren and the Nation He Made*. New York: Riverhead Press, 2006.

Oppenheimer, Martin, "The American Military: What it Does," in Martin Oppenheimer, *The American Military*. New Brunswick, NJ: Transaction, 1971.

Ouimet, Matthew, *The Rise and Fall of the Brezhnev Doctrine in Soviet Foreign Policy*. Chapel Hill, NC: University of North Carolina Press, 2003.

Paret, Peter, *Makers of Modern Strategy*. Princeton, NJ: Princeton University Press, 1986.

Parmet, Herbert S., *Richard Nixon and his America*. Boston, MA: Little, Brown and Co., 1990.

Piffner, James P., *Power Play: The Bush Presidency and the Constitution*. Washington, DC: Brookings Institution, 2008.

Powe, Lucas, *The Warren Court and American Politics.* Cambridge, MA: Harvard-Belknap Press, 2000.

Renstrom, Peter, *The Stone Court: Justices Rulings, and Legacy.* Santa Barbara, CA: ABC-CLIO, 2011.

Richards, Peter Judson, *Extraordinary Justice: Military Tribunals in Historical and International Context.* New York: New York University, 2007.

Rivkin, Robert S., *G.I. Rights and Military Justice: The Draftee's Guide to Military Life and Law.* New York: Grove Press, 1970.

Root, John B., "Howard B. Levy," in Spencer Tucker, ed., *An Encyclopedia of the Vietnam War: A Political, Social, and Military History.* Santa Barbara, CA: ABC-CLIO, 2011.

Rosen, Jeffrey, *The Supreme Court: The Personalities and Rivalries that Defined America.* New York: MacMillan, 2007.

Rossiter, Clinton L., *The Supreme Court and the Commander in Chief.* New York: Cornell University Press, 1951.

Rossiter, Clinton L., *Constitutional Government: Crisis Government in the Modern Democracies.* Princeton, Princeton University Press, 1948.

Rostker, Bernard, *I Want You: The Evolution of the All Volunteer Force.* Santa Monica, CA: RAND, 2006.

Savage, David G., *Turning Point: The Making of the Rehnquist Court.* New York: John Wiley and Sons, 1992.

Schlesinger, Arthur, *Robert Kennedy and His Times.* New York: Houghton Mifflin, 1978.

Schlesinger, Arthur, *A Thousand Days: John F. Kennedy in the White House.* Boston, MA: Houghton-Mifflin, 1965.

Schmitz, David F., *The Tet Offensive: Politics, War, and Public Opinion.* Lanham, MD: Rowman and Littlefield, 2005.

Schreiber, Harry N., ed., *Earl Warren and the Warren Court: The Legacy in American and Foreign Law*, Lanham, MD: Lexington Books, 2007.

Schulzinger, Robert D., *A Time for War: The United States and Vietnam, 1941–1975.* New York: Oxford University Press, 1997.

Schwartz, Bernard, *The Warren Court: A Retrospective.* New York: Oxford University Press, 1996.

Schwartz, Bernard, *How the Supreme Court Decides Cases.* New York: Oxford University Press, 1996.

Schwartz, Bernard, *A History of the Supreme Court.* New York: Oxford University Press, 1993.

Schwartz, Bernard, *The Ascent of Pragmatism: The Burger Court in Action.* Reading, Mass: Addison-Wesley Publishing Co, 1990.

Schwartz, Bernard, *Super Chief: Earl Warren and His Supreme Court.* New York: Oxford University Press, 1983.

Shafer, Michael D., *The Legacy: The Vietnam War in the American Imagination.* Boston, MA: Beacon Press, 1990.

Shilts, Randy, *Conduct Unbecoming: Gays and Lesbians in the United States Military*. New York: Ballantine Books, 1994.

Simon, James F., *The Antagonists: Hugo Black, Felix Frankfurter and Civil Liberties in Modern America*. New York: Simon and Schuster, 1990.

Simon, James F., *Independent Journey: The Life of William O. Douglas*. New York: Harper & Row, 1980.

Sorley, Lewis, *Thunderbolt: General Creighton Abrams and the Army of His Times*. Bloomington, IN: Indiana University Press, 1992.

Sparrow, John, *History of Demobilization in the United States Army*. Washington, DC: Government Printing Office, 1952.

Staab, James, *The Political Thought of Justice Antonin Scalia: A Hamiltonian on the Supreme Court*. Lanham, MD: Rowman and Littlefield, 2006.

Stamps, Theodore Dodson, ed., *A Military History of World War II, Vol. II: Operations in the Mediterranean and Pacific Theatres*. New York: United States Military Academy, 1953.

Stanik, Joseph T., *El Dorado: Reagan's Undeclared War with Qaddafi*. Annapolis, MD: Naval Institute Press, 2003.

Stebenne, David, *Arthur J. Goldberg: New Deal Liberal*. New York: Oxford University Press, 1996.

Stern, Seth and Wermiel, Stephen, *Justice Brennan: Liberal Champion*. New York: Houghton-Mifflin, 2010.

Stone, Geoffrey R., *Perilous Times: Free Speech in Wartime from the Sedition Act of 1798 to the War on Terrorism*. New York: W.W. Norton, 2004.

Strum, P., *Women in the Barracks: The VMI Case and Equal Rights*. Lawrence, KS: Kansas University Press, 2002.

Sullivan, Patricia, ed., *Freedom Writer: Virginia Foster Durr, Letters from the Civil Rights Years*. New York: Routledge, 2003.

Sulmasy, Glenn M., *The National Security Court System: A Natural Evolution of Justice in an Age of Terror*. New York: Oxford University Press, 2009.

Taylor, Telford, *Nuremberg and Vietnam: An American Tragedy*. Chicago, IL: Quadrangle, 1976.

Taylor, Telford, *Grand Inquest: The Story of Congressional Investigations* New York: DaCapo, 1974.

Tushnet, Mark V., *A Court Divided: The Rehnquist Court and the Future of Constitutional Law*. New York: W.W. Norton, 2005.

Tushnet, Mark V., *Making Constitutional Law: Thurgood Marshall and the Supreme Court, 1961–1991*. New York: Oxford University Press, 1997.

Tushnet, Mark V., *The Warren Court in Historical and Political Perspective*. Charlottesville, VA: University of Virginia Press, 1993.

Urofsky, Melvin, *A March of Liberty: A Constitutional History of the United States, Vol. II, From 1877 to the Present*. New York: Oxford University Press, 2002.

Urofsky, Melvin, *The Warren Court: Justices, Rulings, and Legacy*. Santa Barbara, CA: ABC-CLIO, 2001.

Urofsky, Melvin, *Division and Discord: The Supreme Court under Stone and Vinson*. South Carolina, University of South Carolina Press, 1997.
Van Atta, Dale, *With Honor: Melvin Laird in War, Peace, and Politics*. Madison, WI: University of Wisconsin Press, 2008.
Vile, John R., *Great American Lawyers*. Santa Barbara CA: ABC-CLIO, 2001.
Walker, William O., *Drug Control in the Americas*. Albuquerque, NM: University of New Mexico Press, 1989.
Wallerstein, Morton L., *The Public Career of Simon Sobeloff*. Richmond, VA: Marlboro House, 1975.
Ware, Gilbert, *William Hastie: Grace Under Pressure*. New York: Oxford University Press, 1984.
Watt, Richard, *Dare Call it Treason*. New York: Simon & Schuster, 1963.
Weber, Jennifer L., *Copperheads: The Rise and Fall of Lincoln's Opponents in the North*. New York: Oxford University Press, 2006.
Weigley, Russell F., *The Age of Battles: The Quest for Decisive Warfare from Breitenfeld to Waterloo*. Bloomington, IN: Indiana University Press, 1991.
Weigley, Russell F., *The American Way of War: A History of United States Military Strategy and Policy.* Bloomington, IN: Indiana University Press, 1973.
Weigley, Rusell F., *History of the United States Army*. New York: MacMillan, 1967.
West, Luther C., *They Call it Justice: Command Influence and the Court-Martial System.* New York: Viking Press, 1977.
White, G. Edward, *Earl Warren: A Public Life*. New York: Oxford University Press, 1982.
Wiecek, William, *The Birth of the Modern Constitution: The United States Supreme Court, 1941–1953*. New York: Cambridge University Press, 2006.
Wilentz, Sean, *The Age of Reagan: A History, 1974–2008*. New York: Harper and Row, 2009.
Woodward, Bob, *Shadow: Five Presidents and the Legacy of Watergate*. New York: Simon and Schuster, 1999.
Yalof, David Alistair, *Pursuit of Justices: Presidential Politics and the Selection of Supreme Court Nominees*. Chicago, IL: University of Chicago Press, 1999.
Yarbrough, Tinsley E., *Harry A. Blackmun: The Outsider Justice*. New York: Oxford University Press, 2008.
Yarbrough, Tinsley E., *The Rehnquist Court and the Constitution*. New York: Oxford University Press, 2000.
Yarbrough, Tinsley E., *John Marshall Harlan: The Great Dissenter of the Warren Court*. New York: Oxford University Press, 1992.
Yoshitani, Gail, E.S., *Reagan on War: A Reappraisal of the Weinberger Doctrine, 1980–1984*. College Station, TX: Texas A&M Press, 2012.

Articles

Anon., “Plurality Decisions and Judicial Decision Making,” 94 *Harvard Law Review* (1981), 1127–46.

Borch, Fred L., “The Malmedy Massacre Trial, the Military Court Proceedings and the Controversial Legal Aftermath,” *Army Lawyer*, January 2011.

Citino, Robert M., “Military Histories Old and New: A Reintroduction,” 112 *The American Historical Review* (2007), 1070–90.

Delbrueck, Jost, “A European Peace Order and the German Question: Legal and Political Aspects,” 11 Michigan Journal of International Law (1990), 897–924.

Dunlap, Charles, “A Tale of Two Judges: A Judge Advocate’s Reflection on Judge Gonzales’ Apologia,” 42 *Texas Tech Law Review* (2010), 893–912.

Fisch, Jill E., “Retroactivity and Legal Change: An Equilibrium Approach,” 110 *Harvard Law Review* (March 1997), 1055–123.

Gussman, Larry J., “Rethinking Boyle v. United Technologies Corp, Government Contractor Defense: Judicial Preemption of the Separation of Powers,” 39 *American University Law Review* (1990), 391–434.

Hall, Kermit, “The Warren Court: Yesterday, Today, and Tomorrow,” 28 *Indiana Law Review* (1995), 309–15.

Hansen, Victor, “What’s Good for the Goose is Good for the Gander,” 42 *Gonzaga Law Review* (2007), 335–414.

Hutchinson, Dennis J., “The Black-Jackson Feud,” *The Supreme Court Review* 1988 (1988), 203–43.

Kastenberg, Joshua E., “Recent Proposals to Change the Tradition Military Retirement System to Mirror the Federal Service retirement: Eroding Discipline and Civil-Military Relations through Potential Unlawful and Certainly Questionable Acts,” *Creighton Law Review* 2013.

Kastenberg, Joshua E., “Hugo Black’s Vision of the Lawyer, the First Amendment, and the Duty of the Judiciary: The Bar Applicant Cases in a National Security State,” 20 *William and Mary Bill of Rights Journal* (2012), 1–101.

Kastenberg, Joshua E., “A Sesquicentennial Historic Analysis of Dynes v. Hoover and the Supreme Court’s Bow to Military Necessity: From its Relationship to *Dred Scott v. Sandford* to its Contemporary Influence,” 39 *University of Memphis Law Review* (2009), 595–663.

Kaytal, Neal Kumar, “Internal Separation of Powers: Checking Today’s Most Dangerous Branch from Within,” 115 *Yale Law Review* (2006), 2314–49.

Kelly, Albert H., “Clio and the Court: An Illicit Love Affair,” *Supreme Court Law Review* (1965), 119–34.

Kemp, Jack, “Realities of Soviet Power: Two Views,” *AEI Defense Review*, Vol. II, No.3, 22.

Kohn, Richard, “Comment on Professor Yoo, Administration of War,” 58 *Duke Law Journal* (2008), 2213–19.

Lichtman, Steven, "The Justices and the Generals: A Critical Examination of the U.S. Supreme Court's Tradition of Deference to the Military," 65 *Maryland Law Review* (2006), 907–50.

Lusky, Louis, "Footnote Redux: A Carolene Product Reminiscence," 82 *Columbia Law Review* (1982), 1093–105.

Morgan, Edmund, "The Background of the Uniform Code of Military Justice," 6 *Vanderbilt Law Review* (1953), 169–85.

Noval, Linda, "The Precedential Value of Supreme Court Plurality Decisions," 80 *Columbia Law Review* (1980), 756–81.

O'Connor, John F., "Foolish Inconsistencies and the Appellate Review of Courts-Martial," 41 *Akron Law Review* (2008), 175–230.

Pavlik, John J., "Extraordinary Writs in the Military Justice System, a Different Perspective," 84 *Military Law Review* (1979), 7–40.

Reske, Henry J., "Pragmatic White Retires," *ABA Journal* (May 1993), 16–18.

Smith, James W., "A Few Good Scapegoats: The Abu Ghraib Courts-Martial and the Failure of the Military Justice System," 27 *Whittier Law Review* (2006), 672–708.

Strassfield, Robert N., "The Vietnam War on Trial: The Court-Martial of Dr. Howard B. Levy," 1994 *Wisconsin Law Review,* (1994), 839–961.

Sulmasy, Glenn M., and Yoo, John, "Challenges to Civilian Control of the Military: A Rational Choice Approach to the War on Terror," 54 *UCLA Law Review* (2007), 1815–45.

Turley, Jonathan, "Tribunals and Tribulations: The Antithetical Elements of Military Governance in a Madisonian Democracy," 70 *George Washington Law Review* (2002), 649–768.

Turley, Jonathan, "The Military Pocket Republic," 97 *Northwestern University Law Review* (2002), 1–126.

Tushnet, Mark, "Themes in Warren Court Biographies," 70 *New York University Law Review* (1995), 748–71.

Wiener, Frederick Bernays, "The Seamy Side of the World War I Court-Martial Controversy," 123 *Military Law Review* (1989), 109–21.

Wiener, Frederick Bernays, "Courts Martial and the Bill of Rights: The Original Practice," 72 *Harvard Law Review* (1958), 266–304.

Yoo, Christopher S., Calabresi, Steven, and Nee, Laurence D., "The Unitary Executive During the Third Half Century, 1889–1945," 80 *Notre Dame Law Review* (2004), 1–107.

Index of Cases

Avrech v. Secretary of the Navy, 418 U.S. 676 (1974): 68, 83–5, 95, 106, 112–13, 117, 118–24, 142, 143, 182, 186, 223, 229

Bakke v. Regents of the University of California, 438 U.S. 265 (1978): 146–8
Brown v. Board of Education, 347 U.S. 483 (1954): 27, 205
Brown v. Glines, 444 U.S. 248 (1980): 142–4
Burns v. Wilson, 346 U.S. 137 (1953): 11–12, 40, 139, 215, 217–18, 224

Chappell v. Wallace, 426 U.S. 296 (1983): 159–60
Coleman v. Tennessee, 97 U.S. 509 (1878): 8, 47
Craig v. Boren, 429 U.S. 190 (1976): 154
Clinton v. Goldsmith, 526 U.S. 529 (1999): 200–201

Davis v. United States, 512 U.S. 452 (1994): 197–8
Denedo v. United States, 566 U.S. ___ (2009): 218–19
Department of the Air Force v. Rose, 425 U.S. 352 (1976): 139–41
Department of the Navy v. Egan, 484 U.S. 518 (1988): 207–8
Doe v. Carlucci, 488 U.S. 93 (1988): 209
Dynes v. Hoover, 61 U.S. 65 (1857): 6, 107

Ex Parte Mason, 159 U.S. 696 (1882): 7, 47–8
Ex Parte Milligan, 71 U.S. 2 (1866): 7, 10, 17, 37, 47
Ex Parte Quirin, 317 U.S. 1 (1942): 10–11, 215
Ex Parte Vallandigham, 68 U.S. 243 (1864): 7

Feres v. United States, 340 U.S. 135 (1950): 12, 145, 158–9, 164–8, 189, 209–11, 215, 225, 232
Flast v. Cohen, 392 U.S. 83 (1968): 131
Flower v. United States, 407 U.S. 97 (1972): 133–7
Frontiero v. Richardson, 411 U.S. 677 (1973): 147–55, 168, 189, 205, 211
Furman v. Georgia, 480 U.S. 238 (1972): 89–90, 112, 199–200

Gideon v. Wainright, 372 U.S. 335 (1963): 41, 74, 91–2
Gilligan v. Morgan, 413 U.S. 1 (1973): 130–32
Givens v. Zerbst, 255 U.S. 11(1921): 10
Goldman v. Weinberger, 475 U.S. 503 (1988): 160–63, 182–3
Gosa v. Mayden, 450 U.S. 655 (1973): 78–81
Gravel v. United States, 408 U.S. 606 (1972): 129, 132
Greer v. Spock, 424 U.S. 828 (1976): 135–7
Gregg v. Georgia, 428 U.S. 153 (1976): 199
Griggs v. Duke Power Co, 401 U.S. 424 (1971): 12, 68, 146

Hamdan v. Rumsfeld, 548 U.S. 557 (2006):
Harmon v. Brucker, 355 U.S. 579 (1958): 13, 43, 159, 190, 222
Holtzman v. Schlesinger, 414 U.S. 1304 (1973): 103–5

In re Yamashita, 327 U.S. 1 (1946): 11, 227

Johnson v. Eisentrager, 339 U.S. 763 (1950): 11
Johnson v. Zerbst, 304 U.S. 458 (1938): 10
Jones v. LeMond, 396 U.S. 1227 (1969): 34

Kahn v. Anderson, 255 U.S. 1 (1921): 9, 10

Laird v. Nelms, 406 U.S. 797 (1972): 164–5
Laird v. Tatum, 408 U.S. 1 (1972): 107, 125, 128–9, 162, 179
Linkletter v. Walker, 381 U.S. 618 (1965): 75, 77–81, 90
Loving v. United States, 517 U.S. 748 (1996): 198–9
Luther v. Borden, 48 U.S. 1 (1849): 6

McLucas v. DeChamplain, 421 U.S. 21(1975): 82–3
Martin v. Mott, 25 U.S. 19 (1827): 6
Massachusetts v. Laird, 100 U.S. 886 (1970): 100–101
Meritor Savings Bank v. Vinson, 477 U.S. 77 (1986): 184
Middendorf v. Henry, 425 U.S. 25 (1975): 91–3, 136
Miranda v. Arizona, 348 U.S. 436 (1966): 40, 44–5, 57, 74, 76, 80–81, 197
Mitchell v. United States, 386 U.S. 972 (1967): 32
Morse v. Boswell, 393 U.S. 1052 (1969): 34–7

O'Callahan v. Parker, 395 U.S. 258 (1969): 23–53, 56, 71, 76–81
Orloff v. Willoughby, 345 U.S. 82 (1953), 12, 14, 16, 108, 130–31, 139, 142, 156, 159, 190, 207

Parker v. Levy, 417 U.S. 733 (1974): 49, 68, 83–5, 90, 95, 106–26, 140, 142, 156, 159, 181, 186, 196, 199, 211, 213, 217, 223, 229
Parisi v. Davidson, 405 U.S. 34 (1972): 24, 194
Perpich v. United States, 469 U.S. 334 (1990): 203–4
Porter v. McCollum, 558 U.S. 30 (2009): 232

Reed v. Reed, 404 U.S. 71 (1971): 148–9
Reid v. Covert, 13, 46, 87, 176
Relford v. Commandant, 401 U.S. 355 (1971): 75–8, 81, 84–5, 180–81
Ring v. Arizona, 536 U.S. 548 (2002)
Rostker v. Goldberg, 488 U.S. 1306 (1981), 156–9
Rumsfeld v. Forum for Academic and Institutional Rights, Inc, 547 U.S. 47 (2006): 220–21
Runkle v. United States, 122 U.S. 543 (1887): 7, 8

Schick v. Reed, 419 U.S. 256 (1974): 89–90, 199–200
Schlanger v. Seamans, 401 U.S. 487 (1971): 138–40
Schlesinger v. Ballard, 419 U.S. 498 (1975): 152–3
Schlesinger v. Councilman, 420 U.S. 738 (1975): 84–8
Schlesinger v. Reservists Committee to Stop the War, 418 U.S. 208 (1974): 101–3
Secretary of the Navy v. Huff, 444 U.S. 453 (1980): 144–5
Solorio v. United States, 483 U.S. 435 (1987): 172, 178–84
Stencel Aero Engineering v. United States, 431 U.S. 666 (1977): 166–7
Strait v. Laird, 406 U.S. 341 (1972)
Swaim v. United States, 165 U.S. 552 (1897): 9, 114
Sweatt v. Painter, 339 U.S. 629 (1950): 206

United States v. Albertini, 472 U.S. 675 (1985): 137–9, 211, 216
United States v. Causby, 328 U.S. 256 (1946): 164
United States v. Grimley, 137 U.S. 147 (1890)

United States v. Johnson, 481 U.S. 681 (1987): 209–10
United States ex rel Toth v. Quarles, 13, 46, 49, 92, 199
United States v. Hudson and Goodwin, 11 U.S. 32 (1812): 18, 106
United States v. Larionoff, 431 U.S. 864 (1977), 71, 168
United States v. Nixon, 418 U.S. 683 (1974): 70
United States v. Reynolds, 345 U.S. 1 (1953): 11
United States v. Scheffer, 523 U.S. 303 (1998): 201–2
United States v. Shearer, 473 U.S. 52 (1985): 166–7
United States v. Stanley, 482 U.S. 669 (1987): 210–11
United States v. Virginia, 518 U.S. 515 (1996): 204–6

Weiss v. United States, 510 U.S. 163 (1994): 195–7

Youngstown Sheet and Tube Co v. Sawyer, 343 U.S. 579 (1952): 81,126–8

American Civil Liberties Union v. Laird, 463 F.2d 499 (CA 7, 1972)

Calley v. Callaway, 519 F.2d 184 (CA 5, 1975): 24
Champagne v. Schlesinger, 506 F.2d 979 (CA 7, 1974)
Cortright v. Resor, 442 F.2d 245 (CA 2, 1971): 24, 35, 53, 223
Culver v. Secretary of the Air Force, 559 F.2d 622 (CA DC, 1977): 53, 223

Harris v. Ciccione, 417 F.2d 479 (CA 8, 1969): 60

Kauffman v. Secretary of the Air Force 415 F.2d 991 (CA DC 1969): 15–16

Luftig v. McNarama, 372 F.2d 644 (CA DC 1967) 32

Matlovich v. Secretary of the Air Force, 591 F.2d 852 (CA DC 1978): 185
United States ex rel Flemings v. Chafee, 458 F.2d 544 (CA 2, 1972): 79
United States v. Bolton, 192 F.2d 805 (CA 2, 1951)

Index

Abrams, Creighton 98
Afghanistan 58, 166
  Soviet invasion of 74, 154–7, 174, 183
  United States force in 204, 225
Albertini, James 136–8
Alito, Samuel 214–15, 217, 219
"All Volunteer Force" (AVF) 67, 154, 169, 171, 221–3, 230
Aspin, Les 72, 191, 230

Bazelon, David Lionel 110
Black, Elizabeth, 63
Black, Hugo, 10, 23, 27, 30, 33, 43, 45, 48, 75, 81, 88, 219
  challenge to his nomination to the Court, 102–3
  defense of Douglas, 100
  retirement of, 60
Blackmun, Harry 23, 57–62, 75, 77–9, 85, 89–90, 115–17, 120, 127, 130–36, 138–43, 154, 157–62, 165, 167, 178, 196–7, 204, 210, 232
  Burger, Warren, relationship to 59, 134
  equal rights, 148–9
  military service of 59
  military surveillance of citizens, opposition to 126
  standing 102
  Rehnquist, accuses of intolerance 163
  views on the military as a separate society 89–92
  views on "relativism" 123
Boorstin, Daniel, 62
Bork, Robert 66, 86, 113, 119–20, 185
  Nomination to Supreme Court, 186
Boudin, Leonard, 16, 82–3
Boudin, Michael, Judge 222
Brant, Irving 64, 100
Brennan, William J, 27, 33–4, 45, 48, 57, 63, 70, 77, 79–82, 84, 87–9, 92–3, 100, 105, 115, 122, 125, 127–8, 131–2, 136–40, 143–4, 147, 152, 154, 156, 157, 159, 160, 163–4, 166, 181–3, 208–9, 210, 232
  equal protection, 147–9
  influence during the "Warren Court," 23
  relationship to Douglas, 30, 99
  relationship to Stevens, 64–5
  retirement of, 187
  skepticism of military justice, 87
  standing, 102
Breyer, Stephen 178, 189, 190, 200, 202
Brezhnev, Leonid 71–4, 191
Brown, Harold 68
Burger, Warren 2–3, 22, 23–5, 32, 57, 63–4, 68, 76, 83, 85, 89–91, 95–6, 99, 106, 110, 115, 120–21, 123, 125–8, 130, 131, 136–40, 143, 145, 156–62, 167, 180, 199, 214
  and Carter, James 58
  and Eisenhower, Dwight 58
  equal protection 147–9
  and Nixon, Richard 56, 99
  and Reagan, Ronald 59
  retirement 178–9
  standing, 101–3
"Burger Court" 55, 184
Burns, W. Haywood 67
Bush, George H.W. 10, 173, 187–8, 192
Bush, George W. 215–16, 222, 224, 226
  Executive Branch supremacy doctrine 25, 214
  Iraq, justification for military operations, 223

Calley, William Laws 24, 51–3, 61, 96, 98, 107, 213
Cambodia 70–71, 103–5, 193, 226

Mayaguez incident 70
secret United States aerial campaign in 98–9
Carswell, George H., 59, 68
Carter, James 57, 71, 73, 97, 155–6, 161, 172, 174, 184, 189
Burger, Warren, and 58
Selective Service, and 155
Clark, Tom 14, 61, 96, 118
Clifford, Clark 34
Coleman, James P. 134
Cortright, David 72, 104, 122
Court of Military Appeals 16, 19, 50, 78, 82, 87, 92, 112, 179–80
Douglas, William O., and 49
O'Callahan, James and 39–40
Rehnquist, William H., and 64
renamed to the Court of Appeals for the Armed Forces 195

discrimination 56, 66–8, 145–64
Dooling, John Francis, 35
Douglas, William 8, 15, 23, 27, 28, 32, 44, 56, 70, 75, 77–8, 81, 84, 87, 89–90, 96, 99–102, 105, 109–12, 116, 119–31, 133, 138, 140–41, 154, 164–5, 179, 182, 198–9, 204, 221, 226
attempts to block reservists from being ordered to Vietnam, 32–7
and Look Magazine, 29
equal rights 147–8
fear of military influence in civil government 30, 51–3
and Hastie, William 41
influence in *Miranda v. Arizona*, 45
Nixon's dislike of, 100
retirement of, 64
role in *O'Callahan v. Parker*, 47–51
standing, 102–3
Vietnam War, opposition to U.S. involvement 28,
drug, illegal use of in United States Armed Forces 4, 87, 88, 97, 159
anti-drug trafficking operations 191

Edwards, Harry Thomas 161
Eisenhower, Dwight 27, 29, 44, 58, 60, 67, 89, 90, 96, 105, 150
Ehrlichman, John 57
El Salvador 176, 203
Ervin, Samuel 124
Exhaustion Doctrine 21–2

Fisher, Clarkson F. 135
Follmer, Patrick 40
Foreign Intelligence Surveillance Court 58
Ford, Gerald 57, 64, 70, 97, 100, 172, 222
Fouglas, William O., and 112
Fortas, Abe 27–8, 45–8, 55, 59, 100
Frankfurter, Felix 5, 14–15, 21, 30, 42, 59, 61, 64, 69–70, 81, 189, 199, 220–21, 226
Friedman, Lawrence 22
Frontiero, Sharon, 147–50

Ganey, James 40
Gesell, Gerhard 101–3
Ginsburg, Ruth Bader 161, 186, 188–9, 196–7, 202, 206
Goldberg, Arthur 189
Gravel, Michael 133–5
Grenada, United States invasion of 177
Griswold, Erwin 66

Haldeman, H.R. 57
Harlan, John, 23, 27, 44–9, 64, 100, 199, 226
disagreement with Douglas, 44
majority decision to dissent in O'Callahan, 50–51
Rehnquist's incorporation of Harlan's jurisprudence, 80, 181–2
Hastie, William, 40–43
"Hatch Act" 141
Haynsworth, Clement, 36, 59, 68, 164–5
Hebert, F. Edward, 100
Holtzman, Elizabeth 103–5, 226
homosexuality 4, 22, 24, 64–5, 164, 185, 185, 208–9, 217, 219–20, 225, 229–30

Iran 74, 173–5
destruction of passenger aircraft by United States Navy 176, 183, 191
Iraqi military attacks 192
hostage crisis 169–70
United States military forces engage 175

Iraq 55, 175, 183, 188, 213, 223–5
Iraqi military invades Kuwait, in 1990 192
United States forces in 157, 166, 204, 213, 216, 217

Jackson, Robert 44, 63, 81, 188, 218
Rehnquist, William H, and 62
Jefferson, Thomas 18
Johnson, Frank Minis 150–51
Johnson, Lyndon 28, 30–31, 34, 36–7, 40, 48, 50, 66–7, 71, 73, 78, 79, 100–101, 104
and Fortas, Abe, 48
and women in serving in the military, 145
Judd, Orrin G. 103

Kagan, Elena 214, 216–17
Kelley, Albert 3
Kent State University 124, 129–31
Kennedy, Anthony M. 186–7, 196, 198–9, 202, 219
and Reagan, Ronald, 186
Kennedy, John F. 28, 35, 40, 70, 136
Kennedy, Paul 169
Kennedy, Robert 43, 128
King, Martin Luther 67
Kiser, Jackson L. 205
Kissinger, Henry A. 56, 66–8, 71, 98–9, 104
Korb, Lawrence 73
Korean Airlines Flight 007 crisis, 173, 183, 191, 221, 231
Korean War 14, 30, 31, 36, 162

Laird, Melvin 51, 66–7, 69, 95, 98–100, 104, 128, 170, 230
Lebanon 175
Israeli invasion 174
Leventhal, Harold 110
Levy, Howard 49, 107–9
Lex non Scripta, 20–21
Libya 174–5, 192

MacArthur, Douglas 29–30, 62, 141
McFadden, Frank Hampton 150–51
McNamara, Robert 34, 48
Marshall, Thurgood 27–9, 33, 45, 48–9, 65, 70, 77, 79, 84, 87, 89, 93, 99, 102–13, 105, 115, 120, 122, 131, 136, 140, 149, 152, 157, 164, 166, 183, 204, 208–10, 217, 226, 232
and Douglas, William 80–81, 105
equal rights, 148
and Rehnquist, William 63
retirement, 188
Mikva, Abner 163
Mitchell, David Henry 32
Mora, Dennis 33
Morgan, Charles 110–12
Morgan, Glen, 185

Nicaragua 173, 176, 203
Nixon, Richard M. 2, 24, 36, 53, 55–63, 64, 66, 69–70, 93, 97–9, 100, 103, 105, 123–4, 129, 132, 150–51, 172, 178–9, 184–5, 226
Burger, Warren, and 55–6, 99
Calley, William L., and 53, 98
Kissinger, Henry 98–9
Laird, Melvin L., and 67
Vietnam War, and 55–6
Watergate Affair, 69–70, 151, 189
Nugent, Ted 138

Obama, Barack 138, 214–16
O'Callahan, James 38–9
O'Connor, Sandra Day 65–6, 137, 159, 163, 181–3, 196–8, 202, 210, 214, 226
retirement of 215
Orloff, Stanley 108

Panama 176, 192
Pauling, Linus, 133–4
Powe, Lucas 22
Powell, Colin 52

Powell, Lewis 8, 60, 65, 77, 79, 83–7, 92, 102, 115, 121, 123, 127, 130–31, 136, 139, 142–4, 152–3, 163, 165, 169, 172, 180–83, 193, 209–10, 226
  absence from military law scholarly analysis 62
  equal rights 148–9
  influence on Rehnquist 158
  military experience 60–62
  and Rehnquist's judicial ethics, 127
  retirement, 186
Priest, Oscar, 96

Rabinowitz, Victor, 43–4, 82, 222
Reagan, Ronald 57, 59, 65, 97, 155, 186, 188, 191–9, 205, 22
  foreign and military policy of 172–84
Rehnquist, William 2, 3, 8, 25, 55, 66, 77, 79–81, 85–90, 92, 113–15, 120–29, 135–9, 141, 150, 156, 160, 164–8, 178, 180–82, 193, 196, 198–9, 200, 207–8, 210–11, 215, 221, 226, 229, 232
  equal rights, 150–55
  judicial ethics of, 127
  Legislative Branch, deference toward 64
  minority, views on 61, 63, 163
  and Nixon, Richard 62
  Reagan, Ronald, and 179
  reputation as Chief Justice 57
  Rosenberg appeals of Ethel and Julius, 63
  and Standing, 102
  Weinberger, Caspar, and 172
"Rehnquist Court" 23, 184–90, 214
Rein, David, 16, 83, 96
Relford, Isiah 77–8
Resor, Stanley 98
Retroactive Application of *O'Callahan* 40, 56, 74–81
Rheault, Robert 98
Rivers, Mendel, 100
Rives, Richard Taylor 150–51
Rivkin, Robert 3, 51
Roberts, John 25, 214–15, 219,
"Roberts Court" 214
Rodberg, Lewis 134
Roosevelt, Franklin Delano 27–8, 39, 42, 161, 179, 226
Rose, Michael T. 139–41

Scalia, Antonin 10, 25, 178, 181, 184–6, 189, 196–7, 200, 206–7, 209–10, 217–19, 226
Schwartz, Bernard 22, 57
Seitz, Collins, 40
Sotomayor, Sonia 214, 216
Souter, David H. 187–8, 187, 200, 214,
Spock, Benjamin 134–7, 143
Sprecher, Arthur 65
Stevens, John Paul 64–5, 137, 143, 144, 157–9, 162, 180, 196–7, 200, 203–4, 209, 214
Stewart, Potter, 21, 27, 32, 45, 50, 77, 79–80, 85, 93, 100, 102–3, 113, 115, 116, 120–22, 125, 127, 131–2, 135–6, 143, 226, 232
  on equal rights, 148

Tamm, Edgar 125
Taylor, Telford 44
Thomas, Clarence 187–8, 196, 200, 202, 207, 217
Thurmond, Strom 96
Timbers, William 105
tort law suits against the Department of Defense 12, 145, 158–9, 164–8, 209–11, 225, 232
Truman, Harry S. 29–30, 40, 42, 89, 128, 150, 173, 204
Tushnet, Mark 178

Vietnam War 2, 13, 24, 26, 27, 30, 31, 36, 44–5, 49–51, 53, 55–7, 67, 71, 73, 83, 101, 111, 117, 122–9, 132, 168–9, 171–2, 193, 204, 213, 222–3, 226, 230, 232
  Douglas, William O., and 30, 37, 51
  Fortas, Abe advised President Johnson on 28
  judicial response, 20, 43, 100
  Massachusetts Attorney General, and 100

standing to sue the Federal Government over 100–106
United States military forces in, 18, 29, 67, 76
United States service-members seeking redress against transfer to 32–5, 37
United States service-members protesting United States involvement in 95–8, 118

Waite, Morrison Remick 7
Warren, Earl 2, 23, 26, 30, 33–4, 41, 44, 64, 74, 101
complimented Military Justice system, 44–5, 48
disagreement with Douglas on calling reservists for active service in Vietnam, 34
Nixon's dislike of, 55, 100
Warren Court 3, 23–5, 26, 141, 145, 156, 165, 178, 184, 187
conservative attempts to dismantle, 56–8
Justice Powell's opinion of, 62
Watada, Ehren, 222–4
Weinberger, Caspar 172–3, 176, 191, 230
Westmoreland, William 67, 98
Wiener, Frederick Bernays 5, 48–9, 92, 113, 118–19
White, Byron 25, 27, 41, 45, 57, 79, 89, 92, 102, 115, 123, 125, 127, 130–33, 136–7, 143, 152, 154, 157–8, 162–3, 181, 204, 208, 210–11, 226, 232
equal rights 147–8
military service of 28
retirement 189
standing, 102

For Product Safety Concerns and Information please contact our EU representative GPSR@taylorandfrancis.com
Taylor & Francis Verlag GmbH, Kaufingerstraße 24, 80331 München, Germany

www.ingramcontent.com/pod-product-compliance
Ingram Content Group UK Ltd.
Pitfield, Milton Keynes, MK11 3LW, UK
UKHW010959180926
475701UK00004B/451
9781138274037